Encyclopedia of American Cars 1930-1942

By James Moloney

Editing and Design by George H. Dammann

1251 NORTH JEFFERSON AVE. SARASOTA, FLA. 33577

Encyclopedia of American Cars 1930-1942

Library of Congress No. 77-089427
ISBN Number 0-912612-12-6

Published By: Crestline Publishing Co., Inc.
1251 North Jefferson Ave.
Sarasota, Florida 33577

Typesetting by Colonial Cold Type, Glendale Heights, Ill.
Printed in U.S.A. by Wallace Press, Hillside, Ill.
Binding by The Engdahl Co., Elmhurst, Ill.
Cover Design by William J. Hentges, Warren, Mich.

CRESTLINE AGRICULTURAL SERIES

ENCYCLOPEDIA OF AMERICAN FARM TRACTORS
(352 Pages — 1,500 Illustrations)

ENCYCLOPEDIA OF AMERICAN STEAM TRACTION ENGINES
(320 Pages — 1,250 Illustrations)

150 YEARS OF INTERNATIONAL HARVESTER
(416 Pages — 1,900 Illustrations)

CRESTLINE AUTOMOTIVE SERIES

ILLUSTRATED HISTORY OF FORD
(320 Pages — 1,400 Illustrations)

FORD TRUCKS SINCE 1905
(416 Pages — 2,000 Illustrations)

60 YEARS OF CHEVROLET
(320 Pages — 1,650 Illustrations)

THE CARS OF OLDSMOBILE
416 Pages — 2,000 Illustrations)

70 YEARS OF BUICK
(352 Pages — 1,800 Illustrations)

THE PLYMOUTH-DeSOTO STORY
(416 Pages — 2,000 Illustrations)

THE DODGE STORY
(320 Pages — 1,600 Illustrations)

70 YEARS OF CHRYSLER
(384 Pages — 1,950 Illustrations)

ENCYCLOPEDIA OF AMERICAN CARS, 1930-194
(384 Pages — 1,800 Illustrations)

ENCYCLOPEDIA OF AMERICAN CARS, 1946-195
(416 Pages — 2,000 Illustrations)

GREAT AMERICAN WOODIES & WAGONS
(320 Pages — 1,700 Illustrations)

AMERICAN FIRE ENGINES SINCE 1900
(384 Pages — 1,950 Illustrations)

AMERICAN FUNERAL CARS & AMBULANCES SINCE 1900
(352 Pages — 1,900 Illustrations)

Many Thanks

A book of this magnitude certainly couldn't be completed all by myself. At this time, I want to thank Mr. Jim Bradley of the Detroit Public Library; General Motors Photographic; Chrysler Historical Collection; Ford Archives; American Motors Corp.; Automobile Manufacturers Assn.; and Special Interest Autos. I also want to thank the following people who graciously opened their private libraries to help me with this book, including Al Casper, Aubry Behr, Bob Mehl, George Ferris, John Conde, Tom Powels, Art Smith, Bernie Weis, and others who wish to be listed as anonymous.

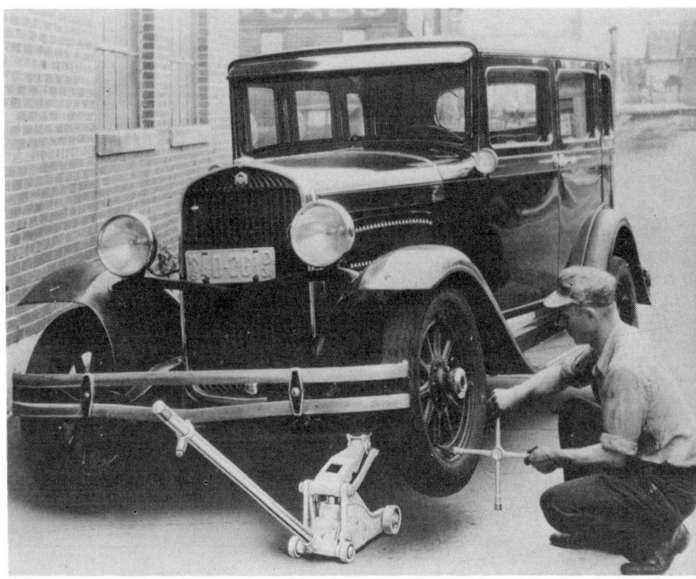

Dedication

I dedicate this book to my 14 children and any other children I happen to adopt before this book is in your hands.

1. Natalie	1941 Buick Super Convertible Sedan
2. Tan Lady	1941 Chevrolet Special DeLuxe Club Coupe
3. Squanto	1941 Pontiac 8 Sedan Coupe Streamliner
4. Woodrow	1948 Chevrolet Fleetmaster Country Club Aero Sedan
5. Mint Julip	1950 Oldsmobile 88 DeLuxe Sedan
6. Buttercup	1951 Chevrolet Bel Air Sport Coupe
7. Grace	1953 Chevrolet Bel Air Sport Coupe
8. Tillie	1956 Chevrolet Bel Air Sport Coupe
9. Soiled Dove	1957 Chevrolet Bel Air Sport Coupe
10. Blue Jay	1958 Chevrolet Impala Sport Coupe
11. Rifka	1958 Chevrolet Impala Sport Coupe
12. Lara	1958 Chevrolet Impala Sport Coupe
13. Inner Sanctum	1958 Chevrolet Impala Convertible
14. La Mont	1970 Chevrolet Monte Carlo

From the looks of this list, you may get the idea I like Chevies. You certainly are right! But my problem is I really like all cars. Just let a car park in my driveway overnight and I'm attached to it.

Many people ask me which car is my favorite. My only reply is a parent should love each child equally. Just because one child is better looking than another is no reason to like that one more. That usually stops them. They either understand, if they like cars, or else they realize I'm completely off my trolley and playing with a half deck.

****Note: Prices shown for the various models are based on the average recommended price for the year at point of manufacture and are for the basic car without accessories, local taxes, or transportation charges. As a general guide, these prices are from 10% to 20% below the true sales price of the car. The weights quoted are dry weights, without gasoline, oil or water, or without such accessories as dual spare tires, air conditioners, or other add-ons.**

FOREWORD

Every decade since the turn of the century has produced a fascinating series of automotive developments. In fact, with only a little effort one can take the entire history of the automobile in America and rather successfully divide it into important segments, each of about 10 years duration.

Take for example the years from 1900 to 1910. During this decade, the automobile graduated from a carriage with a sputtering engine tacked on someplace to a rather sophisticated piece of machinery for a fairly wealthy person to use as a toy. The engines, for the most part, moved from under the seat or from the rear axle to the front of the car – where the horses belonged in the first place. In addition, the gasoline engine was pretty much taking over completely by the end of this decade, though the former popular motive modes of steam and electricity were still hanging in there. And, the gas engines were rapidly multiplying in cylinders, from one and two per car to upwards of six and eight. Yes, this first decade was indeed interesting.

But, the next decade seems even more fascinating. Here the cars went from windblown open toys for the rich to everyday transportation for the middle class. Henry Ford was the pathfinder with this novel idea of providing low-cost transportation for the masses. Maybe by 1920 he still hadn't succeeded in putting every family in a car, but he certainly had most of middle-class America riding in something. Maybe the car wasn't a Ford, and maybe the family only rode for a few miles each Sunday, but an automotive nation had been spawned, and nothing was going to turn it back. And, many of the inventions and innovations of these teen-age years helped to create that situation.

Most notable of these innovations, of course, was the idea of an inexpensive yet reliable car that a good percentage of Americans could afford. This role was filled primarily by Ford, but others, including Brush, Maxwell, Saxon, Hudson, and later, Chevrolet, came on the scene with middle-class transportation. Four other major factors came along in this decade. These were the self-starter; closed body styles; demountable rims; and electric lights. Now for the first time, the little woman could go out in the garage and start the car without cranking – most times. Now for the first time the family could ride in some form of comfort in a closed body style – if they didn't mind being surrounded by acres of plate glass and rattling doors and windows in the rather top-heavy boxes. Now, for the first time, a flat tire could be changed with some relative ease via a demountable rim. If not the best, it was at least better than fighting a tube off a clincher rim at roadside. And lastly, electric lights enabled people to travel further without the fear of getting stranded after dark with only oil or carbide lights for illumination. Now all the country needed was roads that could be travelled after dark.

Those roads came in the 1920s, and so did many other innovations – though overall the 1920s are often overlooked as sort of a temporary levelling off of automotive advancement. The reasons for this are rather nebulous but may lie in the area of styling. The 1920s – the Roaring 20s – were flamboyant in many areas, but not necessarily in the automotive area. In fact, stylewise, it seems almost as if the designers were content to produce a series of look-alike cars year after year. The flamboyance of the 1920s was not relfected in the cars, and therefore many people look at this decade as one of stagnation automotivewise.

Yet, was it? True, for the most part, each year's models were rather square look-alike boxes in blue or green. But certainly there is little comparison between the look-alike boxes of 1920 and those of 1929. Granted, for 10 years, the overall box styling had continued, but during this era the boxes continued to get lower and longer and more sophisticated – sort of like a transition from the cereal box school of design to the shoe box concept.

In addition, one of the most major changes in automotive styling slowly and quietly took place during this era. That was the transition from open touring cars and roadsters to closed coaches and sedans as the primary form of family transportation. At the start of the 1920s, the roadsters and touring cars were by far the most popular styles being manufactured. By the end of the 1920s, these styles contributed very little to the overall automotive production.

The reason for this was a circular advancement of technology. Better engines and chassis were being designed which allowed higher speeds. The higher speeds led to demands for better roads, and the better roads in turn led to still higher speeds. As the speeds increased, so did the discomfort of an open car – especially for passengers in the rear seats. This led to demands for better closed cars and automotive technology was quick to comply. Better door locks and seals were developed. Better window risers were installed. Better metals allowed for faster production which brought the prices down to reasonable levels. And on a few cars, these designs even approached what could be called pleasing. Of course, such design was usually found on the Chryslers, McFarlands, Duesenbergs Lincolns, and other high-price vehicles wearing custom bodies. For the most part, the public was still bumbling about in a bunch of square boxes that varied from each other only in respective size or in the shades of green or blue in which they were painted. But still, Americans were moving about, and doing so in greater numbers each year The point was being reached where all-around, all-weather dependable transportation would be demanded as a right and a necessity, and not simply dreamed of as some future luxury toy.

And that point was reached in the 1930s – the era which is probably the greatest in the overall history of American utomotive development. Here, in the midst of the world's 'orst financial crises, automotive design and engineering oared to unexcelled heights. Here, when the world was omplaining about lack of jobs, poor pay, and general conomic stagnation, more average American families than ver before accepted the automobile as a fact of life that hey would never again be without. And, at this time in istory, when penny-pinching and family budgeting were he rules of the game, the customers made it definitely nown they did not want the stripped models or the mini-ype cars. They wanted the biggest and best cars that they ould possible afford.

For those people with money, the era was an automotive eaven. Beginning in the late 1920s, the custom body era ook a firm hold, and flowered in the early 1930s like it ever had before. Ironically, the flowering was done in ne deepest depths of the depression, and by the late 930s, when the country was definitely in a better nancial condition than it had been a half-dozen years arlier, the custom car business was all but through or good.

But while it lasted, some of the finest examples of utomotive styling and body work were placed on Ameri-an prestige chassis. And what chassis! Just as the stylists xcelled as never before in the body department, so too id the engineers and designers. Wheelbases grew to henomenal lengths, and engine refinements unthought of r technically impossible a few years earlier were now ecoming commonplace – first on the prestige cars and nen on the average vehicles. During this era, the industry w the development of such innovations as the V-block, ompound carburetion, automatic transmissions, pressed eel wheels, safety glass, radios, integral trunks, styled umpers and grilles, alligator hoods – in fact, virtually very modern refinement found on today's cars. Postwar evelopments would include the refinement of almost all f these innovations – but the actual birth of these ideas ame about in the dozen or so years preceding World 'ar II.

Thus, when looking at the entire spectrum of automotive istory, it is difficult to view the 1930s as anything but ne development laboratory for the modern car of today. nd, it is this era which James Moloney has inspected in reat detail, and recorded in chronological sequence on a ar-by-car basis for this book.

Not only does the book go into the major makes, but it so takes a look at those cars whose life span was just bout over when the depression hit. Such cars as the issel, Durant, Elcar, Ruxton, Stutz, and others had just bout finished their automotive careers when the Great epression provided the final straw for their crumbling npires. Yet, because these cars were produced into the 930s, it was felt that they did have a definite place in is book.

Lastly, the final pages of the book are devoted to the non-production cars that, for a variety of reasons, are usually included in lists of American cars. This caused a difference of opinion at Crestline. Personally, I can see no reason why such vehicles as the Parker, the Bornetrager, the Coleman, and others of this ilk should be included in lists of American cars. These home-built vehicles were really no different in concept than any of the well-built hot rods and custom cars that have been on the American scene since the mid-1940s. Thus, my feeling is that if such cars are to be included in lists of American cars, then too, every totally original entry at every custom car or hot rod show should also be included on these lists. Why should one include on the American car lists a vehicle that was hammered together by an old man in New England, and then disregard a much better vehicle that was designed and built by a group of teen-agers in Santa Ana? There is no logical reason, and I for one would have been quite happy to leave out the last dozen or so pages of this book.

Why, then, were these cars included? After long discussion, it was decided that there are just enough pompous puff-bellied automotive pontificators in the world who would start screaming "foul" if these historical pets were not included. So, as a pacification move toward this contingent, we have included these vehicles in the last pages. Along with these cars are some of the more serious automotive projects of the era, such as the Howard, the Tjaarda, and the Mercer, which failed to find suitable financial backing in the depression era. Also, here are some of the strange auto-planes which were proposed as a way of combining flying and driving into a single vehicle.

In this book then, is the entire automotive spectrum of the 1930s and early 1940s. This book has been thoroughly researched and compiled by James Moloney. Jim actually began work on this volume in 1974, though for all practical purposes, much of his work has been done over a life-time love affair with the cars of the Thirties. Undoubtedly, a few mistakes have crept into this work – we defy anyone to produce a volume of this magnitude without some errors creeping in. Hopefully, we have kept these mistakes to a minimum. But, if anyone does spot an error, we would appreciate knowing about it so that corrections can be made in future editions. When writing, please address all questions or comments directly to the author: James Moloney, 430 North Turnpike Road, Santa Barbara, Cal., 93111. Now, please enjoy what we feel is the finest encyclopedia of American cars of the 1930s.

George H. Dammann
Automotive Director
Crestline Publishing Co.

Arrowhead

Of all of the non-production cars that were conceived in the 1930s, the one that probably had the most chance of being successful as a production vehicle was the Arrowhead. Ironically, however, this was the one car that the builders had no intention of producing. A total of six were built by Advance Body Works of Los Angeles strictly as promotional vehicles for the Arrowhead Spring Water Co. of Los Angeles. Once the contract for these six cars was completed, the designs were scrapped and no further efforts were made to build or market additional cars.

The Arrowhead was built in 1936 for the Arrowhea Spring Water Co. of Los Angeles. It was a one-off car use chiefly for advertising purposes. The car had a V-8 engin mounted in the rear from which the drive was carrie forward through clutch, transmission and torque tube int the conventional axle. The Arrowhead used a single rea wheel supported by a circular frame that was rotated by full circle. One of its chief advantages was that it could b turned in a radius that was equal to its own length. The ca was capable of carrying three passengers. It was designe by Mr. W. Everett Miller of Murphy Body fame. However this car was built at the Advance Body Works in Lo Angeles, Calif.

Access to the engine of the Arrowhead was gained by raising the entire rear portion. Engine ventilation came through screened grids, disguised as Arrowhead symbols, located on each side of the engine. Camera distortion in this photo makes the car appear much longer than it actually was. Rearward visibility appears to have been non-existant, doubtlessly making the car a real terror to park at curbside.

A model demonstrates the ease of entry or exit from the Arrowhead car. The low-slung 3-wheeler was teardrop shaped, designed to resemble a drop of Arrowhead Spring Water, no doubt. The driver sat at dead center, with passengers arranged at either side and to the rear of the single operator's seat. All six cars were fully roadable and were registered as passenger vehicles in California. A couple of these cars reportedly still exist.

The stripped chassis of the Arrowhead shows some very refined engineering. Unlike many proposed 3-wheelers of this era, steering was by the front wheels, while power was applied through the single rear wheel. Power was by a Ford V-8, with the radiator located to the rear of the engine. It would seem that changing the rear tire would have been a tremendous project, although some provision may have been made for such an emergency. The frame was tubular steel in a triangular pattern.

Auburn

The Auburn was a product of the newly formed Auburn, ord, Duesenberg empire. At this time it was referred to as ɩe Auburn Automobile Co. of Auburn, Ind. The car as produced from 1900 to 1936 inclusive.

The 1930 Auburn came in three series known as 6-85, ·95, and 125. The 6-85 was a 6-cylinder car developing) HP at 3400 RPM. It used a 120-inch wheelbase. he 8-95s were 8-cylinder cars which developed 100 HP 3700 RPM. They had a 125-inch wheelbase. The 125s ere powered by a 125 HP Eight (at 3600 RPM). They sed a 130-inch wheelbase.

All Auburns used Lycoming engines. Each model had an 8 gallon fuel supply. The tire size for the 6-85 was :50 x 18; 8-95s had 6:00 x 18, and the 125s employed :50 x 18s. Auburns had Lockheed hydraulic brakes in 930.

A total of 17 models were available ranging in price om the $995 6-85 Sport Sedan to the Auburn 125 haeton Sedan for $2,095. A total of 13,149 units left uburn, Ind. this year which put the company in 20th osition.

A 1930 Auburn Model 125 Phaeton Sedan had a 130-inch wheelbase. The engine developed 125 H.P. at 3600 R.P.M. This model sold for $2,095 F.O.B. Auburn, Ind.

The Auburn Model 8-95 Sport Sedan for 1930 had a wheelbase five inches less than its big brother, the 125. It was available on a 125-inch chassis and sold for $1,395. This was a version of a close coupled sedan with seating capacity for five.

The 1930 Auburn Custom-Type Phaeton was the same offering as the Phaeton Sedan except for the more luxurious interior it displayed. Both models weighed 3,990 lbs.

The 1930 Auburn 125 Sport Sedan used the 130-inch chassis and was available only with the 8-cylinder Lycoming engine. It weighed 3,995 lbs. The F.O.B. Auburn, Ind. price was $1,795. Bodies were built by Central Body Co.

The 8-98 Auburn Convertible Cabriolet sold for $1,245 in 1931. Seating capacity for four was allowed by the use of a rumble seat. Silent-Constant Mesh was used in Standard Models. Free Wheeling was offered in all Custom Models as regular equipment.

Auburn

A 1931 Auburn 8-98 Custom Coupe for two is shown with all of its finery. Side mounts, driving light, side mount mirrors and unusual trumpet horns rarely seen in 1931 models make this a beautiful car. Base price for this car was $1,195. The Standard version sold for $200 less.

1931

This year Auburn advertising stated "Five New Bodie on One New Chassis." Gone were the 6-cylinder and large 8-cylinder cars from the line-up. Auburn put all its effort into one new series called the 8-98. This model had an 8-cylinder 268.6 cubic inch engine which developed 98 HI at 3400 RPM. The fuel supply amounted to a 20 gallon tank. The tire size was 6:00 x 17 inches. The wheelbas measured 127 inches.

Auburn's big claims for the year were the use o free-wheeling, silent synchro-mesh transmission, automati Bijur chassis lubrication by the touch of a button on th dash, two way hydraulic shock absorbers and a very beautiful automobile. Mechanical brakes were employed for 1931 after having had hydraulics on the 1930 cars

With five styles available the prices ranged from $79 for the 2-passenger Coupe to $1,545 for a 5-passenge Phaeton Sedan.

Auburn sales amounted to 32,301 cars which gave th company 13th position for 1931.

A 1931 Auburn Custom 4-Door Full Sedan sold for $1,195 as illustrated here. Wire wheels were standard on Custom models and optional at extra cost on the Standard line. Whitewalls were extra throughout the line.

The 1931 Auburn 2-Door Brougham used a 127-inch wheelbase. This model was a 5-passenger car. Its horsepower was 98 at 3400 RPM. The Standard models sold for $945 and in Custom style it brought $1,145.

This 1931 Auburn Full Sedan is shown as a 6-wheel model with the accessory metal tire covers. A cloth canvas top also was available at extra cost, as this model displays.

Auburn introduced the 12-cylinder line of cars for 1932. This example was the 12-160 Sedan which offered free-wheeling, selective ride control, and the synchromesh transmission. The 160 and 16-A cars used a 132-inch wheelbase.

Auburn

932

Auburn for 1932 came in both 8 and 12-cylinder models. 'he Eights carried the designations 8-100 and 8-100A. /hile the Twelves had the designations 160 and 160A fter their 12-cylinder title.

Auburns could be ordered in seven different body styles anging from $945 for the 5-passenger Brougham to well nto the two grand bracket for the Speedster.

Each body style was available in the 100, 100A, 160, 60A series. Wheelbase for the 100 and 100-A was 27 inches while the 160 and 160A carried a 132-inch vheelbase. Tire size was 6:00 x 17 in all but the 160-A, /hich used 6:50 x 17 tires.

These cars featured selective ride shock absorbers, free-vheeling, silent and constant mesh transmission, automatic hassis lubrication, and a dual ratio Columbia rear.

As beautiful as these 1932 Auburns were, the depression ad its hooks well into the car. During its model run of 932, the over-all sales showed a meager 7,937, despite he new V-12 which was supposed to hold its share of the uxury market—such as it was in 1932. Auburn ranked in 8th position for the year.

An Auburn Phaeton Sedan for 1932. It was offered either as an 8-100 for $1,145, or 8-100-A for $1,345. Then, in the 12-cylinder line, the car appeared as a 160 or 160-A.

A 1932 Auburn Boat Tail Speedster on the 160-A Chassis. This model developed 160 H.P. at 3400 RPM. The tire size was 6:00 x 17 inches. Not many of these 12-cylinder Speedsters were sold in the bottom of the depression year 1932.

The 1933 Auburn Cabriolet on a V-12 chassis used a 133-inch wheelbase. This model has the standard production wood artillery wheels. This photo was taken in 1951 when the owner was hoping to get $100 for the car. He settled for $75 from a high school boy.

The Auburn 12-165 Salon Sedan for 1933 came on the 133-inch wheelbase chassis. The 12-cylinder cars employed hydraulic brakes in all models. Sidemount spares with wire wheels was the usual combination. These models had trumpet horns mounted under the headlamps.

A 1933 Auburn Series 12-161 Brougham as shown here sold new for $1,195 F.O.B. Auburn, Ind. This was not considered the most desirable body style for 12-cylinder models. Rarely was one sold without sidemount spares as this one was.

Auburn

An Auburn 8-101 Brougham was displayed during an Auburn, Duesenberg display booth at an auto show in 1933. The engines shown in the foreground were a typical sales display to interest future customers. Note the Duesenberg chassis to the left.

1933

In addition to the 8 and 12 Standard and Custo models which were unchanged, there were two ne models – Salon Eight and Salon Twelve with new bod lines, more luxurious furnishings and more elabora equipment. The Eights continued on the 127-inch whee base and the Twelves rode on a new 133-inch wheelbas The Salon models carried the same Lycoming engines the regular line of 1933 Auburns. Body features of Salc models included a new radiator grille and hood desig single bar vertical Vee bumpers, chromium plated hor under the headlamps, and a Vee windshield. Interiors we upholstered in broadcloth.

The Auburn 8 used a 100 HP engine (3400 RPM). Th 12s used the 160 HP version at the same RPM. Tire si was 5:50 x 17 on all 8-101s, while the 8-105s carrie 6:00 x 17s. All models whether 8 or 12, carried a 2 gallon fuel supply. Braking system for the 8-101 w mechanical while the other series used hydraulics. Th 12-cylinder cars also employed the 6:00 x 17 inch tire siz Body styles consisted of 23 models which started at $74 for the 2-passenger coupe and went up to the 2-passeng Speedster for $1,790.

Auburn dropped one place from its 1932 sales positic of 18th. It now was in the 19th sales slot, selling 4,63 cars for the calendar run.

A bevy of beautiful 1933 Auburns are displayed at an Auburn dealership. In the foreground is a sidemounted 8-cylinder 105 Cabriolet for 4 passengers. This model is nicely equipped with wire wheels, whitewalls, and twin spotlamps.

The 1934 Salon Models continued into the third and last year. This year saw the end of the Salon models. Shown here is a 12-cylinder Series 165 Sedan on the 133-inch wheelbase. This model sold for $1,645.

The 1933 Auburn 8-105 Sedan for 5 passengers rode on a 127-inch wheelbase. It developed 100 HP at 3400 RPM.

.934

For 1934, Auburn presented four brand new lines of :ars, the Standard and Custom Sixes on a 119-inch wheel-)ase, as well as the Standard and Custom Eights on a 126-nch wheelbase. All bodies except for the Brougham came n all-steel construction. Mechanical innovations included a vater pump with an automatically adjusted stuffing box vhich never needed attention, Bendix vacuum-operated :lutch, Bendix vacuum booster for braking, and headlight)eams which stayed at a correct level regardless of)assenger load.

Lycoming engines were used in both series. The Auburn Six had an 85 HP engine at 3500 RPM, while the Standard Eight had 100 HP at 3400 RPM with a cast iron head. All Custom Eights with aluminum heads developed 15 HP at 3600 RPM. Auburn Standard Sixes used :50 x 17 inch tires, Custom Six and Standard Eights rode)n 6:25 x 16 inch tires, and the Custom Eight had :50 x 16s to ride on. Fuel tank capacity in all series vas 20 gallons. All had Bendix hydraulic brakes.

In addition to these four new series, the Auburn V-12 vas continued for the third year, but was phased out by he end of the year. These models used a 133-inch wheel-)ase, rode on 6:00 x 17 inch tires and used the same 160 HP engine at 3400 RPM as in 1933. This series was now eferred to as the 12-165. The Coupe was the only model)f the 12-165 Series which wasn't offered in 1934 as in 1933. Five body styles were now available in this series. A total of 19 models throughout the line were offered, anging from a 5-passenger Brougham for $695 to $1,745 or the 2-passenger Speedster.

Auburn sold 4,703 cars, again putting the company in 8th Position for sales.

A side view of a 1934 Auburn 12-165 Sedan. Five body styles were continued through the year for the V-12 Series 165 models. The company sold 4,703 cars during the 1934 calendar year. Most sales came from the 8-cylinder models, however.

A new model for 1934 was this Auburn Custom 8 Cabriolet for 4 passengers. The sidemounts were optional at extra cost. Four models were available in the Custom 8 line. A wheelbase of 126 inches was employed. This model sold for $1,175.

The Phaeton models were only available in the Custom 6 and 8 models, and sold for $945 and $1,225 respectively. This 6-cylinder version offered the speed-streak hood louvers which gave the car the appearance of fleetness even when standing still.

The Auburn Standard 6 Sedan came on a 119-inch chassis. It used the Lycoming 6-cylinder engine which developed 85 H.P. at 3400 RPM. This model was referred to as the Standard 6-52 and sold for $745.

Auburn

The 1934 Auburn Custom 6 Sedan is shown carrying sidemounted tires. These cars were virtually the same as the Standard Series except for more deluxe appointments. Prices began at $845 for this model.

1935

For 1935, besides the regular 6 and 8-cylinder cars, Auburn brought out some models with a supercharged engine which developed 150 HP at 3900 RPM. If equipped with this engine device, the cars were claimed to do 100 MPH. Eights without superchargers developed 115 HP at 3600 RPM. This series was known as the 851. The Six came with an 85 HP engine at 3500 RPM and was called the 653.

The company's new supercharged line came in five models, including a racy speedster with well skirted fenders, boat tail back and minus running boards. It was the top of this line. The car's fabric top disappeared into a compartment behind the seat. Coming from the hood were four 3-inch exhaust pipes of flexible stainless steel.

Tire size for 6-cylinder cars was 5:50 x 17; the 8-cylinder form was a 6:50 x 16 inch tire. Both series used a 20 gallon fuel tank. Bendix hydraulic brakes were used in both series for the year.

A total of 15 models were available, ranging from a 5-passenger 6-cylinder Brougham for $695 to the Supercharged Speedster for two passengers at $2,245.

Auburn reached 5,163 units for the year, putting the company in 18th Place for sales again this year.

Auburn did offer the public a taxi in the Standard 653 Series for 1935. It was sold only on a fleet sale basis. This model, not in taxi form, sold for $795. The 6-cylinder engine developed 85 H.P. at 3500 RPM.

The Auburn 8 Sedan for 1935 was referred to as an 851 Series. This model cost $1,045. It used the Lycoming 8-cylinder engine developing 115 H.P. at 3600 RPM. It also was available in Supercharged form developing 150 H.P. at 3900 RPM. The Supercharger allowed the car to do 100 MPH.

The 1935 Auburn Custom Six Sedan was available as a 6-wheeled side-mounted sedan. The side mount treatment was optional at extra cost. Hydraulic brakes were used on both 6 and 8-cylinder cars in 1935.

A 1935 Auburn 851 Phaeton Sedan used the 127-inch wheelbase. This model sold for $1.225 in standard form.

1936

The death knell sounded for Auburn this year, after a total of only 1,848 cars left the factory at Auburn, Ind. In reality, the 1936 Auburns were practically the same cars that had been offered in 1935, except for a few minor changes. One such change consisted of a different wheel size on the Sixes – from 5:50 x 17 to 6:00 x 16. Also, there was a change in the model designations, with the Sixes now being called the 654s and the Eights being known as 852s. New for the year was a 7-passenger Sedan in the 852 Series being available in Supercharged version, and a Cabriolet offered for this year only. Altogether, 18 models were available.

Horsepower remained at 85 at 3500 RPM in the 654 Series; 115 HP at 3600 RPM in the 852 Series, and 150 HP at 4000 RPM in the Supercharged models. The fuel supply remained at 20 gallons, and Bendix hydraulic brakes continued to be used on all cars.

Total sales for the year left the company in 18th Position in the sales race, but the 1,848 units sold were not enough to stave off the creditors, and the fine old company had to shut its doors. The attractive home office building remains in the pretty little town of Auburn, and today houses the headquarters and museum of the Auburn-Cord-Duesenberg Club and once a year plays host to the annual meeting of this organization.

A 1935 Supercharged Auburn Phaeton Sedan with rear-mounted spare was used by the Indiana State Police. These cars were used both to benefit the state because of their quick acceleration and as a good ad for the Auburn Co. to help spur along sales. This model wears the full wheel cover discs.

A 1935 Auburn 851 Cabriolet. This unit is displayed with Vogue whitewall tires, sidemount mirrors, factory-installed spot-lamp and a custom mini-trunk nicely arranged on the rear body under the rumble seat. It was priced at $1,175 in stripped form.

The Auburn Speedster was offered both in 1935 and 1936. This example happens to be a 1936 style. Speedsters were only available in Supercharged version, developing 150 H.P. at 3900 RPM. These cars received a dash plaque attesting that Abe Jenkins had tested them at 100 MPH.

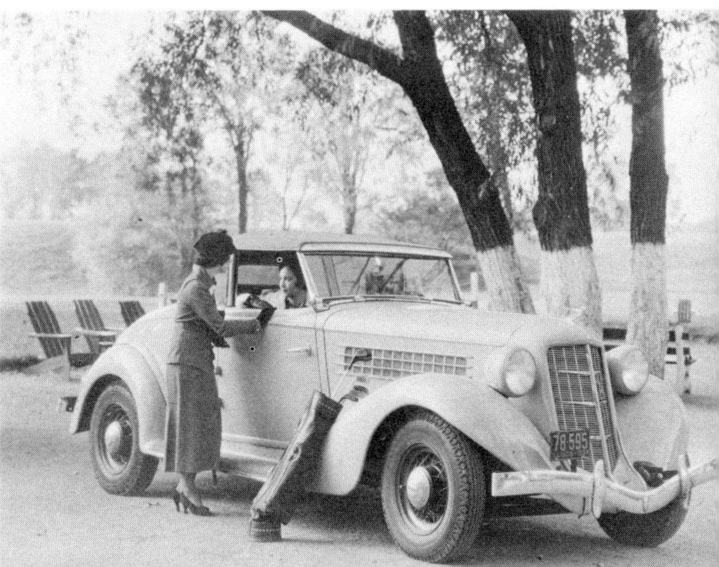
The 653 Cabriolet for 1935 came on a 120-inch wheelbase. It seated four with the aid of the rumble seat. This 6-cylinder model sold for $895 F.O.B. Auburn, Ind. The 653's Series came with painted headlamps. Chrome lamps were available at extra cost.

Auburn

The 1936 version of the Auburn Sedan was virtually the same car offered in 1935. This new model was referred to as an 852 as it showed on the radiator grille. This model is shown wearing full wheel discs and sidemounts with metal covers. It was priced at $1,095 for 5 passengers.

A 1936 Auburn 654 Brougham was a roomy 2-door sedan for 5 passengers. With extra wide doors it made for easy entrance and exit especially for rear seat passengers. It sold for $745.

A twin to the 1936 654 Brougham was the 852 Brougham. This model came on a 127-inch wheelbase with a 115 H.P. engine or 150 H.P. if in Supercharged fashion. It was priced at $995 as an 852 and at $1,445 with the Supercharger.

AUBURN

The 654 1936 Phaeton Sedan is shown above in a rather sporty manner with its top down. This model sold for $995 minus all options.

An 852 Cabriolet for 1936 was available as a comfortable closed model or smart open car at the whim of its owner. In standard version it sold for $1,225. If the Supercharged pipes were added, the price increased to $1,675.

Austin

The Austin was new on the market in 1930. The car came from Butler, Pa. and was manufactured under the title of the American Austin Co. until 1935.

The Austin Automobile Co. of Grand Rapids, Mich. built cars of luxury quality until 1918. The new company in Butler, Pa. was formed by another group of businessmen headed by a James Brandt, formerly of General Motors, who had held the position of vice president in charge of production at Oakland.

The little car carried the radiator emblem of a bantam rooster, which often made people laugh, especially if the owner happened to have fame connected with his name. Many of the Austin owners and admirers were Hollywood celebrities. Among them were: Al Jolson, Buster Keaton, Marion Davies, and Laurel and Hardy.

The Austin had a 75-inch wheelbase and used 3.75 x 18 inch tires. Its 4-cylinder engine developed 13 HP at 3200 RPM. It had a 5 gallon fuel tank. The bodies were designed by Count Alexis de Sakhnoffsky. The Hayes Body Corp. of Grand Rapids, Mich. constructed the body. The body styles for 1930 consisted of a Coupe and Roadster.

The Austin had difficulty getting off the ground at first. Many felt it was a stock selling scheme or swindle on the public. Finally, things took a change for the better, and on May 21st, 1930, the company announced its actual production had started. On June 21st of that year, the newspapers gave the country its first look of the new car. Between June and August the company had over 184,000 unfilled orders. The company had plans for producing 60,000 cars the first year. With business conditions growing worse, these orders never came to be a reality, and the company was dying financially.

The Austin sold for $445 which was almost the lowest priced car in the country at that time.

Austin placed in 28th Position by selling 3,633 cars for its first year of production.

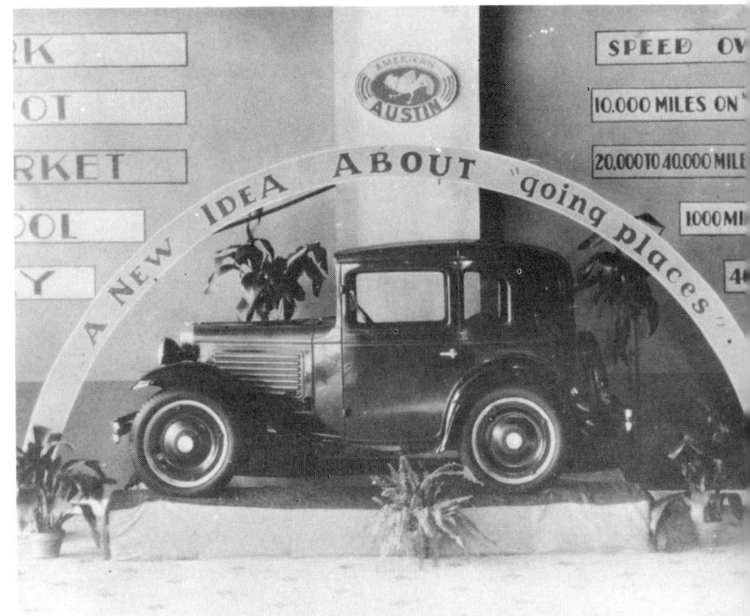

Austin often used unusual types of displays to bring the public forth to see the new models. Here, a 1930 model is shown claiming it can be used for work, going to the depot, market, school, or just as a plaything.

The Austin Roadster for 1930 actually didn't enter the market until October, 1930. It did prove popular, especially with the few more affluent left in the country at that time. It sold for $445 F.O.B. Butler, Pa.

An advertisement for Austin in 1930 told of all the great features this little car had to offer, especially to those over 6 feet tall. It claimed there was plenty of leg room for two 6-feet tall people in the front compartment.

A 1930 Austin Coupe showing its agility on the off-the-path roads where demonstrations often showed their ruggedness. Price tag for this model was $445 F.O.B. Butler, Pa. Licensing agreements with Austin of England called for a royalty payment of $7 for each car produced in the U. S.

Austin

A 1931 Austin Model 138 Business Coupe is being assembled at the Butler, Pa., headquarters. Prices ranged from $445 to $550 for 1931.

1931

Austin remained basically unchanged for 1931. The Roadster body style, which came out late in 1930, had a seat which measured 4 inches wider than the Coupe. Some historians claim this car to have been a 1931 model rather than a 1930. Whichever way, the Roadster came in one of two colors: cream and black or green and black.

The Austin again sold for $445 in Roadster style, and went up to $550 for the DeLuxe Coupe Cabriolet which was of very rare style. This model even carried landau irons.

Sales were becoming scarcer for Austin, and by the end of 1931 only 1,279 cars were built, which placed the company in 27th Position in the sales race.

1932

The Austin for 1932 was beginning its third year of production. From continuing sales that grew worse, the Austin factory closed its doors in the spring of 1932. It reorganized, and a man by the name of Rueben Gill became general manager. Liquidating most of the firm's belongings seemed the only way to go. Roy Evans stepped in and purchased all Austins that were available. He sold these cars for $295 each. After this move, Austin again was reorganized and sold 3,846 cars during the second half of 1932, which put the company in 19th Position.

Austin for the year came in four different models: the Business Coupe for $330, Runabout and Standard Coupe, each selling for $395, and the DeLuxe Cabriolet which brought the astronomical price of $475. All were 2-passenger vehicles and employed a 75-inch wheelbase. These cars weighed between 1,020 and 1,040 pounds and could get as high as 40 m.p.g. The tire size was 3.75 x 18 inches. The brake system was of the mechanical type. Gasoline capacity was five gallons.

Buster Keaton and sons are playing in his 1931 Austin Roadster. These cars carried the Alexis de Sakhnoffsky styling. The bodies were manufactured by the Hayes Body Corporation of Grand Rapids, Mich. A choice of two colors were available – cream with black fenders or green with black fenders. At the end of the year only 1,279 Austins had been built.

This Model 138 Business Coupe for 1931 is ready for delivery. It sold for $445. The interior of these models was done in corduroy.

A truckload of six 1931 Coupes are being delivered to an Austin dealer. All models were assembled in the one factory at Butler, Pa.

Austin

933

Austin was now beginning its fourth year manufacturing ıe sub-compact car designed to give economical trans- ortation during the depression years. Austin for 1933 ʼas basically the same offering as in 1932. The com- ression ratio was changed from 5:00 to 5:10 for 1933. 'here were still four models, but with different names. 'hey were now the Roadster for $305, Business Coupe for 275, Special Coupe for $295, and the Coupe for $315. .ach model carried a lower price tag than in 1932. All were ctually the same vehicles with a 13 HP engine at 3200 .PM. Tire size was still 3:75 x 18. It carried a five gallon ıel tank. Brakes were of the mechanical type.

Sales for the company placed it in 18th Position for the ear, with a total run of 4,726.

934

The company was now starting in its fifth year of roduction. The car was known for its economical trans- ortation, giving as much as 40 m.p.g. from its five allon fuel supply.

The Business Coupe had increased $20 in price, now ·lling for $295 which was the lowest price model. In ddition to this model, there was the Roadster for $305, tandard Coupe for $345, the DeLuxe Coupe for $365, ıd small pick-up and panel deliveries. All models were -passenger vehicles giving out 13 HP at 3200 RPM. Tire ze continued at 3:75 x 18. Braking was of a mechanical ʼpe.

Sales for the year placed it at the lower end, giving it a 2nd Position from 1,057 units being sold.

A 1932 Austin Business Coupe is showing its fleetness, as this advertisement depicts the little car being used in a quick trip to the depot. Economy was one of the big factors, for long or short trips.

The thoughts behind this 1932 photo show the nimbleness of the Austin in being able to park between tiny open spaces. The company advertised that the steering was effortless, which made the little car handle like a polo pony.

Austin was noted for its stunt advertising. This 1933 model was typical of their antics. The car is running on a suspended cable at Pudding River, Barlow, Oregon. Two strands supported the car as it ran under its own power. A third cable steadied the car at the top. The gimmick they were trying to prove was economy, as the car travelled the 120 ft. crossing 1,760 times on a gallon of gas.

More Austins went to new owners in California than in any other state. Many Hollywood celebrities bought these cars for fun and also economy. A Hollywood actress of 1933, Bernice Clare, sits proudly on top of her new acquisition.

Austin

A little face lift was in store for the 1934 models. This DeLuxe Coupe, referred to as the 375, cost $20 more than the Standard Coupe. Its price was $365 which was $50 more than the 1933 models. A total of 1,057 units sold for the calendar year.

THE PANEL

The 1934 Panel Delivery and Pick-up was a very economical means of transportation for small delivery purposes. Grocery stores, pharmacies, florists, and maintenance firms often purchased these vehicles which were priced under $350.

The 1934 Austin Roadster, which many historians state was never built, is shown here in all its glory. The car sold for $305.

1935

American Austin Co., which had been producing cars since 1930, at the end of this year closed its doors to revamp and change its name to Bantam in 1937. It would continue under this name until 1941.

The 1935 model was actually the same car as in 1934. The only change consisted of a $20 increase for the DeLuxe Coupe, making this a $385 car. The other forms were continued starting at $295 for the Business Coupe. Each model used the 13 HP engine at 3200 RPM, carrying a 5 gallon fuel tank and rode on 3:75 x 18 inch tires. Mechanical brakes were used.

Registration figures were not available as so few models were turned out.

THE PONY EXPRESS (Closed)

The Pony Express, as it was called for 1934, was used by the popular door-to-door home vegetable tradesman. Not many of these models were ever produced. It is shown with canopy down in the upper photo and open in the bottom photo.

The 1935 Austins were virtually the same offerings as the 1934 cars. The company closed its doors at the end of 1935 to reorganize for the Bantam, which was scheduled for 1937 but didn't appear until 1938. Seen here was a typical used car lot of a Bantam dealer in 1941 trying to dispose of both new and used merchandise. Note the 1935 DeLuxe being offered as NEW. Next to it is a slightly used model for $25 down.

Bantam

The Bantam for 1937 was from the reorganized facilities ־ the American Austin Co. of Butler, Pa. Actually, the)37 Bantam never was produced even though it was ıtalogued for a Business Coupe, Standard Coupe, DeLuxe oupe, Standard Roadster, Custom Roadster, Cab Pick-up, ıd Panel Delivery. All models were to have a 4-cylinder ıgine developing 20 HP at 4000 RPM from 45.6 cubic ch displacement. The brake system was to be mechanical. he tire size was 5:00 x 15 inches. All models were to use 75-inch wheelbase.

The company advertising claimed it cost less than cents a mile for gasoline, tires, and oil, and stated the ır would travel in excess of 60 MPH. Prices were to range om $380 for the Business Coupe to $492 for the Custom oadster. But the real Bantams didn't begin to roll from ıe assembly line until late 1937 or early 1938, and were gistered as 1938 cars.

The Bantam DeLuxe Coupe interior was available in mohair or velour. Exteriors were available in a choice of colors at no additional cost. This model was to sell for $431.

The 1937 Bantam Standard Roadster was to sell for $431, the same as the DeLuxe Coupe. Safety glass was optional on the 1937 cars at $10 extra.

The top of the Bantam line for 1937 was to be the Custom Roadster at $492. An additional choice of color combinations were to be available for this model. A top speed of 60 HPH was claimed for these cars.

A view of the 1938 Bantam chassis. This chassis would remain basic to the car until its final demise.

The proposed 1937 retail delivered prices of the new Bantam cars F.O.B. Butler, Pa., began at $313 for the chassis alone and increased to $492 for the Custom Roadster. These prices were effective September 15, 1936. The 1937 Bantam Pick-Up Truck sold for $427. The company sales brochures stated it cost less than ¾¢ a mile for gasoline, oil, and tires. Wood side racks were an accessory.

The 1937 Bantam Panel Truck claimed an average of 40,000 miles on a set of tires. It was easy to load, as the rear door was 31 inches wide and 31 inches high. The load capacity could handle up to a quarter ton.

The Bantam Business Coupe for 1937 was to be the ideal car for professional people, salesmen, and business people. It was to sell for $308. But, like the other 1937 Bantams, it was only catalogued and didn't appear until 1938.

Bantam

A perfectly restored example of a 1938 Bantam Custom Roadster was displayed at the Contemporary Historical Vehicle Assn. car show at Buena Park, Cal., in 1974. Note the World War II gasoline "A" coupon sticker on the windshield. This model sold for $479.

1938

The Bantam came on the market in 1938 as a new c It was designated the Bantam 60 and was to sell in t $400 price range. The car did carry some of its p decessor's dimensions, but had been changed in ma ways. The wheelbase was continued at 75 inches. But t four cylinder engine increased its HP to 20 at 4000 RI with a 45.6 cubic inch displacement. The engine used plated Bohnalite Autothermic pistons. The engine w mounted in rubber. The brake system was of t mechanical type. Tread of the front tires measured inches, while the rear consisted of 42-inch tread.

Three body styles in passenger car form were availab each weighing approximately 1,200 lbs. Prices ranged frc $439 for the 2-passenger Business Coupe to $479 for Roadster. Bantam placed 18th in car sales, selling unc 1,500 cars for the year.

Even after the 1938 sales brochures were handed out to prospective customers, along came another change in the fall of 1937 before the actual car was sold. Shown here is a prototype of the 1938 model, with a fixed windshield. The actual cars never used a stationary windshield.

A 1939 Bantam Boulevard Delivery was offered by Bantam as a custom model. Florists used these sometimes as an eye catcher for delivery purposes. Very few of these were ever built. Note the carriage lamps on the rear panels. Fender skirts and whitewall tires were standard equipment.

The 1939 Panel Delivery was often used by small maintenance companies, as it gave economical transportation. Not many of this style were sold during its production.

The 1939 Bantam Coupe was mainly meant to be a 2-passenger car, but if really needed, three could be accommodated. This model was offered in less than half the year's production. It sold for $439.

939

In 1939 Bantam was in its second full year of pro-uction. For this year, the company offered six models at rices lower than the previous year. The company pro-uced the Standard Coupe for $399, which was their owest priced car. This was a reduction of $40 over the 938 model. The top price was $565 for the new 4-assenger Station Wagon. Commercial vehicles were also atalogued by the company.

The Bantam maintained its horsepower at 20 at 4000 RPM. The fuel supply again was a five gallon tank. Tire ize continued at 5:00 x 15 on a 75-inch wheelbase. Tin lated Bohnalite Autothermic pistons were again used, ith rubber engine mounting on all corners. The company laced 20th in sales by selling approximately 1,200 auto-nobiles for the model run.

The 1939 Bantam Station Wagon was available for $565, which was the most expensive model. The bodies were built by cabinet makers and cost an additional $180. These models were very rare even in 1939. They weighed 1,411 lbs.

A view of the 1939 Bantam Roadster and Panel Pick-up outside the factory headquarters in Butler, Pa. The Roadster is fully equipped with skirts, whitewall tires, tonneau cover, fold down windshield, and the very rare "dinner bell gong" center bumper grille guard.

The rarely seen 1940 Bantam Utility Wagon came with an all-steel body and cost $50 less than its wood bodied brother. F.O.B. price on this model was $525. Total passenger capacity was four people. Bantam did catalog a car for 1941. However, the only models that were sold were leftover 1940 cars, as the company closed its doors to passenger and small truck production on June 30, 1940.

The 1940 Bantam Custom Club Roadster was offered for the first time under this model designation. The company advertised it as being smart, thrifty, rugged and able. It sold for $525. Note the different chevron treatment on this model's skirts over the previous examples.

The 1940 Bantam Pick-up changed very slightly from the previous two years. The side panels on the hood are minus the ventilators which some early 1940 models experimented with.

The big news from Butler, Pa. for 1941 was the wartime contract to start and build the Bantam Jeep. An early example of the Bantam Jeep is shown above demonstrating its maneuverability in a tight turn. This experimental model featured 4-wheel steering as well as 4-wheel drive.

One of the first 1941 Bantam Jeeps, dressed in its khaki clothing, ready to do anything it's asked to do. This vehicle put Bantam in the black, showing a profit of $16,965 by June, 1941. A total of 1,500 Bantam Jeeps were produced.

A special-built 1941 Bantam Jeep was designed to carry various pieces of fighting equipment and extinguishers. This model wasn't used in combat.

Bantam

1940

Bantam for 1940 was in its third year of production which also was actually its last year of production. Those models sold in 1941 were leftover cars from 1940 even though the company did put out a brochure in 1941. The 1941 production was only military vehicles.

In 1940, Bantam offered six models as it did in 1939 but body designations were changed to Custom Club Roadster and Convertible Sedan. The other body styles were Roadster, Coupe, Station Wagon, Panel Delivery and Quarter-Ton Pick-up.

The engine had an increased bore, from 2.20 to 2.26 inches, and stroke from 3 to 3-1/8 inches. The improved engine developed 22 horsepower at 3800 RPM. The fuel supply was still a five gallon tank. The tire size was 4:00 x 15 on all models. The brake system again was the mechanical type. The hood locking device was located under the hood. In the engine room was where the battery was located.

The Bantam was priced from $399 for the Business Coupe to $575 for the 4-passenger Station Wagon. Production figures are not available as the company virtually closed its doors at the end of its fiscal year June 30, 1940. It had no working capital. During the 2½ year life span that Bantam did have, approximately 6,700 cars and trucks were produced.

1941

The 1941 Bantams that were sold were really 1940 cars, and it is interesting to note even though the factory doors had closed June 30, 1940, the company did put out a 1941 brochure showing the same offerings as in 1940 only labelling them in the brochure as 1941 cars. All mechanical features stayed the same as the 1940 models and prices were the same too.

Bantam's big news for 1941 was a contract to build the Bantam Jeep for government purposes. In March 1941, the company received a $1,750,000 contract to produce 1,500 Jeeps. By June, 1941, Bantam was in the black for the first time in its four year history, showing a profit of $16,965. In July of that year, the government decided on a standardization policy to have one company build the Jeep. The contract finally wound up at Willys as it could produce more vehicles per day. The final Bantam Jeep was produced shortly before the Pearl Harbor attack. A total of 2,675 Jeeps were produced, which brought an end to the American Bantam Car Co. of Butler, Pa. The company survided the war, building small cargo trailers for Jeeps, and continued with this production for civilian use after the war.

The 1940 Bantam Station Wagon was practically the same car as in 1939 except the bore was increased from 2.20 to 2.26 inches and the stroke changed from 3 to 3-1/8 inches. Prices on this model also increased $10 to $575.

Blackhawk

The Blackhawk was a division of the Stutz Motor Car Co. of America. The company headquarters were located in Indianapolis, Ind. The Blackhawk was built as an automobile, not as a model of Stutz, since 1929. This was its final year of production in 1930.

The Blackhawk was referred to as one word, not two separate words as it was when considered to be just a Stutz model. The Blackhawk, being a junior Stutz, gave a choice of a 6-cylinder Stutz engine or an 8-cylinder Lycoming engine. The Blackhawk Six had an 85 HP engine (3200 RPM) while the Eight developed 90 HP at the same RPM. Both models came on 127½-inch wheelbases and rode on 6:00 x 19 inch tires. The fuel supply in each car was a 20 gallon tank. Lockheed hydraulic brakes were used on these cars.

A total of 20 models were available ranging in price from $1,995 for a 6-cylinder 5-passenger Coupe to $2,655 for the 8-cylinder 5-passenger Deauville. Production was so low it was ranked with Stutz, and figures are not available.

This 1930 Blackhawk 5-passenger Sedan was available both in 6 or 8-cylinder version. The Six used a Stutz engine of 84 H.P. and the Eight had a Lycoming engine that developed 90 H.P. All 6 and 8-cylinder sedans sold for $2,395 F.O.B. Indianapolis.

The 1930 Blackhawk 5-passenger Coupe was available both in 6 or 8-cylinder style and carried the same price tag of $1,995. The 6-cylinder models weighed 4,118 lbs. and the Lycoming 8-cylinder cars weighed 4,255 lbs.

The 1930 Blackhawk 4-passenger Speedster carried a LeBaron Body. Prices began at $2,535 and rose to $2,735 depending on equipment used. All models of the Speedster were available with or without tonneau cowl.

The 1930 Blackhawk Chantilly came with side mounts and sold for $2,595. Its body builder was Weymann. The wheelbase of all Blackhawks was 127½ inches.

The 1930 Blackhawk Deauville had Weymann as its body builder. Prices for either the 6 or 8-cylinder car was $2,655. This was the most expensive model in the line.

Brewster

The heart shaped grille on this automobile could only be the 1934 Brewster Town Car. The Brewster was built from 1934 through 1936. The cars were built under the direction of John S. Inskip, an automotive connoisseur. Most Brewsters used Ford running gear.

Brewster turned out a limited number of luxury cars on a semi-production basis with the Springfield Mfg. Co. of Massachusetts being its headquarters. The car was well recognized by its split front bumpers and heart shaped grille.

Springfield Manufacturing Co. turned out about 300 of these cars from 1934 through 1936. The price ran between $3,000 and $3,500. Most of these cars carried Ford running gear and many Ford body parts, but a few utilized Buick components.

The idea of using Ford parts was decided by John S. Inskip, who was well known as a designer and connoisseur of fine motor cars. Since Brewster had felt the pinch of the depression in its carriage building trade and the Rolls Royce assembly facility in Springfield, Mass. was now practically vacant, this seemed like the ideal spot to produce a new car at a modest price that would be socially acceptable for those who still wished for and could afford the better things of life.

These cars were sold through the Inskip Showroom, then at 32 E. 57th St. in New York City. For the first year of production only the Town Car was available. It was on a 127-inch wheelbase.

This highly unusual vehicle is a one-off Town Car built on a Buick chassis by the famous Brewster Co. of Long Island City, N.Y. The car, which uses a Limited 90 chassis, was sold under the name Brewster, and the Buick name does not appear at all. Other such models were built on Ford and Packard chassis, again with the name Brewster appearing on all exterior surfaces. The company was noted for its fine body work, especially in town cars such as this. For years, its trademark was the heart-shaped grille, snow-plow bumpers, and huge headlights. All body work was custom designed. A few other such models were turned out on Buick chassis this year, but this is the only one to use the Limited 90 chassis. It was originally built for Mr. J. Whitney of the N.Y. Stock Exchange, and is today owned by Noel Thompson of New Vernon, N.J. It is finished in maroon lacquer with black rear fenders and a maroon leather top.

1935

For 1935, the Brewster entered its second year of production. The Brewster continued with its same lines as the previous year, with flared front fenders and heart-shaped grille. For this year, other models were made available: a Limousine, 4-passenger Convertible, and a Coupelet, which actually was a convertible coupe.

Little advertising was ever done on the car, as the home office felt there were people wanting a fine "carriage" who didn't need gaudy sales brochures to entice them to buy.

Besides using Ford running gear, some Brewsters this year were delivered with other make engines and body trim. Among them were Lincoln, Cadillac and Buick.

1936

This was Brewster's final year for building its "flared and heart shaped" Ford. The car, as in the previous two years, came as a Town Car and for the past year as a Coupe, and Convertible Coupe. All sold in the $3,000 to $3,500 price category, and all working gear was Ford at that price category. Many of the body parts rear of the cowl were also Ford. Around 300 of these automobiles were sold to the public, many of whom were the Hollywood, Beverly Hills and New York clientele.

Brewsters used a 127-inch wheelbase and generally used 7:00 x 16 tires. The brakes were Ford mechanical.

Finally, much to the heartbreak of John Inskip, liquidation of the Brewster facility was ordered on June 24, 1936 – one more car that couldn't cope with the depression.

This 1935 Brewster is a 4-passenger Convertible, or as the rare sales brochure listed, a "Coupelet." Besides Ford running gear, some Brewsters were delivered with Lincoln, Cadillac, and Buick components.

Buick

Buick, a product of General Motors Corp., had been built since 1903, with the main factory located at Flint, Michigan.

For 1930, Buick offered three separate models referred to as 40, 50, and 60. All were 6-cylinder cars. The Series 40 developed 80 HP. Series 50 and 60 developed 98 HP, and all at 2800 RPM. The Series 40 used a 118-inch wheelbase and rode on 5:50 x 19 inch tires. The Series 50 had a 124-inch wheelbase using 6:50 x 19 inch tires, and the Series 60 used a 132-inch chassis with 7:00 x 19 inch tires. The Series 40 cars had a 19 gallon fuel tank and the other two series used a 22 gallon fuel supply.

Seventeem models were available among the three series. Prices ran from $1,260 for a Series 40 2-passenger Business Coupe to $2,070 for the Series 60 7-passenger Limousine Sedan.

Buick placed in 3rd position by selling 119,265 units, which also included its companion car, the Marquette, which were referred to as Model 30 cars.

A 1930 Buick 4-passenger Sport Roadster, Model 40 sold for $1,310. It used a 118-inch chassis. The 5:50 x 19-inch tires were used in the 40 Series.

The Buick 60 Series 5-passenger Special Sedan for 1930 sold for $1,695. This model weighed 4,330 lbs. All Series 60 cars had 7:00 x 19-inch tires.

A Series 50 Buick 124-inch wheelbase 4-passenger Coupe. The Series 50 for 1930 consisted of only two models, the Coupe and a Sedan. The Coupe sold for $1,510 and the Sedan version sold for $30 more. This 6-wheel Coupe uses wooden wheels as standard equipment.

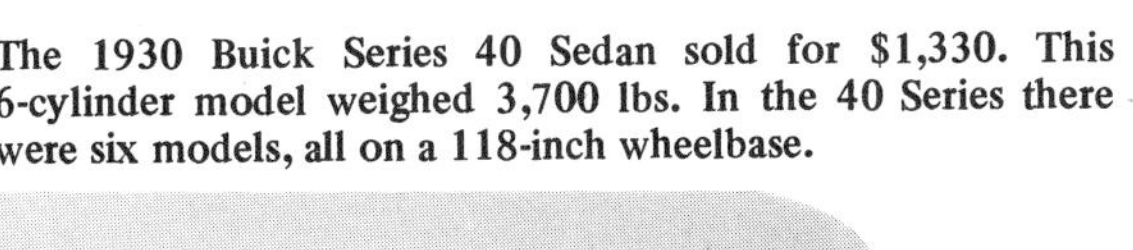

The 1930 Buick Series 40 Sedan sold for $1,330. This 6-cylinder model weighed 3,700 lbs. In the 40 Series there were six models, all on a 118-inch wheelbase.

This 1930 Buick Series 60 132-inch wheelbase Convertible Coupe was a mid-season introduction. Seven body styles were available in this series that ranged from $1,585 to $2,070 F.O.B. Flint, Mich.

Buick

1931

The 1931 Buicks offered three new 8-cylinder cars in four series, with the largest coming on two wheelbases. The use of synchro-mesh transmission, carburetor silencer and oil temperature regulator were Buick's claims for 1931.

The Series designations were 50, 60, 80, and 90. The Series 50 developed 77 HP at 3200 RPM. Series 60 had a 90 HP engine at 3000 RPM and both Series 80 and 90 used the 104 HP engine at 2800 RPM. The Series 50 had a 16 gallon fuel tank. Series 60 used a 19 gallon supply, and the two larger models required 22 gallon tanks. The tire size was 5:25 x 18 inches on Series 50, and the 60 models used 5:50 x 19 tires. The 80 and 90 models used 6:50 x 19 inch tires. The wheelbase was 114 inches on the Series 50, 118 inches on the 60 Series, 124 inches for the Series 80, and 132 inches for Series 90 cars.

A total of 20 models were available ranging in price from $1,025 for a 2-passenger Business Coupe to $2,035 for the 7-passenger Limousine.

Buick sales dropped this year to 88,417 cars which was the first time in over 10 years that Buick sales fell under 100,000 units. This drop put Buick in Fourth Place for sales.

The 1930 Buick 5-passenger Coupe on the 132-inch chassis sold for $1,675 F.O.B. Flint. The wire wheel equipment was extra.

The 1930 Buick Model 60L was a 7-passenger Limousine. It sold for $2,070 which was the most expensive Buick for the year. Buick placed in 3rd position for the calendar year.

A 1931 Buick Series 90 7-passenger Sedan on the 132-inch wheelbase. Wire wheels and side mounts were available, in this series only, at no extra cost. This model weighed 4,435 pounds, but if ordered as a Limousine it was 4,495 lbs. The straight 7-passenger sedan was $1,935 and as a Limousine cost $100 more.

This 1931 Buick 8-50 was the first of the 8-cylinder cars. The 50 Series was considered the low priced line for the year. This Sport Roadster was used in a typical movie of that time. The car sold for $1,055. It was available on the 114-inch chassis.

An 8-90 Buick Coupe for 1931 cost $1,765. The seating capacity of this car allowed for five. The engine developed 104 H.P. at 2,800 RPM both in the 80 and 90 Series. Buick placed Fourth in sales with 88,417 cars being sold for the calendar year.

1932

For 1932, Buick again came in four series: 50, 60, 80, and 90. Price wise, they began with a 2-passenger Coupe for $935 in the Series 50 and rode out to a $2,055 Limousine in the Series 90. Wheelbase for the 50 Series was 114 inches. The cars weighed between 3,275 and 3,510 lbs. Tire size was 5:50 x 18. The 50s had a horsepower rating of 78 at 2200 RPM. Eight models could be ordered.

The Series 60 came in seven different models. They weighed between 3,795 and 3,980 lbs. Tire size was 6:00 x 18. Horsepower was rated 90 at 3000 RPM. The wheelbase was 118 inches.

The Series 80 had only two models. They weighed 4,335 and 4,450 lbs. These two models rode on a 126-inch wheelbase with a tire size of 7:00 x 18. Horsepower was rated at 104 at 2900 RPM.

The Series 90 was classed as Buick's largest series and had nine offerings. They weighed between 4,450 and 4,720 lbs. Tire size was 7:00 x 18. Horsepower was same as Series 80. The wheelbase was 134 inches.

Buick's contribution to the auto industry this year was the synchro-mesh transmission, and a vacuum operated clutch, which were introduced by other manufacturers too.

In 1932, with everything almost at a standstill, Buick's sales slumped by more than 50%, with 41,522 units being built. Buick still had the necessary dealer outlets, 2,105 to be exact, and the third largest dealer organization of GM, but the buyers weren't there. Buick sales slipped to Seventh spot for 1932.

With the depression bearing down hard on Buick's sales, the most popular car of the year had a production run of only 10,803 for domestic sales. It was the Series 50 4-door Sedan, Model 57, which cost only $995 and weighed 3,450 pounds. Wire wheels were an accessory on this car. Silk shades were provided on the rear and quarter windows. This nicely restored example is owned by Gerald Woods of Charlotte, Mich. In addition to regular production, Buick built 504 Series 50 stripped chassis for domestic sales and 140 for export, and also produced 20 body-less Series 50 Phaetons for export.

The new 1932 Series 90 Club Sedan Buick offered was known as Model 91. This series featured the close coupled sedan styling that was becoming very popular at that time. The built-in trunk was standard equipment for this model. The Model 91 sold for $1,820.

A huge yet attractive car was the Series 90 7-passenger Sedan, Model 90, which now used a new chassis of 134-inch wheelbase length. The car cost $1,955 and weighed 4,695 pounds. Buick built 1,368 for domestic sales and 19 for export. In addition, it produced 192 stripped Series 90 chassis for domestic sales and 24 for export.

The most popular car in the Series 60 line was the 5-passenger Sedan, Model 67, which had a run of 9,013 for domestic sales and 47 for export. The large car weighed 3,980 pounds and cost $1,310, with the sidemounts being extra. Upholstery was in gray or taupe mohair or gray whipcord, with heavy velvet carpeting in the rear compartment. Other rear compartment appointments included a folding robe rail, foot rest, assist cords, arm rests and ash trays on each side of the rear seat.

Buick

A fresh new look for Buick in 1932 was offered, as this front view shows. This particular model belongs to the 50 Series. Its lowest priced model began with the $935 Business Coupe. The top of the Series 50 line sold for $1,080 as a Convertible Phaeton. The side mount treatment was optional at extra cost.

1933

For 1933, Buick offered its public 20 different body styles in four series. This was six less than it offered in 1932. Cars ranged in price from $995 for the Business Coupe, Series 50, to $2,055 for the Series 90 7-passenger Limousine. Even though there were fewer models, these cars carried handsome bodies with wheelbases lengthened four to nine inches. All models carried the sloping Vee radiator grille and skirted fenders. A dash button operated the solenoid to the engine starter.

All models carried Delco inertia controlled shock absorbers. Steel spoked wheels were standard on all models. Series 50 cars had an 86 HP engine at 3200 RPM. Series 60 cars had a 97 HP engine at 3200 RPM. Series 80 and 90 cars had a 113 engine at 3200 RPM.

All Series 50 cars carried 6:00 x 17 inch tires. Series 60 used 6:50 x 17 inch tires, and both the 80 and 90 Series rode on 7:00 x 17 inch tires. Wheelbases for these cars were 119 for the Series 50, 127 inches for Series 60, 130 inches for the Series 80 cars, and the Series 90 used a 138-inch wheelbase. Fuel capacity in the 50 Series was a 16 gallon tank. Series 60 used a 19 gallon capacity, and the 80 and 90 Series both used 22 gallon tanks.

Sales position for Buick in 1933 was the Eighth spot, selling 40,620 cars, the lowest production the company had hit since 1914.

The 1933 Buick Series 90 Model 91 Club Sedan. A total of 1,637 of this model were manufactured. Its price remained the same as in the previous year, $1,820. This, being one of Buick's more luxurious models, featured plush mohair interiors with whipcord or a cloth left open for the buyer. Special paint combinations also were available that harmonized with the fender and body treatment.

The 1933 Buick Series 80 Convertible Coupe, known as Model 86-C, came equipped with rumble seat but minus the glove compartment door on the right side. This model sold for $1,575. Only 90 cars were built in this style. The depression didn't warrant many buyers for cars of this luxury.

The 1933 Buick Series 90 5-passenger Victoria Coupe was known as Model 96. This model sold for $1,785. A rear mounted spare tire was standard equipment; however, most models used the side mounts which were optional at extra cost. This was the last year for the Series 96. Only 556 were built.

934

In 1934, Buick offered some firsts such as independent ont wheel suspension, vacuum operated power braking 'stem, heat control and choke, automatic starting, and ı octane selector adjustable from the instrument panel. Among the models available were the Series 40, 50, 60, ıd 90, using wheelbases of 117, 119, 128, and 136 inches spectively. The Series 40 had 93 HP at 3200 RPM. he Series 50 had a 235 cubic inch block developing 88 orsepower at 3200 RPM, while the Series 60 had 100 HP ıd the Series 90 gave 116 HP. Each of these had a 200 RPM rating. Tire size for the Series 40 was 6:25 x 5, Series 50 was 7:00 x 16 and 7:50 x 16s were used on ıe other two series.

Fuel supplies were listed for Series 40 and 50 cars as 5 gallon tanks. Series 60 cars had 19 gallon supplies and e 90 models required a 22 gallon fuel tank. All models ed mechanical brakes, but Series 90 cars were equipped ith Bendix power boosters. For the first time, the public as able to order a factory installed radio.

Buick's production rose this year, thanks to Harlow H. ırtice. He was the one credit must be given to for the ries 40 which helped put Buick on its feet. Sales for e year showed 78,757 cars being turned out. Buick held ghth Position. It had 24 models from Series) through 90.

Buick's low priced model for 1934 was the reintroduction of the Series 40. Shown here is the Series 40 2-door Sedan which sold for $865. It weighed 3,120 lbs. The sidemounts were available at extra cost. It had a built-in trunk, but a luggage rack was also available at an additional cost.

A 1934 Buick Series 90 7-passenger Sedan. The wheelbase for the 90 Series was shortened to 136 inches for the year. The price of this model was $2,055 and in Limousine fashion sold for $120 additional. Side mounts were optional at extra cost. Most all of the 1,151 cars sold had the twin fender spares.

As before, the most popular car in the Series 50 line was the 4-door Sedan, Model 57, of which 12,094 were built for domestic sales and 711 for export. It cost $1,190 and weighed 3,852 pounds. In addition, Buick built 19 Series 50 chassis with cowl. These cost $885 and weighed 2,942.

The 1934 Buick Series 40 5-passenger Sedan was referred to as Model 41. This model sold for $925 and weighed 3,175 pounds. A built-in trunk was standard equipment for this series. The company built 10,953 for domestic use and 542 were shipped abroad. The side mounts and bumper guards on this particular car were optional at extra cost.

The 1934 Series 90 Convertible Coupe, referred to as Model 96-C, weighed 4,511 lbs. and sold for $1,945. The 90 Series used a 22-gallon fuel tank. A total of 68 96-C models were sold for the 1934 model run.

Buick

A Buick Series 60 Club Sedan for 1935 is displayed in a New York dealer's salesroom. This car wears white side wall tires which were not seen too often on cars in this price class during the depression years. Other accessories were the sidemounts and tire covers. The Model 61 cost $1,465. Its weight was 4,288 lbs. A total of 2,762 Series 60 cars were sold during 1935.

1935

Buick production for 1935 models was very low, wit only 53,249 units being produced. With Harlow H. Curtic in the driver's seat, Buick had something great in store fc the public. But it wasn't quite ready, and a car had to b put on the market for 1935. So the 1935 Buicks wei more or less just a slight face lift from the previous yea

Actually, the automatic choke was about the only bi mechanical change. All cars carried the same classificatioi as last year's models – Series 40, 50, 60, and 90.

Prices did take an upswing from 1934, as much as $10 in some cases, but this was needed to defray expense required in building the new car which would follo shortly. In fact, it was the 1936 Buick which helped th 1935 sales picture by its introduction in September, 193 Dealers couldn't get enough of them and Buick sales we in Seventh Position for the year.

A total of 25 models were available, which was on more than 1934. This new model was a Series 40 Co vertible Coupe which came with either tan Bedford clot upholstery or tan leather. This model in this series sol an even 1,000 and cost $925. The public didn't receiv this car too well, as depression buyers were out for mo practical transportation.

A 1935 Buick Convertible Coupe Series 90, Model 96-C, was used for the movie "Desirable" that featured George Brent and Jean Muir. Buick was often chosen as the popular car for many movies of that era. This was the final year Buick would build a Limited Convertible Coupe.

The 1935 Buick Series 90 Phaeton is shown in top-down version. Wire wheels were still used on the 1935 90 Series but most of the models came with the new modern steel spoke wheels as standard equipment. These wire wheels were optional at extra cost.

The 1935 Buick Series 90 Club Sedan came with built-in trunk and side mounts as standard equipment. This body style was referred to as Model 91. A total of 573 were sold. The car weighed 4,666 lbs. and cost $1,965.

The 1935 Buick Series 90 displayed with top up and the new steel spoke wheels with white side wall tires. This, like the Convertible Coupe, was the last year for open models in the 90 Series. Very few cars were sold in open style by Buick in 1935. This car sold for $2,145. Its weight was 4,661 pounds.

36

For the 1936 Buick run, the company had not only e regular numerical designations, but started to refer to e models with special trade names which were held onto til another change was made in 1959.

Four lines of attractive cars were displayed with new dies. This was Buick's first year with the "turret top" steel roof which helped to make it a good seller. n attractive feature of placing the parking lights on the nders, which became a Buick mark of distinction for e next few years, was first seen on these 1936 models. ew for Buick was a divided windshield with windshield pers mounted at the base of the cowl.

These cars gave top acceleration and excellent fuel and l economy. All models were roomier and had longer heelbases. The Special Series 40 came on a 118¼-inch heelbase; Century Series 60 used the 122-inch wheelbase; ries 80, which was the Roadmaster, was 131 inches, and ries 90, known as the Limited, used a 138-inch wheel-se. Tire size on the Special was 6:50 x 16; the Century as 7:00 x 15; the Roadmaster used 7:00 x 16s, and the mited used 7:50 x 16.

All engines turned a maximum of 3200 RPM. The Special ve 93 HP and the remaining models used the 120 HP gines. All models this year used hydraulic brakes. A 5 gallon fuel tank was used in both 40 and 60 Series odels and a 20 gallon supply was used in the top two ries.

Fourteen models were available, from a $765 2-passenger oupe in the Special range to a $1,945 8-passenger mited. Buick enjoyed a good hold of the automotive eld for 1936 by placing Sixth with a model run of 79,533 units.

The 1935 Series 40 Buick was in its second year of production. This is the series which helped Buick stay in business during this crucial two-year period. The Model 47 is what this body style was referred to. It also was phased out in 1936 but did return in 1937, and was a model that the author learned how to drive on. A total of 6,250 of this model were produced and sold for $895.

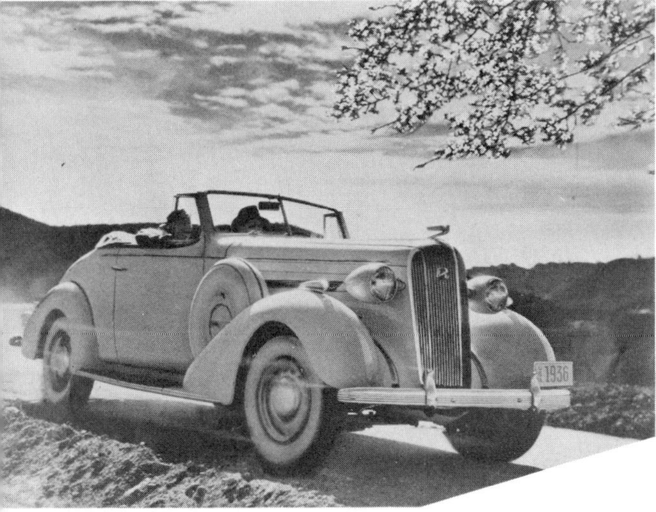

A sporty 1936 Buick Century Convertible Coupe is displayed, wearing whitewalls and side mounts with tire covers. A total of 717 were produced for the home market and 49 were shipped for export. It cost $1,135 and weighed 3,775 lbs.

Buick's most popular car for 1936 was this Special 4-door Sedan. It was known as the Model 41. A total of 77,007 Special Sedans were built in 1936. The spare tire was mounted inside the trunk on this model for the first time. Model 41's sold for $885.

Buick's 1936 Special Business Coupe was a very popular car, especially among professional people who depended on good solid transportation in the medium price class. This model was Buick's lowest price car. It sold for $765. It used the 118-inch wheelbase. A total of 10,912 Model 46 Coupes were produced.

One of the most outstanding models in the four lines of Buick cars for 1936 was this Roadmaster, a 6-passenger sedan with built-in trunk. Fender well equipment was a feature of this model as well as other Buick models but at optional extra cost. This model cost $1,255 and weighed 4,098 lbs.

A 1936 Buick Century, Model 61, is shown here with side mounts. This 4-door sedan weighed 3,780 lbs. A total of 17,806 cars were produced for domestic use and 397 cars went for export. Side mounts were optional at extra cost.

The 1936 Buick Limited Sedan was known as the Model 91. A total of four sedans were available ranging in price from $1,695 for this Model 91 Sedan to $1,945 for a glass partitioned Sedan Limousine.

1937

Building four new series in less than 10 days for complete model change over was no small feat, and Buic was mighty proud of this accomplishment. In the 40 an 60 Series, new frames with I-beam X-members, roomie bodies and an improved hypoid rear axle gearing wer some of the firsts in these two lines. The 80 and 9 models also saw many refinements over 1936. All mode claimed better generators, antenna mountings under th running board, windshield defrosters, and better rid control through stabilizer bars in the front and rea

Design-wise there was a car with a more refinec sculptured appearance than ever offered before by Buicl New fenders showed squared-off ends, a totally new gril had slim bars running horizontally, a narrow pointe hood expanded out toward the windshield, and headlamp were of the same conformity as the fender parking light With lines like these, Buick proved to be a real winner fc the year. This was the first year Buick used some plast appointments for its interior. All door handles, das knobs and steering wheels were done in ivory yello plastic. Buick steering wheels came with a modern hor ring which added class. This was optional in the Speci Series, standard in the three remaining models.

The Special engine developed 100 HP at 3200 RPM. used an 18 gallon fuel tank like the Century but rode o 6:50 x 16 inch tires while Century used 7:00 x 15. Th Special had a 122-inch wheelbase and the Century used 126-inch wheelbase. The Century engine developed 13 HP at 3400 RPM. Roadmasters and Limiteds both use the same engine as the Century but the Roadmaster cam on a 131-inch wheelbase and used 7:00 x 16 inch tire while the Limited came with a 138-inch wheelbase usir 7:50 x 16 inch tires. Both required 20 gallon fuel tank

Twenty-two models were available, ranging from a Seri 40 2-passenger Coupe for $765 to the Series 90 Limousin at $1,995. Production figures kept Buick in Sixth plac with 227,038 units for the calendar year.

Very definitely a special interest car today is this 1937 Buick Special Convertible Coupe. Its model designation was 46-C. A total of 2,265 were built for domestic sales and 134 of this series were sold for export use. It sold for $1,056.

A new model for the Special line in 1937 was this Convertible Sedan, referred to as 40-C. It was the most expensive model in the Special series, costing $1,302. A total of 1,689 Model 40-C's were produced for domestic sales and 256 were for export delivery. Most Convertible Sedans came with sidemounts but they were optional equipment at extra cost. This car also wears the full wheel trim accessory package.

The Model 47 Buick for 1937 holds a special place with the author because he learned to drive on a similarly equipped car that his parents owned. This model had been absent from the Special line-up in 1936, but made its return debut for 1937. A total of 22,312 were built for domestic sales and 205 were for export. This model sold for $995. Wheel trim and whitewalls were optional equipment at extra cost.

A 1937 Buick Century 4-passenger Sport Coupe, Model 66-S, is displaying its large trunk capacity. All Coupe and Convertible Coupes had the rear license mounted on the tail lamp in 1937. The other models mounted it under the trunk license lamp. This 66-S cost $1,187 and weighed 3,600 pounds.

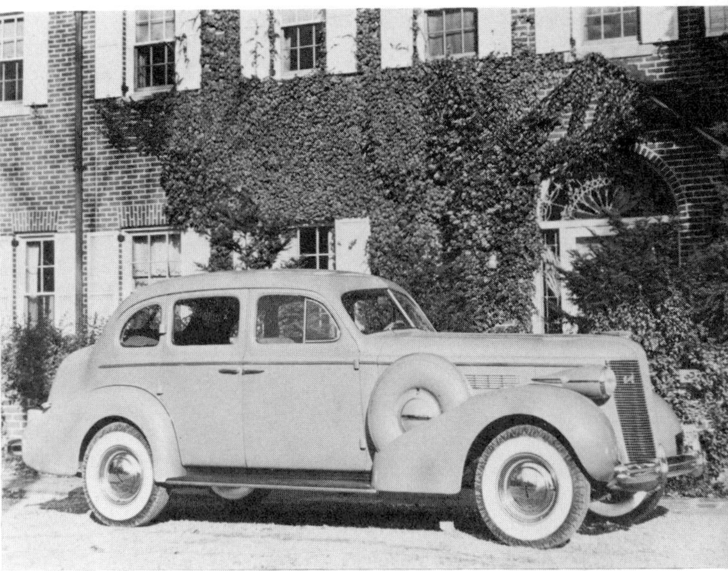

The most popular 1937 model of the Buick Century line was this 4-door Touring Sedan, Model 61. This particular model has the full beauty trim of double whitewalls, accessory wheel trim, and sidemounts. Base price of this model was $1,233. A total of 20,679 cars were built for use in the states and 461 went to other countries.

Buick's most expensive car for 1937 was the Model 90-L that was available only as an 8-passenger Limousine. It came fully equipped with glass partition between chauffeur and passengers, side mounts, wheel trim rings, white side wall tires, radio, heater, and rear seat speakers to the chauffeur's compartment. A total of 720 were built for domestic use and 245 went for export sales. This model sold for $2,342.

Buick

Buick's most popular model for 1938 was the Special 4-door Touring Sedan. This car sold for $1,047 just as it is shown. A total of 79,510 were sold for domestic use and 2,681 were shipped for export sales. Note the accessory dinner bell gong center bumper guard on this car. Early 1938 Buicks had this as standard equipment. Later models offered it only as an accessory.

Only 208 of this Buick Century Convertible Sedan were built in 1938. The model designation was 60-C. This was the most expensive in the Century line, selling for $1,713. A Bob Pipkin of Medford, Oregon was the owner of this beauty until recently.

Buick's 1938 Special Convertible Coupe offered a rumble seat for the last time. This example sold for $1,103. Total production amounted to 2,623 cars. Of these, 152 were destined for overseas use.

1938

Since Buick had a big model change over in 1937, th 1938 models had only a facelifting on an already attractiv car. The suspension was improved with coil springs a around, giving that soft Buick ride for which the cai were noted. As for the engine, it now developed 107 H in the Special and 141 HP in the other three series a 3600 RPM, using turbulator pistons. Buick's ill-fate automatic transmission, which came only on the Special lasted only for one year. Buick did not re-introduce a automatic transmission until 1948 and then only for th Roadmaster models.

The fuel supply was an 18 gallon tank for the Specia and Centurys and a 20 gallon supply on Series 80 and 9 cars. The tire size for the Specials was 6:50 x 16; 7:00 15s were used on the Century; 7:00 x 16s on Roadmaster and 7:50 x 16s on the Limited. The wheelbase for Seri 40 cars was 122 inches. Series 60 was 126 inches, Series 8 took a 133-inch chassis, while the 90 Series came on 140-inch wheelbase.

Body styles amounted to 21, ranging from the $94 2-passenger Special Coupe to a $2,453 Limited Limousin

Even with a general sales slump in 1938, Buick place Fourth, with 173,905 cars being delivered for the calend year.

The big brother to both Buick Special and Century Convertible Sedans was this 1938 Roadmaster Model 80-C which sold for $1,983 complete with all factory equipment as standard. This model weighed 4,325 lbs. Only 350 were sold for home use and 61 went for export sales.

Very similar in appearance to the 1938 Century Convertible Sedan is this Special Model 40-C, with its flat trunk. The 5-passenger Convertible Sedan sold for $1,406 and had a production run of 946 units. Of these 170 were for export sales.

939

For 1939, Buick entered the model run with a car quite ifferent in appearance from its 1938 model. It came ith the first of a new style grille which Buick kept for he next two years. Headlights sat atop the fender catwalk ne, with bullet shaped lamps giving a stylish and massive ɔok to the front end. Two-tone paint was offered in ertain colors and on certain models as a first this year.

Buick made an option item available to those who ished it. Called "Streamboards," these were a replace-ient for the runningboard. Also a first, as standard equip-ient, was the ever popular Buick turn indicator, which 'as mounted on the trunk and gave those behind an idication the driver was planning on either a right or ft turn.

Mechanically, Buick did away with the airplane type iock absorbers in favor of the refillable ones. The frames ere two inches closer to the ground, giving a much lower ffect to the car's general appearance. The Special engine 'as offered with the same 107 HP at 3400 RPM. This eries was on a two-inch shorter wheelbase, being 120 ıches with 6:50 x 16 inch tires. The fuel supply was an 8 gallon tank. Buick offered a taxicab on the Special -door Sedan, which certainly owned up to Buick's eputation for building rugged cars. The Yellow Cab Co. f Los Angeles purchased a fleet of these cars, which were riven all through World War II. The top car for mileage ırned over 717,000 miles with the original engine before eing scrapped in 1946.

The Century for 1939 came on a 126-inch wheelbase. had an 18 gallon tank for fuel. This was the only Series ɔ use 15-inch wheels on a 7:00 size tire. The engine eveloped a 141 horsepower at 3600 RPM, the same as the oadmaster and Limited.

The Roadmaster came on a 133-inch wheelbase. It used :00 x 16 inch tires and had a 20 gallon fuel supply, as id the Limited. The Limited followed the Roadmaster retty much in all respects but wheelbase, which was 40 inches long, and tire size consisting of 7:50 x 16s. 19 models were available. Buick again held the fourth ɔot for sales. The calendar year production was 231,219 ırs.

The most expensive model built by Buick for 1938 was this Limited Limousine, known as the 90-L. It cost $2,453 and weighed 4,653 pounds.

A portion of 1939 Buick Special Touring Sedans that were delivered to the Los Angeles Yellow Cab Co. These cars served well during their years of service. The last one to be retired in 1947 had gone 717,000 miles without any major engine work. Speaks well for the car.

The Sunroof option is shown on this 1939 Special Sedan. This was available on both Special and Century 4-door and 2-door Sedans. Very few were ever sold and they did have a problem of not sealing properly. Without the Sunroof a Special Sedan sold for $996.

The Roadmaster Sport Phaeton as it was called for 1939 was available in either trunk-back style or fast back fashion. The trunk back model, like this car, was more popular, with 311 being built for domestic use and 53 for export sales. Its total price was $1,938. The fender skirts shown here and parking lights were optional at extra cost and very few models saw either as they left the factory.

Buick

The 1939 Special 2-door Touring Sedan sold for $955 and had a sales run of 27,218 cars for the states and 72 additional cars for export duty. This was the year Buick introduced the directional flasher as standard equipment. It only flashed on the rear trunk, however.

The most expensive model for 1939 was this 90-L Limited Limousine which sold for $2,453. The sales amounted to 543 of which 120 went for export. This model was offered only as an 8-passenger with a glass partition between chauffeur and rear seat passengers. A speaking phone also was in the rear passenger compartment.

1940

The return of the Series 50 occurred in 1940 Now known as the Super, it came in four body styles The Super shared the same Torpedo body style as th Roadmaster. However, the Super came on a 121-incl wheelbase while the Roadmaster used a 126-inch chassis In addition to these models were the Special and Century cars which employed the same body style. The Specia grew an inch from 1939 cars and was now on a 121-incl wheelbase. The Century used a 126-inch chassis, whil two series of Limited were available – Series 80 o 133-inch wheelbase and the Series 90 on the 140-incl wheelbase.

The engine compartments of the Special and Super were identical. Each series developed 107 HP at 340 RPM. The fuel supply for these cars was from a 17 gallo tank. Tire size consisted of 6:50 x 16 inches for bot Series.

The Century used the 141 HP engine (at 3600 RPM) a was used on the Roadmaster and Limited. It had a 1 gallon tank as did the Roadmaster. Both Century an Roadmaster employed 7:00 x 15 inch tires.

The Limited in both series used 7:50 x 16 inch tire A 19 gallon fuel tank was used in both the 80 and 9 model cars.

The Super and Roadmaster did away with runnin boards and put chrome moldings in their place. The 194 cars used the directional signal indicators started in 193 Only for 1940, the new devices were not only on th rear trunk, but also the flashing devices were mounte above the headlamps on top of the fenders.

A total of 23 models were available ranging in pric from $895 for the 2-passenger Special Coupe to $2,19 for the Series 90 Limited 8-passenger Sedan.

Buick again placed Fourth position for the year b selling 310,995 units.

A view of the 1940 Buicks at the main Buick retail outlet in Flint, Mich. The Super and Roadmasters were introduced to the public that year with a new body called Torpedo styling.

The new body style for 1940 was introduced as the Super Series. It was offered on a 121-inch wheelbase and weighed 3,790 lbs. The model was the most popular of the Super line and cost $1,109. The company sold 95,875 units for domestic use and 1,351 Super Sedans for export. Two-tone paint became very popular on the Super and Roadmaster models for 1940.

The top of the Buick line for 1940 was this Limited Model 90 8-passenger Touring Sedan. A total of 828 of this model were built in 1940. The price was $2,096 completely equipped with sidemounts, radio, heater, whitewalls and speaker phone compartment to the chauffeur.

The small Limited referred to as Series 80 had a wheelbase of 133 inches. This model was called the 81 and sold for $1,553. It did not continue into the next year as poor sales warranted only a one year stay. This model is minus the side mounted tires.

This 1940 Buick Roadmaster Town Car was to have been a special luxury-built model for the Super and Roadmaster Sedans. However, at the last minute company management decided to hold off on the project, and this is the only one built. The body was done by the Brunn Co. of Buffalo, N.Y.

This Roadmaster Convertible Coupe was known as Model 76-C. The model sold for $1,431 and weighed 4,053 lbs. A total of 612 Model 76-C's were built. This model is using the popular factory installed tear-drop fender skirts, an optional accessory, and has the double white sidewall tires.

A mid-season offering for 1941 was this Special Convertible Coupe Model 44-C. The smaller Special used a 118-inch wheelbase, and was available with compound carburetor, like on the larger series, at optional extra cost. This model sold for $1,138. Buick built 4,309 both for domestic and export use.

This is what the 1941 Buick was to have looked like. Management felt it was too much 1940 as far as the front end goes so a last minute change was ordered to give a more massive front end appearance. This model was actually called the Special Sedanet Model 46 on the GM "B" Series body. It cost $935.

This 1941 Roadmaster Convertible Coupe, Model 76-C, weighed 4,258 lbs. It sold for $1,457 to 1,845 buyers in the states and 24 went to export. Standard equipment as on the 44-C and 56-C was the power operated top and outside rear view mirror.

A 1941 Buick Special 4-door Touring Sedan. This car was being photographed for the press in August of 1940 at the Flint headquarters. This is Model 41 nicely equipped with whitewall tires, Guide Driving Lamps, skirts and stainless steel window reveals. A total of 91,138 were produced for domestic sales and 1,390 went to export. The model sold for $1,134.

The most popular model of the 1941 Super line was the 4-door Sedan, Model 51. It weighed 3,770 lbs. and sold for $1,185. Directional signals on 1941 models were through the parking light on top of the fenders and in the bottom section of the tail lamps rather than on the trunk medallion as had been the case for the two prior years.

An all-time favorite of the author is his 1941 Super Convertible Sedan done in Verde Green. Model designation is 51-C. A total of 467 of this body style were produced for domestic use and 41 went for export. The weight of this model is 4,015 lbs. The price of it was $1,555 complete with radio, heater, and whitewall tires. The fender skirts were optional at extra cost.

1941

The 1941 year was a real banner for Buick. Th company held on in the Fourth sales spot for the year wit one of the sharpest cars it had ever produced.

The 1941 models had dual carburetors on the Super Century, Roadmaster, and Limited models as standar equipment. It was available on both Series of Special at a additional cost. Also new for Buick this year were th new bodies in the Special, Century, and Limited. Th Limited Series 80 had been discontinued at the end o the 1940 model run. Only Series 90 models remained. I mid-year a smaller Buick Special joined the other models It came on an 118-inch wheelbase and was available i four body styles. The sedanet body style of the Series 4 was one of the most popular in the line. It sold well fo families with young children as it offered only two doors It was also popular for businessmen in everyday use

The Specials, if not equipped with dual-carburetion came with a 115 HP engine at 3500 RPM. Otherwise, i developed 125 HP, like the Super, at 3800 RPM. A Century, Roadmaster and Limiteds developed 165 HP a 3800 RPM. All models used an 18 gallon fuel tan except for the Limited which had a 21 gallon supply. Tir size for the Specials and Supers were 6:50 x 16 inches The Century and Roadmaster used 7:00 x 15 inch tire and the Limiteds had 7:50 x 16 tires. The wheelbase fc the two Specials were 118 and 121 inches. The Super als had a 121-inch chassis and 126 inches were on the Centur and Roadmaster. The Limited had a 139-inch wheelbase

All models came equipped with directional signals an wired with an antenna at no additional cost. Also, 2-ton paint was optional at no extra amount. Many people di take advantage of having a 2-tone car.

A total of 36 models were available ranging from th Special Business Coupe at $915 to the Limited Limousir for $2,667.

Calendar year sales kept Buick in Fourth position wit the sale of 316,251 cars.

A dashboard that always gave a look of quality was the 1941 Buick instrument panel. An impressive wood grained effect and engine turned panels around the dials was used in all models from Special through Limited.

Buick

.942

The 1942 line had all the same model designations, but n entirely new body made its debut for the short model un in the Super and Roadmaster Series. Airfoil fenders vere a new feature of the Super and Roadmaster convertibles and sedanets. They gave a new swept-back effect o the sides of these body styles which ran the entire ength of the body until they met the rear fenders. The Special and Super engines were required to be etuned due to new cast iron pistons that were inflicted pon them. This was due to lack of materials available for uto production. In single carburetor version, they eveloped 110 HP at 3400 RPM. With compound carburetion, it offered 118 HP at 3600 RPM. The Century, Roadmaster, and Limited still had the 165 HP engines at 3800 RPM). The fuel supply was a 19 gallon tank on ll models but the Limited, which used a 21 gallon supply. The Century was still the fastest stock car in America t this time.

The tire size was 6:50 x 16 inches for the two models f Special and Super. The Century and Roadmaster models oth shared the 7:00 x 15 inch tires, and the Limiteds had :50 x 16 inch tires. The wheelbases on both Special eries measured 118 and 121 inches. The Super grew aree inches for 1942 and came on a 124-inch chassis. he Century, which was in its last year until 1954, ame in two body styles, both being fast backs. It had a 26-inch wheelbase. The Roadmaster also grew, and used a 29-inch chassis. The Limited had the same wheelbase s in 1941, which was 139 inches.

With production actually beginning in September, 1941, nodel year sales amounted to 94,442 units. But from anuary 1 until February 2, all vehicles produced were irtually minus chrome trim. All that was left in chrome vere the bumpers. All bright work was basically done in a avorable contrasting color to the car's color scheme. Even t that, they were rather drab automobiles and it took ne with a special priority to obtain one. White sidewall res also didn't exist unless a dealer had some stored away.

A total of 23 models were available ranging in price rom $1,046 for a 3-passenger Special Business Coupe to 2,667 for the 8-passenger Limited Limousine. For the alendar year, Buick sold 16,601 cars, staying in the 4th ales position.

The 1941 Roadmaster Touring Sedan, Model 71. This was an early production model minus the rear fender spears as shown on the Super Sedan. Most all Buicks for 1941 came equipped with the antenna mounted directly above the windshield or on the left front fender if it was a convertible Coupe or Sedan. This car sold for $1,364 and weighed 4,204 lbs. Two-tone paint was available in 1941 for all closed cars at no additional charge if the owner wished it.

The top of the line for the Buick Limited Sedans was this 8-passenger Model 90 being photographed for the press in August of 1940. It made its debut in September. This model cost $2,380 and weighed 4,680 lbs. A total of 906 were built for home and export duty. Buick also catalogued many special Brunn bodied Limited cars with convertible tops in some instances. However, GM felt it would be taking sales away from Cadillac so the idea was phased out of production.

One of the most attractive and totally different cars on the road this year was the new Super Convertible, Model 56-C, which used Buick's new swept-back fender styling, decorated with heavy chrome sidebars. It cost $1,450 and weighed 4,025 pounds. Production was 2,454 for domestic sales and 35 for export. The top was electrically operated; fender skirts were standard.

The most popular car in the Buick Super line for 1942 was this 4-door Sedan, Model 51. With the war cries around the corner, only 16,001 were built for domestic use and 264 Super Sedans did manage to be shipped to foreign countries. This model sold for $1,280. All 1942 models after January 1, 1942 were called blackout cars as chrome plating wasn't permitted on the grille, door handles, head and tail lamp doors, etc. The only bright work was on the bumpers.

Cadillac

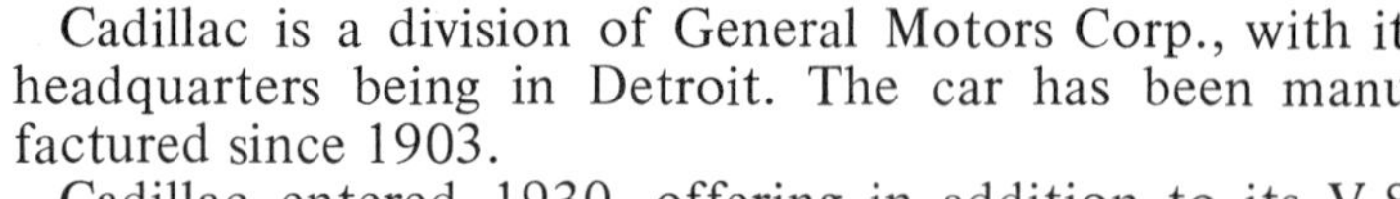

Cadillac is a division of General Motors Corp., with it headquarters being in Detroit. The car has been manu factured since 1903.

Cadillac entered 1930, offering in addition to its V-8 a totally new V-16 with the two banks of its cylinders a an angle of 45 degrees. Each half was nearly a separat engine, having its own carburetor, vacuum fuel supply cooling water and ignition. Its displacement was 452 cubi inches. The brake horsepower was 165 at 3400 RPM. The fuel tank held 25 gallons. The V-16 used 7:00 x 19 inch tires, and had a 148-inch wheelbase.

Later in the year, not to be outdone by any othe manufacturer, Cadillac introduced the V-12 of 370 cubi inches of a similar design. The V-12s developed 135 H at the same RPM. These models had a 21 gallon fue supply. All V-12s rode on 7:00 x 19 inch tires. They ha shorter wheelbases, coming on two different chassis o 140 and 143 inches.

Besides these two new offerings, Cadillac still mad available its V-8 of 95 HP at 3000 RPM. The cars had a fuel supply of 21 gallons also. The tire size was the sam as V-12s and V-16s. It came only as a 140-inch wheelbas car.

All these series used mechanical brakes. A total of sixt models were available ranging from the V-8 2-passenge Roadster for $3,450 to the V-16 7-passenger tow Brougham for $7,525.

Cadillac placed in 16th position by registering 12,07 cars for the model run. For calendar year production recorded with La Salle, a total of 22,559 cars wer produced.

This 1930 Cadillac V-8 Club Sedan was offered for $3,495. Its curb weight was 5,025 lbs. The wheelbase of this sedan was 140 inches. This model wears the wooden artillery spoke wheels which were becoming a bit archaic. Most 1930 Cadillacs were beginning to sport wire wheels.

A 1930 Cadillac V-16 7-passenger Imperial Sedan had the code number of 4375. This was the first year for the 16-cylinder Cadillac. This model sold for $6,525 and had a production run of 438.

The 1930 Cadillac V-16 All Weather Phaeton with body by Fleetwood. The style code for this model was 4380. Technically, it could be referred to as a Dual-Cowl Phaeton with its rear windshield for back seat passengers. A total of 250 of this style were built, with a list price of $6,650. This is a very late production 1930 as noted by the single bar bumper.

The mid-season offering of this 1930 Cadillac V-12 Fleetway All Weather Phaeton came as a surprise to the automotive world since the V-16 had just been announced shortly before. This model was priced at $4,400.

931

For 1931, Cadillac offered again its V-8, V-12 and V-16 nodels. The V-8 came with a 95 HP engine of 353 cubic nches at 3000 RPM. The V-12 offered a 368 cubic inch ngine of 135 HP at 3400 RPM. All V-16s had a 452 ubic inch displacement developing 165 HP, also at 400 RPM. The fuel supplies were 21 gallons for both he V-8 and V-12 and 25 gallons for the V-16s. The vheelbase was 134 inches on all 8-cylinder cars, 140 and 43 inches for the 12-cylinder models, and 148 inches n the 16-cylinder cars. The tire size consisted of 6:50 x 9 inches for the V-8s and 7:50 x 19s were used on the /-12 and V-16 models.

A total of 44 models made their debut for 1931. Prices anged from $2,695 for a 4-passenger V-8 Coupe to $7,525 or the 7-passenger Imperial Limousine.

Cadillac sold 15,012 units for the calendar run which etained them in 16th sales position for the year. These igures are combined with La Salle.

Cadillac's 1930 V-8 7-passenger Sedan was displayed only on the 140-inch wheelbase, which was an increase of three inches over the previous year. This model weighed 5,155 lbs. and sold for $3,795.

This 1931 Cadillac Madam X 5-passenger Sedan was classified in the 4100 Series. This particular model went under code and style number 4130S. A total of 49 were built and sold for $6,950. Bumper equipment was still an accessory but virtually all Cadillacs came equipped with bumpers.

Cadillac offered this 1930 2-passenger Convertible Coupe for $3,595. It weighed 4,845 lbs. One of the new features offered was the non-shatter Security Plate Glass which was standard equipment in all windows of every Cadillac for 1930.

The 1931 Cadillac V-16 2-passenger Convertible Coupe was known as Style No. 4235. A total of 94 were built in that year. They sold for $6,900. This model was catalogued as a 2-passenger car and yet was equipped with a rumble seat, as can be seen by the step pads on the right rear fender.

Cadillac's V-16 5-passenger Phaeton for 1931 sold for $6,500. A total of 85 were built. This car carried a special code in its delivery, having a special mounted windshield. It was referred to as Model 4260.

Cadillac

This was referred to as Model 4276 by Cadillac management, but to the public it was a 1931 V-16 Cadillac 2-passenger Coupe. This model carried a Madam X windshield. It sold for $6,850. The wheelbase was 148 inches on this Fleetwood body style.

The 1931 Cadillac 5-passenger Trans. Town Brougham, as it was technically called, actually was a Town Car. This model carries its roof shelter for chauffeur in place. The car was ordered with a flat windshield, opera seats, and solid rear quarter panels. A total of 6 were produced with a price tag of $9,700.

The 1931 Cadillac V-12 Imperial Sedan sold for $4,345 in 7-passenger style. It weighed 5,435 lbs. and was available on the 143-inch wheelbase only for that body style. Other 12-cylinder cars came on both 140 and 143-inch wheelbases.

An ideal setting for this 1931 Cadillac V-16 5-passenger Imperial Sedan. This model carried a flat windshield and opera seats as a special order. A total of 50 were produced with a list price of $6,300.

Cadillac's least expensive offering in the 1932 models was this V-8 Coupe for $2,795. It came on a 134-inch wheelbase. This six wheel example rides on Kelsey Hayes wire wheels which were optional at extra cost. Most 1932 Cadillacs came with wire wheels even though the wooden artillery wheels were standard equipment.

One of the most popular Cadillac models for 1931 was this 5-passenger Sedan for $2,795. The public at this time was more interested in a conservative looking car rather than an open model. It weighed 4,600 lbs. and was available on a 134-inch wheelbase only.

Cadillac

1932

Cadillac for 1932 offered a vacuum operated clutch, lriver adjusted shock absorbers, silent transmission in all 'orward gears, and for the still style conscious public at he bottom of the worst depression, new bodies which were beautiful to look at, even if the general public couldn't afford to own one. Buyers had a choice of three engines again this year – the V-8 with 115 HP at 3000 RPM; V-12 with 135 HP at 3400 RPM; and the V-16 leveloping 165 HP at 3500 RPM. Brakes were of the mechanical type. Each series carried a 30 gallon fuel tank.

In the V-8 and V-12 body styles, there was a choice of 40 models priced from $2,795 for the 4-passenger coupe to $4,995 for a 7-passenger V-12 Town Cabriolet.

In the V-16 line, 15 models were available, starting at $4,495 for a 4-passenger coupe and ending at $5,945 for either the Town Cabriolet or Limousine Brougham.

Wheelbases for the V-8s and V-12s were 134 inches in Coupes, Roadsters, Convertibles and Sedans. All other models shared the 140-inch wheelbase. The V-16 used a 143-inch wheelbase on the Coupe, Sedan, Convertible Coupe and Roadster, while the remaining 11 models rode on a 149-inch wheelbase. Body makes were Fisher and Fleetwood. Special body builders could be appointed for custom body building. Saleswise, Cadillac and La Salle sold 9,153 units and placed 15th in the sales fight for the year. Tire size was 7:00 x 17 for the V-8s; V-12s had 7:50 x 17s, while the V-16s carried 7:50s and employed an 18-inch wheel.

A 1932 Cadillac V-12 Coupe with rear mounted spare sold for $3,495 and was available only on the 134-inch wheelbase. The golf door was standard on all Coupe models. Most versions still came with the two-tone paint combinations such as this Coupe offered.

A 1932 Cadillac V-16 7-passenger Sedan with deluxe equipment sold for $6,225. A total of 501 were built. The style number was referred to as 4375S.

This 1932 Cadillac V-12 Town Sedan was available for $3,795 in base form. The side mounted tires were optional at extra cost. The new cars offered a vacuum operated clutch, driver adjusted shocks, and synchro mesh transmission in all forward gears.

An example of the 1932 Cadillac V-12 Imperial 7-passenger Sedan is shown here. This model sold for $3,995 with a production run of 83 cars.

This 1932 Cadillac transformable Town Cabriolet was available for $5,795. In 5-passenger style four were built and in 7-passenger version two were produced.

Cadillac

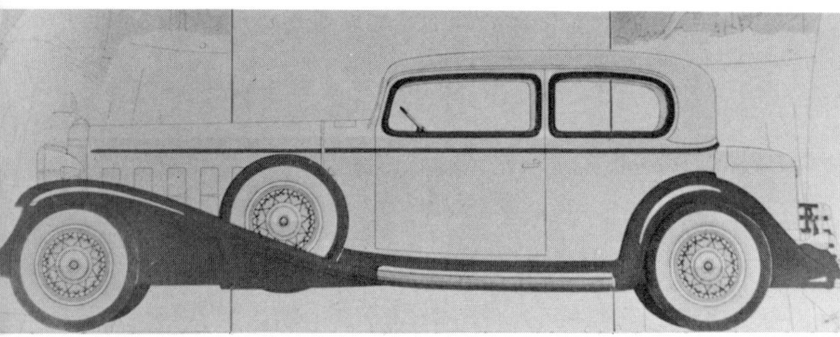

The Town Coupe for 1932 was Cadillac's 5-passenger model also classed as a 2-door Sedan. It sold for $3,395 in 8-cylinder form and $3,795 as a V-12 and was available on a 140-inch wheelbase in either 8 or 12-cylinder version. It was also available in V-16 style for $5,095.

For 1933, Cadillac offered this Roadster in both V-8 and V-12 models. In the V-8 series it was available for $2,795 and as a V-12 it sold for $3,495. The bumpers on some models like this one had triple bar centers with single bar ends. These models had the 134-inch wheelbase. Here it is displayed in open car fashion. Wire wheels had now become standard equipment. In fact, many people chose to cover them with bright chromium disc covers. A five wheel car like this could have the discs for $80. Six wheel models cost $96 for the set.

This 1933 Cadillac V-16 Aerodynamic Coupe was the Chicago Worlds Fair Car. This was the beginning of GM styling which later led to the fast-back styling of the early 1940's. The style code number for this car was 5599. Only one of this car was ever produced in 1933.

1933

For 1933, Cadillac entered the market without any major changes, but with numerous refinements, including more pleasing body lines and Fisher no-draft ventilation. Vacuum operated brakes and clutch control were standard on all models. Only 400 16-cylinder models were built. Body styles in general were fewer than in 1932. Instead of 55 models in the line-up, Cadillac only had 33 coming from the Detroit factory for 1933.

In the horsepower race, Cadillac started out with a 115 horsepowered V-8 at 3000 RPM. The V-12 had 135 HP at 3400 RPM. The V-16 had a 165 HP at 3400 RPM. The 8-cylinder cars had 7:00 x 17 inch tires and the other two series carried 7:50 x 17s. All models used a 30 gallon gas tank. Mechanical brakes were used on all models. Wheelbases were 134 inches for the Roadster, Coupe, and Convertible Coupe in both V-8 and V-12 form and 140 inches in all other models.

Prices began at $2,695 for the V-8 4-passenger Coupe and rose upward to $4,845 for a V-12 Limousine Brougham. With only 400 V-16s being produced, all were on special order, so all prices varied; therefore, no actual price list was available.

Cadillac placed 17th for the year, selling 6,736 units with La Salle's help for the calendar year.

The 1933 V-12 All Weather Phaeton came on the 140-inch wheelbase. This 5-passenger car sold for $4,095. The buyer could also obtain the same car in V-8 style for $3,395.

A beautiful 1933 Cadillac V-16 Imperial Cabriolet with Landau Irons. This was a 5-passenger Sedan by Cadillac's model designations. Only one of this model was built in 1933.

1934

Cadillac received quite a face-lifting for 1934, but basically it was unaltered mechanically from the 1933 models. Its main claims were independent front suspension with a softer ride from the use of coil springs. Two-way hydraulic shocks were used on all 1934 Cadillacs, both front and rear.

Fisher no-draft ventilation was continued with improvements. The cowl ventilator opened in the reverse fashion as Fisher felt that air currents moved forward at that point.

Probably the greatest mark of distinction for these cars as far as design was concerned were the "twin motored" biplane bumpers. These bumpers were equipped with a coil spring bracket so in case of an accident, the bumper would give up to two inches.

Horsepower for the V-8 was 130 at 3400 RPM, while the V-12 gave 150 HP at 3600 RPM and the V-16 produced 180 at 3800 RPM. Tire sizes were 7:00 x 17 on the V-8 and 7:50 x 17 for the V-12 and V-16s.

The fueling system for the V-8 was a 22 gallon supply. The V-12 and V-16 used a 30 gallon tank. Each series used mechanical brakes.

Fifty-two models were catalogued between the V-8s and the V-12s. The V-16 body styles were available, but all were on special order. A total of 400 V-16s appeared in 1934.

Cadillac sold 11,468 cars, placing 13th in the sales picture for the calendar year. Sales, incidentally, were combined with La Salle for the year.

This 1933 Cadillac V-16 Dual-Cowl Phaeton was another example of the one off the assembly line models that Cadillac did produce. Its style code number was referred to as 5559. It was photographed for the press at the Art and Color Division of GM in Detroit.

This 1934 Cadillac Aero Dynamic Coupe came as both V-8 and V-12 weighing 5,300 lbs. and 5,500 lbs., respectively. This body style was taken from the 1933 Chicago Worlds Fair car. It used a 146-inch wheelbase for both models.

The 1933 Cadillac V-8 5-passenger sedan was the most popular offering the company produced in 1933. This 140-inch wheelbase model sold for $2,895 in base form. Sidemounts and wire wheels were optional at extra cost.

Shown here is an impressive 1934 Cadillac Convertible Coupe on the 146-inch wheelbase. It was available either as a V-8 or V-12. The bi-plane bumpers make this car look most impressive and stately. Four bodies of this style were placed on V-16 chassis.

Cadillac

This 1934 Cadillac V-8 Town Coupe, as it was called by the manufacturer, is really a 2-door sedan. It was available on the 128-inch chassis and weighed 4,630 lbs.

Almost a twin to the 1934 Cadillac Town Coupe was the V-8 Town Sedan also on a 128-inch wheelbase. The weight of the Town Sedan was 4,735 lbs. This was a very popular model among families who were able to afford a Cadillac at that time.

The 1934 Cadillac V-12 Sedan for 5 passengers, on a 146-inch wheelbase, appears to be ready for an afternoon outing. Who is opening the door for whom? Or maybe she just wants to see their latest possession. At any rate it is a conservative sedan with wire wheels and metal tire covers.

A well designed 1934 Cadillac 5-passenger sedan on the V-8 chassis sold for $2,895. Its weight was 4,925 lbs. Note the parking lamp lights directly under the headlights.

The 1934 Cadillac Convertible Sedan was available either with V-8 or V-12 engines. The wheelbase measured 146 inches for either car. The V-8 developed 130 H.P., and the V-12 gave 150 H.P. The V-8 weighed 5,580 lbs. and the V-12 weighed 5,790 lbs. This Convertible Sedan wears the full disc wheel covers painted the color of the car matched for harmony.

The 1934 Cadillac Imperial Sedan for 7-passengers on the 136-inch wheelbase. This model wears standard equipped wire wheels with white sidewalls and impressive side mounts which are minus the accessory tire covers. The small flags on the sidewalls appears that this limousine is using Vogue tires.

1935

The main change in all three series for 1935 was more plush interiors than had ever been shown on a Cadillac before. The emphasis was on simplification. Interior hardware on some models had a substance called ducoing, which was to harmonize with the interior of the cars. The instrument panel was etched in a basket weave pattern. For the exterior, little was done to change an already pretty car. The two front fenders appeared to come together under the radiator grille giving a graceful sweep to the massive lines. The radiator emblem was changed to that of a goddess. Gone were the classical biplane bumpers of 1934 in favor of spring bumpers.

Horsepower rating for the three series were 130 HP at 3400 RPM in the V-8, 150 HP at 3600 RPM in the V-12, and 185 HP at 3800 RPM in the V-16.

Tire size of 7:00 x 17 was used in the V-8 and 7:50 x 17 came on all V-12 and V-16 models. Fuel capacities were a 22 gallon tank on the V-8, and a 30 gallon supply on the V-12 and V-16. Mechanical brakes were still being used by Cadillac.

Wheelbases varied in each series. A V-8 could be ordered on a 128, 136, or 146-inch wheelbase in 26 different models with a beginning price of $1,645 for a 3-passenger Coupe. The V-12 could be purchased in 13 styles beginning with a Touring Sedan at $3,145. The wheelbase for these models was 146 inches. The V-16s came on a 154-inch chassis with a base price of $7,450 for a Town Sedan and ending at over $8,000 for a special bodied model. V-16 models numbered an even dozen for the model year.

Cadillac took a 14th seat for the calendar year by putting out 23,559 cars. These figures also represent La Salle sales for 1935.

This is a 1934 Cadillac V-16 Fleetwood Town Cabriolet with style number 5825. Only four of this design were produced in 1934. Altogether during the four year span for this model from 1934 through 1937, nine were built. The list price was $9,250.

The 1935 Shrine Convention was held in Washington, D.C. during June. This white Cadillac V-8 Convertible Sedan was used for the Imperial Potentate Danna Williams. Inspecting the car before its delivery are Nicholas Dreystadt at the wheel, then general manager of Cadillac, and J. C. Chick, general sales manager.

This 1935 Cadillac Convertible Coupe was available in V-8 style on the 128, 136, and 146-inch wheelbases. It was also seen in V-12 fashion on the 146-inch chassis. The above example is on the 128-inch wheelbase. Wire wheels were standard equipment but this car wears disc covers that were optional at extra cost.

For anyone wishing a 2-passenger Coupe of personal distinction this 1935 Cadillac V-8 was the answer. It weighed 4,550 lbs. This was the least expensive Cadillac built in 1935, selling for $2,750. This model was available on a 128-inch wheelbase.

A well balanced 1935 Cadillac V-12 Town Sedan on the 146-inch wheelbase. This car weighed 5,700 lbs. It was also available as a V-8. This model differed from the Close Coupled Sedan in the rear door treatment. The doors on this model open from the rear while the Close Coupled version opened from the front.

Cadillac

A V-8 Cadillac Town Coupe for 1935 was a popular close-coupled model that allowed ample space for three passengers in the rear and two on the individual front seats. A choice of whipcord or broadcloth upholstery was available. The built-in trunk was standard for this model.

The most popular of the 1935 Cadillacs was this 4-door V-8 Sedan. Note very little change took place between the 1934 and 1935 models. The only big difference is the straight bumper for the 1935 cars. This model came on a 128-inch wheelbase and weighed 4,715 lbs.

A streamlined beauty with a luxurious interior was this 1935 Cadillac 7-passenger Sedan. Two auxiliary seats were furnished for rear passengers. When not in use, they folded nicely in back of the front seat cushion. This model was available on the 136-inch wheelbase. It was also available on the 146-inch wheelbase as a V-8 or a V-12.

1936

Cadillac came into 1936 with many new offerings, both in body and mechanical departments. Model designations consisted of three new Eights, two Twelves, and the Sixteen with some improvements.

The V-8s appeared as Models 60, 70 and 75. The Model 60 had a 121-inch wheelbase, a 21 gallon fuel tank, and developed 125 HP at 3400 RPM. Tire size was 7:00 x 16.

Next to this car was the Model 70, using a 131-inch wheelbase, and employing a 25 gallon gas supply. This car, and the Series 75, used a 135 HP engine at 3400 RPM. 7:50 x 16 inch tires were used on both series. The Series 75 had a 138-inch wheelbase, which was really its only difference from the Series 70 cars.

Series 80 and 85 cars were both V-12 models, producing 150 HP at 3600 RPM. Fuel capacity was a 25 gallon tank. Again, as in Series 70-75 cars, the 80 and 85s differed only in wheelbase and models available. The Series 80 came on a 131-inch wheelbase while the 85 used seven more inches. Both used 7:50 x 16 inch tires.

Series 90 cars were the V-16s on a 154-inch wheelbase. Engines developed 185 HP at 3800 RPM. They used a 30 gallon fuel tank, and rode on 7:50 x 17 inch tires. All 1936 Cadillacs used hydraulic brakes except for the V-16 which retained the mechanical device. Models available amounted to 35, ranging from $1,645 for a 4-passenger Coupe to a V-16 Convertible Sedan at $7,950.

Cadillac came in the 14th position selling 28,479 cars for the calendar run. These figures also include La Salle sales for the year.

It looks like this 1936 Cadillac Series 70 is going in for its regular servicing from the local Cadillac dealer. The license plate shows it to be a New York car. Most models came equipped with side mounted spares in 1936 even though they were an accessory. This model was a Fleetwood body. It weighed 4,630 lbs. Its wheelbase measured 131 inches and the price tag was $2,445.

This 1936 Cadillac Fleetwood 7-passenger Sedan was available on a 138-inch wheelbase. It could be ordered as a Series 75 employing a 135 H.P. V-8 or Series 85 using a 150 H.P. V-12. As a V-8 it sold for $2,795 and weighed 4,885 lbs. In the V-12 version it weighed 5,150 lbs. and sold for $3,495.

1937

"New for 1937" was what Cadillac claimed in its advertising. A smart new radiator grille and hood design were used that year. Plush interiors were also offered. The Cadillac 60 for 1937 came with a 346 cubic inch engine, the same as was used on the larger 1936 Eights. The Eights had all steel new bodies equipped with the hypoid rear axle in which the pinion was two inches below the center line of the ring gear. All Eights came with a dual downdraft Stromberg carburetor. The choke used with the carburetor became fully automatic.

The Cadillac V-8 Series 60 came with a 135 HP engine (at 3400 RPM). This series used a 22 gallon fuel tank. These models rode on 7:00 x 16 inch tires, using a 124-inch wheelbase.

All Series 65-70 models shared the same V-8 engine as Series 60 cars, yielding the same power, but were seven inches longer. They required 7:50 x 16 inch tires and a 25 gallon fuel supply. The V-8 Series 75 again was the same car in all respects but was on a 138-inch wheelbase.

All Cadillac V-12s looked like Series 75 cars except when it came to the powerplant. Here were 12 cylinders giving 150 HP at 3600 RPM using a 30 gallon gasoline supply. These models used a 154-inch wheelbase and came with 7:50 x 17 inch tires.

The big improvement for the V-16 was its change over to hydraulic brakes.

There were 27 body styles available for the year, ranging in price from $1,445 for the 4-passenger Series 60 Sport Coupe to the V-16 Imperial Sedan at $7,550. Cadillac placed 15th by selling 45,223 units for the calendar year. These figures also represent La Salle sales for the year.

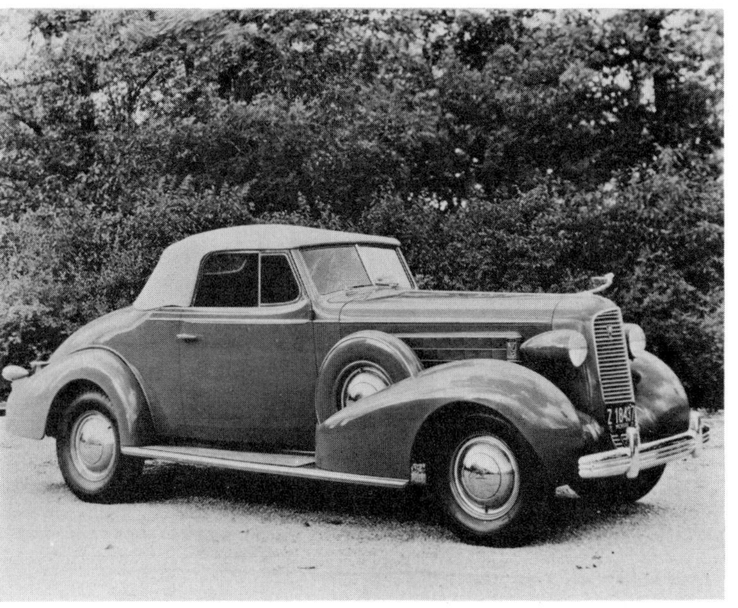

This side mounted Series 60 1936 Cadillac V-8 Convertible Coupe was available for $1,725. A rumble seat was standard equipment on this model. The wheelbase was 121 inches. Seating capacity was for four.

Shown here is a 1936 Cadillac Fleetwood 7-passenger Cabriolet available either as a V-8 in Series 75, selling for $4,445, or $5,145 as a V-12 Series 85. The wheelbase was 138 inches. This model offered a glass partition and a telephone to driver, carried in a slash pocket above the right arm rest. Smoking equipment consisted of ash receivers and lighters. Forward facing auxiliary seats were standard.

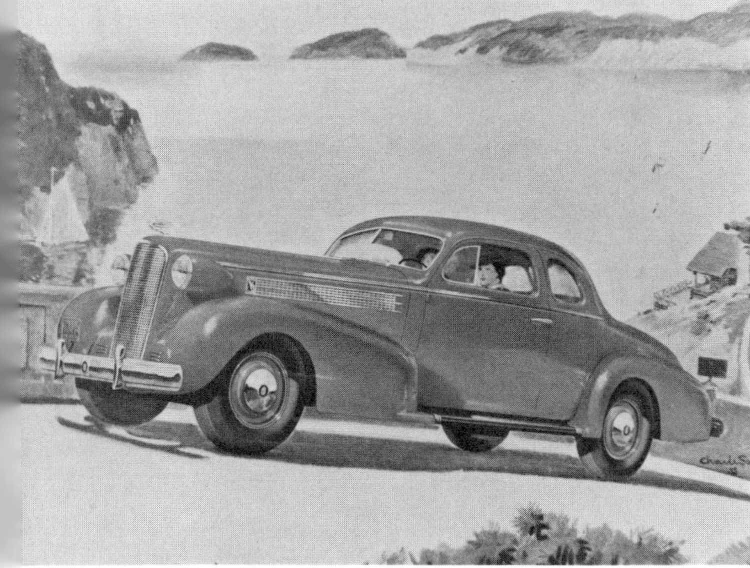

Cadillac's least expensive model in the 1937 line up was this Series 60 V-8 Sport Coupe. It carried four passengers and sold for $1,445. The wheelbase was 124 inches in this series.

The 1936 V-16 Cadillac Convertible Sedan. This style was begun in 1934 and continued through 1937. The style and code number for this car was 5880. A total of 20 were built during the four years. In 1936, six were manufactured. The price was $8,150.

Cadillac

A 1937 Cadillac V-8 Series 60 Convertible Coupe sold for $1,575. It carried four passengers. The rumble seat was still available on this model.

This was the most expensive model in the Series 60. It was known as the Convertible Sedan for five and used a Fisher Body just as did the other Series 60 cars. It sold for $1,885.

The only model available in the Series 65 was this 4-door Touring Sedan for five. A Fisher Body was used in this series, too. It had a 131-inch wheelbase. Most models had fender wells; however, this was one example that escaped this classic looking accessory. Its price was $1,945.

The Cadillac Series 65 for 1938 offered this V-8 Convertible Coupe with a rumble seat for the last time. It came on a 132-inch wheelbase and sold for $2,495. Besides this model, Cadillac also offered a Sedan, Formal 5-passenger Sedan, and Convertible Sedan in the Series 65.

Two examples of this elegant 60's Convertible Sedan were built. Unfortunately neither are around today. Both were experimentals and used by Cadillac brass in 1938.

The real eye catcher of the Cadillac line for 1938 was this 60 Special Touring Sedan with a Fleetwood Body. The wheelbase was 127 inches. Many classed this car as an early hardtop style with the chrome window encasements. It truly was available only in 4-door sedan style. The 60 Special sold for $2,085. Today, the Classic Car Club of America has given full recognition to the 1938 through 1941 60's as Classics.

Cadillac

938

The 1938 Cadillacs made some changes. First off, the -16 came with a new, lighter and simpler L-head engine. he Series 60 had a new low-bodied 4-door sedan with a isher body which caught the eyes of everyone. For the rst time Cadillac offered the gearshift mounted on the eering column as standard equipment. With the change f the V-16 engine, having a 431 cubic inch displacement, adillac felt it wise to discontinue the V-12 Series in 937. The V-8 models consisted of Series 60, 65 and 75. he wheelbases were 127, 132 and 141 inches respectively. he Series 60 came only in one body style, while the 5s were offered in three Fisher bodies. The Series 75 ıed the same body shells as were used in the V-16s, ırrying the same wheelbase of 141 inches. They came 12 models, each carrying a Fleetwood body.

The Series 60 and 65 both used 135 HP engines at 400 RPM. The 75s came with 140 HP at the same RPM. -16 cars used the 175 HP engines at 3600 RPM. The) Sedan had a tire size of 7:00 x 16 while all other odels came with 7:50 x 16s. Fuel supply was a 24 gallon nk in the 60 model, while the remaining three models nployed 25 gallon supplies.

Twenty-eight models were available for 1938, ranging price from $2,085 for a 60 Touring Sedan for 6 ıssengers to $7,170 in V-16 Town Car attire.

Cadillac sold 27,613 cars this calendar run, putting the ımpany in the 14th sales spot. These sales figures also clude La Salle for 1938.

A new device offered on the Model 6119-A and)19-SA was the sun roof. The 6119-A Series built only 2 while the 6019-A Models produced 108 with the ıtional accessory.

A beautiful car with classic lines in 1938, and even more so today, is this 1938 V-16 Cadillac Convertible Sedan. Its style and code number is 9029. This model was built through 1940. A total of 13 were built in 1938 and for the three year span a grand total of 19 were produced. The price of this model was $6,000. Incidentally, all prices introduced in 1938 remained firm through 1940 when the model ceased.

Oddly enough this wasn't the lowest priced 1938 V-16 Cadillac, even though it was classed as a 2-passenger Coupe. Being a car of sporty nature it was more costly by $200 than the 5-passenger Sedan. It sold for $5,335 and was available on a 141-inch wheelbase, just like the 75 Series V-8's.

This 1938 V-16 Cadillac Imperial 7-passenger Sedan sold for $5,420. For the first time all 1938 Cadillacs offered the gear shift mounted on the steering column.

Nicely equipped is this 1939 Cadillac V-8 60 Special Touring Sedan. This model was in its second year and had been accepted very well by the public. Trim changes were the only differences. For 1930 the rear license was mounted on the trunk rather than above the left tail lamp as in 1938. This car is fully equipped with large wheel discs, white sidewall tires, sidemount spares and factory spot light. In base form, this 127-inch car weighed 4,110 lbs. and sold for $2,090. It is rated as a classic today.

A 1939 Cadillac 75 Convertible Sedan for 5 passengers sold for $3,945. This beauty offered side mounts at extra cost. Its weight was 5,075 pounds.

A rear view of the 1939 Cadillac 75 7-passenger Touring Sedan on its 141-inch wheelbase. This model sold for $3,210. In 5-passenger style it was available for $2,995. Both versions had cloth interiors throughout. The Formal Sedans of this version came with a genuine leather front compartment.

The 1939 Cadillac Model 9029 was the same car as offered in 1938, which sold for $6,000. This example is equipped with Trippe road lights and twin mirrors on top of the side mounted spares. In 1939, only four Convertible Sedans were built.

This 7-passenger 1939 Cadillac Town Car sold for $7,175. Five were built. The weight of this vehicle was 9,033 lbs. It was referred to as Style 9053.

1939

An attractively styled new car was what Cadillac brought out in 1939. The line displayed a new hood and grille, and a more squared-off body with the rear license being mounted on the trunk in the Series 60, 61 and 75 models. The Series 65 wasn't offered for 1939.

Better visibility was one of the selling features for that model year. A sun roof was available in the 60 and 61 Sedans as in 1938. The wheelbase on the Series 61 was increased two inches, making it now a 126-inch car. It was practically the same car as the Series 60 except that it used a different body. Both came with the 346 cubic inch V-8 engine developing 135 HP at 3400 RPM. 7:00 x 16 inch tires were required for both models. Each used a 22 gallon fuel tank. The two series used Fisher bodies.

The 75s took an engine of the same displacement but developed 140 HP at 3400 RPM. They rode on 7:50 x 16 inch tires and used a 26½ gallon fuel supply as did the V-16.

All Series 90 cars used a 431 cubic inch V-16 engine with 185 HP at 4000 RPM. The wheelbase was 141 inches, like that of the 75s. Both of these series used Fleetwood bodies.

The V-16 made a rather large change with the 1938 car, so any differences on the 1939 models were minimal.

A total of 29 models were available for the 1939 Cadillacs, ranging in price from $1,610 for the V-8 4-passenger Coupe to $7,175 for the 7-passenger V-16 Town Car by Fleetwood.

Cadillac placed in 15th position by selling 38,520 cars for the calendar run. These sales figures also include La Salle.

This 1939 Cadillac V-16 Formal Sedan was available both in 5-passenger and 7-passenger style. Four 5-passengers and eight 7-passengers were manufactured. Both sold for $6,055.

Cadillac's most popular model for 1940 was the newly designed Series 62 4-door Sedan which weighed 4,032 lbs. and sold for $1,752. This sedan used a Fisher body and rode on a 129-inch wheelbase. It is shown with the full accessory package of fog lamps, sidemounts, twin side mirrors, full wheel covers, whitewall tires, and radio. Equipped like this it brought a few dollars more on the bill of sale. This was the last year Cadillac used sidemounts on its cars.

940

For 1940, Cadillac changed its model designations omewhat. The Model 62s were the lowest priced Cadillacs or the year, beginning at $1,652 for the 4-passenger 'oupe, and ranging upward to $7,175 for a Fleetwood -passenger V-16 Series 90 Town Car. In between these wo series were the 60, 72, and 75, all of which rode on 'leetwood bodies.

All Cadillac 60 and 62 models had a 135 HP engine (at 400 RPM) of 346 cubic inches. The fuel capacity for oth models was a 22 gallon tank. Both shared the 7:00 x 6 inch tires. The Series 62 came on a 129-inch wheelbase nd the Series 60 employed the same wheelbase as the revious year – 127 inches. Two mid-year offerings ecame available. They were both stylish models to add to he 62 line up – a Convertible Coupe, and a Convertible edan.

The Series 72 was also a new addition for the year. It elonged with the Series 75, being offered in six versions f the sedan. Three were 5-passenger Fleetwood Sedans nd the other three were in 7-passenger style. These iodels came on a 138-inch wheelbase. They used a 26 allon fuel supply. The tire size was 7:50 x 16 inches. 'he engines on both Series 72 and 75 models had the 46 cubic inch engine but developed 140 HP at 3400 RPM. The Series 72s had door handles mounted flush vith the stainless steel belt molding, which was different rom the 75 Series.

The Series 75 was mechanically the same car as the eries 72 except the 75 used a ½ gallon larger fuel tank ke the V-16. It also used the same wheelbase as the '-16 of 141 inches. The interior appointments were more vish than the 72 displayed. The 75s weighed roughly 00 lbs. more than the 72 models, and were priced about 300 more.

The V-16 was to play its swan song at the end of the iodel run. It used the same components as had been sed in the 1938 and 1939 cars.

The horsepowér was 185 at 4000 RPM. The tire size 'as 7:50 x 16 inches, fuel supply was 26½ gallons, and it 'as offered in the same 12 models. Altogether, Cadillac ffered 38 different models. Cadillac placed in Fifteenth osition for sales by selling 40,235 cars. These figures, owever, chiefly refer to La Salle as sales figures were nly combined for the year. For the first eight months of ales, Cadillac sold 8,041 automobiles.

In its third year of production, the 1940 Cadillac 60 Special was gaining more popularity. This year four versions were available but most chose the regular Touring Sedan which sold for $2,099 and weighed 4,070 lbs. The other styles were with a division window and two Town Car Touring Sedans. All were built on the 127-inch wheelbase. The top 60 Special sold for $3,829 fully equipped. A sun roof was available at extra cost for this Fleetwood Sedan.

A new 1940 model was this Series 72 9-passenger Touring Sedan. Cadillac felt this model was the ideal answer for funeral homes, as it was just the right size. It had room for three on its auxiliary seats which were regularly required for funeral services. This model came on a Fleetwood body of 138 inches, weighed 4,705 lbs. and sold for $2,795. These cars were used well into the 1950's to haul vacationers from New York City to Catskill Mountains resorts.

Cadillac's 1940 Fleetwood 75 Models were available in 12 styles. This example is the 8-passenger Touring Sedan. It weighed 4,916 lbs. and sold for $3,223. Designed for complete comfort, the seats were made wide and deeply cushioned and upholstered for long wear. Side mounts were optional at extra cost.

The Series 72 Formal Town Car with body by Fleetwood sold for $3,705. It weighed 4,780 lbs. This car had an entirely different rear section than the Series 75. Its tail lamps were mounted high on the trunk compartment as shown in the above photo.

Cadillac

The 1940 Cadillac V-16 5-passenger Sedan rode on a 141-inch wheelbase. This model weighed 5,152 lbs. and sold for $5,140. A total of four were built in 1940. The grand total for the three years this model was manufactured was 60.

One of Cadillac's most popular models for 1941 was this 4-door Series 61 DeLuxe Touring Sedan. It was considered the model that replaced the La Salle in price class. This deluxe model sold for $1,535 equipped with stainless rocker moldings, large wheel covers, and chrome window reveals.

This Cadillac V-16 Convertible Coupe for 1940 sold for $5,440. For the 1940 model run, only two were assembled. During its three year life span, 19 were delivered. This was the final year for the V-16.

Cadillac's only convertible coupe for 1941 was this Series 62 version which sold for $1,645 and weighed 4,055 lbs. The body was by Fisher. This particular car is nicely accessorized with white walls, trim rings, fender skirts, radio and factory spotlight. Hydra-Matic was available on all models at extra cost.

The 1941 Cadillac Series 63 was offered only as a 4-door Touring Sedan. The buyer had his choice of either Fleetwood or Fisher body trim. The 63 model was probably the least popular of all 1941 Cadillacs. It weighed 4,140 lbs. and sold for $1,695.

A beautiful 1941 Cadillac Series 62 Convertible Sedan on the 126-inch Fisher bodied wheelbase. This model weighed 4,230 lbs. and sold for $1,965. Built in fender fog lamps were an accessory that proved very popular in all 1941 models. Fender skirts were optional at extra cost.

.941

For this year the company brought out an entirely new ar which was and has been the most popular car Cadillac as ever built.

New model designations were given pretty much through he line. The lowest priced Cadillac offered was the Series 1 which replaced the La Salle. Next in the line-up came he Series 62 which was the Torpedo style body similar to he Pontiac Custom Torpedo. Olds 98 and the Buick uper and Roadmaster. Following the 62 was a 4-door edan only, called the Series 63. The Series 67 was next which offered four sedans in 5 and 7-passenger style on a isher body. The Series 60, which was first offered in 938, continued in three versions of the 4-door Sedan on Fleetwood chassis. The top of the line was the Series 75 oming in six styles on a 5 and 7-passenger chassis with ody by Fleetwood.

Mechanically, all series were alike. They used a 346 ubic inch V-8 developing 150 HP at 3400 RPM. All odels but the 75 had a 20 gallon fuel tank. The 75 used 24 gallon supply. The tire size on models 60, 61, 62, nd 63 was 7:00 x 15 inches. The Series 67 and 75 used :50 x 16 inch tires. The wheelbase on models 60 through 3 was 126 inches. The Series 67 rode on a 139-inch hassis and the Series 75 came on a 136-inch wheelbase.

Cadillac offered Hydra Matic Drive as another step orward for 1941. It was available in all models. In ddition to this option at extra cost one of the firsts of n air-conditioned unit concealed in the trunk was offered y Cadillac, but very few devices were sold.

Cadillac displayed 24 models ranging in price from 1,345 for a Series 61 5-passenger Sedanet Coupe to 4,045 for the Series 75 Fleetwood 7-passenger Formal edan.

For the calendar year, Cadillac remained in 15th osition from the sale of 59,572 cars.

A 1941 Cadillac Series 67 5-passenger Touring Sedan with a Fisher body weighed 4,555 lbs. and sold for $2,595. This series was available in four models, all on the 139-inch wheelbase. The 7-passenger Imperial Touring Sedan was the top of the line in this series. It sold for $2,800. The Series 67 was new in 1941 and lasted only through the 1942 model run.

Granted classic recognition was the 1941 Cadillac Series 75. It was available in six versions of 4-door sedan ranging in price from $2,995 for a 5-passenger Touring Sedan to $4,045 as a 7-passenger Formal Sedan that weighed 4,915 lbs. Strangely enough, the Series 75's had a 3-inch shorter wheelbase than the Series 67. The 75's were on a 136-inch chassis. This body style continued through 1949.

Cadillac's lowest priced 4-door Sedan for 1942 was this 126-inch Series 61 4-door Sedan that weighed 4,115 lbs. It sold for $1,605. It was only available in Touring Sedan style but had the deluxe options offered in 1941. In an effort to economize, only a Club Coupe and Touring Sedan were offered in the 1942 Series 61 line.

Very few 1942 Cadillacs were sold with World War II shaping up. Most models sold were cars that would give good practical service because no one knew when they'd get another new car. This model came with chrome trim until January 1st, 1942. From that date till early in February, only blackout versions were marketed. The 62 Convertible was $30 shy of hitting $2,000.

A popular model was this 1942 Cadillac Series 62 4-door Sedan. It sold for $1,710 in Touring Sedan style and $1,790 in deluxe fashion with large wheel covers, Hydra-Matic, and special interior decor.

Cadillac

Cadillac's 1942 Series 63 4-door Touring Sedan sold for $1,835. It weighed 4,150 lbs. An unusual piece of equipment on this car are whitewall tires. Very few 1942 models offered this luxury, as the components to make a white tire were being used for defense efforts. This was the final year for the Cadillac Series 63.

The 1942 Cadillac 60 Special resembled the Series 62 a great deal. For the first time in its five year history did it offer a 133-inch wheelbase. The body was entirely changed which seems strange when the management knew that very few models were to be built. The easy identification of a 1942 Series 60 Special are the chevrons placed by the rear quarter vent panes and beneath the fender and door moldings. This model sold for $2,375 in Touring Sedan style and for $2,525 as a Formal Sedan with glass partition between front and rear passengers.

A special bodied Derham Town Car for 1942 was built on the regular 136-inch chassis. Six of this body style were built before the war brought a halt to automobile manufacturing. Fortunately, this one example carries all the brightwork which makes it a beautiful classic.

1942

The 1942 line offered a newly styled front end, fenders and a variety of interior combinations plus som mechanical changes. A new grille which consisted of si large horizontal bars behind which were 14 more thi bars of the same style. Rectangular fog lights, which wer optional, were placed below the headlights and withi the fenders. A more massive bumper with bullet shape guards was displayed. The new fender design offered more streamlined appearance and was available in al models but the Series 75. On the Series 60 through 6 4-door Sedans, the rear fender line extended into the rea doors.

The interiors came with a bullet effect housing on th steering column for mounting the gearshift lever. A entirely new dash with new Lucite trimmed hardware and a new radio grille was displayed.

All 1942 models came with a new hand brake. It was T-shaped handle mounted on the left side of the instru ment panel which was pulled straight out to set the brake To release the brake the handle was pulled to the left

A more sturdy gasoline tank, more effective shoc absorbers, and an improved water pump that gave mor cooling to both banks of the V-8 were used. A new brak drum was introduced that prevented fading even a successive 100 MPH stops.

The same 346 cubic inch engine that developed 150 H at 3400 RPM was still in use. A 20 gallon fuel supply wa on all models but the Series 75 which continued with it 24 gallon tank.

The tire size on all 60, 61, and 63 models was 7:00 x 1 inches. The 67 and 75s used the 7:50 x 16 inch tires. Th wheelbase on the Series 61 and 63 was 126 inches. Serie 62 increased that year to 129 inches. The 60 model used a 133-inch wheelbase, while the 67 models were th longest Cadillacs of the year. They rode on a 139-inc chassis. The Series 75 came on a 136-inch wheelbase

A total of 22 models were available, priced from $1,52 for a Series 61 5-passenger Club Coupe to $4,375 in th 5-passenger Formal Sedan on the Series 75 chassis Cadillac again ranked in 15th Position for the calenda year from the sale of 2,873 cars.

A 1942 Cadillac Series 75 5-passenger Touring Sedan used a 136-inch wheelbase and weighed 4,705 lbs. The body was by Fleetwood. Virtually all Series 75's came with Hydra-Matic Drive. This model sold for $3,225.

Chevrolet

Chevrolet was a division of General Motors Corp. with ıctory headquarters being in Flint, Mich. The car was rst offered in 1911 but officially sold to the public nce 1913.

For 1930, Chevrolet didn't make much of a change, nce 1929 had been the big year for introduction of a -cylinder car. In 1930, the name change from Inter-ational Series to Universal Series was adopted. The tire ze changed to 4:75 x 19 and the car now offered ydraulic shock absorbers, and an electric fuel gauge ıounted on the dash. The engine developed 46 HP at 600 RPM. The fuel supply was an 11 gallon tank. All ıodels came on a 107-inch wheelbase. Mechanical brakes ere used.

Seven models were available ranging in price from $495 or a 2-passenger Roadster to $695 for the Special Sedan or 5.

Chevrolet held the Number 2 place that it had in 1929. roduction figures placed Chevrolet with 683,419 vehicles. old during the calendar year.

This 1930 Chevrolet 4-door Sedan was known as the Universal Series AD. It was very similar to the 1929 International Series but did come with hydraulic shock absorbers and used the slant windshield on all models. This model weighed 2,615 lbs. and sold for $675. In this series 135,193 were produced.

931

For 1931, Chevrolet offered a new body with some dditional models in the line-up. Among them were seen ıe Cabriolet, 5-passenger Coupe, and a Landau Phaeton. he 2-passenger Coupe came in 2-window and 5-window yles. The 5-window version also was available as a Sport oupe with rumble seat.

The new cars were referred to as Independence Series .E. The engine now developed 50 HP at 2600 RPM from s 6 cylinders. The fuel supply was again an 11 gallon ınk. This year's car was 2 inches longer, now being 109 ıches. It again used 4:75 x 19 inch tires. The brake ystem was mechanical. Four Lovejoy shock absorbers ere used, and the steering wheel was a three-spoke hard ıbber type.

Chevrolet offered 10 models ranging in price from $475 or the 2-passenger Roadster to $650 for the Special edan for 5 passengers. The company ranked in First osition from the calendar sale of 627,104 cars.

Chevrolet's Independence Series AE Phaeton for 1931 had a production run of only 852 cars. In basic form it sold for $510 and weighed 2,370 lbs. This particular example is owned by Jim Wesbrooks of Tulare, Cal., and is a national trophy winner continually. It displays all the original accessory equipment then available.

The 1931 Chevrolet International Series AE 2-passenger 5-window Coupe was priced at $545 and weighed 2,490 lbs. This model is displayed for the press, showing off its rumble seat. Double bar bumpers were used on the earlier models such as this car. Later production featured the single bar bumper. All bumpers were optional at extra cost.

The 1931 Chevrolet Independence Series AE offered this 5-passenged Coupe. A total of 20,297 of this model were produced. This model sold for $595 and weighed 2,610 lbs. in basic form. When equipped with sidemount spares it was easier to load and unload the trunk. This particular car is owned by Homer Dotson of Toledo, Ohio.

Chevrolet

A 6-wheeled 1932 Chevrolet Confederate Series BA Special Sedan appeared for the last time this year. Chevrolet produced 52,446 of this body style in both Standard and DeLuxe versions. In Standard form it sold for $615 and weighed 2,800 lbs. The DeLuxe style weighed 2,850 lbs. and sold for $630.

1932

The offerings for 1932 consisted of eleven models from $475 for the Roadster to $660 for the Landau Phaeton. All entries again had a 109-inch wheelbase but with a 60 HP engine at 3000 RPM. Brakes were of the mechanical type. Gasoline capacity was of 11 gallons. Tire size was now 5:25 x 17. The sales picture for Chevrolet was a good one. They held the Number One position as they had done in 1931. The registration figures showed 305,716 units out of dealers showrooms for the calendar year.

There were 117 new improvements for the car. The power plant was now mounted in rubber at six points. A highly ingenious method was devised for mounting the headlamps, fenders and radiator as one unit. These were semi-independent of the frame, but tied to the dash so that they moved with the body and were prevented from wobbling crosswise at high speeds or on rough terrain. A synchromesh transmission with free-wheeling, improved clutch, pressure lubrication to engine main bearings, and a down draft carburetor were a few of the improvements that were found when Chevrolet introduced the new line on Jan. 5, 1932.

This is the 1932 Chevrolet Standard Phaeton that looks pretty plain when compared to the DeLuxe cars of that time. In basic form it sold for $495 and weighed 2,520 lbs. It is debateable whether the Phaeton came as DeLuxe or not. Records indicate it to be not available and yet some have shown up at recent car shows throughout the country. Possibly, owners have added the DeLuxe trim to make them look more sporty.

An introduction to the 1932 line shows off the Queen of the Show in the New York City Auto Show from January 6th to the 13th, 1932. This was a Confederate Series BA Landau Phaeton. A total of 1,602 were built between Standard and DeLuxe models. The Standard weighed 2,700 lbs. and sold for $625. The DeLuxe models sold for $640 and weighed 2,750 lbs. This body style was discontinued at the end of the 1932 season.

A not too popular model at the time was this 1932 Chevrolet DeLuxe Confederate BA 5-passenger Coupe. A total of 7,566 were built in both Standard and DeLuxe models. The Standard models sold for $575 and weighed 2,700 lbs. The DeLuxe line was $590 and weighed 50 lbs. more. Standard equipment in the DeLuxe included assist straps, arm rests, rear quarter window curtains, two ash trays, and a vanity case.

.933

The lines of the 1933 Chevrolet were those of classic .ppeal for the everyday car buyer. It was a sure bet for he Number One sales position once again.

To begin 1933, Chevrolet introduced a 113-inch wheel-ase and referred to it as the Eagle Series CA. It had a loping Vee radiator grille, fenders that were skirted, and 'isher no-draft ventilation. Horsepower was raised from 0 to 65. A starter operated by the use of the accelerator edal, a distributor with an "octane selector" for maximum ower and fuel economy, and an automatic manifold heat ontrol were the new features of this car.

Along in mid-season, something was needed to help the agging sales picture. The model that did it was the 07-inch series called the Mercury. This name was kept nly for one year. Many people refer to this car as the tandard Series, but this title was not given until the 1934 nodels. At a quick glance, both series looked very much like, except for the difference in wheelbase. The Mercury nodels came in three versions: Coach, 2-passenger Coupe, nd Rumbleseat Coupe. Both series used the same engine.

Tire size was now 5:25 x 18. The car had mechanical rakes, and a 14 gallon gas supply. Prices ranged from 445 for the 2-passenger Mercury Coupe up to the Eagle 'abriolet in 4-passenger style for $565. The Town Sedan vas a new model for the year. It was basically a coach, ut had a built in trunk and carried its spare tires in the ender wells. Altogether, Chevrolet offered 11 models.

This year saw 481,134 units built. Of these, 35,848 were f the Mercury Series, and the remaining 445,286 belonged o the Eagles.

A 1932 Chevrolet DeLuxe Confederate Series BA Sports Roadster. This model sold for $500 and weighed 2,480 lbs. The production of this model for the year totalled 8,552 in both DeLuxe and Standard versions. When equipped with sidemounts the car had more appeal to most buyers.

A beautiful 1933 Chevrolet Eagle Series Sedan was a very popular model with families. This model cost $565 and weighed 2,830 lbs. The new name of Eagle was represented by the eagle hood ornament. A total of 162,361 were built for the year.

The press introduction for 1933 Chevrolets took place in Miami, Fl. This is one of the publicity scenes showing a 1933 Roadster that sold for $485. It weighed 2,555 lbs. All Roadsters used the rumble seat compartment for the two extra passengers. A total of 2,867 were built in 1933.

The new suspension system introduced by Chevrolet in 1934 is getting a once over. This new device was called Knee Action by Chevrolet. It was different from the hard riding "I" beam axle that Chevrolet offered before. The Standard did not offer Knee Action at anytime.

Chevrolet

1934

This year Chevrolet also had new independent suspension. Chevrolet's device was referred to as Knee Action, which was to give a superior ride and give added life to tires. In addition to this, the "Cast Iron Wonder" had better lubrication and a different head design with redesigned combustion chambers. This engine was available in Master Series only. The name of the lower priced car, Mercury, was changed to the Standard Series for 1934. A top speed of 80 MPH was claimed.

In the engine compartment, the Standard developed 60 HP at 3000 RPM and the Master produced 80 HP at 3300 RPM. The Standard used an 11 gallon fuel tank while a 14 gallon tank went to the Master Series.

Tire size was 5:25 x 17 on the Standard models and 5:50 x 17 for the big brother. Wheelbases were five inches apart. The Standard came on a 107-inch chassis while the Master used the 112-inch wheelbase.

A total of 13 models were available between the two series. In the Master Series, the Master Sports Sedan with an integral trunk was the newest model available. Prices varied between $465 for the Standard Sport Roadster and $675 for the Master Trunk Sedan.

The 1934 Chevrolet model production run of 620,726 put the company in the First spot once again.

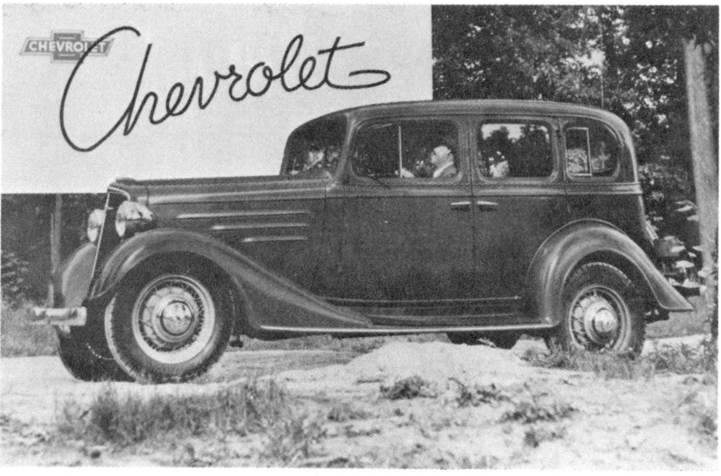

The Master Series 4-door Sedan was Chevrolet's second most popular model. It weighed 3,080 lbs. and cost $640. The total production of this sedan for 1934 was 124,754.

1935

For this year, Chevrolet saw the use of an all-steel ro for the Master. This was called a Turret Top. The Standar didn't acquire this for one more year. Knee action w again talked about and most Master models came with i They were called EA Series with the knees, and witho were known as ED Series. Without knee action, the c cost $20 less.

The Master didn't resemble the Standard at all. It ca with a V-shaped windshield, well rounded fenders, a radiator cap concealed under the hood for the first tim

The Master used the 80 HP engine; 5:50 x 17 inch tire and came on a 113-inch wheelbase, which was an in longer than last year. Fuel supply was again a 14 gall tank. Mechanical brakes were used again in both serie Body styles amounted to six, with a 2-passenger Mast Coupe at the bottom of the price ladder. It cost $58 Top of the model line ran $695 for a Master Sport Seda

The Standard Series was very similar to its 1934 brothe Five models were available, with the Sport Roadster a Phaeton not being built for the entire year. The cars aga came with 5:25 x 17 inch tires, but used a 74 HP engi at 3200 RPM. The fuel supply came from an 11 gall tank. The Standards used a 107-inch wheelbase as on t 1934s.

Prices of these cars went from $465 for a Sp Roadster and ended at $550 for a Standard 5-passeng Sedan.

This year, Chevrolet lost out to Ford for the Numb One sales position. Between the two series, they produc 554,457 units for the model year. The total car productio for the calendar year reached 793,437. Among the figures was Chevrolet's 10-millionth car which was Standard 4-door Sedan.

This 1935 Chevrolet Phaeton was in production for a very short time. A total of 217 were built in 1935 before being phased out. Probably these were the number of bodies left over from 1934 that Chevrolet felt wise to use before dropping the model. It weighed 2,465 lbs. and sold for $485.

Chevrolet's most popular model for 1934 was this 2-door Coach, which weighed 2,995 lbs. and sold for $580. This example is a Master Series which had a production run of 163,948 units.

936

This year Chevrolet introduced some changes. Among hem were: hydraulic brakes, one engine for both series, nd the all-steel "turret top" now available on the Standard odels.

The horsepower developed 79 at 3200 RPM. Chevrolet or the last time offered two separate wheelbases – 109 nches for the Standard models and 113 inches in Master orm. The fuel capacity was a 14 gallon tank in both series. he Standard used a 5:25 x 17 inch tire and the Masters ame with 5:50 x 17s.

Absent in 1935 was a Cabriolet. In 1936 it was used on he Standard Series only. This policy followed through in 937 and 1938, putting a top-of-the-line car out in the tandard axle Master Series only.

A total of 13 models were available this year, seven in he Standard style from the $495 2-passenger Coupe to the 18-inch wheelbase Budd Bodied Touring Brougham for axi and fleet service. The Master Series consisted of six nodels from the $580 Master Coupe up to the $685 Aaster Sport Sedan.

Chevrolet regained its Number One sales position in 936 by selling 975,238 units during the model run.

The most popular model again for Chevrolet was this 1935 Master DeLuxe 2-door Coach of which 102,996 were manufactured. It weighed 3,040 lbs. and sold for $600. The buyer had his choice of standard wire wheels or the new steel spoked wheels if he so chose.

Since it began to look like the country was pulling out of the depression, Chevrolet was trying to interest the public into doubling their families' motoring pleasure by owning two new Chevrolets for 1936. Shown here is the 1936 Master DeLuxe Sport Sedan and the 1936 Standard Cabriolet.

A Master DeLuxe Sport Coupe with wire wheels was a very impressive car in the low priced field. This being a Sport Coupe, the rumble seat was standard equipment but was dropping in popularity. The doors opened from the front only on the 1935 line. It gave a graceful appearance to the entire line but wasn't very popular among those buying a new car. This model weighed 2,970 lbs. and had a price tag of $620.

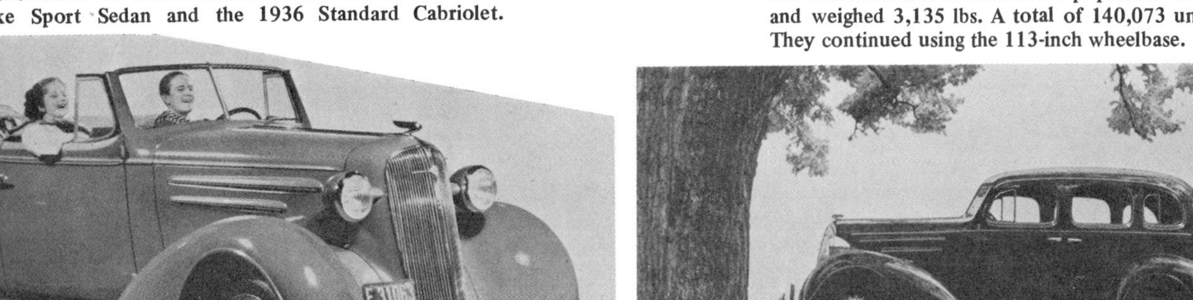

The 1936 Chevrolet Standard Convertible Cabriolet was new for the year since the company didn't put out a Cabriolet or Roadster in 1935. This model came in rumble seat form only. The company sold 3,629 of this model which weighed 2,745 lbs. and cost $595. Its wheelbase was 109 inches.

This 1936 Chevrolet Master DeLuxe Sport Sedan came with the built-in trunk as standard equipment. It sold for $685 and weighed 3,135 lbs. A total of 140,073 units were built. They continued using the 113-inch wheelbase.

Chevrolet

This 1937 Chevrolet Master DeLuxe Business Coupe is a pride-and-joy of the author. It sold new for $685 and weighed 2,840 lbs. This car has the rear large factory wheel covers and fog lamps that belong to 1941 models. It is painted in the original color of Brookhaven Blue metallic.

1937

Chevrolet, like the rest of the General Motors cars, had revamping of the entire line. Chevy came out with a ver impressive line for the year. Model designations we changed to Master for the lower priced car and Maste DeLuxes for the knee action models. Both models use the same new 6-cylinder engine of 216.5 cubic inch using four main bearings rather than three as was the ca in previous years. Horsepower developed was 85 a 3200 RPM in these 112¼-inch wheelbased cars. Fu supply was from a 14 gallon tank. The tire size was 6:00 16 inches in each Series. The Master continued to use th conventional front axle.

In the appearance department, the cars looked mo alike than Chevrolets had ever looked before in differe Series. The Master was shown with less trim than i "gussied up" sister. A plain Master came without du taillamps, double wipers, arm rest for front passenger bumper guards, plain bumpers and minus a heat indicat on the dash panel. All could be ordered but at addition cost.

Twelve models were available beginning at $619 for th Master Business Coupe and ending at $788 for the Mast DeLuxe 4-door Sedan. Chevrolet again took top honors f the No. 1 place in sales by having a model run of 868,25 units.

A 1937 Chevrolet Master DeLuxe Sport Sedan sold for $788 and weighed 2,960 lbs. This was an early press release photo showing only one taillight, as all Master DeLuxes had two rear lamps. Only the Master was equipped with one rear light, on which the license was mounted. The Master DeLuxe had Knee Action in all models.

Obviously, the most popular car in the Master Series continued to be the Town Sedan, a 2-door model with integral trunk. This restored model, owned by Elmer Thomas of North Braddock, Pa., uses the popular accessory chrome wheel covers and dual fog lights. The Town Sedan, which cost $655 and weighed 2,830, had a production run of 178,645. Its companion car, the 2-door Coach, with outside mounted spare and no trunk, had a run of only 15,349. The coach cost $637 and weighed 2,800 pounds.

The only Master Series that really looked like a Master DeLuxe as far as trim goes was this Cabriolet. Strangely enough, one of the top of the line came with the straight axle rather than the highly advertised Knee Action. The Cabriolet sold for $725 and weighed 2,790 lbs. This trim looking car sold only 1,724 units for the 1937 run.

938

Coming out with a major change in 1937, the new nodels for 1938 reflected just minor faceliftings but vere pleasingly done.

Both Series, Master and Master DeLuxe had new grilles sing horizontal chrome bars rather than the vertical attern of the previous year. This gave quite a different ppearance to the car's front end.

The Master continued to use the straight axle in front nd the DeLuxe models came again with knee action.

The engine compartment continued to use the 216.5 ubic inch displacement developing 85 HP at 3200 RPM. The wheelbase was 112 inches, like in 1937, with all nodels riding on 6:00 x 16 inch tires. The fuel capacity gain was a 14 gallon tank.

Twelve models were available ranging in price from 648 for a straight axle Master Business Coupe to the Master DeLuxe Sport Sedan for 6 passengers at $817. Also available was a 7-passenger vehicle with Chevrolet arts but manufactured by the GM Truck Division. This utomobile was not catalogued by Chevrolet, but was eferred to as the General Cab.

Placing First for the year Chevrolet sold 490,447 cars.

This 1938 Chevrolet Master DeLuxe Business Coupe was very similar to the 1937 model both in looks and in mechanical components. It sold well, especially for salesmen or anyone who required a large trunk for keeping supplies. The spare tire was mounted in back of the right front seat. The production of this car was 36,106. Its weight was 2,840 lbs. and it sold for $714.

The heaviest Chevy for 1938 was this Master DeLuxe Sport Sedan that weighed 2,940 lbs. It sold for $817. A total of 76,323 were built. It was also available in Master version for $750 and weighing 2,845 lbs. The Master line sold 20,592 Sport Sedans.

A not very popular car was the Master DeLuxe Sedan with its rear mounted spare. Only 236 were built in 1938. They sold for $797. It was also available in Master style for $730 of which 522 were assembled. The public preferred having a space for luggage with the tire contained inside the trunk.

A 1938 Master Cabriolet was offered for the last time until 1940. Like the 1937 model, it offered the straight axle rather than Knee Action. This model weighed 2,790 lbs. and sold for $775 which was an increase of $50 over the 1937 model.

Chevrolet's most popular model again was this 1938 Master DeLuxe Town Sedan. This photo showed the display floor of the Ingold-Olsen Chevrolet dealership in San Francisco in 1938. This dealership is still in existence at the same location. This Town Sedan in basic form sold for $689 and weighed 2,895 lbs. However, this car with a few goodies like parking lights, fender skirts, and no doubt some deluxe interior appointments, sold for a little higher.

Chevrolet

It looks like a Chevrolet, but says General Cab on the grille. This was actually manufactured by General Motors Truck Co. but did use Chevrolet running gear, had Chevrolet hub caps and Master DeLuxe appeared on the sides of the hood. This 7-passenger sedan used a Fisher Body virtually made up from Chevrolet dies.

1939

Being displayed for 1939, what at first looked like completely new car really wasn't true. The front end wa radically restyled from 1938 with a new hood, grille headlamps and fenders. But behind this was basically th same body as what had been offered for the past two years Here, too, were some face liftings by placing the rea license in the center of the trunk and moving the taillamp up to the body belt line.

Mechanically the car stayed pretty much the same. I did offer, for an additional $10, the vacuum colum shift which nearly every Chevrolet came equipped with

The 216.5 cubic inch engine again developed 85 HP a 3200 RPM. All models used the same 112-inch wheelbas and rode on 6:00 x 16 inch tires. The fuel supply was 14 gallon tank.

For 1939 the new series were referred to as Master 8 and Master DeLuxe. The lower priced Master 85 came wit the I-beam front axle and the Master DeLuxe employe the knee action system with double acting hydrauli shock absorbers.

For the year, Chevrolet dropped the convertible entirel and also at mid-year saw the straight backed sedans i both 4 and 2-door versions phased out as the demand fo the outside spare tire just wasn't there.

Chevrolet offered thirteen models, provided the statio wagon was classed as a passenger car. For the year i placed in first position by selling 648,471 units for th calendar run.

A pair of Master Series 85 1939 Chevrolets. The 4-door Sedan on top minus the trunk sold only 68 versions for $745. The 2-door example below it without trunk sold for $699 and 180 were built. At the end of the model run Chevrolet phased out both models.

This 1939 Chevrolet Master DeLuxe Sport Coupe weighed 2,845 lbs. and cost $715. The production figures for this model were 20,908 units. The body was identical to that used on the Business Coupe which sold for $684. The placing of the gas tank on the right quarter occurred early in the year. Later, all Sport Coupes carried the gas tank mounted on the right rear fender.

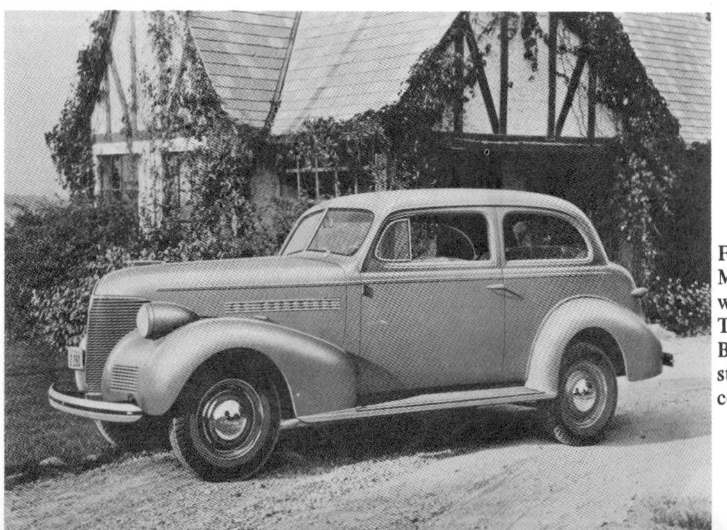

Far more popular than the trunkless 2-door Sedan was the Master 2-door Town Sedan which sold well at $669. It weighed 2,820 lbs. The model run sold 124,059 units. This example is totally stripped of any extra gingerbread. Bumper guards were still an accessory. The floor shift was still standard equipment but could be ordered on the steering column for $10 additional.

›40

For the 1940 line-up Chevrolet offered three separate ›odels known as the Master 85, Master DeLuxe, and the ›ecial DeLuxe which was a dolled up version of the other ʼo.

The Master 85 was available in the same body styles as ›e other two except for a Convertible. Mechanically, it ıs the same car except for having the conventional front ringing. The vacuum shift was standard equipment for . models. Master 85s were delivered minus all optional cessories such as front door arm rests, dual windshield pers, cigar lighter, and bumper guards.

The horsepower remained 85 for the entire line. The ıeelbase increased to 113 inches, but the tire size stayed 00 x 16. The fuel supply was increased to a 16 gallon pacity. Knee action was employed on both Master ›Luxes and Special DeLuxe models.

Chevrolet chose a brand new body for the year, roducing an alligator type hood that was hinged at the ır of the engine firewall. This type of hood locked tomatically and was only able to be released from inside the dash. The car had greater vision, giving an increase two inches to the windshield alone. Sealed beam head-nps were used as standard equipment when the 1940 ›del made its debut.

Some of the deluxe features offered on the Special Luxe line as standard equipment were stainless steel dy belt moldings, shiny metal window and windshield ʼeals, robe cords, ash trays front and rear, deluxe T-spoke ering wheel with a horn blowing ring, and a dash-›unted clock. All of these items were available on the her two models if a customer wished to pay extra.

Chevrolet offered fourteen models among the three ies. Prices ranged from $659 for a 2-passenger Master Business Coupe to $934 for the Special DeLuxe ›assenger Station Wagon. Sales kept Chevrolet in the mber One position by selling 895,734 cars for the endar year. Among those cars was the 25-millionth, ich was a Master DeLuxe 2-door Town Sedan.

A popular car for businessmen as well as the young was Chevrolet's 1940 Special DeLuxe Sport Coupe. This was the first year Chevrolet offered a full bench rear seat rather than the opera auxiliary seats. This model is equipped with the popular grille guard, spot light, accessory goddess on the hood and whitewall tires. The license is a California dealer plate for 1940. Possibly this gentleman is hoping to buy or else allowing a future customer to take his picture. It sold for $750 and had a production run of 46,628.

Chevrolet's first attempt at building a Station Wagon on the passenger car chassis occurred in 1939. This Master DeLuxe version carried its spare tire mounted in the right front fender. A total of 989 were built – 229 in the Master Series. This 8-passenger body was of all wood with a rubberized fabric top.

One of Chevrolet's bread and butter cars for 1939 was this Master DeLuxe 4-door Sport Sedan. This model sold for $766 and weighed 2,910 lbs. A total of 110,521 units were sold. This car was displayed with all Chevrolet's accessories to help encourage those buying a new car to make it look as sharp as possible.

Chevrolet entered 1940 with a new body. The 1940 Special DeLuxe 4-door Sedan in its basic form sold for $802. This was the top of the line Series. The Master 85 was the lowest priced model and the Master DeLuxe was the middle line model. The Special DeLuxe Sedan sold 138,811 units, which was proof the depression was over.

Chevrolet

Chevrolet returned with a convertible in 1940 after having a year's absence. This model was only available in Special DeLuxe style and was called the Cabriolet. It sold for $898 and had a weight of 3,160 lbs. This model was available with every accessory known to man from spinner steering wheel to shark tooth wheel covers. The year saw 11,820 of these models delivered.

1941

The Chevrolet line for 1941 was completely restyl in its two series: the Master DeLuxe and Special DeLux A mid-year offering was made available called the Fleetli which was a Special DeLuxe 4-door Sedan with a mo fancy interior and a hump back trunk.

Mechanically, all models were the same. They had 216 cubic inch valve-in-head engine that now develop 90 HP at 3300 RPM. The fuel supply was contained in 16 gallon tank. The tire size was again 6:00 x 1 Passengers now rode on a 116-inch wheelbase, which w the largest Chevrolet built since the V-8 Series of 191 1918.

The 1941 models continued the vacuum shift introduc two years before. New for the year were 10 MM spa plugs used in place of 14 MM plugs because it was f they stood up better under wide open throttle, warmed more quickly, but ran cooler when the engine was h

As for the appearance, the car caught on immediatel Oblong parking lights were stationed beneath the hea lamps. Running boards were concealed by a gradu outward flare of the doors. Front and rear license plat were mounted in the center. The front mounting w placed between two guards.

If the owner wished, there was hardly an accessory th wasn't available to make this one of the sharpest looki cars on the road.

A total of eleven models were available ranging in pri from $712 for a Master DeLuxe 2-passenger Busine Coupe to $995 for the 8-passenger Special DeLuxe Stati Wagon. The company placed First in sales again from t calendar sale of 930,293 vehicles.

Probably one of the most popular versions of Chevrolet's early club coupes is this 1941 Special DeLuxe Coupe, which the author has owned for about 16 years. It is equipped with most all genuine 1941 factory accessories. In base form it sold for $800 with a weight of 3,050 lbs. According to the original bill of sale, tax, and license, this car sold new in Bellflower, Cal. for $1,075.

Nicely equipped is this 1941 Chevrolet Special DeLuxe Sport Sedan that sold for $851 The factory sold 148,661 of this style. This particular car is equipped with fender skirts, front fender stainless trim, bumper guards, accessory hood ornament, 2-tone paint, radio, and wheel trim rings. This put the price up to well over $1,050 delivered.

A popular photo is this one of Spencer Tracy accepting delivery of his new 1941 Chevrolet Special DeLuxe Station Wagon. Tracy was given this car by the Chevrolet factory in a contest that Chevy sponsored to pick America's favorite actor. This model was only available in Special DeLuxe version and sold for $995 which was the most expensive car for the year. A total of 2,045 were produced.

Chevrolet

942

The 1942 models were to be Chevrolet's last offering ntil 1936. These models were virtually unchanged from 941 except for substitutions such as much plastic to ıke the place of metal components in the car. A new ·ont end was the only big difference displayed. The hood ·as lengthened to conform with the pleasing new grille esign and front fenders blended nicely into the doors. he 1942 Special DeLuxe Convertibles differed from the 941 models in that they offered rear quarter windows hile the 1941s had a concealed quarter panel in canvas.

A new model also made its appearance in the Fleetline ıb-series. This was an Aero Sedan or more commonly ·ferred to as a fast-back 2-door Sedan. The Fleetline -door Sedan also was a sub-series to the Special DeLuxe ne. So, 1942 continued to offer low priced Master De uxe cars and the sub-series Fleetline.

Each series was mechanically the same, and used the 16.5 cubic inch engine that developed 90 HP at 3300 PM. The same 16 gallon fuel tank was used. The tire ze again was 6:00 x 16 inches and the wheelbase was 16 inches.

A total of 12 models were introduced for 1942. Prices ınged from $790 for the Master DeLuxe 2-passenger usiness Coupe to $1,145 for an 8-passenger Special eLuxe Station Wagon. The model year production ·ached 258,795 cars and the calendar year sales were 5,472 units which ended Feb. 2nd.

This 1942 Fleetline Aero Sedan was a subseries of the Special DeLuxe models. This example sold for $880 and weighed 3,105 lbs. The production run for this style was 61,855 cars. This was the first year for this Fleetline Aero Sedan, which was a good seller in its short period of production.

The 1942 Chevrolet Special DeLuxe 4-door Sedan had a model run of 31,441 units before production ceased on February 2nd, 1942. The car sold for $895 and weighed 3,425 lbs.

Only 1,782 Special DeLuxe Convertibles were produced before the war production ban went into effect, and only one is known to exist today. It is this model, shown here with top raised and top lowered. The owner is Dr. John L. Mansell of New Wilmington, Pa. It was built in November of 1941, before the ban on bright trim went into effect, and therefore reflects all of the chrome goodies, including the fog lights and spot light. However, supplies were already becoming scarce, and for that reason, the stainless steel window moldings were omitted. The upholstery is of pleated leather. The car had a base price of $1,080, and weighed 3,385 pounds.

This is a 1942 Chevrolet Master DeLuxe 5-passenger Coupe with the blackout trim that many 1942 cars had to accept. Chromium had to be used in defense work for World War II, so painted grilles and trim were the order of the day. A total of 17,442 were built that sold for $790.

Chrysler

For 1930, this Chrysler Roadster was the lightest car built. It weighed 2,390 lbs. The model was referred to as a Series Six. It came only with a rumble seat. This example came well equipped with accessories of the day such as wire wheels, luggage rack, and side mount tires. It sold for $835.

Chrysler was the main car coming from the Chrysl Corp., with headquarters in Detroit. The car had bee produced since 1924.

The 1930 Chryslers came in five series. They we Chrysler Series Six, Chrysler 66, Chrysler 70, Chrysler 7 and the Chrysler Imperial.

The low priced Chrysler for 1930 was referred to as th Series Six. It had a wheelbase of 109 inches. The c developed 62 HP at 3200 RPM. These models use 19 x 5 inch tires.

The 66s developed 68 HP at 3200 RPM from th 6-cylinder engine. The wheelbase was 112.75 inches. Th model rode on 5:50 x 18 inch tires. The fuel capacit was 11 gallons. The Chrysler 70s and 77s both used th 6-cylinder engine which developed 93 HP at 3200 RP The wheelbases were 116.5 inches for 70s and 124.5 f the 77s. They had 5:50 x 18 inch tires on the 70s an 6:00 x 18s on the 77s. The fuel tanks were 19½ gallo

Chrysler Imperials used 6-cylinder engines developi 100 HP at 3200 RPM. Their wheelbase measured 1 inches. The tire size for these vehicles was 7:00 x inches. Its fuel supply was a 20 gallon tank. All Chrysle had Lockheed hydraulic brakes.

Chrysler cars came wired for the installation of transitone radio. The set was composed of four unit amplifier, speaker, receiver, and batteries. The batteri were carried in a galvanized compartment under th driver's seat. The aerial was concealed in the top of th body, with the lead-in-wire running through the rig windshield post.

Chryslers came in 30 models among the five serie Prices ranged from a Series Six Roadster for $895 to th Imperial Sedan Limousine for 7 passengers at $3,57 Chrysler placed Ninth for the calendar year by registeri 60,199 vehicles.

A beautiful example of the 1930 Chrysler Imperial Town Sedan that sold for $2,975 F.O.B. Detroit. This model weighed 4,310 lbs. Wooden artillery wheels were standard equipment. The sidemount spares which this vehicle has were extra. Chrysler assembled 379 of this style in the two years it was manufactured.

Chrysler's 1931 New Six Series 4-door Sedan was the most popular body style, of which 28,620 were built. This model weighed 2,835 lbs. and sold for $895. This model had a 116-inch wheelbase. Its slanting V-type radiator shell made it a very attractive package.

A Custom bodied 1930 Chrysler 77 Town Car with body by Brewster. This car was available for $4,850 delivered with 6 wire or wood wheels. The purchaser had a choice of color and trim fabric.

Chrysler

For 1931 Chrysler offered more models than it ever had)efore. During the model run, some of these cars were lropped in place of a new series. So, early 1931 cars were ıctually 1930 models but registered as 1931s.

The 1930 Series Six continued into production through)ecember of 1930 with engine numbers going up to CJ-24081. The Series 66 and 70 continued till the end)f May 1931.

New for the 1931 run were the New Series Six, dentified as Series CM. This new series offered a 116.5-nch wheelbase. The engine developed 70 HP at 3200 RPM. The fuel supply was from a 15½ gallon fuel tank. These cars used 5:50 x 18 inch tires.

In addition to the New Series Six were the four new 3-cylinder cars which were the first Chrysler 8s to be)ffered. These cars had an 80 HP engine at 3400 RPM. This series generally has been referred to as First Series CD nodels. They had 5:50 x 18 inch tires and rode on a 124-nch wheelbase. The fuel tanks held a 15½ gallon supply.

The Second Series CD had a 260 cubic inch 8-cylinder ngine which developed 88 HP at 3400 RPM for all early nodels. In April, the engine size was increased to 282 ubic inches developing 100 HP at 3400 RPM. This eries continued to use the 124-inch wheelbase of the arlier First and Second Series CD cars. The fuel supply vas increased to 19½ gallons. The DeLuxe line was ecognized by a split windshield on closed cars. A 4-speed ransmission was used, a screened V-style radiator shell vas employed, and the tire size now was 6:50 x 17 inches.

The Imperial 8 offered a 384 cubic inch engine leveloping 125 HP at 3200 RPM. The fuel tank held a 21½ gallon supply. Tire size for these cars was 7:00 x 18 nches. Later models of the Imperial line used 7:50 x 18 nches.

All Chryslers used "floating power" which was the use of the engine mounted in rubber. All cars had hydraulic rakes and were equipped with free wheeling this year.

Briggs bodies were used on all models unless the request vas made for a special body for the Imperial line. In uch case the services of Waterhouse, Murphy, Locke, or Derham were available.

A total of 52 body styles were available ranging in price rom $745 for a Chrysler Series Six 2-passenger Coupe to $3,145 for the Imperial 8 Sedan Limousine for 7. Prices or special bodies were given on request for the owner only.

Chrysler took 9th place in sales for 1931 with 52,819 ars being sold.

A 1931 Chrysler Imperial Roadster with body by Le Baron. This style cost $3,220 and weighed 4,530 lbs. Le Baron built 100 of this model. The Roadster has a chrome stone guard to protect its radiator grille.

The 1931 Chrysler New Six Series included a Roadster with rumble seat. This car has wire wheels, sidemounts, sidemount mirrors, whitewalls, and Trippe Driving Lights, all considered accessories. It sold for $885 and weighed 2,560 lbs. A total of 2,281 were built.

The 1931 Second Series Eight 5-passenger Phaeton. A Locke body of dual cowl style was used. The tonneau cowl automatically would raise when the rear door was opened. Accessories on this car were sidemounts, trunk, and wire wheels. This car sold for $1,970. A total of 113 examples were built.

This 1931 Chrysler Series CD 4-door Sedan came as an 8-cylinder model. Early examples were called First Series followed by the Second Series which lasted in production until April of 1931. The CD line came on a 124-inch wheelbase. Sidemounts and wire wheels were available at extra cost. This model sold for $1,525 and weighed 3,365 lbs.

Chrysler

This was Chrysler's 1932 Eight 5-passenger Coupe. It came with a split windshield that could be opened individually. This model used the same body as the 1932 Second Series. Trumpet horns were standard equipment for this series. Chrysler built 502 of this model at $1,475.

1932

Chrysler for 1932 offered a vacuum operated clutch floating power, free wheeling, new frames, and improve appearances as some of the innovations for the new mode year. A Six could be ordered with 82 HP, an Eight wit 100 HP and the Imperial and Imperial Custom Eigh both with 125 HP.

The wheelbase of the Six remained at 116 inches. Th Eight increased one inch to 125 inches. The Imperial wa introduced with a new wheelbase length of 135 inches. Th Imperial Custom Eight came out with a 146-inch whee base.

Price wise, Chrysler fell between $885 for a 4-passenge Roadster to the 7-passenger Limousine which came clos to $3,000 when nicely equipped. Fuel capacity in the Si was a 15½ gallon tank, while the Eights carried a 19 gallon tank.

The 6-cylinder cars had six models, the 8-cylinder ca had four models. The Imperial Eights consisted of thre models, and the Imperial Custom Eight shared six differe models.

Chrysler built its own bodies in all models, except fo the 6-cylinder Convertible Coupe which carried a Brig body and a $935 price tag for the 4-passenger ca

Chrysler ranked in 11th Position for 1932 with 25,29 cars rolling off its assembly line. All Chrysler cars use hydraulic brakes.

Chrysler's 1932 CP Series is shown here. It was the most popular model in the 8-cylinder class, selling for $1,475. A total of 3,198 were built for the year. About half carried the rear mounted spare.

A Chrysler Imperial Custom Eight Roadster with body by Le Baron. Only one of this style was ever produced, for use in the Walter P. Chrysler family. Dual air horns were used in addition to the dual electric horns. The small door on the front right fender was a tool box. The front fenders were free standing. This model used a 146-inch wheelbase.

Chrysler's 1933 low priced offering and most popular car in the entire line was the Chrysler Six 4-door Sedan. It sold for $785. Only 13,264 were built because of the depression the world was in. The model is nicely equipped with side-mount spares, trumpet horns, and wire wheels. All were available on the Six for an additional amount.

933

Four impressive lines were introduced for 1933, including ıe Chrysler Six, Royal Eight, Imperial Eight, and Imperial ustom Eight. The new Royal Eight had 3¼ x 4-1/8 inch ylinders, and a displacement of 273.8 inches. This car ınked next to the Six in size and price. The Six and the vo regular Eights were continued for the model run. Features seen on all models were automatic choke, eat control, starter operated by accelerator pedal, Bendix acuum clutch control with pendulum valve, and a new -speed transmission, except for the Imperial Custom Eight hich had a 4-speed transmission with a silent third. endix power operated brakes were optional on the two nperial Eight models.

Chrysler offered 22 models ranging from a $795 2-assenger Business Coupe to a $3,595 Imperial Custom ight Convertible Sedan. The Chrysler Six was now on a 17-inch wheelbase with an 83 HP engine and used a 5½ gallon tank. Tire size was 5:50 x 17. The Royal ight came on a 120-inch wheelbase, using a 90 HP engine. his model used a 16 gallon fuel tank and 6:00 x 17 inch res.

The Imperial Eight developed 103 HP at 3400 RPM and ed a 126-inch wheelbase. This model had the same tire ze as the Imperial Custom Eight – 7:50 x 17. Its fuel pply was a 19½ gallon tank. The Imperial Custom Eight ed a 135 HP engine at 3200 RPM. Its wheelbase easured 146 inches. This model used a 21½ gallon fuel pply in all six of its models. Every Chrysler-built car ed Lockheed hydraulic brakes right from its inception 1924.

Chrysler sales for 1933 put them in Tenth position, with),220 cars being sold.

Also a model of real interest among car collectors today is this 1933 Chrysler CD Convertible Sedan which sold for $945. This was the most expensive 6-cylinder Chrysler built in 1933. The trunk was standard equipment, as were the wire wheels and sidemounts. If the customer chose, he could have a rear mounted spare for $10 less. Of the 207 built, most all came equipped like this car.

The 1933 Chrysler Series 60 Convertible Coupe sold only 677. The 6-cylinder model sold for $795 in basic form. Sidemounts, trumpet horns, wire wheels and whitewall tires were all available on this model but at extra cost. This is truly a special interest car today.

A 1933 Chrysler Eight 5-passenger Sedan was the most popular 8-cylinder built in 1933. This is an early model – note the different style bumpers. The rear bumper was a split design which didn't enhance the rear of the car as much as the later models with the full bumper. This car is minus the trumpet horns which were available at extra cost. The author's family owned one very similar to this. When new, Dad said, "The trumpet horns came off quite easily if just slightly nudged." One could snap them off by hand. Replacements in 1933 cost $2 each.

The Chrysler Eight 5-passenger Sedan is shown with sidemounts and a straight rear bumper. The sidemounts give this CT 8-cylinder sedan a look of more classic design. It sold for $925 and weighed 3,483 lbs. Sidemounts were $10 extra. This model had a run of 7,993 units.

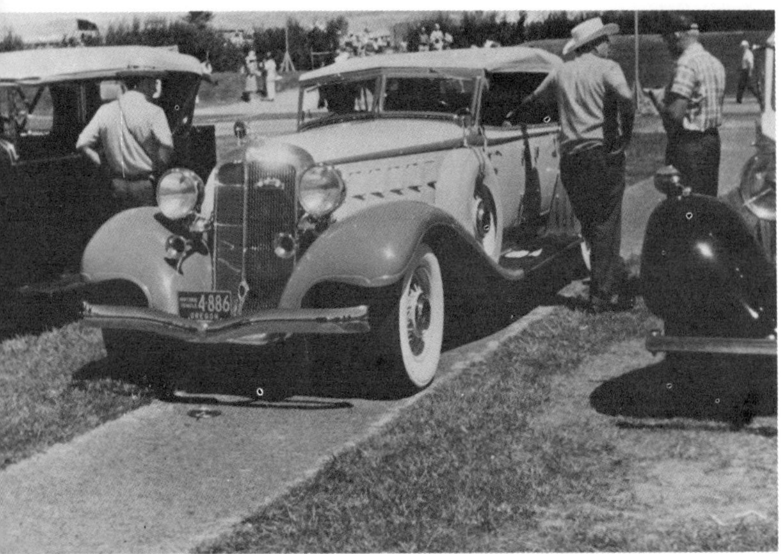

Chrysler's most expensive 1933 model was this Imperial Custom Eight 5-passenger Phaeton by Le Baron. This model cost $3,395 and weighed 4,890 lbs. A total of 36 were made. This example hailed from Oregon and was photographed at a Harrah Car Show in Reno. Note the headlamps are different on this model from most 1933 Chrysler Imperials.

1934

For 1934, Chrysler made some revolutionary changes b introducing the Airflow bodies on the 8-cylinder car Besides these models there was the Chrysler Six in six bod styles on a 118-inch wheelbase with a 93 HP engine a 3400 RPM. Fuel capacity was a 15 gallon tank. The ca used 6:50 x 16 inch tires. Prices for this series began a $795 for the 2-passenger Coupe.

The Chrysler Eight had a 112 HP engine at 3400 RPM Its wheelbase was 123 inches. It had four body styles. Thi car, along with the Imperial Eight, had a 21 gallon fu supply. Tire size was 7:00 x 16 for both series.

The Imperial Eight came on a 128-inch wheelbase usin a 130 HP engine at 3400 RPM. Body styles were thre which was the same for the Custom Imperial Eight whic used a 134 HP engine at 3200 RPM. These models use a 30 gallon fuel supply and rode on 7:50 x 17 inch tire

The Custom Imperial came equipped with automati overdrive and ride stabilizer bar with steel girders covere by structurally strong body panels. The wheelbase wa 146.5 inches. This model only had a curved one-piec windshield, which was the first of its kind on any pr duction car. The 8-passenger automobile had a price ta of $5,145 with very few being sold.

Chrysler again placed Tenth in sales, putting out 36,92 units.

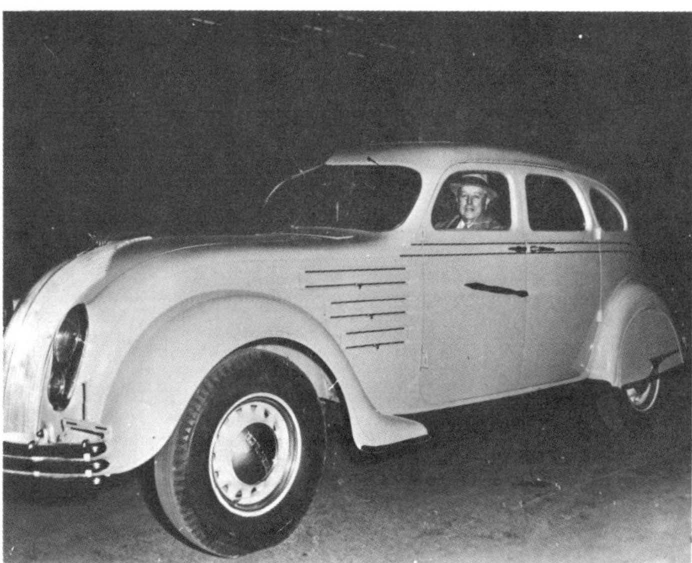

Carl Breer sits proudly at the wheel of The car. He was responsible for creating the Airflow. This is the 1934 Chrysler Airflow Series CU 6-passenger Sedan.

A 1934 Chrysler Eight Airflow Sedan. This was the smallest of the Airflow models coming on a 123-inch wheelbase. It sold for $1,345, weighed 3,760 lbs. This series produced 7,226 cars which was good considering it was a new model of non-conforming lines for the day, and that the depression was still in full swing.

For 1934 Chrysler offered the 5-passenger Sedan in the CA Series. It was only available in this series, on a 117-inch wheelbase. Wire wheels were no longer available on Chrysler; only steel spoked rims, mounted on the 6:50 x 16 inch tires. This model sold for $820 and was the most popular Chrysler for 1934. Chrysler built 17,617 sedans of this series.

935

In 1935, Chrysler offered its public two series of Airflow nd Airstream cars. These were further broken down to ıclude three Airflow Eights and a Six and an Eight in he Airstream models with conventional bodies.

The Airstream Six used a 118-inch wheelbase, had a 3 HP engine (at 3400 RPM) with cast iron head. A 15 allon fuel supply was used. This series came in five styles rom a 2-passenger Coupe at $745 to the 5-passenger 'ouring Sedan for $830. All used 6:25 x 16 inch tires.

The Airstream 8 was available in four styles from $935 ı 4-passenger Coupe style to the $995 5-passenger Touring edan. These models gave 105 HP at 3400 RPM. The fuel upply also was a 15 gallon tank. Tire size was 6:50 x 16 ıches. They rode on a 121-inch wheelbase. All Chrysler ars used Lockheed hydraulic brakes.

Airflow 8s came in three models with prices beginning t $1,375 for a 3-passenger Business Coupe, and $20 more or a 5-passenger Coupe or Sedan. These cars used 7:00 x 6 inch tires and a 21 gallon fuel supply as was true for ll other Airflow models except the Imperial Custom ight which used a 30 gallon tank.

Horsepower rating of the Airflow was now 115 at 400 RPM. These cars again used a 123-inch wheelbase. 'he Imperial Customs again used 130 HP at 3400 RPM 'ith 7:50 x 16 inch tires.

Imperial Customs listed eight different body styles in ither sedan or limousine form. The Imperial Custom ight Limousine used a 146-inch wheelbase and 7:50 x 17 ıch tires. These models used a 150 HP engine at 3200 PM.

All of the same Airflow innovations offered in 1934 ere again available on the 1935 models. Top price for n Airflow Limousine was $5,145.

Chrysler again stayed in 10th Position this year with 0,010 units for the calendar year.

The 1934 Chrysler Imperial's heaviest and most expensive model was this 7-passenger Custom Limousine model CU. It weighed 5,900 lbs. and sold for $5,145. Only 20 of this model were produced. A division window was used to make it a Limousine at the owner's wishes. This series only used the full chrome wheel covers as standard equipment. The car was almost 20 feet long.

The most expensive 6-cylinder Chrysler for 1934 was this Series CB Convertible Sedan which cost $970. It weighed 3,069 lbs. Chrysler only built 450 of these beauties as depression people weren't really looking for sporty cars, just solid transportation. This beautiful restoration hails from Oregon.

The 1935 Chrysler Airstream Six 5-passenger 4-door Sedan was offered with a rear mounted spare for the last time. This car sold for $830 and weighed 3,013 lbs. The production figures showed 6,055 cars being built. This model wears fender skirts which Chrysler used quite heavily on the 1935 Airstream models.

A rarely seen 1935 Chrysler Airflow Eight 6-passenger Coupe. This model also came as a 2-passenger coupe, but only 72 examples were built. The 6-passenger model had a run of 307. Each style sold for $1,245. The wheelbase was the same as in 1934, 123 inches. This coupe is equipped with chromium wheel covers. Fender skirts always were standard equipment on all Airflows.

Chrysler

The most popular 1935 Chrysler 4-door Sedan was this Airstream 6-cylinder trunk sedan. It weighed 3,048 lbs. and was $30 more than the rear spare mounted model. A total of 12,790 were produced. Again, this model is displayed with rear fender skirts that were an accessory. Note, only one windshield wiper was still used on the series.

This 1936 Chrysler Six 2-passenger Coupe was the least expensive model for the year. It sold for $760 and weighed 2,962 lbs. Again, as in 1935, Chrysler stressed fender skirts for the Airstream models. Most models had them when new, but owners of them and often discarded them to scrap drives. They are a much sought after accessory by Chrysler collectors today.

The most popular model in the 6-cylinder line was the 4-door Sedan known as the C-7 Series. It had a run of 12,790 units. that sold for $875. This model weighed 3,137 lbs.

1936

The 1936 models were only slightly restyled from th 1935 cars. All 1936 Chryslers were made more appealin by simply sculpturing out the fine line of the 193 Airflows and Airstreams. The designation of Airstrean was not carried over into the 1936 line. The cars were nov simply called Chrysler Six and Eight. Some of th appealing appointments of both consisted of "torpedo horns which were blended into the catwalks. The rea panels were smoothed out to give a more graceful effec to the rear of the car, and a well designed die cast grill and louvers were used.

The Airflow had a similar design to the 1935s tha helped round out its beauty. Available on Chrysler 8 an Airflow models as standard equipment were carpete floors front and rear.

The Chrysler Six came with the previous year's 93 H engine at 3400 RPM while the Eight had the same 105 H at the same RPM. Airflow 8s now had 118 HP bu Imperial 8 Airflows still were rated at 130 HP, bot turning at 3400 RPM. Wheelbases continued at 118 inche for the Six, 121 inches in the Eight, 123 inches for th Airflow 8 and 128 inches on the Imperial 8. The larg Custom Imperial Airflow was discontinued during the yea

Tire sizes were 6:25 x 16 inches for a Chrysler Six 6:50 x 16 inches in the Eight. Airflow 8s employe 7:00 x 16s and the Imperial Eights used 7:50 x 16 Fuel supplies were 15 gallons on the Chryslers whil Airflows and Imperials both used 21 gallon tanks.

Chrysler dropped to Eleventh place, selling 71,295 unit for the calendar run. A total of 17 body styles wer available ranging from a $745 Coupe in 6-cylinder styl to the Airflow Custom Imperial Limousine for $2,57

This 1936 Chrysler Six Rumble Seat Coupe is stripped of all frills. One taillamp and no bumper guards makes this a real "Plain Jane." Only 750 were built at a cost of $825. It weighed 3,037 lbs.

937

For 1937, Chrysler offered four lines of cars—the Royal ix, Imperial Eight, Custom Imperial Eight and the Airflow ight. The conventional looking cars used some new istinctive features: hoods hinged from the rear and pening from the front. The fenders were wider and more ıassive with a crowned effect. The cars used all-steel roofs ith a larger luggage area. A drip molding over the doors as used for the first time. All models had disc wheels. A more compact overdrive was used. All models except ıe Airflow were continued with knee action front springs ut two way shock absorbers were used at the front ıstead of the built-in type.

The Royal Six again developed 93 HP at 3600 RPM. It sed a 16 gallon fuel tank. All Royals rode on 6:00 x 16 ıch tires and used a 116-inch wheelbase.

The Imperial Eight used a 110 HP engine at 3600 RPM. his series rode on 6:50 x 16 inch tires, had a 16 gallon asoline tank, and a 121-inch wheelbase.

All Custom Imperial Eights used the same 130 HP engine t 3400 RPM. These models had a 20 gallon fuel supply, 40-inch wheelbase, and rode on 7:50 x 16 inch tires.

Airflows also used the same engine as Custom Imperial ights, but had a fuel tank of 21 gallons. These cars used ıe 7:50 x 16 inch tires, too, like the Custom Imperial ight. This was the last year for the Airflow to be built. he company turned out 4,600 of these cars known as -17s for the model run.

Prices for the 1937 models ran from $715 for the Royal -passenger Coupe to $1,475 for an Airflow Sedan. Chrysler placed Tenth in sales, with 107,872 units being old for the calendar run.

The most expensive production Airflow was the Custom Imperial, Series C-11, 7-passenger sedan limousine, which cost $2,575. The car was quickly identified by the divider partition that could be seen through the front windows. Only 37 were built.

Out of production for a year the Convertible Sedan returned in 1936. This example is shown with skirts and sidemounts as accessories. It cost $1,125 as the most expensive model in the 6-cylinder line. It weighed 3,282 lbs. Chrysler advertised this car heavily in magazines during the year but fewer than 500 were sold. As an Eight, 362 were built and sold for $1,265. They weighed 3,495 lbs.

A real little beauty is this 1936 Chrysler Six Convertible Coupe which sold for $925. It weighed 3,053 lbs. A total of 650 were built. Most came equipped with the accessory sidemounts and skirts like this model. The convertibles continued to use the flat one piece windshield, unlike the closed cars.

The 1937 Chrysler Imperial Eight Sedan, as a 5-passenger touring sedan, sold for $1,100. It weighed 3,564 lbs. A total of 11,976 Imperial Sedans were built. The skirts as illustrated were classed as an accessory.

This is the 1937 Chrysler Airflow 6-passenger coupe which sold for $1,610 and weighed 4,225 lbs. Airflows were known as Series C-17 and a total of only 230 were built in this body style, the final year of production.

Chrysler

The new 1938 Chrysler Six 2-passenger business coupe was in the Royal Series. It weighed 3,090 lbs. and sold for $918. The Royal Coupe had a production of 4,840 cars. It was also available as an Imperial Eight Coupe for $1,123 with a production run of only 766.

1938

In 1938, Chrysler again offered three chassis, the Royal, Imperial and Custom Imperial Eight. All models shared a new grille and some mechanical improvements. The headlamps were mounted on the fender catwalks rather than on the radiator shell as on last year's models. This gave the front end a wider and a "happier" looking appearance.

All Royals came on a longer wheelbase of 119 inches, the Imperials came on a 125-inch wheelbase, while the Custom used a 144-inch wheelbase on its two models.

Also increased was the horsepower for the Royals. It came as a 95 HP car at 3600 RPM or with an aluminum head with compression of 7 to 1 for 102 HP. The Imperial Eight developed 110 HP in a cast iron head at 3400 RPM or 115 HP with an aluminum head.

In the Custom Imperial Eight, a 130 HP was available at 3400 RPM.

Tire size on the Royals was 6:25 x 16 inches. The Imperial Eight used 6:50 x 16 inch tires, leaving the 7:50 x 16s for the Custom Imperial Eights. All Royals and Imperial Eights used a 16 gallon fuel tank while the Custom Imperial Eights employed a 20 gallon fuel supply.

Eighteen models were available from a $918 2-passenger Royal Business Coupe to the $1,955 Custom Imperial Eight Limousine. For the year, Chrysler took the 11th Place by selling 41,496 cars.

Chrysler's Custom Imperial Eight was available in three versions – all on the 144-inch wheelbase. They were a 5-passenger sedan, 7-passenger sedan like this model, and a 7-passenger Limousine. This car had two auxiliary seats placed in back of the front seat when not in use. All 7-passenger models weighed 4,510 lbs. A total of 489 Custom Imperials were built in 1938.

Chrysler's most popular car for 1938 was this 5-passenger Royal Sedan, priced at $1,010. A total of 31,991 of this model were produced. Fender skirts were still being pushed by Chrysler dealers, as this sedan features. Windshield wipers were moved to the base of the windshield rather than mounted at the top like on the 1937 cars.

A beautiful design that just had to die from lack of sales was the 5-passenger convertible sedan, seen here in Royal Six form. With highway speeds increasing on an almost annual basis, people no longer wanted the expensive and uncomfortable convertible sedans, despite their beautiful appearance. The model was discontinued after only 177 were built. Priced at $1,425 and weighing 3,450 pounds, it was the most expensive car in the Royal Six Series. In addition to the 119-inch wheelbase models, Chrysler also built 161 Royal Six 7-passenger limousine sedans and 722 7-passenger sedans. These used a 136-inch wheelbase chassis. The sedan model cost $1,235 and weighed 3,450 pounds, while the limousine cost $1,325 and weighed 3,545 pounds.

939

For 1939 Chrysler offered many new advancements, rom freshly styled streamlined bodies to interesting nechanical improvements, including a remote control earshift and an improved overdrive at extra cost called 'Cruise Climb Overdrive" which allowed the driver to eturn to direct drive when the accelerator pedal had been lepressed behind wide open throttle position. The body tyle emphasized a Vee windshield and headlamps of a omewhat heart-shaped design mounted flush in the front enders.

For the model run Chrysler displayed its regular Royal nd Imperial line but also brought out a Royal Windsor vhich had a more fancy interior. The New Yorker and aratoga also bowed as a somewhat sub-line to the mperial. The regular Custom Imperial was also continued.

The Royal and Royal Windsor were 6-cylinder cars using 100 HP engine at 3600 RPM. These models used 6:25 x 6 inch tires and rode on a 119-inch wheelbase, except or the 136-inch 7-passenger sedan. This model used :00 x 16 inch tires. An 18 gallon fuel supply was used on ll Royals and Royal Windsors.

The New Yorker and Saratoga models used the 130 IP 8-cylinder engine at 3600 RPM. These cars had :00 x 16 inch tires and came with a 21 gallon gasoline upply. All New Yorker, Saratoga and Imperial models ame on 125-inch wheelbases.

New Yorkers came in four body styles and Saratogas vith two bodies. Imperials were in four different models. 'ustom Imperials had many cars delivered with Derham odies. All Custom Imperials came with sidemounts for he last time. The Saratoga was offered with a few more nterior grills to give it a $145 higher price tag than the Iew Yorker. It sold for $1,443.

Other Imperials and Custom Imperials employed the ame engine compartments of 323.5 cubic inches. The 'ustom Imperial developed 132 HP, came on a 144-inch vheelbase, and used 7:50 x 16 inch tires. For the Custom nperial, Fluid Drive made its entrance as standard quipment. It was known as Model C-24.

A total of 17 models were available from the Royal -passenger Coupe for $918 to the Custom Imperial -passenger Limousine for $2,695. All body styles again arried Briggs bodies except for the Custom Victoria 'lub Coupes, which used Hayes bodies. The Hayes bodied oupes were a mid-year offering available as a Royal 'indsor, New Yorker, Saratoga and Imperial. All cars ame fully equipped with radio, heater, overdrive, and eluxe wheel trim. A total of 497 units were sold by hrysler dealers as their answer to Mercury's special Hardtop" Club Coupe.

The company placed in 12th Position by selling 7,749 cars.

The 1939 Chrysler Royal offered this 7-passenger sedan on a 136-inch wheelbase. It was also available as a limousine on the same body. The prices were $1,235 for the sedan and $1,325 as a limousine. A total of 821 units were built between the two models. These cars used the 6-cylinder 107 H.P. engine that gave better performance than the regular 6-cylinder engine.

A well streamlined sedan is this 1939 Chrysler New Yorker. It cost $1,298 and weighed 3,695 lbs. It was also available as a Saratoga for $1,443. That weighed 3,720 lbs. The DeLuxe wheel trim and whitewalls were optional at extra cost. This style only enjoyed a one year stay.

Built on a special body is this 1939 6-cylinder Hayes bodied Royal Windsor Custom Club Coupe, or as it was also called, the Victoria Coupe. This body style was built only for one year and was also available in 8-cylinder models. Special broadcloth upholstery was standard equipment. Whitewall tires with special accessory wheel covers and trim rings were standard equipment. A total of 497 Custom Victoria Club Coupes were built for the year.

Chrysler

This 1939 Chrysler Custom Imperial 7-passenger sedan was referred to as Series C-14. It came on a 144-inch wheelbase and weighed 4,620 lbs. It sold for $2,595 complete with skirts, wheel trim, and whitewall tires. Only 95 of this elegant automobile were built.

Chrysler's invitation to luxury came with this 1940 Crown Imperial Limousine for 7 passengers. It weighed 4,365 lbs. and cost $2,445. A total of 210 were manufactured. The Crown Imperials had a 323.5 cubic inch engine that developed 143 H.P.

One of the six 1940 Chrysler Newport dual-cowl phaetons is parked in front of the Lloyd Gregg Chrysler Plymouth dealership in North Hollywood, Cal. This car was built on the 127.5-inch wheelbase, the same as used on the regular 8-cylinder Chryslers for 1940. The Newport was the pace car for the 1940 Indianapolis 500 Mile Race on Memorial Day.

1940

In 1940, Chrysler made a few changes in its mode designations. The popular Royal reappeared but the title of Royal Windsor was dropped in favor of just the Windsor which was a model all its own. New for the year was the traveler which was classed as the low priced Eight. The New Yorker was next in line followed by the Saratoga which was available only as a 6-passenger sport forma sedan with a combination of leather and cloth trim. The Custom Imperial was replaced with the Crown Imperia Eight.

Appearance wise, all models were virtually the same except for the size, quality and variety of trim and equipment. A Highlander trim version was available with Scotch plaid in the Windsor and New Yorker models.

The 6-cylinder cars came on a 122½-inch wheelbase and in 7-passenger version at 139.5 inches. All used 6:50 x 16 inch tires. The 8-cylinder models used a 128½-inch chassis. The Crown Imperial wheelbase became 1.5 inches longe than last year and was now a 145-inch car.

The Royal and Windsors used a 108 HP engine a 3600 RPM. A 112 HP was available at extra cost. Both models had 17 gallon fuel tanks. The tire size wa 6:25 x 16 inches in both series. The Traveler, New Yorker and Saratoga all had 135 HP engines turning over at 340 RPM. Available at extra cost was the 143 HP engine a 3400 RPM. The fuel supply was a 20 gallon tank. The tire size was 7:00 x 15 inches for each series. The Crown Imperial increased its horsepower to 137 at 3400 RPM It too had a 20 gallon fuel tank. The Crown Imperial used 7:50 x 15 inch tires.

Available for the first time at extra cost was Fluid Driv with overdrive for the New Yorker and Saratoga. Th Traveler offered only the overdrive at extra cost with it regular transmission. The Fluid Drive was standard on th Royal or Windsor for one more year.

In addition to the regular line of cars 1940 saw Chrysle come out with two "Idea Cars." These were th Thunderbolt, a 2-passenger car with a retractable hardtop electrically operated windows and deck lid, and push button doors. A total of six cars were built using th optional 143 HP 8-cylinder engine with Fluid Drive.

The other "Idea Car" was the Newport 6-passenge Dual-Cowl Phaeton. It used the Crown Imperial chassis o 145.5 inches and the 143 horsepower engine with Fluid Drive. Six models were built, one of which was used fo the 1940 Indianapolis 500. The company placed in Ninth Position for sales by selling 115,824 units for the calenda year.

The most popular 1940 model in the Royal line of Chryslers was this 4-door sedan that sold for $995. It had a run of 23,274 cars. Its mate, the Windsor, was the same car but had a more expensive interior and sold for $30 more. It had a production run of 28,477 units.

Chrysler

The 1941 models were basically the same offering as ιe previous year but did receive a nice facelifting. All the models that were available in 1940 returned in 941 except for the Traveler. Two new body styles were fered, a 6-passenger Club Coupe in Royal through ıratoga and a 4-door Town Sedan with solid rear ıarters that was available in all models. The Crown nperial Town Sedan was built on the New Yorker chassis ıt carried the luxury appointments of the Crown nperial. The cars with Highlander plaid trim were assed as sub-series to the Windsor and New Yorker odels. The trim package cost $20 extra.

A detailed list of mechanical improvements for all odels consisted of an oil bath air cleaner as standard juipment, new oil pump, improved water pump, and oating type oil screen. The Royal and Windsor models ıcreased the HP to 112 at 3600 RPM. The 8-cylinder odels except for the Crown Imperial developed 137 HP 3400 RPM. The Crown Imperials used the same 323.5 ıbic inch engine but developed 140 HP at the same RPM. he 6-cylinder cars had a 17 gallon tank while the Eights sed a 20 gallon supply. The Royal and Windsor came ith a 121½-inch wheelbase and 139½-inches for the mousine models. All New Yorker and Saratoga cars had a 27½-inch wheelbase. The Crown Imperials had a 145½-ıch wheelbase except for the above mentioned Town edan.

As for tire size, Royal and Windsors employed 6:25 x 6 inch tires and the New Yorker and Saratogas used :00 x 15s. The Crown Imperials came with 7:50 x 6 inch tires.

Late in the model run, a Town-Country 8-passenger tation Wagon was made available in the Windsor line. lso an 8-cylinder version was to be built but only a very ew were ever produced.

Fluid Drive was now available on an optional basis for oyal and Windsor cars at extra cost. Most cars did come juipped with it, and it was standard equipment on all -cylinder models.

A total of 34 models were available ranging in price om $945 for the 3-passenger Royal Coupe to $2,795 or the 8-passenger Crown Imperial Sedan Limousine. hrysler sold 141,522 cars, jumping to 8th Position for ales.

The 1941 Chrysler Club Coupe was available from Royal to Saratoga models. This example happens to be a Windsor, which was considered a new body style that year. It also was very popular, selling 8,513 units in the Windsor line-up at $1,096.

This is the 1941 Chrysler Town Sedan that offered rear doors opening from the back edge rather than the conventional sedans. A total of 2,704 were delivered at a cost of $1,175. This style was available in each Series but were kept as low production units.

Seen here is the 1941 Windsor 3-passenger Business Coupe that was a very practical car for businessmen who required a lot of space to carry their merchandise. The trunks on these coupes were the largest ever offered by Chrysler before or after this style ceased in 1948. The Windsor model sold for $998 to 1,921 customers.

A 1941 Chrysler Royal 4-door sedan was available for $1,051 in base form. Fluid Drive was available at extra cost. in this series and most buyers took it. With the automatic transmission, it developed 112 H.P. The Royal Sedans had a run of 51,378 cars. A like Windsor was available with a fancier interior for $1,125. A total of 36,396 Windsors were sold.

Chrysler

A mid-season 1941 offering was Chrysler's answer to the growing station wagon trend. It was called the Town-Country. It came chiefly as a 6-cylinder car and was offered as a 6-passenger for $1,395 weighing 3,540 lbs. or in 9-passenger style for $1,475 and weighed 3,595 lbs. One 8-cylinder Saratoga was built but, this was the extent of the 8-cylinder wagons for 1941. A total of 796 9-passenger vehicles were built and 200 6-passenger Town-Countrys left the Chrysler factory.

This was a late prototype of the 1941 Chrysler Windsor Convertible Coupe. Note the absence of the parking directional lights above the headlamps and the center bumper guard which the actual model had. This Windsor was available at $1,275. A total of 4,432 were built. It was also on the New Yorker chassis for $1,495. Only 1,295 were manufactured.

1942

For 1942, the models offered new styling and a number of mechanical improvements.

The cars had a new grille with horizontal bars continuing the full width and curving into the sides of the front fenders. The same bar design was used on the rear fenders. Horizontal parking lights were mounted flush with the grille. The running boards were concealed by flared doors. The bumper treatment was more massive than ever offered on a Chrysler before. The front license was mounted in the center between two bumper guards. The bumper bar was equipped with an air slot at the bottom edge which permitted extra air to go into the radiator.

Mechanically, the big improvement for the Six (Royal and Windsor cars) was a change in cubic inch displacement from 241.5 cubic inches to 250.6 cubic inches. This in turn brought the horsepower from 112 at 3600 RPM to 120 at 3500 RPM. The Eight, namely New Yorker, Saratoga and Crown Imperial, all came with the same engine of 323.5 cubic inches which developed 140 HP at 3600 RPM. The 6-cylinder cars had a 17 gallon fuel tank and the Eights used a 20 gallon supply. The Royal and Windsor used 6:25 x 16 inch tires. New Yorker and Saratogas had 7:00 x 16 inch tires, and the Crown Imperials had 7:50 x 16 inch tires. The wheelbase for the 6-cylinder cars was 121½-inches except for the 8-passenger Limousines in both models which came on a 139½-inch chassis. All New Yorker and Saratoga cars had a 127½-inch wheelbase while the Crown Imperials were on 145½-inch chassis. Highlander models were available in the Windsor and New Yorker cars which offered a scotch-plaid interior trim. This was considered a sub-series within each line.

A total of 29 models were available priced from $1,075 for a 3-passenger Royal Business Coupe to $3,063 for the Crown Imperial 8-passenger Limousine. A total of 5,292 cars were produced during the 1942 calendar year putting Chrysler in 12th Position for the year.

A completely new front end enhanced this 1942 Chrysler New Yorker Sedan. This model shared its body with the Saratoga again. Only differences were interior trim and the nameplate at the rear of the front fenders. All 1942 Chryslers used white plastic wheel discs which were a way of economizing before the actual halt of production. This New Yorker sold for $1,475 and production figures amounted to 7,045 before the lines closed in February of 1942.

The most popular 8-cylinder model Chrysler had to offer in 1941 was this New Yorker 4-door sedan at $1,345. Sales figures were combined with the Saratoga which amounted to 15,868 units. Most of these however were the New Yorker Series.

The Continental was 1933's only new mass production car. It was an independent of the Continental Automobile Company, a division of the Continental Motors Corporation. Detroit was the homequarters for production.

It was an attractive little car priced in the $400 class. It had a 101½-inch wheelbase, tread was 56 inches, weight 1,960 lbs. Its 4-cylinder engine developed 40 HP from its 143 cubic inches at 2800 RPM.

Besides the 4-cylinder model, also available was the Light 6 and the Ace Big 6. The former came on a 107-inch wheelbase and the latter came on a 114-inch wheelbase. Naturally, all carried Continental engines under their hoods.

The Light 6 came with a 65 HP engine at 3500 RPM and the Big 6 had 85 HP at 3600 RPM. The Four and Light 6 used 5:25 x 17-inch tires while the Big Six used 5:50 x 17s.

Both Four and Light 6 used a 10½ gallon fuel tank and the Big Six was supplied with a 15 gallon tank. All models carried mechanical brakes. These cars received very good gas mileage, ranging as high as 40 MPG in the 4-cylinder models. Models ranged from a Roadster in 2-passenger style for $355 to the Ace Big Six Sedan at $785. In the three series, 11 models were available.

Continental delivered 2,504 cars for their first year of production. The Sixes were discontinued at the end of this model year. They placed 24th in the sales picture for the year.

The Continental automobile came into being from the assets of the De Vaux-Hall Motor Corporation on February 13, 1932.

The least expensive of the 1933 Continentals was this 2-passenger Roadster known as the Beacon C400. It sold for $355. The 4-cylinder engine developed 40 H.P. This model as well as other Continentals had a new engine cushioning system called "Winged Power." It consisted of coil spring mounts with rubber cores.

A 1933 Continental 2-passenger Coupe sold for $380. This was the business car of the line and was known as the Commercial Coupe. It came on a 101½-inch wheelbase, had an all steel body, and a standard tread of 56 inches.

The pair of 1933 Ace 80 Big Six models are shown here. The Coupe was called a 4-passenger Standard Coupe and sold for $725. The 5-passenger 4-door Standard Sedan was available for $745. Only two body styles were in the top of the line. The Standard models strangely enough came with wire wheels while the DeLuxe cars had wooden wheels.

This 1933 Continental 5-passenger 2-door sedan sold for $380 also. It weighed 2,110 lbs. These Beacon and Flyer models resembled the 1933 Plymouth line of cars. Corduroy velour was used in Beacon models.

A 1933 Continental Flyer 5-passenger Sedan sold for $535. This series was available in four models known as the Flyer C600. It came on a 107-inch wheelbase and used the Continental 6-cylinder engine that developed 65 H.P. at 3500 RPM. It was similar to the Beacon except for wheelbase.

Continental

A 6-wheel 1933 Continental DeLuxe 5-passenger sedan sold for $785. This was the most expensive car Continental built. Standard models used 5:50 x 17 inch tires and DeLuxe cars had 6:50 x 16 inch tires.

1934

This was its final year of production. Continenta made several improvements on the 4-cylinder car. A lon type of wishbone radius rod ran forward from th transmission cross member replacing the parallel rod which had been used in 1933. This increased lengt maintained a more constant castor angle. A single shoc absorber was mounted at the center of the transverse fron spring, so that the chassis could oscillate more freely tha with the previous set-up. Both front and rear springs gav a softer ride. Front engine mounts were in rubber wher previously coil springs with rubber cores were used

Appearance was improved by increasing the width o the fenders and running boards and giving a new depth t the grille. Also, there was a new radiator ornament and more attractive tire cover.

The Continental engine gave 38 HP at 2600 RPM. Th 101½-inch wheelbase car used 5:25 x 17-inch tires. It ha a 10 gallon fuel tank. Mechanical brakes were used. Fou body styles were available priced at $380 for a 2-passenge DeLuxe Sedan. Sales were so few, production and sale figures are unavailable.

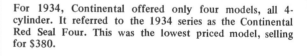

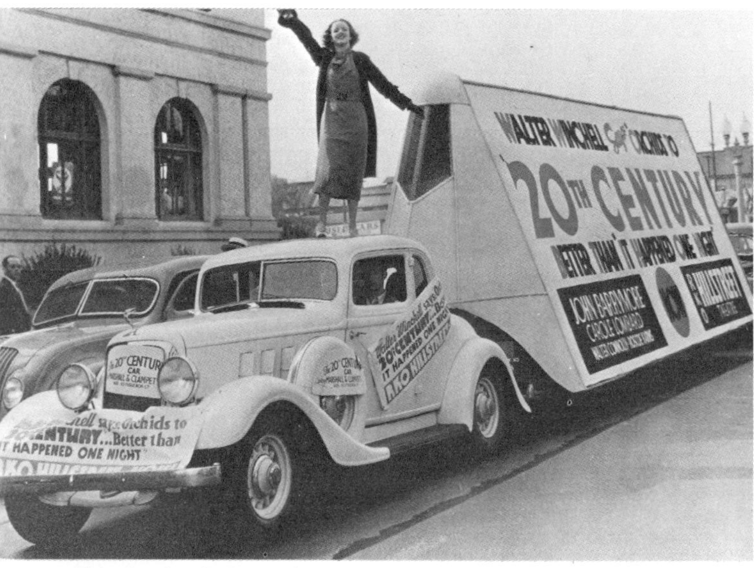

This is the DeLuxe 4-passenger Coupe advertising 20th Century Fox Movie Corp. movie "20th Century." This movie premiered at the R.K.O. Hillstreet Theater in Los Angeles. The Continental Ace came with broadcloth upholstery. This series was discontinued at the end of the 1933 model run.

For 1934, Continental offered only four models, all 4-cylinder. It referred to the 1934 series as the Continental Red Seal Four. This was the lowest priced model, selling for $380.

The 2-door 5-passenger Sedan for 1934 was Continental's answer to the young family with small children. This model cost $380 like the Coupe, which was actually a better buy looking at it from the practicality of the car.

The 1934 Continental was available in two 4-door Sedans. One was the Standard for $393 – the other was the model shown here, in DeLuxe style selling for $460. These models had the true beavertail rear end. Continental ceased production of the cars in July of 1934.

Cord

The 1930 Cord was built by the Auburn Automobile Co. of Auburn, Ind. Production of this series began in late 1929 and thus the series designation of L-29 was used on four models during its years of production from 1929 through 1932. Final Cord production ceased in 1937 with 310,812 models.

The 1930 Cord front-wheel drive had a Lycoming 8-cylinder engine. The car's power plant consisted of a complete unit of differential, transmission, brakes and clutch.

The 8-cylinder engine developed 125 HP at 3600 RPM. The wheelbase was 137½ inches, and tire size was 7:00 x 18 inches. L-29s had a 20 gallon fuel tank. Lockheed hydraulic brakes were used on these cars.

The model designations were Sedan and Brougham for $3,295 and Cabriolet and Phaeton Sedan for $3,295. Production figures of 2,678 cars turned out from August 11, 1929 to December 21st, 1930 placed Cord in the 30th sales position for the year.

One of the 1930 Cord L-29 Cabriolet 2-4 models that was very popular with those who could afford such luxury. This model sold for $3,295.

A 1930 Cord with Sakhoffsky body. This was completed through the Hayes Body Co. of Grand Rapids, Mich. Disc wheels were part of the special equipment on this one-off body style. This car today is fully restored and enjoying life in the Brooks Stevens Museum in Milwaukee, Wisconsin.

This was a special 1930 Cord Speedster, featured with the accessory Wood lights common to many classics of that era.

Complete comfort for five was what Cord advertised for this 1930 Brougham. It sold for $3,095. Serial numbers for all L-29's are found on the front end of the frame on the right side, and on the right side under the front carpet.

Cord

Probably the most popular model for family use was the 5-passenger sedan selling for $3,095. The doors opened with unusual width, giving convenience to its passengers. The height of this sedan is 61 inches.

1931

The same four models as offered for 1930 were again catalogued. They were Cabriolet, Sedan, Phaeton Sedan, and Brougham. They were introduced as 1931 models on January 1, 1931.

For 1931, Cord offered its same front wheel drive Lycoming eight-in-line engine. The cars developed 125 HP at 3600 RPM. The bore and stroke of 3¼ x 4½ inches remained the same for all L-29 Cords. The fuel supply was again a 20 gallon tank. The wheelbase remained 137½ inches and a tire size of 7:00 x 18 inches was employed for all 4 models. Again, Lockheed hydraulic brakes were used on all L-29s.

Basically, all L-29 Cords remained the same during their four years of production.

A total of 1,416 Cords were sold during the 1931 model run. The company placed 26th for the year.

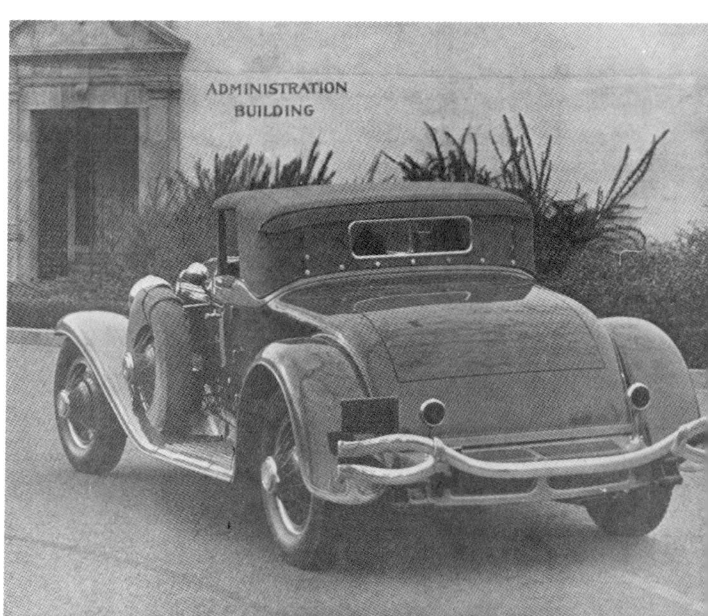

The 1931 L-29 Cord Cabriolet with its rumble seat compartment closed. This model had a taillight on the left and stop and back-up mounted on the right. The rakish lines of the front wheel car will always be loved by admirers of classic cars. Seeing the Administration Building in the background, possibly the proud owner is entering his his Freshman year of college!

A 1931 L-29 Cord Enclosed Drive Phaeton Sedan. This model, like the Cabriolet, sold for $3,295. Every state but Delaware and New Hampshire registered a new Cord in 1931. A total of 1,416 cars were registered.

A factory publicity photo shows a 1931 Cord Brougham. This example is shown wearing a set of whitewalls that could stand a little cleaning for the Concours. It sold for the same $3,095. The tire cover for this model is metal when many used canvas. Also it sports sidemount mirrors. Note the unusual slanting windshield.

932

Cord for 1932 came in four body styles, each carrying entral Bodies. They ranged in price from $2,395 to 2,595. Weight varied from 4,320 lbs. for the Cabriolet 4,620 lbs. for the Sedan. Each came on a 137¾-inch heelbase. The tire size was the same, 7:00 x 18, and all ed Lockheed hydraulic brakes.

The sales picture for Cord wasn't very shattering, with ly 325 cars being registered for the year. The sales cture kept them in the 26th position for the year. This as actually Cord's last year for producing the L-29. hose carried over into 1933 were just leftovers of the maining 1932 models. During the years of the L-29's oduction, 4,429 cars were produced.

For the next three years, as the country wallowed rough the depression, the Cord name was lost to the tomotive public. In late 1935, the coffin-nosed Cord ould make its debut to become quite an attraction.

Posing beside this 1932 L-29 Brougham wouldn't be hard to do, then or today. Prices were reduced in 1932. This model sold for $2,395. The courtesy light above the running-board was standard equipment on all L-29's.

This front right view of a 1932 L-29 Cord Cabriolet demonstrates how comfortable the rumble seat could be. With rumble seat in use, the Cabriolet sat four easily.

This top down version 1932 L-29 Cord Le Grande Phaeton is shown with its Murphy body. Phaeton Sedans measured 58 inches high with top up.

A three-quarter front left view shows off this handsome 1932 Cord L-29 Phaeton. This model has its boot nicely tailored to the lines of the body. Wire wheels were standard equipment on L-29 Cords.

Cord

All lined up together are the Cord Cabriolet, Phaeton, and Sedan for 1932. These cars were constant trophy winners at foreign shows when they were new automobiles. Cord took awards at the Grand Prix, Monte Carlo, Gold Band in Prague, and the Berlin Concours to name just a few. 1932 was really the last of the four years these cars were produced. Any 1933 models were left over from the previous year. A total of 4,429 were built.

1933

For 1933, the Cords that were coming from deale showrooms were really leftover 1932 L-29s. The onl small change seen in the 1933 cars was the change fror Safety Plate glass to Libby Owens Ford. This change wa actually on some cars registered in late 1932. Only earl Cords used Pittsburgh Safety Plate glass. As was stated i the previous chapter, these Cords were really leftover ca from 1932, but registered as 1933 models.

A special built 1932 L-29 Cord Town Car. This example wears double white B.F. Goodrich Silvertowns, and massive front bumper equipment. This model is on display with many other classics of this era.

At an Auburn display in 1939 this L-29 Cord graces the position of honor among its companies products: Auburn, Cord, and Duesenberg. This example sold for $2,595.

A typical California home of the 1930's shows off a 1932 L-29 Cord Sedan parked in the driveway of this Spanish style tile roofed house. This model sports a cadet sun visor. Bumper equipment was still optional but most all did carry this accessory.

1936

Cord now came from the Auburn, Cord, Duesenberg line ɔf cars with its new home being Connersville, Ind. The ːompany was absent from the automotive scene during he 1934 and 1935 model runs. It came back, with the offin-nosed 810 making its debut on Nov. 2, 1935. These ars actually were all hand-built models meant for Auto Shows throughout the country. Due to some difficulties n over-heating, and transmission problems, little was ctually seen of these cars before March of 1936. E. L. Cord, president of the company, promised all the nfilled Cord orders would be completed by Christmas of 935. When Dec. 25th arrived, the Cords were delivered, ut on a different scale. These Cords were 1/32 replicas ast in bronze and mounted on marble for great conversation pieces. With only these items, the Cord picture vasn't too bright, especially for salesmen who felt they eally had something new to offer.

The Cord came on a 125-inch wheelbase, used a V-8 25 HP engine by Lycoming (3500 RPM). The transnission consisted of a 4-speed device with the differential ocated in the front end. Fuel supply was a 20-gallon tank nd the car rode on 6:50 x 16-inch tires. Hydraulic brakes vith centrefuse drums were used.

Four body styles were available for 1936, ranging from 1,995 for the Westhcester Sedan to $2,195 for a Phaeton.

Quote the following from *The Classic Cord* by Dan R. 'ost, page 65 – "Wonder what happened to the 100 handuilt cars that were required before the Cord was allowed n the shows?"

Twenty or thirty were convertibles, and their finish 'as more for the eye than the road. The cost of making hem saleable would have been more than they could have een sold for. These beautiful cars were called in, tripped of parts, and the base body shells were burned. n eye-witness described this bonfire as "a sight to tear our heart out."

The sedans were not as ill-fated, and some are ndoubtedly in use today. These were run through the ne after it was set up, transmissions were installed, and ney were otherwise brought up to date, then sold to uburn auto employees for an even $800 in what was kely the most unusual car bargain sale ever conducted. nterior trims and lacquer jobs on these display units remor the imagination.

Gordon Buehig, the head designer for Cord at that time, ought one – a rust red metallic called "Coppertone." 'opper plating complemented the color by replacing the sual chrome from wheel rims to hood louvers.

Sales put Cord in 22nd place, with 1,174 cars for the ear. Some of these were actually 1937 cars, introduced n November of 1936.

A beautiful classic right from the start is this 2-passenger Convertible Coupe. The 1936 Cords did not have supercharged equipment. This model sold for $2,095 including spare tire, wheel, bumpers, bumper guards, and radio. Whitewall tires were optional equipment. All 1936 models came on a 125-inch wheelbase and developed 125 H.P.

Cord's answer to the Phaeton for 1936 was this handsome 5-passenger model equipped with genuine leather as standard equipment. It sold for $2,195. These 1936 models were secretly photographed for the press at E. L. Cord's home in Beverly Hills, Calif.

A very impressive picture shows what the Indiana State Police thought of the 1936 Cord 810. This model carried the newly designed V-8 Lycoming engine with an improved front wheel drive. This model sold for $1,995 in Westchester Sedan style, the most popular body style available in the 1936 Cords. The Beverly Sedan sold for $2,095. The 4-door model weighed 3,650 lbs.

Rarely seen is an unusual example of a 1936 Cord Phaeton equipped from the factory with dual sidemount tires. The rim of the tire cover barely peaks above the line of the hood. This wheel sidemount somewhat spoils the beautiful fender line this car already had.

1937

The company entered 1937 with the same car it hac offered in 1936 known as the 810.

In addition to this series was the 812, the same car a far as body and interior were concerned, but under th hood it was another story. Any Cord designated as an 81 means it was an 8-cylinder supercharged version tha produced 170 HP. It was available in all models. I addition to these regular models, 1937 also saw a Custon Berline and Supercharged versions of both these models All Custom models rode on a 132-inch wheelbase. If Customer preferred the Custom to come as a Berline, glass partition was available between front and back seat Upholstery combinations were either all broadcloth o broadcloth in the rear with a leather front compartmen at the owner's wish.

1937 production began November 18, 1936, ending i a total of 1,146 cars. Prices ranged from $2,445 for Westchester Sedan to $3,575 for a Supercharged Custor Berline model. The complete line of 1936 and 193 810 and 812 Cords produced numbered 2,320 vehicles putting the company in the 18th position for sale in 1937.

This is an 812 Phaeton for 1937. Shown in top down version, it wears different style wheel covers. In 1937, Cord prices increased and this model sold for $3,060 with Supercharger. Without this equipment it was $2,645.

A 1937 Cord dealership displaying several of the new models. In the foreground is a new 812 Phaeton with the Supercharged pipes and showing its headlamps. Note in the background a 1937 Willys Sedan. Apparently an example of what we have today of a dealer selling a compact car to help out his new car sales.

Chauffeur driven was what often happened when an owner ordered the 132-inch Cord Berline. This example is not Supercharged, and thus lacks the brilliant chrome pipes coming from its coffin-nosed hood. The Custom Berline sold for $3,060. With Supercharger it was Cord's most expensive model selling for $3,575. This was the final year of production, registering 1,146 cars as 1937 models. The two year run saw 2,320 Cords in 810 and 812 style manufactured.

Crosley

Crosley entered the automotive market for the first time in 1939 under the presidency of Powel Crosley Jr. The headquarters were in Cincinnati. The company continued to produce cars through 1952. For 1939 they offered America's lowest priced car.

The models available were a Convertible Coupe for two passengers at $325 and a Convertible Sedan seating four for $350. The cars were sold through Crosley radio and appliance dealers. The company placed in 21st position for sales, selling approximately 1,200 cars.

The automobile used a 2-cylinder air cooled engine with a 3 x 2½" bore and stroke. The head was of cast iron. The engine's horsepower was rated at 12 at 4000 RPM. The direct drive gear ratio was listed at 5:14 and the overdrive at optional extra cost brought it to 5:57. The two models came on 80-inch wheelbases. They had a tire size of 4:25 x 12 inches. A six gallon fuel supply was used.

This Crosley 4-passenger Convertible Sedan was introduced in 1939 for $350. It was America's lowest priced Convertible Sedan for the year. Most of these cars were painted in cream with red wheels. The same offering was available again for 1940.

1940

The 1940 models came in three types: the 2-passenger Convertible Coupe for $325, the 4-passenger Convertible Sedan for $350, and a Station Wagon that was introduced late in the season. All models weighed 925 lbs. on the 80-inch chassis.

Mechanically they were practically the same cars as in 1939. An air cooled 2-cylinder engine developed 12 HP at 4200 RPM, which was a slight increase over the previous year. Mechanical brakes were used, and an overdrive was available at an additional cost. Not many Crosleys came equipped with it as they already gave excellent mileage.

Crosley placed at the bottom of the sales race for 1940 by again selling in the neighborhood of 1,200 cars.

A late season model was this 1940 Crosley Station Wagon. It sold for $445 which included rear seat, spare tire, and wheel. The seating capacity allowed four to sit comfortably. It weighed 1,160 lbs.

The 1940 Crosley interior, showing the dash – strictly functional, minus all frills. It did allow for a small glove box on the right of the dash and in front of the steering wheel the radio could be mounted to balance out its appearances. All gauges were centered directly in the middle.

Crosley

The 1941 Crosley Convertible Sedan looked just about the same as it did in the two previous years. However, the engine proved to be more efficient with a better oiling system and a universal joint connected to the drive shaft. It was available in standard form for $375. A DeLuxe model was also available for $10 more which included better seat material and a variety of paint colors. It weighed 975 lbs. Its standard color was light blue.

1941

Crosley offered 7 body styles in 1941, which include the small trucks for delivery and pick-up purposes Engineering advancements showed a better engine, a more effective oiling system and the addition of a universal join to the drive shaft.

The engine was still a 2-cylinder air cooled 35.3 cubi inch device that developed 12 HP at 4000 RPM. A 6 gallon fuel tank was used for each model. The wheelbas continued at 80 inches and the tire size remained 4:25 x 12 inches. Crosley prices were $299 for a 2-passenge Coupe to $479 for the 4-passenger Station Wagon. Thi year Crosley also sold the cars through automotive dealer ships besides the appliance dealers that sold it durin 1939 and 1940. The company placed in 18th position fo the calendar year selling approximately 2,200 cars.

The Enclosed Panel 1941 Crosley came with rear wooden panels. It was the most serviceable model in the small truck line. It sold for $449 and weighed 1,130 lbs.

The 1941 Crosley Pick-up Delivery was one of the lowest priced models in the entire line for the year. It sold for $399. This model answered the problems of general all-around delivery for loads not to exceed 500 lbs. This small pick-up was ideal for gardeners. Note the spare tire mounted on the rear of the bed.

For 1941 Crosley offered a larger selection of models. The Parkway Delivery was an example of this. It was an all metal delivery car ideal for florists, druggists, and markets. This model sold for $399. The top over the driver was a canvas removable canopy.

1942

Crosley offered pretty much the same package as it did in 1941 except for the all-steel Sedan. Improved acceleration, better brakes, and larger tires of 4:50 x 12 were introduced on the 1942 models. A Crosley designed heater was available in all models at extra cost. A larger and heavier crankshaft and camshaft with refinements in the oil and fuel pump were the main changes for the year.

The engine continued as the same 35.3 cubic inch air cooled 2-cylinder engine of 12 HP at 4000 RPM. The fuel tank held 6 gallons and the models used the same 80-inch chassis. The models available ranged from a $351 2-passenger Coupe to the 4-passenger Station Wagon at $508. So few cars were produced in 1942 that production figures are not available.

A new edition to the Crosley line for 1942 was the Covered Wagon. This model basically was a pick-up with a canvas removable top. It sold for $453 and weighed 1,125 lbs. The seating capacity allowed for four passengers.

Crosley's 1941 Station Wagon was the most expensive model in the line. It sold for $479 and weighed 1,160 lbs. It allowed for four passengers. The rear quarter panels only were done in wood.

The 1942 Crosley 4-passenger Convertible Sedan in standard version used plexiglas window shades which were removable. It sold for $402. Its weight was the same as the DeLuxe line, 975 lbs.

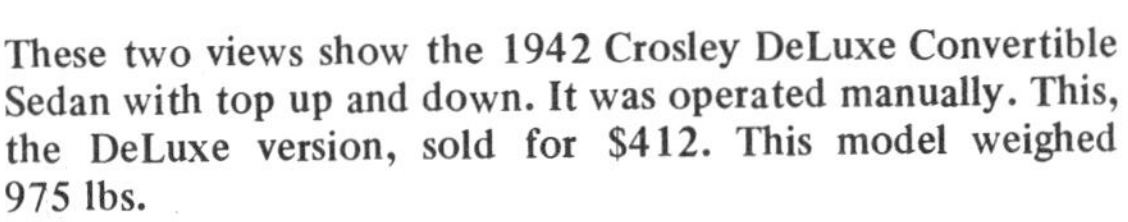

These two views show the 1942 Crosley DeLuxe Convertible Sedan with top up and down. It was operated manually. This, the DeLuxe version, sold for $412. This model weighed 975 lbs.

Cunningham

A top down version of the 1930 Cunningham Roadster. All models were on special order only as Cunningham was working mainly in the ambulance and funeral car trade at this time.

This 1930 Cunningham Semi-Touring was available only as a V-8 developing 110 H.P. at 2500 RPM. It came in this body style on a 132-inch wheelbase. The wire wheels were chrome, at the customer's wish, at no extra cost.

The 1931 Cunningham Roadster Coupe. The only difference showing on this model and the William Seiter Convertible is that this model wears a pair of fog lamps as standard equipment directly above the bumper.

The Cunningham was a product of the Jame Cunningham Sons Co. of Rochester, N.Y. The compan had built cars from 1911 through 1936, but chiefly as custom body builder and hearse and ambulance manufa turer.

For 1930, the Cunningham factory was doing very litt as the depression had taken hold of them quite nicel The company never had a large dealer organization, s many people bought their cars direct from the factor The company did very little advertising and when th depression inched its way in, the passenger car trade wa practically non-existent. Since the firm always had a goo business with building hearse and ambulance bodies, th was continued during the next few years.

The engine consisted of a V-8 with 110 HP at 2500 RPM The wheelbases were 132 and 142 inches, with bodi that were built to order. The wheel size was 7:00 x 2 inches. Mechanical brakes by Bendix were used. A Cunninghams had a 24-gallon fuel tank.

Production was so low that figures are not availabl Since cars were built to order, prices also are not availabl

1931

Most of the business for 1931 dealt with ambulanc companies and funeral homes. Since the public wasn't in position to buy many expensive cars during the depressic years, Cunningham felt the pinch severely. Besides buildi cars on their own bodies the company furnished custo bodies to other companies. Among them were Cadilla La Salle, and Packard.

1932

In 1932, the company built a V-8 car with 140 HP 2800 RPM. It used mechanical brakes and came equippe with 7:50 x 18 tires. The wheelbase measured 142 inche All models carried a 24-gallon fuel supply. Each car leave the Rochester headquarters carried with it a custo body built to order. Production figures were never mac available to the public.

In addition to building high quality custom designe autos, the company continued to be noted for its ve fine line of expensive funeral coaches and ambulance As a result of this business, a great many customers of th auto division were engaged in the funeral business, and ha their first introduction to Cunningham quality via th funeral car trade.

Seated at the wheel of his new 1930 Cunningham Roadster Coupe is William Seiter, the director of pictures at Universal Studios. The purchase was made through Walter L. Elbe, distributor for Cunningham cars in California. There were very few Cunningham dealer outlets at this time. Most transactions were made directly with James Cunningham-Sons of Rochester, N. Y.

Cunningham

933

Since 1924, Cunningham turned out not over 500 cars, o actual 1933 production isn't truly known. Under the ıood was America's largest V-8 engine, with the bore ncreased to 3-7/8 inches from 3-3/4 inches. The stroke vas still 5 inches. It gave a displacement of 471 cubic nches, developing 140 HP at 2800 RPM with a 5 to 1 ompression ratio.

Tire size for this year was 7:50 x 20 inches. The vheelbase remained 142 inches. Fuel supply was a 24-allon tank. Due to the low engine speed, these cars equired only three main bearings, but these were ex-remely large bearings. Its rear main bearing was four nches long. The car's rod bearings were very rugged to andle the thrust coming from each of these large pistons.

Cunningham was still the prestige producer of pro-essional cars in the country, and was widely known as producer of very fine but very expensive funeral cars nd ambulances.

934

The company continued building automobiles strictly n a special order basis for the few who could afford a car f this class in 1934. The only change noticeable over last ear's car was in the tire size which went from 7:50 x 20 o 7:00 x 19 inches.

For 1932, Cunningham dropped its 132-inch wheelbase model to concentrate only on the 142-inch chassis. All models like this 7-passenger Touring car carried a 140 H.P. V-8 engine. Note the double spares on the rear rather than the sidemounts that Cunningham was generally noted for.

This 1933 Cunningham Enclosed Drive Cabriolet is virtually the same car the company had produced in small quantities for the past several years. This example wears the rare whitewalls so few Cunninghams came with. They appear to be Vogue Tyres or B.F. Goodrich with the small red flags on the sidewall. This owner also wished his monograms placed on the rear door belt molding.

A 1931 Cunningham Convertible Cabriolet with landau irons. It's difficult to tell if this beauty has dirty whitewalls or if some black tire dressing is required. This style came on the 142-inch chassis.

The 1931 Cunningham Enclosed Drive Limousine sitting in stately fashion for its 7 passengers. This model was available only on a 142-inch wheelbase.

A 1932 Cunningham 4-passenger Enclosed Drive Sedan. Fewer than 500 of these cars were assembled since 1924. Note the special parking light treatment mounted on the front fender.

Cunningham

The 1933 Cunningham Convertible Town Car is displayed in its ultra conservative styling. Note the speaker horn placed between front and rear compartment for the chauffeur. This model has twin sidemount mirrors placed above the tires.

1935

By 1935, the depression had pretty well taken hold c Cunningham as an actual producer of cars using its ow name. At this time, Cunningham was under contract wit the Ford Motor Co. to turn out some snazzy lookin automobiles. A Ford Fordor V-8 cost $655, but with som Cunningham frills, it turned into a Town Car and wa marketed for $2,600. Enough buyers were there fc Cunningham to keep its doors opened for 1935. Mechani ally, these cars were Ford V-8s.

Besides building the Ford Cunningham Town Car, th company still was doing business in the ambulance an hearse field and also built bodies for Lincoln and Packar mainly that year. The Packards were chiefly on th 120 chassis.

The Cunningham Company claimed to have been in th hearse business for 97 years. It continued through 193 with both the Town Car trade and the turning out c ambulances and hearses.

How much longer could Cunningham continue to find buyers so conservative as to purchase a car that was at least six years behind in styling? This 1934 4-passenger sedan has a carriage type door handle reminiscent of the twenties. Apparently a buyer wished his new model to look like his 1924 car.

1936

This was the year Cunningham decided to close its doo forever. It had been in business since 1838. During th time it built the top quality ambulances, hearses an service cars for funeral homes. With the buyers not the in big enough demand, the firm closed its doors. Th business they did do during 1936 was practically all do with the Ford Motor Co. By changing certain componen of the 1936 Ford into a Town Car, the buyer was sti able to spend $2,600 and have a specially built ca Mechanically, however, these cars still used all For running gear. Actual production figures of the 1936 For Cunningham Town Cars is not fully known, but it estimated that between 100 and 150 left the Rochest facility.

For the funeral car trade, Cadillac, Lincoln and Packar were the main suppliers to Cunningham for ambulanc and hearse vehicles.

Really feeling the pinch, Cunningham decided to discontinue its own line of cars and only build bodies for the elite. This 1935 Town Car carries a Cunningham body but used Ford running gear. The Cunningham Town Car sold for $2,600.

This 1936 Cunningham also shares its parts with Ford. Running gear, front end trim, wheels and bumpers are Ford while the body is by James Cunningham-Sons. This was their final year for producing bodies. The price continued at $2,600.

De Soto

De Soto was a product of the Chrysler Corp. In 1930, he company was beginning its third year of manufacturing utomobiles. The home plant and office were located in)etroit.

The De Soto for 1930 was one of the first cars from the 'hrysler Corp. to use an 8-cylinder engine. This car eveloped 72 HP at 3400 RPM. It had a fuel capacity of 5 gallons. The wheelbase was 118 inches. Its tire size vas 5:25 x 19 inches. The De Soto Six continued to be uilt. It developed 55 HP at 3000 RPM. It had an 11-allon fuel tank. Six cylinder De Sotos rode on 5:00 x 19 nch tires and used a 114-inch wheelbase. Lockheed ydraulic brakes were used on both 6s and 8s.

A total of 14 models were available between both series. Iowever, not all models were available in each series. The s offered a 2-door Sedan which the 8 didn't offer and the)eLuxe Coupe for 5 in 8-cylinder fashion wasn't available ı the 6.

Prices ranged between $845 for a 2-passenger Business 'oupe in 6-cylinder style to $1,015 for the 8-cylinder 'onvertible Coupe for 4 passengers.

De Soto ranked in 13th position by selling 34,889 cars ı 1930.

931

The 1931 models again were offered in 6 and 8-cylinder nes. These cars had a narrower radiator shell in chrome vith distinctive radiator shutters. The nameplate was emoved from the radiator shell and the De Soto coat-of-rms was placed on the headlamp cross bar. Two ventilators vere mounted on top of the cowl. The windshield consisted of the swing out type. New single bar bumpers were sed for the first time on the 6-cylinder models. The 8s sed a split bumper.

The engine room of the De Soto had a 205 cubic inch isplacement, developing 60 HP at 3000 RPM. These ıodels had a 1/8-inch greater bore with cylinder dimenions being 3¼ by 4-1/8 inches. The fuel supply came from 12-gallon tank. The wheelbase was again 114 inches and ıe tire size was 4:75 x 19.

The 8-cylinder cars kept the 75 HP engine at 3400 RPM. 'he cubic inch displacement was 220 inches. The fuel ınk held a 15½-gallon supply. Free wheeling was available s an option. The wheelbase of 8-cylinder cars again was 18 inches and the tire size was 5:25 x 19 inches. With ıe depression putting its marks on the De Soto as well as n the other makes, the 8-cylinder models were disontinued at the end of the year. De Soto didn't return ɔ an 8 again until 1952.

Fourteen models were available for the year. Prices ınged from $795 for a 2-passenger De Soto 6 Coupe ɔ $1,005 for the De Soto 8-cylinder Convertible Coupe ɔr four.

De Soto placed in the 14th position for the year by elling 29,835 units.

Entering the third year of production, this 1930 De Soto 6 Roadster for four sold for $845. It also was available as an 8-cylinder for $915. The Six weighed 2,350 lbs. and the Eight, 2,560 lbs. De Soto used New Departure bearings as represented in this photo.

This prototype 1930 De Soto DeLuxe 6 Sedan sold for $955. This model is a 6-wheel version with one sidemount in the fender and the other mounted on the rear. Some models did use this different arrangement rather than both wheels being fender mounted. The sedan weighed 2,655 lbs. A standard 6 also was available for $855 and weighed 2,645 lbs.

Just leaving the factory after receiving its final inspection is this 1931 De Soto 6 Sedan that sold for $885 and weighed 2,645 lbs. This being the standard model, it offered no accessory frills whatsoever.

De Soto

1932

By this year, De Soto was starting its fifth year o production, and was managing to hold its own, risin from 14th place in 1931 to 9th place for 1932, which wa good for a car fairly new on the market – when it wa actually competing with cars from its own company

De Soto had seven body styles, plus a limited editio Town Car which was built on a Briggs body. Prices bega at $695 for a 2-passenger Business Coupe to $835 for th Sedan on regular production run. The Town Car, full equipped, sold for $1,025. All models came with 5:25 x 1 tires with wire wheels as standard equipment. Engine were all Sixes, developing 75 HP at 3400 RPM. Fue capacity was a 12-gallon tank. A total of 27,441 unit were sold.

This DeLuxe 1931 De Soto 6 Sedan with the 6 wire wheel treatment was owned when new by the author's aunt and uncle, Gertrude and Walter Krebser. The sidemount accessory cost $22 extra. This car sold for $977 new and weighed 2,655 lbs. An 8-cylinder model was available for $1,040. It weighed 2,800 lbs. This was the last year De Soto built an 8-cylinder car until it introduced a V-8 in 1952.

De Soto's 1931 8-cylinder Business Coupe for two was the lowest priced model for the year in the 8-cylinder line. It sold for $975 and weighed 2,690 lbs. The body was by Briggs on all models. A 6-cylinder Business Coupe also was available for $865. It weighed 2,460 lbs. The 8-cylinder had double bumpers to distinguish it from the 6 model.

This 1932 De Soto 6 Roadster is equipped with a set of jumbo 7:50 x 15 Goodyear Air Wheels as a dealer option for $75. By 1933 most manufacturers offered this wheel arrangement. It gave a very comfortable ride to its passengers. The Roadster had a seating arrangement for four. It sold for $875 and weighed 2,520 lbs. All 1932's were known as Model SC6.

A 1932 De Soto Rumble Seat Coupe with 6 wire wheels, with seating for four sold for $925. It weighed 2,580 lbs. This was the deluxe version that sported the trumpet horns and chrome covered sidemounts. The sidemounts were optional at extra cost.

De Soto offered this 6-wheel DeLuxe 1932 Sedan with artillery wheels for $960. The split windshield was on all models for the first time. This Sedan weighed 2,630 lbs. It was the most popular model for the year.

De Soto

)33

For this year, De Soto's design wasn't radically changed om 1932. Artillery wheels were now the rage, along with ırysler's other innovations such as: automatic choke, ıtomatic manifold heat control, a transmission with silent ·lical gears throughout, high speed steel exhaust valve ats to extend valve grinds, and the starter combined on e accelerator were just a few of the many new items at were found on the 1933 De Soto.

A 15½-gallon fuel supply was used on this 114-3/8-inch r. It developed 79 HP at 3400 from its 6-cylinder engine. ıso available was the 86 HP engine with a 6.2 to 1 ımpression Red Head.

This car employed 5:50 x 17 inch tires, but could be dered with 7:00 x 15 inch air wheels.

The braking system was Lockheed hydraulic. Nine odels were available, beginning with the DeLuxe Coupe $695, and going up to the Custom Club Sedan for)75. Saleswise, De Soto slipped down to 12th spot, with ,186 cars registered for the calendar year.

A very rare 1932 De Soto Town Car, with body by Briggs. Fewer than 20 of these were built and price was not available. Note this model wears special wheel covers mounted over its wire wheels. That front bumper isn't bent – this was just the curve line it had in front of the grille.

A 1933 De Soto DeLuxe Sedan is wearing wire wheels rather than the deluxe artillery wheels. It also came without trumpet horns, had only one windshield wiper, and one taillamp. All could be ordered if a customer wished. This model sold for $765 and weighed 3,050 lbs.

A super sport model for the 1932 De Soto line was this Convertible Sedan. It had a seating arrangement for five. The price was $1,115 and it weighed 2,850 lbs. The body was by Briggs for this model and the town car. All other bodies for 1932 were Chrysler built. A total of 278 convertible sedans were manufactured.

This was De Soto's 1933 Custom 4-passenger Coupe that sold for $790. It weighed 2,995 lbs. It was also available in DeLuxe form as a 2-passenger Coupe for $665 and as a DeLuxe 4-passenger Coupe for $735. The DeLuxe models were minus trumpet horns and twin windshield wipers like the Custom models employed.

De Soto did much advertising of the cars in 1933 showing them in distant lands. This example is wearing the standard equipment of the Custom line of twin windshield wipers, artillery wheels, and trumpet horns. It sold for $835 and weighed 3,150 lbs. It is parked by the Cafe de la Paix, getting the final approval from these Parisians.

De Soto

This model was based on the design of the 1933 De Soto Custom Club Sedan that sold for $975 and weighed 3,235 lbs. It was the most expensive De Soto for the year. This particular car, however, was done on an experimental basis, with only one being built. It was almost classed as the first of the hardtops. Both right doors opened minus the pillar between doors.

1934

For the 1934 model run, De Soto, like Chrysler cam out with the Airflow. This automobile was certainl ahead of the time with its streamlined body, from built-i headlamps to shrouded rear wheels. This model wa continued through 1936.

The De Soto only came as an Airflow for 1934, bein built in four different models with a price tag of $1,19 per model. With its streamlined body, it gave comfort an increased width to the interior rather than more speec Its top speed stayed about the same as 1933, which wa about 80 MPH. The windshield provided the best visio up to date with its increase of ten more inches. Interio bordered on being plush with an attractive "freze material. The front seat carried a steel tubing around th back. This could also be used as an assist for rear sea passengers getting out of the car.

Horsepower was rated at 100 at 3400 RPM. Tire siz was 6:50 x 16 and the wheelbase was 115½ inche A 16-gallon fuel tank was used. Brakes were Lockhee hydraulic as in previous years.

De Soto put out 15,825 Airflows for the year, placir again in the 12th position for 1934.

Radically different from the 1933 De Soto was the new Airflow for 1934. All Airflows used the 115½-inch wheelbase. Each of the four models available sold for $1,195. This 5-passenger Sedan was the most popular.

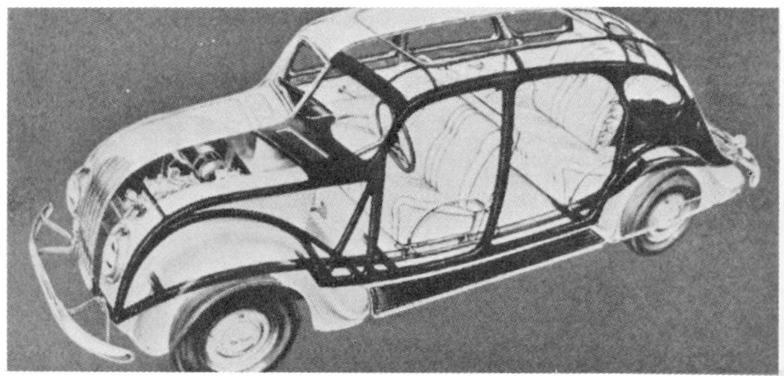

De Soto advertised in 1934 that riding inside the frame, not on it like on conventional cars, gave a far more comfortable ride. The body was one all-steel unit which was 40 times more rigid.

The 5-passenger Coupe and 2-door Sedan carried the same body shell. The Sedan carried the spare mounted on the rear while the Coupe model had it concealed in the rear trunk compartment. Some new features for the year included: Floating Power engine mounts, Flexbeam lighting in the headlights, push button dash starting, and all-steel sound insulated body.

The top of the line as far as giving a little more look of luxury was this 1934 De Soto Town Sedan for 6 passengers. It sold for $1,195 like all the other Airflows for the year. This model offered the enclosed rear quarters windows which gave it a club sedan effect that was becoming popular with many manufacturers at the time.

935

For 1935, De Soto offered two series, the Airstream, hich was new and the Airflow, similar to last year's car. The Airstream developed 93 HP at 3400 RPM, the same the Chrysler Airstream 6. The Airflow used the same igine as the Airstream, but had an aluminum head of 5 to 1 compression ratio and produced 100 HP at 500 RPM. Both models used an air cooled voltage gulator. The Airflow used a push button starter while irstreams used the accelerator pedal. The choke was of e automatic type.

All Airflows came with a sturdy X-frame, with the body eing bolted straight to the frame. The 1935 models ianged the anti-roll stabilizer to the front. All had a ypoid rear axle and optional overdrive transmission which itomatically cut the engine speed by 30% when above) MPH.

The lowest price De Soto was the Airstream 2-passenger oupe at $695. These models went up to $825 for a passenger Touring Sedan. The Airflows came in three odels all selling at $1,195. The Airstreams were ½-inch nger than the Airflows, and had a 116-inch wheelbase. ire size on the Airstreams was 6:25 x 16 while Airflows sed 6:50 x 16s. Both series came with hydraulic brakes. irstreams used a 15-gallon fuel supply and Airflows held ie gallon more.

Sales for the year dropped De Soto to 13th position, ith 34,267 cars built.

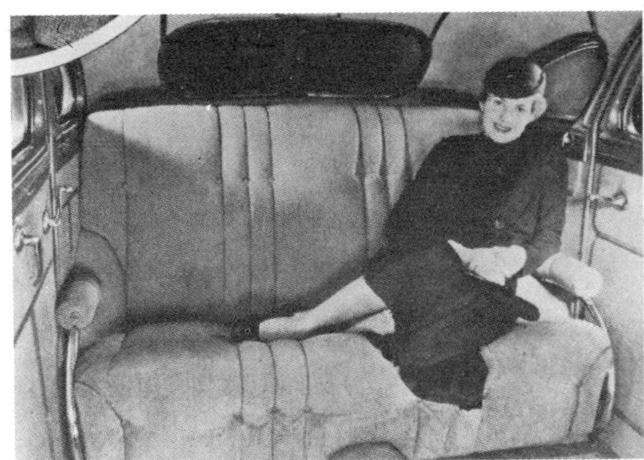

The 1934 De Soto Airflow had an interior quite plush for a medium priced car. This material was "freze" and was of durable quality. Behind this rear cushion is a compartment to place several pieces of luggage.

For 1935 De Soto brought out the Airstream as a companion car to the year old Airflow. This was De Soto's lowest priced model for 1935. It's the Airstream Business Coupe that sold for $695 and weighed 2,829 lbs. It was also available in rumble seat style for $745 as shown here. Not many rumble seat models were sold, however.

The standard version of the 1935 De Soto Airstream Sedan with rear mounted spare sold for $745. Only 6,027 of the model were delivered. It weighed 2,960 lbs. The Airstreams were "SF" models.

A 1935 De Soto Custom Airstream with all the trimmings, which included two-tone paint, fender skirts, whitewall tires, wheel trim rings, and the very unusual fender parking lamps. This model came with built-in-trunk as standard equipment. It sold for $825 in base form and weighed 3,110 lbs.

The 1935 De Soto Airflow Town Sedan gave a more personalized effect, with its enclosed rear quarters. It weighed 3,328 lbs. and used the same 115½-inch wheelbase the Airflows all used. All Airflows had the hand brake handle mounted under the instrument panel and the gear shift lever was placed far forward on the floor board so not to be in the way of front seat passengers. This allowed for three to sit in front in comfort. Toward year end, Airflow prices dropped to $1,015 for all models.

De Soto

The most popular 1935 Airflow was the 5-passenger Sedan. It sold 11,821 models in 1935 at $1,195. Fender skirts were standard equipment on all Airflows. Many people ordered their Airflows with overdrive to give better mileage as the cars were a bit heavy and mileage wasn't outstanding without it.

1936

There was quite a resemblance between the Chrylser and 8 and the De Soto Airstream this year. Both had similar die-cast grille with rakish new hood louvers. Th Airflows were more rounded, giving more style to its tw models. Both models again offered overdrive at a additional cost.

Airstream models came as either DeLuxe or Custo on a 117-inch wheelbase, or 132 inches in 7-passenge form. Seven-passenger De Sotos were often used as taxi DeLuxes came in three models and Customs in fiv

Prices ranged from $715 for a DeLuxe 2-passenger Cou to $835 for the Custom Convertible Sedan. DeLuxe mode carried only one tail lamp, had one windshield wiper, and flat one-piece windshield. Custom models carried doub tail lamps, split windshields and double wipers mounte from the cowl. All De Sotos had steel roof panels bolte to side rails, with the panel being carefully insulated fro the remainder of the body. It also was used as an aeria

Mechanically, De Soto came only as a 6-cylinder. Th Airstream had a 93 HP engine at 3400 RPM, and a 100 H engine at the same RPM was used in the Airflow. Fu supply was again 15 gallons for the Airstream whi Airflows held one more gallon. Tire size of 6:25 x 16 w used in Airstreams, with a 6:50 x 16 size used on th Airflows which had a 115½-inch wheelbase.

Standard compression ratio was 6:1 for the Airstrea and 6.5:1 for the Airflow. An optional aluminum hea was available giving the Airstream 6.5:1 and th Airflow 7:1.

De Soto held its own from the year before with 13 position, selling 52,789 cars during its model run. Airflow were discontinued in 1936.

This was the least popular of the 1935 Airflows. It sold for the same price as the other Airflows, $1,195. Only 3,126 Coupes were manufactured in 1935, which gives them a little edge for popularity today with collectors, due to its rarity. The side view shows its advanced styling of the fast back design that manufacturers tended to imitate in later years. G. M. certainly made use of this style with the Sedanets of the 1940's.

De Soto's 1936 DeLuxe Airstream 4-door Touring Sedan came minus a right taillamp and offered only the driver's side windshield wiper. Upholstery was of a more plain fabric without front door armrests. This model was available for $760. All 1936 Airstream Sedans included the built-in trunk as standard equipment. All 1936 De Soto's were S-1 models.

The 1936 De Soto Custom Coupe came as a 4-passenger model with the rumble seat being used for the rear seat passengers. It sold for $795. In the DeLuxe version it was the lowest priced car for $715. This example sports a rare set of chrome wheel covers. The De Soto Coat of Arms is mounted on the upper portion of the grille. The actual production models carried this emblem on the lower right section of the grille. The coupes and open models used the one-piece windshield.

937

The 1937 De Soto debuted with a roomier body, safety terior, hypoid rear axle and a compact overdrive unit. ll models rode on a new 116-inch wheelbase except for e 7-passenger sedan which used 133 inches.

The car carried a horizontal grille with finely chrome ated bars. Like the Chrysler, De Soto also used a hood nged at the rear and locked in the front by a hood nament. The hood side panels were removable for access the engine when repairs were necessary.

A bumper design used that year was quite the rage and s been used by those wishing to streamline their make, hether it be another make or another year De Soto. The nder design was nicely shaped conforming into the car's neral lines and curving down in the front. The horns ere removed from the fender catwalks and were placed hind the radiator grille. Instrument knob handles were cessed and dash gauges were mounted flush. Door ndles also tapered into a curve, all of which was a part Chrysler Products' safety program for 1937.

De Soto continued its 93 HP 6-cylinder engine. The el supply was a 16-gallon tank. All models used 6:00 x -inch tires except for the Limousines, which required 50 x 16-inch tires. Nine models were available, ranging om a $685 2-passenger Coupe to a Convertible Sedan r $1,220.

De Soto sales put the company in 11th position for the ar, with 86,541 cars during this calendar run.

A 1936 De Soto Custom 4-door Sedan sold for $835. It was the most popular model De Soto Airstream built in 1936. A total of 11,674 Custom sedans were sold. The skirts on this sedan were an accessory, but De Soto dealers pushed this item hard as did Dodge and Chrysler dealers. A divided windshield was new for 2 and 4-door sedans.

A more rounded appearance was quite evident and pleasing to the eye on the 1936 De Soto Airflows. The 1936 Airflows were called S-2 models. The line only offered two models, the 5-passenger Coupe and a 6-passenger Sedan. A total of 13,603 Airflows were built for 1936. They sold for $1,095. This was the last year for these models.

Next to the 1937 De Soto Convertible Sedan in price was this 7-passenger sedan that sold for $1,040. This model used the 133-inch wheelbase and was often seen in taxi service.

De Soto's lowest priced model for 1937 was this 2-passenger Business Coupe that sold for $685. This model has only one taillamp and the trunk mounted lamp to illuminate the license.

Apparently the Police Dept. of Tuckahoe, N. Y., felt the 1937 De Soto to be one of the faster cars on the road at that time. Here the police officer demonstrates his newly installed radio that communicates with local squad cars.

De Soto

The best selling model for De Soto in 1937 was the 5-passenger Touring Sedan that sold for $795. It weighed 3,056 lbs. The wheelbase for 1937 was one inch less than the 1936 models. It was now on a 116-inch chassis.

Not too popular a model in 1937 but a real collector's piece today is this 1937 De Soto Convertible Sedan that sold for $1,220. Fewer than 600 were produced. The centerposts were removable and when all windows and top were down the car had a very stylish appearance. This model has the rare accessory parking lamps mounted on top of the fenders.

1938

The 1938 car just had refinements, as it made a ma body change with the 1937 model. A redesigned front e with headlamps being placed on the catwalks, with fend being flatter at the top than previously and a lon wheelbase were the main appearance changes that public saw.

Mechanically, the car had a larger brake area, steering gear was insulated from the frame by rubber p and the frame was of a sturdier type than ever offe before. The horsepower was 93 at 3600 RPM with 6: compression ratio. The car could be ordered with a 7: aluminum head with 100 HP at the same RPM. The ca fuel supply was from a 16-gallon tank. All models us 6:00 x 16-inch tires except for the 7-passenger sedan wh came with 6:50 x 16-inch tires. The wheelbase was 1 inches except for the 7-passenger sedan which took 133-inch wheelbase.

Seven body styles were available and were considered be in just one series. All models came with the windshi wipers mounted at the bottom of the windshield as v first started with the 1936 De Soto Custom. The cra open windshield also came to an end by now, with c using a cowl ventilating system.

Price tags showed a 2-passenger Business Coupe sell for $870 going up to $1,065 for the Limousine.

De Soto placed 12th by selling 32,688 cars during t calendar run.

One of the least popular models for De Soto in 1938 was this 2-door Touring Brougham for 5 passengers. It sold for $930 and came on a 119-inch wheelbase.

This was De Soto's best seller for 1938. It was called the 5-passenger Touring Sedan and the company sold 14,637 of this body style at $970. The engine developed 93 H.P. at 3600 RPM with a 6:50 compression ratio. A 100 H.P. engine with an aluminum head was also available.

939

This 1939 car bore quite a resemblance to the rest of the mily from Chrysler. It used the remote control column arshift and offered the overdrive similar to what Chrysler d – where pushing the accelerator pedal beyond wide rottle put the car back into direct drive.

These models shared the Chrysler Products' new front d treatment with headlamps being mounted flush in the ont fenders, with the V-shaped windshield and a fast-ck rear end giving a trunk compartment of 23 cubic et. Chromium grille bars were used to show off the front d of the hood and splash pans. The body was finished ith a durable glossy synthetic enamel called Durasheen.

The car employed what was called the "Safety" speed-neter like other Chrysler-built cars, which showed an uminated jewel which turned from green to amber at) MPH and from amber to red at 50 MPH. A conventional dio was mounted to the left of the center radio grille and the right were the newly introduced push buttons to ck up stations the driver liked to hear most frequently.

The 6-cylinder engine developed 93 HP at 3600 RPM. ie car came on a 119-inch wheelbase and also offered e 136-inch limousine again for large families and taxi rvice. Tire size was 6:00 x 16 and 6:50 x 16 for the passenger cars. The fuel supply was an 18-gallon tank.

A total of 13 body styles were available; six in DeLuxe ries and seven for the Custom, which included a special istom Club Coupe with special broadcloth upholstery. iese cars had Hayes bodies from the Hayes Body Co. of rand Rapids, Mich. All Custom Club Coupes came with dio, heater, overdrive and deluxe wheel covers as standard uipment. A total of 264 De Soto Custom Club Coupes ere sold for the only year it was produced. The prices nged from $870 for the De Soto DeLuxe 2-passenger oupe to $1,338 for a Custom Limousine.

De Soto dropped to 14th sales position for 1939 by lling 53,269 cars for the calendar year.

Ideal for larger families was the 1938 De Soto 7-passenger Sedan that used the same 133-inch wheelbase as the 1937 line. Many of the large sedans took advantage of the 100 HP aluminum head engines to give more power to the heavier bodies. It sold for $1,065, but only 2,961 models were produced.

De Soto's most popular model in the 1939 DeLuxe series was the 5-passenger Sedan for $970. It looked exactly the same from the exterior as the Custom but the interior appointments weren't as lavish as the Custom. It weighed 3,174 lbs. A total of 10,237 DeLuxe Sedans were built.

A true special interest car today is this 1938 De Soto 4-passenger Convertible Coupe with rumble seat. This model wears the accessory fender skirts that were still popular on Chrysler built cars. This Convertible Coupe sold for $1,045, but few buyers were there. This was De Soto's last open model until 1940 as the company took a year out in 1939 from building open cars.

The lowest price 1939 De Soto was this 2-passenger DeLuxe Business Coupe that sold for $870. It weighed 3,048 lbs. It was also available as s 4-passenger Opera Coupe in the DeLuxe Series for $925. The Custom line offered two models for $923 in 2-passenger style and for $978 an Opera Coupe could be ordered. All told, the production for the four 1939 De Soto Coupes amounted to 13,427 cars.

De Soto

This was the most popular model of the entire line for 1939. The De Soto Custom 5-passenger sedan sold for $1,023 and weighed 3,179 lbs. A total of 14,352 Custom Sedans were built for the year. This model is nicely equipped with double whitewall tires and the deluxe chrome wheel discs which added to an already pretty car. This body style was available for one year only.

A mid-season offering was this 1939 De Soto Custom Club Coupe with a Hayes body. All of these Club Coupes came equipped with radio, heater, overdrive, and deluxe wheel covers. They sold for $1,145 and weighed 3,164 lbs. A total of 264 De Soto Custom Club Coupes were built during the only year of production.

An extended version for the 1939 De Soto was this 7-passenger model that came both in DeLuxe and Custom series as a Sedan and Limousine. It rode on a 136-inch wheelbase. The prices ranged from $1,195 for the DeLuxe Sedan to $1,338 for a Custom Limousine. All 1939 models were called S6 Series.

1940

For 1940, De Soto had an entirely new car from th previous year. The engine increased its horsepower to 10 at 3600 RPM. The fuel tank was a 17-gallon supply for a models. The tire size was 6:00 x 16 inches for all mode but the 7-passenger Sedans required 6:50 x 16-inch tire The wheelbase was 122½ inches for all models except th limousines which used the 139.5-inch wheelbase.

The model designations for 1940 were DeLuxe, an Custom for the cars with more trim. All models use sealed beam headlamps for the first time. Red warnin signals were used to tell the driver if the fuel suppl water temperature, oil pressure or electrical system r quired attention. The Safety Signal device on the spee ometer which changed color from green to red w continued.

A total of 12 models were available for 1940. Th Convertible, absent in 1939, was reintroduced in th Custom line. It was equipped with a power operated to with a push-pull control on the dashboard.

De Soto lowered its prices for 1940 roughly $35 p model. The lowest price car for 1940 was a DeLu 2-passenger Coupe for $845. The Custom Limousine f seven passengers sold for $1,290. The company so 83,805 cars for the calendar year which jumped them Tenth Position for the year.

De Soto's 1940 DeLuxe 2-door Sedan sold for $905 and weighed 3,066 lbs. This was the first year for this body style, which lasted through 1948. Sealed beam headlamps were used for the first time on the 1940 models.

The 1940 De Sotos were called S7 models. This 1940 Custom 5-passenger Sedan sold for $985. It weighed 3,104 pounds. Two-toning was beginning to come back into style as this model represents. Not too many sedans had this color arrangement, however. It was not available in coupe models.

941

The 1941 De Soto was similar to its offering in 1940 xcept being wider, lower, and 5½ inches longer. The big ews from De Soto was the availability of the Fluid Drive hich was optional at extra cost in both series, which were lled the DeLuxe and the more expensive Custom.

The 228 cubic inch 6-cylinder engine now developed 05 HP at 3600 RPM. The fuel tank held 17 gallons. The re size increased that year to 6:25 x 16 inches. Passengers de on a 121½-inch wheelbase, but the 7-passenger imousine used the 139½-inch wheelbase.

New for the year was a Custom Town Sedan which was 4-window sedan with solid rear quarters. Also new was a passenger Club Coupe in both DeLuxe and Custom odels. A Custom 2-door Brougham was also made ailable with vent panes in the quarter windows.

A buyer had a choice of eight solid colors or four twone paint combinations. Many accessories were available ch as directional signals, underseat heaters, push button dio, cowl mounted swan style side mirrors, beauty and im wheel decor, and wear fender shields to make an ready beautiful car more impressive.

A total of 12 models were available ranging in price om $898 for the 3-passenger DeLuxe Coupe to $1,370 r a Custom 8-passenger Limousine. De Soto placed in)th position for the calendar year from the sale of ,980 cars.

Being absent from the 1939 De Soto line, the 1940 models had this new Convertible Coupe to offer. It sold for $1,095 and weighed 3,329 lbs. It was only available in the Custom line. This model is well equipped with wheel decor whitewalls, trim rings, and stainless wheel covers to add appeal to this sharp open model.

The most popular model in the DeLuxe line for De Soto in 1941 was this 5-passenger sedan. It sold for $995 and weighed 3,254 lbs. Fluid Drive was available in both DeLuxe and Custom models at extra cost. Most all cars came equipped with it.

Another new style for the 1941 De Soto was this Custom 4-door Town Sedan with rear doors that opened to the front. This model sold for $1,095 which was $50 more than the Custom Sedan. Not as many buyers were there as De Soto had hoped for this nice body style. It weighed 3,329 lbs. The 1941 cars were referred to as S-8 models.

A new model was offered for the 1941 season. It was the 5-passenger Club Coupe available in both DeLuxe and Custom lines. This model sold for $985 as a DeLuxe and $1,035 in Custom style. It was a very popular style among Chrysler product enthusiasts. Both models weighed 3,270 lbs. Trim changes were the only differences. The wheel trim rings on this model were an accessory.

The lowest priced offering for the 1941 De Sotos was this 3-passenger DeLuxe Coupe. It sold for $898 and weighed 3,134 lbs. This body style was excellent for people who needed more than ample room for carrying supplies. It also was available in Custom style for $945, weighing 10 pounds more than the DeLuxe.

A 1941 De Soto Custom 7-passenger Sedan was available for $1,295. It weighed 3,649 lbs. An owner also had his choice of buying it in DeLuxe style for $1,255. The Limousine was the most expensive model for 1941 selling at $1,370.

The best looking 1941 De Soto had to be this Custom Convertible for 5 passengers. It was only available in this series and sold for $1,195. It weighed 3,494 lbs. The 6-cylinder engine developed 105 H.P. at 3600 RPM. The outside cowl side mirror was standard equipment on the convertibles. The whitewalls and wheel trim equipment was optional at extra cost but most all convertibles came equipped with this package.

This was the new 1942 De Soto DeLuxe 5-passenger Sedan. It was quite different in appearance from the 1941 model. The hideaway headlamps were quite a change. In fact, De Soto was the only full production car to offer this device since Cord's 1936-37 models. The horsepower was increased for the 1942 models. This car sold for $1,087 and weighed 3,315 lbs.

1942

De Soto made quite a face lift on the 1942 cars. D appearing head lamps with an "S" shaped vertical b grille with parking lights located in the fenders at t outer ends made for a very different looking appearan from the 1941 models. The bumpers, both front and re were more massive than any ever offered before. T running boards curved outward at the bottom and we concealed behind door panels.

A new stop lamp was placed in the center of the tru directly above the license bracket. The tail lamps we mounted flush with the fenders. Both front doors we opened by the ignition key, which saved having to ha two separate keys.

The 6-cylinder engine increased its cubic inch displac ment to 236 inches, turning 115 HP at 3800 RPM. T fuel supply again came from a 17-gallon tank. The ti size was 6:25 x 16 inches and the wheelbase was 121 inches in all models except for the 8-passenger Sedan a Limousine which used the 139½-inch chassis. Fluid dri was again available in both DeLuxe and Custom mode Practically all cars came equipped with it rather than t conventional 3-speed transmission.

The De Soto Fifth Avenue was a new offering within t Custom line. It was a Custom 4-door Town Sedan th offered a more plush interior than on the regular Custo sedan. Exteriorwise, the only difference was a namepla on the sides of the hood that stated it was a Fifth Aven It also had fender skirts as standard equipment.

De Soto offered 14 models ranging in price from $1,0 for a 3-passenger DeLuxe Business Coupe to $1,405 fo Custom 8-passenger Limousine. For the calendar ye De Soto sold 4,180 cars which dropped them in 14th pla for sales.

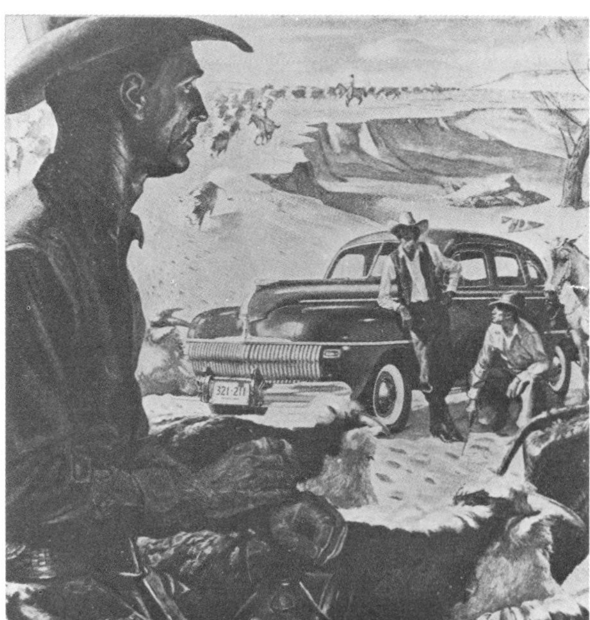

De Soto's new "S" pattern grille was the start of something to follow for the next several years. These 1942 cars were model S10's and this particular Custom Sedan sold for $1,149 and weighed 3,330 lbs. Few 1942 De Sotos came with full bright trim. The substitutions of blackout materials were very common as with all auto manufacturers from January until the plants were turned over to war production. Only 4,186 De Sotos were built for the 1942 model run.

De Vaux

The 1931 De Vaux was a product of independent anufacture coming from the Continental De Vaux Co. f Grand Rapids, Mich. The president of the company as Norman De Vaux who had been the president of urant of Cal. in Oakland, Cal. In 1930, De Vaux decided) branch out on his own to build a car using his name in 931. The company was in business just 14 months hen bankruptcy was called in April of 1932.

This Continental engined car developed 70 HP at 3400 PM from its 214.7 cubic inch engine. The fuel supply ame from a 15-gallon tank. The wheelbase was 113 inches, id tire size was 5:00 x 19 inches. Mechanical brakes ere used during the production months.

A total of 8 models were available ranging in price from 685 for a 2-passenger Coupe to $845 for the 5-passenger ustom Sedan.

For 1931, De Vaux sold 4,315 units which gave them the 3rd slot in sales for the year. During the production run f 1932, it manufactured 1,239 cars and took the 25th iles spot.

One month before the company's demise, it brought out ie De Vaux 80 which was to have been the "shot in the m" that was needed. Bank officials stepped in, and the ompany went into receivership in April of this year.

A well balanced model is this 1932 De Vaux Custom Coupe with wire wheels and sidemount tires. This was standard equipment for the Custom and DeLuxe models for 1932.

Shown with the De Vaux factory headquarters in the background, this 6-wheel 1932 Custom Sedan was one of the last to leave the plant. Only 1,239 were assembled before production ceased in April of 1932. This model sold for $845 and weighed 2,955 lbs.

One of the lowest priced models De Vaux built in 1932 was this Standard 4-passenger rumble seat coupe. It sold for $685 and weighed 2,615 lbs. The freight car in the background leads one to think this model is destined for a shipping trip.

This was De Vaux's lowest priced sedan for 1931. It was the Standard Sedan that sold for $685. It weighed 2,785 lbs. A 70 H.P. engine at 3400 RPM was used in all De Vaux cars.

De Vaux's most expensive model for 1931 was this Custom Sedan. It sold for $845, like the Custom Coupe. The weight of this 113-inch wheelbased model was 2,955 lbs. This series offered sidemounts as standard equipment.

A very stylish car that has true special interest qualities today is this 1932 De Vaux Cabriolet with rumble seat. It sold for $825 and was offered only in the Custom line. The number sold is not known but would be extremely rare to find one today.

Dodge

Dodge's 1930 Series DD 6-cylinder Sedan for 5 passengers sold for $865 and weighed 2,668 lbs. This example came with the cowl parking lamps which makes it a late production. The side mounted spares were optional equipment at extra cost.

The Dodge was a product of the Chrysler Corporatio since 1928. It had been manufactured, however, sinc 1914 by Dodge Bros. Corp.

The 1930 Dodges were offered in both 6-cylinder an 8-cylinder form. The new Six carried the model desig nation of DD6 and the new Eight was referred to as th DC8. In between these two offerings were the regula Dodge 6 and Senior 6 of the previous model rur

The DD6 developed 61 HP at 3000 RPM. This serie used an 11-gallon fuel tank and 5:00 x 19-inch tires. Th wheelbase was 115 inches, the same as on the DC8 Next in line came the Dodge 6 which had a 63 HP engin at 3000 RPM. This series used 5:50 x 19-inch tires an employed a 112-inch chassis. This model used a 12-gallo fuel tank. The third in the series was the Senior developing 78 HP at 3000. These cars used the 120-inc wheelbase and rode on 6:00 x 19-inch tires, This serie had a 15-gallon fuel tank. The new Dodge 8 had a 76 H engine at 3200 RPM, and also used a 15-gallon fuel suppl The tire size was 5:50 x 18 inches. All models use Lockheed hydraulic brakes. A total of 25 models wer available among the four series. Prices ranged from $83 for the 2-passenger 6-cylinder Business Coupe to $1,67 for a Dodge 8 Phaeton for 5.

The company placed in Seventh position by sellin 68,158 cars for the year.

1931

In 1931 Dodge continued to offer both the 6 and 8-cylinder models. This view represents the $845 Dodge Six Sedan. In the background is the Dodge Eight Coupe with sidemounts for $1,095. It weighed 3,094 lbs. A total of 2,181 8-cylinder coupes were sold. The Eights were referred to as Series DG models.

This 1931 Dodge Series DH 5-passenger sedan sold for $845 and weighed 2,820 lbs. The wire wheels on this model were standard equipment. A total of 33,090 models of this body style were built during 1931.

For 1931, Dodge offered a 6 and 8-cylinder line of cars They were considered to have more power and be longe and roomier than any Dodge built up to that date. Thi was the first year of real interchangeability of parts of a Chrysler cars. The new models came with a double dro frame of great stiffness which was reinforced by two addi tional side rails which ran back from the front to a cros member forward of the rear wheels.

The Dodge 6 had a 211.5 cubic inch engine whicl developed 75 HP at 3000 RPM. These cars, along with th 8s had 15½-gallon fuel tanks. The models increased th wheelbase two inches, now riding on a 114-inch chassis The wheel size was 5:00 x 19 inches.

The Dodge 8 used a 220.7 cubic inch engine developin 84 HP at 3400 RPM. This series came on a 118-inch whee base using 5:50 x 18-inch tires.

For the 1931 line, Dodge's famous Ram appeared for th first time. The car's radiator and hood line had a pleasin appearance. The windshield came with a chrome plate frame which opened for additional ventilation. Tw ventilators also were mounted on top of the cow

All 8-cylinder sedans came equipped with rear arr rests, assist cords, ash containers placed in the rear doors and dome and courtesy lights. Wood wheels were standar in both series with wire wheels offered at additional cos The 8-cylinder cars had automatic radiator shutters whil the Six used shutters that were controlled from the das panel. Free wheeling was available as an option.

A total of nine body styles were available, ranging i price from $815 for the 5-passenger 6-cylinder Busines Coupe to $1,135 for the 8-cylinder 6-passenger Sedar

Dodge ranked in the 8th position for the model run b selling 56,003 units.

Dodge

1932

For 1932, Dodge had both Sixes and Eights again for he year. There were five body styles for each series. 'rices started at $795 for the 2-passenger 6-cylinder Coupe ınd went up to $1,395 for the 8-cylinder Convertible ;edan.

Saleswise, Dodge held its eighth position selling 30,216 ınits in its 19th year in the automobile business.

Dodge Sixes now had a 79 HP engine while the Eight leveloped 11 more HP. Both turned a maximum 3400 RPM. The Six was equipped with 5:50 x 18-inch tires ınd the Eight carried 6:00 x 18-inch tires. Both series ıad 15½-gallon tanks. Dodge increased its wheelbase in ›oth series from the previous year. The Six was now riding ›n a 114.5-inch wheelbase, while the Eight was increased 'rom a 118-inch to a 122-inch wheelbase.

The 8-cylinder series DK buyers got a more plush Dodge han had ever been offered before. The seat backs were)f a pleated bolster design. Ash receivers were located ıhead of the rear armrests. Two adjustable sun visors were tandard equipment. Instrument panels and garnish moldıngs were walnut finished. Front seats were adjustable with wo screened ventilators in the top of the cowl. Free vheeling and automatic clutch were standard on the ;-cylinder DK series.

The spirited 1932 Dodge convertible sedan Series DK sold for $1,395 and weighed 3,706 lbs. This was the most expensive Dodge built for the year. The depths of the depression saw only 88 of this model produced.

Dodge's best seller in 1932 was this 6-cylinder 5-passenger sedan known as Series DL. It offered the sidemount equipment and wheel covers at an additional cost. A total of 16,901 of these cars were built.

A rakish appearing 1932 Dodge DK 8-cylinder 5-passenger sedan sold for $1,145 and weighed 3,527 lbs. The Dodge Ram was displayed on the radiator for the first time on the 1932 cars. Wooden artillery wheels were optional at extra cost as wer ethe sidemount spares. Many of this series came so equipped. This 8-cylinder model rode on a 122-inch wheelbase. It offered free wheeling, floating power, sloping windshield, and automatic clutch as standard equipment.

Announced on January 1st was this 1932 Dodge Series DL 6-cylinder. This was the 4-passenger rumble seat coupe that sold for $835. It weighed 2,995 lbs. The company built 1,815 of these models during the calendar year.

Dodge

An early 1933 Dodge rumble seat coupe sold for $640 and weighed 2,541 lbs. These first 1933 models came on the same chassis Plymouth DeLuxe used. This was the 111¼-inch wheelbase. A total of 8,879 of this model were sold.

A more massive appearing Dodge was introduced on April 5, 1933. This is the 1933 Dodge rumble seat coupe on the 115-inch wheelbase. Steel spoke wheels were standard equipment on all models. The sidemount spares were optional at extra cost. This model sold for the same price as the earlier cars.

The Dodge 8 for 1933 was known as Model DO. The prices ranged from $1,115 to $1,395. This 6-wheel 5-passenger sedan sold for $1,145 and weighed 3,580 lbs. Dodge sold 1,173 8-cylinder sedans. The trumpet horns were standard on this series but optional at extra cost on the 6-cylinder models. Note the doors still opened from the rear on the 8-cylinder cars but from the front on the 6-cylinder line. This was the last year for a Dodge 8 until 1953.

1933

The big news from Dodge was its new Six on a 111½ inch wheelbase. Later in the year the wheelbase wa extended to 115 inches. Prices started out at $595 fo the 2-passenger Business Coupe. This model had many o the innovations Chrysler cars were coming with this year A new three speed transmission which was silent through out, a Bendix automatic clutch, free wheeling, "durc chrome" valves to reduce frequency of valve grinds, anc aluminum alloy pistons were a few of the new feature for 1933.

The Six had a 75 HP engine at 3600 RPM, with a com pression ratio of 5.5 to 1. The optional Red Head engin of 6.5 compression developed 81 HP.

The Eight developed 100 HP at 3400 RPM. Tire size varied between the two series. The Six used 6:00 x 1 and the Eight used 6:50 x 17s. Fuel supplies were 6-cylinder, 15-gallon tank; and 8-cylinder, 15½-gallo supply.

There were 9 body styles, four of which were devote to the Six, and the remainder going to the Eights on 122-inch wheelbase. This was the last year for a Dodg Eight until a V-8 was introduced in 1953.

Sales shot Dodge into Fourth Place for the year, wit 91,403 cars being sold.

This is another early 1933 Dodge 6 Sedan on the 111¼-wheelbase. This model sold for $675 and weighed 2,632 lbs. Many people confused this car with the DeLuxe Plymouth as they looked so much alike. In mid-season Dodge management felt it wise to make the car longer to help sales. A total of 104,455 sedans were built for the year.

A very attractive model was the 1933 Dodge Convertible Coupe referred to in the Series DP. This model sold for $695 and weighed 2,541 lbs. The factory sold 1,563 of this body style.

1934

This year Dodge came out with two new cars, both being identical except for the wheelbase. The 117-inch Dodge came in five body styles, being two inches longer than last year's model. The 121-inch Dodge had two styles, the Brougham Sedan and Convertible Sedan. The 8-cylinder car was discontinued.

The engine had 1/8-inch more bore, its dimensions now being 3¼ x 4-3/8 inches. With a 5.6 ratio cast iron head, 82 HP was developed at 3600 RPM. The aluminum head, with 6.5 ratio, developed 87 HP at the same RPM.

Typical features of Dodge were free wheeling, helical gears throughout the three speed transmission, valve seat inserts, and hydraulic brakes. Fuel supply consisted of a 15-gallon tank. Tire size was 6:25 x 16 inches.

Dodge prices began at $645 for the Business Coupe and went up to $875 for the 121-inch Convertible Sedan.

For this year, Dodge again placed Fourth in sales, selling 108,687 cars.

The 1934 Dodge line was referred to as DR and DRXX Series cars in the Standard line and DS models for the DeLuxe line. This was the DRXX model 4-door Sedan, the most popular model of the DR line. It sold well for $745. A total of 9,481 were built. Its wheelbase was 117 inches.

Also available on the DR and DRXX line was the 4-door 5-passenger sedan with sidemounts and factory installed trunk. This 1934 DRXX sold 15,004 models while the DR line produced 78,257 cars. The trunk added greatly to the car's appearance.

The least expensive 1934 Dodge DR Series was this Business Coupe for two passengers. It weighed 2,695 lbs. and sold for $665. It sold far better than the rumble seat version, producing 8,723 units. This series offered the full chrome radiator grille.

This late edition 1934 Dodge DR Series can be identified by its four louvers on the hood sides. All DR models after June 1934 came with the four louver panels. This model sold for $695 and weighed 2,855 lbs. in base form. The Formbuilt trunk was a factory installed accessory.

An attractive 1934 Dodge rumble seat coupe with side mounted tires sold for $690 and weighed 2,745 lbs. A total of only 105 in the DRXX series were built.

Dodge

New for the year was the 1935 Dodge 2-passenger business coupe that became extremely popular with businessmen. A total of 17,800 coupes were built in 1935 selling for $645. It was Dodge's least expensive model for the year.

1935

In this model run, Dodge came forth with a new body and a more comfortable car. It showed off its front design with a pleasing V-shaped grille and more rounded front fenders which included the horns placed flush in the catwalks. A built-in trunk was available in the Sedan and 2-door Sedan at additional cost.

Independent wheel suspension had been abandoned for leaf springs, made from a substance called Mola. Front shock absorbers were two-way hydraulic with single action on the rears.

The engine developed 87 HP at 3600 RPM. The cast iron head gave a compression ratio of 6.5 : 1. All models used an automatic choke this year. Braking was Lockheed hydraulic as in the previous models. Dodge used a 15-gallon fuel tank. All models rode on 6:00 x 16-inch tires.

Eight models were available from a $645 2-passenger Business Coupe to the 7-passenger Sedan for $795.

Dodge again enjoyed Fourth Place sales for the year, with 211,752 cars being shipped. This year marked the 3-millionth Dodge since production began in 1914.

A $715 1935 Dodge 2-door touring sedan that weighed 2,868 lbs. sold 18,069 models. This car differed from the standard styles with the popular addition of the built-in trunk. Note the fancy wheel stripping which Dodge used in this era. This example is on display at the 1935 New York Auto Show.

A happy day at Dodge when this 3-millionth car rolled off the assembly line in 1935. This was the 5-passenger Touring Sedan of which 74,203 were built. This model weighed 2,903 lbs. and sold for $760 which kept the company in the fourth position for sales.

With smooth, attractive styling, the Series DU convertible coupe had a rumble seat. A total of 950 of these sporty little cars were built. All had a rumble seat. Selling for $770 and weighing 2,883 pounds, this model rode on the 116 inch wheelbase and was powered by the 87 horsepower six-cylinder engine.

Not as popular with the public as the trunk sedan was this standard model in the DU Series. Dodge produced 33,118 of this rear mounted spare model. It sold for $735 and weighed 2,861 lbs.

Dodge

936

The car had a new steel top which blended into the oof surface and was also wired for a radio antenna; a ie-cast grille, streamlined horns placed in the catwalks, nd headlights that were mounted on the radiator shell.)n standard models in 2 and 4-door sedans, the luggage 'as reached through the back seat while the touring sedans ad a built-in trunk. Coupes had the spare wheel in back f the front passenger seat. In the 2-door Sedans and 'oupes, a full width adjustable seat with two hinged acks was standard equipment.

Dodge developed 87 HP at 3600 RPM from its 6-cylinder ngine. The wheelbase was 116 inches. It used 6:00 x 16-ich tires. The fuel supply was 15 gallons.

Nine models were available, from the 2-passenger Coupe or $645 to the 5-passenger Convertible Sedan which sold or $995. This used a 132-inch wheelbase.

At the close of the 1936 model run, Dodge again enjoyed ourth Position, shipping 274,904 cars.

The most popular Dodge of the year was this DS 1936 4-door Touring Sedan. Far more buyers were ready to put their money out for this model than the standard style. The trunk sedan sold for $760 and weighed 2,958 lbs.

Dodge's lowest priced car for 1936 was this Series D2 Business Coupe for 2 passengers. It sold for $645 and weighed 2,773 lbs. The company sold 32,952 of this model. The front end was basically the same as the 1935 cars but more rounded to give it a pleasing appearance.

A standard 1936 Dodge Sedan is wearing a rear mounted spare that wasn't seen too often as most buyers were now looking at the built-in trunk models. This car sold for $735 and weighed 2,923 lbs. Dodge only built 5,996 models in this style. This model was equipped with twin windshield wipers and twin taillamps that were both accessories. Yes, that is Shirley Temple on the running board.

This 1936 Dodge 2-door trunk sedan sold for $720 and found 37,468 buyers during the year. It also was available in standard form for $695 but wasn't nearly as popular and found only 2,453 owners. This model is equipped with Goodyear whitewall tires that weren't seen too often on lower priced cars at that time. Double windshield wipers were still classed as an accessory as the factory still felt only the driver's side was all that was necessary. The young lady is apparently a model from the Blue Grass state, displaying the 1936 Kentucky license plate.

Dodge's most expensive model for 1936 was this Convertible Sedan. It sold for $996 and weighed 3,108 lbs. The factory only built 750 of this body style which is definitely a special interest car today. The sidemounts were part of the factory price for this model. Note the back doors open from the rear which was different from other Dodges for the year. This body style was not available in 1935 but aws revived with the 1936 line and lasted through 1938.

Dodge

Dodge's top model for 1937 as far as production goes was this D5 5-passenger Touring Sedan. It sold for $830. The sedan also was available in fast back style for $820. Production between the two styles was entirely different however. In fast back, only 7,555 orders were filled, while touring sedans sold 185,483 units.

1937

For the 1937 models, Dodge followed the appearanc of the other Chrysler-built cars. A new grille design witl several vertical chrome-plated grille bars at its center wer paralleled by wider strips which were completed in th car's body color. Headlamps tended to be larger, witl deeply crowned contours. In the catwalks, the horns ha been removed. They were now placed behind the grille The rear license was placed in the center of the trunk an was illuminated by a well-designed lamp. Disc wheel were standard equipment for each model that yea

Mechanically, the Dodges continued with the 87 H 6-cylinder engine. The fuel capacity now was a 16-gallo tank. The wheelbase was 115 inches in all, but the 7 passenger models, which used the 132-inch wheelbas and rode on 6:50 x 16-inch tires. The regular model came on 6:00 x 16-inch tires.

Ten models were available, ranging in price from $71 for a 2-passenger Coupe to $1,230 for the 5-passenge Convertible Sedan.

Dodge again placed Fourth in 1937 sales by buildin 288,841 cars.

There didn't appear to be too much demand for the rumble seat coupes in any make by 1937. This Dodge Coupe in 1937 only sold 3,500 examples. The car weighed 2,967 lbs. and the price tag was $770. The following year was the last of the rumble seat coupes.

Only 1,345 of the Series D5 convertible coupes were built this year. They sold for $910 and tipped the scales at 3,057 pounds. Perhaps part of their lack of popularity can be attributed to the fact that these cars were equipped with rumble seats, which were declining in popularity.

The largest Dodge of the year was this 1937 7-passenger, available in sedan and also limousine fashion. The limousine offered a leather compartment in front while the 7-passenger sedan came with a cloth interior throughout. The sedans weighed 3,367 lbs. and sold for $1,075. The limousine sold for $1,175 and weighed 3,396 lbs. A total of 2,423 of these 132-inch wheelbased sedans in both lines were built in 1937.

The flagship of the 1937 Dodge passenger car line was the beautiful convertible sedan, with four doors and built-in trunk. The most luxurious of the 115-inch wheelbase 1937 Dodges, only 473 were built. This model was the most expensive of all Series D5 production cars, costing $1,230. It tipped the scales at 3,262 pounds.

938

Basically, the 1938 Dodge was the same car as was the 937, but a little face-lifting made the car look larger, specially in the front end department. The headlamps vere removed from the radiator shell as on all Chrysler-uilt cars that year and nicely arranged in the fenders. The hood louver design had been changed into narrow ɔngitudinal slots with a chrome-plated surface.

Mechanically, the 1938 Dodge was basically the same 937 car. The windshield had an increase of vision by ıounting the glass in rubber molding which required no ıetal frame. The parking brake was mounted on the owl to the right of the driver, giving an easy reach to :lease or pull the brake. All engine mountings were nproved to give longer life and the self-lubricating clutch earing came in a larger size. All 1938 Dodges used the 7 HP 6-cylinder engine and 16-gallon fuel supply. All ıodels again came with 6:00 x 16-inch tires except for ıe 7-passengers which had 6:50 x 16-inch tires. The cars sed a 115-inch wheelbase in eight of the ten models. 'he 7-passenger Sedan and Limousine came on the 132-ıch chassis. Prices ranged between $808 for the -passenger Business Coupe and $1,185 for the Convertible edan. The 7-passenger models were generally employed ɔr taxi use and fleet service transporting to airports or 'ere often seen as mortuary cars.

Dodge sold 106,370 cars during the calendar run, ropping to the Fifth Position for sales.

Dodge's answer for families with small children was this 1938 2-door Touring Sedan with built-in trunk. It sold for $870 to 17,282 buyers. This example weighed 2,957 lbs. Still, Dodge only offered one windshield wiper unless the buyer wished to pay extra for the right one.

A rare model was the 1938 Dodge Station Wagon that was offered for the first time in the passenger car line. The wooden bodies were built by the U. S. Body Forging Co. of Buffalo, N. Y. Only 375 station wagons known as Westchester Suburbans were built in 1938.

Fairly well equipped with accessories that show is this 1938 Dodge Series D8 4-door Touring Sedan. This model sold for $910 in base form and weighed 2,967 lbs. Dodge produced 73,417 of the sedan model. This car is equipped with the accessory grille guard, twin windshield wipers, and wheel trim rings.

It was said that the 1938 Dodge was the "American beauty of motor cars" and this attractive Series D8 convertible coupe with rumble seat shows why. Unfortunately, the rumble seat was now out of fashion and the public was not buying them as they had in the past. Only 701 of these 1938 convertible coupes were built, little more than half of the 1937 model run total for this type. This model tipped the scales at 3,122 pounds and sold for $960.

The most unique model of the year was the low production Custom Club Coupe with body by Hayes. Only 363 of these attractive models were produced for their one year stay. It offered wheel beauty rings, radio and heater as standard equipment. The model sold for $1,055 and weighed 3,075 pounds.

1939

With the unveiling of the 1939 Dodge, the company was to celebrate its 25th anniversary. A new body style and mechanical advancements were offered for the model run. The new line was referred to as the Luxury Liner and Luxury Liner DeLuxe. The cars were entirely different from 1938. The only similarity to the previous year as far as appearance was concerned was the famous "Rocky Mountain Ram" nicely positioned on the hood.

The headlamps were placed in the front fenders and a parking lamp unit could be mounted directly above the lights on top of the fenders as an accessory, which gave additional style to an already sharp looking front end. The V-shaped windshield offered more vision than any Dodge ever before built. It gave a 4½-inch increase in width between pillars. The doors flared out at the bottom which gave a narrower look to the running board when the doors were closed. A new device that was placed on these cars was that of a safety button on the window garnish molding. When the button was depressed the door wouldn't open until the button was lifted, which was a great feature for families with small children.

The engine was the same 6-cylinder of 87 HP at 360 RPM. The fuel tank took an 18-gallon supply. The wheelbase was on a 117-inch chassis for all models but the seven-passenger limousine which employed 134 inches. The tire size was 6:00 x 16 inches on all regular models and 6:50 x 16 for the 134-inch models. Dodge also offered a special-bodied Club Coupe like the De Soto and Chrysler. It was referred to as the Custom Club Coupe with body by Hayes. It came equipped with radio, heater and deluxe wheel trim as standard equipment. A total of 36 units were sold by Dodge for the only year it was produced.

Ten body styles were available – the Luxury Liner 2-passenger Coupe selling at $755 as the lowest priced model. The 7-passenger Limousine sold for $1,195 at the top of the line.

Dodge again placed Fifth in sales by putting 186,47 cars on the road.

A totally different car for 1939 was offered by Dodge. The series was known as the D11 and came in both the Special and DeLuxe Series. This model was the 2-door Special which sold for $815. A 117-inch wheelbase was used on all models but the 7-passengers, which had a 134-inch chassis.

This squadron gray 4-door DeLuxe sedan belonged to the author several years ago. A completely trouble-free car, it sold for $905 new, and weighed 3,045 lbs. This car came with wheel trim rings, whitewall tires, fender mounted parking lamps, and front bumper guard extensions in front of the headlamps. All were accessories available for either series.

Entering as the least expensive body style in the DeLuxe series was the two-door, two-passenger business coupe that cost $803 and tipped the scales at 2,940 pounds. Unlike other models in the 1939 model range, the DeLuxe business coupe came equipped with only a left-hand tail-light.

940

For 1940, Dodge offered a brand new body after doing he very same thing just the year before. The new Dodge, eing a very stylish car, was displayed with high crowned enders front and rear of a similar contour. The radiator rille had finely spaced horizontal bars giving a very culptured look to the front end. Running boards were ptional on all models. Rarely were they not provided in he lower priced Dodge Special. In the DeLuxe Series, uite often they were offered without the boards which ave a more streamlined appearance. Two-tone paint ombinations were available on the DeLuxe Sedans. De uxe cars were called D 14s and the specials were D 17s.

The green, amber and red speedometer offered in 1937 or safety purposes reappeared on the 1940 models. New or the year was the dot on the ammeter, thermometer, il, and gas gauges which turned red indicating to the driver hat trouble may be happening shortly.

Mechanically, both the Special and the DeLuxe were lentical. The only differences were in the trim and nterior appointments.

The 6-cylinder engine still developed 87 HP at 3600 RPM. All models used a 17-gallon fuel tank. The tire size vas 6:00 x 16 on all regular models and 6:50 x 16 for he 7-passenger Limousine. The wheelbase was extended wo inches in 1940. It now was a 119-inch car in regular nodels and 136 inches in 7-passenger version.

Dodge built ten models for the year. They were priced rom $755 for a Special 2-passenger Business Coupe to 1,170 in the 7-passenger DeLuxe Limousine. The company dropped to Sixth Position for the calendar year by elling 225,595 cars.

One of Dodge's lower priced models for 1940 was this Special 2-door Sedan which sold for $815. It weighed 2,942 lbs. An extremely popular model with families with young children, it sold 27,700 units. The Special had a plain pin stripe in place of the stainless steel belt molding as used on DeLuxe models.

A mid-season offering was introduced by Dodge in 1940. It was this two-tone Series D-14 DeLuxe 4-door Sedan. The only two-tone color combination that was available were in two shades of green or maroon and beige combined. Full wheel trim, whitewalls, front bumper guards, and a full chrome horizontal molding through the center of the grille were clues that this was something more than a 4-door sedan. The whole cost an additional $115 and was available only on the 4-door sedan.

This 1940 Dodge DeLuxe Luxury Liner Business Coupe is equipped with front bumper guard trim, rear fender stone guards, and rocker moldings in place of the running board. It sold for $870 to 12,750 buyers.

Perhaps the most beautiful body style in the D-14 DeLuxe series was the convertible coupe. As attractive as it was, only 2,100 were built. They sold for $1,030 and weighed 3,190 pounds. The runningboards seen on this car were now considered optional equipment. Parking lights were now a part of the headlamp bezels, which held the new Sealed Beam lamps in place.

This 1940 Dodge DeLuxe Sedan sold for $905 and weighed 3,028 lbs. in base form. This car came with running boards and no rear fender scuff pads. A total of 84,976 were built of this model.

Dodge

A real looker when equipped with Mopar accessories is this 1941 Dodge Custom Luxury Liner. This car has the full wheel decor, whitewall tires, and front and rear bumper accessory guards. A total of 72,067 Custom sedans were built, selling for $965 in base form.

1941

The new models for 1941 were basically the same cars as the previous year. Only faceliftings were done to add to an already good looking car. For the first time Dodge offered Fluid Drive as an option at extra cost. Most cars came equipped with it. The two new names given to both models were the DeLuxe for the lower priced series and Custom for the more expensive models.

Mechanically, the 1941 models still used the 217 cubic inch 6-cylinder engine but with an increase to 91 HP at 3800 RPM. The fuel supply stayed at 17 gallons. The tire size also remained at 6:00 x 16 inches and the 7-passenger cars used 6:25 x 16-inch tires. The wheelbase was 119½ inches in all models but the 7-passenger Limousine which used a 137½-inch chassis.

Appearancewise the 1941 Dodge had a divided grille. The parking lamps were mounted in the headlamp contour mounted on the outside. Directional lamps were available and they were mounted above the headlamps and designed in a reverse pattern of the tail lamps. Running boards were optional. An alligator style hood which locked from the driver's compartment was new.

Dodge offered a new 5-passenger Club Coupe in both DeLuxe and Custom models and for the Custom line a 2-door Brougham and a 4-door Town Sedan made their appearance for the first time. Altogether, Dodge offered 10 models. They ranged in price from $825 for a DeLuxe 3-passenger Coupe to $1,250 for the Custom Limousine for 8 passengers. Dodge dropped to 7th Position for the calendar year by selling 215,595 cars.

Another nicely equipped 1941 Dodge was this Custom Town Sedan with rear doors opening forward. Just as pleasing in design as the regular four door, the public didn't buy this model as readily. It sold for $30 more than the straight Custom Sedan. Only 16,074 of this model were built. Note the directional signal lights mounted above the fenders. This was an accessory.

Dodge models for 1941 were called the DeLuxe and Custom cars. This happens to be a DeLuxe 2-door sedan referred to as Series D-19. It was available for $880 and had a production run of 34,566 units.

Riding on the 119½-inch wheelbase and using the 217.8 cubic inch engine now of 91 horsepower, the 1941 Dodge sported the best looking lines it had been adorned with in many years. The least expensive car in the DeLuxe series, now the low end of the price scale, was the little business coupe of which 22,318 were built. This two-passenger car cost $825 and weighed 3,034 pounds.

1942

The 1942 models received a facelifting in the front end lepartment. A square effect grille of a more massive ippearance was displayed. The hood was operated by pull outtons below the instrument panel. The running boards were concealed by flared doors at the bottom. True of he entire Chrysler line, the more massive bumpers were used on Dodges line, too. The front license was mounted between two guards on the bumper plate.

Both model names continued – DeLuxe for the less expensive cars and Custom for the higher priced line. The nterior in both series used broadcloth and pile fabric but had a different quality depending in which series it was used. The Custom Town Sedan came with two-tone broadcloth to harmonize with the car's exterior. The Custom Convertible Coupe used leather interiors.

The Dodge engine increased its cubic inch displacement from 217 to 230.2 cubic inches. The horsepower was ncreased from 91 to 105 at 3600 RPM. The fuel supply continued at 17 gallons. The tire size stayed the same at 6:00 x 16 inches in all regular models and 6:25 x 16-inch ires were used on the 8-passenger Sedan and Limousine.

Fluid Drive was again offered in both series on an optional basis at extra cost. Chrysler really pushed this ransmission with all of its dealers and virtually all cars came equipped with it in the Dodge, De Soto, and Chrysler line.

Dodge offered 11 models which ranged in price from $895 for a 3-passenger DeLuxe Business Coupe to $1,395 n the 8-passenger Custom Limousine.

For the calendar year, Dodge produced 11,675 cars which kept them in the 7th Position for the year.

The 1942 Dodge received a facelifted body style with a heavier, more massive frontal appearance. This long deck coupe was the lowest priced Dodge offered for the short 1942 model run. Classified as the DeLuxe three-passenger coupe and part of the D-22 model line, this car cost $895 and tipped the scales at 3,080 pounds. Only 5,257 were built before all passenger car production was suspended due to the war.

Only building 4,685 of the Custom 2-door Brougham made the car fairly rare even when new. This car left the dealership for $1,008. Only the Custom Brougham had the rear window vent panes. The DeLuxe was called a 2-door Sedan and had only a full rear window.

This is a typical 1942 Dodge with the blackout trim which most 1942 cars came equipped with. This model belongs to the Custom line, as told by the fender trim. The DeLuxe models only had trim on the upper front fender going back from the headlight. The Custom Sedan sold for $1,048 and a total of 22,055 were built before automotive production ceased in February of 1942.

Dodge's sharpest car for 1942 was this Convertible Coupe known as a model in the D-22 Series. It sold for $1,245 and weighed 3,485 lbs. on its 119½-inch wheelbase. This car is equipped with factory fender skirts and the white plastic trim rings which had to do in place of whitewall tires that were not generally available on 1942 cars.

Duesenberg

The Duesenberg for 1930 was manufactured under the direction of the Auburn, Cord, Duesenberg empire but this division was known as Duesenberg, Inc. with manufacturing coming from Indianapolis, Ind. Duesenberg production commenced in 1921 under the direction of Frederick and August Duesenberg. In September of 1927 the Auburn Automobile Co. of Auburn, Ind. purchased Duesenberg. The car kept its own manufacturing facility and continued in business through 1937.

Duesenberg sales outlets were not many, but were chiefly concentrated in areas where sales would be the highest. The following were cities where Duesenberg had sales and service facilities in 1930: Chicago, Los Angeles, Miami, New York, Philadelphia, Pittsburgh, and San Francisco. In smaller cities, where Auburn and Cord dealerships existed, often times the dealer made arrangements with the factory to place one Duesenberg on the show floor for a certain length of time during the year. At this time, those who made an inquiry about the Duesenberg were given an opportunity to visit the dealership and make arrangements for a demonstration with a factory representative.

For 1930, the Duesenberg came with a 265 HP 8 cylinder engine of 4200 RPM. All Duesenbergs used Lockheed hydraulic brakes during their entire production. The fuel supply was a 26-gallon tank. The tire size was 7:00 x 19 inches. For this year, the wheelbase was a 142½-inch chassis. Duesenberg bodies were built on special order. The company employed 14 different coachbuilders to place their talents on a Duesenberg chassis. The Walter M. Murphy Co. of Pasadena, Cal., was one of the main contenders for Duesenberg bodies. The company supplied approximately 125 bodies to Duesenberg and also dealt directly with many separate chassis owners who preferred dealing directly with the Murphy Co.

Prices for Duesenberg ran between $14,750 and $17,950 F.O.B. Indianapolis. Exact sales figures for Duesenberg are not available.

This 1930 Duesenberg came from the Indianapolis factory in chassis form for $8,500. Advertising claimed this model could be built as a Limousine with top up, partition, and side glass. As a Town Car it was available if the owner wished the front of the top rolled back, and lastly it could be an open Phaeton with top down and partitions removed.

This 1930 Derham bodied Duesenberg Model J was referred to as a Tourster. It was built for the late Gary Cooper. Gordon Buehig was the chief designer at Duesenberg from 1929-1933 and he had a special part in this car's first life. At that time it was painted Goldenrod Yellow with Pale Green fenders. Later, a boattail rear end was built to replace the trunk.

Looking quite similar to the 1930 Derham Tourster is this 1929 Murphy Dual-Cowl Phaeton. Murphy did much of the special body business for Duesenberg.

A 1930 Duesenberg Model J with Rollston Body. This car was owned in the late 1950's by James Aiken, an Oldsmobile dealer in Westwood, Cal. It was photographed by the author in 1956 at the famous Pebble Beach Concours in Carmel, Cal.

This was Duesenberg's 1930 Town Cabriolet which developed 265 H.P. from its 8-cylinder engine. This same model was available with virtually no changes until Duesenberg closed its doors in 1937.

This photo was taken of Gary Cooper in 1931 as he sits behind the wheel of his year-old 1930 Duesenberg Tourster. In this photo the rear windshield is in the down position. Apparently he had plans of driving it alone on that sunny day in 1931.

Quite similar to Gary Cooper's 1930 Tourster is this 1931 Derham example wearing double whitewall tires, twin side-mounted side mirrors, and the full chrome plated wheel covers. This ebony black Tourster came with a red leather interior which cut quite a figure for its owner, actor Joe E. Brown.

This was Murphy's answer for the 1930 Convertible Roadster. The company files listed it as design number 22301.

An interior view of the 1930 Town Cabriolet could very well be a 1932 as far as that goes. All bodies were practically the same. Note all the fine detailing this beautiful automobile gives: the embroidered pillow, seat piping, vanity case, and the tassle assist cord.

Duesenberg was the 1930 winner of an elegance rally held at both Cannes and Paris, France. The car competed with 150 of the world's most expensive automobiles and this was the vehicle chosen for its elegance at the concours.

A 1931 Duesenberg Formal Town Car was offered by Rollston. Its body design number was 9731002. The purchaser had a choice of several interior appointments such as silver inlaid circasian walnut, bone fitted hardware, cloisonee vanity case, and two opera seats. This style used an unusual Vee windshield.

Duesenberg

Registered as a 1931 is this Rollston Close Coupled Sedan. The wheelbase measures 142½ inches with a 265 H.P. 8-cylinder engine. Wire wheels most often were done in chrome as this model displays.

1931

All 1931s had the same original 8-cylinder engine o 420 cubic inches which developed 265 HP at 4200 RPM The fuel supply was still a 26-gallon tank. Lockheed hydraulic brakes were always used on Duesenberg. These cars used a 142½ or a new 153-inch wheelbase. The tir size was 7:00 x 19 inches.

August Duesenberg was not as active in the company a was Frederick at this time, though he had been very muc a partner prior to the time when Auburn became th owner. The Duesenberg Corp. still built no bodies of it own but did order them from a select group of body builders. Among the most famous were Murphy, Derham Weymann, Bohmann-Schwartz, Rollston, Le Baron Willoughby and Judkins. The man behind all these designs to be arranged with different body builders, was Gordo M. Buehig, who also was responsible for building th beautiful later Cords.

Le Baron also did a great deal of work for Duesenberg. This 1931 Model J Dual-Cowl Phaeton is a good example. This model wears a special driving light mounted in front of the radiator grille. Le Baron prices began at $14,750.

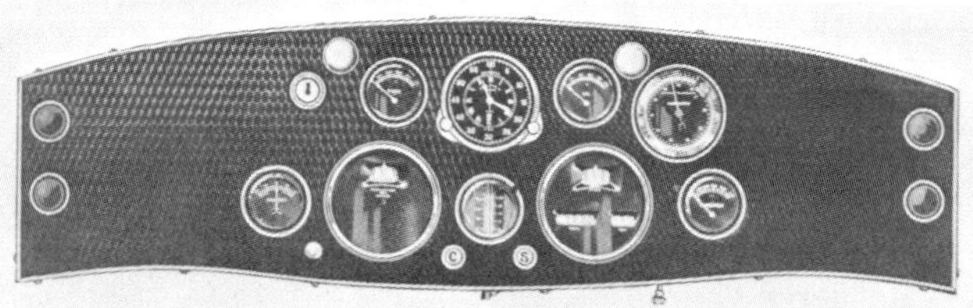

All gauges were mounted right in the center of the dash—easy for the driver to see. The gauges included brake pressure, ammeter, tachometer, oil pressure, the split second stop clock, 150 MPH speedometer, altimeter, barometer, gasoline gauge, water temperature gauge, ignition lock, carburetor control, and starter control. Also included for ease of the driver's mind were automatic lights that called for changing the oil and chassis lubrication at the right time. All these instruments were on every Duesenberg from beginning until the 1937 close.

This 1931 Duesenberg J with Rollston body looks like it was printed backwards in the photo. Actually not, this car was built for service in Europe, thus the right hand drive. Note the license is mounted on the right, under the taillamp. Chrome wire wheels, whitewalls, and spot lamp make this a beautiful classic.

A very rare 1931 Duesenberg was this Boattail Speedster. This car was actually built for the 1930 Salons and was the first speedster on the J chassis. By the time production fully started, this car was classed as a 1931. The top, deck, and belt molding were done in polished aluminum. The hood and body were completed in silver lacquer to make quite an impression. Not more than four of these examples were built on the 142½-inch wheelbase.

932

The real spirit of Duesenberg, Inc. died when Frederick . Duesenberg passed away in July of 1932 of compli-ations resulting from an automobile accident a few weeks rior.

The cars themselves, being built for this year, were cars hat had special bodies built to order for the patrons. The)uesenberg still had a 265 HP engine of 4200 RPM.)uite frequently, these cars were the same automobiles 'ear after year, as far as running gear was concerned, but ad newer bodies placed on them from time to time until he doors closed in 1937. A good number of Duesenbergs 'ound up with the socially elite of Hollywood and Beverly Iills. Many owners were the same people who bought ustins, as was mentioned under the Austin section of this hapter, but this is the only comparison between the cars.

If 265 HP wasn't enough, another thrill took place in he middle of 1932 when Duesenberg offered the Super-harger giving 320 HP with a maximum speed in second ear of 104 MPH. Full speed when in high gear has never een fully determined.

Another fine example of a 1931 Duesenberg with a stationary top and landau irons. The body also is by Letourneur et Marchard. Note the different arrangement of mounting the door handle below the belt line in the center of the door. Disc wheels were optional, and this beauty chose the rare equipment.

Duesenberg also had foreign body builders besides those at home. This 1931 Club Victoria with the landau irons is a Letourneur et Marchard example. This model came with canvas covered sidemount covers and wears special monograms on the doors.

An engine that was truly prêcision made is shown here. This is the 265 H.P. version of a Duesenberg engine. The supercharger models showed in mid 1932.

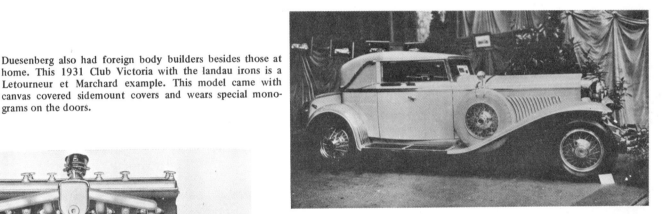

This was the first year for the S. J. designation which showed it was a supercharged model. Practically all Duesenbergs from 1932 on came so equipped. Featured here is a 1932 Murphy bodied Phaeton with top down.

The 1932 Murphy Phaeton is shown here in all its splendor, wearing its chrome supercharger pipes, chrome rimmed sidemount covers, sidemount mirrors, chrome wire wheels, and whitewall tires. Note the sleek angle of the windshield. Murphy bodied cars began at $16,500.

The 1932 Duesenberg SJ Murphy creation was called a Beverly model. It came in the $16,500 price range. The cloth top and cloth covered trunk were done to a customer's specifications. This Murphy model has front doors opening from the front which isn't true of all Murphy bodies. The SJ had been a part of the D. Cameron Peck collection.

Another of Duesenberg's special foreign bodies was this 1932 Fernandez bodied model. Featured here in this 1932 setting was Prince Sahibzada Nawob Azum of Hyderabad, India, with the Princess.

A top down version of the 1932 Duesenberg SJ Murphy Convertible Coupe. This was a factory publicity shot taken in the Hollywood Hills of Cal. Note the typical tile roofs on the homes in the background, being of the Spanish architecture of that era.

The Rollston bodied 1932 Duesenberg SJ Twenty Grand, or as it first was known, the Arlington Sedan. This title of the Arlington was catalogued as a two-window model in 1931. So, from this designation it was changed to the Twenty Grand. This model employed a sharply styled Vee windshield with a harmonizing leather covered roof. This 4-passenger model had four individual chairs. Its interior was paneled in burl walnut with a silver inlay. Rear seat passengers also were given an instrument panel on the back of the front seat. It included a speedometer, compass, and a split second watch. The title Twenty Grand appropriately applied to its price.

A perfect setting for this 1932 Rollston Convertible Coupe is displayed above. This SJ version wears the disc wheel covers with the chrome wires underneath, easily removable at the owner's wish. The rear fender line is more accentuated at teh bottom than on many earlier Duesenbergs. Rollston prices went between $14,750 to $17,950 depending on the model and equipment specified by the buyer.

933

After the first of 1933, a downdraft manifold was onsidered standard equipment. Many earlier Duesenbergs hanged over to this more satisfactory device later on. /hile Derham was in charge of design, the body depart- ıent had been staffed with designers for sketching new ıodels. Gordon Buehig had been Duesenberg's chief esigner until 1933. At this time, he was given the omplete directorship in designing the 1936 Cord.

Of all the coachbuilders who had a part in producing ıese cars, the Walter M. Murphy Co. of Pasadena, Cal., layed a prominent part. The Murphy Co. often was eferred to as "The Young in Heart" body builder. His esigns make this statement quite clear to understand. mong those who played an important part were Frank pring, George McQuarry, and Franklin Hershey of the Iurphy staff. Murphy supplied about 125 bodies during ıe nine year span of Duesenberg production under A.C.D. ther prominent builders consisted of Willoughby with pproximately 50 bodies, and Derham and Rollston each ırning out approximately 40 bodies. Judkins, Weymann, nd Le Baron also built bodies, along with several other uilders who also turned out some impressive looking cars.

Mechanically, the Duesenberg came again with its 265 IP car, or the SJ with 320 HP at 4200 RPM.

Resting in the restoration department of Harrah's Auto Museum in Reno, Nev. is the 1933 yellow-black Weymann bodied "Fish Tail" Speedster. Gordon Buehig was responsible for the car's construction. The automobile certainly wasn't waiting for restoration with only 10,000 miles, but received a little detail work for a Harrah car show.

A rear view of the 1933 Weymann bodied Duesenberg at a Grand Classic Show several years ago. Note the Nevada license on the Fish Tail Speedster which rode on the 153½-inch wheelbase.

With top nicely fastened in the up position for inclement weather, this 1932 Murphy SJ bodied Convertible Coupe is ready for winter driving.

Another 1933 Duesenberg Speedster from the Harrah auto collection. This one carries a Schwartz body with the SJ 320 H.P. engine. Note the enclosed side hood panel on the left leaving the supercharged pipes on the right do their work most efficiently.

Duesenberg

This was an example that Fernandez and Darrin built in 1933. It also was a one-off model. About all that appears as a Duesenberg are the headlamps, wheels, and radiator grille. The fender line had extreme cut off points at the bottom. Spare tires were mounted on the rear.

1934

For 1934, Duesenberg offered a convertible that had i top completely sealed when lowered. This model wa known as the Riviera Phaeton. It was built by Brunn fc the New York Auto Show in January, 1934. The car wa built on the short chassis. It had a somewhat sloping rea deck to contain its disappearing top. Shortly after th Riviera Phaeton was exhibited, a later display had a identical car being shown, but it was given a new desi nation as the Convertible Sport by Brunn. A total of thre of this style were made for the year.

Mechanically, the Duesenberg was the same car as i previous years. It came with a 265 HP engine in the Series; or, as a Supercharged SJ model it developed 32 HP at 4200 RPM. Top speed was over 130 MPH

Built by Murphy of Pasadena, Cal., is this early 1934 Duesenberg J Club Sedan on the 153½-inch wheelbase. An option not seen too often on Duesenbergs were the twin taillamps which this model displays. Being a true club sedan, the rear quarter panels are enclosed for privacy.

Rarely seen after 1932 were those Duesenbergs minus the supercharged pipes coming from the hood panel. This was an example of one, however. It is a 1933 Model J with Murphy body on the 153½-inch wheelbase.

This is the exhaust side of a 1934 supercharged Duesenberg, minus its hood and fenders. All engine components were done in polished aluminum. This king of the highways developed 320 H.P. with supercharger.

A left side view of the 1934 supercharged engine. It looks quite easy to work on when compared with today's cars.

935

The 1935 model run, actually begun in late 1934, saw ɔme body and trim changes that were recognizable for ıe first time since Cord took the reins. The changes ere mainly shown on Rollston bodies. Some of the ıceliftings included a shorter running board apron which ıve way to the redesigning of the battery carrier and tool ɔx to permit a lower door line. Also shown were bullet-ıaped taillights finished with the color of the fenders ıd minus the back-up light feature of earlier cars. hese lights were used in dual installation with long veeping skirted rear fenders. Most of these models came ith 17-inch wheels and were designated as Models JN r SJN with the supercharger. Smaller bullet-shaped eadlights, in keeping with the same tail lamp design, ere fitted by factory personnel rather than being done a dealer installation. On several of these cars, cowl mps were omitted according to body builders' or the ıstomer's desire.

When a "Duesenberg Special" was built in 1935 for b Jenkins, a blower for this car was designed with two rge carburetors. The regular manifold was eliminated. ı place of this was used a small manifold without ater jackets. Superchargers placed on cars after this time sed this system but were equipped with carburetors of ılf the capacity as earlier models.

The car was basically the same except for the above entioned items. The 265 HP engine at 4200 RPM was ill the standard engine and the 320 HP version was ailable with supercharger. These were still called the Series.

Lockheed hydraulic brakes were used, with 7:00 x 18-ch wheels being used along with 7:00 x 17-inch models. he wheelbase was still 142½-inch or 153½-inch, pending on the model desired. Top speed would show 30 MPH.

The majority of Duesenbergs sold in the U.S. were iced in a range up to $16,500. There were models nging from $17,000 to $19,500 and cars in this price acket were considered by Duesenberg executives to be the "upper" price class.

Bodies were by special order and production figures ere not available.

The 1934 Duesenberg J, Brunn Riviera Phaeton was introduced to the public on January 6, 1934. Brunn built six bodies for Duesenberg. This style was one of the last creations. This fantastic phaeton, in like-new condition, is owned by Walt Shearer of Thousand Oaks, Cal.

A late 1934 Duesenberg SJ Convertible Coupe with the Rollston body. Some refer to this late edition as the 1935 model but actually this one was registered as a 1934, with the minor face lifting of 1935 cars. These changes are noted as a more skirted front fender, which many earlier models had done when sent back to the factory for alteration. Seventeen inch wheels were also used on this model. Rather than double bar bumpers, this model wears a single plate bar which wasn't too common for Duesenberg.

Here is a 1935 Rollston SJ Convertible Coupe with semi-modern fender line but not fully skirted front fenders. It offers the new bullet shaped taillights which Duesenberg displayed until the end in 1937. Disc wheels were also being used on these last models, too.

A beautiful 1935 J Series Duesenberg with the late fully skirted fenders. It also wears a badge bar of car clubs it belongs to. Headlights do not appear to be Duesenberg equipment, but probably Lucas.

Nicely parked is a 1935 Duesenberg Town Car with Rollston body. It has the full metal wheel covers, bullet shaped taillights, but not the optional skirted front fenders. Rollston town cars sold in the neighborhood of $17,750 to $17,950 in 1935.

1936

With Duesenberg making some faceliftings in 1935 this year's models were unchanged. The faceliftings tha were done were mainly on the Rollston bodied versions c 1935-1936. Generally speaking, from 1929 to 1937, ver few major changes ever took place. But, during thes years various engine and body components did underg some refinements and modifications.

A short wheelbased 1936 Duesenberg SJ Roadster came on a 125-inch chassis. It was formerly owned by D. Cameron Peck and today is in the Briggs Cunningham stable of cars at Costa Mesa, Cal.

Bohmann-Schwartz of Pasadena, Cal. were a little more modern with the taillamp, headlamp, and disc wheel treatment on this 1936 Duesenberg 7-passenger limousine. This example, however, doesn't have the skirted front fenders. Only two bodies were executed by Duesenberg to be built by Bohmann-Schwartz. Individuals took their cars to them later for work.

Another work of art by Rollston of New York was turned out in 1936 when this Duesenberg Convertible Coupe model SJN sold for $17,500. This photo was taken by the author at a recent Harrah car show where this vehicle was on display.

This beautiful 1936 Bohmann Schwartz formal Town Sedan was one of the last creations for Duesenberg. This was a J Series, as can be noted by the lack of pipes coming from the hood. Skirted fenders were optional.

37

Duesenberg closed its doors in 1937. As for prices of ese cars, most were in the range up to $16,500. There s been recognition of the two Duesenbergs that did sell w for $25,000. One of these cars was a 1934 3-passenger upe built on a 142½-inch wheelbase. The other model ıs built on the West Coast and came on a special 178-ch wheelbase. The car was a Landaulet.

Most Duesenbergs weighed approximately 4,900 lbs., and came equipped pretty much the same with a vertical gle to the steering wheel for ease of driving and comfort. earshift and brake lever stood at a high position for ease handling. Headlamps, parking lights and bumpers all nformed in the usual Duesenberg pattern for the sake of rmony. These models as well as earlier ones continued use the combination tail-back-up-light of an 8-inch ameter, unless the owner requested the more modern al bullet-shaped taillights, which many did have changed keep up with the times.

Standard equipment always included six chrome wire ieels with the spares mounted in the front fender wells, pplied on 17 or 18-inch wheels with whitewalled 7:00-ch tires. Duesenbergs employed the same straight 8-linder engine developing 265 HP at 4200 RPM. The J. Ns were also available with 320 HP and the same PM rating. The fuel capacity always was a 26-gallon tank. l models used the 142½-inch wheelbase or the 153½-ch wheelbase, depending on the model.

Probably the last Duesenberg to ever be produced didn't tually come from the Indianapolis factory in 1937. The r was completed in Chicago and inspected by Augie ıesenberg. All arrangements for its delivery were made rough the Chicago branch Duesenberg dealership where e chassis was completed in 1937 at a cost of approx-ately $20,000.

A Rollston Convertible Sedan made its debut on November 14, 1936. It is debateable whether this Duesenberg was a late 1936 or one of the last 1937 models. It was extremely modern for a Duesenberg, coming with fully skirted fenders, front and rear, and bullet shaped head and taillamps.

One of the last Duesenbergs to be displayed on a sales floor when new was this 1937 SJ Phaeton with the full skirted front fenders and chrome wheel discs. Note the special mesh grille cover over the actual radiator.

Truly the last Duesenberg built was this model. Even though Duesenberg had gone out of business, a Mr. Rudolph Bauer of Berline, Germany, had ordered the car before the company closed its doors. With war conditions developing for Germany it actually took Mr. Bauer till 1940 before the car was completed by Rollston of New York. It cost $20,000. Later, this car was on display at Pettits Museum of Motoring Memories at Natural Bridge, Va.

This 1937 Duesenberg SJ Convertible Sedan was restyled at the wishes of its owner, Henry J. Topping Jr. before he took delivery of it. It was designed with a trunk back and sloping grille. All that truly resembled the Duesie were hub caps, hood emblem, and the supercharged pipes.

du Pont

This 1930 Du Pont Series "G" Sport Sedan was offered to those with individual preferences. The Continental 8-cylinder engine developed 140 H.P. This series rode on a 141-inch wheelbase. Only four distributors handled the sale of du Ponts in 1930. They were located in New York, Philadelphia, Baltimore, and Los Angeles.

A 1930 Series "E" du Pont Speedster was guaranteed to exceed speeds of 100 MPH. This line, which produced fewer than 20 automobiles, offered advanced styling for the company in its last days. The special Wood-lites were an option available to du Pont owners. Many cars came with them.

The du Pont for 1930 was from the du Pont Moto Mfg. Co. with headquarters in Wilmington, Del. The c was built from 1919 through 1932. During the years production, only 537 du Ponts were produced.

The car came from the genius of E. Paul du Pont, wh planned for several years for the hand assembling of truly classic automobile.

The body builders responsible for turning out th du Ponts were chiefly Merrimac, Waterhouse, and Derha

Most 1930 du Ponts were delivered with the Model "C inscription on the body plate. They had an 8-cylinder 3 cubic inch Continental engine that developed 140 HP 3200 RPM. The wheelbase was 141 inches. These ca had hydraulic brakes, hydraulic shock absorbers, and ext long springs with rubberized shackles which didn't requi lubrication.

The Series E was also built in 1930 but fewer than were produced. This series sold for approximately $3,75 Model Gs sold from $4,360 to $5,750.

With fewer than 537 cars being built during fourte years, exact sales and production figures for 1930 a unobtainable.

Another Series "E" du Pont Speedster for 1930 was this 4-passenger model. Note that this example carries its spare tire mounted freely on the brackets attached to the side of the hood panel rather than in a fender well. Fender design was similar to motorcycle fenders. These models sold for $3,750.

Merrimac was one of du Pont's main body builders, as all the work was strictly done with special coach workers. This 1930 du Pont Town Cabriolet was available for $5,750 with coach work and finish left up to the owner's wishes.

A 1931 Series "G" du Pont Speed Sedan was identical to the 1930 rendition. This car carried coach work by Merrimac and was available only on the 141-inch wheelbase. Note the rakish angle of the windshield. Distributors for du Pont were narrowed to two for 1931. In New York, A. J. Miranda held the position and on the west coast it was E. A. Van Trump Jr. of Los Angeles.

Du Pont called this model the transformable Berlin in 1930 through 1932 sales catalogues. It was ideal for town or country, offering the passengers comfort that only the hydraulic shock absorbers could give through their air cushions. This model "G" sold for $4,690 fully equipped.

931

The 1931 du Ponts were sold mainly through the istributorship of the A. J. Miranda Co., which only andled the elite foreign cars such as Maybach Zeppelin ıd Delage in New York City. On the West Coast, E. A. an Trump was the distributor.

The offerings for 1931 were practically the same as in 930 – the Model H as it was referred. Only three cars ere produced in the series. It was practically the same car the G Model in every way except for its chassis, which ıd a 146-inch frame rather than 141 inches.

The same 8-cylinder Continental engine of 322 cubic ches was used in both G and H models.

The exact number of Model Gs for 1931 isn't certain, ıt there were 273 of these models built between July, 928 and the company's close in 1932.

932

For 1932, the du Pont was practically a grand name to remembered. As the depression grew worse and many mpanies had to close their doors, du Pont followed eir paths. Without having a sub-line to fall back on, e company felt it wise to cease production rather than sorry later for having introduced a cheap line which ould have brought disgrace to a top-line classic builder.

Some of the noted personalities among the 537 owners om 1919 till the end were Jack Dempsey, Charles ckford, Peter Helck and Will Rogers. January of 1932 v the last du Ponts being hand assembled.

The last du Ponts were identical to the models that preceded them in 1931. This 1932 4-passenger convertible Victoria was only illustrated in catalogue renderings for prospective purchasers.

A 1932 du Pont Club Sedan on the Merrimac body sold for $4,800 and up depending on interior options and exterior appointments. This was the last year for the du Pont, which closed its doors in January of 1932.

Du Ponts were rare even when new, and the Series H introduced during the 1931 model run is even rarer than the G Series. Only three cars were produced. It was available only on a 146-inch wheelbase, but mehcanically both cars were the same. Each used the 322 cubic inch engine that developed 140 H.P.

The 1931 du Pont Victoria Cabriolet with a Waterhouse body seated four passengers. All interiors on sport models were done in leather but at the wishes of the customer as to design and quality. This model sold for $4,500. Du Pont never built more than two cars per day and during the last four years of survival only 273 vehicles were built.

A true sport model was the 1932 Speedster for 4 passengers. It used the Continental 8-cylinder engine developing 140 H.P. just like the Series G cars. The fender line of the Speedster was the epitome of class in 1932, even if it did splash mud all over the lower portion of the body. Charles Bickford, of movie fame, owned one of these models.

Durant

Durant's lowest priced offering for 1930 was the 2-passenger business coupe in the Standard 6-14 Series. It sold for $645. This model had room for luggage to be placed in the rear compartment. A rumble seat model also was available for $670. The business coupe weighed 2,680 lbs. and the rumble seat cars weighed 2,710 lbs.

The 1930 Durant was manufactured by the Durar Motor Co. of Muncie, Indiana. The car was in existenc from 1921 through 1932. It was named after its founde William C. Durant, former president of General Motor At this time Durant had some reshuffling of its executiv board, and new personnel were hired to put Durant in more solvent position.

With a more competent executive staff, the compan went on to develop two new 6-cylinder cars to be sol below the $1,000 bracket. These cars were to have mo durability, comfort, and appearance, and would b superior to anything Durant produced before.

The model designations were 6-14 and 6-17. The 6-1 came with a 6-cylinder Continental L-head engine develo ing 58 HP at 3100 RPM. These models had a 3-spee transmission. The fuel capacity was 12 gallons. The ti size was 5:00 x 19 inches. They came on a 112-inc wheelbase.

The 6-17s used a Continental 6-cylinder L-head engir also, but it produced 70 HP and had 3000 RPM. Th 6-17s had seven main bearings with pressure lubricatic to the main, rod, and camshaft bearings. All 6-17s used 4-speed transmission with a silent internal geared thi and standard shift. They had a 14½-gallon fuel suppl These models also used a 112-inch wheelbase but roc on 5:50 x 19-inch tires.

The best way to distinguish a 6-14 from a 6-17 was th all 6-14s did not have parking lights on the fenders, a all 6-17s did. All models used mechanical brakes. Th body styles amounted to 14 models ranging in price fro a 6-14 2-passenger Coupe for $645 to the 6-17 5-passeng DeLuxe Sedan for $785. The company's slogan was " Good Car."

Durant placed in 18th Position by selling 20,183 uni that calendar year.

The most popular 1930 Durant in the 6-14 Standard line was the 5-passenger sedan which weighed 2,780 lbs. and sold for $695.

Six wire wheels gave a look of distinction to the 1930 Durant DeLuxe 6-17 4-door sedan. This model, even though using the same 112-inch wheelbase, offered a heavier engine than the 6-14. It weighed 2,945 lbs. and sold for $785.

)31

By the time the 1931 Durants were introduced, the .ndwriting was pretty much on the wall as to the rection sales would go for the next year. The 1931 odels offered a novel-type bed of sorts, referred to as a 'ullman attachment" which could be made into a full ngth reclining couch. This was only available on the odel 6-12 and 6-14 5-passenger Sedans. For this year, irant continued the Continental 6-cylinder engines of '9 cubic inches developing 58 HP at 3100 RPM in both 12 and 6-14 models. The 6-12s used 4:75 x 19-inch es and 6-14s had 5:00 x 19-inch tires. In addition to ese, a 4-cylinder car came on the market with a 50 HP gine at 2800 RPM. This series used 4:75 x 19-inch tires o. The fuel supply in each series was a 12-gallon tank. ie wheelbase was 112 inches for all three series. Six models were available among the three series which nsisted of a Coupe and Sedan for each class. Prices gan at $675 for the 4-passenger, 4-cylinder Coupe and ded at $775 for the Durant 6-14 5-passenger Sedan. Durant sold 7,000 cars during the model run which t them in the 19th Position for 1931 sales.

Not as popular when new as the sedan was this 1930 Durant DeLuxe 6-17 Phaeton weighing 2,875 lbs. and selling for $765. It may not have been as popular as the sedan when new, but wouldn't a collector love to own it today?

32

Being one of the independent manufacturers hard hit by : depression, Durant only produced a 5-passenger Sedan ling for $695 this year. It was referred to as the 6-19. came on a 109-inch wheelbase, weighed 2,710 lbs., d travelled on 4:75 x 19-inch tires. The 71 HP 6-cylinder gine of Continental design produced 3300 RPM. Fuel pacity consisted of a 12-gallon tank.

A carryover from 1931 was Durant's novel Pullman achment which turned the interior into a full length ıch similar to Nash's bed of a few years later.

So few 1932 Durants were sold that production figures · not available.

Durant for 1931 offered the 6-10, 6-12 and the 6-14 as three separate Seires. Shown here is the 6-12 5-passenger sedan that featured a "Pullman attachment" which turned the interior into a full length reclining couch. This model came on a 112-inch wheelbase, weighed 2,765 lbs. and sold for $725.

A neat looking little 6-wheel 1930 Durant DeLuxe Coupe in the 6-17 Series weighed 2,825 lbs. as a rumble seat model and sold for $750. Durants were noted for their durable chrome plating.

Elcar

The Elcar was of independent manufacture, bein produced in Elkhart, Ind. The company had been i existence since 1908, but 1930 was the next to final ye of production.

For 1930, Elcar was offered in four series, the 75, 9 96 and 130.

The Elcar 75 developed 61 HP from its 6-cylind Lycoming engine at 3000 RPM. This model used 5:00 19-inch tires and had a wheelbase of 117 inches. The fu capacity was 19 gallons, the same as in the other thr series. Lockheed hydraulic brakes also were used throug out the line.

The 95 and 96 models developed 90 HP from 8-cylind Lycoming engines. Both models rode on 123-inch whe bases and had 5:50 x 19-inch tires. The only differen between these two models was that the 96 series offere a far more plush looking car than the Series 95.

The Elcar 130 offered a Lycoming 8 which develop 140 HP at 3300 RPM. This series used 6:50 x 20-in tires. Its wheelbase was mentioned in its model des nation – 130 inches.

A total of 32 models were available ranging in pri from the 75 Roadster for 2 passengers for $995 to t Elcar 130 7-passenger Sedan for $2,465.

The 1930 Elcar 75 Roadster was the company's lowest priced car for the year. It sold for $995 in 2-passenger style and weighed 2,558 lbs. This model used the 6-cylinder Lycoming engine that developed 61 H.P. at 3000 RPM. Its wheelbase was 117 inches.

An Elcar Series 96 4-passenger Roadster was available for $1,635 and weighed 3,300 lbs. Both the Series 95 and 96 were cars on the same chassis. The difference was seen in a fancier interior that the 96 models offered. Both series had 8 models to choose from ranging in price from $1,295 to $1,895.

A similar model to the Series 75 is this 1930 Elcar Series 95 4-passenger coupe. This model fit between the low priced 75 Series and the more expensive Series 96. It rode on the same 123-inch wheelbase as the 96, but cost only $1,465. This car used the wooden artillery wheels and rear mounted spare as its basic equipment.

This 4-passenger Convertible Coupe that Elcar offered in the Series 96 sold for $1,665. It weighed 3,413 lbs. The 8-cylinder Lycoming engine developed 90 H.P. at 3000 RPM. As a Series 75 the identical car sold for $200 less.

Elcar's 4-passenger Coupe for 1930 is shown above in the Series 75. In base form it sold for $1,165 and weighed 2,942 lbs. This model is well equipped with optional accessories such as wire wheels, sidemount spares, and the luggage rack.

Very similar in all respects was the 1931 line of Elcar automobiles. This 1931 4-passenger Series 75-A Roadster weighed 2,658 lbs. and sold for $1,145. The 1931 line was referred to as 75-A to distinguish it from the 1930 cars.

)31

In 1931, Elcar offered the same line of cars as in 1930 these models: the Series 75-A, Series 96, and Series 30. The 90 HP Series 95 was no longer available, but the car 140 made its entrance to compete with the Chrysler nperial, Cadillac V-8, Packard Series 833, and the erless.

The Series 140 offered a 322 cubic inch Lycoming cylinder engine which developed a 140 HP at 3300 PM. This series had a 19-gallon fuel supply like the her models. It came on a 135-inch wheelbase, using 50 x 20-inch tires like the Elcar 130 Models.

The Series 75-A used a 6-cylinder Lycoming engine of 35 cubic inches which developed 61 HP at 3000 RPM. nis series had a 117-inch wheelbase and rode on 5:00 x)-inch tires.

The Series 96 had a 246.7 cubic inch 8-cylinder engine veloping 90 HP at 3000 RPM. These models used 50 x 19-inch tires and had a 123-inch wheelbase.

The Series 130 used the same engine components as the 40s except the 130s had a 130-inch wheelbase.

The depression kept Elcar from completing a full year of oduction and so another fine old line of cars couldn't ranked among the regulars for the next model run. Production and sales figures were too low to be corded for the 1930 and 1931 statistics.

Rarely seen when new was a 1931 7-passenger Elcar on the 75-A chassis. The 75-A Sedans began at $1,195 and went up to $1,395 in 75-A 7-passenger style. This series continued to use a 6-cylinder engine.

The Series 130 Elcar was one of the top lines for 1931. It had the same 140 H.P. engine as the Series 140, only it rode on a 130-inch wheelbase. Elcar's advertising, which was very little, stated it was the car with the Shock-less Chassis. It sold for $1,995 and weighed 3,980 lbs.

The most expensive Elcar in 1931 was the Series 140 Convertible Sedan. It sold for $2,750, weighed 4,375 lbs. and used the 135-inch wheelbase. Its companion was this 5-passenger touring, which sold for $2,465. In a last gasp, Elcar produced the Series 120, which was a cross between the 130 and 140.

The 1931 Elcar 5-passenger Princess Sedan, Series 140, with landau irons came on a 135-inch wheelbase, sold for $2,645 and weighed 4,375 lbs. This car was introduced in 1931 to compete with the upper middle class cars. With the depression getting worse very few were sold.

Erskin

This was the Erskine Dynamic Coupe for 1930. It was a 2-passenger model that sold for $895. Also available as a rumble seat coupe for four, it sold for $945. The 2-passenger model came with a leather interior while the rumble seat version offered a mohair interior with leather seats in the luggage compartment.

The Erskine was a product of the Studebaker Cor poration of South Bend, Indiana. The car was manu factured in the Detroit assembly plant of Studebaker fror 1927 to 1930.

The 1930 Erskine was not produced for the full yea As the depression deepened, the Studebaker Corporatio felt the car wasn't producing enough sales to warran its continuing.

The car carried a 6-cylinder engine developing 70 HP a 3200 RPM. The Erskine used a 14-gallon fuel tank. It wheelbase measured 114 inches and the tire size wa 5:25 x 19 inches. All models used Bendix mechanica brakes.

A total of eight models were available ranging fro $895 for the 2-passenger Coupe to $1,095 for a Reg Land Sedan for 5. Production figures placed Erskine i 23rd Position, selling 8,757 cars for the year.

The Erskine for 1930 also came as a Tourer for $965. It was also available in Regal Tourer style for $1,065. The regular Tourer models came with wooden wheels as standard equipment, with wire wheels an accessory. The Tourer models also came with a fold down windshield as part of the sporty appearance.

Erskine's top sedan of the line sold for $1,095 and was called the Regal Land Sedan. The customer had his choice of a mohair or broadcloth interior on deep springs. A rear seat center armrest was part of the luxury package this model offered. Also included as standard equipment were six wire wheels with side mounted spares, folding luggage rack, and rear quarter panel landau irons. This was Erksine's last year.

Erskine's best sellèr for 1930 was this 5-passenger sedan that sold for $965. This model came with six wire wheels and folding luggage rack as standard equipment. A customer also had a choice of wooden wheels.

A 1930 Erskine Club Sedan for five sold for $895. This was basically the 2-door sedan that came equipped with adjustable front seats. The steering column also was adjustable, which was one of the first in a production car. The interior was done in a fine mohair.

The Essex was a product of the Hudson Motor Car o., Detroit. It was in production from 1917 to 1932. The title for the 1930 car was Essex Super 6. It had a 0 HP engine at 3600 RPM. The car had a 113-inch heelbase and rode on 5:00 x 19-inch tires. It had an 1½-gallon fuel tank. Mechanical brakes were used on the ssex Super 6.

A total of nine body styles were available ranging from ne $675 5-passenger coach to the Speedabout Speedster or $945.

Essex sold 64,502 vehicles which placed it in the 6th osition for the year. Calendar year production is placed ith Hudson, where it ranked in 4th Position with 13,898 cars sold.

931

The 1931 cars entered the market with a great reduction price, though the series was still called Essex Super 6. he engine displacement was 175.3 cubic inches, and the cylinder now developed 60 HP at 3300 RPM. Bendix echanical brakes were used on the 1931 Essex line. The heelbase remained 113 inches and the models still used 00 x 19-inch tires. Only six models were available for 931, beginning at $595 for either a 2-passenger Business oupe or a 5-passenger Coach. The top of the line was a 775 5-passenger Touring Sedan.

Essex and Hudson took the 7th seat by selling 57,825 nits during the 1931 model run.

This was the 1930 Essex Super 6 4-passenger Sport Roadster that sold for $725. This model, like all 1930 Essex cars, rode on a 113-inch wheelbase.

A rare model was the 1930 Essex Super 6 Speedabout Speedster that sold for $945. This example carried a body by Biddle-Smart. The 6 wire wheels and sidemounts were standard equipment.

This 1930 Essex Brougham for 5 passengers was the most expensive closed model for the year. It sold for $775. The enclosed rear quarter panels gave this little car a special look of elegance. The trunk rack, sidemounts, wire wheels, tire cover, and landau irons all were part of the package of standard equipment. Essex was one of the first to put accessories out classed as a group package.

The Sunsedan was Essex' name for this 2-door 5-passenger Phaeton. Essex used this car to publicize its fleetness. For example, it was given a special run from Michigan Central Station to Chicago Central Station, a distance of 272 miles. The car completed the run in 4 hours and 32 minutes. Note the twin spot lamps and the siren in the center of the radiator compartment.

Essex

Barney Oldfield stands by the 1931 Essex 2-passenger business coupe, giving it a once over approval. Being the "king of the throttle boys," this was quite a fete to have him extol the car's virtues. This was the lowest priced offering for the year at $595.

1932

At the end of this year, Essex was phased out for th Terraplane. In July, when this car was introduced for th remainder of the year, it was known as the Essex Terr plane. It had a 106-inch wheelbase, but still used th same engine as the former Essex.

Essex started out 1932 by jumping from 7th Place t 4th in the sales picture. They sold fewer cars than in 193 but did register 57,550 vehicles for the year combine with Hudson. The company produced eight models fc the year, all on 113-inch wheelbases. These cars ha 6-cylinder, 70 HP engines of 3200 RPM. Tire size w 5:25 x 18. Fuel capacity was a 12-gallon tank. Thes eight models began with a price tag of $695 for 2-passenger Coupe, ranging upward to $895 for th 4-passenger Convertible Coupe.

Body lines and interiors were wholly new, of bedfor cloth in brown, green and blue to match the exterior c the car. This was the work of Frank Spring, former chi body designer of Walter Murphy Body Co. of Pasaden Cal. The splash apron under the radiator blended with th fenders and radiator shell and the headlamp contou were carefully selected to fit the picture. The radiatc core was concealed by a vertical grille instead of shutter which rounded out the front end.

Essex' best selling car for 1931 was the 4-door sedan at $695. It carried a 6-cylinder engine under its hood that developed 60 H.P. at 3300 RPM. This was the last year for this body style.

An early 1932 Essex Super 6 Town Sedan on the 113-inch wheelbase sold for $745. This model carried the parking lights by the front door. Later Essex Terraplanes had them mounted on the front fenders. The total Essex models produced were 17,425 units for their part of the year.

This was the 1932 Essex Super 6 coach for 5 passengers. This model sold for $705. All Essex models on the 113-inch wheelbase were phased out in July of 1932 to make way for the Essex Terraplane.

Essex Terraplane

The Essex Terraplane was a product of the Hudson Motor Co., Detroit. This was the only year of production or the Essex Terraplane. It was announced on the market in July of 1932 as a mid-season unit, and was replaced in 1934 by the Terraplane.

The Essex Terraplane was offered in two engines, the 0 HP Six (3200 RPM) with a standard compression ratio f 5.8 to 1, or 80 HP with an optional head giving 7.1 atio. The Terraplane Eight offered 94 HP at 3200 RPM with a standard ratio being 5.8:1 compression.

The wheelbases consisted of 106 inches in the Six and 13 inches for the Eight. Tire sizes were 5:25 x 17 for the ix and 6:00 x 16 on the Eight, with this being optional or the Six. Fuel capacities for the two cars were 11½ allons in the Six and 16 gallons in the Eight.

Body styles listed 16, with 11 going to the Terraplane 6 nd the remaining five for the 8-cylinder cars. Prices went rom $425 for a Terraplane Six 4-passenger Roadster to 725 for the Terraplane Eight Sedan.

Essex Terraplane sales dropped one place this year to eventh Position. They sold 40,982 cars. These calendar ear sales also include Hudson.

A 1932-33 Essex Terraplane Phaeton for 5 passengers sold for $495. This model didn't prove too popular with the public in 1932 or 1933. Very few exist today. The Essex Terraplane name was phased out at the end of 1933 and became just the Terraplane for 1934.

A mid-season offering was this 1932-1933 Essex Terraplane Business Coupe for $470. It carried 2 passengers on its 106-inch wheelbase. It weighed 2,135 lbs. The models all used wire wheels as standard equipment.

Good publicity for the 1932-1933 Essex Terraplane was to have someone of prestige standing by the newly introduced model, or have them taking delivery of it. Here, it is the famous aviatrix, Amelia Earhart, posing by the new model which sold for $590 as the Special Sedan. It weighed 1,250 lbs. Note the parking lamps are mounted on the fenders of this model.

Very similar in appearance to the 2-passenger coupe was the Essex Terraplane Sport Coupe for 1932-1933 which carried 4 passengers with the aid of the rumble seat. It weighed 2,190 lbs. as a 6-cylinder and 2,490 lbs. as an 8-cylinder. The 6-cylinder sold for $550 and the 8-cylinder for $695. Note these coupes must have been early production, without the fender mounted parking lamps that later Essex Terraplanes came equipped with.

FOR FURTHER INFORMATION, SEE TERRAPLANE SECTION

Ford

Theodore Luce, the Lincoln-Ford dealer in New York City, offered this 1930 Ford Model A to its customers for $1,200. Not only the most expensive model for the year, it also weighed the most at 2,525 lbs. It was available only on special order.

Ford is a product of Ford Motor Co. of Dearborn, Micl The car has been in production since 1903.

In 1930, Model As were beginning the third year c production. During the 1930 model run, the 4-milliont Model A left the Dearborn factory since its inceptio in 1928.

The 4-cylinder Model A developed 40 HP at 2200 RPM The car had a 10-gallon fuel tank and averaged abou 25 MPG. The tire size was of 4:50 x 21 inches. Thes models had a 103½-inch wheelbase.

In 1930, a new model was displayed. This was th DeLuxe Phaeton which had genuine leather upholster and a trunk rack. The biggest seller for the year was th Tudor Sedan. Introduced late in the model year was th 2-door close coupled Victoria with body by Briggs whic appeared with a tan canvas top. This model became a goo seller at $625.

Ford sold 1,155,162 cars for the year placing them i 1st Position for the model run.

A practical car for the businessman was this 1930 Ford DeLuxe Coupe for $550. It weighed 2,248 lbs. Note how the windshield opened for ventilation.

This is the 1930 Ford Model A Standard Coupe which sold for $50 less than its DeLuxe brother. The only external difference between the two is the lack of parking lights on the cowl.

One of Ford's best sellers for 1930 was this Standard Fordor Sedan. It weighed 2,419 lbs. and sold for $600. It was also available in a DeLuxe model for $25 more. It weighed 2,497 lbs.

The 1930 Ford Model A Convertible Cabriolet with top down made a very nice open car for those who enjoyed the fresh air. This model weighed 2,339 lbs. and sold for $645.

Ford

931

During the 1931 model run, Ford produced its 20-illionth car, which was a Town Sedan for 5 passengers. : sold for $630.

The 1931 4-cylinder Model A, which had a 205.5 cubic ıch engine, developed 40 HP at 2200 RPM. The fuel apacity for the little car now was an 11-gallon tank. The 'heelbase remained 103½ inches. Model As used mech-nical brakes.

Actually Ford produced 23 different models, if the arious styles of Roadsters are classed as separate models. he same held true with the Cabriolet. The Victoria style 'as available as a steel roofed car or with fabric over the :eel, which was an early rendition of today's vinyl tops. The Model As ranged in price from $430 for a Standard -passenger Roadster to $1,200 for the DeLuxe Town Car edan which held 4 passengers comfortably. These Fords sed both Murray and Briggs as their body builders at ıis time.

The 1931 models were the last of the Model As. During ıe four years of its production, over 5 million Model As 'ere placed on the highways.

Ford placed 2nd for the calendar year by selling 41,615 units.

Always a favorite with young families was the 1930 Standard Model A Ford Tudor Sedan. This example sold for $500 and had a seating capacity for five. It weighed 2,348 lbs. Cowl lights were not on the Standard models.

A popular car in the 1931 Ford Model A Standard line was this Fordor Sedan. It was available for $590. The DeLuxe models sold for $630. Both used bodies built by Briggs and Murray. Ford sold its 20-millionth car in 1931.

The 1931 Ford Model A DeLuxe Roadster with rumble seat and side mount spares sold for $495 and weighed 2,275 lbs. It was also available in a trunk model for $20 less. Note this example wears the accessory quail radiator ornament, which is very popular among Model A buffs today.

A 1931 Ford Model A Standard Phaeton was available for $440. It weighed 2,212 lbs. The DeLuxe Phaeton brought a price tag of $625 and weighed 2,285 lbs.

The lowest priced car for the 1931 Ford line was this 2-passenger Roadster which sold for $430 and weighed 2,155 lbs.

Ford

Not considered factory equipment but seen on many 1931 Ford Model A's were the General Jumbo Tires. These tires offered a shockless ride to its passengers. The tires were filled with 12 lbs. of air. They sold for an additional $60.

Ford's Model A DeLuxe Sedan for 1931 differed from the regular Ford line of sedans with the enclosed rear quarter panels. This model weighed 2,475 lbs. and sold for $660.

Introduced late in the model run of 1930 was this close-coupled Tudor Sedan known as the Ford Victoria. This example is a 1931 version that sold for $625. The canvas top was part of its standard equipment. The body builder of this cute little model was Briggs. Note its accessory quail radiator cap.

Ford offered this right hand drive version for its customers in England. It was classed as a Convertible Cabriolet and sold for $595. in the states. The only differences, in addition to being a right hand vehicle, are the fender mounted parking lights and right hand mounted license and taillamp assembly.

This 1932 Ford Station Wagon was a 4-cylinder Model B which sold for only $10 less than its V-8 counterpart. These cars weren't in demand like the V-8 series, which sold for $600.

A beautiful car when new and just as pretty today is the 1932 DeLuxe Roadster with rumble seat that sold for $500. This same car was available in trunk style.

Ford

1932

The pride and joy of Henry this year was his totally new car, carrying a brand new V-8 engine for the first time. Full details of this car were given in over 2,000 newspapers on March 29, 1932, when the V-8 bowed to the public for the first time. Ford did everything possible in this "bottom of the depression" year to get Americans to come forth and buy its products. In over 6,000 theaters, Ford put on free shows to start prosperity drives. More than 5½ million people visited Ford dealers' sales floors the first day the V-8s were shown. By the first part of March, 1932, deposits had been placed on more than 100,000 Ford vehicles. Better than 70% of these were for the V-8.

Body styles numbered 18 for the year in both the 4-cylinder Model B and the V-8. Prices ranged from $430 for the Model B 2-passenger Roadster to $650 for the 5-passenger Town Sedan.

These cars had a 106-inch wheelbase and a 50 HP 4-cylinder engine or the V-8 which produced 65 HP. The Model B had an 11-gallon fuel tank while the V-8 had a 14-gallon tank. Both models used 5:25 x 18-inch size tires. The brake system was Ford's own mechanical device. For the year, Ford sold 232,125 units, placing second in the sales race.

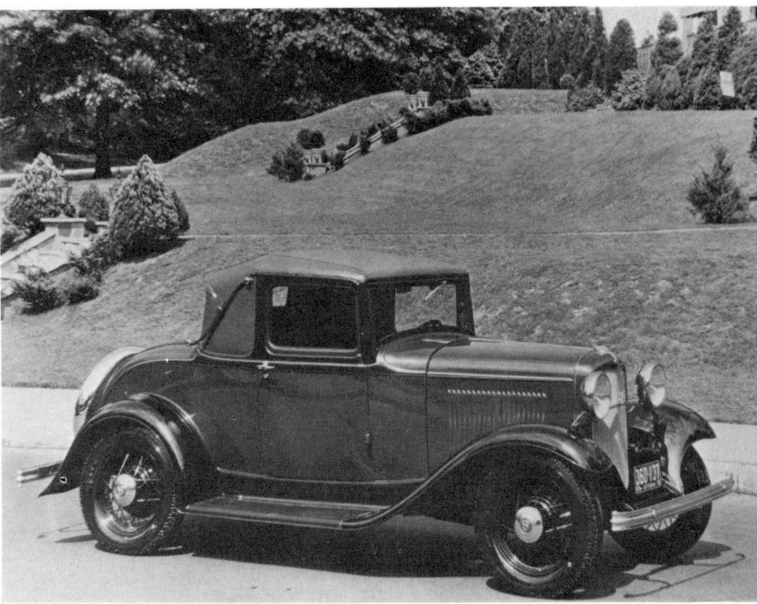

A car always in demand–when new, as it grew older with the hot rod boys, and today, as a collectible among the Ford V-8 fans. This 1932 Sport Coupe, with the stationary landau irons, came either as trunk model or with rumble seat as shown here. This being a DeLuxe model, with its chrome tire cover as standard equipment, sold for $535.

This was the new 1932 Ford DeLuxe Phaeton displayed with top and windshield in the down position. As a V-8 it sold for $545.

The Convertible Sedan retained its roof rails, giving it a rather strange appearance when the top was down. It sold for $650.

The DeLuxe Tudor turned out to be the popularity leader for the year at $550.

The Convertible Cabriolet could be had with either trunk or rumble seat for $610.

Ford

1933

Not registered as a passenger car in 1933 was this Ford Station Wagon. Ford classed these vehicles and catalogued them as light panel trucks or surveyors trucks. At any rate, it's a passenger car by today's standards. It sold for $640.

This, the second year of V-8 production, was a complet sell-out for the Eight cylinder cars. Not quite the sam was the story for the Model B, as it was dropped at th end of the model run.

The wheelbase for 1933 brought out the longest For yet built, which was 112 inches. Body styles numbere eighteen. The same body in the Model B could also b ordered in the V-8. The lowest price Ford on the mark for 1933 was the 2-passenger Roadster in Model B for which sold for $410. The most expensive Ford at th time was the DeLuxe Fordor Sedan for $610. Tire siz was 5:25 x 18 for both series with a 14-gallon fuel tan listed for both models. Brakes were of the mechanic type in each series. Horsepower for the Model B w 50 at 2800 RPM, and for the V-8, 75 HP at 3400 RP

Production kept Ford in the Number 2 Position for th calendar year, with 334,969 cars sold.

A real sharp looking 1933 Ford Victoria is being used by the Wrigley Co. It sold for $550 as a Model B and $600 with the V-8 engine. This particular car is equipped with Vogue Whitewall Tyres and twin spot lamps which makes it a trim looking little unit. Note the Wrigley poster in the rear window compartment and the company inscription lettered on the door.

Ford's lowest priced car for 1933 was this sharp looking Model B 4-cylinder Roadster. This example cost $410. It weighed 2,131 lbs. It was available as a V-8 for $50 more. The tire cover, right taillamp, and whitewall tires were not part of the price, as all of these items were classed as accessories.

Becoming more popular all the time was the Cabriolet. The 1933 Ford Cabriolet sold for $560 as a Model B, weighing 2,295 lbs. The roll up windows offered a more solid feel to the car and also kept out the moisture on inclement days.

Very popular as a fleet car with companies was the 3 or 5-window coupe. This typical example of the 5-window coupe was used by Gerber Baby Foods as a company car. In Standard version it sold for $440 as a Model B. As a V-8 the price was $490. It seated 2 passengers.

934

This year, Ford started its third year of manufacturing he V-8. It had now seen its millionth V-8 come from the ssembly line. The 1934 Fords were chiseled out a little nore to make an already pretty car just a little more of a ooker.

Since the 4-cylinder Ford was gone, this allowed Ford nore time to devote to the V-8. Horsepower was now ncreased to 85 at 3800 RPM. Tire size was 5:50 x 17 nches. A 14-gallon fuel supply was used. Wheelbase was 12 inches again.

Twelve body styles were available this year, ranging from he Standard Five Window Coupe for $515 to the DeLuxe -passenger sedan for $625. A station wagon was also nade available but in 1934, this body style was cate-orized under commercial vehicles. It sold for $660.

Also new on 1934 cars were fenders painted in the ame color as the body on all DeLuxe cars, as well as on Standard models if they were painted green or grey.

Some custom body builders were now beginning to feel he pinch of the depression and felt a Ford V-8 was a ood way to go with their custom bodies. Brewster was ne of the first to choose Ford. Later, Cunningham also elt it a good way to keep the doors opened.

Ford took Second Place in 1934 by selling 563,921 ars for the year.

A factory publicity photo shows this 1934 Ford 3-window Coupe in a typical California setting with banana palms and Spanish style architecture. This is the DeLuxe version which sold for $555. A Standard model, not as popular, sold for $515.

A very popular model with the American family proved to be this 1934 DeLuxe 5-passenger Ford Sedan for $625. It weighed 2,425 lbs. The wheelbase was 112 inches. Fenders were painted the same color as the body on all DeLuxe cars, and could be ordered this way as a special order on Standard models.

Ford offered the 1934 Phaeton as a DeLuxe line for $550, an increase of $55 over 1933 models. The weight of this model was 2,369 lbs. A leather interior was standard equipment on the Phaetons, Roadster, and Cabriolets for 1934. Only the Phaeton had both doors hinged at the center.

This 1934 Ford Victoria offered a built-in trunk connected with its spare tire carrier. Not much could be carried in the back but at least it did offer a closed compartment which was seen on many cars as standard equipment in 1934. The Victoria had a $10 increase over 1933 models. It now sold for $610. The belt line stripe was standard equipment on all DeLuxe models.

Ford

1935

This special built body was turned out by Derham Body Co. of Rosemont, Pa. for special customers. This was not part of the Ford trade, but in 1934 body builders did use Fords as they were peppy and made a fast, smooth running car for those who had money and wished something a little extra.

1935 was the year Ford had been striving for. This year they outsold their No. 1 competitor, Chevrolet. Sales figures put them in the First Place, with 942,439 units being sold for the calendar year.

This year Ford looked larger but still rode on the same 112-inch wheelbase. The engine and seats had been moved forward 8½ inches, with the bodies being widened as much as 5½ inches to allow three to ride comfortably in the front seats. Also new to Ford were an improved clutch and brakes which were redesigned to provide improved action and less pedal pressure. The alloy drums had additional cooling ribs which increased the radiating surface by about 40%. The brake system was still mechanical.

On June 2nd, the 2-millionth V-8 came from the assembly floor. The engine gave an 88 HP reading at 3800 RPM. It fuel supply was 14 gallons. The tire size was 6:00 x 16 in both the Standard and DeLuxe versions.

DeLuxe models came in 10 styles ranging from a 5-window Coupe with trunk for $560 to a $750 DeLuxe Convertible Sedan. At the other end of the ladder was the Standard 5-window Coupe with trunk for $495 minus all unnecessary chrome trim. The Standard Fordor sold for $575. In this series was the Station Wagon, although Ford did not class this model as a passenger car. It was known as a commercial vehicle. Three models were available in Standard form, but including the Station Wagon would then give four models. Ten were listed in the DeLuxe Series making a total of 14 models to choose from.

This is a 1935 Ford DeLuxe Fordor Touring Sedan with built-in trunk as standard equipment. It sold for $655. The trunk model was not available in the Standard Series. The DeLuxe Fordor Sedan without trunk sold for $635 but was not nearly as popular as this Touring model.

As near a classic design that Ford ever produced was displayed on this 1935 DeLuxe Phaeton which sold for $580. From the looks of the pavement it's good to have the top up. Only DeLuxe models had the chrome radiator and shell.

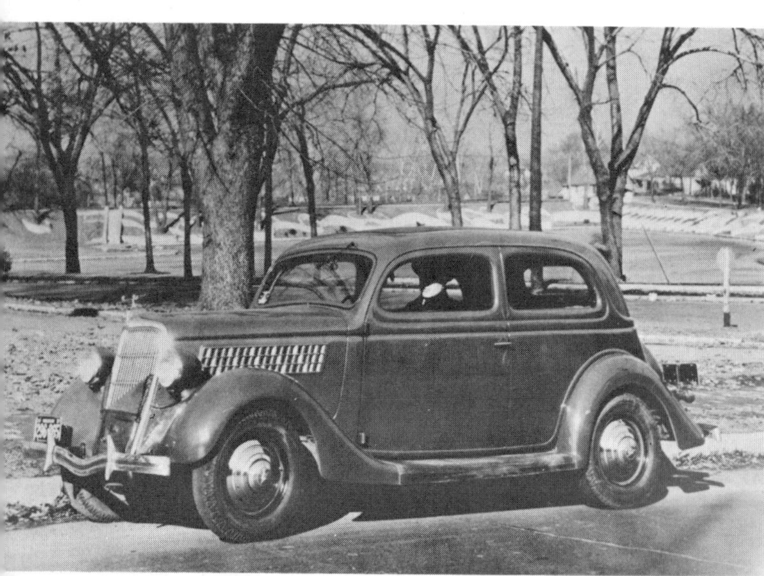

This is the 1935 Ford DeLuxe Tudor Sedan that sold for $575 in base form. This model appears equipped with more than just the regular options, such as the rare full wheel covers and the accessory radiator grille screen used on cars that saw winter driving. This body style was popular with families with young children.

1936

Ford in 1936 brought out a family of real lookers in 8 different models, including the Station Wagon, which as referred to as a commercial vehicle. Twelve models ere offered in the DeLuxe line and the remaining six owed up as Standards. Pricewise, these cars ranged etween $510 for the Standard 5-window Coupe and 780 for the DeLuxe Convertible Touring Sedan. This ear's cars offered trunks as an option on the Tudor and ordor Sedans as well as the Convertible Touring Sedan.

All models received faceliftings, with a nicely restyled ille, hood and fenders, along with the use of steel ressed wheels. Interiors were more attractive with taupe lored mohair and Bedford cord available on closed eLuxe models. Leather was used on open cars. The onvertible Phaeton also could have Bedford cord if the uyer preferred. Standard models used a special Bedford ord suitable to the body style.

All models used a V-8 engine of 90 HP at 3800 RPM. he fuel supply was a 14-gallon tank.

Brakes were of the mechanical type. Tires consisted of :00 x 16 inches on all models. The wheelbase remained 12 inches. During the year, Ford sold its 3-millionth V-8 nce introduction in 1932. Still, this was not quite enough keep the number one sales spot earned in 1935, and us the company returned to its Number Two Position y selling 791,812 cars.

The 1935 Ford Station Wagon was classed with the small trucks, but today it is definitely placed with the passenger cars. This particular wagon must have been an early one as it is minus the front bumper guards which were considered standard equipment on DeLuxe models. Ford sold this wagon for $670. Roll-up windows were part of the bargain for front seat passengers. All other windows had the plexiglass shades which snapped in or out of place with snap buttons.

This 1936 Ford DeLuxe Tudor Sedan sold for $565 and was quite popular. Still, more people preferred the Tudor Touring Sedan for $35 additional. A Standard Tudor also was available for $520 which sold well to fleet users.

Probably the most well accepted model with the general public was this 1936 Ford DeLuxe Fordor Touring Sedan that came with the chromed grille, chrome horn rings, and chromed front fender welting. Even though it did offer a neat trunk compartment, storage wasn't the best feature. The car sold for $650.

Popular when new and a real collector's piece today is this 1936 Ford 5-Window Coupe. It was available as a trunk model for $555, or $580 for the rumble seat version. Few were being delivered with rumble seats, as the public appeared to be tiring of the air blowing in their faces.

An early 1936 Ford Convertible Sedan looked a great deal like the Phaeton for that year with its rear mounted spare. About the only external difference was the partition placed between the wind-up windows on the Convertible Sedan. The Phaeton used plexiglass curtains which were removable. Late in the model run Ford decided to put a trunk in place of the outside spare on the Convertible Touring Sedan. This made an entirely different looking car. It was the most expensive model built by Ford for the year and sold at $780.

Ford

Ford was always popular with its open models and this 1936 DeLuxe Roadster was no exception. It sold for $560 and came in the DeLuxe style only with a rumble seat.

A new offering for Ford in 1936 was this Convertible Club Cabriolet. This was the beginning of Ford selling an open car that contained all passengers enclosed, and without using a rumble seat. Its top was much longer than on the regular 2-door convertible. The Club Cabriolet sold for $675.

Fully equipped, which not too many sedans had the privilege of, is this nicely dolled 1937 DeLuxe Fordor Touring Sedan. The car's accessories include the ever popular spider wheel covers, whitewall tires, radio with roof mounted antenna (which Ford started on the 1937 models and continued to use through 1948), and the factory installed fender skirts. In base form the car sold for $760.

1937

1937 marked a fairly big year for Ford as far as change were concerned. Two engines were offered, the regular V-8 plus a new smaller 60 HP engine that was available in the Standard Series.

As for style, it resembled its cousin, Lincoln Zephyr a great deal, especially in the front end appearance with the V-shaped grille and sunken headlights stationed in the catwalks of the fenders. The hood was hinged by the cowl and raised from a center handle for easy access to both sides.

Ford continued the 85 HP engine for DeLuxe cars The Standard Series had a 60 HP engine at 3500 RPM Fuel capacity was a 14-gallon tank in both series. The 60 models used 5:25 x 16-inch tires and the DeLuxe took 6:00 x 16s. Both series used the 112-inch wheelbase Mechanical brakes were still being used on Fords. This was the first year that Ford had its battery mounted in the engine room, which made it convenient for servicing Eighteen body styles were available with a base price of $585 for the Standard 5-window Coupe to the top of the line, the Convertible Sedan listed at $860. Ford again took Second Place in sales this year by turning out 848,608 units.

The 1937 Ford Tudor Sedan was available in two versions: the Standard and DeLuxe. In Standard style it could be ordered with either the 60 H.P. engine or the 85 H.P. version. The DeLuxe models only had the 85 H.P. engine. This model is the 60 H.P. Standard model that sold for $610.

Quite a change from the 1936 models is evident in this DeLuxe Fordor Sedan that sold for $735. The DeLuxe line included the stainless steel trim rings as standard equipment and twin windshield wipers. The double whitewall tires were an accessory at extra cost. The complete face lifting this model received in 1937 certainly gives it the appearance of a baby Lincoln Zephyr.

)38

This was the last year Ford would use mechanical :akes. There was quite a difference between the 60s and 5s in appearance. The wheelbase was the same in both ·ries – 112 inches.

Ford lessened its body styles more in 1938 than had ɜen the case in some while. Including the Station Wagon, ıere were only 12 models being assembled. They ran om $625 for a Standard 5-window Coupe to the top of ıe DeLuxe line, a $900 Convertible Sedan.

Ford again placed Second for the model run by selling 10,048 vehicles.

Not too popular in 1937 but a real special interest car today is the 5-passenger Convertible Sedan. This was the most expensive Ford model for the year. It sold for $860. A model looking quite similar but minus the center posts was the DeLuxe Phaeton for $750.

At the top is the 1938 Standard Tudor Sedan in the fastback style which sold for $650. It was also available as a Tudor with bustle back trunk at $665. Either the 60 H.P. or 85 H.P. engines were used in the Standard models. The DeLuxe 85 H.P. Sedan beneath the Standard model sold for $770 and was the most popular Ford for 1938.

Now in its second year was the 1937 5-passenger DeLuxe Club Cabriolet which sold for the same price as the DeLuxe Touring Sedan, $760. Today, it is a rare model and is worth many times more than the sedan. The factory fender skirts were not part of the base price.

This was the DeLuxe Tudor Sedan that came with more frills than its Standard model sister. This series used only the 85 H.P. engine and had more chrome around the windshield, grille moldings, and the stainless steel wheel trim rings. It sold, in base form, for $725 and was a good buy with families with small children.

Again, the DeLuxe 5-Window Coupe was the answer for businessmen and those who were young that liked a peppy V-8 engine. This model sold for $685. It used the same wheelbase as the Standard models, which was 112 inches.

Ford

Even though it was still classed as a commercial car in 1938, today it is registered as a passenger vehicle. Starring with the 1938 models, all Station Wagons had sliding glass windows in each window panel. This 8-passenger vehicle sold for $825.

Ford's most expensive and their rarest model for the 1938 season was this Convertible Sedan. It sold for $900. Also available for the last time was the Phaeton, which sold for $820 and continued to use its canvas side curtains.

This was Ford's DeLuxe Fordor Sedan for 1939 that sold for $790. The big news Ford had to tell was that it now had switched over to hydraulic brakes. Ford was the last of the "Big Three" to do so. Note that windshield wipers were still mounted from the top of the windshield on the Coupes, Tudor and Fordor Sedans.

1939

Ford introduced its line of 1939 models, showing 1 styles among the three lines offered. The nomenclatur of the Standard Ford was not used in 1939. The low price Ford was called the Ford V-8 and came either with 60 HP or an 85 HP engine. The DeLuxe Ford was offere with only one engine, the 85 HP V-8. The Ford 60 an 85 of plain trim were offered in four styles each, includin the Station Wagon. The DeLuxe 85 was displayed in si styles.

Big news for Ford this year was its change over t hydraulic brakes. On the DeLuxe line the ammeter wa replaced with a new instrument referred to as the batter condition indicator. It explained at a glance the conditio of the battery generator circuit with a maximum chargin rate of 30 amperes.

The fuel supply of the 1939 Fords was a 14-gallon tan in all models. The tire size for the lower priced car wa 5:50 x 16, while the DeLuxes rode on 6:00 x 16

The price range for the year started at $640 for the For V-8 60 HP 3-passenger Coupe and ended at $920 for th Convertible Sedan and the DeLuxe Station Wagon.

Ford placed in Second Position for the calendar yea selling 532,152 automobiles. During the year, the 2 millionth car was built.

Ford's answer in 1939 for families looking for good, solid, economical transportation was this Standard Tudor Sedan that carried a $680 price tag. The 1939 Standard models resembled the DeLuxe line of 1938 a great deal, especially in the contour of the grille and headlights.

Ford offered a Standard and a DeLuxe version in the Station Wagon line for 1939. Shown here is the DeLuxe model which seated 8 passengers. It was priced for $920. In the Standard model it sold for $840.

940

The Ford line for 1940 was made up of Standard and eLuxe models. It was a very good year for Ford, as they ırned out a very stylish looking car. This was particularly ue in the DeLuxe Coupe line. Mechanically, the 1940 ırs were very similar to the 1939 models. They had a eering column gearshift, two spoke steering wheel, ealed beam headlamps, window ventilators as standard quipment, and a fixed windshield with wipers mounted the bottom of the windshield. These were a few of the im changes that were made.

The V-8 engines were 60 HP at 3500 RPM available only the Standard models or the 85 HP version at 3800 RPM hich was available in the Standard and in the DeLuxe ne. The fuel tank had increased now to a 15-gallon ıpply. The Standard line continued with 5:50 x 16-inch res and the DeLuxe again used 6:00 x 16-inch tires. The heelbase for both Series was 112 inches.

Ford offered a total of 10 models between the Standard ıd DeLuxe line. The Standard Station Wagon model was ıly available as a V-8 of 85 HP.

Prices ranged from $660 for a 3-passenger Standard 0 HP Coupe to $950 for the DeLuxe Station Wagon. ord placed in 2nd Position for the calendar year by elling 599,175 cars.

Ford's most popular car in 1940 turned out to be this DeLuxe Sedan weighing 2,856 lbs. and selling for $810. The whitewalls were extra but the wheel trim rings were standard equipment on the DeLuxe line.

Very popular both in 1940 and today is the 1940 DeLuxe Convertible Coupe. This open model sold for $853 and weighed 2,846 lbs. It seated four comfortably. This was the only open model Ford offered in 1940. The Convertible Sedan ended in 1939 and the 1940 Standard models only came as closed cars.

Strangely enough, this 1939 DeLuxe Ford Convertible Coupe sold for the same price as the DeLuxe Fordor Sedan, which was $790. The open models like this one had the windshield wipers mounted on the base of the windshield. The 1939 Convertible Coupe was the last Ford to offer the rumble seat.

Probably one of the best liked Ford V-8's of all time was this popular 1940 DeLuxe 5-window Coupe. It came as both a Business Coupe and a Club Coupe. The Business Coupe sold for $725 and weighed 2,681 lbs. and the Club Coupe brought $745 and weighed 2,721 lbs.

This was the DeLuxe 1940 Ford Tudor which weighed 2,854 lbs. and sold for $765. It was also available in Standard version carrying either a 60 H.P. engine or the 85 H.P. engine of the DeLuxe line, the same as in the other Ford models for 1940.

Ford

Ford's most expensive model for 1940 happened to be this DeLuxe 8-passenger Station Wagon. It sold for $951 and weighed 3,141 lbs. A Station Wagon also was available in the Standard line, however, only with the V-8 85 H.P. engine.

1941

For 1941 Ford offered a completely new car both i body and in engines. The model names were also replaced The Special was the series that took the Standard name The DeLuxe was in name only the same as last year. I actually was a new series coming in five models with les trim than the 1940 DeLuxe. The Super DeLuxe actuall replaced the DeLuxe of last year. As for engines, th V-8 221 cubic inch was offered in the Special DeLux and Super DeLuxe developing 90 HP at 3800 RPM. Th 60 HP V-8 was discontinued and in its place was 6-cylinder 226 cubic inch 90 HP engine at 3300 RPM It was available only in the Standard and DeLuxe. A models used a 15-gallon fuel tank. The tire size was 6:00 16 inches for each series. All rode on 114-inch chassi

A new model offered in the Super DeLuxe line was th sedan coupe, mainly known as a Club Coupe. It became very popular car with the younger generation.

A large array of accessories were available to make thes cars quite attractive. Such items as bumper and gril guards, spot, fog, and back-up lights, wheel trim an fender stainless steel trim really put the final touches o the cars.

Ford built 15 models ranging in price from $674 for Standard 3-passenger 6-cylinder Business Coupe to $1,01 for a Super DeLuxe 8-passenger Station Wagon. The con pany continued to place in 2nd Position for the calend year, with the sale of 600,814 cars.

An entirely new body style was offered by Ford in 1941. This was the new series called the Super DeLuxe Sedan Coupe. It weighed 3,052 lbs. and sold for $838.

The 1941 Ford Super DeLuxe Convertible Coupe was only available in that series. It weighed 3,187 lbs., selling for $935. This model doesn't carry the stainless fender trim molding later Super DeLuxes came equipped with. It was optional at extra cost at that time. The cowl side mirror was standard equipment on the convertible.

New line for the year was the Super DeLuxe range, of which this is the three-passenger Five Window Coupe at $775.

The DeLuxe Station Wagon used sliding glass in all but the front doors. The "horsey set" still was its prime market. Price, $965.

942

The 1942 Ford was practically the same car as the 1941 odel except for a front end change. It also was one inch wer because of a redesigned front axle and the use of a ansverse front spring. The headlights were flush with the ont part of the front fenders and the parking lights were f a horizontal type mounted above the grille.

A 6 or 8-cylinder engine was offered in the DeLuxe and uper DeLuxe models while the Special only came as a 6. his was truly an economy package coming only in black, ith one tail lamp, one windshield wiper, one sun visor, d no cigar lighter or armrests.

The horsepower on the 6-cylinder models was 90 at 300 RPM. Its engine size was 226 cubic inches. The -8s had a 221 cubic inch engine that developed 90 HP : 3800 RPM. Both 6 and 8-cylinder models used a 15- llon fuel tank. The tire size was 6:00 x 16 inches in all odels. The wheelbase again was 114 inches.

A total of 13 models were available for this short lived odel year. Prices ranged from $780 for a Special 3- assenger Business Coupe to $1,080 for a Super DeLuxe onvertible Coupe.

Ford again placed in 2nd Position for the year from the le of 43,407 cars.

Ford's 1942 Super DeLuxe Sedan sold for $60 more than its 1941 counterpart. With war tones being heard, this car had many small items deleted which were put to work in defense material. All models after January 1, 1942, were called blackout models due to the substitutions and lack of chrome on the bodies.

The Super DeLuxe Tudor, $885.

The Super DeLuxe Coupe was a three-passenger model, selling for $850.

Nice body lines were evident on the Super DeLuxe Station Wagon.

The U.S. Government was a large scale buyer of Standard Fordors, most of which went into the military services. The civilian version of this Army model sold for $850.

Franklin

This is a 1930 Franklin, Series 145 DeLuxe Sedan, wearing the typical Ryan headlamps which Franklins were noted for. The body builder for this model, as with most Franklins, was the Walker Body Co. This model came on the 125-inch chassis, weighed 3,930 lbs., and sold for $2,485.

The Franklin was an air-cooled car built by the Frankli Automobile Co., with headquarters in Syracuse, New York The car began production in 1902 and ended in 1934 The company was noted throughout its life for buildin only fine air-cooled models.

Franklin offered two series in 1930. They were calle the Series 145 and 147. The 145 Series were generall known as the Pursuit Models, and the 147s were th Pirate Series. Each series developed 95 HP at 3100 RPM This year a new cylinder head of aluminum with bronz valve seats was featured on the 274 cubic inch engine Each Series employed a 20-gallon fuel tank. The Pursui models had a 125-inch wheelbase and rode on 6:50 x 19 inch tires as did the Pirate models. The Pirate used 132-inch wheelbase. Both series used Lockheed hydrauli brakes.

A total of 21 models were available between the tw series. Eight were available in the Pursuit 145 models an 13 were in the Pirate 147 series. Prices ranged from $2,48 for a 5-passenger Model 145 Sedan to $7,500 for th Model 147 Convertible Sedan.

Franklin placed in 24th position for the year b selling 7,511 automobiles.

Franklins also were delivered to prominent families throughout Europe. This is another example of a 1930 Series 145 on an endurance run in France. Note the flags for our country and France mounted on the front bumper.

The 1930 Franklin Pirate Phaeton in the 147 Series seated 7 passengers, came on the 132-inch wheelbase, weighed 4,120 lbs., and sold for $2,870. This model has its tonneau windshield in the up position. The body builder for this car was Merrimac.

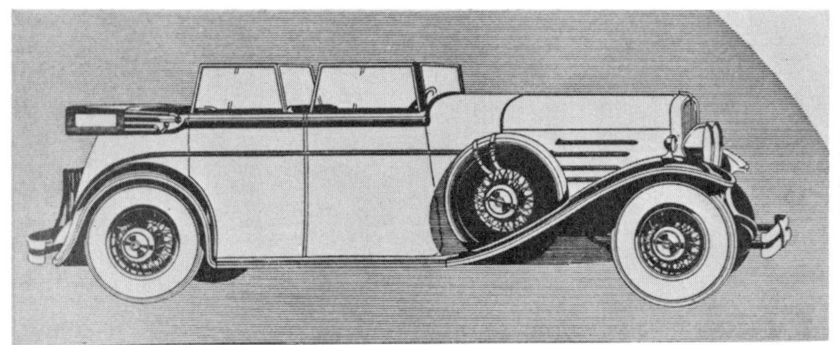

An artist's conception of the 1930 Franklin Series 145 Close Coupled Convertible Sedan. It weighed 3,750 lbs. and sold for $2,670. This was a late 1930 model with horizontal hood vents.

)31

For 1931, Franklin offered the Trans Models and the eLuxe models. Both were classed as Franklin 15s. The 74 cubic inch 6-cylinder air-cooled engine now developed)0 HP at 3100 RPM. A 20-gallon fuel supply was again ;ed as were Lockheed hydraulic brakes. The two models ;ed 5:50 x 19 and 6:50 x 19-inch tires depending on the odel. The Trans line of cars used a 125 and 132-inch heelbase depending on the style. All DeLuxe models de on the 132-inch wheelbase.

A total of 21 models were available with prices beginning $2,345 for the 4-passenger Roadster and ending at 3,345 for a 4-passenger DeLuxe Speedster. Franklin sold 881 cars for the year which kept them in 24th sales)sition.

This is a 1930 Franklin Pursuit Phaeton in the Series 145 which used the 125-inch wheelbase, weighed 3,750 lbs., and sold for $2,670. This photo was taken several years ago at a Grand Classic Car Show in California.

An early 1931 Franklin Airman Series 145 Touring Sedan. Some refer to this model as a DeLuxe. It came on the 132-inch wheelbase, weighed 4,220 lbs., and sold for $2,695.

This 1931 Franklin Pursuit came on the 125-inch wheelbase and sold for $2,495. This model wears a rare license frame with the name FRANKLIN printed above the frame. This was in the Series 15 group of cars.

An early 1931 Franklin, still referred to as a Series 14, was this example for European delivery. It had a right-hand drive. The body is by Deauville. Its owner is the Franklin authority, Tom Hubbard, of Tucson, Arizona.

Franklin

On display at a Franklin showing is this 1931 special bodied model with body by Merrimac. Note the special body molding beneath the door handles. The convertible top also is a bit unusual.

1932

Important features for the 1932 Franklins include more attractive bodies, a silent synchro-mesh transmissio with free-wheeling, Delco Remy shock absorbers adjuste by the driver, and the use of a "supercharger." Th company reported a marked increase in the car performance.

The car came in eight different body styles ranging fror a $2,345 5-passenger Coupe to $4,695 for a V-1 Limousine. All models came on the 132-inch wheelbas A 144-inch wheelbase with the V-12 came out later i the year. Tire size was 6:00 x 19 on the 6-cylinder 10 HP model (3100 RPM). The V-12 used 7:50 x 17s on th 150 HP model (3100 RPM). Fuel tanks were a 20-gallo supply for the Six. The V-12s used a 28-gallon fuel suppl Brakes were of the hydraulic type on all models.

The sales picture for the year showed Franklin movir up to 23rd place in the race. They sold 1,577 cars for th year.

A 1931 Franklin early Series 14 Sport Phaeton with body by Merrimac. This model used the 132-inch wheelbase and sold for $2,895 in base form. The wire wheels were optional equipment at extra cost. Very few were equipped like this car, with the rear mounted spare.

This was one of the attractive 1932 Franklin Six Supercharged Airman Coupes. The model was known as a Series 15, selling for $2,345. It rode on the 132-inch wheelbase.

The 1931 Franklin Series 15 Club Sedan on the DeLuxe chassis of 132 inches. This example weighed 4,160 lbs., and sold for $2,745. Its air-cooled engine developed 100 HP at 3100 RPM.

933

The news from Franklin this year was its addition of a ·ss expensive running mate in the form of the Olympic ix which came as a Sedan, Coupe, and Convertible Coupe. hese cars began at $1,385 with the Convertible bringing 1,500. Altogether, Franklin offered 16 models. The most xpensive and luxurious was the 7-passenger Limousine ›r $4,185.

Wheelbases ranged from the 118-inch Olympic to 144 ıches for the 12-cylinder models. In between was the new ranklin Airman Six on a 132-inch wheelbase. The lympics used 6:00 x 17-inch tires. Airman Six had :50 x 18s and the Twelves used 7:50 x 17s. Brake ystems on all three cars continued to be Lockheed ydraulic. The Olympic and Airman Six employed a)-gallon fuel tank and the Twelves came with a 28-gallon ıpply. The Olympic and Airman Six both carried 100 HP ıgines (3100 RPM) which were identical in all respects. he Twelves gave 150 HP at 3100 RPM. The cars, as in revious years, used air-cooled engines. The Supercharger as continued in 1933.

The sales picture by this time was not good for Franklin, the depression worsened and the public showed less ıthusiasm toward air-cooled engines. They ranked again the 24th position for the year, selling 1,180 cars which as 397 less than the previous year.

The Franklin Six displayed here was a late 1932. It was often referred to as a 1932-1933. Technically, the car was a Convertible Sedan with body by Merrimac. Very few of this special order were produced at that time.

Franklin's lowest priced car in 1933 was this Olympic coupe. It sold for the same price as the 5-passenger Sedan– $1,385. The Olympic models rode on a 118-inch wheelbase. The front seat was upholstered in whipcord, while the rumble seat was leather covered. The interior also featured a package tray behind the front seat, a pocket in the right door, and a dome light.

The 1933 Franklin Olympic Sedan was known as a Series 17. It used the same engine as the Franklin Six, developing 100 HP at 3100 RPM.

This was the most expensive 1933 Franklin in the Olympic series. It sold for $1,500. The body was the same as that used on Reo in that time, which was built by Hayes Body Co.

Franklin

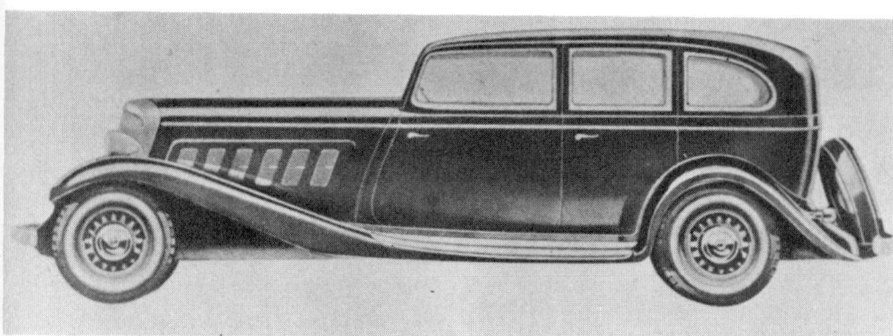

In 1933, Franklin continued with its V-12. This Limousine was a supercharged model on the 144-inch wheelbase. It weighed 5,870 lbs., and sold for $4,185. A Club Brougham and a 7-passenger Sedan also were available.

Franklin showed this 1934 Airman 6 in five body styles. This is the 5-passenger Sedan on the 132-inch wheelbase. It weighed 4,420 lbs. and was available for $2,185. This model is equipped with wire wheels and sidemounted spares which were extra equipment.

1934

For this year, Franklin brought out the new Airman and continued with the Olympic 6 and the V-12 mode
The Airman 6 had some styling to resemble the Twel
The grille took on a Vee-shaped sloping design. The wir shield took on the same slope that the grille had. T fenders all became skirted. Four body styles we available – two 7-passenger Sedans, one 6-passeng Sedan, and one Club Sedan. Prices began at $2,185 for t series. Safety glass was used throughout. All four mod used a 132-inch wheelbase and 7:00 x 17-inch tires. F capacity was a 20-gallon tank in both this series and t Olympic. Horsepower in both series was 100 at 3100 RP
The Olympic rode on 6:00 x 17-inch tires. Three mod were available at a starting price of $1,435 for the passenger Sedan. Wheelbase for this car was 119 inch It featured electrolock with the Startix switch, frame wi X-member and box construction, free-wheeling housi integral with the transmission case, and a six point pow plant support.

The Twelves were unchanged from 1933, producing 1 HP at 3100 RPM, using a 28-gallon fuel tank and riding 7:50 x 17-inch tires. Each series used Lockheed hydrau brakes.

Twelve models were offered throughout the entire li this year.

The most expensive Franklin 12 for this year was t 7-passenger Limousine selling for $3,185. Less than 1,0 cars were produced and sold. This was the last ma produced air-cooled engine the United States indus would try until Preston Tucker experimented with Tucker automobile in 1948.

Franklin's last year was 1934. This Series 18 V-12 Limousine was one of the last cars to come from the Syracuse factory. Prices were reduced drastically on these models. This example, as a 7-passenger Limousine, sold for $3,185.

The Series 18 for 1934 was what Franklin referred to this Airman 6 Club Sedan as. It weighed 4,425 lbs., and sold for $100 more than the regular Sedan at $2,285. The same fuel supply was used on this model as the Olympic– which was a 20-gallon tank.

Gardner

The Gardner, a product of independent manufacture by ardner Motor Car Co., was produced from 1919 through)31. The company headquarters were located in St. ouis, Mo.

The 1930 Gardners offered four lines of cars for the ar. The 136, 140, 150, and the front-wheel-drive car, hich was new for the year. Both 6s and 8s used Lycoming gines. The 136 models had a 70 HP 6-cylinder engine 500 RPM). These cars as well as the 140 Series had 50 x 19-inch tires. All models had 16-gallon fuel tanks d Lockheed hydraulic brakes.

The Series 140 had a 6-cylinder 90 HP engine at 3300 PM. This line used the 125-inch chassis. The 150 models veloped 126 HP at 3300 RPM. This series used 6:50 x 3-inch tires and had a 130-inch wheelbase.

The new car with the front-wheel-drive came on a 133-ch wheelbase and weighed 3,000 lbs. This model was fered only as a Sedan in 6-cylinder form developing HP at 3000 RPM. This series used 6:00 x 18-inch tires. e large wheelbase for this car was due to placing the insmission, differential, and clutch ahead of the engine ich explains the long hood line.

This model had the gearshift placed in the center of the strument panel. A long narrow battery was mounted tween the frame and crankcase on the right side of the gine. The running boards of this model were mahogany ished wood, molded with chrome strips.

A total of 25 models were available among the four ies. Prices ranged between $1,195 for a 5-passenger ries 136 Sport Sedan and $2,345 for the 7-passenger ries 150 Sedan.

Sales were so low for the year that the car was only ted among the miscellaneous as far as sales and pro-ction figures are concerned.

This was the 1930 Gardner display at the New York Auto Show, held from January 4th to the 11th, 1930. The models displayed were the Series 140 Sport Phaeton for five passengers, weighing 3,290 lbs. and selling for $1,695, and the Club Brougham Series 140 weighing 3,400 lbs. and selling for $1,645. A 7-passenger Sport Phaeton also was available for $1,945 in the 140 Series.

A Series 150 Gardner for 1930 was offered on the 130-inch wheelbase in 5 and 7-passenger models. This example happens to be a 7-passenger model, which weighed 4,210 lbs. and sold for $2,345.

A side view of the 6-cylinder Lycoming engine as used in the 1930 Front-Wheel-Drive Gardner. Note the position of the battery placed between the frame and crankcase, and the unusual mounting of the belt-driven fan.

New for 1930 was Gardner's Front-Wheel-Drive model which only came as a sedan on the 133-inch wheelbase chassis. This was a 6-cylinder car developing 80 HP at 3000 RPM. It weighed 3,000 lbs. and sold for $2,045.

Gardner

This Series 148 Gardner for 1931 was the Phaeton, on a 125-inch wheelbase. It only was available as a 5-passenger model weighing 3,290 lbs. The model sold for $1,845 which was a $150 increase over the 1930 model.

A 1931 Gardner Series 158 Sedan. For the final year no 7-passenger models were produced. This is just a 5-passenger version weighing 3,890 lbs. and selling for $2,170.

Appearing more deluxe than most Gardners for 1931 is this Series 148 Sedan on a 125-inch wheelbase and weighing 3,500 lbs. The sidemount tire equipment and wire wheels were optional at extra cost. In base form this model sold for $1,845.

1931

The 1931 Gardner was assembled chiefly from parts o other manufacturers. 1931 was the final year o production.

The series designations for this year were 136, 148, 158 and the front-wheel-drive 4-door Sedan. Each series use Lycoming engines. The 136 had a 70 HP 6-cylinder engine a 122-inch wheelbase, and used 5:50 x 19-inch tire The 148 used an 8-cylinder engine developing 100 H at 3300 RPM. It used the same tire size as the 136s. Th wheelbase was 125 inches.

Gardner 158 models had 126 HP 8-cylinder engines a 3300 RPM. They used 6:50 x 18-inch tires and had 130-inch wheelbase. All models had 16-gallon fuel tank Gardners used hydraulic brakes in each series.

The front-wheel-drive Gardner, continued from 1930 were the same cars that were offered in that year. The developed 80 HP at 3000 RPM from the 6-cylinde engine. The wheelbase was 133 inches.

Gardners sold between $1,270 for a Series 13 5-passenger Sport Sedan and $2,770 for the Series 15 5-passenger Sedan.

Gardner made use of the funeral and ambulance trad for the year as its 8-cylinder engine performed exceptio ally well, especially for low speed driving. The Lycomir engine was also noted for its responsiveness to quic acceleration when required.

The final year of production was 1931 for passeng car business. However, the company did continue fc one more year building ambulances and hearses whic came with an 85 HP V-8 engine.

Production and sales figures were too low to be recorde They ranked among the miscellaneous makes for the yea

The 1931 Gardner Series 148 with the Lycoming 8-cylinder engine was priced from $1,795 to $1,845. This model wears the optional extra cost stone guard protector over its radiator grille. The cloth cover over the sidemount tire was often furnished by the dealer with the inscription of his dealership for advertising purposes as this model appears to have.

The last of the Gardners was this 1931 Front-Wheel-Drive model. It appears to have been identical to the 1930 cars. Possibly these were just carryovers from 1930, retitled as 1931 vehicles.

Graham

The Graham was a product of the Graham Motors ɔrp. of Detroit. The company had been producing cars ıce 1927. Production ended in early 1941 with the troduction of the 1941 model. The title of Graham-ıige was discontinued in 1929, and was used for later ıck production only.

Graham had a complete line of cars for 1930 ranging ɔm a Standard 6 to the Custom 8 "137." The Standard offered a 66 HP, 3200 RPM car in 8 body styles. This ɔdel had a 115-inch wheelbase, and rode on 5:25 x 19-ɔh tires. Next in the line was the Graham Special 6 ıich developed 76 HP at 3400 RPM. This model was on e same wheelbase but used 6:00 x 19-inch tires. Both ies had 12½-gallon fuel tanks.

Graham's big news for the year was the Standard and ecial 8 moedls. These cars came with a 298.6 cubic inch gine which developed 100 HP at 3400 RPM. They ered either a three or four-speed transmission as tional equipment. The gear ratio was 4:45 or 3:90. The eelbase measured 122 inches. Tire size was 6:00 x inches.

n addition to these 8s were the Custom 8 127 and stom 8 137 models which employed wheelbases of that gth. Both Custom Series had 120 HP engines (at 3200 M). The tire size was 6:50 x 19 inches. The fuel acities in all 8-cylinder cars was 18½-gallons. All hams used Lockheed hydraulic brakes.

he Graham bodies were redesigned so that practically wood parts formerly held by screws, were now held by ts and bolts easily placed and readily reached by ning back the interior trim fabric. All Graham bodies the front section made of steel.

ll 1930 Grahams made their debut wearing a new iator contour. It was deeper, with a curved top and tom core lines which came forward to a slight point. total of 36 models were available ranging from a ndard 2-passenger Coupe for $1,350 going up to the tom 8 Limousine for 7 at $1,975. Graham sold 560 vehicles for the year which put them in the h sales position.

Graham's 1930 Standard Six Coupe in 2-passenger style was the lowest priced model for the year. It sold for $1,350. This car weighed 2,915 lbs. and used the 115-inch chassis. Eight models of the Standard Six were available.

This was the 1930 Graham Special Six 4-door sedan, on display in a Graham agency. The car is showing the advantages of having safety plate glass against plain plate glass. "It shatters but won't splinter" is what the display cards tell prospective customers. The Special Six came in two models only–Coupe and Sedan, selling for $1,395 and $1,410 respectively.

A late model introduction for the 1930 Graham line was this Special Eight Convertible Sedan. This model came on a 122-inch wheelbase. There were four body styles in the eries. The Convertible Sedan weighed 3,700 lbs. and sold or $1,725.

An early 1930 Graham dealership display room. Some historians would actually refer to these models as late 1929 cars as they were referred to as Graham Paige. The Graham Paige title wasn't used on true 1930 examples.

Graham

The most popular model of the 1930 Special Eight Grahams was the 4-door Sedan. The Special Eights developed 100 HP at 3400 RPM. The company lowered the price on this series to entice more upper middle class families into buying a Special Eight model. This example sold for $1,595. Special Eights had vent panels or doors on the hood, as this model shows, while the Sixes had traditional louvers on side panels.

Available in both Standard and Special Six models was the 1931 Graham Coupe. The Standard model sold for $1,145, which was quite a drop from the previous year, and the Special model was priced at $1,185.

Apparently being put into demonstrator use for 1931, from the looks of the Dealer License plate for that year, is this Special Six Sedan, also called the Prosperity Six Sedan. This example came on a 115-inch wheelbase, weighed 3,095 lbs. and carried a lower price tag than its 1930 counterpart. It sold for $1,375 but did not include the wire wheels and sidemount options. It wears the single bar bumper where early examples had double bars. This is a late model.

1931

Graham's big news for the year was the Special Eigh This model replaced the Special and Standard Eights 1930. It used a 248 cubic inch engine that develope 85 HP at 3400 RPM. The model had a five main beari crankshaft. It used an 18-gallon fuel tank like the Custo Eight. The tire size was 6:00 x 17 and the model used 120-inch wheelbase.

The Graham Standard and Special 6 had a 76 HP engi (at 3400 RPM) and a 12½-gallon fuel tank. These tw series both used 5:50 x 18-inch tires. The wheelba consisted again of 115 inches for both models.

The Custom Eight came with the 100 HP engine. T tire size was 6:50 x 18, and they rode on a 134-in wheelbase.

All models except for the Standard Six used a four-spe transmission with a quiet helical third and a sile synchro-mesh shift to third and fourth gear.

A total of 13 models were available ranging in pri from $1,145 for the Standard 2-passenger Coupe $1,800 for the Graham Custom 8 Limousine for passengers.

Graham dropped many of its body styles for 1931 the public just wasn't there for many of the offeri that were available in 1930. The company placed in 19 position from the sale of over 15,000 vehicles this ye

The 1931 Graham Roadster was available only as a Standard Six model. It weighed 2,870 lbs. and sold for $1,160. The sidemounts, wire wheels and luggage rack were extra.

The close coupled 1931 Graham Town Sedan could be ordered in either a Standard or Special Six model. Exteriors were virtually the same but the interiors were more plush in the Special models. Prices were $1,200 for Standard models and $1,275 for the Special Town Sedan. This model is equipped with the regular artillery wheels.

932

For 1932, the Graham Blue Streak Series was considered ıe style pace-setter for the year. Graham retained its odels of 1931 but also had the new Eight. The Eights ere where the interest was shown. Body lines for the mes were a bit unusual, but nothing as extreme as in 938. The most interesting feature, mechanically speaking, as the whole new frame design with the springs mounted ıtside the side rails. The advantages were lowness and eater stability.

Prices went from $765 for a 6-cylinder, 2-passenger oupe to $1,170 for the 8-cylinder Convertible Coupe. The Sixes had 5:50 x 17-inch tires while the Eights ere equipped with 6:00 x 17-inch tires. The Six had a) HP engine at 3200 RPM, and the Eight had 90 HP 3400 RPM.

Fuel capacity for the Six was 12½ gallons – the Eight ıd an 18-gallon gasoline supply. Both series came ıuipped with Lockheed hydraulic brakes. The car's lines owed in a pleasing unbroken sweep from front to rear. ıe radiator grille curved rearward from a Vee point until met the molding along the top edge of the hood. The lash aprons blended smoothly into the fenders. The r's headlamps contoured well with the radiator shell ıd fender curves. The headlamps were lacquered to ırmonize with the body except for a rim around the edge the headlight which was chromium plated.

Saleswise, the company sold 8,001 cars, which placed in 17th position for the year.

The 1931 Graham Six Sedan with rear mounted spare was available in both Standard and Special models. The wooden artillery wheels were standard equipment; however, many buyers preferred the optional at extra cost wire wheels. This car sold for $1,175 in the Standard style and $1,250 for the Special model.

Graham's top of the line for 1931 was this Custom 7-passenger Sedan called the Eight Thirty-four. This model used the 134-inch wheelbase and 8-cylinder 100 HP engine. It sold for $1,800. The sidemounted spares allowed space for the rear luggage rack. Sidemounts, rack, and wire wheels were all options.

The DeLuxe version of the Blue Streak 8-cylinder Graham for 1932 is this sidemounted model with skirted fenders that sold for $1,120. This model weighed 3,175 lbs. and, in spite of the depression, was the most popular Graham for the year. Graham is credited with popularizing skirted fenders.

This is considered the second series Graham for 1932. It carried the title of Blue Streak models. This 4-door sedan in Standard 8 form sold for $1,045. It had a 123-inch wheelbase. The designer of the Blue Streak models was Amos Northrup.

Graham

Not too popular with buyers at the bottom of the depression was this 8-cylinder 1932 Graham DeLuxe Convertible Coupe. The car weighed 3,234 lbs. and was available only in the deluxe line for $1,170. It was the most expensive Graham.

Graham's Custom 8 Sedan for 1933 came on a 123-inch wheelbase and sold for $125 less than its 1932 running mate. The price was $995 and it weighed 3,182 lbs. The sidemount tire equipment was optional at extra cost, but even with the public being concerned over money matters, most all Custom 8 models were so equipped.

1933

For 1933, Graham offered two Eights and a Six. Tl Standard Six and Standard Eight were referred to as tl new chassis models. The latter had the identical engine the Custom Eight which was continued from the 19: model run. With a different manifold and carburetio the horsepower for the Six was increased to 85 while tl Eights went up to 95 at 3400 RPM. An aluminum cylind head permitted the compression ratio of 6.5:1 witho requiring the use of premium fuel.

Body lines were rounded out a little to make a st more graceful car. The front bumper was split, havi two graceful plated pieces which blended well to recei the slope to the radiator grille. Chrome strips were us along the running boards, going forward along the fro fenders and curving slightly up the rear fender.

Interiors of the cars were more plush than ever befo The dash gauges were neatly arranged within the spe ometer housing. Grouped in this case were the odomet ammeter, oil pressure gauge, gasoline gauge, a thermometer. The Graham Standard 8 and Custom were the same except in the fancier trim departme where the Custom 8 did shine.

Tire size of the Standard 6 was 5:50 x 17, while Eights used 6:00 x 17s. Brakes were Lockheed hydrau Fuel capacity for each series was the same, 18 gallo

Body styles numbered eleven, ranging from the Stand 6 2-passenger Coupe for $745 to the Custom 8 Sedan $995.

Graham climbed the ladder two spots from 1932. T year saw 9,069 cars sold giving them 15th position the industry.

With a split bumper and a chrome strip along the running board, it was easy to tell the difference between a 1932 and a 1933 Graham model. This is the Standard 8 Convertible Coupe selling for $925. It was only available in the Standard 6 or Standard 8 for the year. The wheelbase measured 123 inches for 8-cylinder cars.

The 1933 Graham Blue Streak continued into the new year with very little change except for the split front bumper as shown in the view of this model. Also, it was now available in 6-cylinder form on a 113-inch wheelbase. Graham claimed in their ads that the new car was wider than it was high. This 6-cylinder sedan sold for $795.

·34

For 1934, Graham offered four series, the Standard 6, ›Luxe 6, Standard 8, and the Custom 8.

The big news from Graham was its advanced super-arger for the Custom 8 only. The new device offered 5 HP at 4000 RPM which was unheard of on any other r in this price class. All 8-cylinder cars had 1/8-inch ger valves. The Standard 8 used an updraft carburetor. ch model used the push-button starter on the dash panel. The 6-cylinder cars came with an 85 HP engine at 00 RPM and the Standard 8 had a 95 HP engine at 00 RPM. Sixes used 6:25 x 16-inch tires. Standard 8 had 6:50 x 16s and Custom 8 employed 7:00 x 16s. The es used a 116-inch wheelbase while both Eights came the 123-inch version.

All series used an 18-gallon fuel supply. Lockheed draulic brakes were used in each series. Twenty models re available. Prices began at $695 for the 2-passenger upe up to $1,025 for a supercharged Custom 8 Sedan. A total of 11,430 units were sold, giving Graham the nor of 14th position.

The 1934 Graham Standard 6 Convertible Coupe with the 116-inch wheelbase. This model sold for $745 with a seating capacity for four. Graham claimed the highest compression ratio of any stock car that used regular fuels at that time.

Graham's lowest priced car for 1934 happened to be this Standard 6 Business Coupe for 2 passengers. It sold for $695. It was also available with the rumble seat option for $20 more.

This was one of Graham's first sedans to be offered with a built-in trunk. The model is a DeLuxe 6 which sold for $810 with the sidemounted wheel equipment. Many Grahams at that time offered two-tone paint combinations. This model appears to be one of them.

The instrument board of the 1934 Graham was pleasing but simple. All dials were located directly in front of the driver. Next to the dials were three aluminum door panels. The windshield ventilation was operated by the center window crank.

A 1934 Auto Show scene shows the 1934 Graham DeLuxe 6 on display. This model carried a finer array of interior appointments than the Standard 6 models. It sold for $750. Note the De Soto Airflow Sedan in the background.

Graham

For 1935, Graham introduced this new model on the 111-inch wheelbase. It was called the Graham 6 and came in two versions–the 2-door Sedan for $625, shown here, and a 4-door style.

New for 1935 was this Graham 6 Sedan which used a 60 HP engine at 3500 RPM. This little car had a built-in luggage compartment behind the rear seat. It sold well for $640. The rear design showed strong European influence.

This was the 1935 Graham Six in the First Series. This model continued the fresh lines Graham had offered for the past three years, only rounding out the streamlined graceful appearance the car already had. It came in the Special 6 Series on the 116-inch wheelbase and sold for $810 as it did the previous year.

This is the 1935 Graham Special 6 sedan in fastback styling. It sold for $790. It was also available as a Graham 8 and a Supercharged 8 on the 123-inch wheelbase.

1935

For this model run, Graham introduced a brand ne Six and offered it in the lowest price range. The moc came on a 111-inch wheelbase and was offered in bo 5-passenger Sedan and 2-door Sedan. Wheel and tire si consisted of 5:25 x 17 and developed 60 HP at 3500 RP. This series only used Bendix hydraulic brakes. The oth models came with Lockheed hydraulic systems. The lo priced car offered a 12-gallon fuel tank.

In addition to this car, the company offered the Spec Six at 85 HP (3400 RPM). The Graham Eight came witl 95 HP engine at the same RPM and the supercharg Eight developed 140 HP at 4000 RPM.

The Special Six used 6:00 x 17-inch tires and the t Eights came with 6:50 x 16s and 7:00 x 16s in that ord Special Six used a 116-inch wheelbase, an 18-gallon tai and was offered in four body styles. The Graham Ei was sold in four models and used a 123-inch wheelba and the same fuel supply as the Special Six. This also v employed in the Supercharged version. The Supercharg models had the same body dimensions as the regu 8-cylinder line, but differed with its increased power fr the charger. This was the last year for the 8-cylinder c

Prices varied from $625 for the 111-inch car to $1,0 for the Supercharged Custom Eight Sedan. The three series came equipped with aluminum cylinder heads. small series used an iron alloy head. All models had do draft carburetors for the first time.

The year saw Graham take a 16th position in sales w 15,965 cars produced.

A 1935 Graham 8 rumble seat coupe for four was available for $895. In the Supercharged version it sold for $1,010. Very few Supercharged models were produced in 1935, however. Vent windows were standard equipment.

The 1935 Graham 8 and Supercharged 8 were the same car until the hood was raised. A Supercharged Convertible Coupe like this model sold for $1,015. Very few buyers were there to purchase a car of this quality, however. The 8-cylinder models were discontinued at the end of the 1935 model run.

36

Gone was the Graham Eight. The company now offered ree Sixes, one with a supercharger that was quite nilar to what was available on the previous Eight. The low price line was called the Crusader Six, Series 80, the 111-inch wheelbase, yielding 70 HP at 3500 RPM, th a 12-gallon fuel supply. Brakes were hydraulic. These rs used 5:25 x 17-inch tires.

Next in the line was the Cavalier, Series 90, using an HP engine with an RPM rating of 3300. These models, e the top of the line, used a 15-gallon fuel supply and draulic brakes. Tire size was 6:00 x 16.

The Supercharger, Series 110, was practically the same r as the Series 90 except the Supercharged version veloped 112 HP at 4000 RPM. These models carried a e of 6:25 x 16. The wheelbases of the Series 90 and 110 re 115 inches. These two models used pistons of aluminum alloy and were equipped to handle an overdrive ich reduced engine speed 30% above 45 MPH.

Models available numbered ten, ranging from a $640 usader 2-door Touring Sedan to $895 for a Supercharged 0 4-door Touring Sedan. The company held the 16th les Spot for 1936, and sold 16,439 cars during the del run.

Four-Door Touring Sedan with Trunk

The Crusader Six, which was the Series 80 for 1936, came only in the 2-door and 4-door Touring Sedans shown here. The 2-door model was Graham's lowest priced car for the year, selling at $640.

Three-Passenger Coupe with Rumble Seat

The middle series for Graham in 1936 were the Cavalier models, commonly called Series 90 cars. These were quite similar to the most expensive models for the year except the interiors were not as elaborate and the Supercharger was not available. The 3-passenger coupe with rumble seat sold for $710 and the 4-door model brought a price of $750. This was a major change year for Graham.

Graham offered quite a facelifting on the 1936 models, with their Hayes-built bodies. This example was the Supercharged 2-door sedan in the Series 110. It developed 112 HP at 4000 RPM. The price for this model was $850. Not many 2-door sedans were sold with the Supercharger option.

A sleek looking coupe was offered by Graham in 1937. This example happens to be the Cavalier 6 Business Coupe for three. It sold for $725. A Sport Coupe was available also for five passengers at $775. Graham still retained the trumpet horns under the headlamps on its 1937 models.

Graham

This was Graham's Cavalier Six-95 Sedan for 1937. A similar car to this attained 23.95 MPG during the Gilmore Economy Run for the year and was the winner in its class. This Touring Sedan was available for $775, and in deluxe fashion with a fancier interior, sold for $805.

A rare model was this 1937 Graham Supercharger Series 116 2-door sedan. This car was available either as a fastback or in this hump back version. This model sold for $895. It was also available with dual sidemounts.

1937

The 1937 Graham claimed instantaneous lubrication c the six-cylinder walls, especially for cold weather startin; This was the first device ever to lubricate the pistons wit the first movement of the starting engine, which prevente scuffing or abrasive wear.

Graham offered four series: Crusader Six "85," Cavali Six "95," Supercharger Six "116," and the Custo Supercharger Six "120."

The Crusader Series used the 70 HP 6-cylinder engi (at 3500 RPM), Crusaders rode on a 111-inch wheelba and used 6:00 x 16-inch tires like the Cavalier and regul Supercharged models. This series used a 12-gallon fu tank.

All Cavalier cars came with a 6-cylinder 85 HP engi (at 3300 RPM). This series used a 15-gallon gasoli supply and a 116-inch wheelbase.

The 6-cylinder "116" Supercharged Graham develop 106 HP at 4000 RPM. It also used a 15-gallon gasoli tank and the same 116-inch wheelbase.

The top of the line was the "120" Custom Supercharg using a 116 HP 6-cylinder engine (at 4000 RPM). The cars had 6:25 x 16-inch tires and were on 116 and 12 inch wheelbase chassis.

Graham used the cars in the California Gilmore Econon Runs at this time and always did very well in their cla

For the year, 20 models were available, ranging from $595 Crusader Six Sedan up to the Custom Supercharg "120" Trunk Sedan for $1,095.

Graham placed 17th for the model run by selli 13,987 automobiles.

Graham's most expensive line for 1937 included this 5-passenger Touring Sedan in the Custom Supercharger Six Series 120. The sidemount equipment was additional and very few were ever built with it. This model sold for $1,025 in basic form.

Very few 1937 Graham Supercharged Six Series 120 Convertible Coupes were built. It is felt fewer than 100 were produced before Graham changed its body dies for the 1938 line of cars. This model sold for $1,015.

38

Just looking at a 1938 Graham made one think some-ing new was going on. The public either felt they loved or they had an intense dislike for it right from the ırt. The grille and fenders more or less leaned forward ring the effect of speed. The headlamp lenses were of a uare style placed at the forward edges of the front ıders. A stainless steel belt molding was mounted from e front of the grille nose to the trunk side panels. rakish rear fender shield concealed the rear wheels. e tail lamps were placed at the upper part of the rear e panels above the belt molding. There was less chance breakage, being placed at this position.

Two series were available, the Special 6 with a 90 HP gine (at 3600 RPM) and 6:00 x 16-inch tires, and the percharged Six version, yielding 116 HP at 4000 RPM. ese models carried 6:50 x 16-inch tires. Other than the percharger, they carried the same options and used the ne 120-inch wheelbase and 16-gallon fuel supply. thin the Supercharger model was a "dolled up" Custom percharger, equipped with items ordinarily classed as tra equipment. They included air foam cushions, peting front and rear, electric clock, special plastic ıjo steering wheel, and a deluxe type of upholstery. \ device optional for each model was the short con-ıient gearshift lever mounted at the base of the dash, uum mechanism to help take over in the shifting of ırs.

All series offered three models, Business Coupe for 3, mbination Coupe for 6, and Sedan for 6. Prices ranged ween $940 in Special 6 form to $1,225 for a Custom lan. Graham placed 17th for sales, selling 4,139 units its model run.

This was the 1938 Graham Coupe. It was the lowest priced car available from Graham in that model run. As a Special 6 it sold for $940. It also came as a Supercharger 6-97 for $1,125 and as a Custom Supercharger 6-97 for $1,200.

The 1938 Graham Special 4-door Touring Sedan introduced an entirely new car. Their advertising played with the descriptive title of "Spirit of Motion." These new cars introduced hidden door hinges, a built-in trunk, and standard equipment fender skirts. This model sold for $985. It was a very radical car for the era.

The most expensive model Graham offered for 1938 was the Custom Supercharger 4-door Touring Sedan. This series was offered for $1,225 and was well equipped with many items classed as accessories on other makes.

The lowest priced model Graham offered in 1939 was this Special Six-96 Combination Coupe. It sold for $940. The customer had a choice of the gearshift being mounted in one of three places–on the floor, steering column or a dash-mounted device.

Basically, the 1939 Graham was the same car as the company offered in 1938. Changes included the addition of rubber skuff shields on the rear fenders and the enclosed running boards under the doors. This model is the Special Six-96 Custom Sedan for $1,095.

Graham

Graham even offered a custom bodied Town car in 1939. This model had a Derham body with a genuine leather top and sliding roof compartment for the chauffeur. The fender skirts were standard equipment just as on the other Grahams from 1938 through 1940.

1939

The 1939 Graham was practically the same car as w offered the previous year. Few appearance changes we made. The running boards were enclosed under the doo The customer had a choice of the gearshift being plac on the steering column (rather than on the dashboa mount) or still placed on the floorboard. The upholste combinations were of a better grade of cloth.

The dashboard came in a plastic solid color trim a round control knobs in the Custom models, and marbl plastic with flat knobs in the Special Series. Both Custo and Specials had the radio and speaker placed in the cen of the dashboard. The push button radio was classed an accessory.

The Graham Special was offered with a 6-cylin 90 HP engine (at 3600 RPM). However, it also came a Custom Special with 90 HP or with the 116 HP Sup charger. The top car of the line had a 116 HP engine 4000 RPM. This was the Custom Supercharger.

All Specials used 6:00 x 16-inch tires and the Sup charged versions used 6:25 x 16s. The fuel supply each series was a 16-gallon tank. The wheelbase w 120 inches for each model.

The body styles amounted to three types with a s series within each style if a customer wished a m expensive interior. The lowest priced model consisted the Special Combination Coupe for $940. The Custo Supercharged Sedan for five was listed at $1,225.

The company placed in 19th position with the sale 3,876 cars for the calendar run.

This 1940 Graham sedan was available in the Special line as a DeLuxe for $993 and as a Custom for $1,130. The same car was also available in the Supercharger line as a DeLuxe for $1,130. The top sedan sold for $1,268 as a Supercharged Custom model.

Graham catalogued this convertible coupe as a new model for the 1940 model run. Whether any were ever built is not known. The combination coupe for 1940 was offered at $993 in the Special line and ranged upward to $1,268 for the Custom Supercharged model–the same as the 4-door sedan. In later years, all 1938 to 1940 models became known as "shark nosed" Grahams. However, the unique and radical styling proved to be too advanced for the era, and by 1940 the company was in financial trouble.

The lower priced 1940 Grahams were the Clipper series in the mid-season offering. The sedan sold for $925. It used a 6-cylinder engine of 85 HP at 3800 RPM. The Clipper Convertible was extremely rare. Some records indicate fewer than 40 were built; others claim it was only catalogued and never produced. The Hollywood line also was to have a Convertible Coupe but records don't say how many if any, were ever built. Possibly the figure of 40 cars might refer to both series.

)40

For 1940 the company continued to produce the Special The Supercharger 6 was the new name for the Custom odels of 1939. Both series were practically the same as e previous year. The Carter carburetor of 1939 was placed with the Marvel unit on 1940 models. The horse-)wer on the Specials was increased from 90 to 93 at 300 RPM. The supercharged series now had 120 HP at)00 RPM. The only other real change was an increase in ice of approximately $35 per car.

In addition to these two Series a mid-year model was troduced. This was the car that used the Cord body es bought from the defunct Hupp Motor Co. This eries came in two versions. The Graham Clipper, which as the less expensive model, had a 199 cubic inch engine at developed 84 HP at 3800 RPM. The fuel supply was e same in each Series – 14½ gallons. The more expensive ersion to the Clipper was the Graham Hollywood, which so was a more popular car with its supercharged 120 HP igine at 4000 RPM. This engine had 217.8 cubic inches ith a bore and stroke of 3¼ x 4-3/8 inches. The tire size the Hollywood models was 6:25 x 16 while the Clippers sed 6:00 x 16-inch tires.

Prices ranged from $925 for the newly introduced raham Clipper Sedan to $1,268 for either the Custom edan or the Hollywood Sedan. A total of 16 models ere available among the Specials, Supercharger 6, Clipper id Hollywood models. Graham sold only 1,856 cars for e model run, which placed them in 19th position.

1941

The Graham company ceased production during the middle of the year.

The only models offered for 1941 were the Clipper and the Hollywood. The Clipper was the less expensive car using a 199 cubic inch engine that developed 85 HP at 3800 RPM. The Hollywood used the Supercharger device and had a 217.8 cubic inch engine that gave 120 HP at 4000 RPM. Both models used a 14½-gallon fuel tank. The Clipper had a 6:00 x 16-inch size tire and 6:25 x 16s were used on the Hollywoods.

A total of 4 models in Convertible and Sedan form were available in the two series. Prices ranged from $925 for the Clipper Sedan to $1,268 for a Hollywood model with Supercharger equipment. The only appearance difference offered between the 1940 and 1941 models were two-tone paint options at no additional cost if the buyer preferred. So few cars were sold in 1941 that calendar year sales are not available.

This Graham Hollywood is recorded as being a 1941 model. Actually, it may very well have been a 1940 as appearance-wise there wasn't any difference. The 1941 cars offered two-tone paint combinations which was their one big difference. This car, however, has no rear fender gravel shields as do the other Clipper and Hollywood models. It sold for $1,268 again in 1941.

This 1941 Graham Hollywood Sedan was one of the last cars to come off the line as the company ceased production in mid-1941. This car wears the accessory factory approved grille guard and also has a side cowl mounted antenna. Following the demise of Cord, the 810 Series body dies were modified slightly and used by both Graham and Hupmobile as their "swan song" models. Thus, three great makes of cars all faded from the American scene displaying one of the most unique and beautiful body designs ever to roll from American assembly lines.

Whether it was a prototype or one of the few Graham Convertibles built for 1940-41, it's mighty sharp looking, with the Cord body that it displays. This model wears different front bumper guard equipment from the other Clipper and Hollywood models. Possibly, these were factory accessory guards. Note the Convertible has its windshield wipers mounted at the base of the windshield while sedans used the Cord version of mounting at the roof over the windshield.

Hudson

A 1930 Hudson Landau Brougham was available on the 126-inch chassis for $1,195. The wooden artillery wheels were standard equipment on all Hudsons for 1930.

Hudson was a product of the Hudson Motor Car Co with headquarters in Detroit. The car was produced fror 1909 through 1957. Its last years of production were i merger with Nash. From 1955 it was part of America Motors.

The Hudson Eight was introduced to replace the Supe Six in 1930. The new car was called the Great Eight. I was offered in 9 models. The car came with a new body hood, and radiator of well designed proportions. The bi event at Hudson was the introduction of the 2-door Su Sedan. This car was a 5-passenger open model with foldin front seats for entrance and exit of the rear seat passenger. It resembled the early Victoria type body styles of sever manufacturers which followed shortly, among them bein Ford, Chrysler, and Chevrolet.

The Great Eight developed 80 HP at 3600 RPM. Th cars came on two wheelbases of 119 and 126 inches. Th fuel supply was a 16-gallon tank. All models used Bendi mechanical brakes.

Prices ranged from $875 for the 2-passenger Coupe t $1,475 for the 7-passenger Limousine. Hudson sol 113,898 cars, combined with Essex, placing them in 4t position for the calendar year.

This was Hudson's 1930 Sport Roadster, referred to as the Model T. It was available only on the 119-inch wheelbase. These 8-cylinder models suffered in sales as the depression took its grips on the company. This car sold for $995.

This was Hudson's lowest priced sedan for 1930. It was an 8-cylinder car on a 119-inch wheelbase, referred to as the Standard Sedan. It sold for $995. Sidemount equipment was optional at extra cost.

Hudson's Town Sedan for 1930 came on the 126-inch wheelbase. It was known as the Model U and sold for $1,145. A similar model attained 25.5 MPG in an economy run of 480 miles from Wellington to New Plymouth, New Zealand, during that year.

1931

The new model displayed a more attractive sturdier ody with new frame and 1/8-inch larger bore.

The only model was an 8-cylinder which developed 7 HP at 3600 RPM. The fuel supply was a 16-gallon tank. he tire size used was 5:50 x 18 and the wheelbases were 19 inches and 126 inches.

A total of 13 models were available, between $875 for ne 2-passenger Coupe and $1,450 for a 7-passenger amily Sedan. The 126-inch cars had adjustable front and ear seats and assist cords as standard equipment.

Hudson and Essex sold 57,825 cars in the calendar year hich gave them the 7th sales position.

In 1930 Hudson built this special model, a Convertible Sedan with a Le Baron body. The wheelbase was 119 inches. It was referred to as the Great 8 Series and sold for $1,325. Note the adjustable sun visor over the windshield. Wire wheels were standard on this special built model only.

This was Hudson's 1931 Family Sedan, which was a 7-passenger model on a 126-inch chassis. The device at the bottom of the radiator grille is the horn. This 8-cylinder model developed 87 HP at 3600 RPM. It sold for $1,450.

Hudson offered two coupes in 1931 on the 119-inch chassis. This one was the 2-passenger version that sold for $875. The 4-passenger model with rumble seat sold for $925. Wire wheels were now standard equipment. The whitewalls were a rare piece of equipment on middle priced cars of that era. Note the chrome spare tire cover.

A 1931 Hudson 8 Club Brougham, with the landau irons on the rear quarter panels and a canvas roof, made a very special looking sedan. This sedan wears the new wire wheels which were classed as standard equipment. The whitewall tires and sidemount equipment were accessories. In base form it sold for $1,195.

Hudson

The 1931 Hudson Touring Sedan sold for $1,495. It had a 126-inch chassis. This model featured adjustable front and rear seats along with pull straps and assist cords which were available on all Hudsons with the 126-inch wheelbase for 1931. Note the unusual "X-braced" horn mounting.

1932

For 1932, Hudson offered far more attractive bodie and more luxurious interiors, as did the little sister, Essex Greater power, new double drop frames with X-bracing anti-flood choke, intake silencer, adjustable shocks fron the dash, silent synchro-mesh transmission, and free wheeling were but a few of the more flattering qualities LIke the Essex, Hudson shared the Frank Spring stylin department.

Hudson was only built as an 8-cylinder car in 1932 leaving the Six to the Essex. Thirteen body styles wer available. Prices ranged from $995 for a 2-passenger Coup up to $1,595 for the 7-passenger Sedan. All models wer on a 119-inch wheelbase, except for the Suburban an Special Sedan which shared the 126-inch wheelbase, an the Touring Sedan, Club Sedan, Brougham, and 7 passenger Sedan which came on a new 132-inch wheelbase These cars rode on 6:00 x 17-inch tires except for th 132-inch models which were on 6:50 x 17-inch tires. A cars carried a 101 HP engine (3600 RPM). They wer supplied by a 16-gallon tank.

With all these improvements, sales weren't as good as ha been shown the previous year. Delivered units amounte to 8,192 cars. Hudson slipped from its 1931 sales positio but made up for it with the Essex sales. Combined sale from the two cars amounted to 57,550 units which gav them the 4th sales position.

A custom model offered by Hudson in 1931 was this Special Convertible Sedan with a Murphy body. It sold poorly as people just didn't have the money to spend for expensive vehicles. In addition to this model, the Phaeton body style was also available with a body by Biddle-Smart. Note the accessory Wood-lites that this Convertible Sedan wears. It also has a 1932 style grille.

This 1932 Hudson 8 Brougham Sedan was classed as one of the more expensive models for the year. It rode on a 132-inch wheelbase and sold for $1,495. The sidemount equipment was optional at extra cost but most cars in this series came with it. It had brilliant exterior colors, complemented with interiors in pastel shades. The hardware appointments were in silver and ivory.

The 1932 Hudson 8 Coupe with the rumble seat made this a compact 4-passenger car. It was also available as a 2-passenger trunk coupe. The models sold for $995 and $1,045, respectively. Both were on the 119-inch wheelbase chassis.

933

The big news was a new Hudson Super Six. The Eight vas continued, showing improvements in the body lines nd mechanical details. All series showed off the popular kirted front fenders and Vee-shaped grilles. Hudson came vith a Bendix vacuum-operated automatic clutch control s standard equipment. On the 8-cylinder cars, a vacuum-perated power brake unit also was a regular item. Bendix wo-shoe, duo-servo brakes were used on all models.

Horsepower was listed as 73 for the Super Six (3200 RPM), but an optional ratio gave seven more horsepower t 3600 RPM.

The Hudson Eight was able to produce 101 HP at 600 RPM when equipped with the regular 5.8:1 ratio ead, or 110 HP at 7:1 compression.

The Super Six was equipped with 5:25 x 18-inch tires nd the Eight wore 6:00 x 17s. Wheelbase on the Super ix was 113 inches for all models while the Eight came s a 119-incher in four models and 132 inches on the emaining five models. All cars carried mechanical brakes, nd used a 16-gallon fuel supply.

Prices varied from $995 for a Super Six Coupe to $1,595 or the 7-passenger 132-inch Hudson Eight Sedan. Alto-ether, fifteen models were available. The company fell to th place, selling 40,982 automobiles. Those calendar ear sales are combined with Essex-Terraplane.

A 1932 Hudson 8 Pacemaker Special Sedan is shown with optional sidemount equipment, at extra cost, and whitewalls on the wooden artillery wheels. Note the parking lamps are of the same contour as the headlamps, which employ the famous Hudson triangle design. It also employs the outside windshield visor which later models didn't have. This model sold for $1,445.

Coming on a 113-inch wheelbase for 1933 was the Hudson Super Six series. This 4-door sedan sold well for $1,025. All 1933 Hudsons had skirted fenders for the first time. The Super Six line offered only side vents in the hood while the 8-cylinder models used ventilating doors. Unlike the 2-door sedan, this car has cowl parking lights.

The 1932 Hudson 8 Sedan in 7-passenger style was the top car of the year and also brought the highest price of $1,595. This model, like all 1932 Hudsons, carried the Frank Spring styling.

Hudson's lowest priced Coach for 1933 was this Super Six model for 5 passengers. It developed 73 HP at 3200 RPM. This was the introduction of the Super Six line again after being absent for many years. It sold for $995 like the Super Six Coupe. This example does not have cowl lights—apparently it was an early model.

Hudson

For 1933, Hudson rounded out the body lines on an already sharp looking car. This example was the Hudson 8 Model T rumble seat coupe for 4 passengers. It sold for $1,175. It was the only Coupe available in the 8-cylinder line.

Hudson's 1933 Model T 4-door sedan came on the 119-inch wheelbase and sold for $1,200. A total of four models were available in this 8-cylinder series. Side hood ventilating doors were used for these 8-cylinder cars.

This 1933 Hudson 6-wheel sedan was referred to as the Pacemaker Eight Sedan. The company advertised it as the car with "draftless ventilation." The contour of the rear fender appears out of proportion with the wheel opening, but this is an optical illusion caused by shadow and camera distortion. This sedan brought a price of $1,295.

It was rare when new, so what is it today? Just never seen! That's the 1933 Hudson 7-passenger sedan on a 132-inch wheelbase that definitely carries classic lines. The sidemount wheel equipment and whitewall tires were optional at extra cost. The 132-inch cars came in four models and the sedans had rear-opening back doors. It sold for $1,595, as the most expensive 1933 Hudson available.

Hudson returned to only 8-cylinder cars for 1934, dropping the Super Six line. This Standard 1934 Coupe came on a 116-inch wheelbase and was the lowest priced Hudson for 1934 selling at $760. The new style lacked the grace of the 1933 models.

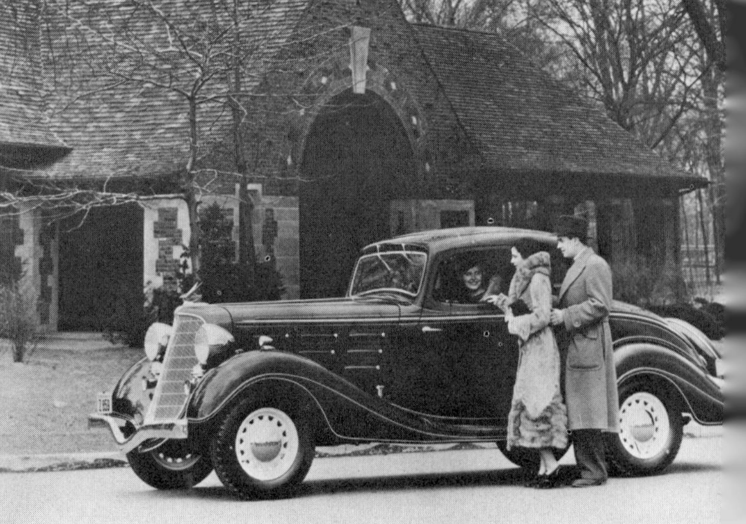

934

For 1934, the Hudson was again built only as an 8-ylinder car, leaving the Six for Terraplane. The Standard ludson Eight with a cast iron head yielded 108 HP at .75 compression ratio at 3800 RPM. The DeLuxe ludson Eight at 3800 RPM gave 113 HP, while the 7:1 ompression ratio gave 121 HP at the same RPM. Cars vith this compression required premium fuel. All series sed the 15½-gallon fuel tank.

Standard Hudson took 6:00 x 16-inch tires and the)eLuxe Models used 6:50 x 16s.

Eighteen different models were available, ranging from he 116-inch wheelbase Coupe for $760 to the DeLuxe ight Brougham on 123-inch wheelbase at $1,195.

Hudson far surpassed 1933, producing 85,835 cars which ave them the 5th place for the calendar year. Sales are ombined with Terraplane for the year.

This 1934 Hudson Eight, in deluxe style, was called the Model LU. It used the 116-inch wheelbase and sold for $935 in base form. The built-in trunk was good to keep the spare tire from having to weather the outdoor elements but didn't offer too much storage space. Note the unique bumper guards mounted inside of the bumper.

Hudson, like all automobile manufacturers, enjoyed having a celebrity appreciate the merchandise. Here is news commentator Lowell Thomas taking delivery of his new 1934 Hudson 8 DeLuxe Sedan on the 123-inch wheelbase. It cost $1,195 in basic form.

Hudson's lowest priced car for 1935 was the new Hudson 6 Business Coupe that sold for $695 on a 116-inch wheelbase. The same model was available as an 8-cylinder for $760. Strangely enough the Eight had a wheelbase that was only one inch longer than the Six.

Being displayed in front of a Hudson-Terraplane dealership is the 1935 Hudson Six Sedan which sold for $770. A like model in Special Eight style sold for $840. The 1935 Hudsons came with an all-steel roof for the first time. The sidemount equipment was a factory installed accessory which was quite common on the sedan models.

Hudson

A young movie starlet by the name of Patricia Ellis proudly enjoys being photographed in her new 1935 Hudson Big Six Convertible Coupe. This car came with wire wheels which were not as common as the steel pressed wheels for 1935. It also has the impressive factory fender skirts which Hudson frequently used on their cars in that era. The model was a 4-passenger that sold for $790.

Hudson's top car for 1935 was this Custom 8 Brougham which sold for $1,195. The new Electric Hand was standard equipment on this series and extra cost on the other models. This was a pre-selective shifting device.

Hudson made a fastback version of the Touring Brougham for 1936 that sold for $845 in 8-cylinder style. For $10 more, the built-in trunk could be ordered. Both styles sold about equal.

1935

Hudson's big news for 1935 consisted of the "Electri Hand," which permitted owners to shift by touching tiny lever with the tip of a finger. This innovation wa standard equipment for the Custom Hudson 8 and at extr charge was available on other models. This product wa supplied through the Bendix Co. It could be ordered eithe with or without a vacuum-operated clutch. Eliminatin the conventional gear shift and moving the emergenc brake to the left of the driver gave ample room for thre in the front seat.

Appearancewise, the all-steel roof not only looke better, but was much safer for the passengers.

For the year, Hudson offered a totally new, 116-inc Hudson Big Six, as a Special and as a DeLuxe; a 117-inc Hudson Eight, and the 124-inch Custom Hudson Eigh which came in two models – Custom Club Sedan an Custom Brougham. These two models were fully equippe including full wheel covers, dual tail lamps, radio, exteric dual trumpet horns and the "Electric Hand."

Tire sizes for the Hudson Six was 6:00 x 16; Hudso Eights had 6:25 x 16, and the Big Hudson Eight ha 6:50 x 16s. Brakes were mechanical in all series, and 15½-gallon fuel supply was used throughout the lin

The cast iron heads produced 93 HP at 3800 RPM for Hudson Big Six; Hudson Eight gave 113 HP at 3800 RPM The aluminum head developed 100 HP in the Six 3800 RPM and 124 HP with 4000 RPM in the Eigh

Hudson offered 17 body styles among the four serie ranging in price from $695 for a 2-passenger Coupe t $1,195 for the Custom Club Brougham Eight.

The company placed 8th in sales for the year by sellin 101,080 automobiles. These calendar figures also represe Terraplane sales.

For 1936, Hudson offered cars similar in appearance to 1935 models and yet different enough to give a nice face-lifting. A Vee-shaped windshield was used for the first time as this model displays. The 6-cylinder model was called the Touring Brougham for five. It sold for $795. Fender skirts added nicely to the rear of the car's appearance.

Hudson

936

For Hudson in 1936, the new front spring suspension 'as of great importance, along with the new Duo-Servo ydraulic brake system which was a simple linkage llowing the pedal to operate the rear shoes in case of a ydraulic brake failure.

For 1936, Hudson had a die cast grille, a Vee-windshield, n all-steel roof, and deeply crowned fenders. The Six eveloped 93 HP at 3800 RPM, while the Eight developed 13 HP at the same RPM. Both offered an optional ompression ratio with aluminum heads, increasing HP to 00 on Sixes and 124 for Eights. Otherwise, compression 'as 6:25 for the Six and 6:00 in the Eight. Both shared a 6½-gallon fuel supply in the 120-inch wheelbased cars. lso available was a Custom Eight with a 127-inch wheel-ase.

Tire size for the Six was 6:00 x 16, and 6:25 x 16 on ie Eights. Hudson's "Electric Hand" was changed some-'hat. Its appearance on the steering column was improved y streamlining. Even as early as 1936, Hudson used red ash lights in place of gauges to warn when the generator 'asn't working or the oil pressure was low.

Hudson offered 15 models in both series with the ludson 6 3-passenger Coupe selling for $710 as the lowest rice, ranging upward to the Hudson Custom 8 for $990. he company had the 8th sales position, selling 123,266 ırs for the calendar run. These sales figures also include erraplane.

Coming down the line for their final inspection are a group of 1936 Hudsons and Terraplanes. Both makes were assembled on the same assembly line.

Wilbur Shaw, the famous race driver, appears here accepting the trophy for the Hudson that won the 1936 Gilmore Oil Company Economy Run to Yosemite, Calif. The car averaged 22 MPG. Hudson always entered these economy runs and usually won in their class.

This was the Hudson 8 Convertible Coupe on the 120-inch chassis. It seated five. It did not sell too well during depression days, but brought a price of $960. It also was available as a Six for $795.

Another famous personality who enjoyed driving Hudsons was British race driver, Sir Malcolm Campbell. He is seen here with his new 1936 Hudson Custom Eight Sedan. The 127-inch wheelbase car sold for $990.

Hudson

Hudson offered this 1937 Victoria 4-passenger coupe in both DeLuxe and Custom models for $695 and $720 in the 6-cylinder line. An 8-cylinder model on the same 122-inch wheelbase was available for $770. Fender skirts were again an accessory.

1937

Hudson entered 1937 with its three lines of cars restyle in front, and having new interiors, more power and wit some mechanical refinements.

Continued was the "Electric Hand" shift lever tha didn't require lifting to engage into reverse. The revers slot was placed left of low gear so that there was n mistake of going into the wrong gear. The 1937 model stored the battery in the engine room and made use of dual carburetor system new to the industry at that time It came with an automatic choke and an anti-percolatin device which supposedly gave a better average fuel pe mile.

Hudson's unique front suspension was continued wit its soft springs shackled at both ends and held in positio by steel radius arms mounted to the frame by rubbe bushings.

The Six models used 101 HP engines (at 4000 RPM) o an aluminum head version at 7:1 compression. This gav 107 HP. The Eights came with 122 HP at 4200 RPM A 7:1 head was available in this model too, giving 12 HP. The Six used 6:00 x 16-inch tires while 6:25 x 16 were used on the Eights. Fuel supply was the same in bot models – 16½ gallons. Wheelbases were 122 inches fo both Six and Eight and a 129-inch wheelbase model wa available in the Hudson 8 and Custom 8 Series in the forr of a Sedan and Touring Sedan. A total of 23 models wer catalogued ranging from a $695 3-passenger Coupe in th Hudson Six line to $1,040 for the Custom Eight Tourin Trunk Sedan.

Hudson took an 8th seat this year with combined sale from Terraplane reaching 111,342 units for the calenda year run.

A 1937 Hudson 6-passenger Touring Sedan was the most expensive model in the 6-cylinder line, selling for $815. All of the Sixes used a 122-inch wheelbase. This same model came as an Eight for $890.

The 1937 Hudson Convertible Brougham was available in both 6 and 8-cylinder lines selling for $785 and $840 respectively. This model offered the comfort of a 2-door Brougham and the pleasure of convertible driving. Note that side curtains were used in the rear quarters.

Hudson did much export business to Europe. This 1937 Custom 8 Touring Sedan is a good example. Note the right-hand drive. In the States, this model sold for $1,040 in base form. This example wears factory accessory wheel covers, rare sidemount tire equipment, and fender mounted parking lamps. Trumpet horns were only used on export models, but could be ordered as accessories.

938

For 1938, Hudson was offered in six separate models. ince the Terraplane was no longer classed as a separate ar, the company now referred to it as the Hudson Terra-lane, coming in DeLuxe and Super styles. Next was the ludson "112," Hudson 6-84, Hudson 8, and the Hudson ustom 8.

Each of these cars could be optionally ordered with ludson's Selective Automatic Shift, except the "112." his was originally termed "Electric Hand" from 1935, ut through improvements the company gave it this new ame, feeling it was more automatic than previously escribed in the literature.

The Hudson 112 was introduced early in 1938 and was neant to take the place of the Terraplane which would be hased out shortly. The 112-inch car had an 86 HP engine f 6 cylinders that turned a maximum 4000 RPM. It used 12½-gallon fuel tank, and rode on 6:00 x 16-inch tires.

The Terraplane Series came on a 117-inch wheelbase. n engine with 96 HP at 3900 RPM was used in the eLuxe Series while the Super Terraplanes employed a -cylinder engine developing 101 HP at 4000 RPM with a ompression ratio of 7:1.

The Hudson 6-83 employed the same engine as used on ne Super Terraplanes, but were on a 122-inch wheelbase. he Hudson 8 and Custom 8 gave 122 HP with a 6.25:1 tio at 4200 RPM. These cars were on 122 and 129-inch heelbases, using 6:50 x 16-inch tires. The other models l used 6:00 x 16-inch tires. Each series used a 16½-gallon uel tank.

Available from Hudson were 47 different styles, ranging price from a 3-passenger Hudson "112" Coupe for 745 to the Hudson Eight Custom Touring Sedan on 29-inch wheelbase for $1,219.

Hudson placed in 8th position by selling 51,078 cars.

This fully equipped 1937 Hudson Eight DeLuxe Custom Country Club Sedan came only on the 129-inch wheelbase and sold for $1,020. Manual brakes functioned when the hydraulic system failed. This double acting brake, now in its second year, had gained in popularity with Hudson owners.

This 1938 Hudson Terraplane DeLuxe Sedan offered a 96 HP engine. In the Super Series it employed the 101 HP, 6-cylinder engine. This DeLuxe Sedan sold for $864.

This 1938 6-cylinder Hudson Coupe was referred to as a model 6-83. It sold for $909. The 8-cylinder version was model 6-84 and was available for $990. Both series offered the Selective Automatic Shift at extra cost.

The lowest priced Hudson Sedan for 1938 came on the market shortly after January 1st, 1938. It was called the Hudson 112 and was just basic good transportation. It sold for $806 as the Touring Sedan, which weighed 2,712 lbs.

Hudson

Hudson's lowest priced cars for 1938 were the newly introduced Hudson 112s. This model is the Touring Brougham on the 112-inch wheelbase. This series came in five models and was available for two years only.

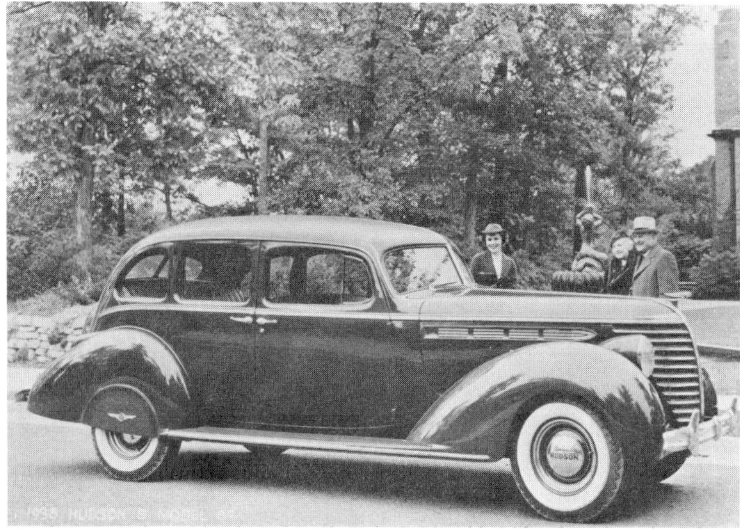

The 1938 Hudson Custom 8 Sedan was referred to as Model 87 with a fastback trunk. This example sold for $1,199 and was available only on the 129-inch wheelbase. Factory fender skirts were an accessory for this car but most in this series were equipped with them.

1939

The new Hudsons for 1939 offered three features that were new to the Hudson line. They were: a steering column gearshift as standard equipment in all models but the 112 (where it could be ordered as optional equipment at extra cost), "Auto-Poise" which was a steering control that brought the wheels right back into position after hitting a rut, and airfoam seats which gave new comfort for the car's passengers. This year saw Hudson offer five lines of cars. The Hudson "112" was offered now in its second year with an 86 HP engine at 4000 RPM. The car used 6:00 x 16-inch tires and had a fuel supply of 12½ gallons. The Series was available in five models.

Second in the line was the Hudson Six, developing 96 HP at 3900 RPM. It offered six models on a 118-inch wheelbase that also rode on 6:00 x 16-inch tires. The fuel tanks held a 16½-gallon supply.

The Hudson Country Club Six was like the Country Club Eight in all respects except it had an engine that developed 101 HP at 4000 RPM. This series used 6:25 x 16-inch tires and also had a fuel supply of 16½ gallons. The wheelbase was 122 inches, the same as the Country Club Eight. Body styles were six in the Hudson Six and Country Club Eight.

The Country Club Eight offered a 122 HP engine at 4200 RPM and rode on 6:50 x 16-inch tires. This series also used a 16½-gallon fuel supply.

The fifth in the Hudson line was a sub-series of the Country Club Eight. It was the same car in all respects as the 122-inch sedan, but used a 129-inch wheelbase and was only built as a Touring Sedan for six.

Prices ranged from $745 for the 3-passenger "112" Coupe to $1,174 for the 129-inch wheelbase Country Club Eight Sedan.

Hudson celebrated its 30th anniversary this year and shipped 82,161 cars for the calendar year. It placed 9th for the year.

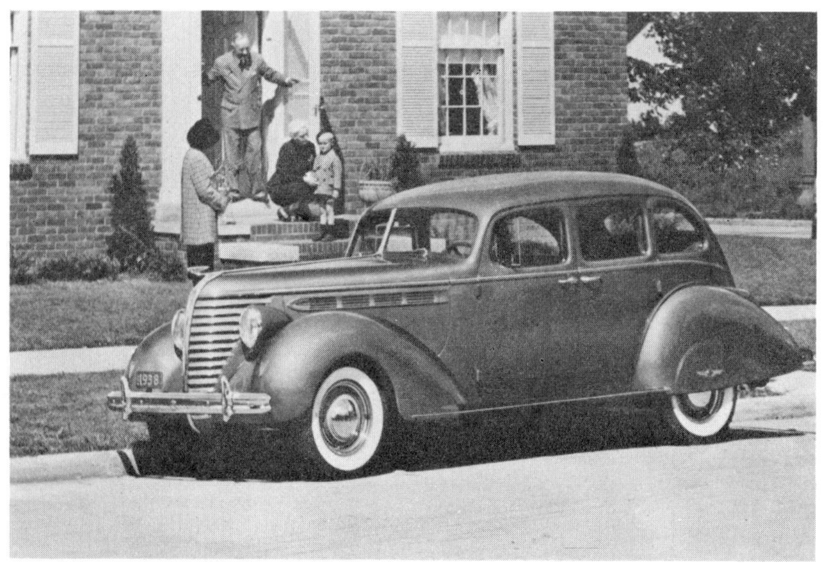

Available as either a Six for $984, or as an Eight for $1,060 was this 1938 Hudson fastback sedan. This 122-inch model is equipped with whitewall tires, factory wheel trim rings, and fender skirts, all at extra cost.

Hudson's lowest priced 4-door sedan for 1939 was this model which sold for $806. This series was the 112, and the name was received from its 112-inch wheelbase. The sedan weighed 2,712 lbs. and was virtually the same car as in 1938 except for its front end facelift with different appearing grille.

1940

The 1940 Hudson offered three basic lines of cars with ub-series in the line. Two Sixes and one Eight were available at reduced prices over the previous year. All models vere equipped with independently sprung front wheels vhich Hudson introduced on the 1939 models. A Warner overdrive was available on all models at extra cost.

The lowest priced offering was the Hudson 6-40 which eplaced the Hudson 112. This Series had a 6-cylinder ngine developing 92 HP at 4000 RPM. It had a 12½-gallon uel tank and was available on a 113-inch wheelbase. The ire size was 6:00 x 16 inches. A total of eleven models vere available ranging from the Traveler 3-passenger Coupe or $670 to the DeLuxe Convertible for six passengers t $955.

The Super Six was next in the line. This Series offered a 02 HP engine at 4000 RPM and used a 16½-gallon fuel upply. A 118-inch wheelbase was used and the same tire ize as the 6-40 Series was employed. Six models were vailable ranging in price from $809 for a 3-passenger Coupe to $1,030 in the Convertible style.

The Hudson Eight was available with a 128 HP engine at 200 RPM. It too used a 16½-gallon fuel tank. The wheelbase was 118 inches as in the Super Six. Six models ranged n price from $860 for the 3-passenger Coupe to $1,122 or the 8-cylinder Convertible.

The sub-series were classed as Country Club Six, and Country Club 8 using the same mechanical components as he Super Six and Eight, only coming on 125-inch wheelbases. A Touring Sedan for five, and a 7-passenger Sedan vere available. They ranged in price from $1,018 for he Country Club Six Touring Sedan to $1,330 for the Country Club Eight Sedan for seven passengers.

Hudson placed in 12th position for the calendar year by selling 79,979 automobiles.

This was the 1939 Hudson 6 Business Coupe known as the Series 6-92. It used a 118-inch wheelbase. It weighed 2,757 lbs. and sold for $823.

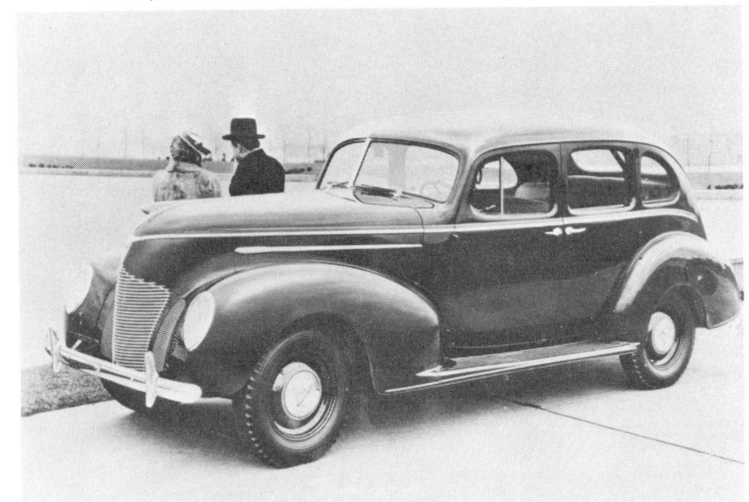

Hudson's most popular model for 1939 was this Country Club Sedan known as Series 6-93. It came on a 122-inch wheelbase and sold for $995. It weighed 3,023 lbs. A trademark began with the 1939 models with the small light at the front end of the chrome spear on the side of the hood. Hudson used this side hood light for many years to follow. Later models displayed it in the form of their famous triangle.

This 1939 Hudson Convertible Brougham was available in both Country Club 6 and 8-cylinder cars. As a Six it weighed 3,193 lbs. and sold for $1,195. In the Eight line it weighed 3,307 lbs. and was priced at $1,201. Both series rode on 122-inch wheelbases. Sidemount spares were extremely rare by 1939. Side curtains were still used.

The lowest priced Hudson for 1940 was the 6-cylinder Traveler Business Coupe. It came on a 113-inch wheelbase, weighed 2,800 lbs. and sold for $670.

Hudson

"America's lowest priced straight Eight" was what the company called this 1940 Hudson 8 Sedan. It weighed 3,185 lbs. and sold for $952 as a Touring Sedan.

A car similar to this 1940 Hudson 6 Sedan set an AAA record for endurance in 1940 by traveling 20,327 miles at an average speed of 70.5 MPH. This model was called the Super Six and offered a 102 HP engine at 4000 RPM. It weighed 3,050 lbs. and sold for $870.

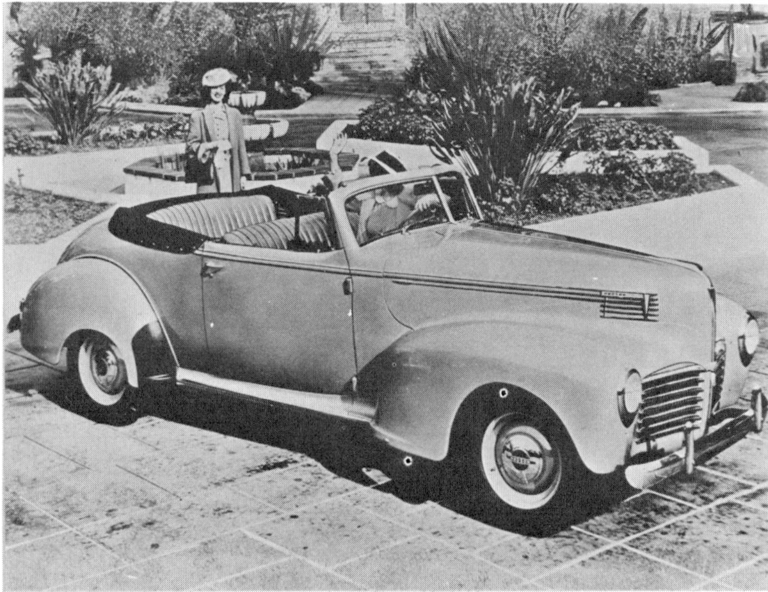

A mid-season option for the 1940 Hudson 8s were the rear fender scuff pads like this Convertible Coupe displays. Also note the triangle parking light affixed to the front side portion of the hood. This was a Hudson trademark on their cars during that era. This model came on a 112-inch wheelbase and sold for $1,122.

The lowest priced model for 1941 was the Hudson Traveler 3-passenger coupe which sold for $695. It came on a 116-inch chassis and weighed 2,790 lbs.

This was the lowest priced series of the year. It was called the Hudson Six and was offered in nine models referred to as Traveler or DeLuxe models. This is a DeLuxe Touring Sedan that weighed 2,950 lbs. and sold for $856.

941

For the 1941 models Hudson offered three basic chassis vhich were used to provide five series of cars. These ncluded the Traveler which had a 175 cubic inch -cylinder engine developing 92 HP at 4000 RPM, a 16-inch chassis and a 12½-gallon fuel tank. Within this eries was the DeLuxe Traveler which came with more eluxe appointments. Both models used 5:50 x 16-inch ires. The Super Six was next in line with a 212 cubic inch ngine that developed 102 HP at 4000 RPM. This series ised a 16½-gallon fuel supply, rode on 6:00 x 16-inch ires, and had a 121-inch wheelbase. A Convertible Coupe vas the only addition that wasn't available in the Standard raveler Series.

After the Super Six was the Commodore Series being ffered both as a Six and Eight on a 121-inch wheelbase. 'his series replaced the Country Club models of 1940. Aechanically, the Commodore Six was the same as the uper Six except it weighed 50 pounds more and had :25 x 16-inch tires. The Commodore Eight had a 254 ubic inch engine that developed 128 HP at 4200 RPM. t was the same car in all respects as the Commodore Six xcept for its 8-cylinder engine. The top of the line was he Custom Commodore Eight which used the same ngine as the regular Commodore Eight. The difference in his car was a more plush interior, a 128-inch wheelbase, nd 6:50 x 16-inch tires. In the Custom Commodore line vas an 8-passenger Sedan. A total of 30 models were vailable ranging in price from $695 for a 3-passenger raveler Business Coupe to $1,438 for the Commodore Custom Eight Sedan. Hudson sold 79,529 units for the alendar year which placed them in the 13th sales spot.

The most popular 1941 Hudson Sedan was the 6-cylinder Super Six model on the 121-inch wheelbase. Its engine developed 102 HP at 4000 RPM. This sedan weighed 3,050 lbs. and had a price tag of $932.

Being new to Hudson was the 1941 edition of the Station Wagon. Hudson had a wagon in 1936 on a low production basis and did not return with it until 1941. This model was available on the Commodore Six and Eight chassis of 121 inches. The Six developed 102 HP and the Eight gave 128 HP. Not many wagons were sold by Hudson in 1941. The Hudson 6 Commodore wagon weighed 3,315 lbs. and sold for $1,236. The Commodore 8 was offered for $1,312.

The 1941 Hudson Custom Commodore Touring Sedan was available only on the 128-inch chassis. This was by far the most impressive Hudson for the year. It came only with the 128 HP 8-cylinder engine and weighed 3,400 lbs. It sold well at $1,232. The bumper trim guard, wheel covers and whitewalls were standard equipment on this series only.

In place of the 1941 Hudson Traveler this 1942 Hudson Sedan belonged to the Series known as the 6-20. A DeLuxe version was also available. This model weighed 2,940 lbs. and sold for $945.

Hudson

The 1942 Hudson Super Six Club Coupe sold for $1,126 and weighed 3,010 lbs. This was an early 1942 model built before January 1st, 1942, as it offers full chrome and the rare whitewall tires that very few 1942 cars were able to be equipped with.

1942

The 1942 models offered a new device called Drive Master that was available in all models at extra cost. It included a conventional clutch and transmission which could be operated either manually or semi-automatically. It was available with or without overdrive. The automatic clutch, which had been a Hudson feature for a few years, offered a vacuum cylinder control that was operated by a governor switch that shifted the transmission from second to high when the speed exceeded 13 MPH and the accelerator pedal released. As long as the accelerator pedal was depressed the car was in second gear no matter how fast it was driven. With Drive Master, the car shifted automatically from high into second if the speed dropped to 10 MPH and the throttle was closed.

In place of the Traveler Series of 1941, the model was known as simply the 6-20 and 6-20 DeLuxe. It offered the same 175 cubic inch 6-cylinder engine that developed 92 HP at 4000 RPM. The fuel supply was a 12½-gallon tank; it rode on a 116-inch chassis, and used 5:50 x 16 inch tires like the 1941 Traveler.

The Super Six used the same 212 cubic inch engine that developed 102 HP at 4000 RPM. It used a 16½-gallon fuel supply. All Super Six models had 6:25 x 16-inch tires, a 121-inch wheelbase like the Commodore Six and Eight.

The Commodore Six was the same car in all respects except for a fancier interior. The Commodore Eight used all the same body components except that it had the 254 cubic inch 8-cylinder engine that developed 128 HP at 4200 RPM and used 6:50 x 16-inch tires. The Custom Commodore Eight mechanically was the same as the regular Commodore but it was available only in four styles. The 3 or 6-passenger Coupe on a 121-inch wheelbase, and the 6 or 8-passenger Sedan available only on a 128-inch chassis.

A total of 30 models were available ranging in price from $866 for a 3-passenger 6-20 Business Coupe to $1,467 in the 8-passenger Custom Commodore Sedan. Hudson ranked in 11th position for sales during the calendar year from the sale of 5,396 vehicles.

Oddly enough, Hudson termed this 1942 model a Convertible Sedan even though it was strictly a Convertible Coupe. This model is the Commodore Six on a 121-inch wheelbase. It weighed 3,280 lbs. and sold for $1,253. A total of five convertibles were catalogued for 1942 among the different series.

All dressed up in its finery is this 1942 Hudson Commodore 8. The full wheel covers were standard equipment and whitewalls had to be classed as extra equipment due to their rarity on 1942 cars. This model was built between September and December, 1941, with all its bright chrome work glistening. This model weighed 3,280 lbs. and sold for $1,254.

Hudson offered its last Station Wagon in 1942 with the Super Six being the only model available. It was an 8-passenger model on the 121-inch wheelbase that weighed 3,315 lbs. It sold for $1,282.

Hupmobile

The Hupmobile came from the Hupp Motor Car Co. of)etroit. The car was produced from 1908 through the ummer of 1940.

Hupmobile came in 3 Series for 1930. They were known s Series "S," "C," and "H."

The Hupp "S" was a 6-cylinder car developing 70 HP t 3200 RPM. This model used a 15-gallon fuel tank. The heelbase was 113½ inches. They rode on 5:50 x 18-inch ires.

Series "C" cars offered 8-cylinder engines of 100 HP at 200 RPM. This model used an 18-gallon gasoline tank, he wheelbase was a 121-inch chassis which used 6:00 x 9-inch tires.

The Model "H" was also an 8-cylinder car but was of a rger cubic inch displacement of 365.6 cubes. These eveloped 133 HP at 3400 RPM. This series used a 125-nch wheelbase riding on 6:50 x 19-inch tires. The fuel upply came from a 21-gallon tank.

A total of 13 models were available. The company anked in 17th position for the year by selling 22,183 nits. The cars sold from $995 for a 2-passenger 6-cylinder Coupe to $2,145 for a Series "H" 7-passenger Phaeton.

Accelerating from 0 to 50 MPH took only 16 seconds for the 1930 Hupmobile Straight Eight Coupe. This model was on a 121-inch wheelbase and called Series C. The wire wheels were optional at $45 extra. The model sold for $1,595 as a 4-passenger coupe.

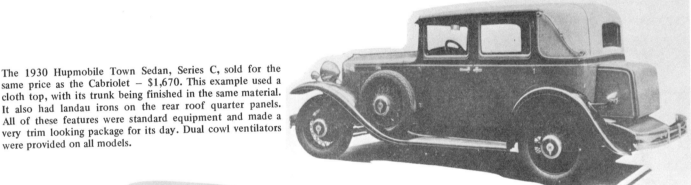

The 1930 Hupmobile Town Sedan, Series C, sold for the same price as the Cabriolet – $1,670. This example used a cloth top, with its trunk being finished in the same material. It also had landau irons on the rear roof quarter panels. All of these features were standard equipment and made a very trim looking package for its day. Dual cowl ventilators were provided on all models.

A side view of the 1930 Hupmobile Series C convertible Cabriolet for 4 passengers. It sold for $1,670. This model and the Coupe did not come with an outside visor as did the sedan models. Series C cars could hold a steady 80 MPH.

Hupmobile's most popular model in the 1930 Series C cars was the 5-passenger Sedan which sold for $1,595. Only an 8-cylinder engine was used in Series C cars. Disc wheels were standard equipment. The sidemount tire accessory was only available at extra cost, as were the wire wheels.

Hupmobile

For 1931, the lowest priced Hupmobile was the Century 6 Coupe for 2 passengers. It sold for $995 and came on a 113½-inch wheelbase. It weighed 2,745 lbs. It was also available as a 4-passenger rumble seat coupe at the same price, but weighed ten pounds more and had a large luggage compartment, reached through a side quarter panel compartment. Hupmobiles were regarded as relatively high speed cars.

1931

The 1931 cars came in five series. The Century Six Century Eight, Hupmobile "C," Hupmobile "H" and the Hupmobile "U." The last four models were all 8-cylinder cars.

Hupmobile's big news for the year was its free-wheeling which greatly reduced oil and fuel consumption. By using the free-wheeling device the clutch operation also was reduced about half of its normal wear. It was available in all models.

The Century Six developed 70 HP at 3200 RPM. Its fuel supply was a 15¼-gallon tank, the same as on the Century Eight. The wheelbase was 113½-inches. Tire size was 5:50 x 19, and the same was true of Century Eights. The Century Eight developed 90 HP at 3200 RPM. Their wheelbase was 118 inches.

Hupmobile Series "C" developed 100 HP at 3200 RPM. An 18-gallon gasoline tank was used. The tire size was 6:00 x 19 inches and all Series "C" models used a 121-inch wheelbase.

Hupmobile "H" and "U" Series developed 133 HP at 3400 RPM. The fuel supply came from 21-gallon tanks. They both used 6:50 x 19-inch tires. Series "H" cars had a 125-inch wheelbase and Series "U" cars came with a 137-inch chassis. All models used mechanical brakes.

Twenty-seven different models were available during the year. The prices ranged from $995 for a 2-passenger Century Six Coupe to $2,295 for a 7-passenger Series "U" Sedan Limousine.

Hupmobile took its 15th position for the calendar year by selling 17,456 cars.

Available in Series C models was this 1931 Victoria Coupe on a 121-inch wheelbase. It weighed 3,535 lbs. and sold for $1,615. This 5-passenger coupe offered a plush interior of mohair. The body was by Murray.

A 1931 Hupmobile Century 8 Phaeton sold for $1,350. It weighed 3,150 lbs. and was one of six models in that series. Note this model is equipped with the disc wheels and tire cover rather than the wire wheels.

Hupmobile's 1931 Century 8 Cabriolet was the most expensive model in that series. It sold for $1,350 and weighed 3,055 lbs. There was passenger room for four, using the rumble seat. Unlike the Phaeton, it had roll-up windows.

This 7-passenger sedan was Hupmobile's finest offering for 1931. It came on a 137-inch chassis and weighed 4,270 lbs. It was classified as Series U and was available in three models, all selling for $2,295.

932

For the middle priced field, Hupmobile had two Eights vith unusually pleasing lines. Although not radical, these ew cars had enough different appearance to catch the eye f anyone who entered a Hupmobile dealership. Spare tires vere carried in the fender wells. The front fenders, instead f sweeping gradually rearward, curved around the front vheels and then reversed this curve at the base to meet ıe running board with an unbroken line.

The tie between frame and body was unusual and was ıtended to give great strength. Other features new to [upmobile were silent synchro-mesh transmission, free-'heeling, and hypoid rear axle gearing. Automatic shock bsorbers made a dash adjustment unnecessary.

Besides building an 8-cylinder car, the company offered 6-cylinder car in various models. A 114-inch wheelbase ıodel for $765 in Roadster form was called the 214. lso shown were the 216, 218, and 221. Wheelbases were 16, 118, and 121 inches in that order.

For the 8-cylinder cars, model designations were 222, 26 and 237. Prices varied from $1,295 for a 4-passenger oupe to $1,700 for the 137-inch 7-passenger Sedan. Tire sizes for the Sixes were 5:50 x 18 and 5:50 x 19. he Eights had 5:50 x 19, 6:00 x 19, 6:00 x 17, 6:50 x 19, :50 x 17 and 6:50 x 19. Fuel capacities varied: The Sixes ıd 218 Series used 15-gallon tanks. The 221 used an 8-gallon tank, and the 222, 226 shared a 20½-gallon tank. he 225 and 237 Series both used 21-gallon tanks. orsepower ratings were as follows: Series 214 had a) HP Six (3200 RPM); 216 had a 75 HP Six (3200 RPM); 18 had a 90 HP Eight (3200 RPM); 221 had a 100 HP ight (3200 RPM); 222 had a 93 HP Eight (3200 RPM); 25 had a 133 HP Eight (3400 RPM); 226 had a 103 HP ight (3200 RPM); and the 237 had a 133 HP Eight 400 RPM).

Hupp saw 10,476 cars go to their customers. They ere in 14th position for sales this year.

This is Hupmobile's 1931 Century 8 Sedan that came on a 118-inch wheelbase, weighed 3,175 lbs. and sold for $1,295. The wire wheel equipment was standard for this series.

New for the year was this ultra smart body style which Hupmobile offered for the first time in 1932. The special cycle fenders were very handsome indeed and were part of the styling on all Series 222, 225, 226 and 237 models. Sidemounts were standard equipment on all in these models. This car is the Series 226 Sedan on the 126-inch wheelbase. It sold for $1,595.

Known as the 214 Series for 1932, Hupmobile offered four models in this line. This Roadster was the lowest priced model, available for $765. It weighed 2,855 lbs. and came on a 114-inch wheelbase.

Only two inches longer than the Hupmobile 214 was this 1932 216 Coupe which sold for $995. This series used a 75 HP engine at 3200 RPM. These cars were noted for their smartly colored paint combinations.

Hupmobile

Available in Series 222 and 226 only was this 1932 Hupmobile Cabriolet Roadster. This particular car is a model 222 on a 122-inch wheelbase. It sold for $1,395. As a 226 Series, it cost an additional $300. Very few of this body style were sold in 1932 as the depression took hold of Hupmobile quite well.

Hupmobile's lowest priced line for 1933 was the 321-A Series. Shown here is the 4-door Sedan for $895 on its 121-inch wheelbase. Mechanical brakes were used on these cars. Note the unusual louver arrangement on the hood panels.

The 1933 Hupmobile Victoria Coupe for 5 passengers was available in Series 321, 322 and 326. Wheelbases were identified by the last two digits in the series designation. This model was the 326 on a 126-inch chassis. It sold for $1,510. This car was also called the Silver Anniversary Victoria.

1933

This model run saw last year's two Eights with a fe improvements and a new Six. All three series had di tinctive lines which followed the basic design of th beautiful 1932 car. The series designations were 321A 321, 322, and 326.

The Six could be bought for $895 in either a 4-passeng Coupe or a 5-passenger Sedan. Prices went upward t $1,545 for a 3-passenger Cabriolet in the 326 Series. A models came equipped with an automatic choke and aut matic manifold heat control. The main new devices on th 1932s were again on the Eights and incorporated into th Sixes. These items were the X-frame, double Vee bra rods running from the cowl to the cross members of th radiator, tubular front axle, and hypoid rear axle. The Si carried a 90 HP engine at 3800 RPM with a 5.75: compression ratio as standard equipment and 5.25:1 as a optional device. The Eights developed 93 HP at 3600 RP with a 5.47:1 compression ratio, and the larger series ga 109 HP at 3500 RPM with a compression ratio of 5.43:

Fuel capacities consisted of 15 gallons for the 321 Serie and 20½ gallons for the other two series. The car's braki system was mechanical. The last two digits in the seri designation applied to the wheelbase. Thus, a 321 had 121-inch wheelbase, 322 had 122 inches, and the 32 had a 126-inch wheelbase. The 321A, 321, and 322s use 6:00 x 17-inch tires and the 326 carried 6:50 x 17s. total of 12 models were made available, and 51,316 ca were built for the model run, dropping Hupmobile Space 16 for the year.

Buyers looking for good value certainly got their answer with this beautiful Series 322 Coupe that sold for $1,195. Sidemount tire equipment was standard on this model, as were the twin trumpet horns and dual wipers.

At $1,445 this 1933 Hupmobile Series 326 was available with true classic lines, yet it was still difficult to find buyers and this body style was discontinued at the end of the model run.

1934

This year Hupmobile built three distinct cars: The low-priced Six beginning at $725, called Model 417, the "Aerodynamic" Six, Model 421, with a beginning price of $795, and the "Aerodynamic" Eight, Model 427, with a starting price of $1,145. Within the 421 and 426 Series were the sub-series given designations as 421-J, 422, and 427. These were models having extra frills. The last two numbers referred to the car's wheelbase as they had done previously. A 427 wheelbase was 117 inches, and a 426 had a 126-inch wheelbase.

The low-priced Six used the 80 HP engine of 3400 RPM. The 421 Six used a 90 HP engine; the peppier version carried a 93 HP engine at the same RPM. The 426 Eight developed 109 HP at 3500 RPM, and the 427 Model used the most powerful engine, 115 HP with the same RPM. Tire sizes varied among the models: 6:00 x 17 on the lighter cars, 6:50 x 16 for medium Aerodynamics, to 7:00 x 16 on the largest Eight. Fuel capacity varied from a 15-gallon tank on the low-priced Model 417 to 19 gallons for Series 421 and 20 gallons in the 426. Brake systems were mechanical throughout the line.

Models available numbered 23 among the three major series.

For the year, Hupmobile sold 9,420 cars which gave them the 15th position for sales.

The most expensive model for the year was this 1933 Hupmobile Series 326 Cabriolet. It sold for $1,545 but fewer than 100 of this model were produced.

"A Car for the Careful Investor" was what Hupmobile told its buyers in 1934 when they came to look at the Model 417. This was the lowest priced series, selling for $795 in touring sedan form.

The 1934 Hupmobile 4-passenger Coupe was the only other model in the 417 line. It sold for the same price as the sedan, $795. Note the difference of the side hood vents from the sedan. The coupe was an early photographic sketch of the proposed car.

The Series 421 rumble seat coupe for 1934 sold for $895. It was available as a commercial car by the removal of the rumble seat to provide extra cargo space.

This was Hupmobile's swanky 1934 Cabriolet Roadster in the 421 Series. The disc wheel covers were of stainless steel and were optional equipment. This model weighed 3,235 pounds and sold for $995. A more deluxe version on a 122-inch wheelbase, called the 422, sold for $1,145.

Hupmobile

Hupmobile's truly new car for 1934 was this Aerodynamic car called the 426 and 427 Models. A sweeping airspeed line combined a new concept of comfort and beauty in this 4-passenger coupe. It weighed 3,795 lbs. and sold for $1,145. This was a rumble seat model.

1935

Hupp's big news for the public was the new offering t be sold between $700 and $800. This car was of th Aerodynamic design, had a wheelbase of 118 inches, an was called Model 518. It developed 91 HP at 3500 RPM The car came chiefly as a 4-door Sedan and replaced th Series 417. The Models 521 and 527 were continued, bot sharing the Aerodynamic design. The 521 used a 101 H engine at 3600 RPM, while the Hupp 8, called Series 52 gave 120 HP at 3500 RPM. Tire size on the new smaller ca was 6:00 x 16, 521s used 6:50 x 16s and the 527 use 7:00 x 16s.

Fuel capacity on the 518s was a 15-gallon tank, whil the other two used a 19-gallon supply. All models use mechanical brakes for the year. Body styles consisted c seven models. The 521 models used a 121-inch wheelbas and the 527s came with a 127½-inch wheelbase. The las two numerals in the model designations referred to th car's wheelbase.

Hupmobile sales came in the 17th position. They sol 9,346 cars for the year.

For 1935 the Hupmobile Series 521 was displayed again, only this year the 121-inch model was delivered on the Aerodynamic chassis. It weighed 3,325 lbs. and sold for $1,095. All 521 models used a 6-cylinder engine.

Looking down on a car with an Aerodynamic design certainly shows its appeal for fleetness. This 426 Hupmobile Sedan for 1934 came on a 126-inch wheelbase, weighed 3,845 lbs., and sold for $1,145 as did the Coupe. The handle above the spare tire cover was for opening the trunk. It really wasn't the most spacious trunk for carrying luggage but it at least kept it protected from the weather.

Factory executives look pleased with their new 1935 offering of the Series 518 which actually was to take the place of the former Series 417. It was offered only as a 4-door sedan and sold for $795.

1936

Even though the Aerodynamic design was basically ıchanged, the Six and 8-cylinder models did come forth ıth a more pleasing line and had more plushness to the teriors. The cars showed off a new chrome-plated grille ith the hood louvers being formed into a more stream-ıed effect. Also new was an automatic overdrive as ›tional equipment at extra cost. The unit was placed at e rear of the transmission, which really made it an .tomatic two-speed transmission in series with a three-eed transmission.

The 6-cylinder model had a 118-inch wheelbase, and ıs equipped with a 101 HP engine at 3600 RPM. It used 00 x 16-inch tires and a 16-gallon fuel supply, as were ed in the Eight. Six models were available in the 618 ries. Prices were $795 for the 3-passenger Coupe to ;90 for the Touring Sedan.

Eight cylinder models came as 121-inch cars, with :0 HP at 3500 RPM. This series, called the 621, used 50 x 16-inch tires. The models available numbered five, ıging from the $995 Sedan to the Touring Trunk Sedan r $1,075. All Hupmobiles used hydraulic brakes this ar.

Hupmobile placed 20th for the model run, selling 1,556 rs. The company did not present a new car for 1937 as ey reorganized and retooled that year for the 1938 car.

Hupmobile's most expensive line for 1935 was the 527. It was available in three body styles all selling for $1,395. This sedan weighed 3,700 lbs. The 527 only used 8-cylinder engines developing 120 HP at 3500 RPM. At the end of the year, the Series 527 was discontinued.

Even though there were only two series for 1936, more models had become available. This Series 518 Hupmobile Coupe was available either as a Business Coupe for $795 or in Rumble Seat Coupe style for $840.

New for the year was the 1936 Hupmobile Series 521 Touring Sedan that sold for $1,035 as an 8-cylinder. It could also be purchased in the 518 Series as a 6-cylinder for $850.

Available in the 1936 Hupmobile line was this 4-door Sedan as a Series 518 for $850, or on the 521 chassis for $995.

Hupmobile

Within each series of the 518 and 521 models was the Custom model which offered a more finely appointed interior and small exterior appointments as standard equipment. This 518 Sedan is an example, showing the rear fender skirts which were extremely rare even when this car was new. It sold for $880 equipped.

1938

The 1937 model didn't appear as Hupmobile was goi through a reorganization period and had plans of comi out with a different car for 1938. The company continu to build cars through late summer of 1940. Som historians claim these to be early 1941s.

Hupmobile offered its customers a 6 and an 8-cylind car. Its appearance wasn't quite as radical as the Aer dynamic models of the last body style but the car d tend to be rather streamlined for the time. The gearsh mounting could be ordered on the steering column but w optional at extra cost. A pleasing dash was arranged wi the start of many plastic appointments in the interi Unfortunately, these warped, discolored and cracked af a few years, as was true with all early plastic on ca

The engine developed 101 HP at 3600 RPM in the and the 8s produced 120 HP at the same RPM. Tire si on the 6 was 6:25 x 16 and 6:50 x 16s were on the A 122-inch wheelbase was used on the 6s and three mo inches were used on the 8s. Both models used a 16-gall fuel tank.

The body styles available were two Sedans. One ha flat back while the Touring Sedan employed a bus back trunk version. Both 6s and 8s came in the sa styles; the only difference was in wheelbases.

Hupmobile took the 19th seat this year by sell 1,020 units.

The newly styled Hupmobile for 1938 offered two versions of the sedan. One was with the bustle back trunk, the other had the flat back trunk as on this model. As a 6-cylinder it sold for $1,095 and as an 8-cylinder had a price tag of $1,245. The wheel trim rings this car wears were standard equipment on all 1938 Hupps. This model does not have the full standard equipped bumper guards that the 1938 Hupmobile finally had when delivered.

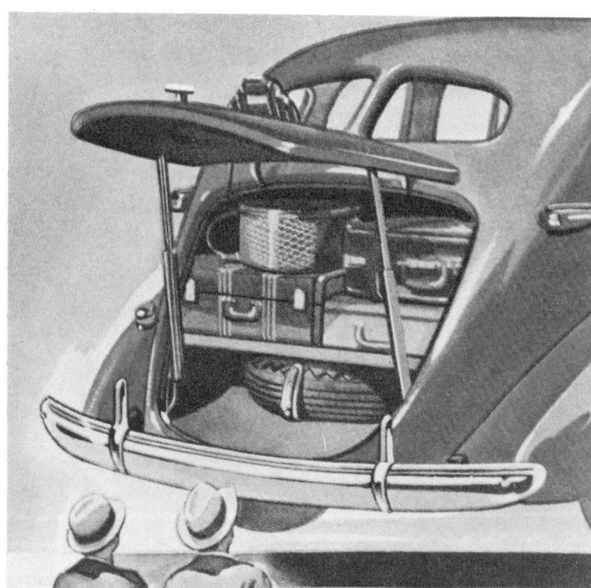

A trunk view shows the luggage capacity the 1938 Hupmobile flat back sedan could carry. Two sturdy trunk supports held the deck in a rigid position when opened. The spare tire always was carried beneath the luggage shelf.

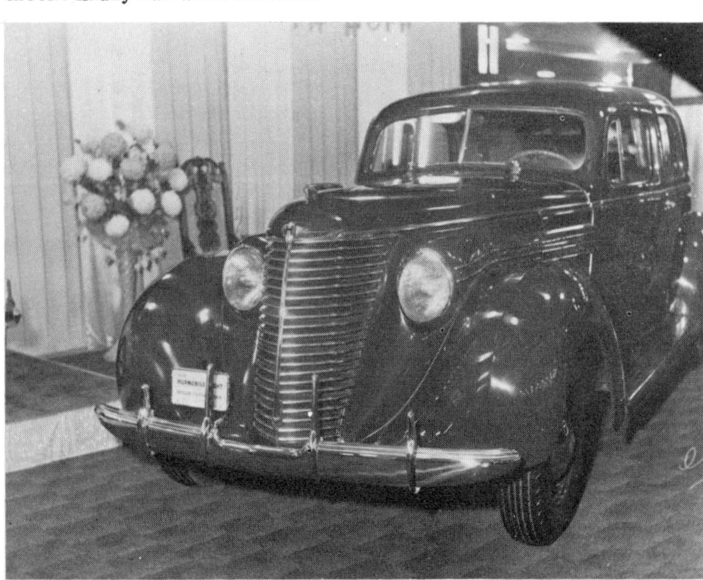

A front view of the 1938 Hupmobile Sedan on display at an Auto Show. This example is featured with two bumper grille guards and two smaller guards spaced further out. This was considered standard equipment on all models for the year.

939

The 1939 Hupp was offered in two radical styles, either resembling the other. Hupp bought the dies from ie Cord Corp. and built an ultra-modern new creation. ne new model came on a 115-inch wheelbase and used ie same 6-cylinder engine that was offered on the larger upmobile Six which developed 101 HP at 3600 RPM. his model used 6:00 x 16-inch tires. A 14-gallon fuel tank as supplied. Hupmobile offered only a sedan in two rsions, Sport Sedan and Custom Sedan. The car did not tain the Cord front-wheel drive but used its own rear rive. The company had planned on building this car also a 4-cylinder model. This didn't materialize, however. was priced at $995 in Sport Sedan version. Hupp's lditional models were the Senior Six and Eight. The Six sed the 101 HP engine and as an Eight developed 120 HP 3500 RPM. The Six came with 6:25 x 16-inch tires on a 22-inch wheelbase. The Eight used a 125-inch wheelbase ith 6:50 x 16 tires. Both models had a 16-gallon fuel ipply. Fewer than 1,400 cars were produced, again utting them in the 19th position for sales.

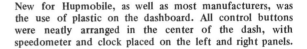

New for Hupmobile, as well as most manufacturers, was the use of plastic on the dashboard. All control buttons were neatly arranged in the center of the dash, with speedometer and clock placed on the left and right panels.

Hupmobile introduced this new car on the market in late 1939, calling it the Skylark. It used Cord body dies from the 1936-37 models. This particular version was called a Sport Sedan and sold for $995. The side panels differ from the models that were finally produced and came off the assembly line in Spring of 1940.

A side view of the 1939 Hupp Skylark Custom Sedan. Actual models did not have the squared off effect to the hood that these early prototypes came with. The more conventional 1938 Hupp continued to be sold into 1939, and approximately 1,400 cars were built before the Senior Hupps were discontinued.

A front view of the proposed 1939 Hupp Skylark. It was to have used front-wheel drive but last minute changes brought about the conventional rear drive train. This example wears different side panel trim from the earlier prototype for 1939.

Hupmobile

1940

The Hupmobile production ended in late 1940. Som historians claim these cars to be 1941s, but those tha were actually sold in 1941 were leftover 1940 model:

Only one series was available. It was the Hupmobi Skylark which came from the dies of the Cord Cor There were to be available three models, the 5-passeng Sedan, a 5-passenger Phaeton, and the Sportster, 3-passenger Convertible. Although photos have shown th Sportster, it is debateable if either the Phaeton or Sportst ever were produced beyond two or three models.

The 6-cylinder L-head engine developed 101 HP at 360 RPM. A 14-gallon fuel supply was used. The wheelba was 115 inches. The tire size was 6:00 x 16 inches. Th Skylark Sedan weighed 3,000 lbs. and was priced at $99 Following Hupp's demise, the Cord dies were bought b Graham and were used to produce that company Hollywood models.

The 1940 Hupmobile Sportster was a 3-passenger convertible cabriolet with an automatic top nicely concealed behind the seat when lowered. This car was to sell in the $1,000 bracket but it is doubtful if more than three were ever produced.

To be built on the same body style as the 1936-37 Cord Phaeton was the 1940 Hupmobile 5-passenger model called the Corsair Phaeton. Even though catalogued for 1940 it is doubtful if any were ever built.

This is the 1940 Hupmobile interior, showing off the dashboard with its airplane-like instrument panel. The customer had his choice of two-tone upholstery, in flat cloth or in mohair, and of five exterior colors.

Often referred to as the Flagship Series, this 115-inch Hupp sedan for 1940-41 is appropriately positioned in front of the plane with the same inscription. Note the hood lines were rounded off more than on the prototypes, which gave a pleasing appearance. This was one of the last Hupmobiles to be built. It sold for $995.

Jordan

The Jordan was a product of the Jordan Motor Co. ıe car was manufactured from 1916 to 1931 at eveland, Ohio.

The 1930 Jordan came in different series, all using cylinder Continental engines. The Series were called , 90, 93 and the Special Speedway. The Series 80 used 80 HP engine, 5:50 x 18-inch tires, and came on a 0-inch wheelbase. They used a 17½-gallon fuel supply e the larger models which came on 6:00 x 18-inch tires d employed a 125-inch wheelbase.

The 90 and 93 Series had an 85 HP engine at 3200 PM.

A total of 11 models were offered for the year ranging price from $2,095 for the 4-passenger "80" Coupe, to ,500 for the Speedway Series. The Speedway Series ed the 114 HP engine at 3200 RPM.

This was Jordan's next to last year of being manuctured. Output was so low that production and sales gures are listed with the miscellaneous makes for 1930.

One of Jordan's lower priced cars for 1930 was this rumble seat coupe for $2,095. This was known as the Series 80, which rode on a 120-inch wheelbase. Dummy landau irons gave a classy flair to the leather-covered top.

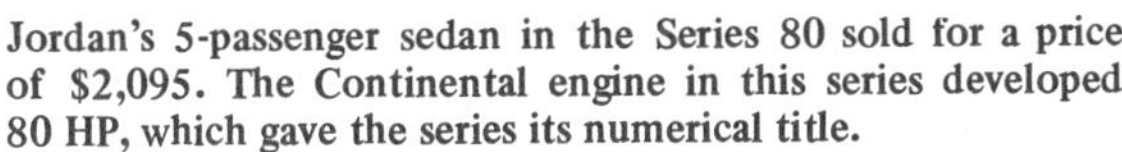

Jordan's 5-passenger sedan in the Series 80 sold for a price of $2,095. The Continental engine in this series developed 80 HP, which gave the series its numerical title.

The Series 90 Jordan Speedboy for 1930 was actually a dual-cowl phaeton. This example came with contrasting two-tone paint. This model used a 125-inch wheelbase and sold for $2,895. The spotlight and wind vane equipment was standard on this car.

Jordan

This close-coupled Jordan sedan for 1930 was classed as the Sport Sedan for 4 passengers. It came only in the 90 Series on a 125-inch chassis. It weighed 3,600 lbs. and sold for $2,695. The canvas top, side mount covers, and canvas covered trunk were all part of the package price.

1931

Two series, both 8-cylinder models, were available i 1931. They were the Jordan "80" and Jordan "90. The 80 Series came with a 246.7 cubic inch engine whic developed 80 HP at 3000 RPM. They used 5:50 x 18-inc tires and had a 120-inch wheelbase. Both series use hydraulic brakes.

The 90 models came with a 268.6 cubic inch engine c 85 HP at 3200 RPM. They had 6:00 x 18-inch tires, an rode on a 125-inch wheelbase. Both models used 17½ gallon fuel tanks. Only two models were available in tl 80 Series, a 4-passenger Coupe and 5-passenger Seda Both cars sold for $1,795. The 90 Series offered ni models ranging in price from $2,295 for a 4-passeng Coupe to $2,795 for the 5-passenger Phaeton.

Jordan sales were not listed other than among tl miscellaneous cars for 1931.

Jordan offered this Series 90 Playboy in limited production for $2,595. The special trunk, sidemount mirrors, tire covers, spotlight, and wire wheels all were considered regular equipment for this Playboy. It was only available on the 125-inch wheelbase and weighed 3,540 lbs.

The 1930 Jordan 7-passenger Limousine offered solid comfort with an enclosed front compartment in leather, two folding jump seats, and a deeply cushioned main rear seat. It allowed for five in the rear and two in the front. This was the one exception in the Series 90 cars to use a 131-inch wheelbase. It sold for $2,795.

Rarely seen was the Series 93 Jordan for 1930. This example offered a more expensive interior than the Series 90 models and sold for $100 more than the Series 90 Coupe at $2,495. Five could sit comfortably in this car – three in front and two in the rumble seat. All Jordans featured an adjustable driver's seat.

Kissel

The Kissel was a product of the independent Kissel :otor Car Co. of Hartford, Wis., from 1906 through 1931. Kissel was available in both 6 and 8 for 1930. The 6- linder Model 73 had a 70 HP engine at 3500 RPM. 15-gallon fuel tank was used in this series. The tire ze was 6:00 x 18. It used a 117-inch wheelbase. Model 95 had an 8-cylinder engine that developed 95 HP 3400 RPM. They also used a 15-gallon fuel tank. The re size was the same as in Model 73. The wheelbase for ese cars was 125 inches. The top car of the company as Series 126 which was an 8-cylinder car developing 26 HP at 3300 RPM. This series rode on 7:00 x 18-inch res and came on two wheelbases of 132 and 139 inches. ll Kissels had Lockheed hydraulic brakes for 1930. hese cars used a 24-gallon fuel tank. The 1930 Kissels me in 19 different models ranging in price from $1,595 r a 5-passenger Brougham Sedan to $3,885 in 7-passenger rline Sedan fashion.

Kissel production and sales figures were so low that ey were not available. The Kissel was listed among the iscellaneous cars for 1930.

31

Kissels for this year were offered in three series – the , 95, and 126.

The 73s offered an 8-cylinder, 185 cubic inch engine veloping 70 HP at 3500 RPM. The fuel supply came om a 15-gallon tank. The wheelbase was 117 inches and is model used 6:00 x 18-inch tires.

The 95 Series used an 8-cylinder engine of 246 cubic ches that developed 95 HP at 3400 RPM. A 15-gallon el tank also was used. A 125-inch wheelbase was used d 6:00 x 18-inch tires were also employed.

The luxury 126s used a 298 cubic inch engine developing 6 HP at 3600 RPM. They used a 24-gallon fuel tank. e tire size was 7:00 x 18 inches. Two wheelbases were ed, the 132-inch Speedster and Roadster and the 139- ch Sedans of different styles.

Nineteen different body types were available among the ree series. Prices ranged from a $1,595 5-passenger ougham Sedan in Series 73 to $3,885 for a Series 126 rline Sedan for 7 passengers.

Kissel sales and production figures for 1931 were only nked among the miscellaneous cars for the year.

The 1930 Kissel Series 73 All-Year Coupe Roadster came on a 117-inch wheelbase. It weighed 3,132 lbs. and sold for $1,695. Its seating capacity allowed for 4 passengers – two in front and two in the rumble seat. The top would fold down, and the landau irons were functional.

Kissel offered this 1930 Brougham Sedan in all three of its series. This model happened to be the 8-cylinder Series 95. It came as a 125-inch vehicle that weighed 3,664 lbs. and sold for $2,595. The "73" Brougham was $1,995 and the "126" Brougham came in an all-year style for $3,185, and a deluxe version sold for $3,275.

The Kissel sport model for the 1930 year came on the 95 Series chassis for $2,195 and on the 126 Series chassis for $3,275. The wheelbases were 125 inches and 132 inches respectively. This was a semi-custom car, available on special order only. The car was often referred to as the Kissel Gold Bug.

Kissel's top of the line cars for 1930 were the Series 126. This 7-passenger sedan weighed 4,680 lbs. and sold for $3,785. A Berline Sedan was also available in 7-passenger style. It weighed 4,743 lbs. and sold for $3,885. Very few of these 7-passenger models were ever produced. The 126 models were known as the White Eagle Series.

La Fayette

A new make for 1934 was introduced by Nash. It was called the La Fayette. This was the 2-passenger Coupe which was La Fayette's lowest priced model. It sold for $585 and weighed 2,925 lbs. A 4-passenger rumble seat coupe also was available in the deluxe line for $700.

The least popular La Fayette for 1934 was the 5-passenger 2-door sedan for $650. This model weighed 3,030 lbs. It came only on a 113-inch wheelbase.

New for the year was the La Fayette, a product c Nash Motors Co. of Kenosha, Wisconsin. This car took it name from the V-8 La Fayette which was built from 192 to 1923. That car also was owned by Nash, only unde separate manufacture. The 1934 La Fayette was buil through 1939, and sold only through Nash dealer:

This new Six used a 113-inch wheelbase chassis and cam in eight body styles ranging from the 2-passenger Coup for $585 to the 5-passenger Town Sedan Brougham fc $745. Brakes were of the mechanical type in all model: Free wheeling was available, but wasn't included in th base price. The fuel system consisted of a 16-gallon tanl Tire size was 5:50 x 17 with 6:50 x 16 being used a optional equipment. Wheels were either steel artiller or wire. The car developed 75 HP at 3200 RPM. Its engin was mounted in rubber at four points and there was rubber mounted stabilizer at the rear of the transmissioı

Standard equipment included safety glass windshielc package compartment, vacuum operated windshield wipe one adjustable sun visor, disappearing ash tray on th dash panel, non-glare rear view mirror, and built-in radi antenna. Factory equipment at extra cost were bumpe: with guards, metal spring covers, metal spare tire cove and spare tire lock.

Optional equipment at extra cost consisted of indepen ently sprung front wheels, air wheels, free wheelin detachable trunk, radio, heater, and safety glass in sid windows.

Cars could be equipped with a plentitude of delu accessories such as cigar lighter, dual windshield wipe double sun visors, outside side-mirror with thermomet attached, chromium plated trumpet horns, special stainle steel wheel covers, and driving lights. These were classed Royal equipped, Regal equipped, or Crown equipp cars, depending on the prescribed equipment.

La Fayette produced 28,664 units, putting them in tl 11th sales slot for 1934. These calendar year figures a combined with Nash.

The most popular model 1934 La Fayette was the 5-passenger sedan, available for $620 as a completely stripped car for $670, with more trim but still in the standard line, and $720 as a deluxe model. The deluxe line came with a built-in trunk as standard equipment. Note the vent panels on the side of the hood for engine cooling control.

La Fayette's 1934 5-passenger touring sedan came equipped with a built-in trunk and received many more orders than its 2-door sedan sister model. It sold for $700 and weighed 3,030 lbs. Note the factory striping on the pressed steel wheels. This was a Nash-La Fayette trademark during those years. A deluxe version of this car sold for $750.

935

For the model run, the car came in eight body styles nging from $585 for the 2-passenger Coupe up to 750 in 5-passenger Sedan body style. All models rode n 6:00 x 16-inch tires with 6:50 x 16s optional at extra ost. The engine developed 80 HP at 3200 RPM. The fuel nk carried 16 gallons. Its wheelbase was the same as st year, 113 inches. Brakes hadn't become hydraulic as ey did for Nash. Free wheeling was not available this ear.

The car's new features included softer front springs quipped with a new insert cushion. Hood louvers were designed to give more engine cooling capacity, and a ew radiator filler cap was used to seal the radiator from e overflow pipe unless enough pressure rose per square ch. At that time a spring-closed valve would open. This ew device was an aid to prevent water from evaporating well as boiling in high altitudes.

La Fayette sales for the year showed 44,637 units, acing them in 12th position for the year. These figures so represent Nash for 1935.

A front view of the 1935 La Fayette shows the headlamps perched on brackets in the fender catwalks. There was hardly any change in this car's appearance from the 1934 models. The engine received better cooling from newly designed hood vents. The horsepower was increased from 75 to 80 on the 1935 line.

A 3-passenger business coupe was La Fayette's lowest priced model for 1936. It sold for $595 and weighed 3,025 lbs. These cars were noted for their excellent gasoline economy–but certainly drew no raves from other automotive stylists.

This was the 1935 La Fayette 5-passenger trunk sedan, commonly called the Brougham. For the factory, it was known as Model 3513. The F.O.B. price was $750, an increase of $30 over the 1934 model.

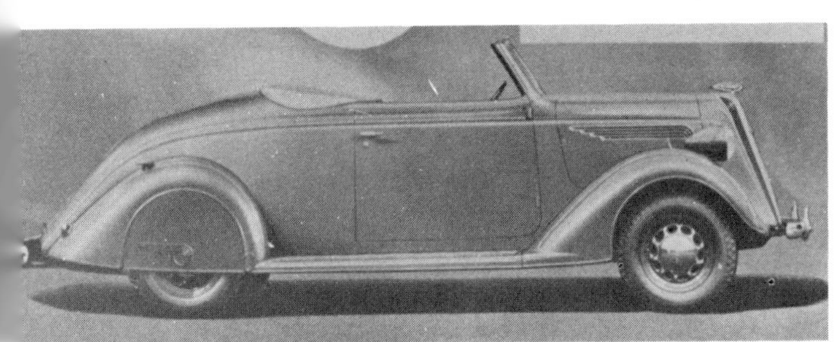

Technically, this rare open model was known as the Sport Cabriolet. It weighed 3,125 lbs. and sold for $675. During the year, Nash-La Fayette made a profit of $1,020,708 on sales of $30,965,894.

La Fayette introduced a new body style. This was called the Victoria with trunk. It weighed 3,075 lbs. and sold for $625. The fender skirts this model wears were a factory accessory.

La Fayette

Model 3618 was the technical name for this 1936 La Fayette Sedan that weighed 3,075 lbs. and sold for $675. To work on the engine of these little cars a hood release lifted the entire hood from the front. The wheelbase continued to be 113 inches.

For $25 more than the sedan, a buyer could have this 6-passenger trunk sedan for $700. It weighed 3,075 lbs. Most people preferred it, as it tended to be the most popular model for the year. The La Fayette was billed as "The big car in the low priced field for 1936." It also was the last year to be called a straight La Fayette. Beginning in 1937 all models were called Nash La Fayette 400's, and continued this way through 1939.

This 1938 Nash La Fayette 6-passenger, 2-door sedan was a very popular model in the low priced market. It weighed 3,290 lbs. and sold for $855. This model evidently was put into dealer use by the looks of the California demonstrator license fastened to the bumper support bracket.

1936

The 1936 La Fayette debuted with a sloping Vee-shape grille with cross bars both at top and bottom of th vertical barred grille. The cars were sold jointly in Nasl La Fayette dealerships.

Mechanically, the La Fayette came with a new cylinder 83 HP engine at 3200 RPM. The fuel capacit was 15 gallons. The car used 6:00 x 16-inch tires. Brake were of the hydraulic type by Bendix. All models rode o a 113-inch wheelbase. Models available numbered seve ranging in price from a $595 3-passenger Coupe to $700 Touring Trunk Sedan.

La Fayette placed 13th for the year by selling 53,03 cars. This was the last year La Fayette would go under tl straight nomenclature of La Fayette. In 1937, it w referred to as the Nash La Fayette 400. These sales figur also include Nash for the calendar year.

This 1938 Nash La Fayette 4-door sedan was technically called Model 3818. By this time the horsepower had been raised to 95 at 3400 RPM. The wheelbase was now 117 inches. The sedan weighed 3,300 lbs. and sold for $900.

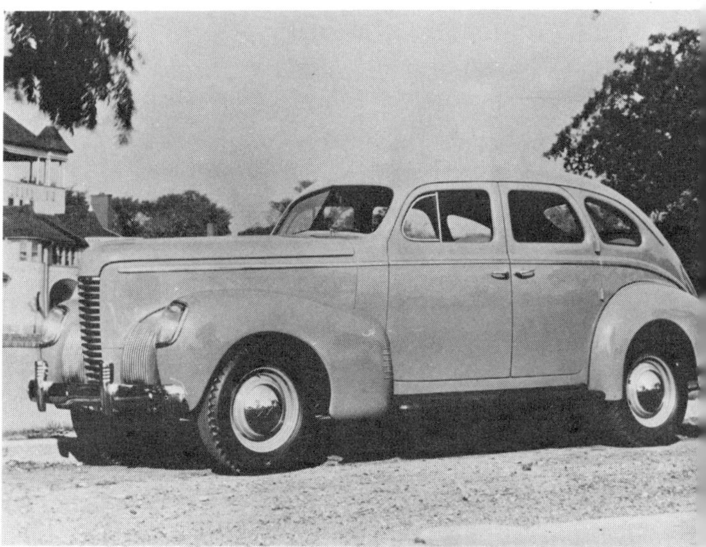

This was the 1939 Nash La Fayette 4-door sedan which was one of many of the 1939 line to show a price reduction. This car sold for $885. The corporation saw a loss of $1,573,524 by the end of their fiscal year which was Sept. 30.

La Salle

The La Salle was a division of General Motors Corp.,)etroit. The car was always considered a sub-series of 'adillac. Production began in 1927 and ceased in 1940.

For 1930, La Salle offered a V-8 engine developing 0 HP at 3000 RPM. This engine was 340 cubic inches. 'he car had a 23-gallon fuel supply. Its wheelbase was 34 inches. The tire size was 6:50 x 19 inches. Mechanical rakes were used on La Salles for 1930.

Thirteen models were available during the year. Prices ınged between $2,385 for a 4-passenger Phaeton upward ↄ $3,825 for a 4-passenger Sedanet.

The company had entered its fourth year in the automotive market and ranked in 16th position by selling 2,559 cars. Its calendar year sales are placed with Cadillac.

La Salle referred to this 1930 model as the Phaeton. It was the lowest priced car. It sold for $2,385, had a seating capacity for four passengers and weighed 4,060 lbs. This body style had a vee-shaped windshield which was an early departure from the one-piece windshield. This model had a Fleetwood body.

The 1930 7-passenger La Salle Touring came on the 134-inch wheelbase, weighed 4,057 lbs., and sold for $4,057. The body was by Fleetwood. The wooden artillery wheels were standard equipment. Note the coat-of-arms on the canvas tire covers.

A close-coupled sedan, that La Salle referred to as the Town Sedan, weighed 4,660 lbs. and sold for $2,590. The wooden artillery wheels which this 1930 model sports were standard equipment. The sidemount tire equipment and trunk were available at extra cost. Most of this body style were equipped like this car.

La Salle's 7-passenger sedan used the regular 134-inch chassis that weighed 4,725 lbs. and sold for $2,775. This car used a Fisher body. A 7-passenger Imperial Sedan by Fleetwood also was available for $2,925.

This was La Salle's best seller in 1930. It was simply called the 5-passenger sedan and weighed 4,645 lbs. This body style in base form brought a price tag of $2,565. The wire wheels were no-cost optional equipment, but the sidemount tires were classed as an accessory. The body was by Fisher.

La Salle

The 1930 La Salle Sedanette Cabriolet for 1930 used a Fleetwood body and was often referred to as the "Fleetwing" model. Like all other 1930 La Salles it employed 6:50 x 19-inch tires with the optional wire wheels. It sold for $3,725. It had a seating capacity for 4 passengers. This roof line would almost make one think it was the original "hardtop." It weighed 4,081 lbs.

La Salle's 1930 Sedanet weighed only one pound more than the Sedanet Cabriolet, coming in at 3,182 lbs. But it sold for $100 more at $3,825. The body also was by Fleetwood. This model employed the vee-shaped windshield like the Phaeton.

The lowest priced La Salle in 1931 was this 2-passenger coupe with body by Fisher. Even though referred to as a 2-passenger model, the rumble seat arrangement allowed for two more passengers. A neatly placed golf compartment was arranged on the right side quarter panel. Disc wheels were available as standard equipment. This model weighed 4,470 lbs. and sold for $2,195.

Being displayed at a car show is this beautiful 7-passenger 1931 La Salle Touring. The car weighed 4,440 lbs. and sold, when new, for $2,345. This example is fully equipped and has the correct wooden artillery wheels. The bumper mounted fog lights were accessories.

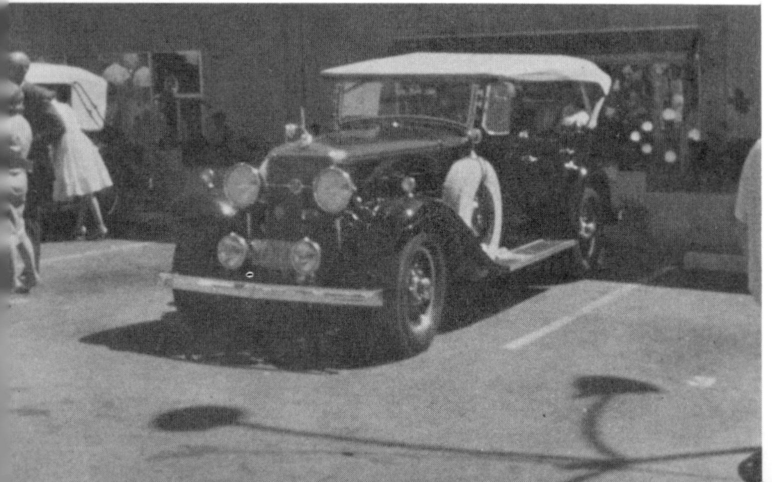

1931

La Salle now offered a 353 cubic inch V-8 that develope 95 HP at 3000 RPM. This car was practically the sam automobile as the Cadillac V-8.

Surprisingly enough, the La Salle offered a two-gallo larger fuel tank (23 gallons) than the Cadillac V-8. Th tire size also was different from the Cadillac, as it rode o 7:00 x 18-inch tires. It weighed ten pounds less at 4,65 pounds in 4-door sedan version. Mechanical brakes wer used on La Salles at this time.

A total of 12 body styles were available with price beginning at $2,195 for the 4-passenger Coupe to $3,24 as a Sedan Cabriolet for 5 passengers.

La Salle and Cadillac sold 15,012 cars, which place them in 16th position for the calendar year.

1932

La Salle offered its followers pretty much the sam package as did Cadillac. La Salle for 1932 resembled th Cadillac V-8.

La Salle now came with a 115 HP V-8 (3000 RPM) ju as did the Cadillac V-8. They had the same tire and whe size of 7:00 x 17. Fuel tank capacity was 30 gallon Wheelbases differed slightly from the Cadillac V-8. L Salle used a 130-inch wheelbase or a 136-inch wheelbas on the 7-passenger Sedan.

Seven basic models were offered ranging from th $2,395 4-passenger Coupe to $2,745 for the Imperi 7-passenger Sedan. La Salle, with Cadillac, sold 9,158 uni during this year putting it in 15th slot for sales positio

The 1931 La Salle 5-passenger all-weather Phaeton with body by Fleetwood weighed 4,675 lbs. and sold for $3,245. The wire wheels were optional equipment. A glass division separated the rear seat passengers from the front passengers if the owner desired, but could be lowered by a window crank on the back of the front seat compartment. The center pillars folded out of sight when the side windows were lowered.

1933

Like Cadillac, body styles were quite similar to 1932. Grilles had a Vee-shape to round out the frontal appearance, fenders were given a more skirted effect, and the rear of the car was streamlined into a nicely proportioned body. The beautiful hood ornament was one which stood chiefly as a stationary piece of art, as the filler opening was placed under the hood. As is true with Cadillac, Fisher no-draft ventilation was made standard equipment, with windshields being permanently placed.

La Salle offered seven body styles, ranging from a 4-passenger Coupe for $2,245 to the Imperial 7-passenger Limousine for $2,645. Wheelbases were 130 inches for four models and 136 inches for the larger sedans. All models used 7:00 x 17-inch tires. The engine was the same as the Cadillac V-8. The La Salle weighed 4,860 lbs. in its 4-door version while the Cadillac tipped the scale with its 4-door V-8 at 5,015 lbs. Fuel capacity was a 30-gallon tank. Vacuum-operated brakes, as used before on Cadillacs' larger series, were now offered for the first time on the La Salle as standard equipment. The Bendix vacuum-operated clutch control was still optional equipment on all models.

La Salle showed 12th position with 6,736 cars being sold. These figures are combined with Cadillac for the calendar year.

La Salle's most popular car in 1931 was this 5-passenger sedan weighing 4,650 lbs. It sold for $2,345. It was powered by a V-8.

Offering a flare of individuality was the 1931 La Salle Town Sedan with body by Fisher. This model weighed 4,665 lbs. and sold for $2,345. The trunk and additional luggage rack were standard items on this car, as were the sidemounts.

This was referred to as La Salle's Town Coupe for 1932. It used the 130-inch chassis and sold for $2,545. The disc wheels which this model portrays were optional equipment at extra cost, but the built-on trunk was standard.

This 7-passenger Sedan, offered by La Salle in 1931, used a Fisher body. It weighed 4,750 lbs. and sold for $2,475. An Imperial 7-passenger model also was available. It weighed 4,825 lbs. and sold for $2,595. Non-shatter Security-Plate glass was used in all La Salle windows this year.

La Salle offered this 1932 2-passenger Coupe with rumble seat as their lowest priced model for $2,395. This model used the Fisher body mounted on a 130-inch chassis. The driver's half of the seat was adjustable forward and back which made it more pleasant for the driver. Five wire wheels were standard equipment.

Nicely equipped for a Sunday outing is this 1932 La Salle Convertible Coupe for 4 passengers. This example wears the sidemount wheel equipment, sidemount mirrors, luggage rack, and white sidewall tires, all extra equipment. It sold in base form for $2,495.

La Salle

La Salle's best seller for 1932 was this 5-passenger sedan. Strangely enough, it sold for the same price as the Town Coupe, $2,545. The sidemount tire equipment was optional at extra cost. Wire wheels, however, were standard equipment.

1934

The highlights for the 1934 La Salles consisted of streamlined new bodies and independently sprung front wheels. This year La Salle came with Fleetwood bodies and a new L-head straight-Eight engine developing 90 HP at 3700 RPM. The car used a 119-inch wheelbase and 7:50 x 16-inch tires carrying only 22 lbs. pressure. These new models weighed approximately 3,750 lbs.

La Salle's fleeting design made it look about 20 inches longer than it actually was. Streamlined fenders and headlamps had always been notable features of this car. Bi-plane bumpers were another feature of the 1934 La Salles. All La Salles used a 20-gallon fuel supply. They were one of the first G.M. cars to switch over to hydraulic brakes.

Five body styles were available this year, ranging from $1,495 for the Coupe to $1,675 for the 5-passenger Club Sedan.

La Salle took a 13th position by selling 11,468 cars. These calendar year figures are also including Cadillac. In 1934, La Salle was the pacesetter for "Indy 500."

Offered only on the 136-inch chassis was this 1932 7-passenger La Salle sedan which sold for $2,645. It also was available as a 7-passenger Imperial sedan for $2,795. Five wire wheels were standard, but the sidemounts were extra.

La Salle's 1933 Town Coupe was available for $2,395. This example has the trunk, luggage rack, and sidemount equipment all at extra cost. Two-tone paint was quite common on La Salles in 1933 but wouldn't be seen again until the 1940 models.

La Salle's lowest priced car for 1933 was this 4-passenger rumble seat coupe that weighed 4,389 lbs. and sold for $2,245. Wire wheels were standard equipment but the sidemount equipment with tire covers were optional at extra cost. Whitewalls were also classed as special equipment.

The most popular 1933 La Salle was the 5-passenger sedan. It came on a 130-inch chassis and sold for $2,395, the same as the Town Coupe. This model shows off the new vent panes in the front door glass, which became available in 1933 on all G.M. cars. It was called Fisher's No-Draft Ventilation.

.935

For the model year, the same as held true for Cadillac ılso applied to La Salle. The car virtually was the same ıutomobile as the year before.

Mechanically, about all that appeared different was an ıncrease in power from 90 to 95. The RPM also changed ›y dropping 100 to 3600. Wheelbase was 119 inches again; ire size was 7:00 x 16 for the year; the fuel system was ?0 gallons again, and the hydraulic brakes, being a selling 'eature in 1934, were again advertised as the best available.

In appearance, the 1934 and 1935 models were ›ractically identical except the 1934 biplane bumpers vere gone in favor of the one-piece steel bumpers with pring strengtheners behind the bumper bars.

Five models again were displayed – all were straight 8 :ngine cars. They earned a sales spot of 14th by selling ?3,559 cars in the calendar year. These figures also are for Cadillac sales. Prices were lowered and a 5-passenger Sedan :ould be purchased for $1,295.

The 1933 7-passenger La Salle Limousine came only on a 136-inch chassis, and sold for $2,495. It also was available as a 7-passenger Imperial Sedan, selling for $2,645. A rear-mount spare was standard. The sidemounts and luggage rack shown here were accessories.

La Salle entered the 1934 model year with an entirely different car both in appearance and with a straight eight engine developing 90 HP. This example also was offered with a much lower price of $1,495 for the 4-passenger rumble seat coupe.

With top up, this 1934 La Salle Convertible Coupe sits proudly with new lines to appeal to all. The bi-plane bumpers were an attraction of the 1934 La Salle line. It sold for $1,595.

Getting ready for May 30, 1934, at the Memorial Day Indianapolis 500 is the Pace Setter for the race. It's a 1934 La Salle Convertible Coupe. Note the accessory chrome wheel discs.

La Salle's most popular entry for 1934 was this 5-passenger sedan for $1,650. The painted disc wheel covers were part of the standard equipment. On the base of the hood was mounted the familiar La Salle hood ornament. The car used a 119-inch wheelbase.

La Salle

The same 5-passenger La Salle sedan for 1934, when fitted with the sidemount tires, had a look of more length. A 5-passenger club Sedan, with enclosed rear quarter panels, was the most expensive model selling for $1,675. Note the Chevrons mounted on the front crown of the fenders. This became a La Salle trademark for the next few years.

1936

For 1936, La Salle just made improvements over the 1935 car. Appearance differed only slightly, with a new radiator grille. Front doors were no longer of the suicide type, hood parts became more streamlined, and the instrument panel was very similar to the Cadillac V-8. Interior appointments also differed from the preceding model with the hand brake lever being mounted on the left side under the cowl. This was the last year for La Salle to use a straight Eight engine. In 1937, it would return to the V-8.

The engine was a 105 HP L-head 8, (3600 RPM). The fuel capacity was 18 gallons. Hydraulic brakes were used. Tire size was 7:00 x 16 on the 120-inch car. Four models were available with a starting price of $1,175 for the 2-passenger Coupe and going upward to $1,255 for the 4-passenger Convertible Coupe.

La Salle placed 14th for the year, selling 28,479 cars. These figures also represent Cadillac calendar year sales.

Virtually unchanged from the 1934 line was the La Salle Coupe for 1935. This model was a 4-passenger coupe with rumble seat. It weighed 3,815 lbs. but carried a lower price tag than the previous year. It sold for $1,225.

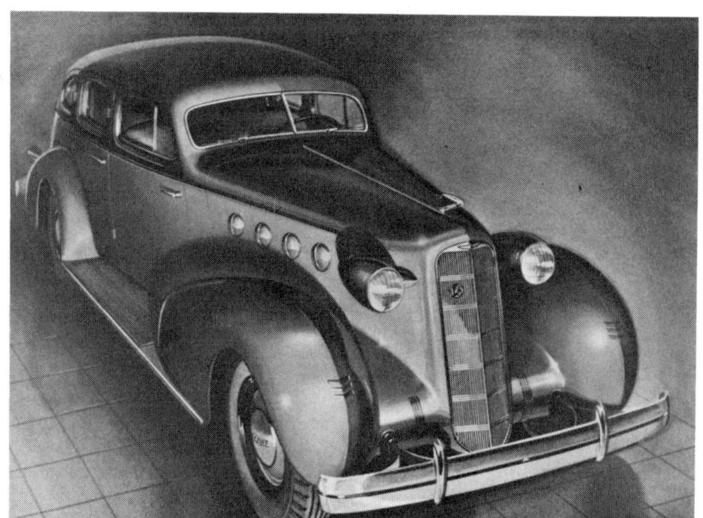

This was the most popular model La Salle offered in 1935. It's a 5-passenger sedan that weighed 3,995 lbs. and sold for $1,295. A single bar bumper was used on the 1935 cars in place of the popular bi-plane design of 1934.

Very trim looking is this 1935 La Salle Convertible Coupe with the optional at extra cost sidemount equipment. It weighed 3,780 lbs. and was available for $1,280 with the straight-Eight engine. Note that taillights and headlights are of the same pointed contour.

The 2-door Touring Sedan was how La Salle referred to this 1935 model. It weighed 3,925 lbs. and sold for $1,260. The horsepower was increased to 95 at 3600 RPM.

937

La Salle came back with a V-8 for the 1937 model run hich was the same engine as used in the Cadillac Series 0 of 1936. Both La Salle and Cadillac 60s were very ose in the similarity of their specifications.

The La Salle came with hypoid rear axle in which the inion was two inches lower than the center line of the ng gear.

Appearance of the 1937s was a very beautiful car with stately narrow grille and well-crowned fenders. The front nders had three V-shaped chevrons placed at the center f the crown. Headlamps were placed on the mountings f the radiator grille.

Mechanically, this V-8 model developed 125 HP at 400 RPM. This model came with 7:00 x 16-inch tires on 124-inch wheelbase. The fuel supply was a 22-gallon nk. Five models were available which ranged in price om $995 for the 4-passenger Coupe to $1,620 for the onvertible Sedan in 5-passenger form.

La Salle placed in 15th sales position this year by selling 5,223 cars. These figures also include sales from Cadillac or the calendar year.

The 1937 V-8 La Salle was the car chosen for the pace-tter of the Memorial Day Race at Indianapolis.

For 1936 La Salle's lowest priced car was this Coupe which sold for $1,175. It weighed 3,815 lbs. and was basically the same offering as in 1935 except the engine now developed 105 HP at 3600 RPM.

This stately 1936 La Salle Convertible Coupe offered sidemount tire equipment as an extra cost item. This was the last year the company would build a straight-Eight engine. This Convertible Coupe sold for $1,255, the same as the sedan, but weighed 3,860 lbs.

Gone were the suicide front doors on the 1936 La Salle models. This 2-door Touring Sedan also was known as a Touring Coupe. It sold for $1,185 and weighed 3,853 lbs.

Back was the V-8 for La Salle in 1937. This model was the lowest priced offering for the year. It sold for $995 F.O.B. Detroit. The wheelbase increased to 124 inches on all models. This model wears the accessory full wheel covers similar to Cadillac.

La Salle

The 1937 La Salle 2-door Touring Sedan weighed 3,710 lbs. and sold for $1,105. This was the least popular of the closed La Salle models for 1937.

1938

The 1938 La Salle was displayed with a somewha restyled car from the 1937s. The bodies were roomier an a lower chassis was used. The grille resembled the Cadillac' a great deal as it was much wider than any La Salle befor or after. The well-crowned front fenders gave the car more massive appearance in the front end. The openin device for the hood was no longer placed on the side of th hood panels but was now used on the front hood emble by pulling upward. When closed the hood was held by a automatic catch in addition to the lock operated by th ornament.

The V-8 La Salle again used the 125 HP engine (340 RPM) with a compression ratio of 6:25. All models rod on 7:00 x 16-inch tires and came on 124-inch wheelbas The fuel supply was a 22-gallon tank. A total of fiv models were available. Prices varied from $1,300 for th 2-passenger Coupe to $1,820 for a 5-passenger Convertib Sedan. Available for the first time in limited quantity wa the sun roof. It was available only on the 4-door Seda Model 5019A. A total of 72 were produced.

La Salle sold 27,613 units during the calendar ru which placed them in 14th position for the year. The figures also represent calendar sales from Cadillac for 193

La Salle's most expensive offering for 1937 was this 5-passenger Convertible Sedan. It sold for $1,620 in base form. This example wears the six-wheel equipment, tire covers, wheel trim rings, and white sidewall tires at extra cost. This was the last year for La Salle to display the three chevrons on both front fenders, which they introduced in 1934.

This 1937 La Salle 5-passenger 4-door Touring Sedan was the company's best selling car for the year. It sold for $1,145 and weighed 3,740 lbs. The 125 HP V-8 engine was very similar to what was used in the 1936 Cadillac Series 60.

Again La Salle had the honor of having its Convertible Coupe be the Pacesetter for the Indianapolis 500. The pace car was similar to this 1937 model, priced at $1,290 in base form. This model wears the six-wheel package, wheel trim rings, and white sidewall tires as optional equipment at extra cost.

For 1938, this $1,300 La Salle Coupe was the lowest priced car. It resembled Cadillac a great deal, with its wider grille and more massive front end. It weighed 3,615 lbs.

939

The 1939 La Salle and Cadillac Series 61 were very ose in all their specifications. The wheelbase for the 939 model was lessened by four inches, making it 120 ıches, but it still offered a body that was 1-9/16 inches nger than the Cadillac. The front appearance showed a Salle's return to its tall, narrow and stately grille with ullet shaped headlamps mounted to the radiator panels. 'ell-crowned fenders, which were a La Salle feature in the revious models, were very effective on the 1939 models. ll series carried the license plate on the rear mounted on ie trunk for the first time, with an illuminated lamp nder the license bracket which also included the trunk andle. The La Salle Convertible Coupe no longer offered rumble seat, as small opera seats were now stationed ehind the driver's seat.

Mechanically, the La Salle came as a V-8 with 125 HP 3400 RPM. The models all used 7:00 x 16-inch tires. 22-gallon fuel tank was offered again for that year. Again, an optional accessory at extra cost that was ailable for the La Salle 2 and 4-door Sedans was the n roof. Turning the crank slid this device backward. his was also available for Cadillac 60 and 61 Sedans and as also used on Buick and Oldsmobile models.

La Salle was offered in five body styles for the year, nging in price from $1,240 for the 4-passenger Coupe to ,880 in the 5-passenger Convertible Sedan. All models ere referred to as Series 50 cars.

La Salle placed in the 15th position for the calendar ar by turning out 38,250 cars. These sales figures also clude Cadillac for 1939.

The top of the line for the 1938 La Salle was the Convertible Sedan. It sold for $1,820 in base form. The sidemount equipment, white sidewalls, and large wheel covers were frequently seen on this model but still were available only at extra cost.

An entirely different looking car was offered by La Salle for the 1939 model run. This 4-door Touring Sedan sold for $1,320 and weighed 3,750 lbs. An optional sunroof was available on this model. A total of 404 4-door sedans had this accessory and 23 2-door sedans carried the extra cost option.

With headlamps neatly placed in the catwalks the 1938 La Salle looked larger than previous models since 1934. This example sold for $1,380 as the popular 5-passenger 4-door Touring Sedan. The white sidewall tires and large wheel covers were optional at extra cost.

This 1939 La Salle Convertible Coupe weighed 3,715 lbs. The wheelbase was lessened to 120 inches. Comfortably, it would seat four. It sold for $1,395.

La Salle's most expensive car in 1939 was the Convertible Sedan that brought a price of $1,880 F.O.B. Detroit. It weighed 3,780 lbs. and carried a Fisher body like the other models for the year. Streamboards were a new option at no additional cost if a customer preferred them in place of the running boards.

La Salle

The most popular 1940 La Salle was this Series 50 4-door Touring Sedan. It weighed 3,770 lbs. and sold for $1,360 F.O.B. Detroit. A sunroof option was available in this model as well as on the 2-door Touring Sedan. Only nine sunroofs were built in the 2-door style but 140 were sold in the 4-door model. This model has the full running board so the rubber scuff pads on rear fenders aren't used.

1940

This was the last year the La Salle was manufacture The 1940 La Salle was a very impressive car. In fact, it h often been said that this is probably the only car that w ever discontinued when sales were at an all-time hig La Salle, being considered the junior Cadillac, was takir too many sales away from the smaller Cadillacs. S management felt it would be wise to concentrate on a ne series of Cadillac models for the next year and phase o the name La Salle with the 1940 car.

Two series were available. They were the Series 5 which was less expensive, coming in five body styles, ar the Series 52 coming in the Torpedo body version ar being offered in four new models.

Mechanically, both Series were the same. The engi compartment held a 322 cubic inch V-8 developing 1 HP at 3400 RPM. The fuel supply was a 22-gallon tan Both series rode on 7:00 x 16-inch tires and had a 12 inch chassis.

La Salle prices began at $1,240 for a 4-passenger Cl Coupe and ended at $1,905 for the Series 52 Converti Sedan for 5 passengers.

The calendar year sales were generally joined wi Cadillac. However, La Salle took the 15th position f sales. For the first eight months of the 1940 model ru La Salle sold 16,599 cars.

New for the 1940 model run was the La Salle Special, technically called the Model 52. This car was considered to be the companion car to Cadillac's Sixty Special. It used the same body as the Series 62 Cadillac; however, it used the same 123-inch wheelbase as the Series 50. It sold for $1,450 F.O.B. Detroit.

La Salle's Series 50 Convertible Sedan sold for $1,825, which was less than the comparable model of 1939. Rear fender scuff pads are used on this car due to the use of streamboards in place of the runningboards.

Only 50 of this Series 52 La Salle Special Convertible Sedan were built. Each sold for $1,905. It was only offered as a mid-season car with the "52" Convertible Coupe, and thus, is quite rare today. This example has the factory accessory grille guard, full wheel covers, and whitewall tires as additional equipment. This was the last year that La Salle was built.

The 1940 La Salle Special Convertible Coupe, referred to as Model 52, did not make its debut with the regular 1940 line but was offered as a short run mid-season model. This car wears an accessory grille guard, double white sidewall tires and wheel trim rings as its extra equipment. It sold for $1,825.

The Lincoln was the luxury car of the Ford Motor Co. he main headquarters were located in Dearborn, Mich. he Lincoln first was displayed on the automotive scene ; a 1921 car on September 14, 1920. These cars were eland built Lincolns. During 1922, the Ford Motor Co. ɔok over the ownership of Lincoln and has owned it ⁄er since.

This was Lincoln's final year for the Model L which ad a 90 HP V-8 of 384.8 cubic inches, at 2800 RPM. he fuel supply was a 20-gallon tank. The tire size was :50 x 19 inches and the car measured 136 inches on s chassis.

Few changes were made in this last year of "L" roduction since plans for the Lincoln K were to start in ıst a few months. Appearance of the 1930s were ractically the same as the previous year but the fenders 'ere of matching body color, which helped to modernize ıe vehicles. Natural canvas tops and tire covers were ffered for open cars. All models shared mechanical brakes.

Sales were extremely low due to both the depression ıd Lincoln's not stressing sales too much for the advent f the Series K. A total of 20 models were available ınging from $4,200 for a 5-passenger Sport Phaeton to 7,200 for the 7-passenger All-Weather Cabriolet rougham.

Lincoln sold 4,356 cars, which put them in 26th sales osition.

Available for European sales was a plan offered by Lincoln even during the depression years. This 1930 Coupe with a Locke body is equipped with right hand drive and rear license mounted under the right tail lamp. This example weighed 5,245 lbs. and sold for $5,000 stateside.

Technically speaking this Lincoln Le Baron Sport Sedan was built in late 1929. Most were sold as 1930 cars. This model sold for $5,500 and came equipped with broadcloth headliner and seats. The door panels were done in leather with pockets in each panel. The top material was covered with Landau leather. This example is well-equipped with double white sidewall tires, twin spot lamps, monograms placed on the front door, deluxe tandem wipers, and a small extra lamp mounted above the tail lamp. The gentleman seated on the running board is a young Buster Keaton.

This 1930 Lincoln Dietrich Convertible Coupe came only as a 4-passenger model and sold for $6,200. This version weighed 4,900 lbs. Only 42 examples were built of this body style. Obviously, the landau irons were functional.

Lincoln's 1930 Convertible Sedan with Dietrich body was technically called Model 182. It sold for $6,600 and weighed 5,000 lbs. Only 40 of this style were built.

Lincoln

Offered as a 7-passenger Semi-Collapsible Cabriolet, this 1930 Lincoln Brunn sold for $7,200 and weighed 4,950 lbs. On this body style the rear quarter was collapsible and the forward compartment top became removable. The chauffeur received weather protection via a snap-on leather or leatherette top and roll-up windows.

The Le Baron All-Weather Cabriolet for 7 passengers was how Lincoln referred to this 1930 model. It sold for $6,900. In this series Lincoln offered an All-Weather Brougham, and an All-Weather Landaulet also. The entire series accounted for only 49 cars. The divided windshield was a feature of these models.

The late 1931 Lincoln Series K Sedan with a Le Baron body sold for $5,500. The hood louvers were similar to those which would appear on the 1932 models. The lower splash aprons gave the car a much longer appearance. Note the license plate was mounted incorrectly on the headlamp bar. All 1931's were placed directly in the center of the bumper. This hood was an experiment to see how a cowl-less design would look. Lincoln decided against the design, though the vent doors were adopted in 1932.

1931

The big news offered from Lincoln this year was i new car called the Model K. The Model L had bee discontinued with the 1930 line. The Model K engine di resemble the L engine a good deal as it carried the sam bore and stroke as the previous engine. The V-8 had 384. cubic inches developing 120 HP at 2900 RPM. The com pression was increased on this engine. A double downdra carburetor led gas into an improved manifold which di result in a better mixture to make the engine operate mo efficiently. The fuel tank held 28 gallons. The wheel siz on these cars was 7:00 x 19 inches, but if the own wished, an 18-inch wheel was available as option equipment. The wheelbase was 145 inches. Available we 23 styles ranging from a $4,400 Sport Touring in passenger fashion to the $7,400 5-passenger Broughar

With the depression letting Lincoln know it was ther only 3,311 cars were sold during the model run which pu them in 25th sales position.

1932

In 1932, Lincoln bowed with its new Series KB on 145-inch wheelbase chassis that used a 150 HP 12-cylind block with a 65-degree angle. Besides the KB, the V-8 wa continued, and used KA as its identifying symbol. Th quickest way to identify a KB from a KA is that the K identifying emblem was done in blue, while the KA wa shown in red. The KA was a less expensive car than i larger brother. Its bodies were largely production versio by both Lincoln and Murray.

The Eight had a 125 HP engine while the KB used 150 HP powerplant of 12 cylinders (3500 RPM). Th main difference appearancewise was that the KA retaine the earlier Series K radiator shell while the KB had a mo rounded effect to its radiator. Thirty body styles we available ranging from a $2,900 Rumbleseat Roadster the KA Series to the $7,200 KB 7-passenger Cabriole

All used 7:50 x 18-inch tires. The KA had a 136-inc wheelbase while the KB had a 145-inch wheelbase. A models had mechanical brakes by Bendix and a 28-gallo fuel supply. Between the KA and KB, only 3,388 ca were sold, putting the company in 21st place for the yea

This was the 1931 Lincoln Model K 3-Window Town Sedan, Model 204B, which sold for $4,600 and weighed 5,205 lbs. The total production run of this model was 447 units.

Lincoln

933

The big news from Lincoln at announcement time was ıat the V-8 was discontinued and the company was evoting its efforts to a smaller V-12 along with the larger B being continued. This smaller car received the desigation of KA as had been bestowed upon the V-8 in 932.

The horsepower of the KA was 125 at 3400 RPM. Its ig brother carried a 150 HP engine basically unchanged om what it was in 1932. This, however, was to be the st year for the KB Series. The production for this series ame to only 2,210 units.

The KA rode on a 136-inch wheelbase and the KB used ıe 145-inch wheelbase. Both models came with mechical vacuum booster brakes which featured a lever on ıe steering column for variable pressure adjustments. he fuel supply was a 28-gallon tank.

In the middle of the year, Lincoln sent out memos to ıe dealers that skirted fenders would be used on all future 933 Lincolns. If anyone who purchased a 1933 before ould prefer the change, the Ford Motor Co. would oblige.

Sales for 1933 showed only 587 KB models being roduced and 1,420 KAs coming off the line. Lincoln ook the 22nd seat for sales in 1933.

With a reduction in price this 1931 Lincoln Convertible Roadster, Model K sold for $4,700. This model was equipped with rumble seat and tire covers for the side-mounted spares. It weighed 4,810 lbs. The body was by Le Baron.

The 1931 Lincoln Series K All-Weather Cabriolet, Model 208, carried a Brunn body. It was available either with collapsible or non-collapsible top. It sold for $7,400. Only 30 examples were built in 1931.

The 1931 Willoughby Panel Brougham Lincoln Series K was classed as one of the most expensive models for the year. It sold for $7,400 and weighed 4,985 lbs. Willoughby produced Lincoln's highest styled models throughout the life of the Series K.

This was the least expensive 1932 Lincoln. Referred to as the KA Series, this model was built with a Murray body and sold for $3,200. This car used Lincoln's V-8 of 125 HP rather than the new V-12 of the KB Series.

A classic in every sense of the word was this 1932 Lincoln Convertible Roadster with body by Le Baron. In its rumble seat version it sold for $4,600. Its weight was 5,535 lbs.

Lincoln

Quite similar in many respects to the previous year is this 1933 Lincoln KA 5-passenger sedan. This sedan also sports a Murray body. It weighed 5,089 lbs. and sold for $3,200. The sidemount equipment and white sidewalls were accessories, however. The major difference, however, was that this year all KA Lincolns had a new V-12 instead of a V-8.

1934

With only a two-year span for the Lincoln KB and one-year show for the KA, both models were dropped fc 1934. A new model and engine, referred to simply a Series K, was introduced to the public. This new ca employed a V-12 engine of 414.1 cubic inches. At 340 RPM it developed 150 HP. It was a larger engine than th KA, and gave horsepower equal to that of the KB. Th engine was developed with a 67-degree slant, and a bo and stroke of 3-1/8 x 4.5. It used aluminum head

Models rode on 136-inch wheelbases and were designate as the 521 Series, still commonly called KA. The 145-inc wheelbase cars were still known as KB, and were used fc full-custom and semi-custom bodies, generally 7-passeng models. This series was factory known as 271. A Roadst or Phaeton design was available, but only on special orde

Early cars had louvered hoods at first, but during th year, these were discontinued in favor of thermostaticall controlled doors. A new ventilating system known "Clear Vision" was employed for all closed cars. consisted of screened cowl ventilators and a new bod ventilation system. A new overdrive unit was available fc all 136-inch wheelbase cars, and was standard on the 27 Series. Braking system was an improved mechanic two-shoe servo brake unit with vacuum booster. Tire siz was 7:00 x 18 inches on all models. Each series used 26-gallon fuel supply.

Twenty models were available ranging in price from 136-inch wheelbase 2-passenger Coupe for $3,200 to 145-inch wheelbase 7-passenger Brougham for $6,80 These cars had bodies built by Brunn, Judkins, LeBaro Willoughly, and Dietrich, as well as three of Lincoln own bodies.

Production rose slightly for the year, with 2,149 uni being delivered. The company placed 20th in sale

This elegant 1933 Lincoln Series K has a Le Baron body. It sold at a reduced price of $4,400. The gentleman standing by the trailer, circa 1934, is none other than the late movie comedian W. C. Fields.

Appearing very similar to the KA Series is the 1933 KB 7-passenger Sedan known as Model 257A. The big difference in this model over the KA line is the additional length of this car, which rode on a 145-inch wheelbase chassis. Only 110 of this model were produced at a cost of $4,700 in base form.

The 1934 Lincoln Willoughby 4-door Sport Sedan was a new offering for the year. This sedan weighed 5,661 lbs. and was available for $6,800. It used the 145-inch wheelbase chassis. The rear doors opening from the reverse made it a rather novel looking car for that era. The roof has a special ventilator, an attraction many cars were beginning to experiment with during 1934.

935

With the coming of something special from Lincoln in ıst a few months, the company wasn't too worried about ıe slow sales from the Series K. Still, time was ripe for a ·vamping. Both 136 and 145-inch cars were retained in incoln's lineup with the larger models referred to as eries 321s and the smaller models known as Series 541, least to Ford Motor Co. personnel.

The new Ks were more rounded out, with still the true assic appearance that was true of Lincoln. Stylewise, ıe radiator cap had been removed from the shell and aced less conspiculously beneath the hood. The grey-ound mascot stood in a stationary position from now on. place of the louvers of the past two seasons, horizontal oors graced the hood side panels.

Mechanically, the 35 Ks used 150 HP V-12 cylinder ıgines. A 26-gallon fuel tank was used. Brake system was Bendix mechanical type. All models used 7:50 x 17-inch res with wire wheels being standard equipment. The enter mounted emergency brake was used only on early 935s. Later models mounted it left of the driver on the ıder-dash panel. At this same time, space was made ailable for a radio to be mounted on the dash panel.

The production of Series Ks amounted to only 2,370 ır the year. The 145-inch wheelbase cars accounted for 232, while the remaining 1,138 were 136-inch chassis. Nineteen models were available, ranging from a $3,200 -passenger Coupe to the $6,800 7-passenger Brougham.

On June 25, 1935, the big surprise from Lincoln was to egin. This was the manufacturing of the new Lincoln ephyr which was to be introduced in November of 1935. his car was later hailed as the first successfully stream-ıed designed car in America by the Museum of Modern rt.

Lincoln held its same place as last year in the sales race, hich was position 20. The calendar year sales showed ,370 units being delivered.

Built only on the 145-inch wheelbase Lincoln chassis was this 1934 4-passenger Sport Phaeton. Only two of this style were actually built. The rear compartment had curved wind deflectors which would lower into the doors, and the car's tonneau windshield could be lowered into a compartment in back of the front seat. This model sold for $5,800.

Brunn was the builder of this 1934 Lincoln Convertible Victoria. It weighed 5,045 lbs. and sold for $5,600. The model came with painted head and parking lamps with contrasting wheels. Sidemount equipment was standard for this model. It used the 145-inch wheelbase chassis.

936

The Series K retained its unchanged V-12 of 414 cubic ches which developed 150 HP at 3400 RPM. The Ks used 26-gallon fuel supply. All Series K models rode on 7:50 x 7-inch tires. These cars used 136 and 145-inch wheelbases ı all 18 production and semi-production body styles. he body builders for the year were: Brunn, Judkins, e Baron and Willoughby in addition to the regular incoln-built series.

Some styling changes were seen with new fenders being ore rounded, stamped steel wheels replacing the wire heels and a different grille using small rectangles of ırome steel.

The Ks placed in 21st sales position. The company sold 523 of this series in 1936.

For 1935, Lincoln's most popular model appeared to be the 7-passenger Sedan, Model 303A. This sedan used the 145-inch wheelbase, weighed 5,535 lbs. and sold for $4,754. A total of 351 of these beauties were sold during the year.

A 1936 Lincoln Brunn Convertible Victoria, Model 328, was available on the 136-inch wheelbase. This true classic sold for $5,500 to only 10 customers. It was available on special order only. It is shown here on the old Storm King Highway between West Point and Cornwall, N. Y.

A handsome 7-passenger Limousine by Willoughby is this 1936 Lincoln. It was considered the most popular semi-custom style of the year. It weighed 5,661 lbs. and sold for $5,700. A total of 62 orders were placed. It is seen here in New York City's Central Park – apparently in this era, one could still travel through Central Park at night.

Judkins was the builder of this 1936 2-Window Berline, Model 337A. This sedan weighed 5,561 lbs. and sold for $5,500. The car was built only on the 145-inch chassis. A total of only 51 were built for the year.

Lincoln

1937

The Series K again developed 150 HP at 3400 RPM These automobiles used a 26-gallon fuel tank. Dependin on the model, the wheelbase sconsisted of 136 or 14 inches. The tire size was 7:50 x 17. All Series Ks use mechanical brakes.

A total of 18 body styles were available in factory an custom form. The custom body builders were: Brunn Judkins, Le Baron and Willoughby. The appearance c the new Ks saw a new grille, and body doors being almos lengthened to the running board. All sedans built by th factory had a flush rear deck where the spare tire wa housed. This gave a more streamlined effect. Also new fo the Ks was a two-piece windshield of a vee-style in mos models.

They received the 19th sales position by selling 96 cars for the model run.

Prices ranged between $4,200 for the 5-passenger Coup to $7,050 for the Willoughby Panel Town Brougham

1938

The Series K cars were very similar to the 1937 model mechanically speaking. The appearance also showed marked resemblance except for the trunk end of the ca in sedan form where they had a bustle back.

The Lincoln K again used a V-12 engine developin 150 HP at 3400 RPM. These models came with eithe 136 or 145-inch wheelbases. The tire size used wa 7:50 x 17. The Ks used a 26-gallon fuel tank. Mechanic brakes were employed on this mode, too. Body styles i the K line amounted to 22. Some styles were built as ju one model. The body builders in addition to Lincoln we Le Baron, Brunn, Judkins and Willoughby. Prices range from $4,546 for a 5-passenger Sedan to $7,400 for th Willoughby Panel Brougham, of which only six were buil

A total production of 398 Ks left the Dearborn assembl line in 1938, placing them in the 20th spot.

Lincoln offered this 1937 Series K, Model 365 Judkins Sedan Limousine for $5,950 which was $1,100 more than the regular Lincoln-built models. This model weighed 5,940 lbs. The sidemount tire equipment was an accessory. Only 27 purchasers were found for this model.

939

This was actually the last year of production for the ›ries Ks. Those that were sold in 1940 were actually cars ft over from 1939.

All 1939 Series Ks were identical to the 1938 models hich used the 414 cubic inch engine developing 150 HP 3400 RPM. These models used 7:50 x 17-inch tires ıd came on 136 or 145-inch wheelbases. The same body ıilders other than the Lincoln Division were still available. ıe names of Brunn, Judkins, Le Baron and Willoughby ere still catalogued.

A total of 29 models were available, but only 120 ›ries Ks were sold for 1939. They placed in 22nd ›sition for the calendar year.

The Willoughby Panel Brougham, Model 373 was the technical name for this 1937 Series K Lincoln. It was priced at $7,050 for the four orders it received that year. Strangely, this car is without white sidewall tires.

940

As was stated, the 1939 Lincoln K was truly the last of .e series. However, a few did dwindle along into 1940 ith the only change being a black cloisonne grille emblem place of the blue emblem as used in prior years. Some storians felt this was done to signify the end of Lincoln automobiles.

Mechanically, the cars had the same 414 cubic inch ıgine that developed 150 HP at 3400 RPM. All models ›ed 7:50 x 16-inch tires and rode on either the 136 or 45-inch wheelbase. All cars were built on a special order ısis, and were available again from Brunn, Judkins, Baron, and Willoughby.

A total of 29 models were catalogued, as in 1939. ›oduction figures are not available, as so few cars were ›oduced.

Brunn designed this 1938 Lincoln K and called it the Cabriolet. It was available with semi-collapsible and non-collapsible tops. This was the semi version, which sold for $7,000 and weighed 5,716 lbs. Only 5 of this style were built and 6 were available with non-collapsible tops.

Lincoln's most popular semi-custom design was this 1938 Willoughby 7-passenger Limousine which weighed 5,826 lbs. It sold 46 examples. The price tag was $6,200. It offered a leather front compartment, glass division window, inter-com phone and had a genuine leather covered roof.

The least expensive of the 1939 Lincoln Series K's was this 5-passenger sedan. This 3-window model sold for $100 less than its 1939 counterpart. The price now was $4,800, and it weighed 5,735 lbs. This was actually the last of the Series K models. Any that were sold in 1940 were cars left over from 1939 but registered as 1940 models and having black rather than red hub caps and grille emblems.

Lincoln Zephyr

The newly introduced Lincoln Zephyr for 1936 offered this 2-door sedan as the lower priced car. It sold for $1,725, and weighed 3,239 lbs. This style was referred to as the Model 903. Interior appointments included an electric clock, cigarette lighter, ash tray, and a locking glove. compartment as standard equipment.

The Lincoln Zephyr was a product of the Ford Motc Co., Dearborn, Mich. The Zephyr was actually put int production in June of 1935. The car was introduced to th public in November of 1935 to compete with Buick Oldsmobile, Chrysler and Studebaker.

For being a rather expensive car in the time of depression, it was received rather well. The Zephyr cam in two forms, a 2-door Sedan and a 4-door Sedan sellin for $1,275 and $1,320. Each model came on a 122-inc wheelbase. The cars employed a small V-12 engine c 267.3 cubic inches developing 110 HP at 3900 RPM. Th fuel capacity was 20 gallons. Each model rode on 7:00 16-inch tires. The Zephyr used mechanical brakes.

The car began its career following the John Tjaard design, Briggs-built, rear engine car that Ford displayed i 1933 at the Century of Progress exhibit in Chicag However, with the country in a depression, the compan decided against the rear engine plan, but used the Brigg bodied design.

The 1936 Zephyrs placed 17th by having a productic run of 13,635 units for the calendar year. Of this numbe 908 cars were for export.

With doors wide open this 1936 Lincoln Zephyr Sedan shows the comfort and room offered for six passengers. Note the chrome rail bars piped on the sides of the seats.

Practically the same car as the previous year, this 1937 Lincoln Zephyr 4-door Sedan had 5 chrome strips horizontally placed on the grille, front fender ornaments, and bumpers without quite as much of a vee to the center. Other than that, it was basically the same offering. The sedan had a $55 price reduction over 1936 models and sold for $1,265. The weight was the same, 3,349 lbs. A total of 23,159 were built.

This was the more popular of the two 1936 Lincoln Zephyrs offered that year. It was technically called Model 902, cost $1,320, and weighed 3,349 lbs. Home production amounted to 12,727 units and export sales were 908, making a calendar year run of 13,635 units.

This was the 1937 Lincoln Zephyr 3-passenger Coupe which was both the newest model and the lowest priced model for the year. It sold for $1,165, weighed 3,323 lbs., and had a production run of 5,199 units. Note this apparently was an early production model as it doesn't wear the small fender ornaments above the headlamps.

Lincoln Zephyr

37

There was not too much difference from the previous odel, as the car being new in 1936 didn't need much of change this year.

Two new models were introduced, the Coupe and the wn Limousine. The latter consisted of a sedan body th a divider partition and more refinements in the terior. All Zephyr models displayed a revamping of the struments on the control panel, and the placing of small naments above the headlamps in contour with the grille. e bumpers were of a more straight type rather than the ght Vee pattern of 1936.

The Zephyrs continued the V-12 of 110 HP. The fuel pply consisted of 19 gallons. The cars continued on the 2-inch wheelbase which rode on 7:00 x 16-inch tires. e brake system was still of the mechanical type.

A total of four body styles were available ranging in ice from $1,165 for the 3-passenger Coupe to $1,425 r a 7-passenger Town Limousine. All models carried yes bodies.

Lincoln Zephyrs received the 16th sales position by ling 28,333 cars for the model run.

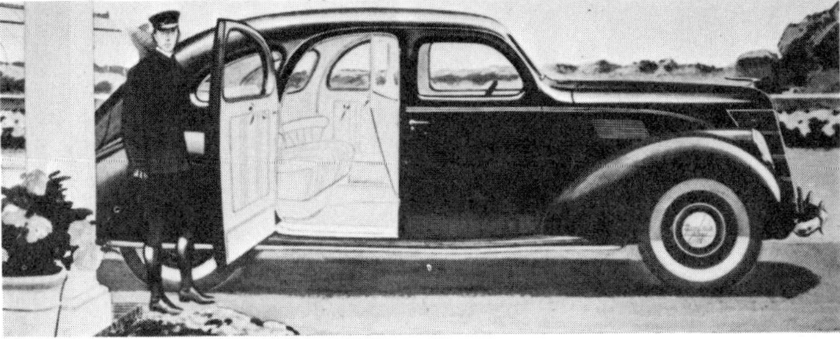

Least popular and most expensive of all Zephyrs was the Town Limousine, Model 737. Only 139 were built. The car cost $1,425 and weighed 3,507 pounds. Note how the glass partition curves into the rear compartment. In addition to the cars shown, Zephyr also produced three experimental convertible sedans.

One of Zephyr's best known ads shows the newly introduced Coupe-Sedan, Model 700, in Brewster green. The car weighed 3,289 pounds and sold for $1,245. Since only 1,500 were built, the model is relatively rare today. Zephyr production this year reached 30,000, with all bodies built by Briggs.

For 1938, Lincoln Zephyr's lowest priced model was this 3-passenger Coupe selling for $1,295. Production was down from 1937 models and only 2,600 units were built. This style weighed 3,294 lbs. and was technically called Model 720.

Out for a country ride is this 1938 Lincoln Zephyr Convertible Coupe wearing a California demonstrator license. This model, known as a 760 B was new for the year. It weighed 3,489 lbs. and sold for $1,650. Only 600 were built for the year, making it a rare car today.

Lincoln Zephyr's most popular car for 1938 continued to be the 4-door Sedan for $1,375. It weighed 3,444 lbs. The sedan production for the year totalled 14,520 units. The car is shown here near the lake at Greenfield Village, Mich.

Lincoln Zephyr

1938

The Zephyr, now in its third year of production, w displayed in 1938 with an attractive facelifting. The fro end appearance had a divided grille coming into a pointe center piece. Also new for the Zephyr were a Convertib Sedan and a Convertible Coupe which made a total of s models.

The Lincoln Zephyr came with a hypoid rear axle ar offered its gearshift lever mounted under the dash to gi ample room for the middle front seat passenger to ride comfort.

The 1938 Zephyrs used the V-12, 110 HP engine, no at 3800 RPM. The new 128-inch wheelbased cars car with 7:00 x 16-inch tires. These models had a 19-gallc fuel supply. Mechanical brakes were still being use

Prices for the six models started at $1,295 for tl 3-passenger Coupe going up to $1,790 for the Convertib Sedan.

The production figures of 19,751 units put them in tl 16th sales position for the calendar year.

Brunn built this one-off custom Town Brougham, using the standard Zephyr 4-Door Sedan as the basic body. The conversion could be special-ordered at a cost of $7,000, which included the price of the basic Zephyr, but there were no further takers. The leather covered top is a solid unit, and the landau irons are strictly decorative, though drawings indicate that a semi-collapsible version was at least considered.

The otherwise smooth lines of the new Zephyr 4-Door Convertible Sedan were spoiled somewhat by the rather cumbersome top-folding arrangement. Still, the car far surpassed in beauty virtually every other upper-medium range convertible sedan of the year. Lincoln produced a total of 461.

Displayed at the factory home office in Dearborn, Mich., is the 1938 Lincoln Zephyr 4-door Convertible Sedan. This model was new for 1938 and was not offered in the remaining years of Zephyr life. The body style was known as Model 740. It weighed 3,724 lbs., sold for $1,790, which was the most expensive Zephyr to date, and had a production run of only 461 units.

The Zephyr Town Limousine, Model 737, continued to be the basic 4-Door Sedan with an interesting glass partition between compartments. On some models, leather upholstery was used in the front compartment, while others had the upholstery throughout in the berline tradition. The car was the least popular Zephyr, and only 130 were built. It was priced at $1,550 and weighed 3,474 pounds.

Zephyr continued to call its 2-door sedan the Coupe-Sedan, Model 700. The car was priced at $1,355 and weighed 3,409 pounds. Eight hundred were built.

939

For 1939 the Zephyr again developed a 110 HP at 800 RPM. The tire size was 7:00 x 16 inches, and they retained the 19-gallon fuel supply that they had previously.

During this model run nine models were offered. The ig news, which was greeted with much enthusiasm, was that now they had hydraulic brakes in place of the mechanical devices. The new cars came with concealed doors that flared out at the bottom to cover the runningboards or the first time. The handbrake received a new mounting to the left of the driver, by the cowl. The Zephyr also employed the battery condition indicator in place of the battery ammeter which told the condition the battery was operating under.

The Lincoln Zephyr placed in 17th position, selling approximately 22,000 vehicles.

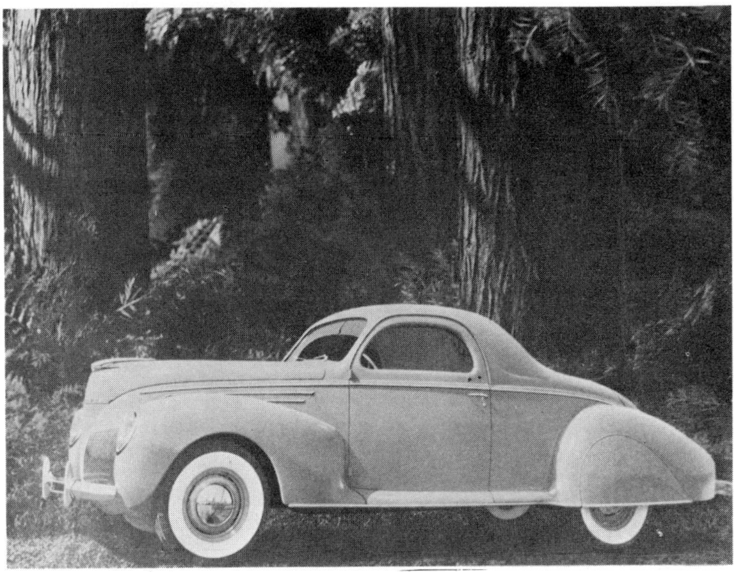

Lincoln Zephyr displayed this 1939 3-passenger Coupe, Model H-72 in dealer showrooms for $1,320. A production run of 2,500 was attained, making it the second most popular model for the year.

The 1939 Lincoln Zephyr Coupe-Sedan Model H-70 was in its last year of production with only a run of 800 units. It sold for $1,330 and weighed 3,600 lbs.

Again being offered as the most popular Zephyr for the year was the 1939 Sedan, which saw a production run of 16,663 cars. It weighed 3,620 lbs. and sold for $1,360. This sedan was technically called the H-73.

A prototype of nice things to come was unveiled in Florida in 1939 when this Continental was delivered to Palm Beach for Edsel Ford's personal use. Two more models quite similar were built for Henry Ford II and Benson Ford, who were Edsel Ford's sons.

The least popular Zephyr continued to be the Town Limousine, Model H-22. The 6-passenger car was basically the 4-Door Sedan with a modified interior and a $1,700 price tag. It drew 95 orders. The car weighed 3,670 pounds.

Lincoln Zephyr

Briggs continued to produce the body for the low production Zephyr Convertible, Model 76. With the 4-door convertible being discontinued, this was Zephyr's only remaining open style, yet only 700 were produced. It cost $1,770 and weighed 3,760 pounds.

1940

The Lincoln Zephyr for 1940 entered its fifth year production with an entirely new body. Also, for 194 the Continental was classed as a model within the Zeph line and the name "Continental" did not appear on t car. It was just generally known as the Lincoln Co tinental.

Mechanically, the 1940 Zephyrs increased their hors power from 110 to 120 at 3900 RPM. They continued t use the 19-gallon fuel tank. The tire size stayed at 7:00 16 inches. The Lincoln Zephyr used a 125-inch wheelba for 1940.

The main changes came in a bigger car, offering mo room for heads, legs, and shoulders. Also, the lugga compartment was increased 30% in all models. Th steering column adopted the gearshift and a fresh ne dashboard was improvised with all dials, directly in fro of the driver. Sealed beam headlamps were offered for t first time on the Zephyrs.

A total of six models were available ranging in pri from $1,393 for the 3-passenger Coupe to $2,910 for t 6-passenger Continental Cabriolet.

Lincoln Zephyr took the seventeenth position for sal in 1940 by selling 24,021 units.

A new design for the year was the Zephyr Club Coupe, Model 77, which replaced the former 2-door sedan. It was Zephyr's second most popular style, with 3,500 being produced. The $1,400 car weighed 3,590 pounds.

Briggs' big contract was producing bodies for the Zephyr 4-Door Sedan, Model 73, which enjoyed a production run of 15,764, making it by far Zephyr's most popular style. The car weighed 3,660 pounds and cost $1,400.

The real thing saw production beginning in October of 1939 when this 1940 Continental made its debut. Actually, it was still classed as a model in the Lincoln Zephyr line for 1940. It weighed 3,850 lbs. and sold for $2,783. Most models were hand-built with interiors done in leather with fabric seat inserts. A total of 350 Coupes were built.

Of even lower production than the Continental Coupe was the Continental Cabriolet or Convertible, of which only 50 were made. It cost $2,840 and weighed 3,740 pounds. Many were produced with Columbia two-speed rear axles. The convertible tops were raised and lowered automatically by a vacuum-powered mechanism. Actually, this year, these cars were considered part of the Zephyr line, and the name "Continental" did not appear until the 1941 model year.

941

The Lincoln Zephyr and Continental were the only ıxury cars the Ford Motor Co. had to offer now. The ephyr had been on the market since June of 1935. The ontinental was now a series of its own as the Zephyr tle was dropped from the car.

A larger model, which was basically a Zephyr, was the incoln Custom. It had the same powerplant as used in the ther two series but came on a 138-inch wheelbase. It was ffered in Sedan and Limousine version only. The ontinental was basically the same as its 1940 rendering ith a few exceptions. Flush pushbutton doors were troduced, parking lamps were mounted on top of the eadlights, and directional signals were now employed. roduction of these cars was kept low, and buyers were ept on a waiting list. Fewer than 1,300 Continentals were uilt for the calendar year. This makes them a much ought after car by classic car collectors today.

All Lincolns used the 282 cubic inch V-12 engine eveloping 120 HP at 3500 RPM. The fuel supply was a 9½-gallon tank in each series. The tire size was 7:00 x 6 inches and the wheelbase measured 125 inches for the gular Zephyr and Continental.

A total of 17,756 units left the Dearborn plant, putting em in 17th position for the calendar year.

New for the year was the 1941 Lincoln Custom 7-passenger Sedan, Model 31. This V-12 model filled the gap between the former Zephyr Town Limousine and the Lincoln Series K. It weighed 4,250 lbs., sold for $2,622, and had a production run of 355 units.

Zephyr's big production leader continued to be the 4-Door Sedan, Model 73, which had a run of 14,469. It cost $1,493 and weighed 3,710 pounds. This car, the Club Coupe and the 3-Passenger Coupe also could be ordered with custom or luxury interiors. In the 3-Passenger Coupe, this cost $75 more, while in the Club Coupe and Sedan, the fancy interior cost $124 more.

Zephyr's second most popular style continued to be the 5-Passenger Club Coupe, Model 77. The nicely styled car had a production run of 3,750. It cost $1,493 and weighed 3,640 pounds.

Lincoln achieved an apex of automotive beauty this year with the Continental Convertible Cabriolet, Model 65, an outstandingly beautiful car priced at $2,778. Only 400 of this model were built. Although the 3,860 pound car bore close resemblence to the 1940 models, a number of refinements had been made.

The pretty Zephyr Convertible saw a production run of only 725 this year. Designated the Model 76, it weighed 3,840 pounds and cost $1,801, thereby making it the heaviest Zephyr of the year, and also the most expensive.

1942

Actually, three series were available. They were th Zephyr, Continental, and Custom. Mechanically, all seri were the same. They had a larger engine than the previou year, which was a 305 cubic inch V-12 that develope 130 HP at 3800 RPM. The fuel tank was again a 19½ gallon supply. The wheel size changed for 1942 model the new size being 7:00 x 15 inches. The Zephyr an Continentals had a 125-inch wheelbase and a 138-inc chassis went to the Lincoln Customs which was onl available in 8-passenger style.

An important new feature which Lincoln introduce was an option at extra cost called Liquamatic Drive. consisted of a fluid coupling, conventional clutch an transmission with overdrive that shifted automatically each gear except for low or reverse, where the clutch w required. For normal driving, the gear lever was placed high gear and left there unless low or reverse were neede All driving was done by the use of the accelerator peda When the car stopped it automatically shifted from hig to second so that starts were made in the latter gear eve though the gearshift lever stayed in high position. Th transmission really never had a chance to prove itself the war halted it shortly after being introduced and fe were ever put into use.

Model production began October 1, 1941 and ende February 2, 1942, showing approximately 1,276 Zeph and Custom cars and 336 Continentals being assemble Lincoln had eight models to offer, ranging in price fro $1,748 for a 3-passenger Coupe to $3,248 for a Custo Limousine for 8 passengers, of which only 66 were bui Lincoln placed in 16th position for sales.

The Custom series appeared for the last time, and would not be reactivated after the war. It again consisted of two models, the Custom 7-Passenger Sedan, Model 31, shown here, and the Custom Limousine. The sedan version weighed 4,380 pounds and cost $3,117. Only 47 of the big sedans were built.

The Zephyr Club Coupe, Model 77A, continued to take the place of the former 2-Door Sedan, but had only a limited production of 253 this year. It weighed 3,810 pounds and cost $1,801. With the optional Custom Interior, it cost $1,901.

The large "covered wagon" top was continued on the Continental Convertible Cabriolet, and it enhanced the car's lines greatly. The convertible this year weighed 4,020 pounds, and before production ceased, it sold for $3,174. However, because of war-time scarcity, by 1943 these cars were commanding better than $6,000 on the black market, and the price went still higher in 1944.

Nicely equipped was this 1942 Lincoln Zephyr 4-door Sedan. This car was a real early production model sporting all the deluxe chrome goodies which most 1942 cars were lacking. Seen on this sedan are the rare white sidewall tires. full factory installed deluxe wheel trim, fog lamps, spot lights, and deluxe style license frames. The fender skirts were standard equipment as on all previous Zephyrs. Only 4,418 1942 Zephyr Sedans were built and of those only 1,276 were in the 1942 calendar year. This model weighed 3,980 pounds and sold for $1,801.

Marmon

The Marmon was a product of the Nordyke-Marmon Co. The company headquarters were in Indianapolis. The car was manufactured from 1903 to 1933.

A total of three separate lines were offered for Marmon in 1930. They were Series 8-69, 8-70, and the Big 8. Both the 8-69 and 8-70 were roomier than the 68 and 78 Series of 1929. Each car came with an 8-cylinder engine using Marmon's "Double Dome" L-head combustion chamber which had more power per cubic inch than other cars of a like size.

The appearance department gave more pleasing body contours than the 1929 models. Radiator shutters were added to both 8-69 and 8-70 models. These were manually controlled on the 8-69 and automatically operated on the 8-70 as in the Big 8.

The 8-69 developed 84 HP at 3200 RPM. This series had a 114-inch wheelbase and rode on 5:50 x 19-inch tires. The series had a 14-gallon fuel tank.

All 8-70s developed 107 HP at 3250 RPM. They came on a 117-inch wheelbase using 6:00 x 19-inch tires. Their fuel supply was a 22-gallon tank.

The Big 8 had a 125 HP engine at 3400 RPM. This series rode on a 136-inch chassis and used 6:50 x 19-inch tires. They used the same fuel supply as the 8-70s. All series had mechanically operated brakes.

The body styles available amounted to 16. Prices ran from $1,465 for a 4-passenger Coupe in the 8-69 Series to $2,995 for a 7-passenger Big 8 Limousine.

Marmon placed in 19th position by selling 13,262 vehicles.

For 1930, Marmon offered this 2-passenger Convertible Coupe for $1,505. It had an 8-cylinder engine developing 84 HP at 3200 RPM. This sharp looking model offered weatherproof coupe comfort in wet weather but could be converted to an open model at a minute's notice. The interior was upholstered in leather, as was the rumble seat.

This was the 1930 Marmon Series 70 4-passenger Victoria. It was described as a safe vehicle for families with small children and also a utilitarian value as well. It offered ample luggage space in its trunk compartments as well as a handy parcel shelf in back of the driver's seat. It sold for $1,490. The 8-cylinder engine produced 107 HP at 3400 RPM.

Marmon's senior line of cars for 1930 were called the Big Eight Series. This was the 2-passenger Standard Coupe that rode on a 136-inch chassis. It sold for $2,700. The Big Eight offered many conveniences for the owner, including standard equipment such as a dome light operated by a switch on the window pillar, curtains on both rear and rear quarter windows, and a trunk rack. The rumble seat was opened by a lever located inside the car.

Designed for the typical family who could afford a car of such luxury was the classic looking 1930 Marmon Big Eight 4-door Sedan. Dome lights operated when either front or rear doors opened and automatically were stopped when the doors closed. Deep cushioned seats were a standard feature, with elastic pockets placed in each door panel. This model sold for $2,895. In 7-passenger style it sold for $2,995.

Marmon

This 1930 Marmon Big Eight 5-passenger Brougham offered the ultimate in comfort and quality throughout. This model came with a khaki colored top carried out down the rear quarter panels with matching tire covers done in the same material. The interior was finished in broadcloth with a figured worsted lace. It sold for $2,925. Most models were sold only on special order.

For 1930 this Weymann-bodied Marmon was built only on special order. Production figures aren't available nor was the price, but it is safe to say fewer than five were sold. This ultra-light body was built of fabric laid over a wood framework.

1931

Five separate series were displayed for 1931. They we the 68, 69, 78, 88 and the 16. The Series 68 and 69 we virtually the same car except for more deluxe appoin ments in the 69 Series. An 8-cylinder engine developi 76 HP at 3400 RPM was used in both lines.

The Marmon 78 was an 8-cylinder car with a 211 cub inch engine giving 86 brake horsepower at 3400 RP A 15-gallon fuel supply was used for this series. The ti size was 5:50 x 19-inches, and the wheelbase measur 112¾ inches.

The Marmon 88 used an 8-cylinder engine of 125 HP 3400 RPM. The engine displacement was 315.2 cub inches. A 22-gallon fuel tank was used, as were 6:50 19-inch tires. The wheelbases measured 130 and 1 inches for the six models offered.

The Marmon V-16 was offered as a new line for t first time. The aluminum engine was at a 45 degree inclin angle developing 200 HP at 3400 RPM. The cubic d placement was 291 inches. It contained a 29-gallon fu tank. The wheelbase measured 145 inches and the ti size was 7:00 x 18 inches.

The Marmon 16 didn't make its debut as early in t year as the 8s. It wasn't until April of 1931 that the fi of the 16-cylinder cars started off the line. Producti difficulties kept the company from making the first re showing of Marmon 16s until the middle of the summ of 1931.

The 16s were continued through until the compa closed its doors in May of 1933. Fewer than 400 Marm 16s were built during its production run.

A total of 18 models were catalogued for the year wi prices ranging from $1,465 for a 4-passenger Coupe $5,500 for the V-16 7-passenger Limousine.

Complete sales figures placed Marmon in 21st positi from the sale of 5,263 cars.

A neat and compact model was the 1931 Marmon 69. Shown here is the Convertible Coupe with rumble seat which gave a seating capacity for four. Khaki top and sidemount covers were of the same high quality material. This car sold for $1,525. Sidemount equipment was extra.

Marmon's lowest priced line for 1931 was the Series 68. This 5-passenger Sedan had an 8-cylinder engine developing 76 HP at 3400 RPM. It sold for $1,500. Sidemount tire and luggage racks were classed as extra equipment.

932

For 1932, there was a new striaght Eight with 125 HP 3400 RPM, on a wheelbase of 125 inches, with an tractive new body and many interesting features such as vacuum operated clutch, synchro mesh transmission, ıd shock absorbers adjustable from the seat. This series ıd an attractive V-shaped radiator sloping to the rear ıghtly, a long, high hood, slanting windshield, and full own fenders.

The new bodies were upholstered in mohair or whipcord lged with leather piping. The steering column was ljustable to two positions. The rear compartment had mfortable arm rests. All instruments were arranged in ont of the driver for easy visibility. The speedometer dicated engine RPM as well as MPH. All control buttons ere in the center of the dash. The standard version me with five wire wheels and the deluxe had six wire heels, two being in the fender wells. Tire size was 00 x 18. This was the only year this 8-cylinder was built.

The Marmon Sixteen continued to please its patrons th some refinements including chrome-plated radiator utters, new radiator ornament, cowl lights on front nders, upholstery edged in leather, ash receivers built to the arm rests, and a new assist cord which slid on a r above the rear quarter. The Sixteen had a 145-inch heelbase and was equipped with 7:00 x 18-inch tires. ıese cars had a 200 HP engine that turned over at 00 RPM.

The 8-cylinder cars came in Coupe, Convertible Coupe d Sedan. The Sixteens were built in eight body styles. The sales position was 24th, producing 1,309 cars.

Marmon's new 1931 model 78 had a 211 cubic inch 8-cylinder engine developing 80 HP at 3400 RPM. The model offered light easy handling as one of its main features. Wire wheels were classed as standard equipment, but the sidemounts were optional at extra cost. It sold for $1,625.

The 1931 Marmon 88 came with an 8-cylinder engine developing 125 HP at 3400 RPM. The price of this example is not available as so few cars were being produced.

This was the newly styled Marmon V-16 5-passenger Victoria for 1931. It was known as Model 143. The car developed 200 HP at 3400 RPM. It weighed 5,150 lbs. and sold for $5,270. This example was not equipped with the optional hood ornament. These were truly outstanding cars.

Available in three body styles for 1932 was the new Marmon 8-125. This 5-passenger Sedan offered all deluxe appointments from vanity cases to twin horns mounted beneath the headlamps. Still, with all of its quality the buyers just weren't there and the 8-125s were discontinued at the end of the model run.

This 1932 Marmon 2-passenger DeLuxe Convertible Coupe came on the market known as the "8-125" chiefly because of its 8-cylinder engine and 125-inch chassis. Full leather interior was used for this model. This year Marmon offered a new automatic clutch control.

Marmon

Very similar to the 1931 Marmon V-16 Victoria was this 1932 version. Only identifying changes were the chrome-plated radiator shutters, cowl lights not shown in this artist's sketch, and ash receivers built into the rear arm-rests.

1933

For 1933, Marmon came out only as a 16-cylinder ca Prices were reduced as much as $925 with the base beir $4,825 for a 5-passenger Sedan and also for the 4-passeng Coupe. Altogether, eight models were offered with tl 7-passenger Limousine bringing a healthy $5,175 p copy at the top of the line.

The wheelbase on all these models was 145 inches. Tl tire size was 7:00 x 18. The chief body builder was I Baron for all eight body styles. The braking system w mechanical with vacuum booster. Each of these 1 cylinder cars carried a 29-gallon fuel tank. Horsepow was rated at 200 at 3400 RPM.

Only having eight models to pick from was not a he to the company. Others who also were in financial troub kept up a good front by offering their patrons as many 30 bodies at a time to choose from. So few cars were so in 1933 that sales records are not available.

Marmon's 1932 7-passenger Sedan, Model 146, is shown wearing its chromed full wheel covers. It weighed 5,440 lbs., and in 1932 sold for $5,900.

1934

Actually, 1933 was the last true year the car was bui but this year a few cars were turned out from the Indiar polis factory, so they can actually be classed for 193

In 1934, Marmon again came out as a 16-cylinder c only. Prices remained the same for the eight mode available: from $4,825 for a 5-passenger Sedan to $5,1 for the 7-passenger Limousine.

The wheelbases for all eight models were the same 145 inches. Tire size was 7:00 x 18. Each model aga used a 29-gallon fuel tank. Horsepower was 200 at 34(RPM. Mechanical brakes with a vacuum power boost unit were employed for each model.

The car's chief body builder was Le Baron. With so fe cars being sold for 1934, sales records again were n available.

The 1932 V-16 Marmon 5-passenger Club Sedan came on a 145-inch wheelbase and weighed 5,335 lbs. Prices fluctuated as in all Marmon V-16s from introduction to demise. In 1932, it sold for $5,800. The very next year, and its last year, the same model sold for $4,925. The huge all-aluminum engine developed 200 horsepower.

The last year for Marmon was 1933, but what a way to say good-bye. This beautiful example is on display at Harrah's Auto Museum in Reno, Nevada. It is an aluminum body, known as Le Baron Convertible Coupe Style No. 144. The weight is 5,100 lbs. and its price was $4,975, which was an $875 decrease from the previous year. About the only visual difference in the 1933 models from earlier V-16 Marmons were the streamlined parking lamps in comparison to the 1932 oval lamps.

Marquette

The 1930 Marquette was a product of General Motors orp. and was considered a car in the Buick sub-series. was built during 1929 and 1930 in Flint, Mich. The Marquette carried a 6-cylinder L-head engine of 2.8 cubic inches. It developed 67 HP at 3000 RPM. 16-gallon fuel tank was used. The car rode on 5:25 x 3-inch tires and used a 114-inch wheelbase. Mechanical akes were used on Marquettes.

A total of six body styles were available ranging in price om $990 for the 2-passenger Business Coupe to $1,060 r the 5-passenger Sedan. The Marquettes were classed as ries 30 cars under the Buick series. These cars being subries to Buick were actually classed in Buick production d sales figures for the year. A total of 119,265 units ere listed with Buick. However, if listed separately, ,007 Marquettes are placed by themselves.

Marquette's lowest priced car for 1930 was this 2-passenger Business Coupe, Model 38. All Marquettes were classed as a sub-series to Buick and were referred to as Series 30 cars. This model weighed 2,760 lbs. and sold for $990.

This 6-cylinder 1930 Marquette Sedan was the most popular model within the line selling for $1,060 and weighing 2,925 lbs. The sidemount equipment was optional at extra cost, as on all Marquettes.

The 1930 5-passenger 2-door Sedan that Marquette offered was Model 30. It was fairly popular within the line but never did sell as well as Buick-Marquette dealers would have liked. It weighed 2,850 lbs. and sold for an even $1,000.

Selling for the same price as the Sport Roadster and Sport Coupe was this 1930 Marquette 5-passenger Phaeton referred to as Model 35, which had a price of $1,020. This example weighed 2,670 lbs. The Marquette ceased to produce cars at the end of 1930.

Looking very much like a Buick was this 1930 Marquette 4-passenger Sport Roadster. It came only on a 114-inch wheelbase, selling for $1,020. This model had a weight of 2,640 lbs. Wire wheels were optional equipment which most came with.

Martin

One of the few nearly successful automotive ventures in the life of James V. Martin was the production of the Martin Dart. The Austin-like mini-car was developed in 1928 and 1929, with production slated to begin in 1930. Plans called for an annual run of 250,000 Darts, to be sold for $200 each, plus $50 freight. The freight charge included a large wooden shipping crate with doors, which would then act as the Dart's garage. The 60-inch wheelbase car, engineered by Miles Carpenter of Phianna fame, was to have been built in Hagerstown, Md., by the M. P. Moller Co., which had produced the Dagmar car and commercial bodies for other makes. However, the whole idea seems to have simply faded after a half-dozen or so prototype Darts were hand-built. The car was readvertised as the Dart (without the name Martin attached) in 1931, but shortly after this the entire project disappeared. The car would have used a 4-cylinder air-cooled Cleveland motorcycle engine.

The name Martin was used on eight different car ventur from 1898 through 1954. This company began business i 1926 and continued into 1932. Its president was J. V Martin, with the firm name of Martin Aeroplane Co. o Garden City, N.Y. The company had plans on sellir 250,000 models known as Darts during 1930 for $25 They were to have been sold by mail and shipped by rai The owners could use the wooden crate the car came in a garage for the vehicle. The cars were to be built Hagerstown, Md. In addition to this line were aerodynam three-wheel models that the company claimed could atta a speed of 110 MPH. One model used a 4-cylind Continental engine in the rear that developed 60 HP. Th other car came with an American Austin engine that w mounted across the back which drove the single rear whe by twin belts. Neither model proved successful and th company discontinued manufacturing automobiles in 193 A revival was attempted after World War II for these mi cars, but it, too, was unsuccessful.

Although this book covers only the years 1930 to 1942, and although this Martin Stationette was not introduced until 1950, there is a reason that it is included here. That reason is a strong belief on the part of many that this is really the same 3-wheel Martin Aerodynamic that J.V. Martin introduced in 1932, only now sporting an attractive wooden body built by Biehl Auto Body of Reading, Pa. Before introducing this car, Martin had introduced another 3-wheeler in 1948, under the name of Martinette. That car was very similar to the 1932 version, except that it sported a large port-hole window in the rear quarter and had a larger rear window. It was also fitted with Martin's curious patented airless tires, which proved to be anything but successful. It is very probable that the Martinette was simply an updated version of his original 3-wheeler, brought out in the hopes of introducing the car-hungry nation to back production. Finding no backers, Martin withdrew the vehicle, only to introduced the Stationette in 1950. The attractive wood-bodied car now sported conventional wheels, and was powered by a rear-mounted 4-cylinder Hercules industrial engine of 47 cubic inches. The transmission was now by the Martin Magnetic Fluid Drive (whatever that was) and the price was to be $1,000. A top speed of 80 MPH was claimed. The car moved around for several years, then surprisingly, was awarded the grand prize at the World Motor Sports Show in 1954. It was then sold to another firm, which kept it around for a couple of years, after which the entire project was dropped. This car, and the 4-wheel Aerodynamic sedan still survive, but none of the Darts are known to exist.

A very advanced car for its era was the Martin Aerodynamic, built in 1932. Powered by a Continental 4-cylinder engine, the car reportedly had a top speed of 110 MPH. Its body styling resembled the center-door concept of the late teens, whereby all passengers entered into the rear compartment, then squeezed between the front seats to gain access to the front compartment. The car did not use a conventional chassis, but instead was constructed on a laminated wood and aluminum platform. The engine was located in the rear, and drove the rear wheels through a transaxle supported by Martin's patent aviator-cord suspension system.

The 1939 Mercury was the new car for the year,)ming from the Ford Motor Co. in Dearborn, Mich. For its debut, the Mercury filled a slot that had always :en vacant in the Ford Motor Co. field. The car was 'iced between the Ford DeLuxe and the Lincoln Zephyr.

The 1939 Mercury came with a 95 HP engine (at 3600 PM). It carried 6:00 x 16-inch tires on a 116-inch wheel-ıse and had a 14-gallon fuel tank. It used Ford's newly lopted hydraulic brakes. The car came with a more xurious interior and a roomier body than the Ford. he appearance resembled the Ford a great deal. Its grille ıd horizontal bars while Ford carried vertical ones. The p and side pieces of the hood were made in one unit and ıd a hinge at the rear, lifting from the front, alligator shion.

In some respects it carried components similar to the ncoln, too. It used a torque tube and rear axle similar to e Zephyr and its transmission carried a blocker type nchronizer of the Zephyr type. A new type of steel panded rings were employed on the 1939 Mercury, ıich aided compression and oil consumption.

Four body styles were available – a 4-door Sedan, door Sedan, Convertible Coupe and Sedan Coupe. Convertible Sedan also was shown for press release ıotos, along with some prototypes.

The lowest priced Mercury for 1939 was the $916 2-door dan. The Convertible Coupe carried a tag of $1,018 as e most expensive model on catalog listed production. ercury placed in 11th position and sold 76,198 vehicles, cluding those which were built in late 1938 but were tually 1939 cars.

Mercury's first year of production brought this low priced 2-door Sedan on the market for families with small children. It sold for $916 and weighed 2,997 lbs. This example is an early model as the hub caps still state "Ford-Mercury." Later models had the inscription "Mercury" only on the cap, when it was decided that the car would stand as a separate make rather than as a top series of the Ford line.

Shown with its top down is the pretty Mercury Convertible, the style leader of the totally new car that Edsel Ford conceived, named, and placed on the market. Designated the Model 76, the car was priced at $1,018 and weighed 2,995 pounds. It was the most expensive Mercury.

Mercury's most popular car for 1939 was this 4-door Town Sedan, Model 73. It weighed 3,013 lbs. and sold for $957. The wheel trim rings were standard equipment, but white sidewalls were only available at extra cost.

Historians aren't quite sure if only a few 1939 Mercury Convertible Sedans were built or if a prototype only was produced. At any rate it gave an inkling of what was to come in 1940 when the true one-year production of Convertible Sedans was introduced.

Mercury

Well-received in 1940 by the public was this Mercury Convertible Coupe, Model 76. The buyer had his choice of leather interiors and a variety of colored canvas tops to choose from. A total of 9,226 of this style were sold during the year for $1,079. This car weighed 2,996 lbs. The top was power operated.

1940

This was the second year that the Mercury was i production, and for the new year, Mercury didn't mak any changes in the year-old car. Some of the improv ments included sealed beam headlamps, two-spoke steerir wheel with a steering column mounted gearshift, windo ventilators, and a stationary windshield with wipe mounted at the bottom.

The Convertible Sedan was truly offered in the 194 line, but only 979 cars were built, which has made it model highly sought after by car collectors today.

Mechanically, Mercury offered the 95 HP V-8 engi of 239.4 cubic inches at 3600 RPM. The fuel supply w increased to a 17-gallon tank. The tire size was 6:00 x 1 inches, and a 116-inch chassis was used again.

A total of five body styles were available ranging price from $951 for the 2-door Sedan to $1,217 for t 6-passenger Convertible Sedan.

The company placed in 11th position for the calend year by selling 82,770 cars.

A little more rounded out than the 1939 car, this 1940 Mercury 4-door Town Sedan featured sealed beam headlamps and a gear shift lever mounted on the steering column as standard equipment. This model weighed 2,992 lbs. and sold for $987 – an increase of $30 over the previous year.

A totally new style for the year, excepting the prototypes produced in 1939, was the Mercury 4-Door Convertible Sedan. At 3,138 pounds and $1,212, it was Mercury's heaviest and most expensive model. Sadly, the car was not continued in 1941, and the style was dropped after a total run of somewhere between 975 and 1,000.

A pretty little car was the 5-passenger Mercury Sedan Coupe, Model 72. At $978 and 2,919 pounds, it proved to be solid, nice handling, and relatively economical.

941

The Mercury, being a member of the Ford family, nderwent much restyling. The bodies were new and oomier, with a wheelbase two inches longer than the 940s. It now was a 118-inch car with 6:50 x 16-inch tires. 'he fuel supply remained at 17 gallons. The same 239.4 ubic inch engine was used. It developed 95 HP at 600 RPM.

Two new body styles made their appearance: a 3-assenger Business Coupe and the Station Wagon. The 'onvertible Sedan stopped with the end of the 1940 line-p. Two-tone paint was seen on many Mercurys for the rst time. It consisted of fenders different colored from ie body.

Mercury placed in 12th position for the calendar year om the sale of 80,085 cars. A total of seven models were vailable ranging in price from $914 for a 3-passenger 'oupe to $1,146 for the 8-passenger Station Wagon.

Proving very popular with businessmen and young couples was the 1941 Mercury Club Coupe, or, as it was technically called, the Coupe Sedan. It was referred to as Model 72, weighing 3,310 lbs. and selling for $981.

A very popular car was the Mercury 2-Door Sedan, Model 70, which weighed 3,169 pounds and sold for $950.

The only open model Mercury offered in 1941 was this Convertible Coupe, Model 76. Full leather interior was standard equipment. It weighed 3,207 lbs. and sold for $1,104.

Mercury's big seller in 1941 was the 4-door Town Sedan, Model 73. The car weighed 3,026 lbs. and sold for $991 F.O.B. Dearborn. The white sidewall tires were optional at extra cost as on all 1941 models.

New for the year was the Mercury Station Wagon, an 8-passenger vehicle using the same basic wood body as used on the Ford wagon. Designated the Model 79, it weighed 3,453 pounds and cost $1,145, thereby making it the heaviest and most expensive Mercury of 1941.

Mercury

Fully equipped with a host of 1942 Mercury factory approved accessories is this Convertible Coupe, Model 76. It weighed 3,288 lbs. and sold for $1,288. The accessories included are bumper tip guards, fog lamps, spot lamp, radio, and white sidewall tires. The swan style side mirror was standard equipment on Convertibles and the wheel trim rings also were classed as regular equipment.

1942

The big news for Mercury was the fluid coupling and automatic shift which was called Liquamatic. Drive. This was the same automatic drive that Lincoln offered. Neither produced very many, as the war stopped all production shortly after the beginning of the year. It was not too successful a transmission and Mercury did not offer another automatic until 1951 when they introduced Merc-O-Matic.

The appearance changes for the 1942 models included a restyled grille, bumpers, and fenders. The grille consisted of a broad design of two groups of horizontal bars. The parking lights were of the horizontal type placed above the grille near the hood. Directional signals were available at extra cost. Both front and rear bumpers were of a more massive type. The fenders were more squared off and had two small stainless steel trim pieces that ran the entire length of the fender.

The same 239 cubic inch V-8 engine was employed but the horsepower was increased to 100 at 3800 RPM. The fuel supply was 17 gallons. The wheel size changed to a 15-inch rim, now using 6:50 x 15-inch tires. The wheelbase continued at 118 inches.

A total of 6 models were available for 1942. The 5 passenger Coupe was discontinued as the sales weren't as plentiful for this model as they were in other body styles. Prices ranged from $1,056 for a 3-passenger Business Coupe to $1,336 for the 8-passenger Station Wagon. Mercury took the 13th sales position for the calendar year with 4,430 cars being sold.

The 1942 Mercury 4-door Town Sedan was the most popular model for the year. It sold for $1,130 and weighed 3,263 lbs. This example was an early production model without any "blackout" trim which many 1942 cars were equipped with.

Because of the war, the country was becoming military minded, and this was reflected in most auto ads this year – such as this one for the Mercury 3-Passenger Coupe, Model 77. The car weighed 3,073 pounds and cost $1,056. This year, the rear quarter windows could be opened for ventilation. Features were a one piece seat, large package compartment behind the seat, and armrests on each door.

The Mercury Station Wagon, Model 79, was the heaviest and most expensive of the line. It weighed 3,528 pounds and sold for $1,336. The wood body was identical to that used on the Fords this year. Roll-up windows were used in all doors, but the rear quarter windows were of the sliding type. The rear door was divided horizontally, with the lower portion folding down in tailgate style while the upper portion folded up. The spare was mounted outside on the lower portion of the rear door.

Nash

Nash was a product of the Nash Motors Co. with eadquarters in Kenosha, Wis. The company began under ne direction of Charles W. Nash in 1916. The first Nash vas built in 1917. Nash purchased the company of 'homas B. Jeffery. Before Nash's directorship, the com-any was Jeffery and prior to that it was called Rambler rom 1900 to 1913.

For 1930 Nash offered three series of cars – the Single , Twin Ignition 6, and the Twin Ignition 8. On the 1930 iodels Nash introduced a clutch pedal starter that was a Iash feature for many years to follow. The purpose of iis arrangement was to remove the possibility of "in-gear" tarting.

The Single 6 developed 60 HP at 2800 RPM from its -head engine. This series had a 13-gallon fuel tank. A 14-inch wheelbase was used and these models rode on :25 x 18-inch tires. Mechanical brakes were used on this eries as well as the two higher priced lines.

The Twin Ignition 6 was introduced in mid-1928 as the 929 model. This car continued into 1930 as an overhead alve Six which had two spark plugs for every cylinder. t came with two sets of points, two condensers, two coils, nd a single distributor. This engine developed 74 HP at 800 RPM. The fuel supply was from a 15-gallon tank. ll Twin Ignition 6s came on a 118-inch wheelbase and ode on 5:50 x 19-inch tires.

The Twin Ignition 8 was new for 1930. It was similar to ie Twin Ignition 6, but developed 100 HP at 3200 RPM rom its 298 cubic inch engine. This series used nine main earings, with aluminum alloy pistons and full pressure ibrication. A 19-gallon fuel supply was used. A 124 and 33-inch chassis were used. The tire size was 6:50 x 19 iches.

A total of 32 models were available ranging from a 935 Single 6 5-passenger Sedan to $2,385 for the 7-assenger Twin Ignition 8 Limousine. A total of 54,605 ars were produced, placing the company in 10th position or the year.

This was Nash's 1930 7-passenger Twin Ignition 8 Touring. It was available also as a Single Six Touring for 5 passengers and a Twin Ignition Six. In the style shown, it sold for $2,045 and weighed 3,950 lbs. The car was listed as the Model 498.

The Cabriolet for 1930 that Nash offered came as a Single 6, Twin Ignition 6, and this Eight which had a nine main bearing engine developing 100 HP. It weighed 3,840 lbs., seated 4 passengers, and sold for $1,875 in this form.

Nash offered this 1930 Twin Ignition Ambassador, which was a Club Sedan in every sense of the word. It had enclosed rear quarter panels which gave a sense of privacy to rear seat passengers. This model sold for $2,095 and was available in the 8-cylinder cars on a 133-inch wheelbase, weighing 4,050 lbs. The version shown here is fitted with the extra cost Regal package, which included sidemounts and covers.

Posed for a 1930 publicity shot was this Nash Model 490. This 8-cylinder car offered twin-ignition for its new models introduced that year. It sold for $1,775. The 124-inch Sedan weighed 4,000 lbs. even.

Nash

The least popular of the 8-cylinder 1930 Nash models was this 2-door Sedan wearing standard wooden artillery wheels. It sold for $1,675, came only on the 124-inch wheelbase, and weighed 3,950 lbs. The trunk was standard.

1931

Nash offered four lines of cars in 1931. They were called the 6-60, 8-70, 8-80, and 8-90. Even in the midst of a depression these four series, which offered 24 models, earned $4,808,000 for the company.

The 6-60 was Nash's lowest price car. It was a 6-cylinder, with a 201.3 cubic inch engine that had a maximum horsepower of 60 at 2800 RPM. The fuel supply was a 12-gallon tank. Its wheelbase measured 114½ inches and it rode on 5:00 x 19-inch tires.

The 8-70 came next in line with an 8-cylinder engine of 75 HP at 3200 RPM. Its displacement was 227.2 cubic inches. This series had a 15-gallon fuel tank. The 8-70s used 5:25 x 19-inch tires and had a 116¼-inch chassis

Nash 8-80s had a 240 cubic inch 8-cylinder engine of 85 HP at 3200 RPM. They had a 16-gallon fuel supply These models had 5:50 x 18-inch tires and the wheelbase was 121 inches.

The senior car in the Nash line was the 8-90 which had a 298 cubic inch engine developing 115 HP at 3600 RPM This series used a 20-gallon fuel tank. The tire size wa 6:50 x 19 inches. Two separate wheelbases were used – 124 inches for the regular 5-passenger Sedan and 13 inches for the remaining seven models of the 8-90 Series.

The 1931 Nash prices began at $795 for a 2-passenge 6-60 Coupe and worked upward to $2,025 for the 7 passenger Limousine in the 8-90 Series.

Nash produced 39,616 cars for the year which gave them the 12th position for sales.

The 1931 Nash 870 was one of 24 models made available. Wire wheels were optional equipment in 1931 and most cars came equipped with them. However, this model had the wooden artillery ones. In this series was a Special Sedan for $955, like this car, and the more deluxe version for $995. Both weighed 3,000 lbs.

Nash made this little 1931 sedan-delivery available on the 6-60 chassis for anyone who had a delivery service such as drug stores, markets or hardware stores. It proved fairly popular at $795. Take out the enclosed side window, remove the door from the back of the car, attach the spare tire equipment and you had a 2-door Sedan.

This is Model 881 in the 1931 Nash lineup. Rather unusual for Nash were the disc wheels which this example is wearing. This photo shows the 1931 Nash line at the New York Auto Show, beginning Jan. 2 through Jan. 8, 1931.

Nash

1932

In the 1932 model run, Nash emphasized silence. All bodies were carefully sound-proofed, running gear was insulated with rubber brushed spring shackles, and the synchro-mesh transmission used in all models had a silent second gear. The public was offered five models in the 960 Series beginning at $795 for the 2-passenger Coupe. The same was offered in the 970 Series beginning at $945 for the same model. The 980 Series began with a $1,245 Coupe. In Nash's luxury line, there were ten choices starting with the 990 Sedan for $1,565.

Wheelbases for the cars were 114¼ inches for the 960 Series, 116¼ inches for the 970 Series, 121 inches for the 980 Series, and 124 inches for the 990 Sedan and 133 inches and 142 inches for the remaining 990 models. The 960 came with 5:00 x 19-inch tires, the 970 had 5:25 x 19s, the 980 had 6:00 x 18s, and 990 had 6:50 x 19s. Fuel tanks for these cars were as follows: 960 had a 12-gallon tank, 15-gallon tank for the 970, 980 had a 16-gallon tank, while the 990 used a 20-gallon tank. The 960 came with a 65 HP engine at 2800 RPM. The 970 had a 78 HP at 3200 RPM. The larger cars had a 94 HP at 3400 RPM in the 980 Series and the 990 came out with 115 HP at 3600 RPM.

Sales were quite good, showing 17,696 cars being registered, placing Nash in 13th position for the year.

The beautiful 1931 Nash Model 897 Town Sedan, on a 121-inch wheelbase, sold for $1,375 and weighed 3,400 lbs. This car had a 220 cubic inch 8-cylinder engine that developed 85 HP at 3200 RPM.

Being displayed in front of the Dodson Vogue Tyre Distributor in Los Angeles, is this 1932 Nash Model 971 Convertible Coupe. It naturally wears the Vogue Tyres, twin spot lamps, and twin side mirrors. This model sold for $1,075 and weighed 2,950 lbs., the same as the Convertible Sedan in that series. The Vogue Tyre Distributor is still going under the name of Dodson today and is located at the same place in Los Angeles. Vogue Tyres were an additional piece of equipment not included in the factory base price.

This handsome white 1932 Nash Sedan was Model 994. The gentleman posing proudly with hand on the window sill is the Mayor of Chicago, Anton J. Cermak. The other man has reason to be proud as he is Charles W. Nash. This car weighed 4,100 lbs. and sold for $1,825. The car was used as one of Chicago's official limousines for transporting important guests.

Equipped with just about every conceivable accessory of the day is this 1932 Nash Coupe in the 990 Series. It sold for $1,695 in 2-passenger style and for $1,745 as a 4-passenger Coupe. This example wears a center driving light, twin fender guides, sidemount tire equipment, twin side mirrors, white sidewall tires, and rear fender mud flaps which were quite popular at that time. It was used as an official car of Chicago Motor Club, and is shown in front of the Club's headquarters on Michigan Ave.

Nash

This was the largest Nash ever built to date and it was one of the most expensive cars of the year, too. This 1932 Ambassador Eight came on a 142-inch chassis. Weighing 4,050 lbs., it sold for $1,825. As a 7-passenger Limousine it was available for $2,025. Needless to say, in depression days not too many were sold.

A display floor view of two handsome 1933 Nash Advanced Eight Sedans selling for $1,320. This model weighed 3,870 pounds and this series 8-cylinder engine developed 100 HP at 3400 RPM.

Nash's lowest priced 1933 4-door Town Sedan, Model 1127, had an F.O.B. Kenosha, Wisconsin, price of $695. This model weighed 3,100 lbs. For 1933, Nash introduced the light dimmer switch on the floor between the brake and the clutch.

1933

For 1933, Nash offered five lines of cars which included the new Standard Eight. This car ranged between $830 and $845. It delivered 80 HP at 3200 RPM.

All models featured synchro-mesh transmission, free wheeling, dual mufflers, and X-frames. The additional models to the new Standard Eight – Big G, Ambassador Special, the Advanced Eights – offered dash regulated ride control as a standard feature.

These models changed their designations from 1932. The Special Eight had been the Standard Eight. The Special Eight of 1932 became the Advanced Eight and the Advanced Eight became the Ambassador Eight which could be ordered as a 133 or 142-inch wheelbase car.

In addition to the Standard Eight's 80 HP engine, there was a 75 HP Six at 3200 RPM; Special 8 of 85 HP at 3200 RPM; Advanced 8 with 100 HP at 3400 RPM, and the Ambassador 8 of 125 HP at 3600 RPM.

Tire sizes were 5:50 x 17 on the Six and Standard 8. 5:50 x 18 were used for the Special 8; the Advanced 8 used 6:50 x 17s, and 7:00 x 18s went on the Ambassador 8.

Fuel systems started with a 14-gallon tank for the Special 8 and 16-gallon for the Big Six and Standard Eight and a 19-gallon tank for the Advanced 8 and Ambassador Eight. Mechanical brakes were used throughout.

Prices began as low as $725 for a 2-passenger Coupe and ended at $2,055 for the 7-passenger Limousine on the Ambassador Eight. Wheelbases started at 116 inches and ran between 121, 128, 133, and finally 142 inches.

Sales held at 13th space with 14,973 cars being produced for the calendar year.

This was Nash's 1933 advanced Eight Convertible Sedan on the 128-inch wheelbase. It sold for $1,575 and weighed 4,000 lbs. It carried a Seaman Body like other Nash's of that era.

34

In 1934, Nash produced three series of cars: Big 6, lvanced 8, and the Ambassador 8. The Big 6 started out $765 for the 2-passenger Coupe. Five models were built this series. Wheelbase was 116 inches. All used 5:50 x -inch tires and had an 88 HP engine at 3200 RPM. The Advanced 8 used a 100 HP engine at 3400 RPM; 50 x 16-inch tires, and had five models ranging in price om $1,035 to $1,085. Wheelbase was 121 inches. The Ambassador 8 came equipped with a 125 HP engine 3600 RPM. Wheelbase was 133 inches, or 142 inches the Brougham, 7-passenger Sedan and Limousine. ve models were available. Tire size for this model was 00 x 17. Prices ranged from $1,575 for a 5-passenger 3-inch Sedan to $2,055 for the 7-passenger Limousine. l models used a 19-gallon gasoline supply and came uipped with mechanical brakes.

During 1934, Nash produced its millionth car. Even ough Nash sales improved in 1934, the company lost ,625,078 on sales amounting to $19,679,777. The cars oduced amounted to 28,664 units, which put them in 11th position for the year. These figures also represent fayette sales.

An Advanced Eight 1933 Nash Cabriolet seated four and sold for $1,395. This example weighed 3,750 lbs. The wire wheels were standard equipment, but wood artillery wheels also were available.

One of Nash's most expensive models for 1933 was this Ambassador Eight 7-passenger Sedan. It came only on a 142-inch wheelbase, weighed 4,600 lbs., and sold for $1,955. It also was available as a Limousine for $2,055. The side-mount tire equipment and trunk extension were optional and most came equipped with it.

This scene, used in what is probably Nash's best known color magazine ad, shows a 1933 Nash Ambassador Eight Brougham. The car used a 142-inch chassis, weighed 4,470 lbs. and sold for $1,820. It carried five passengers comfortably. This series used a 125 HP engine at 3600 RPM.

Proudly standing by the car that bears his name is Charles W. Nash. This 1934 Nash Sedan marked the 1,000,000th Nash to leave the assembly line.

Nash

This shows the ample space provided in the trunk compartment of this 1934 Ambassador Eight Sedan Brougham. The bumper guards were classed as an accessory even for this model. Note the attractive pressed steel design used on the fender skirts.

This is the 1934 Ambassador Eight 5-passenger Brougham, which came on a 142-inch wheelbase. This model sold for $1,820 and weighed 4,460 lbs. The rear fender skirts were a factory accessory available on any Nash model this year for a slight extra cost.

The 1934 Nash Big 6 Coupe came on a 116-inch wheelbase. It weighed 3,290 lbs. and sold for $765. Even with an upswing in sales the company took a loss of $1,625,078 this year.

1935

In 1935, Nash reduced the line of models to tw 6-cylinder cars and four 8-cylinder body styles. Pric varied between $895 for the Advanced Six Victoria $1,290 for the Ambassador Eight Sedan.

Sweeping lines showing off a sloping rear, deep skirted fenders, new hood louvers, slanted Vee radiat grille, and steel artillery wheels pretty well summed up t modern package Nash offered in 1935.

The wheelbase had been increased to 121 inches in t Six and to 125 inches for the Eight. Both series us all-steel body construction, which gave more head roo along with the cars being four inches lower. The Sixes us 6:25 x 16-inch tires and 6:50 x 16s went to the Eigh Both series were now equipped with Bendix hydrau brakes and used 19-gallon fuel tanks. Horsepower for t Six was 88 at 3200 RPM and 100 for the Eight at 34 RPM.

Nash sales for 1935 put them in 11th position, selli 44,637 cars. These figures also represent Lafayette f 1935.

The 1934 Nash Ambassador Eight Sedan was available in a variety of models ranging in price from $1,575 to $2,055. The wheelbases were 133 and 142-inches. This example was the 7-passenger Sedan selling for $1,955 and weighing 4,590 lbs. This and the limousine used a 142-inch wheelbase chassis.

Nash cut back drastically in the number of models available in 1935. This example was the lowest priced offering for the year. It was referred to as the Advanced 6 Victoria, Model 3525, selling for $895. It used a 120-inch wheelbase chassis and a 90 HP six-cylinder engine.

Looking practically the same as the Advanced 6 Victoria was this Advanced 8 Victoria, only wearing a pair of factory approved fender skirts. It sold for $1,125 and came on a 125-inch wheelbase chassis. It used a 102 HP Eight.

36

)n October 27, 1936, Nash and Kelvinator merged, t January 4, 1937 was the actual date the merger became ective.

Nash was offered in three series and one sub-series – sh 400, DeLuxe Nash 400 Six, Nash Ambassador Six, d Nash Ambassador Eight. The models were distin- shed as in 1935 by the sloping grille and hood. The 0 had a narrower grille than was used in 1935, with the tical bars curving upward over the top to join into the od. The Ambassadors bore a resemblance to the 1935s, t showed a more graceful pattern. A more attractive ver design was displayed on each of the series. The 400 used a 90 HP engine (at 3400 RPM), a 15- lon fuel tank, and 117-inch wheelbase. The tire size s 6:00 x 16. Brakes were of the hydraulic type on all dels. The 400 DeLuxe had more trim than the Nash). Ambassador Sixes used 93 HP engines and a 19- lon fuel supply. These cars used 6:25 x 16-inch tires l a 125-inch wheelbase, which was also used on the nbassador Eight.

All Eights were similar to Ambassador Sixes except for larger engine. Both Ambassadors turned over at 3400 M. The Eight developed 102 HP. Body styles consisted 16 models ranging from a $665 3-passenger Coupe in 400 Series to the Ambassador Eight Sedan for $995. sh's big news for Sedan owners was its convertible bed. e rear seat and trunk area were quickly adaptable to double bed.

Nash settled for the 12th position this year by selling ,038 cars from its joint Nash-LaFayette dealerships. Fayette calendar year sales are also included.

Nash's most expensive model for 1935 was the Ambassador 8 Sedan selling for $1,290. The slope of the rear end of this model gave it the name of "aero-form design." Fender skirts were a factory accessory and practically all Nash's came with them in 1935.

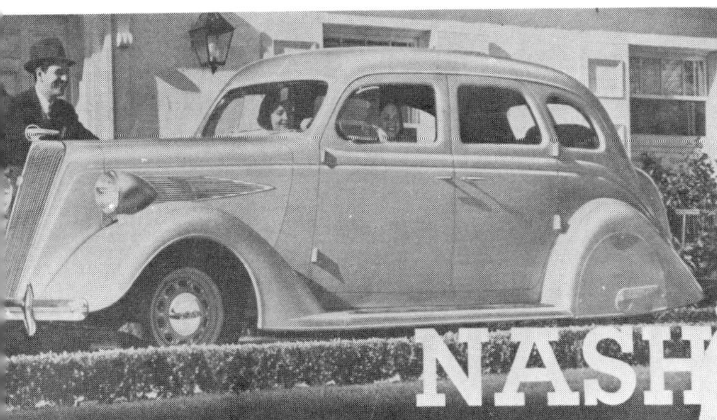

In 1935 Nash offered this "400" Sedan in Touring style for $765. It weighed 3,150 lbs. A straight sedan without the bustle back trunk also was available for $740, weighing 3,100 lbs.

The "Beaver-tail" back was an early rendition of today's fastback design. This was the Advanced 8 Sedan, Model 3580, for 1935 which sold for $1,165.

This was basically the same model as the 1936 Nash "400" but was referred to as DeLuxe "400" selling for $790 as a Touring Sedan. Due to more trim throughout, it brought about a higher price. Note the three fender skirt bolts required to remove the skirt. Again, Nash went heavy on selling this factory accessory to its customers.

Nash

NASH AMBASSADOR SEDANS
WITH BUILT-IN TRUNKS
125 INCH WHEELBASE
$835 to $995

The top of the line for 1936 was the Ambassador, on a 125-inch wheelbase and available as either a Six or an Eight. The Six sold for $895 and the Eight brought $995.

1937

Nash was now a product of the newly formed Nas Kelvinator Corp. with the automotive headquarters sti being in Kenosha, Wis.

For the year the name Lafayette as an individual c had been dropped and the name Nash Lafayette 400 h been adopted. A selection of three series was introduce the above mentioned 400, the Ambassador Six, ar Ambassador Eight. All received new bodies and a delivere price less than the previous year.

The new Nash Lafayette 400 came on a 117-in wheelbase like its predecessor. This series used a 90 H 6-cylinder engine at 3400 RPM and rode on 6:00 x 1 inch tires. A 20-gallon fuel tank was supplied. The seri came in five models, starting at $595 for a 3-passeng Coupe up to $740 for a Cabriolet. Overdrive was option in this series as well as in the other two series.

The Ambassador Six used a 121-inch wheelbase ar 6:25 x 16-inch tires. It developed 105 HP at 3400 RP and used a 20-gallon fuel supply like its smaller ar bigger brothers. Five models were available with a starti price of $755 for the 3-passenger Coupe up to $866 f the Cabriolet.

The Ambassador Eight came on a 125-inch wheelbas The 105 HP 8-cylinder engine had the same RPM as t other two series. Tire size consisted of 7:00 x 16 inch for each of the five models available. The price range we from $855 for a 3-passenger Coupe to $960 for Cabriolet.

Nash placed 12th for the 1937 calendar run by produci 85,949 cars. These figures also include Lafayette sal

For 1937, Nash incorporated the name of La Fayette into its models. So this 1937 6-passenger Victoria Sedan technically was a Nash La Fayette that cost $655. It was one of five models available. This 2-door model wears the pressed steel wheels that have the wheel openings to give cooling to the brake drums.

This was the 1937 Nash La Fayette, Model 3718, "400" 4-door Sedan which came on a 117-inch wheelbase. This 6-cylinder sedan seated six passengers and sold for $700.

Babe Ruth, the famous baseball player, was photographed with his new 1937 Nash Ambassador Eight Sedan. The car sold for $945 F.O.B. Kenosha, Wis. It weighed 3,720 lbs.

38

'or 1938, Nash offered three cars – the Nash Lafayette ning in two series, Master and DeLuxe; the Ambassador : and Ambassador Eight. These models made up a total 18 body styles for the three series.

Iash offered many improvements. Among them was a v heating system referred to through the years as 'eather Eye," along with a shortened gearshift lever that :ended from the instrument panel.

'he Nash Lafayette Master came with a 6-cylinder, HP engine (at 3400 RPM). The wheelbase was 117 hes. Three models were available: Coupe, 2-door Sedan 1 4-door Sedan, all on 6:00 x 16-inch tires. These dels used the 20-gallon fuel supply, the same as the ibassadors.

'he DeLuxe Lafayette was the same car as the Master :ept it offered more refinements and deluxe equipment, s two additional body styles.

'he Ambassador Six used a 105 HP engine of the same M as the Lafayette. Its wheelbase consisted of 121 hes, and it used 6:25 x 16-inch tires. Five models were ilable.

'he top line consisted of the Ambassador Eight, which d a 115 HP engine at 3400 RPM. These models came a 125-inch wheelbase and rode on 7:00 x 16-inch tires. ey also offered five models. Prices for the entire line from $770 for a 3-passenger Lafayette Master Coupe $1,240 for a 5-passenger Ambassador Eight Cabriolet. Iash placed 13th for sales by selling 32,017 units during 1938 calendar year.

The Model 3781 was this 1937 Nash Ambassador Eight Cabriolet that came on a 125-inch wheelbase. It sold for $900. This well-equipped car has the factory approved fender skirts, wheel trim rings, spot light, and hinge mounted side mirror. The gentleman standing by the car is Charles W. Nash, who was then elected Chairman of the Board.

A front view of the 1937 Nash Ambassador Eight Sedan Model 3788. This was the year Nash merged with Kelvinator Corp. The two gentlemen are Charles Nash and the company's new president, George W. Mason.

This 1938 Nash Ambassador Six Sedan came on a 121-inch wheelbase and sold for $1,050. This fender skirted sedan apparently was put into demonstrator use by the largest California Nash dealership at that time. The license plate frame inscription says Nash California Co. of Los Angeles.

This 1938 8-cylinder Nash Ambassador Sedan had a price tag of $1,200. It was referred to as Model 3888. The sedan weighed 3,790 lbs. and was the most popular model in the 8-cylinder lineup. Nash introduced its famous heating system that year called "Weather-Eye," which probably wasn't necessary on this particular car living in southern California.

Nash

The most expensive model in the 1938 Nash Ambassador Six line was this 121-inch wheelbase 5-passenger Cabriolet. It sold for $1,090.

The most expensive 1938 Nash was this Ambassador Eight Cabriolet. It sold for $1,240. This model came equipped with factory approved fender skirts, wheel trim rings, and radio with side cowl-mounted antenna. It weighed 3,620 lbs.

This 1939 Nash Ambassador Six came as both a 3-passenger Business Coupe for $925 and also as a 5-passenger All-purpose Coupe for $960. Both models were identical from the outside, using a 121-inch wheelbase. The same story was true in the Nash La Fayette DeLuxe Series and the Ambassador Eight. The model is well-equipped with factory fender skirts, wheel trim rings and the grille guard assembly.

This 1939 Nash Ambassador Eight came both as a "Slip-stream Back" model and with the bustleback trunk known as the Touring Sedan. Both models sold for the same price – $1,235. The 8-cylinder engine developed 115 HP.

Completely new for 1939, the Nash Ambassador Six Cabriolet, Model 3921, weighed 3,430 lbs. and sold for $1,035. A similar Ambassador Eight was also available, only on a 125-inch wheelbase.

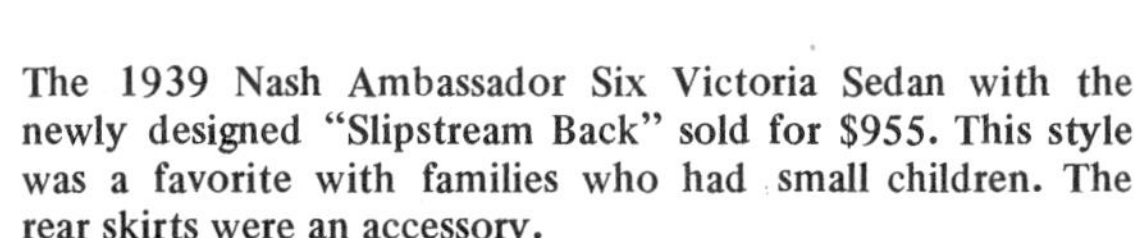

The 1939 Nash Ambassador Six Victoria Sedan with the newly designed "Slipstream Back" sold for $955. This style was a favorite with families who had small children. The rear skirts were an accessory.

1939

New Nash features for the year included a triple front ıd grille design with two of the grilles being vertical yles in the fender catwalks and the center one being a horizontal fashion. The headlamps were placed in a ısh mounted design in the fenders. All models came ith the conventional gearshift lever as standard equipent but a remote control lever was available as optional uipment.

As in 1938, three chassis were available: the Nash ıfayette, Ambassador Six, and Ambassador Eight, ranging 22 styles from the $770 Nash Lafayette 3-passenger ısiness Coupe to the Ambassador Eight Cabriolet for ,295. Prices were reduced as much as $68 from the evious year in some models.

All the new models used a hood design referred to as an igator type which opened from the front. New door ːiker plates were introduced to make for surer closing. ıe upper hinges on front doors were concealed, which ded in the lines of the body. All models shared better shions, making softness one of the key selling points. ıe Ambassador Eight used rubber cushion pads which ded to comfort on a long trip.

The Nash Lafayette Six developed 99 HP at 3400 RPM. ıey used 6:00 x 16-inch tires on a 117-inch wheelbase. ıis series as well as the other two models used a 20-llon fuel tank.

The Ambassador Six developed 105 HP at 3400 RPM. ıis series came on a 121-inch wheelbase with 6:25 x -inch tires.

All Ambassador Eights came with a 115 HP engine the same RPM. They used 7:00 x 16-inch tires on theiı 5-inch chassis.

The Nash sales picture for 1939 kept them in 13th sition by selling 65,552 units for the calendar run. Yet company felt a fiscal loss of $1,573,524 for the year ıich ended September 30, 1939.

Nash's 1940 Ambassador 8 Touring Sedan weighed 3,710 lbs. and sold for $1,195. A total of six models were available in this series. This example came equipped with white sidewall tires, full wheel trim, radio, and bumper guard equipment. The front license plate should be mounted on the right side.

Nash introduced this 1940 4-door Sedan, Model 4080, emphasizing its practical purpose with the convertible bed for those who enjoyed outdoor living. It was available in the Nash La Fayette and Ambassador 6 and 8 Sedans. This model is the Ambassador 6 Sedan which weighed 3,380 lbs. and sold for $985.

This 1940 Nash All-purpose Cabriolet was mounted on the Ambassador Six chassis which weighed 3,410 lbs. It sold for $1,085 F.O.B. Kenosha, Wis. The Cabriolet was also available in the La Fayette series in Ambassador Eight style for $1,295.

This is the 1940 Nash Ambassador Eight Cabriolet, Model 4081. It weighed 3,640 lbs., its price was listed as $1,295. Universal Studios featured the 1940 Nash Convertible in many of their pictures, and used some, including this vehicle, as company cars.

Nash

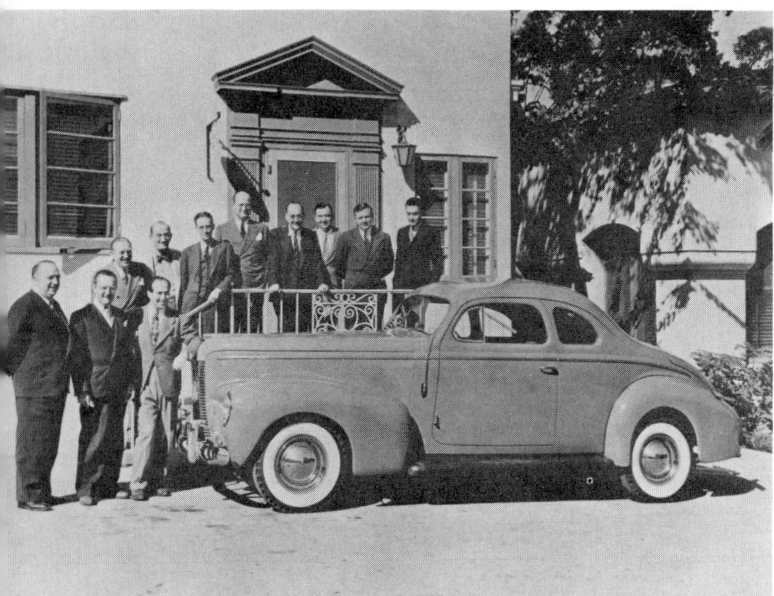

Universal Movie Studios production manager, Martin Murphy, happily accepts the keys to his 1940 Nash Ambassador Eight Coupe that was presented to him on his 25th anniversary with the movie studio. This car is well-equipped with factory accessories. In base form it sold for $1,170. A 3-passenger Business Coupe also was available for $1,135.

1940

For 1940 Nash presented three lines that were reduce in price $20 to $50. They were the Lafayette (Ambassador 6 and 8. The most important new featu for the year were the independently sprung front wheel The kingpin supports were linked to the frame by cros levers with shock absorbers forming the inner mountin of the upper levers.

Nash continued its Weather Eye heating system, onl perfecting it by placing it directly ahead of the instrumen panel. Air foam seating became standard in both th Ambassador 6 and 8 Series. It was optional at extra cos for the Lafayette. All sedan models were offered wit either fastback trunks or humpback trunks at no addition cost.

The Nash Lafayette offered a 6-cylinder engine c 99 HP at 3400 RPM. The Ambassador Six came with dual ignition 6-cylinder engine, which had the famili two spark plugs per cylinder arrangement. It develope 105 HP at 3400 RPM. The cubic inch displacement c this engine was 234 inches, the same as in the Lafayett models.

The Ambassador Eight developed 115 HP at 3400 RPM It had a 260 cubic inch engine that required 7 quarts of oi

Tire size for the Nash Lafayette was 6:00 x 16. Th Ambassador Six used 6:25 x 16 inches and 7:00 x 1 inch tires were used on the Ambassador Eight. A models used a 20-gallon fuel tank. The wheelbase of th Lafayette models was 117 inches. The Ambassador Si came on a 121-inch chassis, and the Ambassador Eigh used the 125-inch chassis.

A total of 18 models were available ranging in pri from $795 for the Lafayette 3-passenger Business Cou to $1,295 for an All Purpose Ambassador Eight Cabriole

Nash placed in 14th position for the calendar year b selling 63,617 units.

A classic all its own is this 1940 Nash Special that was created by Count Alexis de Sakhnoffsky. This model received its new styling from a standard Nash Cabriolet. Note the low swept door line. Approximately 50 of these beauties were built during the 1940 model run.

A new model and a new design were offered by Nash in 1941 when this economical 2-door Sedan was introduced. It was called Model 4146, or the Nash "600." The term "600" meant 600 miles to a 20-gallon tankful of gasoline. This model was advertised for $810.

The higher priced Nash for 1941 was the Ambassador, available as either a 6 or 8. Both models used the 121-inch wheelbase. The Ambassador Six Touring Sedan sold for $1,030 while the same car could be ordered in the Ambassador Eight for $1,101.

•41

Nash introduced a new model which replaced the Nash ıfayette of 1940. This new car was referred to as the ash 600. Its purpose was to compete with the Big Three the low price range. It offered a full size body that was nilar in most dimensions with the larger car, but still it ıly weighed 2,550 lbs. due to its unit body construction ıth box section side rails that were welded to the body llars. The 6-cylinder engine of 173.6 cubic inches veloped 75 HP at 3600 RPM. This L-head engine with otional overdrive offered 25 to 30 MPG. The fuel tank r this series as well as the larger Nash was 20 gallons. ıe tire size was 5:50 x 16 inches and passengers rode on 2-inch chassis.

In addition to this series were the Ambassador Six and nbassador Eight. Both of these were twin-ignition odels, as Nash had offered since mid-1928. These two ries were identical except for a 234.8 cubic inch cylinder engine that developed 105 HP at 3400 RPM d rode on 6:25 x 16-inch tires in the Ambassador Six. ght cylinder cars used a 260.8 cubic inch engine that veloped 115 HP at the same RPM. The wheelbase in th series was 121 inches. Nash's "Bed-in-a-Car" was ain available in all Sedans and Broughams. A total of 21 odels were available, ranging in price from $710 for the 0 3-passenger Coupe to $1,215 for an Ambassador briolet. Nash placed in 11th place from the sale of ,408 cars.

The most expensive and least popular model in the 1941 Nash Ambassador 6 and 8 line for the year was the Convertible Cabriolet. The 6 weighed 3,430 lbs. and sold for $1,095. The Ambassador 8 weighed 3,581 lbs. with a price tag of $1,215.

Nash claimed this 1941 Model 4140 – or as it was better known, the Nash "600" – was the first completely revolutionary car in the past ten years. This was the first Nash with "unitized" construction which featured a single welded steel body for greater strength. This 4-door DeLuxe Sedan weighed 2,660 lbs. and sold for $860. Note this model wears accessory bumper wing tips, white sidewall tires, and wheel trim rings.

This was what Nash had been advertising during the year – ECONOMY FROM THE NASH "600." The little car proved just that on the Gilmore Economy Run to the Grand Canyon in 1941 by averaging 25.81 MPG. The Nash distributor in Los Angeles was the Nash California Co. who claimed they'd deliver this car for $954 including standard equipment and federal tax.

The least expensive 1942 Nash Sedan was the "600" Sedan with a fastback trunk. It sold for $940 and weighed 2,655 pounds. The wheelbase measured 112 inches and the six-cylinder engine developed 76 HP at 3600 RPM.

Nash

This 1942 Nash 4-door DeLuxe Touring Sedan offered stainless fender trim only on the early models built before Jan. 1, 1942. This model also wears the rarely seen white sidewall tires for 1942. It weighed the same as the straight "600" Sedan, 2,655 lbs., but cost $25 additional at $965.

1942

The 1942 models were virtually the same offering as 1941 except for some trim changes which included lower horizontal grille with moldings extending into th fenders. The compression ratio was raised from 6:30 6:50 on the Ambassador Six and the torque increased fro 195 lbs. to 203 lbs. The overall length of Ambassado increased to 205½ inches and the 600 Series increased 196½ inches.

The 600 models had a 172 cubic inch engine th developed 76 HP at 3600 RPM. The Ambassador S used a 234 cubic inch engine of 104 HP at 3400 RPM. Th Ambassador Eight came with a 260 cubic inch engi that developed 115 HP at 3400 RPM. All series used 20-gallon fuel tank. The 600's had 5:50 x 16-inch tire while the Ambassador Six used 6:25 x 16s and th Ambassador Eight used 6:50 x 16-inch tires. The 60 Series had a 112-inch wheelbase and the remaining tw came on a 121-inch chassis.

A total of 15 models were available for the year rangi in price from $890 for a 3-passenger 600 Business Cou to $1,176 for the Ambassador Eight Touring Sedan. Na did not offer any convertibles in the 1942 lineup. Th placed 10th position for the calendar year from 5,4 sales.

This 1942 Nash Coupe came as both 6 or 8-cylinder in the Ambassador line, using the 121-inch wheelbase. The Ambassador Six had a 105 HP engine and the Ambassador Eight developed 115 HP at the same 3400 RPM. As a Six, it sold for $1,051 and as an Eight, the price was $1,101. Note this example is minus all frills. It doesn't have the directional signal lights mounted in the fashionable fender spears like the other 1942 models displayed here.

A typical 1942 "Blackout" car is this Nash Ambassador 8, Model 4280. This 4-door Sedan in fastback styling weighed 3,440 lbs. and sold for $1,151. Much plastic was used in these cars as a substitute for metal. This was the last year Nash built an 8-cylinder car, until they merged with Hudson in 1955.

Last one off the line for the duration of the war. Sporting all of its "Blackout" trim, it did manage to obtain a set of white sidewalls, however, to help brighten it up. The model happens to be the most expensive 1942 Nash built, which was the Ambassador Eight 4-door Touring Sedan that sold for $1,176. This scene took place on the afternoon of Feb. 4, 1942.

The 1930 Oakland was a product of General Motors ɔrp., built at Pontiac, Mich. It was sold with Pontiac ıd classed as the higher priced car in the Pontiac family. aklands were built from 1907 through 1931. The ɔmpany was originally formed by Edward Murphy, and ıilt cars under his directorship until purchased by G.M. ı April 9, 1909.

The 1930 Oaklands were built as V-8 cars, and were 'fered in the low priced field, hoping to help increase les which had been slipping the past few years due ainly to their own competition from the Pontiac line. The V-8 developed 85 HP at 3200 RPM. It used a ;-gallon fuel tank. The Oakland rode on 5:50 x 18-inch 'es and used a 117-inch wheelbase. Mechanical brakes ɜre used. Seven body styles were available ranging from ,145 for a 4-passenger Roadster to $1,345 for the passenger Custom Sedan.

Oakland placed in 5th position for sales by selling ;,225 units. These calendar year figures also include ɔntiac sales.

Oakland's 1930 2-door Sedan offered a mohair interior as standard equipment as did all 1930 closed models. The sidemounts and wire wheels were available at extra cost. It sold for $1,205. Lovejoy hydraulic shocks were used on all Oakland models this year.

For 1930, Oakland offered this 5-passenger 4-door Sedan for $1,250 in base form. It also was available as a Custom Sedan with a more lavish interior for $1,345. Sidemounts and a rear luggage rack added tremendously to this car's looks.

This 1930 Oakland Sport Roadster was the company's lowest priced model, selling for $1,145. It used a V-8 engine developing 85 HP at 3200 RPM. Sidemount equipment and wire wheels were optional at extra cost. A side door on the right gave access to a compartment for golf clubs, packages, etc.

More popular than the Business Coupe was this 1930 Oakland Sport Coupe which had a seating capacity for four. This 1930 model came equipped with what they called safety indicator lamps on the front fenders. The head and tail lamps and cowl band were brilliantly chrome plated. The natural wood artillery wheels were standard equipment. This model sold for $1,180. Note the package door just ahead of the rear fender for access to a rear storage compartment.

Oakland

The Oakland Phaeton for 1930 was a very impressive looking car with its genuine leather interior and door panels in fabrikoid. The Phaeton emphasized its fleetness by a sloping one-piece forward folding windshield and a top that could be lowered and tucked away in a boot that was provided. It sold for $1,325. Oakland still considered bumpers an added cost accessory, as were sidemounts.

1931

The year 1931 saw the Oakland offer its final model only as a V-8 of 251 cubic inches. The maximum bral horsepower was still 85 at 3400 RPM, and the wheelba remained 117 inches. The tire size again was 5:50 x 1 inches. Mechanical brakes were used on these model

The car offered a synchro mesh transmission for tl first time with a quiet second gear. The rear end had bee made sturdier with a gear ratio of 4.55 instead of 4.4

The Oakland's appearance was impressive with tl continued use of fender lamps mounted on top of tl front fenders. A Vee-type front splash apron was offere for the first time.

Oakland offered one less model this year than last, no coming only in six styles. The prices were lowered fro 1930 with hopes to increase sales but the buyers werer buying in 1931. The lowest priced Oakland was tl 2-passenger Coupe for $1,015. The top of the line, f $1,225, was the 5-passenger Custom Sedan. Oakland ar Pontiac sales amounted to 86,307 units which gave the the 5th place again.

For 1931, Oakland displayed this Convertible Coupe with landau irons, leather interior, and wire wheels as standard equipment for $1,160. Few buyers were ready to purchase this open model.

The practical Business Coupe is what Oakland referred to this 1931 Coupe. It rode on a 117-inch wheelbase, weighed 2,970 lbs. and sold for $1,015. This car was equipped with a large rear trunk area instead of a rumble seat. With rumble seat, it was known as the Sport Coupe.

The final Oakland appeared in 1931 with its same V-8 engine as was offered in 1930. Very few changes were apparent in the 1931 cars. The single bar bumper was one of the few noticeable differences over the previous year. This Sedan was one of two offered. The DeLuxe Sedan like this sold for $1,150 and the Custom model was available for $1,225 with enclosed rear quarter panels.

Oldsmobile

Oldsmobile, a division of General Motors Corp., has its adquarters in Lansing, Mich. The car has been built ice 1897.

The new car for 1930 offered only the L-head 6-cylinder gine developing 62 HP at 3000 RPM. Its engine dis-acement was 197.5 cubic inches. A 15-gallon gasoline pply was used. The wheelbase measured 113½ inches. 1 models rode on 5:25 x 18-inch tires.

A total of six body styles were available for the year. ices ranged from $895 for the 2-passenger Coupe to ʼ95 in 5-passenger Sedan style.

Even though the sales picture was bleak, Oldsmobile gineers were out trying to better the car with new road sts. One such experiment took place in South Africa in e Kalahare Desert during 1930, when two Oldsmobile oresentatives took a car over land which had never been iven on before. The Oldsmobile wouldn't quit. From ovember 23rd to November 29th, 1930, the Oldsmobile avelled over 1,000 miles of unexplored terrain, which lped Oldsmobile prove the durability of the cars. Oldsmobile came in for 12th position this year by ling 49,886 units.

The 1930 Oldsmobile Convertible Cabriolet oddly enough was more expensive by $30 than the 1930 Phaeton. This Cabriolet sold for $995. With the rumble seat, it seated four.

On display at an auto show in 1930 is this Oldsmobile six-wheel trunk sedan that sold for $995 in base form. Oldsmobile still painted the headlamps on the 1930 cars, as is shown in this photo.

Oldsmobile's 1930 Phaeton for five had its sleek lines enhanced by the fold-down windshield. The interior was finished with leather seats and fabrikoid door panels and trim. This Phaeton sold for $965, and 76 models equipped like this were sold. The wire wheels, sidemounts, and bumpers were all extra cost accessories.

This 1930 Oldsmobile Rumble Seat Coupe was available for $965. The model seated four and came on a 113½-inch wheelbase. The 6-cylinder engine developed 62 HP at 3000 RPM.

The 2-door Sedan that Oldsmobile offered for 1930 sold for $895–the same as the Business Coupe. These were the lowest priced models for the year. The wire wheels and sidemount tire equipment were optional at extra cost, as were the bumpers. Note the Oldsmobile cdat-of-arms on the canvas tire cover.

Oldsmobile

1931

The 1931 car offered some improvements that t public accepted quite well. Among them were the adopti of synchro-mesh transmission, a new down-draft carbure which gave better mileage and better performance, and stronger and stiffer frame.

Oldsmobile came as a 6-cylinder car offering a 19 cubic inch engine with a new maximum brake horsepow of 65 at 3350 RPM.

The fuel supply was a 16-gallon tank. The tire size s was 5:25 x 18, and the wheelbase still measured 11 inches.

Again, six models were available for the year. Th ranged from $845 for a 2-passenger Business Coupe $960 for the Patrician Sedan. The company sold 48,0 units for the 1931 model run which placed the compa in 11th position for the year.

Ranked among the lowest priced Oldsmobiles for 1931 was this 6-cylinder 2-door Sedan that sold for $845. The wooden spoke artillery wheels were standard equipment for this year.

Sleek looking was the 1931 Oldsmobile Convertible Roadster with the standard functional landau irons. The wooden artillery wheels were standard equipment but sidemounted spares were an accessory. This example sold for $935, and a total of 1,179 were sold.

The 1931 Oldsmobile 5-passenger 4-door Sedan sold for $925 in base form. The sidemount spare equipment, tire cover, and spot light were all classed as factory approved accessories. A total of 4,383 were built. In addition to this model there was a more deluxe sedan referred to as the Patrician Sedan for $960.

This 1931 Oldsmobile 2-door Sedan is equipped with the accessory wire wheels which gives the car a look of more grace and style. It also wears an accessory spare tire cover with a chrome rim.

A nice facelifting was done when the 1932 Oldsmobile was displayed. This 6-cylinder 2-door Sedan developed 71 HP at 3200 RPM. It was ranked among the lower priced models for the year, selling at $875. A total of only 784 of this body style were built.

›32

Oldsmobile really turned on the lines for its new owings this year. A new L-head Straight Eight was fered, giving 82 HP at 3200 RPM. The new Six had HP at the same RPM. The automatic choke made an teresting development this year. Another new device hich was standard for Olds were shock absorbers justable from the seat. Both series rode on the same assis with a new 116½-inch wheelbase. The length of e hood had been lengthened three inches to accomodate the new Eight. These features gave the appearance a really big car.

The front end was rendered more attractive by the proved radiator contour, single bar bumper chrome ated headlights, and chrome plated trumpet horns rectly beneath the classic appearing headlamps. Parking nps had curved glass so that the light was visible from e side. The public had a choice of wood or wire wheels no extra cost. Wheels and tire size measured 6:00 x 18. x models were available in each series. Prices began at 75 for the 2-passenger Business Coupe in the 6-cylinder odel and went up to $1,090 for the 5-passenger Patrician dan. These cars came with a 16-gallon fuel tank and used echanical brakes.

With all its charm in the looks department, saleswise, ds slipped from 11th to 12th spot, delivering only ,933 units for the year.

A fashionable deluxe 1932 Oldsmobile Sport Coupe, equipped with 6 demountable wood wheels, sold for $925 as a 6-cylinder. As an 8-cylinder, it had a price tag of $1,025. In the six line, a total of 420 were built, while 163 were made in the eight cylinder series.

At almost the top of the line pricewise in both 6 and 8-cylinder series was the fleet looking Convertible Coupe. This 5-wire wheel model sold for $955 in the 6-cylinder line, producing only 88 examples. Even fewer were turned out with the rear mounted spare in the 8-cylinder line. A total of 35 were shipped to Oldsmobile dealers, selling for $1,055.

This 1932 Oldsmobile 4-door Sedan was available in both 6 and 8-cylinder models, using the 116½-inch wheelbase. As a 6, with sidemount equipment and wire wheels, a total of 1,295 were built for $955. In the 8-cylinder, with the same equipment, only 507 were produced, selling for $1,055. A special Patrician series was also available in both 6 and 8-cylinder models which sold for $35 additional.

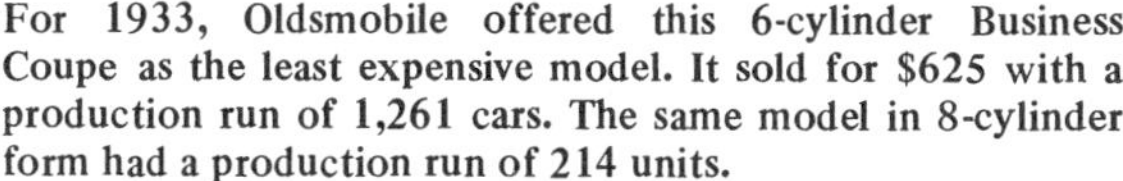

For 1933, Oldsmobile offered this 6-cylinder Business Coupe as the least expensive model. It sold for $625 with a production run of 1,261 cars. The same model in 8-cylinder form had a production run of 214 units.

Oldsmobile

Oldsmobile displayed this 1933 6-cylinder 6-wheel side-mounted Convertible Coupe for $675. The steel pressed wheels were standard. A total of 119 were built. In the 8-cylinder line, only 115 Convertible Coupes were built.

1933

Two series again were offered for 1933, a Six and Eight. These came in thirteen models, seven Sixes, a six Eights. The wheelbase for the Six was 115 inch while the Eight was a four-inch longer car.

Tires on the Six were 5:50 x 17s and the Eights ca with 6:00 x 17s. The brake system was Bendix mechani for both series. Both models used a 16-gallon tank. T Six developed 80 HP at 3200 RPM and the Eight produc 90 HP at 3350 RPM. Prices ran from $625 upwa

Stylewise, the Olds came equipped with the comm Vee-shaped grille that most cars were now beginning use, skirted fenders, and the beaver tail rear end. St spoked wheels which blended into the car's design w used in both series as standard equipment.

Oldsmobile took the 9th position by selling 36,3 cars for this calendar year.

The Indianapolis Pacesetter for 1933 happened to be the 1933 Oldsmobile 8-cylinder Convertible with the rear mounted spare. This model used the 119-inch wheelbase. Production figures show 146 five-wheel convertibles being built. The pace car was light gray in color.

This 8-cylinder 1933 Oldsmobile Touring Sedan with side-mounts proved to be one of the more popular 8-cylinder cars. Rare wire wheels were available at extra cost, but most chose the steel pressed wheels like this model has.

A rare car when new was this 1934 8-cylinder Oldsmobile 6-wheel Convertible Coupe. Only 367 were manufactured. In the 5-wheel version, 536 were delivered.

Oldsmobile offered this 6-cylinder 1934 Touring Coupe for 5 passengers as one of their lower priced cars for the year. The built-on trunk was standard equipment for this model. It was the most popular style among the Touring Coupes. A total of 11,717 were built as five-wheel models. As a six-wheel version, only 551 6-cylinder Touring Coupes were sold. Note the rare factory approved spotlight.

34

New this year was the feature all of General Motors as claiming. This was the independent front suspension rmed "knee action." Also a first for Olds were hydraulic akes used on both Sixes and Eights.

In the engine compartment, the Six was reduced 1/16-ch to a new dimension of 3-5/16 x 4-1/8 inch bore and roke, giving a horsepower rating of 84 at 3450 RPM. he Eight gave out the same horsepower as 1933 models, hich was 90 at 3350 RPM. Top speed of the Six was 7 MPH and the Eight could deliver 84 MPH. Gasoline ileage was considered good. The Six at 50 MPH eraged 17 MPG and an Eight at the same speed delivered 4 MPG.

The wheelbases for the Six and Eight were 114 and 19 inches. Tire size on the Six was 5:50 x 17 and the ight drove on 7:00 x 16s. Both used steel spoked heels. Fuel capacity was 15 gallons on the Six and an 8-gallon supply for the Eight. Body styles numbered 13, nging from $625 for a 2-passenger Coupe in the Six to 860 for the Eight cylinder DeLuxe 5-passenger Touring edan.

Oldsmobiles style improvements showed a wider radiator ell, new grille contours, torpedo louvers for the hood, nger bodies, sloping rear panels, built-in trunks on ouring models, bullet shaped taillamps on the Eights, nd bullet shaped headlamps for both the Six and Eight. Olds came in Sixth with 80,911 cars being sold this alendar year.

This 1934 Oldsmobile 6-wheel Touring Sedan ranked as the most expensive Oldsmobile for the year. It sold for $860. Only 3,339 were built for the states and 76 more went for export.

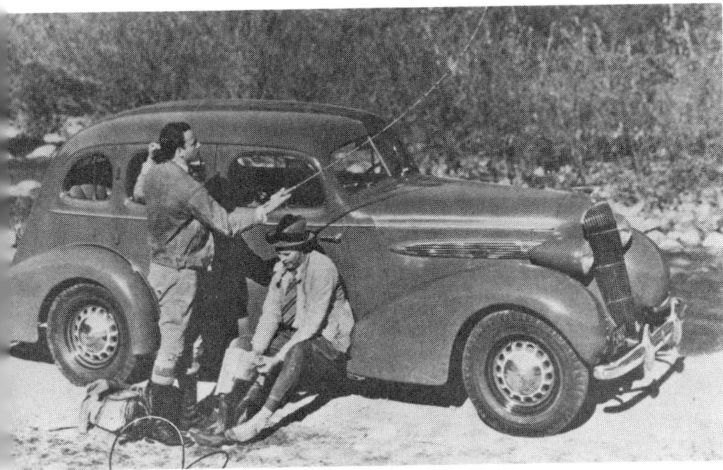

Oldsmobile enjoyed a huge gain in sales of approximately one hundred thousand over the previous year. This F-35 1935 Oldsmobile 5-passenger Sedan was one of the popular reasons. It sold for $790, weighed 3,380 lbs. A total of 12,807 6-cylinder flat-back sedans were sold for home use and 50 were for foreign delivery.

The top of the line for 1935 was this L-35 5-passenger Touring Sedan in 8-cylinder form, on a 121-inch wheelbase. It sold for $970. A total of 16,500 were built for home use and 52 were overseas bound. This photo, from one of Oldsmobile's best known ads, showed the car in gun metal gray finish.

Rarely seen wearing the sidemounted tires is this 1935 6-cylinder Oldsmobile Touring Coupe. A total of 191 were built like this. In the 8-cylinder line only 2 were assembled with sidemounts. In base form this 6-cylinder sold for $755.

Oldsmobile

1935

Olds came forth with a line of cars more refined tha before, showing off the all-steel Turret Top. No-dra ventilation was improved over last year, a smart Vee-shape windshield was permanently sealed, hood louvers co sisted of six narrow chromium plated slits on horizont bars, and a nicely crowned chromium-plated die-cast gril added to the car's frontal appearance and also added the radiator cooling capacity.

The engine and body were moved five inches forwa which not only added to the improved riding qualitie but gave way to the additional luggage space. The whee base on the Six was now 115 inches while the Eights we six inches longer.

Tire size was 6:25 x 16 for the Six. The Eights use 7:00 x 16s. Fuel supply consisted of an 18-gallon tank both series. The Six used a 90 HP engine and the Eig developed 100 HP both at 3400 RPM. Bendix hydrau brakes were now in their second year for Oldsmobi

The same seven body styles were available for bo series, beginning at $675 for the Business Coupe as a S and ranging to $970 for the Eight Cylinder Touring Seda From these fourteen body styles Olds claimed the fif place in sales by selling 183,153 cars for the calendar ye

The lowest priced 1936 Oldsmobile was this 6-cylinder Business Coupe. It sold for $675 and weighed 2,998 lbs. The wheelbase measured 115 inches. A total of 19,284 were built, all for delivery in the states. None went for export.

Oldsmobile's most expensive model for 1936 was the L-36 5-passenger Touring Sedan which sold for $970. It weighed 3,400 lbs. Production figures show 26,379 5-wheel sedans being built and 1,916 sidemount sedans assembled. For export delivery 78 of both 5 and 6-wheel models were shipped.

Just rounded out a little with the absence of the suicide doors is this 1936 Oldsmobile 6-cylincer Convertible Coupe. A total of 2,056 five-wheel models were produced and 63 sidemounted 6-cylinder Convertibles were sold. For foreign delivery, a total of 47 in both 5 and 6-wheel versions were sold.

A 1936 Oldsmobile Eight L-36 Touring Coupe sold for $900. It weighed 3,355 lbs. A total of 224 4-wheel models were produced and 155 5-wheel models were manufactured. This unit, owned by the Lansing, Mich., police has been fitted with an early two-way radio unit.

936

New for Oldsmobile in 1936 were a stiffer frame and ngine mountings, and aluminum pistons. The Six deeloped 90 HP and the Eight came with a 100 HP engine, oth turning over at 3400 RPM. Each model used an 8-gallon fuel tank. Again, the wheelbase on the Six was 15 inches, while the Eight was six inches longer. Both ars used hydraulic brakes. Tire size of the Six was now :50 x 16 while Eights used 7:00 x 16-inch tires. Body tyles were the same in each series.

Lines were more rounded over the good-looking 1935s. 'he die-cast grille of last year was continued with a wide hrome strip running down the center of the grille. Headmps were mounted higher on the radiator shell and were itted closer together so that their streamlined brackets lended into the grille. Gone were the suicide doors of 935.

The Sixes began with a $675 2-passenger Coupe. The op of the Six line was the Touring Trunk Sedan for $820. 'he Eights began with a 2-passenger Coupe for $860. Top ar for the Eights was the $970 Touring Trunk Sedan. A otal of 14 models between both series were available. Oldsmobile placed Fifth this year by selling 187,638 nits.

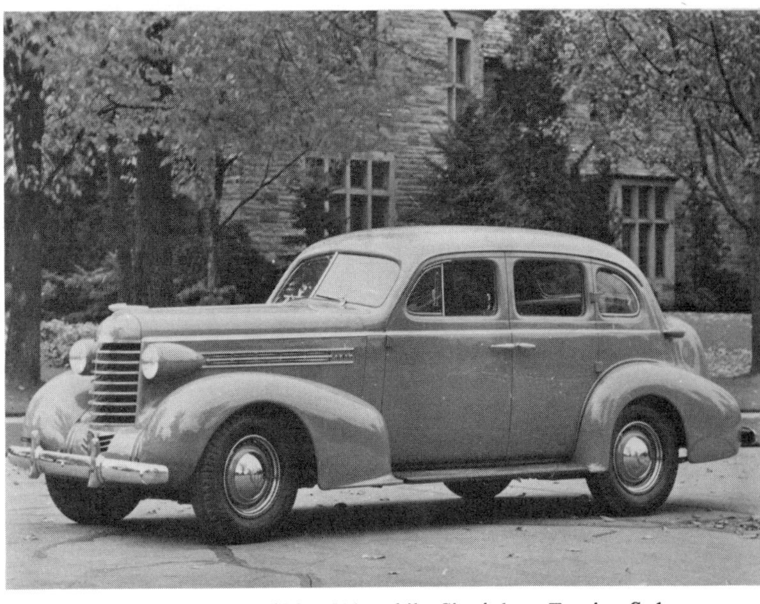

This was the 1937 Oldsmobile Six 4-door Touring Sedan, nicely equipped with accessory trim rings and the owner's monograms neatly placed on the hood side panels between the two longer chrome strips. This model weighed 3,290 lbs. and sold for $945. Olds built 59,794 for home delivery and 3,139 of both right and left-hand drive for overseas use.

This L-37 1937 Oldsmobile Eight Business Coupe once was owned by the author. This 110 HP model weighed 3,400 lbs. and sold for $935 in base form. The car was quite well equipped with mostly genuine accessories from the era. A total of 2,018 were produced for stateside use. Only one left-hand and one right-hand drive model were sent for overseas shipment.

Viewers could easily compare the 1937 Oldsmobile Six in the foreground with an 8-cylinder 2-door Touring Coupe on the left, with cut-aways of the new models at the New York Auto Show which was held from Nov. 11 to 18, 1936.

Not as popular as the Touring Sedan model was this 1937 Olds Eight 4-door Sedan. It sold for $1,025, weighed 3,480 lbs. Only 477 were built for home delivery; one saw duty as a left-hand drive model for overseas use; and just nine six-wheel models were built for U.S. usage.

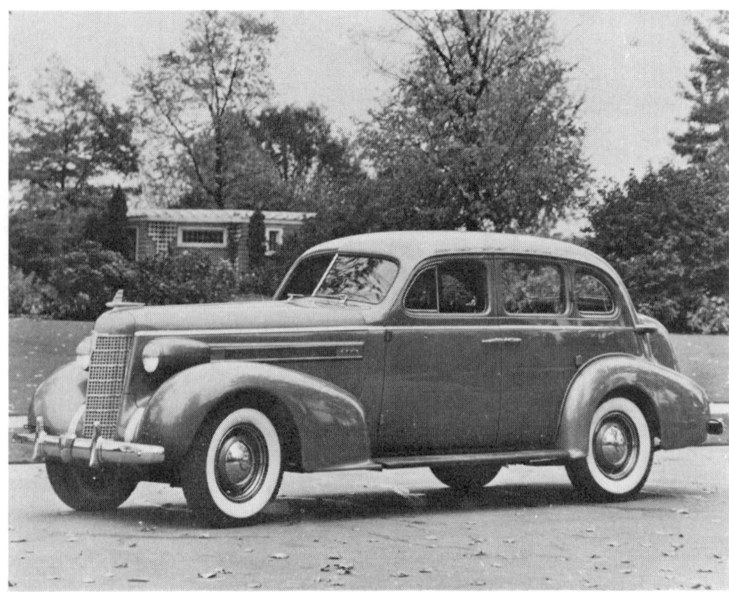

A car with real sleek lines similar to this was owned by the author's parents from 1937 to 1950. Only one word described it – Dependable. It sold for $1,050, weighed 3,490 lbs. and was known as the 4-door Touring Sedan. The factory built 28,203 of this model, making it the most popular 8-cylinder Olds for the year. For overseas delivery 288 were built in both right and left-hand drive. This model is equipped with double white sidewall tires, wheel trim rings, and owner monograms placed on the hood side panels.

1937

Oldsmobile came into 1937 with two brand nev offerings. Both cars were completely revamped from 1936 offering larger bodies, more powerful engines, I-bear X-member frames, and the first of an automatic trans mission. This, however, was only available on the Eight

Appearancewise, the Six and Eight for the first time didn't resemble each other at all. The Six had horizont grille louvers, done in chrome, while the Eight used square mesh grille design of cadmium. Both carried th taillamps mounted high at the body belt molding, wit the license mounted on the trunk with a chrome plate illuminated lamp above it. Head and taillights on the Si were of a rounded type and the Eights had their lights c a square design tapering in a modernistic style for that er

The Six used a 117-inch wheelbase with an increas from 90 to 95 HP at 3400 RPM. Tire size was 6:50 x 1 inches. The fuel supply in both series came from a 18-gallon tank. Seven models were available for the Si from $825 for the 2-passenger Coupe to $995 for 4-passenger Rumble Seat Convertible.

The Eight had a 124-inch chassis developing 110 HP 3600 RPM, which was ten more horses than offered i 1936. The tire size was 7:00 x 16 inches. The Eigh offered seven models, too, from $935 for the 2-passeng Coupe to $1,105 for the Convertible Coupe with rumb seat.

Oldsmobile placed in the Seventh spot this year b selling 212,767 cars for the calendar year.

Oldsmobile for 1937 turned out only 95 Convertible Coupes in the 8-cylinder line with sidemounts. A total of three in both right and left-hand drive were for export. This model weighed 3,530 lbs. and was the most expensive Olds for the year, selling at $1,105.

Oldsmobile's lowest priced sedan for the year was this 1938 6-cylinder flat trunk Sedan. It sold for $920 and weighed 3,285 lbs. The factory only built 1,458 of this style plus 19 for export.

Far more popular with the public than the flat trunk sedan was this 6-cylinder Touring Sedan which sold for $945 and weighed 3,290 lbs. A total of 27,257 were built plus 3,657 which were for export.

938

Again in 1938, Oldsmobile offered two distinct lines of .rs not resembling each other at all. The Six was offered ith a different type of grille with wide openings between ırs. It came on a 117-inch wheelbase. The Eight used a 24-inch wheelbase. with a squared angle type of grille ith fine lined chrome bars.

Safety was one of the features Olds used in their adver- ing for the year. Since the car mechanically was similar the 1937s they needed a way to bring the public to the ealerships. Safety was the method they chose. The instru- ent panel had all gauges conveniently placed in front of e driver where safety was the byword. The interiors nphasized safety with deeply piled cushions where sharp lges weren't confronting the passengers. Lastly was the tomatic Safety Transmission, as it was called then, hich cost $40 extra. It was available on the Six and the ght.

Mechanically, the Six came with a 95 HP engine at 400 RPM, while the Eight registered 110 HP at 3600 PM. The fuel supply was an 18-gallon tank for both ries. The Six used 6:50 x 16-inch tires and the Eight rode 1 7:00 x 16s. Each series had seven models ranging in ice from an $825 2-passenger 6-cylinder Coupe to 1,105 for the 8-cylinder Convertible Coupe.

Oldsmobile sold 93,705 cars in this depression dip year, hich put them in Seventh place for sales.

The most expensive Oldsmobile Six for 1938 was the Convertible Coupe with rumble seat. It sold for $995 and weighed 3,360 lbs. The factory built 1,001 for home use and 183 for export sales as both right and left-hand drive models. Offered in both the six and eight-cylinder cars this year was Oldsmobile's new automatic safety transmission.

Oldsmobile offered this 1938 8-cylinder 4-door Touring Sedan for $1,050 in base form. It weighed 3,490 lbs. The model year production saw 13,950 assembled plus 374 right and left-hand drive models go to other lands.

Oldsmobile's lowest priced car for the year was this "60" Series Business Coupe which sold for $777. It weighed 2,870 lbs. and came only with a 6-cylinder engine developing 90 HP. Oldsmobile produced 5,539 for state use and 36 for export.

The Oldsmobile "60" 4-door Sedan was a new offering for 1939. It shared the Chevrolet and Pontiac Quality Six Chassis. The car weighed 3,000 lbs. and sold for $889. A total of 14,554 were built for this country's usage and an additional 1,404 went for export.

The middle line Oldsmobile for 1939 was the "70" Series. This Coupe came on a 120-inch wheelbase and was available as a Business Coupe for $840 and as a Club Coupe for $891. As a Business Coupe 5,188 were built and as a Club Coupe 4,653 were sold. Between the two models a total of 165 in left and right-hand drive went for overseas duty.

The most popular version of the 1939 Oldsmobile 8-cylinder Touring Sedan was this example. It sold for $1,043 and weighed 3,340 lbs. A total of 12,242 regular Touring Sedans were built. In addition to this model a 4-door Touring "Sun" Sedan like Buick, La Salle, and Cadillac was available. A total of 84 were produced and 770 DeLuxe Touring Sedans were built for various dealer displays. These were Sedans with virtually every Oldsmobile factory accessory on them for the 1939 model run.

1939

For the 1939 model run Oldsmobile introduced thr separate lines referred to as Series 60, 70 and 80. The c ranged in price from $777 for the 60 Series Busin Coupe to $1,119 for the Olds 80 in Convertible Cou form.

From the front view all three lines resembled ea other, but the Olds 60 shared the Chevrolet and Ponti Quality Six body. The Olds 70 and 80 used the Ponti DeLuxe and Buick Special body. All 60 and 70 cars used 6-cylinder engine developing 90 HP at 3200 RPM for t 60 and 95 HP for the 70 at 3300 RPM. The Series came only with the 8-cylinder engine developing 110 H at 3500 RPM.

Oldsmobile's big claim for 1939 was the continu refinement of the Safety Transmission, which by 19 had many improvements over the past two years. Th transmission was available in the 70 and 80 Series cars on

As these new 70 and 80 models were built low runningboards were not needed unless the owner st preferred them. All 70 and 80 cars carried rubber sto deflectors on the forward bottom section of the re fenders for protection from rocks defacing the fende Actually the only outward differences on the 70 and cars were the Roman numeral designation VIII on t grille for 80 cars and a bumper plate in the center for t 8-cylinder models. The wheelbase for the 60 models wa 115-inch chassis while the other two series used the 12 inch wheelbase. The 6:00 x 16-inch tires were used on and 70 models while the 80s came with 6:50 x 16s. models used 17-gallon fuel tanks.

Oldsmobile offered 14 different models for the ye The sales position remained Seventh, as in 1938. Th sold 158,560 cars for the calendar year.

For 1939, Oldsmobile offered this 120-inch chassis in both the Series "70" and Series "80". This happens to be the "70" Series Convertible Coupe, evidenced by the lack of the VIII emblem on the grille and the special bumper center plate. It sold for $1,045 and weighed 3,230 lbs. The factory built 1,509 on the "70" Series chassis for home use and 205 for export sales.

The Series "60" 1940 Oldsmobile 2-door Touring Sedan sold for $853 and weighed 3,065 lbs. It was only available as a 6-cylinder model on a 116-inch wheelbase. The 1940 production figures for this model amounted to 27,220 which made it the most popular model in the "60" Series.

Even though prices did increase over 1939 models, the buyer got a nice looking unit with the 1940 Oldsmobile line. Shown here is the lowest priced model, the Business Coupe for 2 passengers, selling for $807, weighing 3,030 pounds and having a production run of 2,752 cars. Oldsmobile did not have a general export division beginning with the 1940 line.

40

The Oldsmobile for 1940 offered three entirely new ıes known by the same first two series as in 1939. That ıs Series 60 and 70. Both lines had entirely new bodies. ıe Series 90 was a brand new offering in the G.M. style a "Torpedo Body" which was shared with the Pontiac ›rpedo Eight, Buick Super and Roadmaster, La Salle : and Cadillac Series 62. Oldsmobile offered this body ell in four models.

Mechanically, Oldsmobile put the improved transmission at had been offered since 1937 on the market now as ydra-Matic Drive. This new four-speed transmission was ailable for all models for $57 extra. This new marvel to e industry taught many people how to drive and was a eat aid to anyone who might have a difficulty in shifting.

The Oldsmobile Six in 60 and 70 Series developed 95 ? at 3400 RPM. The Series 90 had a 110 HP engine at 00 RPM. A 17-gallon fuel tank was used in all models. ıe tire size was 6:00 x 16 for Series 60, 6:50 x 16 for ries 70, and 7:00 x 15 for the Series 90 car. The wheel-ses were 116 inches for the 60 models and 120 inches r the 70 models, while the Series 90 had a 124-inch ıeelbase.

Oldsmobile offered 15 body styles ranging in price from 07 for a Series 60 2-passenger Business Coupe to ,570 for the Series 90 Convertible Phaeton.

Oldsmobile again ranked in Seventh position for calendar ar sales by selling 215,028 cars.

Something new for Oldsmobile was added in the middle of the year. It was this Station Wagon on the Series "60" chassis. It used a Hercules body and sold for $1,042, making it the most expensive model in the Series "60" line. This wagon weighed 3,255 lbs. and seated eight passengers. A total of only 633 were built.

The middle group of Oldsmobile for 1940 was the Series "70." Among the models available was this 4-door Touring Sedan on a 120-inch wheelbase. It weighed 3,220 lbs. and sold for $963. Being the most popular model in this series, a total of 41,467 units were produced.

Being very proud of their accomplishments are the factory workers and top brass at Oldsmobile as they produce the one millionth car since November of 1933. The model happened to be a 1940 Series "90" Custom Cruiser 4-door Touring Sedan that sold for $1,131. This model weighed 3,555 lbs. A total of 33,075 were built making it the most popular model in the "90" Series.

Offered for the 2nd year was the Series "60" 4-door Touring Sedan which had a price tag of $899. This example weighed 3,100 lbs. The factory produced 24,422 of this model.

Oldsmobile

Selling the fewest in the 1940 Oldsmobile "70" Series was the Convertible Coupe. A total of only 1,070 were built. They weighed 3,240 lbs. and sold for $1,045.

Building only 290 1940 Oldsmobile Series "90" 8-cylinder Convertible Coupes made this a rare model to start with. It weighed 3,590 lbs. and sold for $1,222. This Torpedo body style was new for the year, coming only on the "90" Series. The Convertible Coupe did not make its introduction until mid-season.

The rarest Oldsmobile of all was this 1940 Series "90" Convertible Sedan. It, like the Convertible Coupe, wasn't officially shown until mid-year. Only 50 of this body style were built, weighing 3,750 lbs. and selling for $1,570.

A popular car with businessmen was the 1941 Oldsmobile Club Coupe, available as a Series "66" or "68". As a Six, it sold for $893 and as an Eight, for $935. The 6-cylinder line sold 23,796 units and the 8's sold 2,684 cars. The same body style was available as a Business Coupe but only 6,433 Sixes were manufactured and as an Eight, only 188 were built.

A new body style was used on the 1941 Oldsmobile Special which was made available either with a 6 or 8-cylinder engine on the low priced series for the first time. As a six, it was referred to as a Series "66" weighing 3,230 pounds, selling for $945, and producing 25,889 units. As an eight, it was called Series "68", weighed 3,360 lbs., sold for $987, and had a production run of 3,831 cars. This sedan was a Hydra Matic model by the nameplate denoting it, directly beneath the hood.

941

In 1941, Oldsmobile offered three attractive lines on wo wheelbases. The 60 and 70 Series were completely estyled while the Custom 90 only received a facelifting. ll three series offered both a Six or an Eight. They were asily detactable by the Eight nameplate on the trunk, nus a 68, 78, or 98, or a 66, 76 or 96. The wheelbase on ne 60 Series cars was 119 inches, while 70 and 90 cars sed the 125-inch wheelbase.

A mid-year model in the 60 Series, available in March, 'as a 4-door Sedan with the hump trunk effect like the eries 90 cars. This model was referred to as the 4-Window own Sedan and sold for the same price as the regular -door Sedan, $945.

Mechanically, the 6-cylinder engine was increased to 00 HP at 3400 RPM by enlarging the bore from 3-7/16 ıches while the stroke stayed at 4 inches. The 8-cylinder ngine continued to develop 110 HP at 3600 RPM. The ıel supply was a 19-gallon tank for either 6 or 8-cylinder ars. The tire size on the 60 models was 6:00 x 16 inches; ne 70 models had 6:50 x 16-inch tires, and the Custom 0s used 7:00 x 16-inch tires.

The Hydra-Matic Drive continued without any changes xcept the linkage on the starter pedal moved the range ver back to neutral whenever the starter clutch was epressed. This was for safety purposes to prevent the ır from jumping away once the engine was started.

A total of 24 models were available in a choice of 6 or -cylinder engines. Only in two models was the choice not ven: The 6-cylinder Station Wagon and the 8-cylinder onvertible Phaeton. The cars were priced from $852 for ı Olds 66 3-passenger Coupe to $1,575 for the 98 6-assenger Convertible Sedan. Oldsmobile ranked 6th from ıe sale of 230,701 cars.

Not only did the "60" Series receive a new look but the "70" Series came with fastback styling and was referred to as Dynamic Cruiser. It was available also as either a Six or Eight. The "70" Series came either as a 2-door Sedanette or 4-door Sedan in both standard and deluxe versions. This 1941 Oldsmobile is a 6-cylinder Series "76" in standard form. A quick way to identify the difference is the lack of chrome trim shields both on front and rear fenders and the smaller hub caps. A total of 39,938 were built, weighing 3,325 lbs. and selling for $954. In deluxe style 6,947 were produced.

Only available as an 8-cylinder car was the 1941 Oldsmobile Convertible Phaeton. It was the most expensive model for the year selling at $1,575. The factory produced just 119 of these beauties.

In its second year for this body style, the 1941 Olds Custom Cruiser 4-door Sedan was available as a Six or an Eight. This car, being an Eight, was referred to as a "98". The price tag was $1,135 and it weighed 3,500 lbs. It was the most popular model in the top of the line. Oldsmobile produced 22,081 cars of this style. Fender skirts were also classed as an accessory for this model.

A 1941 Oldsmobile 8-cylinder Dynamic Cruiser, Model "78" in deluxe style, brought 7,534 sales. The car weighed 3,500 lbs. and sold for $1,045. Chrome trim shields and larger hub caps were standard equipment. Hydra Matic Drive, which this car has by the nameplate beneath the hood, white sidewall tires, and fender skirts were optional at extra cost.

Oldsmobile

1942

The new models for 1942 offered a new body on tl 98, a new streamlined fender contour going into tl front doors, and a radically changed front end in a models.

The series designations for 1942 were Special, either as Six or an Eight. The Dynamic Cruiser also was availab in either Six or Eight, and the Custom Cruiser w offered only as an Eight. Each series was also known a 4-door Sedan, 2-door Club Sedan, and a Convertib The hood of the Custom Cruisers extended almost to t windshield, eliminating the cowl ventilator. Instead it h two ducts on each side of the dash for fresh air. All models offered Hydra-Matic Drive as standard equipme

All 6-cylinder models came with a 238 cubic inch engi that developed 100 HP at 3400 RPM. The 8-cylinder ca had a 257 cubic inch engine that gave 110 HP at 36 RPM. The fuel supply in all models was a 19-gallon tan The tire size was 6:00 x 16 inches in the Special 66 Seri All 68, 76, and 78 models shared the 6:50 x 15-inch ti which were new for the year. The 98 continued to use t 7:00 x 15-inch tires. The Specials used a 119-inch whe base. Dynamic Cruiser models came on a 125-inch chass and the Custom Cruisers employed a 127-inch chass A total of 27 models were available from a $992 passenger 66 Special Coupe to the 98 Custom Crui Convertible Coupe for $1,561.

Oldsmobile placed 6th for the calendar year from t sale of 12,230 vehicles.

All 1942 Oldsmobiles in the "90" Series were 8-cylinder cars, consequently they were referred to as "98" models. This "98" 4-door Sedan was typical of many 1942 cars, showing all its "blackout" trim. Hydra Matic was available in all lines for 1942. The Series "98" offered a brand new body for its short lived life. A total of 4,672 "98" 4-door Sedans were built for 1942. This model weighed 3,705 lbs., and sold for $1,376 F.O.B. Lansing, Mich.

Certainly not the weather to have the top down, a rare 1942 Oldsmobile "98" Convertible Coupe sits in a bleak, slushy countryside. Note the use of both cloth and leather for the seats, which was the tendency then and directly after the war. This model sold for $1,561 with only 216 being built before the halt to automotive production took place.

The 1942 Oldsmobile Dynamic Cruiser was basically the same car as the 1941 model except for front end appearance. The model illustrated is the "76" Standard 4-door Sedan that weighed 3,465 lbs. and sold for $1,153. A total of 9,166 of this model were built before the lines had to close for the duration of the war.

Introduced as a mid-season model in 1941 and continuing into 1942 production was this Town Sedan, available only on the 119-inch wheelbase. It was available in either 6 or 8-cylinder version. As a Six it weighed 3,350 lbs. and sold for $1,089. The Eight weighed 3,455 lbs. and had a price tag of $1,130. Total production of both "66." and "68" Town Sedans numbered 3,888 units.

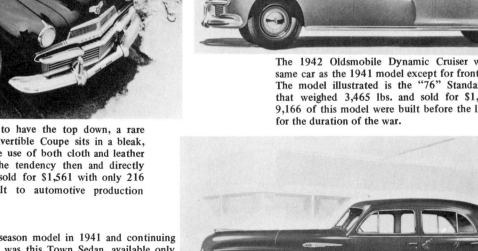

Packard

The Packard was a product of independent manufacture ith its factory headquarters being in Detroit. The car was roduced from 1899 through 1958.

For 1930, as for all Packards since June of 1923, these ars were referred to by series rather than by year. So, 930 models are known as Seventh Series cars. These ehicles were classed in three groups – the Standard Eight hich was produced from August 20th, 1929 to August 4th, 1930; the Speedster Eight was in production from eptember 29, 1929 to August 14, 1930 producing only 50 cars; and lastly, the Custom and DeLuxe Eights, roduced from August 20, 1929 to August 14, 1930.

The Standard Eight developed 90 HP at 3200 RPM, and ame in two models – the 726 and 733. The two models ed a 25-gallon fuel tank. The 726s came on a 127½-inch heelbase while the 733s used a 134½-inch chassis. All 26s used 6:00 x 20-inch tires and the 733s came with 50 x 20-inch tires. The Speedster Eight, known as odel 734, developed 145 HP at 3200 RPM. These cars so used a 25-gallon fuel tank. The wheelbase was 34 inches, and the tire size was 6:50 x 20 inches.

The Custom and DeLuxe Eights had a 106 HP engine at 200 RPM, a 28-gallon fuel supply, and 7:00 x 19-inch es. A 140½-inch wheelbase was used on the Customs hile the DeLuxe models employed a 145½-inch wheelse.

A total of 38 models were available in the Seventh Series. ices ranged from $2,375 for a 5-passenger Model 726 dan to $5,350 in Sedan Limousine style on a 745 eLuxe 145½-inch chassis. Packard placed in 15th position selling 28, 177 units at the end of their year.

The 1930 Packard DeLuxe 8 Phaeton had a 106 HP engine at 3200 RPM. This 7th Series model came on a 145½-inch wheelbase, making it the longest Packard for the year. It weighed 4,645 lbs. and sold for $4,585. A total of 8,102 cars in this series were built in 1930.

Being referred to as the Dual-Cowl Sport Phaeton for 1931, this handsome classic was delivered to only 97 customers. It weighed 4,535 lbs. and sold for $3,790.

This 1931 Packard was classed in the 840 Salon group of cars. It was model 1879, better known as a Victoria Convertible, weighing 4,418 lbs. It sold for $5,175.

Packard's 1931 Series 840 Phaeton was referred to as Model 471. It came on a 140½-inch wheelbase, weighed 4,439 lbs. and sold for $3,490. It was in production from Aug. 14, 1930 to June 23, 1931. A total of 114 of these Phaetons were built.

Packard

Known as the 1931 Packard Convertible Sedan with body by Dietrich. This car technically used the body number 1881. The weight was 4,674 lbs. and its price tag was $5,275. The sidemounted spares, luggage rack and six mounted wire wheels brought an additional $208 to the price. Practically all came equipped like this.

1931

The 1931 Packards technically are referred to as Eight Series cars. They came in four separate series known a 826 which came only as a 5-passenger Sedan. Next in lin was Series 833, 840 and 845.

Production this year started Aguust 14, 1930 and ende June 23rd, 1931 for all models.

The 826 and 833 shared the same engine of 320 cubi inches. The horsepower reached a maximum of 100 a 3200 RPM. These models, as well as the other serie employed a 25-gallon fuel tank. The tire size for 826s an 833s was 6:50 x 19; The 826 Series used a 127½-inc wheelbase while 833s had a 134½-inch chassis.

Packard 840s used the 384.8 cubic inch displaceme engine developing 120 HP at 3200 RPM. These cars use 7:00 x 19-inch tires and had a 140½-inch wheelbas

The 835 Series, being Packard's Senior line, had th same engine as the 840 but came on a five-inch long wheelbase of 145½ inches.

Packard production of Eighth Series cars ended early i the year because of their unveiling the new Ninth Seri 1932 cars in June of 1931.

The company sold 13,123 units for Packard's model ru of ten months. They placed 18th in sales for the yea

An 8th Series 1931 Packard, Model 845 using the 145½-inch wheelbase. This being the largest series, it weighed 5,010 pounds and sold for $4,150. Its model designation was 474.

Packard's 1931 Standard Eight was the lowest priced model for the year. It came on a 127½-inch wheelbase, weighing 4,479 lbs. and selling for $2,385. This 926 was known as Model 463 and was only available as a 4-door Sedan.

A 1932 Packard Ninth Series, Model 904, was available as the Individual Custom Stationary Coupe by Dietrich. The white sidewall tires and wire wheels were classed as accessory equipment. It's interesting to note that this same body also was popular on Lincoln Series K chassis.

This 1932 Packard 5-passenger Sedan was the newly re-introduced Twin Six on a 142½-inch wheelbase. It was classed in the 905 Models that were displayed on June 17, 1931, and continued until June 1, 1932. It weighed 5,635 lbs. and sold for $3,745 during its first months of production, but oddly enough, increased rather than decreased its price on Jan. 9, 1932 to $4,245.

Packard

1932

As it had typically done before, Packard didn't date the cars as 1932, or any other year for that matter. A true Packard devotee never refers to the car by year; it is always by series. So was the case for 1932 – these cars and are known today as Ninth Series cars no matter whether it's a Light Eight Coupe for $1,795 or a Model 906 Landaulet Town Car at $7,950 per copy.

The Ninth Series cars differed from the Eighth Series in that they had synchro-mesh. The Standard and DeLuxe Eight made their 1932 debut on June 17, 1931. Other models were exhibited later in the year.

These early Ninth Series cars were bigger and more powerful than their predecessors. They had longer wheelbases and an entirely new frame. The cars which had used the 4-speed gearbox now relied on a 3-speed unit, but a 4-speed device could be arranged.

Big news of the Ninth Series was the reintroduction of the V-12 Twin Six, which caused much excitement and enthusiasm among those who were still well-to-do. On the New York Stock Exchange, Packard took a spurt in a direction it hadn't seen for months. When first introduced, this car could only be ordered with a semi-custom body at a price of $6,600 and up F.O.B. Detroit. In January, however, Packard began to build its own bodies. A Ninth Series Twin Six can always be identified by its "Twin Six" inscription on the hub cap, and non-skirted fenders.

Packard followers had a choice of 67 models for the year. The Light and Standard Eight had 110 HP engines at 3200 RPM. The DeLuxe Eight had 135 HP at the same RPM. The Twin Six had a 160 HP engine also at 3200 RPM.

The sales picture saw 16,613 Packards delivered to owners from June 1931 till the Tenth Series Packard was unveiled.

Packard received a 16th sales position for the year. For the 1932 calendar year Packard sold 8,018 units.

A Ninth Series Packard for 1932 in Town Car styling was this body style 4002 in the Model 906 Custom Cars. The wheelbase was 147 inches, its weight was 5,490 lbs., and it sold for $7,550. Only the Landaulet Town-Car was more expensive than this model. Note the wooden wheels even for this model were considered standard equipment. Most all chose the optional at extra cost wire wheels which gave the car a far smarter appearance.

A 1932 Packard Light Eight Convertible Coupe in the Ninth Series. This vehicle was used in the Banacek T.V. shows. It was classed as a 559 in the 900 Models. It weighed 3,930 lbs. and sold for $1,795. It was produced from Jan. 9, 1932 to Jan. 5, 1933.

A Model 906 Packard 7-passenger Sedan for 1932 with sidemount equipment and white sidewall tires weighed 5,765 lbs. It sold for $3,995 until prices increased during the model run to $4,495.

This was the 1932 Packard Ninth Series Individual Custom Convertible Sedan with body by Dietrich. It was technically a 2070 in the Model 904's. Its weight was 5,100 lbs. and it sold for $6,250. The wheelbase measured 147½ inches.

Packard

1933

The new features for 1933 was more power, a new ventilating system, and power brakes. Engines were actually the same as before but an increase in power was shown by the use of dual carburetors.

The Eight gave 120 HP at 3200 RPM rather than 110 as in 1932. The Super 8 developed 145 HP and the Twin Six produced 160 HP. Both had the same RPM as the Packard Eight.

Packard's ventilating system was all their own development. The front door window glass was pivoted top and bottom at the front instead of sliding up and down. The rear section of this window glass was similarly pivoted at the rear. The front part was swung out by a knob while the rear part was moved by hand. Rear quarter windows had ventilators like used on the front windows.

Packard's braking system was the Bendix vacuum operated device, with four adjustments on the dash to provide from a light pedal to heavy pressure.

The Packard Eight used a 20-gallon fuel tank. Super 8s came with a 25-gallon supply, while the Twelves used a 32-gallon fuel tank. Packard 8 and Super 8s used 7:00 x 17 inch tires and the Twelves came with 7:50 x 17s.

A total of 42 body styles were available among the three series. These cars, being considered Tenth Series, went into production in January of 1933, completing the model run in August of 1933. Among the three series, 4,800 cars were produced on wheelbases ranging from a 127½-inch Eight Sedan at $2,150 up to a 147-inch wheelbase $7,000 All Weather Le Baron Town Car. Packard placed well earning 14th position for 1933 sales. A total of 9,670 cars were sold during the year.

This beautifully equipped 1932 Packard Ninth Series Twin Six Phaeton was the proud possession of movie actress Jean Harlow. It was body style 571 in the Model 905. This car weighed 5,275 lbs. and sold for $4,290. Note the factory spotlight, windwings, six wire wheels, sidemount covers, grille stoneguard, deluxe flying lady, fender mounted sidemirror, and Packard inscribed license frames, all considered extra-cost equipment.

This 1933 Packard Phaeton was 8-cylinder Model 1002, body style 611. It weighed 4,270 lbs. and sold for $2,370. The horsepower was increased to 120 at 3200 RPM for the year. A total of 2,980 Tenth Series Packard Eights were produced from Jan. 5, 1933 to the end of 1933 production on Aug. 21, 1933.

The Dietrich Convertible Victoria for 1933 seated 4 passengers and sold for $6,070, which was $1,580 more than the regular 12-cylinder Convertible Victoria. Its weight was 5,175 lbs. These special bodied Packards were chiefly available from Dietrich and Le Baron. Note the skirted fenders on the 1933 models.

Coming on a wheelbase of 142 inches was the 1933 Packard Super Eight Club Sedan for 5 passengers. This car had body style number 656, Model 1004. It weighed 4,795 lbs. and sold for $2,975.

The Tenth Series 1933 Packard Dual-Cowl Phaeton had a Dietrich body. This was Model 1006 and body style 3069. It weighed 5,160 lbs. and sold for $5,875. The number of Packard Twelves built in 1933 was 520.

Packard

1934

For 1934, Packard hosted its Eleventh Series, which ıctually began production August 21, 1933. These cars were almost identical to the 1933 or Tenth Series cars. The differences were shown in mechanical devices ;uch as an oil pressure regulator incorporated to show oil pressure, which could be adjusted from outside the engine; a full-flow oil filter, and an oil temperature regulator permitting use of the same oil thickness the full year around and regulating the temperature of the oil to suit the current driving conditions. The radio panel was in the center of the dash. Another was a heavy duty air-cooled generator to aid the heavy electrical load on many of these cars.

Both front and rear fenders were more skirted than ast year. Front fenders were extended down above the front bumper. Rear fenders followed the wheel lines closely. The running board mats came with chromium strips for the Eleventh Series models.

Actually, three series were available: the Packard 8, Super 8, and 12. The Eight gave 120 HP at 3200 RPM; Super 8 gave 145 HP, and the 12 had 160 HP. Each of the ast two also turned a maximum of 3200 RPM. The Eight and Super 8 both used 7:00 x 17-inch tires while the 12s ame with 7:50 x 17s. Wheelbases for the Eight were 29 and 136 inches. The Super 8 and 12 used 135, 142, and 147-inch wheelbases. The fuel supply for Eight and uper 8s was a 25-gallon supply. The 12s had a 32-gallon apacity. All models used mechanical brakes.

Production for 1934 lasted just one year, from August 21, 1933 to August 30, 1934. Production of 6,071 automobiles provided the 17th position for sales this year.

Thirty-eight models were available. Prices ranged from $2,350 for a 5-passenger Sedan on the 8-cylinder chassis to $4,750 for a 12-cylinder Convertible Sedan.

This Packard Eleventh Series Twelve with body by Le Baron was referred to as Model 1106, Speedster Runabout. It had body style number 275. This 2-passenger car had a shipping weight of 5,400 lbs. and sold for $7,746. Le Baron constructed a very similar car for Walter P. Chrysler, using a Chrysler chassis, of course.

Packard's lowest priced 4-door Sedan for 1933 was this Tenth Series Model 1001 body style 603. It weighed 4,335 pounds and sold for $2,150 in base form. This model sports the sidemount equipment and sidemount mirrors as optional equipment at extra cost.

The 1934 Packard Twelve Sport Phaeton by Le Baron as Model 1107, body style 741. It weighed 5,400 lbs. and the delivered price was $7,613 with standard equipment. Equipped with wheel covers, fender skirts and white sidewall tires, the model sold for $7,771.

This handsome 1934 Packard Boattail Speedster had a Le Baron body. It weighed 5,370 lbs. Some historians claim it to be a one-off car. Price is not available. Note that non-skirted fenders were used on this model.

Packard

This 1934 Packard Twelve Town Car with body by Bohman-Schwartz of Pasadena, Calif. was built especially for the late Jeanette MacDonald. It is definitely a one-off custom of undisclosed price.

The Eleventh Series Packard Twelve, Model 1108, body style 734 was available only as a 7-passenger Sedan. It sold for $4,603 with standard equipment and in the deluxe version, like this model, brought $4,762. The wheelbase was 147 inches and its weight was 5,700 lbs. A total of 960 Packard Twelves were produced from Aug. 21, 1933 to Aug. 30, 1934.

Something new was stirring at Packard for the 1935 cars. This was it, the Packard 120A, which received its name from its 120-inch wheelbase. The body number of the 4-door Touring Sedan was 902. It weighed 3,550 lbs. and sold for $1,095. This was truly the first year since Packard introduced their cars as Series that they technically could be referred to as a year model as well as a Series.

1935

The company came forth with a new smaller 8-cylinde car which was to have been Packard's answer to th depression. This car was the Series 120. A decision to bring this car out was made in 1933. It came on a 120 inch wheelbase, where it received its name, and develope 110 HP at 3850 RPM. An aluminum head of 6.5: compression ratio was standard. The optional ratio, wit an aluminum head was 7:1 compression. Tire size wa 6:50 x 16. Bendix hydraulic brakes were used. Fuel suppl was a 20-gallon tank.

Seven models were available, ranging in price from $98 for a Business Coupe to $1,095 for the Touring Sedan Production of these cars began the first week of Januar 1935, and saw 30,759 cars sold during the model yea

For the Packard 8, Super 8, and 12, the followin applies: Packard 8 had a 130 HP engine, used Bendi mechanical brakes, rode on 7:00 x 16-inch tires, had a fue tank of 25 gallons, and came on 127, 134, and 139-inc wheelbases depending on model, which amounted to 1 body styles being priced from a $2,385 5-passenger Seda to $3,255 for a 5-passenger Formal Sedan.

The Super 8 used a 150 HP engine, Bendix mechanica brakes, the same fuel supply and tire size as the Packard 8 and came in a dozen body styles ranging from $2,88 for a 4-passenger Coupe to $3,910 for the 5-passenge Convertible Sedan. This series used 132, 139, and 14 inch wheelbases.

The Packard 12 was offered with a 175 HP engine, sam braking system as the Eights, but used a 30-gallon tan These cars had 7:50 x 17-inch tires. Twelve models we available in this series, ranging from $3,820 for a passenger Coupe to $6,435 for the All Weather passenger Town Car by Le Baron.

All Eights, Super Eights, and Twelves began productio on August 30, 1934 ending it on May 21, 1935 making production run of 6,894 cars being sold for the model ru With the help of the 120, Packard showed 9th positio for the model year. The total calendar year sales f Packard amounted to 52,256 cars mainly due to the 12 sales.

A 1935 Packard Twelve special-bodied Le Baron Sport Convertible. It isn't certain the exact number of this style produced. The Twelfth Series Twelve had a total production run of only 721 models. Note the chrome chevrons placed beneath the doors and the auxiliary light to help passengers. Disc wheel covers were beginning to come into their own by this time.

Packard

Enjoying one of the first 1935 Packard 120 Convertible Coupes to be delivered is the late Lawrence Tibbet, who was associated with the Metropolitan Opera Co. The body style number was 899 for this series. It weighed 3,385 lbs. and sold for $1,070.

Packard offered this 1935 Super Eight Victoria from Aug. 30, 1934 to May 21, 1935. The company produced 1,392 Super Eights during 1935. This model weighed 5,000 lbs. and sold for $3,760. It was classed among the 1203 Models under body style 847, which had a 132-inch wheelbase. Disc wheels were optional equipment for the Super Eight.

The longest wheelbase of the 1935 Packards is displayed here in this 1935 Twelfth Series Model 1207 Sedan. It has a 144-inch wheelbase chassis, with a 12-cylinder engine that developed 175 HP. This car came in the 1208 Model, and was body style 834. It weighed 5,800 lbs. and sold for $4,285. A distinguishing mark on the Twelves, from the other models, are the double row of hood louvers.

This 1935 Packard Twelve All-Weather Town Cabriolet with body by Le Baron sold for $6,290 and weighed 5,930 lbs. It was the Model 1207, with body style 195. It used a 139-inch wheelbase and was also available on a 144-inch chassis, known as Model 1208. That form sold for $6,435. This particular model was built for a W.K. Jewett of Pasadena, Cal.

Being introduced later than the Senor Models for 1936, the Packard 120 made its debut on Sept. 23, 1935. For this model run all cars were classed as Fourteenth Series so that no one who might be superstitious would be driving a "Thirteenth Series Bad Luck Car." The 120 models accounted for 55,042 units with this Touring Sedan being the most popular. It weighed 3,560 lbs. and sold for $1,115. This type of steel pressed wheel wasn't commonly used, but was available at no extra charge if the customer preferred it.

Posing nicely on the door ledge of her 1936 Packard 120 Convertible Coupe is the movie starlet Dixie Dunbar of the 1936 era. This model used the body style number 899. It weighed 3,525 lbs. and sold for $1,110. Note the factory mounted spotlight and the specially equipped Vogue Tyres.

Pasadena, Cal., was always a Packard town. The author lived there as a boy and remembers seeing more of the classic Packards than any other marque of that class. Shown here is the Fourteenth Series Twelve Model 1408 Convertible Sedan on its 144-inch wheelbase parked in front of the Annandale Country Club which is a suburb of Pasadena. The body style number was 973 on this beauty. It weighed 5,945 lbs. and sold for $5,050.

1936

Since Packard referred to their cars by Series rath than year, 1936 Packards were referred to as Fourteen Series. Thirteenth Series Packards don't exist becau Packard management felt No. 13 shouldn't appear their advertising program as it might be unlucky. Packa was just now beginning to see the return from the hu investment of tooling for the 120. The car, being a gre success, was just what was needed at this time.

The 1936 Packards were not all introduced at the sar time as was the case in previous years. The Eight, Sup Eight, and Twelve all were announced on August 10. T 120 Series made its showing September 23, 1935.

All 120 models now came with 120 HP engin (3800 RPM), used a 20-gallon fuel tank, had a 120-in wheelbase, and used 7:00 x 16-inch tires. Only in th model were hydraulic brakes being used. The number body styles available were eight beginning at $990 for 2-passenger Business Coupe, and ranging upward to $1,3 for the Convertible Sedan.

Packard Eight came with a 130 HP engine at 3200 RP used a 25-gallon fuel tank, and measured 127, 134 a 139 inches. It used 7:00 x 17-inch tires and mechanic brakes. The number of body styles available were seve teen, ranging from a $2,385 127-inch wheelbased sedan $5,385 for the All Weather Le Baron Town Car.

Packard Super Eight came with a 150 HP engine 3200 RPM. It also used a 25-gallon gasoline supply. T wheelbases for this group of cars were 132, 139, and 1 inches. These models also used 7:00 x 17-inch tires a mechanical brakes also were employed. The same body styles were used. Prices began at $2,990 for a 13 inch Sedan and ended with a $5,815 All Weather Le Bar Town Car of 144 inches.

Packard sales resulted in 10th position, with 80,699 ca being purchased during the model run.

Parked in front of the Sleepy Hollow Country Club in New York's Westchester County is this 1936 Packard Twelve Convertible Victoria Model 1407, body style 927. It weighed 5,585 lbs. and sold for $4,890. A total of 682 1936 Packard Twelves were produced.

Always a popular body style was the Packard Club Sedan. This Fourteenth Series 12-cylinder 5-passenger version was no exception. It weighed 5,640 lbs. and sold for $4,060. The wheelbase measured 139 inches, its body style number was 936 and was classed as a 1407 Model. It is shown parked in front of the exclusive Indian Hill Club of Winnetka, Ill.

The 1936 Packard Twelves were produced from Aug. 10, 1935 to Sept. 3, 1936. This Model 1408 Le Baron Town Car was classed as body style 295 which weighed 5,590 lbs. and was offered for sale at $6,435.

37

ackard's "claim to fame" in 1937 was shown at the tional Automobile Show during the week of October 1936, when the new Packard Six made its debut. kard sold 65,400 of these 115-inch wheelbase cars and de quite a name for itself.

he horsepower for the Six was 100 at 3600 RPM. They d 6:50 x 16-inch tires and had a fuel supply of 17 lons. These models as well as all other Packards now re using hydraulic brakes.

he 120 Series, the companion to the Six, sold 50,100 s. These 8-cylinder cars developed 120 HP at 3800 M. The wheelbase was still 120 inches, using 7:00 x 16-h tires. The fuel supply consisted of a 20-gallon tank.

he third car in Packard's line for 1937 was the Super ht coming on three wheelbases: 127, 134 and 139 hes. It used a 135 HP engine at 3200 RPM. Fuel supply s from a 25-gallon tank. This series rode on 7:50 x 16-h tires.

he Packard Twelve, classed in the Senior Series, eloped 175 HP at 3200 RPM. These cars had two eelbases of 132 and 144 inches, and rode on 8:25 x 16-h tires. The fuel supply was 40 gallons. There were re 1937 Packard 12s sold than in any other year of its duction.

ll Packards for the year were called Fifteenth Series s. A total of fifty models were available among the four ies which ranged between $795 for a 2-passenger upe in 6-cylinder form to $5,900 for a Le Baron All ather Town Car.

roduction for these cars commenced September 3, 1936 l ended September 29, 1937, except for the Twelve ich stopped August 9, 1937. Packard placed ninth in es chiefly due to the 6 and 120s which accounted for % of the sales. The run gave Packard 109,518 cars sold ring the calendar year.

Being in its third year of production is this 1937 Packard 120 Touring Coupe, body style 1094. It weighed 3,435 lbs. In standard form it sold for $1,010 and the deluxe version brought a price of $1,200. This car closely resembled the Packard Six except the 120 model used a wheelbase of 120 inches and the Six came with a 115-inch wheelbase.

Packard's 1937 Model 120 Touring Sedan weighed 3,520 lbs. and sold for $1,060 in base form. A deluxe version was available for $1,250. In the 120 Series, total production for 1937 was 50,100 cars.

Arrangements were made with Dietrich for this Convertible Sedan to have the "Body by Dietrich" nameplate mounted on the lower right body section by the front right door. Actually, the body was built by Murray, even though the design was by Dietrich. This true Special Interest Car weighed 3,630 lbs. and sold for $1,355. It also was available for $1,550 with a more deluxe trim. This model sports the accessory Flying Lady hood ornament and a Packard approved grille guard. Sidemounts were optional at extra cost on the Convertible Sedans in 1937, but most every owner ordered them.

The 1937 Packard Twelve in 7-passenger Sedan style weighed 5,600 lbs. and was available at $3,885. It could be completely equipped like this model, with sidemounts, whitewalls, and the regular Packard deluxe equipment for $4,270.

Packard

This 1937 Packard Twelve Convertible Sedan came on a 144-inch wheelbase as the Model 1508 with body style 1073. It weighed 5,680 lbs. and sold for $4,650 in this fashion. A deluxe version was available for $5,150. Strangely, this car is devoid of any special equipment that generally would go with an open model.

In the 1937 Packard Twelve line, the total production was 1,300 automobiles. This Fifteenth Series Model 1507, body style 1036 Club Sedan was available for $4,045 completely equipped. It weighed 5,520 lbs. The Packard Twelves for 1937 were in production from Sept. 3, 1936 to Aug. 9, 1937.

This was a Sixteenth Series Packard Six Model 1600, Touring Sedan, body style 1182. This model demonstrates how easy it was to park a Packard in tight quarters. The sedan weighed 3,525 lbs. and sold for $1,070.

1938

For this year the Packards were known as the Sixteen Series. The company claimed it was one of the largest a richest of the automobile companies in America. This w mainly due to the sales from the Six and the 127-in wheelbase Eight.

Packard introduced the new line of 6s and 8s September 30, 1937. These cars showed a new styling the lower priced line, and were called the Packard S and Packard Eight.

For the Senior Series, consisting of the Super Eight a Twelve, the general body construction was similar 1937. However, they came with a Vee-shaped windshie and a center divider, and a more modern instrume board with dials being placed across the panel in a we designed manner. An ivory deluxe steering wheel w employed in both series as standard equipment, as we built-in defrosters and a built-in four-position lighti system for Park, City, Drive and Drive Pass as new featu offered for the Senior line.

Horsepower was 100 at 3600 RPM for the Six, on a 12 inch wheelbase, using 6:50 x 16-inch tires. The Six had 18-gallon fuel tank. They offered five body styl

The Packard Eight used the same 120 HP engine fro 1937. The wheelbases for this model were 127, 139, a 148 inches. They came with 7:00 x 16-inch tires. The fu capacity was a 21- gallon tank. A total of eleven sty were available.

The Super Eight used a 130 HP engine at 3200 RP with a 24-gallon fuel supply. These models used 7:50 x 1 inch tires. Super Eights came in fifteen models with th different wheelbases: 127, 134 and 139 inches.

The Packard Twelve used the 175 HP engine at 32 RPM, with a fuel supply of 30 gallons. These models came with 8:25 x 16-inch tires and used the 134 and 1 inch wheelbases.

Some models were still being offered as special bodi cars by Briggs with a Le Baron body plate. Brunn a Rollson also were catalogued for the Senior cars.

Prices ranged from $1,075 for the 2-passenger Packa Six Coupe to $8,110 for a 139-inch 12-cylinder Weather Brunn Cabriolet. The Twelve began producti September 10, 1937, ending for the year September 1938.

Sales amounted to 50,260 units which placed them ninth sales position.

Packard's lowest priced car in the Sixteenth Series was the 1938 Packard Six Business Coupe, Model 1600, body style number 1188. It was in production from Sept. 20, 1937 to Sept. 20, 1938. A total of 30,050 Packard Sixes for 1938 were produced. This model weighed 3,450 lbs. and was priced at $975.

Packard

For this year only Packard did not refer to this example as a 120, but it was known as a Packard Eight. A total of 22,624 Packard Eights were built in 1938. This model came as either an eight passenger Sedan or a Limousine. The eight passenger Sedan weighed 4,195 lbs. and cost $2,110. The Limousine weighed 4,245 lbs. and brought a price of $1,955. Both used the 148-inch wheelbase and were classed as Model 1620's.

This 1938 Packard Twelve, Model 1607, body style 1127 Convertible Victoria is commonly referred to by Packard afficionados as being in the Sixteenth Series. This series was in production from Sept. 10, 1937 to Sept. 20, 1938. A total of 566 Packard Twelves were produced in 1938. This model weighed 5,345 lbs. and sold for $5,230. Note the antenna mounted under the running board.

Packard prices were generally reduced on the 1939 models. This Seventeenth Series Packard Six sold for $944 as a Club Coupe. It weighed 3,365 lbs. The car was in production from Sept. 20, 1938 to Aug. 8, 1939. A total of 24,350 six-cylinder automobiles were produced during this time.

Well equipped with 1938 Packard approved accessories is this 134-inch wheelbased Model 1607 5-passenger 12-cylinder Touring Sedan. Its body style was 1133. The car weighed 5,525 lbs. and sold for $4,155. This example includes sidemounted tire equipment, twin sidemount mirrors, driving lamps, grille guard, license frames, and full wheel decor as its additional equipment. Note the courtesy light at the base of the rear fender.

This 1939 Packard Six 2-door Touring Sedan weighed 3,390 lbs. and sold for $964. It was in the Model 1700, and its body style was 1284.

The 1939 Packard Super 8 did not have the classic lines of the previous Super 8's. They used the body of the Packard 120, on a 127 and 148-inch wheelbase. They were known as Model 1703 and 1705. This 4-door Touring Sedan carried body style 1272. It weighed 3,930 lbs. and sold for $1,732 which was quite a reduction from the previous Super 8's. A total of 3,962 Super 8's were produced.

Packard

An early experiment of great things to come was this 1939 Packard Darrin. The man responsible for its beauty is sitting behind the wheel – Howard "Dutch" Darrin.

A 1939 Packard 120, as it was again referred to, sold for $1,196 as the 5-passenger Touring Sedan. The 120 Series were known as Model 1701, which came on a 127-inch wheelbase. This example carried body style 1292. The "120" models that were built amounted to 17,647 units.

Packard referred to this 1940 110 2-door Sedan as the Family Sedan. Technically, it was an Eighteenth Series, Model 1800, with a body style of 1384. It weighed 3,190 lbs. and was available for $944 in standard form or $964 with deluxe features including air-foam seat cushions, cigarette lighter, twin sun visors, and arm rests on both front doors.

1939

The 1939 Packards were introduced to the public as th Seventeenth Series. Production began September 20, 193 and the model run lasted until August 8, 1939.

For the year, Packard models ranged from the 100 H Six at 3200 RPM to the Packard 12 developing 175 H at 3200 RPM. Between these came the 120 at a 360 RPM giving 120 HP and the Super 8 with 130 HP a 3200 RPM.

In the lineup, the Super 8 had a reduction in pric from $835 to $1,370. All Sixes and Eights were equippe to handle an overdrive unit called Econo-drive, and th gearshift was now mounted on the steering column. press-button radio with the Packard nameplate was avai able at optional extra cost.

All Packard Sixes came on a 122-inch wheelbase usin 6:50 x 16-inch tires. They had an 18-gallon fuel suppl

The Packard 120 as it was again referred to, used 127-inch wheelbase, or 148-inch chassis if it was th 7-passenger Sedan or Limousine. These models use 7:00 x 16-inch tires and had a 21-gallon fuel tan

All Super 8s came on the same wheelbase, used th same tire size and fuel supply as the 120. They appeare in six models whereas the 120 came in eight style

The Twelves used a 134 or 139-inch wheelbase and rod on 8:25 x 16-inch tires. They developed 175 HP at 320 RPM. The Packard 12 had a 30-gallon fuel supply

Thirty-four models were available in the 12s, with th Rollston and Brunn Companies still being Packard's chie outside body builders. They built these bodies on speci order mainly for the 12-cylinder trade.

Prices ranged between $888 for the 2-passenger Packar Six Coupe to $8,355 for the 12-cylinder All Weath Cabriolet by Brunn.

Packard sold 76,573 units during the calendar yea which put them in the 10th position for 1939 sale

This 1940 Packard 120 4-door Touring Sedan was classed as Model 1801, body style 1392. It weighed 3,450 lbs. and sold for $1,166. As displayed in this photo, the 120 Sedan sports an accessory grille guard and the factory approved Flying Lady often used on the 120 line.

940

The 1940 Packards were displayed as the Eighteenth eries. There were four chassis models available – the 110 hich replaced the name for the 1939 Packard Six, the 20, the 160, and the 180. The latter two both had a new ıgine of 160 HP at 3500 RPM. This engine succeeded the ackard Twelve of the previous year. The 110 had a 100 P engine at 3200 RPM. The 120 used a 120 HP engine at 600 RPM. The fuel supply for the 110 was a 17-gallon ınk and the remaining three used a 21-gallon supply. ire size for the 110 was 6;25 x 16 inches. The 120 used :50 x 16-inch tires and the 160 and 180 models used :00 x 16-inch tires on all 8-cylinder models. Air conitioning was also available.

The wheelbase for the 110 remained at 122 inches. The ıree eights used a 127-inch wheelbase while the 160 and 80 also came on 138 and 148-inch wheelbases. The latter heelbase was employed only on 7-passenger cars. In ldition to these various wheelbases, special order cars on ıe 120 and 160 chassis came with a 160-inch wheelbase ɔr ambulance and hearse bodies.

The Packard Darrin had been displayed as a sampler in 938 but really didn't make a full debut until the 1940 ıodels came out. It was available in Sport Sedan, onvertible Sedan, and a Two Door Convertible Victoria. he Darrin bodies were built in Connersville, Indiana ɔr 1940 only.

There were thirty models available priced between 867 for the 3-passenger 110 Business Coupe to $4,575 ɔr a 7-passenger All Weather Town Car with body by ollson.

Packard placed in 13th position from the 66,906 cars ɔld during the calendar year.

The Eighteenth Series 1940 Packard Super Eight 160 Convertible Coupe was technically called Model 1803, body style 1379. It weighed 3,795 lbs. and was available for $1,797. The 160 models were introduced Aug. 8, 1939 and were produced through July 1, 1940, with 5,662 units being built.

The Convertible Sedan was offered on the 1940 Packard 120 Series. This model had a 127-inch wheelbase and an 8-cylinder engine that developed 130 HP. It weighed 3,640 lbs. and sold for $1,573. This model helped only slightly in the production run of the 120. It is truly a Special Interest Car today. Sidemount tires were available at extra cost. Total production for the 120 Series in 1940 was 28,158 units.

This unique looking station wagon was offered by Packard in 1940 on both the 110 and 120 chassis. This example happens to be the 110 model, with a body style of 1383. It weighed 3,380 lbs. and sold for $1,200. The wheelbase measured 122 inches. The 120 wagon sold for $1,407 and weighed 3,590 lbs.

A sporty appearing 1940 Packard was the Super Eight 160 Club Coupe, body style 1375, in the Model 1803. The 160 Series designation was given because the model developed 160 HP. This example weighed 3,735 lbs. and sold for $1,614. The sidemount equipment was optional at extra cost.

Packard

The top of the line 1940 Packard was the Super Eight 180. These cars were referred to as Models 1806, 1807, and 1808. This particular car was a 7-passenger Touring, Model 1808, with body style 1351. It weighed 4,510 lbs. and sold for $2,541. The wheelbase was 148 inches and the horsepower was 160, as on the 160 Models. Total production of the 180 was 1,900 cars for 1940.

Body style 700, Model 1806, was this Convertible Victoria by Darrin. It was hand-built in the Darrin factory in California for 1940 only. The weight was 4,121 lbs. and it sold for $4,570.

Offered in both the 110 and 120 Series was this Nineteenth Series 1941 Packard Station Wagon. The only real difference between the two models was the 8-cylinder engine in the 120 and wheelbase. The body was by the Hercules Body Co. The 110 weighed 3,460 lbs. and sold for $1,231. The 120 version weighed 3,720 lbs. and sold for $1,436 in standard style. A Deluxe model was available weighing 6 lbs. more and selling for $1,496.

Introduced to the public Sept. 19, 1940 and continuing through until Aug. 25, 1941 was the Packard Super Eight 160. The model designations were 1903, 1904, and 1905. This one was body style 1470 in the 1905 Series. It weighed 4,570 lbs. and sold for $2,334 as a 7-passenger Touring Limousine. A total of 3,525 cars were produced in the 160 line for 1941.

This Nineteenth Series 1941 Packard 160 Convertible Sedan used the 127-inch chassis with an 8-cylinder engine that developed 160 HP. It came as Model 1903, body style 1477, weighing 4,140 lbs. and sold for $2,180 as a standard model. A deluxe version equipped like this model with sidemounts and fender skirts, was available weighing 4,160 lbs. It sold for $2,405.

Introduced in the middle of the season was this eye-catching Clipper, Model 1951, body style 1401. It weighed 3,725 lbs. and sold for $1,375. A total of 16,600 Clipper Sedans were built from April 1, 1941 to August 25, 1941.

941

For 1941, Packard was referred to as the Nineteenth ›ries and offered the 110, 120, 160, and 180. In the ›ring of the year they came out with the famous ipper Sedan.

Looking at the front of the car, all models resembled ›ch other. In all models but the Clipper the radiator side illes were larger and hoods were longer. The catwalks ›re flush with fender tops and the headlamps were ounted in front of the fenders, which were highly owned. Running boards were optional at no additional ›st.

A smooth automatic clutch called Electromatic was troduced this year. The air conditioner was in its second ar and was available in all 8-cylinder cars. It sold r $275.

Two-tone paint was offered in a variety of harmonizing lors which were separated by a continuous chrome belt olding that went around the rear of the car from the belt e at the rear of the hood.

Power windows were standard on all 180 cars but could ordered on all other models at additional cost.

The Packard 110 offered a 245.3 cubic inch engine that veloped 100 HP at 3600 RPM. It had a 17-gallon fuel ık. The wheelbase was 122 inches and the tire size ›asured 6:50 x 15 inches. The 120 models used an cylinder engine that developed 120 HP at 3600 RPM. is model had a 20-gallon fuel supply. The wheelbase ıs 127 inches and it used 7:00 x 15-inch tires. All 160 d 180 cars used the 282 cubic inch Eight that developed 0 HP at 3500 RPM. Their wheelbases were 127, 138, d 148 inches depending on the body style. The fuel pply was a 20-gallon tank. These cars used 7:00 x 16-ch tires.

The Packard Darrin for 1941 was built in the Special ckard body division in Detroit rather than Connersville, diana as its predecessor had been. The Clipper Sedan ıde its debut in early Spring of 1941 and became an mediate success. Mechanically, it was pretty much the ne car as the 120 models, except that it developed 5 HP rather than 120. It weighed 190 pounds more than 120 4-door sedan and cost $114 additional, selling : $1,375.

A total of 41 models were available, ranging in price ›m $907 for a 110 2-passenger Business Coupe to $5,550 the Le Baron Custom Super 8 180 Limousine for passengers. Packard ranked in 14th position from the e of 66,906 cars for its calendar year.

Offered as a semi-custom was the Nineteenth Series 180 Packard Sport Brougham, Model 1907, by Le Baron. Its body style number was 1452. This example weighed 4,450 lbs. and sold for $3,545. Air conditioning was available for $1,080 additional. Not many cars came equipped with it either.

Designated as the Nineteenth Series 180 Model 1906, body style 1429, this 1941 Packard Darrin Convertible Victoria was built in Connersville, Ind. on a low production basis. It weighed 4,040 lbs. and sold for $4,595. It was a part of the 930 Custom Super Eight 180 models that were produced.

The newly introduced Clipper of 1941 was brought out in the 6-cylinder line for 1942. This was the Twentieth Series, Model 2000 coming in both Special and Custom styles. This example was the Club Sedan weighing 3,415 lbs., selling as a Special for $1,215. The Custom had a price tag of $1,285. The 1942 Packards were introduced Aug. 25, 1941 and ceased production Feb. 7, 1942.

Virtually the same offering as the 1941 Clipper was this 1942 8-cylinder Model 2001 Touring Sedan. In 1942, this body was available in three different styles. In addition to 2001, were the 2011 and 2021 Models. The body style of this car is 1512, weighing 3,585 lbs. and selling for $1,305. The deluxe version brought $1,373. A total of 19,199 models in this 8-cylinder line were produced.

Packard

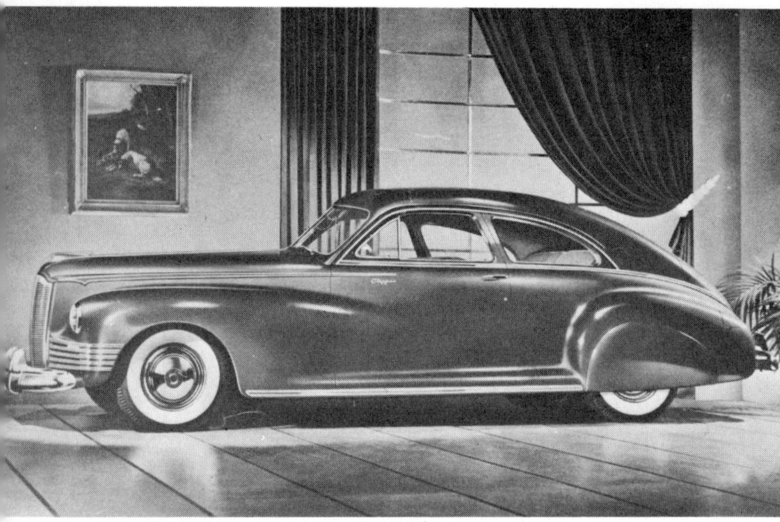

The Twentieth Series 1942 Packard Super Eight Custom 180 Clipper Club Sedan came on a 127-inch wheelbase. The car weighed 4,010 lbs. and sold for $2,244. All 1942 180 production ended Dec. 30, 1941. There was no "blackout" models among the 180 Series. A total of 672 were built in this series.

1942

With the late arrival of the 1941 Clipper, and with i immediate success, the factory decided to offer the models both as a 6-cylinder and in the three versions the 8-cylinder models. They were available in both 2-do fast back styling and 4-door Sedan.

In addition to the Clipper styles, also available were t regular 160 and 180 models of the 1941 convention style. Also available, but in limited production, were t 6-cylinder 110 models and 120 Series in a Convertib Coupe of the body style used in 1941. These were le over bodies from that year. They were built on t 160 chassis, however.

The engines remained basically the same as last ye except that the compression ratio was increased to 6:86 1. The use of aluminum pistons was available at the sta of the 1942 model run and were continued on the 1 and 180 models. When supplies became short, cast ir pistons had to be used in the 110 and 120 models. T Packard 110 used a 245 cubic inch engine with an increa in horsepower to 105 at 3600 RPM. The Clipper 120 us a 282 cubic inch engine that developed 125 HP 3600 RPM. The Super 8 and Custom Super 8 both shar the same engine of 356 cubic inches that developed 1 HP at 3600 RPM. The 110 models used a 17-gallon fu tank and a 20-gallon supply was employed in all 8-cylind cars. The 110 and 120 models both used 6:50 x 15-in tires and the 160 and 180 cars used the 7:00 x 15-in tires. The wheelbase measured 120 inches for the 110 a 120 models, 122 inches for the 110 and 120 Convertibl 127 inches for the Clipper 160 and 180 models, and 1 and 148 inches on the custom cars.

A total of 29 models were available for the year rangi in price from $1,180 for a Clipper 3-passenger 6-cylind Business Coupe to $5,795 for a Custom Super 8 1 Touring Limousine for 8 passengers. Packard's calend year sales for 1942 amounted to 6,085 cars which p them in 9th position.

Retaining its body lines of the previous year is this 1942 Super Eight 160 Convertible Coupe. It was referred to as Model 2023, body style 1579. This 127-inch wheelbase car weighed 3,905 lbs. and sold for $1,795. A total of 2,580 160 models were built for 1942.

The 1942 Packard Super Eight Custom 180s were classed as Models 2006, 2007, and 2008. This example happens to be Model 2007, body style 1532, better known as a Formal Sedan weighing 4,390 lbs. selling for $3,201 F.O.B. Detroit. About the only difference in its appearance are the horizontal chrome bars on each side of the grille where the 1941's had vertical bars.

The last of the Packard Darrins were to appear on the 1942 Custom Super Eight 108 Series. This was Model 2006, body style 1529. This example weighed 3,920 lbs. and for 1942 the price increased $188, selling for $4,783. Note that even a car like this didn't rate whitewall tires due to material shortages.

Peerless

The Peerless was a product of independent manufacture ›ming from the Peerless Motor Car Co. of Cleveland, hio. The company had been in business since 1900. The ıal year of production was 1932.

For 1930, Peerless offered three new and attractive head 8-cylinder cars along with the 6-cylinder Model .A.

The 6-cylinder car had a 62 HP engine with a maximum 3000 RPM. This series used a 15½-gallon fuel tank. ıe wheelbase measured 116 inches and rode on 5:25 x -inch tires.

Peerless Standard 8 used a 90 HP engine at 3200 RPM. ıey also used the same fuel supply as the 6-cylinder odels. A 118-inch wheelbase was used, and this series ıd 5:50 x 19-inch tires.

The Master and Custom 8s both had 120 HP engines 3200 RPM. These models used a 125-inch wheelbase r the Masters which came on 6:00 x 19-inch tires, and 8-inch wheelbase for the Custom 8s which had 6:50 x -inch tires. A fuel supply of 24 gallons was used. All odels had mechanical brakes.

A total of 14 models were available. The 8-cylinder cars .d Hayes built bodies designed by Alexis de Sakhnoffsky. ices ranged from $1,445 for a 4-passenger 6-cylinder ›adster to $3,145 for the Custom 8, 7-passenger mousine. Sales and production put Peerless in the 'th position for the year. They sold 3,642 cars.

Peerless offered this new model called the 61-A in 1930. It developed 62 HP at 3000 RPM. The wheelbase for this series was 115 inches. The car, depending on the model, sold from $50 to $200 less than its 1929 predecessor. This sedan sold for $1,485.

This was a rare production model of the 1931 Peerless Close Coupled Sedan with body design by Alexis de Sakhnoffsky. This model was in the Master Series which came on the 125-inch wheelbase and used the 120 HP engine. Prices were not available on this model.

1931

The 1932 Cars were offered in the following series: The Standard 8, Master 8, Custom 8 and the one-off Murphy bodied aluminum Sedan.

The Standard 8 had a 246.7 cubic inch engine developing 85 HP at 3200 RPM. The fuel supply consisted of a 15½-gallon tank. This series used 5:50 x 19-inch tires and had a 118-inch wheelbase.

The Master 8 shared the same engine as the Custom 8, which had a displacement of 322 cubic inches and a maximum horsepower rating of 120 at 3200 RPM. The fuel tank held 24 gallons. Tire size on the Master 8 was 6:00 x 19 inches. The Custom 8 carried 6:50 x 19 inches. The wheelbase was 125 inches for the Master 8 and 138 inches for the Custom 8. Mechanical brakes were used throughout.

Peerless had plans to produce a V-16 line of automobiles with aluminum bodies from Alcoa and built through the Walter M. Murphy Co. of Pasadena, Calif. However, only one V-16 Peerless is known to have been produced. It carried a 170 HP engine of 3600 RPM. This car used 6:50 x 19-inch tires and had a wheelbase of 145 inches.

Peerless sales and productions were so low that they were listed among the miscellaneous makes for the year.

1932

Peerless, having been in business for over 30 years and known for being one of the famous "Three P's," (Packard, Peerless, and Pierce Arrow), couldn't cope with the depression any longer. Finally, it had to close its doors in 1932.

This year, Peerless built cars known as the Master 8 for $1,995 in a Sedan version, up to $3,145 for the Custom 8 Limousine. The Master 8 was offered in four body styles and had a 125-inch wheelbase. All used 6:00 x 19-inch tires except for the Cabriolet which came with 18-inch rims. Body styles for the Custom 8 numbered five. Both series had 120 HP 8-cylinder engines with a maximum of 3200 RPM. All had a 24-gallon fuel supply. All custom bodies came equipped with 6:50 x 19-inch tires. They had Bendix mechanical brakes for all models. Production was so low, figures were not available.

Virtually the same car as the 1930 model was this 1931 Peerless Custom Eight. It was a large, luxurious automobile on a 138-inch wheelbase. It developed 120 HP at 3200 RPM.

Pierce Arrow

A beautiful 1930 Pierce Arrow 7-passenger Tourer, classed under Group A, rode on a 144-inch wheelbase. Note the spotlight mounted on the windshield post. This model sold for $3,975. The tonneau windshield and sidemounts add a touch of elegance.

The Pierce Arrow was a product of independent man facture coming from the Pierce Arrow Motor Car Co. Buffalo, N.Y. The company was in existence from 1901 1938, but started the 1930 era by being under the directc ship of Studebaker Corp.

The 1930 Pierce Arrows claimed greater power fro their 8-cylinder engines, a new transmission, three chass and four wheelbases. More acceleration and ability f climbing hills in high gear was one of the big claims for t year. Horsepower was 115 for the Series C; 125 for Seri 132 and 134 cars, and 132 in the 139 and 144 mode All were rated at 3000 RPM.

The transmission differed considerably from 1929. T gearing was referred to as herringbone gears. In high ge the cars had a ratio of 4.42.

The transmission had 7:00 x 18-inch tires, and all mod used a 24-gallon fuel tank. Mechanical brakes were us throughout the line.

Pierce Arrow chose letter designations to identify t cars. Series C were the lower priced vehicles whi included three models beginning at $2,595 for 5-passenger Club Brougham. These models had a 132-in wheelbase. The models classed as Series B listed 9 bo styles. They rode on 134 and 139-inch wheelbases. Pric here began at $2,975 for a 4-passenger Roadster. The t of the line was Series A which had 5 models on a 144-in wheelbase. The top price was a 7-passenger town Cabrio for $6,250.

Pierce Arrow sold 6,795 cars this year, placing in 25 position for sales.

In Group B was the 1930 Pierce Arrow 4-passenger Tourer that came on a 134-inch wheelbase and had an 8-cylinder engine developing 125 HP. This model used the optional drum headlights which were not common to Pierce Arrow. The Tourer sold for $2,975.

On display at an auto show in 1930 is Pierce Arrow's most expensive model for the year, a 7-passenger Town Car in the Group A division, selling for $6,250.

A 1930 Pierce Arrow 5-passenger Club Berline in the Group B class used the longer wheelbase of 139 inches in that series. This model sold for $3,550. The sidemount equipment was optional at extra cost. This model had demountable rims rather than demountable wheels.

Pierce Arrow's 1930 Group B 5-passenger Victoria Coupe came on the 139-inch chassis with an 8-cylinder engine developing 125 HP. A total of nine models were available in the Group B cars. This close coupled Victoria Coupe sold for $3,350.

31

'or 1931, Pierce Arrow offered the following Series: 42, and 41. The higher number designations meant the vest priced car in the Pierce Arrow lineup for 1931. 'he Series 43 had an 8-cylinder 366 cubic inch engine t developed 125 HP at 3000 RPM. The fuel supply was 0-gallon tank. Tire size was 6:50 x 19 inches and the eelbase was on two chassis of 134 and 137 inches. ll Pierce Arrow Series 42 and 41 cars used the larger ylinder engine of 385 cubic inches developing 132 HP 3000 RPM. They used 28-gallon fuel tanks in both ies. The tire size was 7:00 x 18 inches and the wheel-e measured 142 and 147 inches. The 147-inch models re referred to as the Custom Group with Le Baron lies.

larger selection of body types were offered for 1931. cars were offered for the first time with free-wheeling ich acted as a part of the 3-speed transmission. Also ilable was a 4-speed transmission with silent third as ional equipment.

he style was quite similar to 1930. However, the nning board apron was narrower, the radiator had a ater vertical pitch, and the bottom of the doors were h with the body sills.

ierce Arrow offered 21 models ranging in price from 685 for the 4-passenger Coupe Model 43 to $6,250 a 7-passenger Model 41 Town Car.

'he company sold 4,522 cars for the model run, cing in 22nd position.

Before getting their check book out to pay for it, these "young ladies" felt it wise to at least try out the comfort of the seats in this 1930 Pierce Arrow Group B Convertible Coupe. This also was one of the few drum headlamp Pierce Arrows built. It sold for $3,250 using only the 134-inch wheelbase. Models equipped with the free-standing headlights used the fender-mounted parking lights, while models using Pierce Arrow's traditional fender-mounted headlights had free-standing parking lights mounted on the front fender tie bars.

For 1931, Pierce Arrow did not refer to their cars by letter designations but called them in a numerical sequence of 43, 42 and 41. This example happens to be a Model 41 on a 147-inch wheelbase. It was called the 4-passenger Convertible Coupe of the Salon Group. It sold for $4,275. Being the top of the line it was the only Convertible Coupe for the Series 41 cars. The Salon Group consisted mainly of semi-custom or limited production body styles.

The Group C 1930 Pierce Arrow 4-passenger Rumble Seat Coupe came on a 132-inch wheelbase with an 8-cylinder engine that developed 115 HP. This example sold for $2,750. The landau irons were decorative.

Elegance is the only word for this 1931 Pierce Arrow Sport Phaeton for 4 passengers. This model came on a 142-inch wheelbase, selling for $3,750 F.O.B. Buffalo. Note the courtesy light above the running board to aid passengers and the well equipped matching trunk and top boot. This series continued to use the double bar bumper while the Senior 41 models had a single bar bumper.

This beautiful 1931 Classic Pierce Arrow Convertible Town Cabriolet, with body by Le Baron, is on the Series 41 Chassis with a 147-inch wheelbase. This great Pierce Arrow is owned by the famous Phil Hill of racing fame. It has been in his family since new. Price when new was $6,250 F.O.B. Buffalo, N.Y.

The 4-passenger Convertible Victoria with body by Le Baron. This 1931 version came on a Series 41 147-inch chassis. Without the ever popular sidemount equipment, this model appears to have an exceptionally long front end. The lines are clean and massive. Note even owners of Pierce Arrows paid extra for the spare tire equipment.

Showing off its beautiful front-end with the fender-mounted headlamps that Pierce Arrow was well noted for, is this 1931 Convertible Coupe for 4 passengers. It sold for $4,275 as a Series 41 with a 147-inch wheelbase. Note the free-standing parking lights on the fender tie-bar.

Shown above is one of the lower priced 1932 Pierce Arrows. This example happens to be an 8-cylinder Model 54 5-passenger Club Brougham which sold for $2,385. This model developed 125 HP at 3000 RPM. Wire wheels and sidemount tire equipment was available at extra cost.

This 1932 Pierce Arrow Model 53 Convertible Sedan rode on a 137-inch wheelbase and sold for $3,750. It used the V-12 engine developing 140 HP at 3100 RPM. Note the twin horns on the tie-bar, a new innovation this year.

For 1932, Pierce Arrow offered this Model 53 5-passenger Club Sedan for $3,450 in base form. Its 12-cylinder engine developed 140 HP. This model used the 137-inch wheelbase. Demountable wheels were now used on all models.

Pierce Arrow

32

Pierce Arrow for 1932 showed two Twelves and an ght. They came out with new bodies and frame uctures. A 3-speed transmission was used with free eeling at the rear.

Models were designated as 51, 52, 53, and 54. The ghest number was the 8-cylinder model with the other mber designations being for the Twelves. The lowest ice Series 54 was a Coupe for $2,385, with prices up to ,300 for the All Weather Town Cabriolet. Listings owed 37 different models.

Wheelbases for the Series 53-54 were 137 and 142 ches depending on body style. The Series 52 rode on a 2 or 147-inch wheelbase depending on the model. The ries 51 came only as a 147-inch wheelbase car. Braking all models was by Bendix mechanical brakes. Tire size the 54 was 6:50 x 18, while the other three series ne equipped with 7:00 x 18. The free-wheeling unit was Warner product. All Series 54s carried a 22-gallon tank l the 51s, 52s, and 53s used a 30-gallon supply. The rsepower ratings were 125 at 3000 RPM for the ylinder cars, 3100 RPM with 140 HP for Series 53, l 150 HP at 3100 RPM in the Series 51 and 52. Pierce Arrow again saw position 22 for the year, and istered 2,481 new vehicles for 1932.

A 1932 Pierce Arrow V-12 Enclosed Drive Limousine for 7 passengers. This was Model 51, on a 147-inch chassis only, which sold for $6,300 F.O.B. Buffalo. Note the divided windshield on this Limousine.

Photographed at the Bonneville Salt Flats in 1932 was this Pierce Arrow V-12 Roadster that maintained a 112 MPH average for 24 hours. When seen without fenders, the standard size hood appears to be relatively short.

Always a favorite with Pierce Arrow followers was the Convertible Coupe-Roadster. This 1932 example is a Model 53 on the 137-inch wheelbase. It sold for $3,450. This model wears the rear-mounted spare, not seen too often on this body style.

Ab Jenkins, the noted race driver, stands proudly beside his new 1933 Pierce Arrow V-12 Convertible Coupe outside the Pierce Arrow factory at Buffalo, N.Y. The car displays a 1933 Utah license plate where Jenkins did much of his Pierce Arrow speed achievements. Note the windshield placed in a downward manner which helped give the car a look of fleetness.

Very much at home in its setting of Bloomfield Hills Country Club at Bloomfield, Mich., is this 1933 Pierce Arrow 12-cylinder Convertible Victoria Coupe with body by Le Baron. The car was classed as Model 1247 using the 147-inch wheelbase. It sold for $5,200.

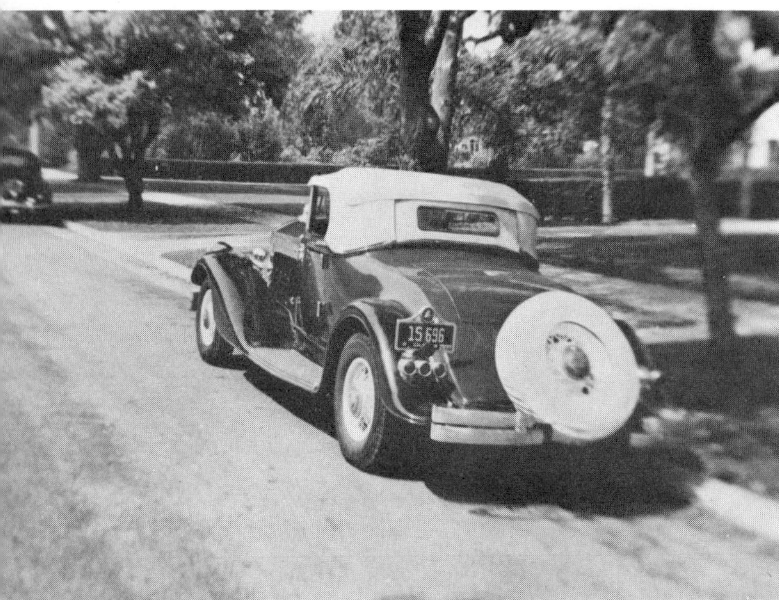

A rare 1933 Pierce Arrow V-12 Custom Convertible Coupe on the 147-inch wheelbase. The rumble seat aided in carrying extra passengers. It developed 175 HP like all Custom 12's. It sports the half-rear bumpers which were optional for the last year on Pierce Arrows. This model sold for $5,600.

1933

This was the year which saw Pierce Arrow bring out streamlined Pierce Silver Arrow on a very limited pı duction of approximately six cars. Price of this vehi was $10,000. Its designer was Phil Wright. Basically, t car was of aerodynamic design, which was popular w other companies at this time though only on an expe mental basis.

During this year, Pierce Arrow regained its independen from Studebaker, which sold the unprofitable compa for $1 million to businessmen from Buffalo.

For the year, Pierce Arrow came as an Eight and a Twelve with a new body and some interesting mechani features. Some of these items were Stewart-Warner pov brakes, automatic manifold heat control by thermost automatic choke, automatically adjusted brakes, a Startix carburetion system.

Horsepower was 135 at 3400 RPM in the Eight. T Standard 12 gave 150 HP at 3400 RPM and the Custom developed 175 HP with the same RPM.

Fuel capacities were 25 gallons for the Eight a Standard 12 and 30 gallons in the Custom 12. Tire s was 7:00 x 17 inches in the first two series and 7:50 x in the Custom 12. Wheelbases began at 136 inches for and Standard 12s. Then there were 137, 139, 142, a 147-inch wheelbased models. All told, there were models ranging in price from a $2,385 8-cylinder C Brougham to a $7,200 Enclosed Drive 7-passen Brougham.

Pierce Arrow showed 1,776 cars being sold, rankin 23rd position for the calendar year.

An aerial view of one of the six famous 1933 Pierce Silver Arrows. This photo was taken outside the Pierce Arrow facility at Buffalo, New York.

A close-up right angle view of the 1933 Pierce Silver Arrow V-12 Sedan. It developed 175 HP at 3400 RPM. The Silver Arrow was the proud work of Phil Wright. Note the opening in the right front fender was where the spare tire was housed. This car sold for $10,000. Only six were built.

Famous Pierce Arrow authority Bernard Weis once owned this mint conditioned V-12 5-passenger 1933 Pierce Arrow Sedan on the 137-inch wheelbase. It was referred to as Model 1242.

934

For 1934, many of the streamlined effects of the Silver rrow were incorporated. The company brought out two ghts, one of 135 HP for the 136-inch wheelbase car hich was Pierce Arrow's answer to the depression. This r was available in two body styles, a 5-passenger Sedan d 5-passenger 2-door Club Brougham. Prices started at 2,195. These were referred to as Model 836A.

The other models were the 139-inch and 144-inch heelbase Eights. These cars employed the 140 HP engine 3400 RPM. They used 7:00 x 17-inch tires and were mmonly known as Model 840A. These cars were ailable in eight body styles with prices beginning at 2,795 for the 5-passenger 2-door Club Brougham. The p of this line sold for $3,350 as the Enclosed Drive mousine for Seven Passengers.

Next in line was the Model 1240 A using the 175 HP -12 engine. These models used 7:50 x 17-inch tires and ere available in the same body styles as the Eight. Prices ere from $3,195 in 2-door Brougham style to $3,750 r the 7-passenger Limousine.

The top of the line were the 147-inch wheelbase models, nsisting of two standard Pierce Arrow bodies of 7-ssenger style, along with special custom bodies that were ferred to as Model 1247. They used the same V-12 gine as the Series 1240A. Fuel capacities in each series nsisted of a 26½-gallon supply. They were priced at ,295 to $4,495.

New car registrations for 1934 showed 1,740 Pierce rows registered, which gave them the 21st sales position.

An extremely rare 1934 Pierce Arrow 8-cylinder 7-passenger Sedan on the 144-inch wheelbase. It was technically referred to as Model 840-A, that sold for $3,200. The drum headlamps were virtually never used on the later model Pierce Arrows. This example belongs to Dr. Roland Scheuchzer of Birmensdorfzurich, Switzerland.

Ready for an evening's drive is this 1934 Pierce Arrow 12-cylinder Sedan on the 1247-A chassis. This model came only in the 7-passenger line. This version sold for $4,295.

Pierce Arrow's answer to the depression was this 1934 Model 836-A 4-door Sedan. It carried an 8-cylinder engine of 135 HP under its hood and rode on a 136-inch chassis. This model is equipped with accessory sidemounts. The built-in trunk compartment carried only a minimal amount of luggage. Prices began at $2,195.

A smart looking 1934 Pierce Arrow Convertible Roadster, as factory brochures referred to it, is displayed here. The 1934 line, except for the 836-A's, used side panel louvers to aid in keeping the engine room cool. This example was Model 1240-A on a 139-inch wheelbase. It sold for $3,395. Note the golf compartment door on the rear quarter panel.

Pierce Arrow

Technically, this car is supposed to be a 1935 Pierce Arrow 836-A according to the original owner who purchased it in April of 1935. If so, it was an early production model, by the absence of the hood louvers. The front end had a very pleasing appearance that kept in good taste with the true Pierce Arrow design. This 8-cylinder model sold for $2,295 as a 5-passenger Sedan.

The 836-A Model 1935 Pierce Arrow 2-door Brougham sold for $2,195. It was the lowest priced car for the year and was discontinued at the end of the model run.

1935

Pierce Arrow offered the low-priced package for th second year in a row. This model carried the same seri designation of 836-A and again came in the same bodi as last year. Prices were $2,195 for the Brougham an $2,295 in Sedan form. The car came on a 136-inch whee base. It used the 135 HP engine at 3400 RPM and 7:00 17-inch tires.

The 845s listed eight models from $2,795 for a Clu Brougham to $3,495 in Silver Arrow 2-door 5-passeng version. These cars came as Eights, developing 140 HP a 3400 RPM. Tire size was 7:00 x 17, using 139 and 14 inch wheelbases, depending on model.

Fuel capacity was a 26½-gallon tank in each of th series.

The 12-cylinder cars were classed as 1245 and 125 models, giving 175 HP at 3400 RPM. Tire size wa 7:50 x 17 on all 12s. Mechanical brakes by Stewart we used for the year on all models. The 1245 Series came i eight models ranging from $3,195 in Club Brougham sty to $3,895 for a 2-door Silver Arrow. The 1255 mode numbered two types, Sedan for seven passengers a $4,295 and Enclosed Drive Limousine for $4,495.

Wheelbases on the 1245 were 139 and 144 inches. Th 1255s used only the 147-inch chassis.

Pierce Arrow gave the owner of a 1255 an almost infini variety of color and upholstery choices. Buyers of th 1245 were given a selection of 17 color choices and 1 different upholstery options. The 845 had 11 color optio with three different fabrics. The 836 models came wit seven color choices and a Bedford upholstery choice i two colors.

Cars registered for 1935 numbered 875, placing Pierc Arrow in the 21st position for the model year.

On display at the New York Auto Show, which opened its doors Jan. 5, 1935, is a V-12 1935 Pierce Arrow Model 1245 Club Sedan on the 138-inch wheelbase. This example is displayed wearing a set of Vogue Tyres which were quite common on cars of this class at that time. It was available for $3,395.

The 1935 Pierce Arrow Model 845 5-passenger Sedan used the 138-inch wheelbase. This 8-cylinder model developed 140 HP at 3400 RPM. It weighed 4,965 lbs. and sold for $2,895.

Pierce Arrow

)36

For the 1936 models, Pierce Arrow offered three ıproved lines including the 8-cylinder models with 139 ıd 144-inch wheelbases. The Twelves came on the same ıassis, but also had a 147-inch wheelbase Limousine. The ight was increased in HP from 140 to 150 at 3400 RPM. ıe Twelves were rated at 185 HP this year at the same PM by adopting an aluminum cylinder head with higher ımpression ratio and mufflers which reduced back essure. Both 8s and 12s used a 6.4 to 1 compression tio.

Free wheeling in all gears was a feature in direct drive ıt was locked out in overdrive. Both free wheeling and erdrive could be locked out by operating a knob on the strument board if the driver so desired.

All models came with a mechanical brake system and a)-gallon fuel supply. The 8s used 7:00 x 17-inch tires ıd 12s came with 7:50 x 17s. Sixteen body styles were ailable. The 8 and 12 in Salon style were identical ccept for engine. Custom 12s came only in three sedan rms. Prices started at $3,195 for a 4-passenger 8-cylinder oupe and ending at $5,795 for a 7-passenger Brunn Town ır.

For the year, Pierce Arrow placed in 23rd position by gistering 787 cars.

Looking almost like a twin to the 845 Pierce Arrow was this 1935 Club Sedan. It does have its differences though – there are no vent windows in the rear window compartments like on the Club Sedan. It sold for the same price. This was a factory press release photo for 1935. Apparently backgrounds didn't enter into it when the company already had a beautiful car to offer. The name on the gasoline station claims it to be of the American Oil Company.

This was Pierce Arrow's most expensive car for the 1935 regular production run. It's a 147-inch Town Car with a Brunn body. It sold for $4,495. Pierce Arrow only produced 875 cars for the year.

Pierce Arrow's lowest priced car for 1936 was the 4-passenger 8-cylinder Coupe which sold for $3,195. A horsepower increase was seen on the new models. The 8 developed 150 HP and the 12 performed with 185 HP. This model has wire wheels which were rarely seen on the last Pierce Arrows, even though the customer still had his choice. This model still used the rumble seat for two of its four passengers.

It's hard to believe this classic-appearing 1935 Pierce Arrow 9-passenger Sedan could be called a Commercial Sedan. Strangely enough, this car went against all of Pierce Arrow rules. It was a Model 1255 which regularly carried only the 12-cylinder engine. This example came with the 8-cylinder engine developing 140 HP. Its wheelbase measured 147 inches. It came with the plain radiator cap, full chrome tire covers, a chromed grille shell, and chromed hood doors which were all options Pierce Arrow made available for customers. It currently is owned by a Lawrence Birstos of Denver.

Looking very similar to its "big brother" Model 1245 is this 1935 Pierce Arrow 845 8-cylinder Club Sedan which sold for $2,995 F.O.B. Buffalo. The only difference between the two models was in the engine compartment. This car was restored by Perry Fowler of Bremerton, Wash., and now resides at Harrah's Auto Collection in Reno, Nev. Note the special full chrome wheel cover this model sports. It was an accessory, as was the sidemount itself.

Pierce Arrow

The most sporty Pierce Arrow for 1936 was the Convertible Coupe, which like all 139 and 144-inch models was available either as an 8 or 12-cylinder. This model happens to be the 8-cylinder version on a 139-inch wheelbase, weighing 5,590 lbs. and selling for $3,295. The 12 weighed 5,800 lbs. with a price tag of $3,695. This model wears the rare accessory wheel covers.

1937

Pierce Arrow was practically the same car that w produced in 1936. The dashboard had some minor change and some new models were offered. New for the 193 Pierce Arrow 8 and 12s were the Club Berline, Convertib Sedan and Formal Sedan, which were not catalogue for 1936.

The 1937 Eights developed 150 HP at 3400 RPM while the Twelves developed 185 HP at the same RPM Tire size was 7:00 x 17 for the Eights and 7:50 x 17 in th V-12s. Fuel capacity was a 30-gallon tank for both serie The wheelbases were 138, 144 and 147 inches. Th 147-inch models were primarily offered in the Custom 1 line in 7-passenger Sedan and Limousine form only

Pierce Arrow placed in 20th position by selling 16 cars for the model run.

The 1936 Pierce Arrow Club Sedan weighed 5,600 lbs. in 8-cylinder style and sold for $3,295. The 12-cylinder Club Sedan weighed 5,850 lbs. and was available for $3,795. The sidemount equipment was available as on all 1936 Pierce Arrows at extra cost, and practically every car came equipped with the factory option. Notice the famed Pierce Arrow archer hood ornament.

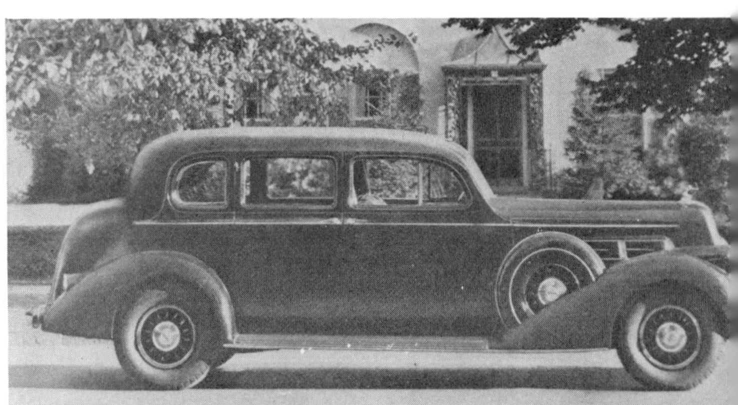

Pierce Arrow's 1936 Enclosed Drive Limousine was available only on the Custom 12, which had a 147-inch wheelbase. This example weighed 6,145 lbs. and sold for $4,995. Pierce Arrow produced only 787 cars for the 1936 model run.

A beautiful 1937 Pierce Arrow 7-passenger Limousine on the 147-inch wheelbase weighed 6,145 lbs. and sold for $4,995 F.O.B. Buffalo. The Limousine also is equipped with factory accessory wheel covers which were rare even when new.

A new model not seen in 1936 was this 1937 Convertible Sedan, available either as an 8 or 12. This model happens to be a 12-cylinder version which weighed 5,920 lbs. It sold for $4,650 and was available only on the 144-inch chassis. This model is equipped with the rare factory chrome wheel covers.

)38

The Pierce Arrow entered 1938 only for a very short n with practically no changes whatsoever. The license ate on the rear was placed on the trunk, but only on e Sedans, with a well-designed license light above it. ıis light was what Oldsmobile used on their 1937 ght Series. It had a small trade name placed on the top ying "Opco," which is exactly what Oldsmobile's said. xteriorwise, this was about it.

The Eights used the 150 HP engine at 3400 RPM and velves used the 185 HP plant at the same RPM, while 00 x 17 tires were used on the Eights and 7:50 x 17 es were on the Twelves. Both series used 30-gallon fuel nks. The wheelbases consisted of 138, 144 and 147 ches. The 138 and 144-inch wheelbases were used on gular models while the 147-inch cars belonged to the ıstom Twelves, which amounted to two models – passenger Sedan and Limousine.

Production figures were so low that they vary from fferent sources. Fewer than 100 cars were sold it's safe say, which puts them toward the last on the list as r as sales go.

Another new body style offered for 1937 was the Pierce Arrow Club Berline. As an 8-cylinder model it sold for $3,495 and as a 12 the price was $3,945. Its wheelbase was 139 inches for both models. Very few of this special Club Sedan styling were produced, as the factory only built 166 cars for the model run.

A special built 1937 Pierce Arrow Model 1703 Town Car on the 147-inch wheelbase. The car weighed over 6,000 lbs. Price was not listed, but it was high.

Pierce Arrow offered this same Metropolitan Town Car with body by Brunn in its last three years of production. It was a 7-passenger 147-inch wheelbase car that weighed 6,085 lbs. The price was $5,795, making it the most expensive model for the three year run.

This was the final year for Pierce Arrow. This 1938 example is a 7-passenger Limousine on the 144-inch wheelbase, weighing 6,105 lbs. Pierce Arrow dealers sold it for $4,150. Fewer than 100 cars were sold as 1938 models during the few months they were still operating.

Plymouth

Plymouth is a product of the Chrysler Corp., wi headquarters in Detroit. In 1930 the car was beginning i third season and was now being sold by Chrysler, De So and Dodge dealers.

The 1930 Plymouth offered a 4-cylinder engine 175.4 cubic inches that developed 45 HP at 2800 RPM These cars used Lockheed hydraulic brakes. All mode rode on a 109-inch wheelbase. The tire size was 4.75 x 1 The Plymouth had an 11-gallon fuel supply for all mode The 1930 line consisted of seven models which ranged price from $655 for a 2-passenger Coupe to $745 for t 5-passenger De Luxe Sedan.

Plymouth sold 67,658 cars for the year which put the in the 8th place for 1930 car sales.

Plymouth's 1930 5-passenger Touring weighed 2,355 lbs. and sold for $695. Plymouth was the only one of the big low priced three to come with hydraulic brakes this year. The Touring Car was called the Phaeton in Plymouth sales literature.

A show room of 1930 Plymouths with the Deluxe version of the Roadster and a 2-door Sedan in the foreground. Both of these models are equipped with the accessory wire wheels, and the Roadster has sidemount equipment. The parking lights were featured only on the deluxe models. The Roadster is the more expensive version.

This 1930 Plymouth Standard Roadster weighed 2,265 lbs. It sold for $675 in base form. Oddly enough, being a standard model it still is equipped with the wire wheels which were an accessory for this model. The Plymouth Roadster was really a true convertible, with full windows rather than curtains.

The 1930 Plymouth 2-door Sedan was available only in standard style. It weighed 2,475 lbs. and sold for $675. It proved to be very popular with young families with small children. Its 4-cylinder engine developed 45 HP at 2800 RPM.

Enough of a change was made in the 1931 Plymouth so that buyers knew the company had come out with a different car. This model was the popular 2-door Sedan in Standard fashion. It offered the same 4-cylinder engine only with a larger displacement of 196 cubic inches. The 109-inch wheelbase model weighed 2,595 lbs. and sold for $535. Note this model is minus the cowl parking lamps and has painted headlamps.

Plymouth

31

The 1931 line offered a 4-cylinder car with a 196 cubic :h engine which developed 48 HP at 2800 RPM. The fuel pacity was from a 12-gallon tank. Lockheed hydraulic ıkes were used on Plymouth cars right from the first ar of production.

The tire size was 4:75 x 19 inches, and the wheelbase s 109 inches.

For the 1931 line, Plymouth offered "Floating Power" ıich meant that the engine was mounted in rubber at ır points. Also available was free wheeling for the first ıe.

Eight body styles were available with prices ranging m $535 for the 2-passenger Roadster to $695 for a passenger Convertible Coupe.

Even with the depression weakening all manufacturer's es, Plymouth managed to move up to the 3rd place in es by selling 106,259 cars for the calendar year.

32

Plymouth was a product of the Chrysler Corp., with adquarters in Detroit. They were beginning their fifth ır in the automobile industry.

This was the first Chrysler-built product to have floating wer, an improved engine mounting which made a Four smooth as an Eight. A vacuum operated spark advance l a silent second gear with free wheeling at the rear re other noteworthy points. These cars carried a 56 HP ylinder engine (2500 RPM). It had a 12-gallon fuel ply. The wheelbase was 109-3/8-inches in each of the ıt models offered, with a tire size of 4:75 x 19. The kes were hydraulic. Models ranged in price from $535 the Roadster up to $695 for the 7-passenger Phaeton. The sales picture put Plymouth in third position for the r, building 121,468 units.

A deluxe 6-wheel version of the 1931 Plymouth 5-passenger Sedan sold for $625 in base form and weighed 2,670 lbs. The chrome headlamps and cowl parking lamps were standard equipment on this model. Note the small flags imprinted in the tire sidewalls. These were a trademark of Goodyear tires, which all Chrysler products used for years. Rear quarter windows were equipped with roller shades, as evidenced by the shade-pull tassels showing in these windows.

The 1932 Plymouth offered a vacuum operated spark advance and a silent synchro-mesh transmission. This Coupe came as a Business model for $565 and as a Rumble Seat version for $610. The weights were 2,550 lbs. and 2,645 lbs., respectively. Note how this model received additional fresh air by the aid of the windshield opening. All Plymouths of this era were equipped with hinged windshields.

A very famous car is this 1931 Plymouth 4-cylinder Phaeton for 5 passengers. Its owner was President Franklin D. Roosevelt who used the car on his estate at Hot Springs, Georgia. This model weighed 2,340 lbs. and sold for $625. The President's car was equipped with special hand controls so that F.D.R. could do his own driving.

Often referred to as the "PB" 1932 Series, this 1932 4-door Sedan weighed 2,880 lbs. and sold for $635. This model is on display at a recent Plymouth car club outing in Detroit. Note additional Plymouths parked next to it.

Plymouth

1933

In 1933, Plymouth offered a choice of two wheelbase 107-inch and 111-inch, but one engine. The Standard ar DeLuxe Plymouth Sixes more than doubled the previo year's production by selling 255,564 cars and also he onto its number 3 sales spot.

Some of Plymouth's features for the year were floati power, X-frame, Bendix vacuum-operated clutch, sile second transmission, free wheeling and hydraulic brake

The 70 HP engine (3600 RPM), was used for both serie All had a 15-gallon fuel supply. Tires used in both seri were 5:25 x 17. Wire or wood wheels could be ordered no extra charge, but if Airwheels were ordered with eith wire or wood rims, there was an extra charge. Mod available were nine, four in the Standard Series beginni at $495 for a 2-passenger Coupe, and five addition models in the DeLuxe Series going to $595 for the Co vertible Coupe.

An extremely rare Plymouth even when new was the "PB" 7-passenger Phaeton, which sold for $695, making it the most expensive Plymouth for the year. Note the jump seats for extra passengers in the rear compartments. This attractive Phaeton is parked in front of the former Plymouth Executive Offices in Detroit.

Plymouth offered this 1933 Standard Coupe on a 107-inch wheelbase. It weighed 2,418 lbs. and was available for $495. It was one of the models which helped Plymouth more than double its sales from the previous year.

This is the earlier 1933 Plymouth PC 6-cylinder Sedan that was offered on the 111-inch wheelbase. It sold for $575 in base form. This model wears the rare wood spoke wheels with steel rims. Note the difference in the early front end appearance over the later PD Series.

A larger rendition of the 1933 Plymouth Coupe came on a 111-inch wheelbase. Wire or wood wheels were available at no extra cost. This example was called the Plymouth PD Business Coupe. It was a late version of the earlier Plymouth PC. The headlamps were tapered more in the back, and a more rounded grille and larger hood ornament were offered. It sold for $495.

A very attractive little car was this 1933 Plymouth Standard Sedan for 4 passengers. This example had lines very similar to the new Continental car of 1933. The 107-inch sedan weighed 2,553 lbs. and sold for $545. It used the same 6-cylinder engine in both series. Shown in this car is Ann Lee Doran, a rising starlet of the era.

)34

1934 saw two improved Sixes giving independent front heel suspension and a more powerful engine. The andard Plymouth, introduced in 1933, continued using ; 107-inch wheelbase, but the DeLuxe Series was creased to 114 inches. Horsepower was 77 with the andard 5.8:1 compression head. Also available was a 5:1 aluminum head producing 82 HP. Both turned a aximum 3600 RPM. Fuel supply came from an 11-gallon nk. The standard tire size was 5:25 x 17 with either wire heels or stamped steel spoke wheels as standard uipment – 6:00 x 16-inch tires could be ordered at tra cost.

In the DeLuxe line, a generator with automatic voltage gulator was used to allow the battery to be charged ster. Brake drums were made two inches wider.

Front doors had ventilating windows and sedan versions so had rear quarter windows that opened. A disappearing h tray was mounted in the center of the dash panel. his could be removed for the installation of controls and als for the Philco Transistor radio. Brakes continued to the Lockheed Hydraulic mechanism.

On August 10, 1934, Plymouth turned out its millionth r after being in business for only six years. This was nsidered remarkable for a new car which spent most of ; time being manufactured under the clouds of a pression. There were 351,113 units registered in 1934, hich kept the company in Third Position. Four body yles were available for the Standard and five for the eLuxe. Prices began at $565 in Standard form, ranging ward to $685 for a DeLuxe.

What three inches can do to a car! With the start of the 1934 Plymouth Deluxe line, the car became larger than ever before. This Deluxe 5-passenger 2-door Sedan sold for $670, the same as the Rumble Seat Coupe.

A very appealing looking car to anyone interested in open models was this 1933 Plymouth PD Convertible Coupe with rumble seat, It sold for $595, making it the most expensive production model offered this year. There is a great similarity in the lines of this car and the other Chrysler products of 1933. Note the fold-down windshield that was still available on the 1933 line open cars.

Plymouth dabbled slightly in custom cars in the 1930's. Shown here is one of the few 1933 Plymouth Town Cars that was turned out by Derham. Note the special hub caps on this example. A sliding division window was used between rear passengers and chauffeur. The price is not available. Despite depression economies, these cars were not successful.

A typical scene of how Plymouth Coupes were put to work as business cars for companies was this Deluxe 1934 Plymouth Coupe. It was available as a Business Coupe for $645 or as a Rumble Seat Coupe for $670. The wheelbase was increased to 114 inches on this new model. Note the new style hood vent doors with the louvers, which gave additional cooling to the engine. This year Duplate Safety Plate Glass was available, but as an extra-cost option.

Plymouth continued to use the 107-inch wheelbase on its Standard models for 1934. Four models were available in this series. This was the 4-door Sedan which sold for $575.

Plymouth

Referred to as the 1934 Plymouth "PE" 5-passenger Sedan, this Deluxe model came on the 114-inch wheelbase. It used a 77 HP 6-cylinder engine at 3600 RPM. This model sold for $685 in base form. Note the wheel trim rings, which were optional factory accessories.

1935

For 1935, the Standard and DeLuxe version came on th same 113-inch wheelbase. The Standard only had thr models, Coupe, Sedan, and 2-door Sedan. Prices began $565 for the Coupe. The DeLuxe line included six mode beginning at $630 for the Coupe ranging up to $685 f the Touring Trunk Sedan. All models used the 82 H engine (3600 RPM). Fuel tanks were 15 gallons. The ca rode on 6:00 x 16-inch tires. Hydraulic brakes were alwa a part of Chrysler cars right from the first mode

Stylewise, the 1935 Plymouths were clean looking ca with a high, narrow, sloping grille similar to the oth Chrysler products for the year. They featured ne louvered hood side panels for better air circulation to t engine, had a more sloping windshield, and a more skirt effect on the fender line.

Mechanically, the Plymouth engines had new wa jackets that extended the length of the cylinder bor They also had balanced weight distribution with a n ride stabilizer bar which was initiated for Chrysler cars 1934 and was made available to Plymouth for this mod year.

Sales for Plymouth kept them in 3rd position, selli 442,281 cars.

A 1935 Deluxe Plymouth 5-passenger Sedan, with the rear mounted spare, weighed 2,785 lbs. and sold for $660. This model came equipped with full chrome headlamps as optional equipment, which virtually all Deluxe models claimed. The Touring Sedan sold for $685 with its built-in trunk.

A typical 1935 Plymouth that was used for fleet purposes. This example was the Standard Coupe which weighed 2,650 lbs. and sold for $565. This account went to Swift Meat Co., painted in their company colors of red body and black fenders. The Standard Series did not offer the Plymouth Mayflower hood emblem or hood side panel trim. It does have the factory accessory bumper guards, however.

Little difference is shown between the 1935 Plymouth Standard Coupe and this Deluxe version. Circular hood vent trim and the Mayflower hood emblem are about the only apparent changes. This model weighed 2,705 lbs. and sold for $630 in Business Coupe style. With a rumble seat, it sold for $645. The wheelbase measured 113 inches for both series this year.

Plymouth

1936

For 1936, Plymouth resembled its bigger brothers, with the same style treatment as was shown in the other cars. The new Plymouth showed off a smart new grille design with vertical bars. Horizontal hood louvers added to the streamlined design. Two series were offered, the Standard coming in three models and the DeLuxe being shown in eight models, plus the Station Wagon. Prices ranged from $565 in Standard Coupe form to $700 for a 7-passenger Sedan.

The wheelbase was 113 inches in all but the 7-passenger, which used a 132-inch chassis. Tire size was 6:00 x 16 in all but the 7-passenger which employed 6:50 x 16s. Horsepower was 82 at 3600 RPM. Fuel supply consisted of a 15-gallon tank. Plymouth was the first car in the low-priced market to offer rubber insulated body mountings.

The two-millionth Plymouth rolled off the assembly line in Fall of 1936. However, being in the model change over season, the car actually was a 1937 style.

Plymouth again took the Third sales position, selling 527,177 cars for the model run.

Plymouth's 1936 5-passenger 2-door Sedan was a good seller at $650 and a better buy for a family than the Rumble Seat Coupe for $10 more. This model featured a built-in trunk and weighed 2,820 lbs.

Almost the same car, as far as appearance goes, was the 1936 Plymouth. This Deluxe Business Coupe came on the same 113-inch wheelbase, weighed 2,705 lbs. and sold for $640, a ten dollar increase over the previous year. The rumble seat model sold for $660.

The most popular Plymouth for 1936 was the 5-passenger Touring Sedan weighing 2,850 lbs. and selling for $695. The 1936 line had an engine that developed 82 HP at 3600 RPM.

One of the less popular models in 1936, but worth more than any other 1936 Plymouth today, is this Deluxe Convertible Coupe with rumble seat. It weighed 2,810 lbs. and sold for $715. Note the twin windshield wipers are mounted from the base of the windshield rather than at the top like all the other 1936 Plymouth models. Bumper guards were even an accessory for the deluxe line.

This 1937 Plymouth 2-passenger Coupe was completely changed from the previous year as far as appearance was concerned. Mechanically, it was quite similar to 1936 cars, but it did offer many new safety features. This completely original automobile was on display at a recent Harrah Car Show in Reno, Nev. New, it sold for $575.

Plymouth

The 1937 Plymouth Deluxe 2-door Sedan came on a 112-inch chassis, weighed 2,840 lbs. and sold for $670. A lower priced offering was the Business Six, which weighed 2,770 lbs. and sold for $550. Plymouth this year claimed 18 to 24 miles per gallon.

1937

The 1937 Plymouth offered a number of safety feature such as a safety panel with recessed controls with rounded bottom edge raised enough for knee clearance and door handles curving inward to prevent tearing o clothes.

Mechanically, the car offered hypoid gearing whic resulted in the floor of the car not being quite so bulky Rubber mountings were carried on brackets attached to th frame which helped in the car's insulation against roa noises.

Plymouth came on a 112-inch wheelbase this year i all models except the Limousine, which was offered onl on a 133-inch chassis. The hood in all models was longe with the fenders having a deeply crowned slope to then The wheels were changed to discs, having three slots in th wheel like in the other Chrysler products for 193

Placed on these cars were drip moldings, inconspicuousl styled, to prevent water trickling onto the passengers they exited from the car.

They offered an 82 HP engine at 3600 RPM. All mode rode on 6:00 x 16-inch tires except for the Limousin which used 6:50 x 16s. A 16-gallon fuel tank was used i all models.

Plymouth offered a Business Six in three styles an priced from $510 for the 2-passenger Coupe up to 5-passenger Sedan for $595.

The DeLuxe Six came in eight styles from the $57 2-passenger Coupe to $775 for the 7-passenger Limousin

Chrysler's "bread and butter" car again placed third th year by selling 514,061 units. In the Fall of 1936, with th introduction of the 1937 line, Plymouth celebrated th production of its 2-millionth car.

As in previous years, in 1937 the Plymouth Deluxe 5-passenger Touring Sedan was the most popular model. It weighed 2,840 lbs. and sold for $680. The all-steel roof became a part of all Chrysler products in 1937.

Looking very similar to the 1937 Plymouth, this Deluxe 1938 5-passenger Touring Sedan only received a facelifting by adding four inches to the hood and redesigning the hood lines. It weighed 2,840 lbs. and sold again for $680 F.O.B. Detroit.

This was Plymouth's 1938 Model P-6 Convertible Coupe with rumble seat. It was only available in the Deluxe line, weighing 2,840 lbs. and selling for $695. It was the least popular model for the year as the depression seemed to take its hooks a little deeper into the auto industry again in 1938. Unlike the closed models, the Plymouth Convertible did not have a windshield that would open.

938

The 1938 Plymouths used a four inch longer hood, ermitted by redesigning the grille in an upward manner. 'his not only gave more engine room space but also gave he car a more massive appearance. Like the other Chrysler uilt cars, the windshield was now permanently placed nd ventilation to passengers was by a ventilator placed on he cowl. The interior of the 1938 Plymouths followed he safety features introduced on last year's model. The and brake was hung from the cowl as it was on other 'hrysler built cars for the year.

An accessory that Plymouth offered, that wasn't made oo well, was a rear seat radio speaker which attached to he back of the front seat.

The engine developed 82 HP at 3600 RPM both in its 3usiness Car models and the DeLuxe Series. The fuel tank ıeld a 16-gallon supply. Each series used the 112-inch vheelbase except for the Limousine, which came on a 32-inch chassis. The Business models used 5:50 x 16-inch ires while the DeLuxe used 6:00 x 16-inch tires. A total of 12 models were available ranging from a $510 Business Aodel Coupe for 2 passengers to $875 for the Limousine.

Plymouth placed third in sales again for the year by elling 297,572 units for the calendar run.

Plymouth offered a brand new body in 1939. These were used only for one year. This was the Roadking P-7 Business Coupe, which weighed 2,724 lbs. and had a price tag of $645. This series continued to use the floor-mounted gear shift but a column shift was available at an additional cost.

The longest Plymouth built up to date was the 1939 7-passenger Sedan and Limousine. It weighed 3,374 lbs. As a Sedan, it sold for $1,005, and in Limousine fashion it brought a price tag of $1,095.

A very compact looking car was the 1938 Plymouth Deluxe Coupe. It was available as a Business Coupe for $575, weighing 2,765 lbs. and also as a Rumble Seat Coupe for $625 with a weight of 2,810 lbs.

A very practical car for large families, funeral homes, and taxi use was this 132-inch 1938 Plymouth 7-passenger model. It was available as a Sedan weighing 3,324 lbs. and selling for $926. A Limousine was also available weighing 3,371 pounds. It sold for $970.

Truly a Special Interest Car today and highly sought after by car collectors is the 1939 Plymouth Convertible Sedan. It had only a one-year production. The interior was done in leatherette, while the top was finished in a khaki material.

Plymouth

A very attractive style was produced in 1939. It was the Plymouth P-8 Convertible Coupe with a rumble seat. This was the last year a rumble seat was available on a Plymouth chassis. This year the wheelbase was extended to 114 inches. The car weighed 3,044 lbs. and sold for $895. Full wheel covers and whitewall tires were considered standard equipment for the Convertible Coupe. For the first time, Plymouth offered a power-operated top.

1939

The 1939 Plymouths debuted as an entirely new line o cars for the year. Some of the new features were inde pendent springing which moved the wheels forward tw inches, giving the car a longer wheelbase now measurin 114 inches in both Roadking and DeLuxe Series. Th seven-passenger models used a 134-inch wheelbase.

With that change also came an additional ten inche placed on the hood, and a vertical radiator grille. For th first time Plymouth used a Vee windshield, which als gave length to the car's general appearance. Windshiel wipers continued to be mounted on the top of the wind shield. The headlights and taillamps were mounted flus in the fenders, which added greatly to the car's appearance

All DeLuxe Plymouths came with the column mounte gearshift while Roadkings continued to use the floo mounted lever. All models had the safety speedomete which lighted green to 30 MPH, amber to 50 MPH, an red after 50 MPH, as was done on all Chrysler car for 1939.

Both models had an 82 HP engine at 3600 RPM. Th fuel tank was increased to 18 gallons, which gave 2 mor gallons than the 1938 models. The tire size was 5:50 x 1 for the Roadking and 6:00 x 16 in the DeLuxe models

Plymouth offered a total of fifteen models, five bein in the Roadking Series and 10 in the DeLuxe models

Prices ranged from a $645 2-passenger Roadking Coup to $1,150 for the DeLuxe Convertible Sedan. Incidentally this was the only year Plymouth ever offered a Convertibl Sedan.

Sales again put Plymouth in third place with 350,04 cars being sold during their calendar year.

Plymouth offered this Station Wagon Suburban for 1939 on a regular production basis, using the 114-inch chassis. It seated eight passengers. Previous to this, different body builders did produce wagon bodies for Plymouth on a limited basis, but these were not cataloged as they were not Plymouth sales projects. This model weighed 3,089 lbs. and sold for $930. Only one sapre was mounted in the right front fender well.

Plymouth offered this 1940 2-passenger Business Coupe in both the Roadking and Deluxe Series. The Roadking sold for $645 and the Deluxe was $725. A 4-passenger version was also available in the Deluxe line for $770.

The 1940 Plymouth 2-door Sedan was available in the P-9 Roadking Series, weighing 2,834 lbs. and selling for $699. The Deluxe P-10 line also carried the same model, but with more deluxe equipment. It weighed 2,849 lbs. and sold for $775. This model used streamboards in place of the running boards. Consequently, the rubber scuff shields on the rear fenders were standard equipment.

Plymouth

940

Plymouth, like the other Chrysler products, again ffered an entirely new car after having had a complete hange just one year before. The 1940 models had more oom for the passengers. Front and rear fenders had the ame contour. Both were curved at front and rear and gave igh backs that were near horizontal which accentuated he length and lowness of the car. The fender catwalk to he rear of the radiator shell was combined with the ide pieces of the hood. The top panel of the hood was inged at the top center line and when lifted, it was utomatically held in position. Vacuum windshield wipers hat were located on top of the windshield in 1939 were tationed at the bottom on all 1940 models.

Both models, Roadking and DeLuxe, now had the gear-hift mounted on steering column.

Mechanically, both series were the same. They offered n 84 HP engine at 3600 RPM. The fuel tank was a 17-gallon supply. Tire size was 5:50 x 16 for the Roadking nd 8:00 x 16 for the DeLuxe, and the chassis had a 3½-inch gain over the previous model. It now was 17½ inches except for the Limousine which used a 37-inch wheelbase.

Plymouths were offered in eleven models, ranging in price from $645 for the Roadking 2-passenger Coupe to $1,080 for a DeLuxe 7-passenger Limousine.

From the sale of 509,735 cars the company again placed third for the year.

One of the highlights on the 1940 Plymouth Convertible Coupe was the use of the automatic controlled top. With just the touch of a button it was lowered or raised. This 4-passenger model weighed 3,049 lbs. and sold for $950.

Beginning to gain in popularity was the 1940 8-passenger Plymouth Station Wagon. It weighed 3,144 lbs. and sold for $970. Windshield wipers were mounted at the base of the windshield on all models for the first time.

This 1940 Plymouth 7-passenger Sedan or Limousine used the 137-inch wheelbase. The Sedan weighed 3,359 lbs. and sold for $1,005. The Limousine was 3,405 lbs. and was offered for $1,080.

Plymouth's most popular 1940 model was the 4-door Touring Sedan available in both series. This Sedan is in the Deluxe line, with the 117-inch wheelbase, weighing 2,924 lbs. and selling for $805. The less expensive Roadking offered it for $740.

This is the 1941 P-12 Plymouth Special Deluxe Coupe with all the trimmings. It apparently was a very early production model, by the Plymouth inscription on the front fender side panel. All in this series had the nameplate Plymouth Special Deluxe. Only the low priced P-11's had the inscription Plymouth. This Special Deluxe model weighed 2,866 lbs. and sold for $760 as a 3-passenger Coupe. The 5-passenger Coupe weighed 2,936 lbs. and sold for $805.

Plymouth

1941

The 1941 models were basically the same cars, appearancewise, as offered in 1940 with only some trim changes. Mechanically, the improvements included a more powerful engine which developed 87 HP at 3800 RPM due to higher lift cams and an intake manifold with milder curves at the branches to the cylinder ports. The gear ratio of the rear axle had been changed in the sedans from 4.1 to 4.3 and from 3.9 to 4.1 in the coupes. The fuel supply was a 17-gallon tank. The wheelbase was 117½ inches for all models except the 7-passenger models which were 137½ inches. The tire size was 6:00 x 16 inches and the 7-passenger cars employed 6:25 x 16-inch tires.

The three lines of cars offered were the Plymouth, the DeLuxe, and the Special DeLuxe, which included the Convertible and Station Wagon. There were 11 standard color choices available and in the Special DeLuxe models four two-tone combinations were available on 2 and 4-door Sedans.

A total of 13 models were available among the three lines. Prices ranged from $685 for the Plymouth 3-passenger Coupe to $1,045 for a Special DeLuxe 8-passenger Sedan. For the calendar year, Plymouth took 3rd seat from the sale of 429,869 cars.

A well equipped 1941 Plymouth Special Deluxe P-12 2-door Sedan weighed 2,941 lbs. and sold for $810. This version is equipped with the factory approved fender skirts and the deluxe wheel covers. It also was available as a P-11 for $739 and a Deluxe P-11 for $779.

Wearing a Calif. Plymouth dealer demonstrator license plate, this handsome 1941 Convertible weighed 3,166 lbs. and sold for $970 F.O.B. Detroit. This model is equipped with the optional streamboards and rear fender scuff pads which were gaining in popularity on the 1941 Plymouths. The Convertible was only available on Special Deluxe models.

This is a 1941 Plymouth 5-passenger Convertible Coupe equipped with all the genuine factory approved accessories like radio, wheel trim covers, white sidewall tires, and fender skirts. The swan cowl sidemirror was standard equipment on the Convertibles, as were the separate vent panes. This model was favorably received with the public.

The best seller for Plymouth in 1941 was the Special Deluxe 4-door Sedan. It weighed 2,956 lbs. and sold for $840. Two-tone paint combinations were becoming quite popular on the 1941 Plymouths as this example represents. The bumper end tips were standard equipment on Special Deluxe models but classed as an accessory on the other two series.

Proving its popularity with large families was the 1941 Plymouth 8-passenger Station Wagon which came only in the P-12 Special Deluxe models. The wagon weighed 3,194 lbs. an had a price tag of $995. A leatherette material was used in the full interior. Many states still considered station wagons as commercial vehicles.

Plymouth

1942

The 1942 models were lower and had a more massive pearance. Two models were offered, the DeLuxe and ecial DeLuxe. The car's driving comfort was increased locating the brake and clutch pedals directly in front the driver. Dual air-horns were standard on all models. e horn could not be blown when the ignition key sn't on. The running boards were practically flush with e door. An air scoop under the front bumper added more for the radiator.

The engine offered a larger cubic inch displacement of 7 cubic inches which developed 95 HP at 3400 RPM. e fuel tank was a 17-gallon supply. All models used the 00 x 16-inch tires. The wheelbase stayed the same as t year, which was 117 inches.

lymouth offered cars, as did all the other manufacrers beginning January 1st, 1942, known as black-out odels that had painted chrome trim. With war scares ound the corner, Plymouth eliminated some models at weren't as popular sellers as others. A total of 11 odels were available that ranged in price from $715 for DeLuxe 3-passenger Coupe to $1,030 for the 8-passenger ecial DeLuxe Station Wagon.

The company again placed third for the calendar year om the sale of 25,113 cars.

This 1942 Plymouth P-14 Special Deluxe 3-passenger Business Coupe weighed 2,955 lbs. and sold for $815. Looking almost like the same car was the Deluxe with a less fancy interior. It weighed 2,930 lbs. and brought a price of $740.

Looking very similar to the 1942 Dodge was this 1942 Plymouth 4-door Sedan, available either in Deluxe or Special Deluxe style. The Deluxe model weighed 3,025 lbs. and sold for $835. The Special Deluxe weighed 3,060 lbs. and had an $895 F.O.B. Detroit price on it.

This 1942 Plymouth P-14 2-door Special Deluxe Sedan was fairly popular with those who didn't want a rear door opening for the children. It came in both Deluxe and Special Deluxe style, selling for $820 and $865 respectively. All Plymouths built after Jan. 15, 1942 were considered "blackout" cars due to the lack of chrome trim.

A new model for 1942 was the Plymouth Club Coupe which resembled the other Chrysler product Club Coupes, which were introduced in the 1941 line. This 1942 Plymouth Club Coupe was available on the Deluxe Chassis, weighing 2,990 lbs. and selling for $785. The Special Deluxe version, with a more detailed interior, weighed 3,035 lbs. and sold for $855. It was received better, and for $70 more was the better buy.

Another new body style offered for this short production year was the 1942 Plymouth 4-door Town Sedan. This is the same body style that had back doors opening from the rear, like those offered on the other 1941 Chrysler products. It was available only in the Special Deluxe line, weighing 3,085 lbs. and selling for $935.

Pontiac

This was the most popular model Pontiac for 1930. It used the 110-inch wheelbase, like all Pontiacs of the year. It weighed 2,702 lbs., had a 6-cylinder 60 HP engine, and sold for $895.

The Pontiac was a division of General Motors Corp. wi headquarters in Pontiac, Michigan. The Pontiac was sc with the Oakland and considered a series of it. Producti began in 1926.

The 1930 Pontiac was introduced as the Pontiac I Six. The company was hoping to interest those whc formerly driven Ford, Chevrolet, and the newly se Plymouth into their corner with a car that had ma refinements. Among these items were tin plated pisto metric spark plugs, a more rigid crankcase with hea ribbing at its base, four point engine mountings complete insulated with rubber, and a new semi-automatic start

The car had a 60 HP engine with a maximum of 30 RPM. A 13-gallon fuel tank was used in all models. T size was 5:00 x 19 and the wheelbase was 110 inch Mechanical brakes were used.

Seven body styles were available with prices starting $745 for the 2-passenger Business Coupe to $925 for t 5-passenger Custom Sedan.

Pontiac placed in 5th position for the year by selli 86,225 cars. These figures also include Oakland for th calendar year.

Pontiac's most expensive model for 1930 was the Custom Landau Sedan which allowed the rear quarter section to be lowered. It weighed 2,717 lbs. and brought a price of $925. Surprisingly, Chevrolet also offered one of these high-styled models in 1929.

Referred to as the Pontiac Big Six for 1930, this Coupe came in a 2-passenger Business model for $745 and as a 4-passenger Rumble Seat Coupe for $775. Both models weighed within 5 lbs. of each other at 2,532 and 2,537 lbs., respectively. The sidemount equipment, wire wheels and Indian hood ornament were optional at extra cost.

Being received quite well was the 1930 Pontiac Sport Roadster which seated four. It weighed 2,342 lbs. The interior was finished in Spanish leather and fabrikoid. The door curtains were done in single pyralin panels, opening with the doors. The wire wheels and sidemount equipment on this model were available at extra cost. In base form the car sold for $780.

The 1930 Pontiac 2-door Sedan sold well, helping to put Pontiac into the 5th sales position for the year. This model weighed 2,595 lbs. and sold for $860. The doors were 35 inches wide, allowing for eash rear seat entrance.

1931

The Pontiac was offered only as a 6-cylinder car with a displacement of 200 cubic inches. The maximum horsepower developed was 60 at 3000 RPM. The fuel capacity came from a 13-gallon tank. The tire size was 5:00 x 19 inches and the wheelbase was advertised as 112 inches for all models.

The new models used rubber-bushed shackles and the connections between rear springs and axle were fully insulated by rubber pads placed above and below the springs. Pontiac used steeldraulic brakes which had a greater mechanical advantage and clearance between the lining and drums, with a result that less pedal pressure was required for stopping.

Pontiac replaced the Sport Roadster with a Convertible Coupe and eliminated the Phaeton this year. A total of six models were available. Prices started at $745 for the 2-passenger Businessman's Coupe and ended at $925 for the Custom Sedan for 5 passengers. Pontiac and Oakland sold 86,307 cars this year, taking again the 5th position in company sales.

The 1931 Pontiac looked quite similar to the previous models and offered no great mechanical changes for the year. Its wheelbase was increased two inches to 112 inches. This was the lowest priced model, called the Business Man's Practical Car. It weighed 2,650 lbs. and sold for $745. The Rumble Seat model cost $775 in base form.

Pontiac offered the 1931 5-passenger Sedan for $850, which was a $10 reduction from the previous year. It weighed 2,680 lbs. The wire wheels were optional at extra cost.

Pontiac offered two sedans for 1931. This 5-passenger model called the 401 sold for $875 and the more plush Custom Sedan was available for $925. For 1931, one-piece bumpers were fitted on the front and a split bar bumper was used on the rear. The cowl lamps were replaced by the ever popular fender parking lamps which Pontiac displayed through 1935.

A rare 1932 Pontiac Convertible Coupe on display at Harrah's Auto Museum in Reno, Nevada. This car sold new for $575 in base form with a 6-cylinder engine developing 65 HP. Its wheelbase was 114 inches.

Pontiac

Using the leftover engines from the 1931 Oakland, these 1932 Pontiacs had a V-8 engine developing 85 HP. This was the only year Pontiac used the V-8 engine until it introduced its 1955 cars. This V-8 Sport Coupe rode on a 117-inch wheelbase, and with the aid of the rumble seat was able to seat four passengers. It weighed 2,800 lbs. and sold for $635.

1932

The company was now beginning its seventh ye building automobiles. It was still considered the ba sister to Oakland, which was now being phased ot

The new 8-cylinder Pontiac was actually a V-8 whi had been taken from the Oakland line of the previous ye Very few were sold an the V-8 would not be seen in Pontiac again until 1955.

The Pontiac Six was the chief seller for the year. Bod in both series were very attractive, much like the others the G.M. family for the year. Standard features in bo series consisted of a silent synchro-mesh transmissic free wheeling, and shock absorbers adjustable from t front seat. Gasoline capacity for the Six was 15 gallo while the Eight carried a 20-gallon tank. All cars ca with wire wheels as standard equipment. The Six h 5:25 x 18-inch tires, the Eight had 6:00 x 17s.

Horsepower for the Six was 65 at 3200 RPM and t Eight had an 85 HP engine at 3400 RPM. The braki system was Bendix mechanical on all four wheels. T Sixes were assembled on a 114-inch wheelbase while t V-8s were three inches longer, giving a 117-inch wheelba Six body styles were available and were quite similar appearance. Prices vareid between $555 for a 2-passeng Coupe to $715 for the Custom 5-passenger Sedan in V form.

This made the last year for the Six until 1935. Ponti sold 46,594 cars for 1932 and kept for itself the Numb Five spot on the sales market.

This was the 114-inch 1932 Pontiac Six 2-door Sedan. It sold for $585. It didn't prove to be as popular as the 4-door Sedan. Note the new vent doors to aid in the engine cooling.

The most popular 1932 Pontiac was this 4-door Sedan, available as a Six for $625 or as a V-8 for $695. A Custom Sedan was also available in both series for $20 additional. The cloth interiors in all closed models were of a heavy and durable mohair.

Coming out with an entirely new car in both looks and with a new straight-eight engine, the company managed to hold onto its number five sales position. This 1933 Pontiac Eight 2-door Sedan came on a 115-inch wheelbase. It weighed 3,110 lbs. and sold for $635.

)33

In this model run, Pontiac dropped the Six, and its Eight ›came a straight Eight rather than the V-8 of 1932. ıis 115-inch wheelbase car used a 77 HP engine. Turning ·er at 3600 RPM, it claimed a top speed of 80 MPH. ıel supply came from an 18-gallon tank. Its tire size was 50 x 17. It came with mechanical brakes.

Pontiac used the Vee-shaped radiator grille of its others and sisters throughout the industry. All models ıme with skirted fenders and a beaver tail rear. Fisher)-draft ventilating system was used on the front windows the closed cars and safety glass was employed in windield. Libby Owens Ford Glass could be ordered in all indows at an additional cost.

Seven models were available starting at $585 for the port Roadster and ending at $710 for the 5-passenger ›uring Sedan. Pontiac sold 85,772 cars for the calendar :ar, keeping them in Fifth Position.

This very rare 1933 Pontiac 8 Convertible Coupe was photographed at an eastern car show several years ago. This example wears the double trumpet horns which were classed as accessories and the General Jumbo tires and air-ride wheels which did add to the car's riding qualities. The price on this model was $695.

Pontiac's 1933 5-passenger Sedan sold for $695 F.O.B. Pontiac, Mich. The example is equipped with the side-mount tires and covers which were an optional piece of equipment at extra cost. This model weighed 3,138 lbs.

Looking quite similar to the previous year's models, the 1934 Pontiac did offer new improvements, making it a heavier and still a faster car with a top speed of 85 MPH. This model in base form sold for $715. This was an increase that didn't help the Convertible sales, as buyers were not interested in flashy cars during the depression years. This model is equipped with accessory wheel trim rings and sidemount spares with metal covers.

Pontiac offered the 1934 models only as Eights again, but on a 117¾-inch chassis with an engine developing 84 HP. This 4-passenger Rumble Seat Sport Coupe sold for $650, which was a $20 reduction over the previous year. Note the front license plate was mounted directly to the fender rather than have a bracket attached to the bumper brace. The sidemount equipment was available at extra cost.

Pontiac

This 1934 Pontiac 5-passenger Sedan sold for $725 and was the most popular model for the year. A 5-passenger Touring Sedan with fender wells was also available but did not prove to be as popular as this model Sedan. Pontiac sales slipped in 1934, putting the company in the 7th Sales Position.

1934

Pontiac made claim to the independently sprung fro end for its new cars as did the other divisions of G.M Besides this, Pontiac also was larger, heavier, faster, mo economical, and more powerful. Coming only as an Eigh it developed 84 HP at 3600 RPM. Top speed was abo 82 MPH.

Tire size for all models was 6:00 x 17 inches. Mechanic brakes were still considered ample for 1934. Fuel supp consisted of an 18-gallon tank on these 117¾-inch whee based cars.

The car was accentuated by lengthening the hood seve inches so as to almost overlap the cowl. Its Vee-shap grille had an inch more slope than the 1933 car. Fro fenders continued further down in back of the bumpe The cars used more massive chromium plated bumpe with bumper guards as standard equipment. All mode came equipped with wire wheels as standard equipmen

Models available consisted of seven, ranging from 4-passenger Sport Roadster for $615 to $765 for t 5-passenger Touring Sedan.

Sales for the year put Pontiac in Seventh Place wi 79,803 cars being built.

This 1935 Pontiac Seluxe Six 4-door Sedan rode on a 112-inch wheelbase, weighed 3,445 lbs. and sold for $735. The 6-cylinder engine developed 80 HP at 3600 RPM.

One of the lower priced Pontiacs for 1935 was the Standard Six 2-door Sedan which sold for $635. This model was equipped with the bare necessities and weighed 3,372 lbs. It came with the Knee Action as did the other G.M. cars of the year.

Pontiac offered the Deluxe Cabriolet in both Deluxe Six and Eight versions. The Six sold for $725 and the Eight brought a price of $805. Interiors were finished in leather, with fabrikoid door panels. The Six rode on a 112-inch wheelbase while the Eight employed a 116-5/8-inch chassis.

935

Pontiac brought back the 6-cylinder car, closely resem- ing the Eight in style. Also new was the start of a trade ame which stayed with Pontiac for a number of years. he name was "Silver Streak." To help the effective name, ost Pontiacs carried many chrome strips down the hood d continued these over the trunk line.

The 1935 Pontiac Six carried Knee Action, as did the ther G.M. cars. It used an 80 HP engine at 3600 RPM, :00 x 16-inch tires, and a 15-gallon gas tank. Wheelbase r the Six was 112 inches, while the Eight was 116-5/8 ches. In addition to the Standard Six, there was a eLuxe Six which had the refinements of the Eight. he Standard Six came without any frills – one sun visor, e tail lamp, one windshield wiper, etc. It was a car eant for the economy minded. Pontiac Eights had an 4 HP engine at 3800 RPM, used 6:50 x 16-inch tires, and 18-gallon gas supply. Bendix hydraulic brakes were used roughout the line. Eight-cylinder cars listed eight models, hile Sixes came in 12 styles ranging from a $615 Pontiac tandard Coupe to the $835 Touring Trunk Sedan for five.

In 1935, Pontiac produced its millionth vehicle. The car as a 2-door DeLuxe Pontiac Six Sedan, made in June of 935. The model run showed 175,268 units sold this alendar year, placing in Sixth Position.

Reintroduced after its disappearance in 1932 was the 6-cylinder Pontiac. For 1935, it was available as a Standard Coupe for two at $615, or in the Deluxe line as a 2-passenger Coupe for $669, and a Sport Coupe with rumble seat at $705.

The 1935 Pontiac 8-cylinder Sedan rode on a 116-5/8-inch chassis and developed only four more horsepower than the Six, which brought it to 84 HP. This model weighed 3,570 lbs. and sold for $810. A Touring Trunk Sedan also was available for $835. The fender well spare tire equipment was indeed a rare accessory, and virtually none exist today.

Pontiac offered this 1936 4-door Sedan, commonly referred to as one of the Silver Streak models in both 6 and 8-cylinder styles. This example happens to be one of the more popular 6-cylinder Deluxe Sedans. It weighed 3,315 lbs. and sold for $770. As an Eight, it weighed 3,430 lbs. and brought a price of $815.

A 1936 Pontiac Deluxe Eight 2-door Sedan weighed 3,400 lbs. and sold for $770. A trunk back version was also available for $815, weighing 30 lbs. more. Similar models were also available in the Pontiac Six, and Deluxe Six for the year.

The most popular body style for the 1936 Pontiac was the Touring Sedan, available in the Six, Deluxe Six, and 8-cylinder models. This version happens to be the 116-5/8-inch 8-cylinder version model which weighed 3,430 lbs. and sold for $840, making it the most expensive Sedan model for the year.

1936

Having made a big change in 1935, Pontiac chose to onl make refinements for 1936. A distinctive chrome plate set of grille bars swept back over the hood, with outer ba done in lacquer the color of the car. Suicide doors we eliminated in favor of placing the hinges at the front pa of the front door. The nose of the car was rounded rathe than being flat, which gave a look of fleetness to its desig

A line of three series were available: the Pontiac Maste 6, DeLuxe 6, and DeLuxe 8. The Master 6 and DeLuxe were very similar except for trim differences. Both DeLux models came with knee-action while the Master 6 use straight axle design.

Horsepower for the Sixes was 80 at 3600 RPM. The had a 15-gallon fuel supply, and 6:00 x 16-inch tires. A models used hydraulic brakes from here on. A total of 1 models were available between the two Sixes. Wheelbas was 112 inches. Prices ran from $665 for the 2-passeng Master Six Coupe to $795 for a DeLuxe Six Touring Trun Sedan.

Pontiac Eight used an 87 HP engine at 3800 RPM, a 18-gallon fuel tank, and 6:50 x 16-inch tires. They had 116-5/8-inch wheelbase. A total of six models we available, with the Cabriolet absent in the Eight lin Prices ranged from a $730 2-passenger Coupe to an $84 Touring Trunk Sedan.

Saleswise, Pontiac picked the Seventh Position by sellin 178,496 cars for the calendar year.

The 1937 Pontiac Eight 2-door Touring Sedan appeared, looking practically the same as the 6-cylinder version except for its longer wheelbase of 122 inches and the raised Indian head among the hood "Silver Streaks." This model weighed 3,412 lbs. and sold for $950.

This 1937 Pontiac Convertible Cabriolet on the 6-cylinder 117-inch chassis was the property of Cornelius Vanderbilt. This car apparently was sold through the Pontiac dealership in Beverly Hills, Cal., known as Beverly Motor Co. Note all the Pontiac approved accessories such as grille guard, Guide fog lamps and a Guide Spot Lamp. This model sold for $975 in base form.

A rare 1937 Pontiac Six Convertible Sedan with top in the folded position. This model developed 85 HP at 3500 RPM. It weighed 3,479 lbs. and sold for $1,085. It also came on the market later in 1937 as an 8-cylinder model weighing 3,565 lbs. and selling for $1,245, which was Pontiac's highest priced model for the year.

937

For 1937 Pontiac offered a new line of cars, as was done / the other G.M. divisions. These cars were wider, longer id more powerful than Pontiacs previously built. A total ' 19 models were available ranging from the Standard Six three models to nine versions of the DeLuxe Six and ven models of Pontiac Eight. The Convertible Sedan on e 8-cylinder chassis didn't appear until late in the season. ices ran from $815 for the 2-passenger Six Coupe to 1,245 for an Eight Convertible Sedan.

The Pontiac Standard Six came as the plain version in the ie. It offered no deluxe trim. For example: one tail lamp, ie windshield wiper, one sun visor, one arm rest on the ont left door, no cigarette lighter, and the trunk Silver reak chrome strips were omitted. These cars were chiefly ld for fleet and taxi service. Mechanically, it was the me car as the Pontiac Six.

The new center point steering introduced on all 1937 ntiacs was one of the main selling points. The knee-tion suspension also proved to be a big sales factor. The andard series did not come with the knee-action, owever.

The Pontiac Six developed 85 HP at 3500 RPM. The ghts used a 100 HP engine at 3800 RPM. The Six had 00 x 16-inch tires and Eights used 6:50 x 16s. Both odels used 18-gallon fuel tanks. The wheelbase of the x was 117 inches and the Eight was 122 inches.

The 1937 Pontiacs placed Fifth by selling 235,322 cars r the calendar year.

Pontiac decided to enter the Station Wagon market in 1937 for the first time with this model. It was only available with the 6-cylinder engine. Very few were sold and there was a price of $952 for this unit. It managed to seat 8 passengers, which was a bit of a load for the 85 HP when filled to capacity.

As in previous years, the 4-door Touring Sedan proved to be the most popular model for Pontiac. This 1937 8-cylinder version weighed 3,461 lbs. and sold for $995.

Pontiac offered this 1938 Sport Coupe both as a Six and as an Eight. The Six sold for $891 and the Eight brought a price of $955. The only apparent differences were the 117 vs. 122-inch wheelbase on the two models. The Eight carried a special nameplate on its bumper, parking lamps on top of the headlamps, and a larger Indian Chief on top of the hood.

The 1938 Pontiac Six 4-door Sedan sold for $916. It wasn't as popular as the best selling model in the line, the Touring Sedan, which sold for $942. Comparable models were available in the 8-cylinder line for $980 and $1,006, respectively.

Now in its second year was the 1938 Pontiac Station Wagon, available only as a 6-cylinder model. The wagon model was offered only in a maroon or brown paint color rather than a large array of paints. This year the wagon model price increased to $1,110.

Pontiac

Available as a 6 or 8-cylinder model, the 1938 Convertible Cabriolet was the last to use the rumble seat. The owner had his choice of an interior done in taupe whipcord, or Spanish grain leather available in six colors. The top fit nicely in a well concealed boot. As a Six, it sold for $993 and the Eight brought $1,057.

The most expensive model in both the 6 and 8-cylinder 1938 Pontiacs was the Convertible Sedan. The Six sold for $1,310 and the Eight had a price tag of $1,353. Both increased considerably over the previous year. This also was the last year for Pontiac to build a Convertible Sedan. The interior materials followed the same patterns as on the Convertible Coupes. Sidemounts were still available on this model, but were a seldom seen accessory.

Known as Model 26 was the 1939 Pontiac Deluxe 2-door Sedan which developed 85 HP at 3420 RPM. This model weighed 3,115 lbs. and carried a sticker price of $871.

1938

Since Pontiac made a complete change in 1937, the ne car for 1938 just saw refinements.

New for Pontiac, as with many car manufacturers, w the change of the gearshift control. Pontiac placed thei on the steering column for an additional $10.

Exterior appearance included a grille with wider ba being done in chrome and with a more rounded appea ance. The Silver Streak appearance with chrome strips c the hood and trunk were continued. The Eight also ha parking lamps placed on top of the headlamps and larger Indian Chief stationed on the hood.

The Six developed 85 HP at 3500 RPM while the Eig used a power plant of 100 at 3700 RPM. The fuel suppl consisted of an 18-gallon tank in both models. The S used a 6:00 x 16-inch tire size leavinf the 6:50 x 16 the Eights.

The wheelbase for a Six was 117 inches and for the Eig it was 122 inches.

Eight body styles were available for the year in bo series. The Pontiac Six Coupe for 2 passengers was liste for $835. At the top of the line was an 8-cylind Convertible Sedan selling for $1,353.

Pontiac had 95,128 sales for the calendar run, to dr them to Sixth place for the year.

The most popular model in the 1939 Pontiac Quality Six line was the 4-door Sedan. It came on a 115-inch wheelbase weighing 2,995 lbs. and selling for $866. Note the absence of the right taillamp for this model. It was available but only as optional equipment at extra cost.

Pontiac's 1939 Quality Six Coupe came as a Business Coupe weighing 2,880 lbs. and selling for $785 and also as a Sport Coupe which weighed 2,930 lbs. and sold for $809. Pontiac placed in Sixth position for the year. The Quality Six was called Model 25. The Sport Coupe featured two folding seats behind the front seat.

Pontiac

39

For 1939 Pontiac offered three lines. New for the year ıs the Quality Six, a body style offered in five versions. ıis model shared its body with Chevrolet and the Olds). The wheelbase was 115 inches. Continued from pre- ɔus years were the DeLuxe Six and DeLuxe Eight, both ling on 120-inch wheelbases.

The DeLuxe lines were identical in appearance except for medallion denoting the DeLuxe Eight, mounted on the ımpers. All models offered the gearshift mounted on .e steering column as standard equipment for 1939. In the DeLuxe line the windshields were wider, and ıstomers had a choice of narrow runningboard skirts or ll width boards. Pontiac in the DeLuxe line offered a ɔdy style the same as the Olds "70" and "80" and the ıick Special, which helped the corporation cut costs ɔnsiderably by giving three different makes all the same ɔdy.

Pontiac retained its Silver Streak appearance with ırome strips going down the center of the hood. For the :st time the alligator hood design was offered with nge mountings at the back end of the hood.

The Quality Six and DeLuxe Six each shared the 85 HP ıgine at 3520 RPM. Each used 6:00 x 16-inch tires. The ɔLuxe Eight came with a 100 HP engine at 3700 RPM ıd used 6:50 x 16-inch tires. All models came with a 5-gallon fuel tank.

A total of fifteen models were available, five models cluding the Station Wagon in the Quality Sixes, and ve each for the DeLuxe Six and DeLuxe Eight. Prices ere $758 for the Quality Six Business Coupe to $1,046 r the DeLuxe Eight Cabriolet.

Pontiac again took the Sixth Position in sales by selling 70,698 units during the calendar year.

Pontiac's 1940 Deluxe 4-door Touring Sedan was available with either the 6 or 8-cylinder engine on the 120-inch chassis. As a Six it weighed 3,210 lbs. and sold for $932. As an 8-cylinder, it weighed 3,300 lbs., with a price of $970. This model came with the streamboards and rear fender scuff shields as optional equipment. Note the unusual accessory vent between the right door and hood side panel. It also had wheel trim rings and white sidewall tires as part of its accessory equipment.

The only real difference in this 1939 Deluxe Pontiac was the engine. The Deluxe Six Model 26 carried the 85 HP engine and the Deluxe Eight Model 28 employed the 100 HP engine at 3700 RPM. This model in 6-cylinder fashion weighed 3,160 lbs. and sold for $922. As an 8-cylinder it weighed 3,255 lbs. and cost $970.

In its third year of production was the 1939 Pontiac Station Wagon. Its price was decreased $120 from the 1938 models and it sold for $990. The spare tire was mounted on the rear panel. It was available only on the 115-inch Quality Six Chassis.

This well accessoried 1939 Pontiac Cabriolet was actually a prototype in the last stages before production began. Note the lack of a belt molding, rounded tail lamps, and no Indian medallion in the center of the bumper. The well shaped fender skirt may have been used but many Pontiac authorities doubt if it was truly available. This model in 6-cylinder fashion weighed 3,155 lbs. and sold for $993. In 8-cylinder style it weighed 3,250 lbs. and sold for $1,046, making it the most expensive 1939 Pontiac.

Pontiac

This 1940 Pontiac Special Six received a brand new body on a 117-inch wheelbase. It was available as either a Business Coupe or Sport Coupe. This happens to be the Sport version weighing 3,045 lbs. It sold for $819. Note the factory approved fender skirts.

1940

Four models were available for 1940. They consisted two Sixes and two Eights. Pontiac's newcomer to the li was a 122-inch Torpedo Eight model which resembled tl Olds "90," Buick Super and Roadmaster, and the Cadill "62". Windows were larger and seats wider than ar Pontiac offered before. All offered running boards on optional basis. The Torpedo came as a Sport Club Cou and a Touring Sedan. The chassis was the same as tl DeLuxe Six and Eight, except for its frame. The Speci Six was Pontiac's low priced car and it came in fi models on a 117-inch wheelbase.

Mechanically, the Pontiac Six increased its horsepower 87 at 3520 RPM and the Eights developed 103 HP 3700 RPM. The fuel supply was a 16-gallon tank for ea Series. The tire size was 6:00 x 16 inches on the Speci Six and DeLuxe Six. Both DeLuxe and Torpedo Eigh used 6:50 x 16-inch tires.

Pontiac offered a wide range of accessories, includi two types of heaters, either under dash or under seat wi control knobs mounted under the radio grille. A fi time offering by Pontiac were directional signals operat by a steering column lever. Parking light bulbs we replaced with a 21-3 candlepower bulb for the larg filament used for flashing. Also available were rear whe shields, driving lamps, back-up lights, spot light, two typ of radio, door scuff pads, stainless steel wheel cover and seat covers.

A total of 17 models were available, ranging in pri from $783 for a Special Six 3-passenger Coupe to $1,0 for the Torpedo Eight Sedan. Pontiac sold 249,303 ca for the 1940 calendar year, putting them in Fifth pla for sales.

This 1940 Pontiac Torpedo 8-cylinder 4-door Sedan used the new body style which proved very popular. It developed 103 HP at 3700 RPM. This example is fully equipped with factory accessories such as wheel trim rings, wheel center covers, whitewall tires, fender skirts, and radio. It weighed 3,475 lbs. and sold for $1,072.

In its first year in 1940 was the Pontiac Torpedo Series. It rode on a 122-inch chassis and weighed 3,390 lbs., selling for $1,016. The Torpedo line came only in two models.

Available for 1940 was the Pontiac Special Six Station Wagon which seated 8 passengers. It weighed 3,295 lbs. and sold for $1,015. A single sidemounted spare in the right fender well was standard equipment. None was available on the left side. The body was by Hercules Body Co.

41

ᶠor 1941, Pontiac offered a complete fleet of Torpedos, sed on the success of the 1940 Torpedo models. The yer had a choice of either a Si l or an Eight-cylinder in e three series of DeLuxe Torpedo on a 119-inch wheel-se, a 122-inch Streamliner Torpedo, or the 122-inch stom Torpedo.

The front of these cars gave a massive, sturdier appear-ce with a wider grille that extended from headlamp to adlamp. The bumper design was more tastefully done an on any Pontiac before. Bumper tip guards and trunk ard were offered as an accessory, which gave a nice ich to an already good-looking car. Gravel guards came ont and rear on all models as standard equipment. rrow running boards were concealed by flared doors on models. A new type of door hinge was offered in all odels. It held the door fully open without having to ld it.

The Six-cylinder car had a 239 cubic inch engine that veloped 90 HP at 3200 RPM and the Eights had a 8 cubic inch displacement that developed 103 HP at 00 RPM. Both Sixes and Eights had a 17-gallon fuel pply. The tire size on the Sixes was 6:00 x 16 inches and ght models employed 6:50 x 10-inch tires.

Pontiac offered a wide range of accessories, from road hts to venetian rear window blinds, and in between were Luxe or Custom radios, heater, wheel trimming, fender irts, trunk light and exhaust deflector, plus many more.

Pontiac offered a mid-season model on the DeLuxe assis. Known as the Metropolitan 4-door Sedan, it was comparable model to Chevrolet's Fleetline, Oldsmobile's wn Sedan, and Buick's small 118-inch wheelbase Special.

A total of 14 models were available either in Six or ght-cylinder version. Prices ranged between $907 for a passenger DeLuxe Six Coupe to $1,250 for the Custom rpedo Eight 8-passenger Station Wagon with a Hercules dy.

Pontiac sold 282,087 units for the calendar year, which pt them in 5th position for the year.

Making its 1941 debut, the Pontiacs offered this Deluxe Torpedo with either a 6 or 8-cylinder engine. The 6-cylinders were classed as Model 25s and 8-cylinders were Model 27s. As a 25 it weighed 3,235 lbs. and sold for $921. Model 27 weighed 3,285 lbs. and sold for $946.

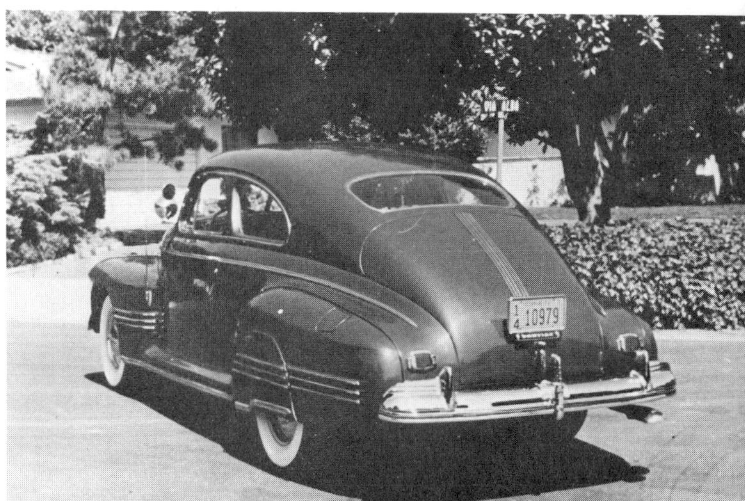

This 1941 Pontiac Streamliner Torpedo Super Sedan Coupe with 8-cylinder engine is owned by the author. It is fully equipped with all 1941 Pontiac factory approved accessories. The car barely shows 35,000 original miles and has the original color Allendale Green Metallic. Its weight is 3,385 lbs. and in base form it sold for $994.

For 1941, Pontiac placed the Station Wagon in the Custom Torpedo class. The 6-cylinder wagon was Model 24, while the Eights were called Model 29. The Six weighed 3,665 lbs. and sold for $1,225. The Eight weighed 3,730 lbs. and had a price of $1,250. The Hercules Body Co. supplied the station wagon body. It rode on a 122-inch chassis.

The 1941 Pontiac Streamliner Torpedo 4-door Sedan in standard style used the 122-inch chassis. It weighed 3,425 lbs. and sold for $1,005. A deluxe version was available for $1,051.

Pontiac

Coming out as a mid-season unit was this 1941 Pontiac Metropolitan 4-window sedan. In 6-cylinder version it sold for the same price as the regular 6-window model, but weighed five lbs. less. As an 8-cylinder, the price was the same as the 8-cylinder 6-window sedan, but it weighed 10 lbs. additional, at 3,295 lbs.

Pontiac's top of the line 1941 Custom Series came also in 6 or 8-cylinder versions. The Six, Model 24, 4-door Touring Sedan weighed 3,355 lbs. and sold for $1,052. The Eight, Model 29, had a weight of 3,430 lbs. and sold for $1,077. The 8-cylinder model was by far the more popular. With shortages on the next year models, the Custom Series was not continued in 1942.

The most popular Pontiac Eight Sedan for 1942 was this Streamliner Chieftain Sedan which weighed 3,460 lbs. and sold for $1,164. A less expensive version as a straight sedan sold for $1,087. Similar models were available with 6-cylinder engines beginning at $1,013. The fender skirts and front bumper accessory guards were optional equipment which most came with until automobile production ceased in February of 1942.

1942

The models offered a more massive look to the front e by having longer fenders which were carried back into door line. The hood also continued back to the co eliminating the former vent door. Venting now ca through ducts that were operated from the dash. Only t series were available, the Torpedo and the Streamlin both being offered in a Six or an Eight. The shortage materials for 1942 cars kept the Custom Torpedo fr being offered.

The 6-cylinder models used the 239 cubic inch eng that developed 90 HP at 3200 RPM. The 8-cylinder mod had a 248 cubic inch displacement that offered 103 HP 3500 RPM. The Eight cost $25 additional. The fuel sup for both series was a 17-gallon tank. All Torpedo mod used 6:00 x 16-inch tires and the Streamliners h 6:50 x 16-inch tires. The wheelbase stayed the sar 119-inches for the Torpedo and 122-inches for Streamliners. A total of 26 models were offered if 6 and are classed in the each series. Prices began at $940 for Torpedo 6-cylinder Business Coupe and ranged upward $1,280 for the Streamliner 8-cylinder Station Wagon. T Station Wagon was previously classed as a Custom Torpe but with its elimination for the year, the company plac it in the Streamliner Series. Pontiac placed in 5th positi for the calendar year from 15,404 sales.

Since the Custom Torpedo line for Pontiac in 1942 had been discontinued, the factory put the 1942 Station Wagon in the Streamliner class. It still carried a 122-inch wheelbase and had a Hercules Body. As a Six, it weighed 3,689 lbs. and sold for $1,285. The Eight weighed 3,779 lbs. and carried a price tag of $1,325, making it the most expensive Pontiac for the year.

Pontiac made a rather big facelifting on the 1942 models. This is the Streamliner, available as 6 or 8-cylinder model. As a Six, it weighed 3,400 lbs. and sold for $1,082. The Eight weighed 3,460 lbs. and had a price of $1,107. Note the fender skirts and bumper accessory guards which this Sedan Coupe is equipped with.

Reo

The Reo was a product of the Reo Motor Car Co. of nsing, Michigan. The Reo Company began to produce 's in 1904 and continued into 1936. The name was rived from the initials of Ransome E. Olds, originator d first president of the company.

For 1930, Reo offered three series of cars known as ries 15, (same car as in 1929), and the Series 20 and 25 ich replaced the Flying Clouds of 1929.

The Series 15 used a Continental L-head 6-cylinder gine of 60 HP at 2800 RPM. This series employed a -gallon fuel tank. It came on a 115-inch chassis and used)0 x 18-inch tires.

The Series 20 had its own 6-cylinder engine which was pable of 80 HP at 3200 RPM. These cars had a 21-gallon el supply. All Series 20 models used the same size tire Series 15 but had a 120-inch wheelbase.

The Series 25s were the same car practically as the 20s, chanically speaking. However, they had a 125-inch eelbase and used 6:50 x 18-inch tires. All 1920 Reo's ed Lockheed hydraulic brakes.

The 1930 Reo catalogue listed seven models ranging m a $1,125 2-passenger Series 15 Coupe to $1,845 for 5-passenger Series 25 Sedan.

Reo took the 22nd seat for 1930 by selling 11,499 cars.

This 1930 Reo Model 15 Coupe came as a 2-passenger car on a 115-inch wheelbase, selling for $1,125, and also as a rumble seat version for four, available at $1,175.

With five more inches added to its chassis, this 1930 120-inch wheelbased Reo Model 20 Rumble Seat Coupe sold for $1,595. Reo featured the silent second transmission for the 1930 cars. This car is equipped with the six-wheel sidemount accessories which were classed as extra-cost items.

The top of the line car for Reo in 1930 was this Model 25 which used a 125-inch wheelbase. Basically, it was the same car as the Series 20 except for its longer wheelbase and 6:50 x 18-inch tires. This model had its parking lights mounted on the fenders rather than on the cowl as did the Series 15 and 20 cars. This Model 25 sold for $1,845.

Reo's 1930 Model 20 4-door Sedan was available for the same price as the Sport Coupe – $1,595. This version used the 6-cylinder 80 HP engine at 3200 RPM. The trunk and sidemount spares were available as extra equipment, as were the wire wheels.

For 1931, Reo again used the name Flying Cloud. The cars were available in 6 or 8-cylinder form. This version is a 5-passenger Model 30 Sedan which weighed 4,375 lbs. It sold for $1,995. Its 8-cylinder engine developed 125 HP at 3300 RPM.

This 1931 Reo Royal 5-passenger Victoria came in the Series 35 cars on a 135-inch wheelbase. It weighed 4,475 lbs. and sold for $2,485. All Reo models used the Murray body of totally new design, which provided the cars with a very modern appearance. In addition, the longer wheelbases allowed for much better fender and body line treatment.

Reo's 1931 Royale Convertible Coupe offered one shot lubrication as did all the other models in both Series 30 and 35 cars. This series is ranked among the classics, with the Classic Car Club of America. When folded, the top stored flush with the car's door line.

Virtually the same car as it was in 1931, this Reo Royale for 1932 came on a 135-inch wheelbase. It weighed 4,650 lbs. and sold for $2,445.

1931

Reo offered five lines of cars in 1931. The lowest pr series was the Reo 15. It was followed by the Series 2 25, 30, and 35.

The Reo 15 had a Continental 6-cylinder engine 214.7 cubic inches, with a maximum horsepower rating 60 at 2800 RPM. The fuel capacity for this car was 15-gallon tank. Its tire size was 5:50 x 18 with a wheelba of 116 inches.

The Series 20 and 25 shared the same 6-cylinder engi of 268.3 cubic inches developing 85 HP at 3200 RP They used a 20-gallon fuel supply. The tire size for t Series 20 was 6:00 x 18 with a 120-inch wheelbase. T Series 25 used 6:50 x 17-inch tires and had a chassis 125 inches.

Reo 30s and 35s had identical engines of 356 cul inches developing 125 HP at 3300 RPM. They used 2 gallon fuel tanks. The tire size was 6:50 x 18 inches both Series. The Reo 30 had a 130-inch wheelbase and t 35s had a 135-inch wheelbase. All Reo models employ a hydraulic brake system.

A total of 23 models were available, which ranged fron $900 Series 15 2-passenger Coupe to $2,485 for the Ser 35 models which consisted of 3 body styles all selling the same price.

Reo ranked in 20th position this year by selling 6,0 cars.

1932

The big news from Reo for 1932 was the vacuu controlled clutch. This was the start of so-call "automatic driving." The outstanding advantage claim by Reo was that it didn't depend on engine speed or up the movement of the accelerator for its action. It allow the driver to hold the clutch in any desired position fro full release to full engagement or to engage or release with the same control that was possible with the foot the clutch pedal. The new automatic clutch butt controlled the action of the clutch in a manner entir similar to the method that clutches have been control for years on most cars. The clutch pedal remained in pla and could be used at any time if the driver so desir

Reo came as a Six with 85 HP at 3200 RPM or in t 8-cylinder versions offering 90 HP or 125 HP at 3300 RP The Sixes had 6:00 x 18-inch tires. The Eights, known 821 and 825, came with the same tire size, but had inch rims. All Series 831 and 835 Eights had 6:50 x inch tires. Each series came equipped with Lockhe hydraulic brakes.

Prices ranged within a $2,000 variance, from $995 fo 6-cylinder Sedan to $2,995 for a Convertible Cou Altogether, there were 20 models available. Reo sold 3,5 cars and placed 20th in the sales race for the year. 835s are recognized as true classics today by the Clas Car Club of America.

This 1932 Reo Royale with rumble seat weighed 4,500 lbs. and sold for $2,445. This model offered a package compartment behind the front seat. Note the step pad on the left fender for entrance to the rumble seat.

933

For 1933, Reo lessened its number of models available y fourteen. This year, there were only six cars – three eo "S" and three Royales.

Prices varied from $795 to $2,425 for the Royale 8 edan. The S Series was mainly known as Flying Cloud x. Both this car and the Royale 8 had the Vee-sloping diator grille. The radiator shell and front splash aprons ere remolded. A curve in the front bumper added to the r's already pleasing appearance. The front fenders were irted and running boards were curved at outer edges.

Along with modern styling, the Flying Cloud had four bber mounted cushions for its engine while the Royale ed six mountings. Both had redesigned transmissions, ee wheeling, a down draft carburetor, automatic choke, d automatic heat control.

Wheelbases consisted of 117½ inches for the Flying oud and 131 for the Royale. Tire sizes were 6:00 x 17 r Flying Cloud and 6:50 x 18 in the Royale. The brake stem was Lockheed hydraulic. Fuel supplies were less an in 1932, but still ample with a 21-gallon supply being ed in the Flying Cloud and a 24-gallon tank going to the oyale rather than the 32-gallon supply used the previous ar.

Horsepower showed 85 at 3200 RPM in the Flying Cloud d 125 at 3300 RPM in the Royale 8.

Reo sold 3,082 cars, giving it a sales position of umber 20 for the year.

Reo's 1932 Five Passenger Victoria offered a spacious interior and easy access to the rear seat. This model weighed 4,475 lbs. and sold for the same as the Coupe and Sedan – $2,445. The rear and quarter windows were equipped with roller shades.

The most expensive Reo for 1932 was the 8-35 Royale Convertible Coupe. It sold for $2,995 and weighed 4,440 lbs. This model had a top which fit snugly into its well, which kept the same classic aerodynamic streamlining. Hand-buffed leather upholstery harmonized with the car's exterior finish.

Reo's lowest priced car for 1933 was this "S" Series Flying Cloud Six Coupe. It sold for $795 as a standard model. An 85 HP engine, at 3200 RPM, was used in this series.

This was the 1933 Reo Royale 8 Elite 5-passenger Victoria. This model claimed the seating intimacy of a coupe and the capacity of a sedan. A low hinged rear deck emphasized Reo's "Air-Stream" design. It could be removed for installation of a smart custom built trunk used as storage space with the regular rear deck. This model was available for $2,385.

This classic-appearing 1933 Reo Royale 8 Sedan offered an automatic clutch for its second year. Free wheeling, down draft carburetor, automatic choke, and automatic heat control also were shown on the new 1933 cars. This model sold for $2,425.

Reo

1934

Reo began its 31st year in the automobile business l coming out with an increase of eight models this yea A total number of 14 body styles were available rangi from $795 for the Reo 65 Coupe for four passengers the Reo Royale Custom Coupe for five at $2,44

Reo's big news for this year consisted of the Se Shifting Transmission. This device was exhibited wi great emphasis at car shows throughout the country. cost $75 additional. One of the selling features was th three could now sit comfortably in the front, with t elimination of a floor shift lever and the emergency bra moved to the left of the driver.

Horsepower was 85 at 3200 RPM in the S Series a 125 at 3000 RPM in the Royale. Tire size consisted 6:00 x 17 for the S's and 6:50 x 18 for Royales. Fu capacity was 21 gallons in the S and 24 gallons for t 8-cylinder car. Brake system was Lockheed hydraulic both series with free wheeling still available in both lin

Wheelbase consisted of 118 inches for the Six and 1 and 135 inches for the Royales.

Reo was able to gain the 19th position, selling 3,3 cars for the calendar year.

The Elite Convertible Coupe was the name Reo gave to the "S" Series 1933 Flying Cloud Six. This 4-passenger Convertible Coupe used a 117½-inch wheelbase. It sold for $995 and was available only as a deluxe model. Fender well equipment and tire covers were optional at extra cost.

Reo's lowest priced car for 1934 was this 1934 Flying Cloud 3-passenger Coupe. It weighed 3,500 lbs. and sold for $795. Technically, it was referred to as the Reo "65." A feature of this year's Reos was the self-shifter automatic-type transmission.

This 5-passenger Reo Sport Coupe for 1934 sold for $845. All models came equipped with artillery pressed steel wheels as standard equipment, which added to the car's smart appearance. Sidemounts were part of this model's regular equipment.

For 1934, Reo offered this more deluxe version of the 6-passenger sedan, calling it the Sport Sedan. It was equipped with built in trunk, but had twin sidemounts with metal covers, and also had twin sun visors. This model weighed 3,620 lbs. and sold for $845.

The 1934 Reo Flying Cloud 6-passenger Deluxe Sedan weighed 3,590 lbs. and sold for $795. Standard features included a built in trunk, twin horns, safety glass in the windshield, and twin windshield wipers, which made a nice package for the buyer in 1934.

935

Reo offered two styles for 1935. A new model was ıdded called the Reo "6A," also known as the Flying loud, which came as a moderate priced Six in two body :yles on a 115-inch wheelbase using 6:25 x 16-inch tires. he car developed the same horsepower as Reo "S," hich was 85 at 3400 RPM. Fuel capacity also was shared ı the "6A" and "S" Series. This was a 15-gallon tank. rakes were hydraulic for both. However, the "6A" used Iidland Products and the larger series had Lockheed ydraulics.

Prices for the Flying Cloud were $845 and $795 for -door Coach and Sedan body styles. Styling of the Flying loud was actually more modern than the "S" Series. It onsisted of a high sloping radiator grille with a fastback esign to the trunk area. This model was equipped with an uminum head giving a 7:1 compression ratio. The "S" ıodel had 5.4:1 compression ratio. The standard trans-ıission consisted of three speeds with synchronized ıifting into second and third. Also available, but at extra ost was the Reo self-shifter for both series.

The "S" model sold for $100 more than the Flying loud in Sedan form and went to $995 for the Convertible oupe. The cars carried a wheelbase of three inches more ı length and a tire size of 6:50 x 16.

The company placed 19th that year selling 3,894 cars

Reo offered this new body shell on the 1935 line of cars. It was referred to as Model "6A." It was available for $795 as a 2-door sedan. The body builder was Hayes, who also supplied bodies to Graham in 1936 and 1937, thus accounting for the similarity of appearance between the two cars.

A rear view shows the pleasing fastback styling of this 1935 Reo "6A" 4-door Sedan. Its Hayes-built body brought a price tag of $845. Note that all four doors opened rearward.

Reo's 1935 4-door Sedan in the Series "6A" sold for $845. Generally, this series was known as the Flying Cloud. Reo sold 3,894 cars during the 1935 calendar year. This model was the best seller. Approximately 2,200 of this style were produced. Note the sharp V of the front bumper.

Less popular than the 1935 Series "6A" was this Reo "S7" Sedan. This model came on a 118-inch wheelbase, and used the same body dies as the 1934 models. A total of four models were available selling for $100 more than the "6A" Series. This example sold for $945. The public preferred the "6A" Series over this body style, as it wasn't nearly as attractive by 1935 standards.

Reo

New for 1936 was Reo's 2-door Deluxe Brougham. The bustle back trunk gave additional luggage space which buyers did appreciate. It sold for $845. Note the rubber tipped cushions on the bumper guards, which helped in keeping the guards from getting scratched or dented.

1936

Reo of Lansing, Mich., was an independent compan The car began production in 1904. During this year R would close its doors forever to passenger cars, but wou continue its fine line of trucks. Reo tried to hold on wi some innovations but the buyers just weren't ther

The new car had a three speed transmission with sile gearing in all speeds and synchronization for second a high. A grille of die-cast design was improved over previo years and streamlined headlamps were attached to t radiator. Fender parking lamps of the same design we available at extra cost. Also new were interior desi upholstery, fresh styling of the instrument board, a extra large glove box. Extra appointments like rad control provisions, cigar lighter, dual ash receivers fro and rear, fully carpeted floors front and rear (DeLu Models only), and red leather piping on seat edges we some of the refinements, but still the public wasn't ther

The car had an 85 HP engine at 3400 RPM, used 115-inch wheelbase, rode on 6:25 x 16-inch tires, h hydraulic brakes, and used a 15-gallon fuel supply. Tw Standard Flying Clouds and two DeLuxe versions appear as 2 and 4-door sedans from $795 to $895. The compa placed 18th by selling 3,146 cars in its last year production.

This 1936 Reo Deluxe Sedan was available for $845 with the flat trunk styling. It offered many deluxe appointments such as dual ash receivers, cigar lighter, twin wipers, fully carpeted flooring, and fender mounted parking lamps as standard equipment.

Reo's 1936 Deluxe Touring Sedan came with the bustle back trunk, which was available only on the 1936 models. This sedan sold for $895 and was the most popular model for the year. The company placed in 18th Sales Position for its last year building passenger cars. After this, Reo would continue to build a fine line of medium and heavy trucks right up until the company's final production year of 1975.

Reo's lowest priced car for 1936 was this 2-door Coach which sold for $795. It came on a 115-inch wheelbase with 6:25 x 16-inch tires. The body builder for the final year of Reo passenger cars was Hayes Body Co. of Grand Rapids, Michigan. Note that the extreme front bumper of 1935 was now replaced with a conventional style unit.

Rockne

The Rockne was a division of the Studebaker Corp. with adquarters being in Detroit. The car entered the tomotive market in mid-1931.

The Rockne resembled the Studebakers a great deal, pecially in its front end appearance. The new car was st offered as a 5-passenger Sedan and later in the year me a 4-passenger Coupe. The line was simply called the ckne Six. It had a 189.8 cubic inch engine developing HP at 3200 RPM.

A 12-gallon fuel tank was used on these cars. The tire e was 5:25 inches with a 110-inch wheelbase. Free-eeling and a silent second synchromesh transmission re offered. The line was offered at $585 in Standard rm, which was the only way it came.

Sales and production figures were not available as they re grouped with Studebaker.

Coming on the market as a late season car was this 1931-32 Rockne. Shown here is the Rockne 4-passenger Rumble Seat Coupe, with fender well spares, which sold for $585 in base form.

Rockne offered this 1931-32 Model 65 on its 110-inch wheelbase. Five body styles were available with a 189.8 cubic inch engine developing 65 HP at 3200 RPM. This model was available for $585.

Rockne had a Series "65" Sedan on the 110-inch wheelbase chassis. It sold for $585. Also offered was this 114-inch Sedan in the Series "75" for $735. This example wears a California dealer demonstrator license plate from Paul G. Hoffmann, the California Studebaker Rockne Distributor at that time.

Offering a more rounded out line of cars for 1932 was this Rockne "75" 2-passenger Coupe on the 114-inch wheelbase. This model sold for $685. Sidemount tire equipment was optional at extra cost, but the chrome plated Klaxon horn was standard.

A sharp looking 1932 Rockne Convertible Coupe Series "75" sold for $675. It was a mid-season offering, with fewer than 800 cars being built during the 1932 model run.

Rockne

This 1932 Rockne Convertible Victoria was a late model entry, not available until June, 1932. It sold for $695, but few buyers were present. Note the rakish angle of the spare to give the car an additional few inches of length. It carried a Briggs body not unlike the convertible sedan body being built for Ford.

1932

Named for the great football coach of Notre Dan University, this car had pleasing lines and resembled t Studebakers a great deal.

It offered free-wheeling and a silent second gear. Tv series were available, the 65 and the 75. The 65s on came in two models which were both 5-passenger Seda starting at $585. They had a wheelbase of 110 inche These sedans had 5:25 x 18-inch tires while the 75 seri carried 5:50 x 18-inch tires. The 65s were mainly us in fleet service. It carried a 12-gallon fuel supply. received its numerical designation because of its 65 H engine which turned over at 3200 RPM maximu

The Series 75 carried seven more horsepower and 14-gallon fuel supply. This series had a 114-inch wheelbas All models had mechanical brakes. The Series 75 came six body styles ranging from the $685 2-passenger Cou to the $780 5-passenger DeLuxe Sedan.

For its second year of production, Rockne help Studebaker out by selling 15,244 cars. It came in 6 place in sales, combined with Studebaker, selling a total 44,325 units for the calendar year.

This dealer is demonstrating Rockne's rigidity and ability to maintain equal balance minus one of its wheels. This 1933 2-door Sedan in its Standard form sold for $595.

This was Rockne's 1933 Standard Business Coupe for 2 passengers. It used the 110-inch wheelbase chassis and sold for $585. It was the lowest priced Rockne of the year. The Series 75 was dropped. leaving only the Series 65 for 1933.

Rockne's 1933 Rumble Seat Coupe for 4 passengers was a favorite for the young who enjoyed Studebaker products. This example sold for $620. Note the canvas covering over the rear mounted spare tire.

933

This was the car's third and last year of production due financial problems at Studebaker.

For this year, the model designations were Standard and eLuxe. Standards ran as low as $585 for the 2-passenger oupe without rumble seat. Top of the line went for 740 in the form of a Convertible Sedan. A total of 12 odels were available.

The lines were very similar to the 1932 offering, but st smoothed out enough to make it still a more desirable ckage. The wheelbase was 110 inches but the bodies ere made roomier, especially in the rear seat, which was ½ inches longer.

By coming out with 5:25 x 17-inch tires, the car had a wer overall appearance than in 1932. A sloping radiator d hood also gave a look of style.

The mechanical devices to its credit consisted of electro-ated pistons, a counter balanced crankshaft with four unterweights, an engine that was cushioned in four aces by rubber, free-wheeling, and synchromesh trans-ission. The fuel supply was a 12-gallon tank. All models ed mechanical brakes. The whole line rode on a 110-inch heelbase and used a 70 HP engine with a maximum of 00 RPM.

The DeLuxe version had two chromium plated horns, unk rack, wire wheels with fender wells for two spares, d fenders and aprons painted to match.

Studebaker and Rockne sold 43,024 cars for the calendar ar, putting it in 6th position.

This was the Deluxe 1933 Rockne 2-door Sedan, complete with sidemount tires and twin bugle horns. The base price of this car was $640. Rockne used Budd bodies on all but the convertibles this year.

A 1933 Rockne Deluxe Convertible Roadster wears its luggage rack and sidemount tire accessories as standard equipment. This 6-cylinder model came with the regular 70 HP engine at 3200 RPM. It sold for $720.

Rockne's most popular model for 1933 customers was this 6-wheel sidemounted sedan in the Deluxe line. The twin bugle horns and wire wheels were part of the deluxe package available only in this series as standard equipment. This model sold for $680. Rockne production ended in July, 1933.

A prototype of the never to be produced 1934 Rockne. This was a factory mock-up of the Convertible Sedan which was discarded when Studebaker decided that it had already lost too much on its Rockne project.

Roosevelt

Roosevelt offered this 1930 8-cylinder 5-passenger Sedan for $995 in base form. This car was built by Marmon. The Eight was priced close to the average Six of the day.

The Roosevelt was a product of the Nordyke a Marmon Co. with headquarters in Indianapolis, India The Roosevelt was built during 1929 and 1930 and v generally classed as the baby Marmon.

The 1930 models offered an 8-cylinder L-head eng of 201.9 cubic inches. It developed 72 HP at 3200 RP The wheelbase was 112 inches and tire size was 5:00 x inches. A 14-gallon fuel supply was used. Mechani brakes were employed on the Roosevelt as on the lar Marmons.

Four body styles were available with a beginning pr of $995 for a 4-passenger Coupe to $1,095 for 4-passenger Convertible Coupe.

Roosevelt sales were included with the Marmon wh ranked in 19th position. The calendar year sales w 13,262 units. This was the final year of production Roosevelt cars.

For 1930, Roosevelt offered this 2-passenger Standard Coupe as its lowest priced model. It weighed 2,601 lbs. and sold for $965. The fender well equipment was available only at extra cost. The car was rumble seat equipped.

Offered for those who enjoyed both the comforts of a closed coupe and the smartness of a convertible was this 1930 Roosevelt Cabriolet Coupe. It weighed 2,591 lbs. and sold for $1,095. It was offered with either a rumble seat or a trunk.

This Roosevelt 8 Sedan is equipped with all the deluxe accessories of the day. It is shown with wire wheels, side-mount tire equipment, and rear mounted trunk rack. The 8-cylinder engine developed 72 horsepower.

Showing its stamina at a non-stop endurance rally is this 1930 Roosevelt Sedan. It is flashing by the stands at the famous Indianapolis 500 Race Track. The car performed for 440 hours in over 18 days without a single stop except for refueling.

Ruxton

Che Ruxton was first displayed in prototype form in 29. The car came out just as the 1929 crash occurred d everything fell apart for the initial company. Many tomobile companies were to build Ruxton. Some of ese firms were Hupp, Gardner, Kissel and Marmon. oon finally merged with Ruxton since their car was continued in 1929 and the company needed financial p at that moment. The new corporation was referred as New Era Motors with headquarters in New York City. ien production finally got started it was the Moon otor Co. of St. Louis, Mo.

The Ruxton used a Continental 8-cylinder L-head engine 85 HP at 3000 RPM. It was of 268.6 cubic inches. ont wheel drive was employed on all models. A 15- lon fuel supply was used. They used Lockheed hydraulic ikes. The standard wheelbase was 130 inches, but for ecial bodies, 140 inches was used.

The body styles were chiefly a 5-passenger Sedan and adster for 4 passengers. Both sold for $3,195.

Special built cars by Ruxton were: Phaeton, Cabriolet, wn Car, and Limousine.

The manufacturers of Ruxtons were: The Moon Motor r Co. of St. Louis, Mo., where most all cars were built. ssel Motor Car Co. of Hartford, Wis. then built 25 units der a contract with New Era Motors of New York City. Production of Ruxtons actually lasted from June 1930 November of 1930. Approximately 500 cars were oduced. The company took the 31st sales position.

The Ruxton Roadster is shown with top up and rumble seat open. It sold for $3,195. The Continental L-Head 8-cylinder engine developed 85 HP at 3000 RPM. The car was trimmed in Textileather throughout.

Probably one of the more popular body styles displayed on the 1930 Ruxtons was the 4-door Sedans, also selling for $3,195. Front wheel drive was standard equipment on all Ruxton automobiles.

Shown in a rakish fashion is this 1930 Ruxton Roadster with its top in the down position. This example is displayed with the popular Woodlites, common to cars of the Ruxton caliber. Note the large Griffin emblems on the hub caps.

An interior view of the 1930 Ruxton Sedan shows the width of the seats and lavishness of its interiors. Note the mounting of the gear shift lever beside the dashboard controls, and the flat floor due to the front-wheel drive components.

The most impressive of the 1930 Ruxtons had to be this Phaeton, which used a 140-inch wheelbase. Like the Roadster, it also wears a pair of special Woodlites. The parking lights were of the same contour. Note the rear mounted windshield for rear seat passengers. Both windshields could be placed in the down position to give the car an additional feel of speed and lowness to the ground.

Showing off its "owl eyes" in this three-quarter front view is the 1930 Ruxton Sedan. Hydraulic brakes were used on all Ruxton cars.

Scarab

The Scarab was the product of William B. Stout, wl was president of Stout Engineering and also headed tl Society of Automotive Engineers. This car was talked being produced in 1935, but it wasn't until the 19 models started to debut that the experimental Scarab w first seen. The car was to have been built in Dearbor Mich., but Stout was unable to get enough financial he to actually produce the car. As far as is known, only o car actually was produced.

The engine was a V-8 Ford giving 90 HP at 3800 RPl The car was meant to take seven passengers seated in div and easy chairs which could be placed at the owne discretion. Sleeping arrangements could also be provide

The car's suspension was by coil springs and airplane-ty oleo-shocks. The flooring made rear door entrance eas The engine was in the rear, and the radiator grille extend up into the roof to aid in proper cooling.

Stoud had plans for building 100 cars during the year a cost of $5,000 each, but funds didn't come forth. In l advertising, it was claimed that within three years, manufacturers would have followed the Stout design f automobile production.

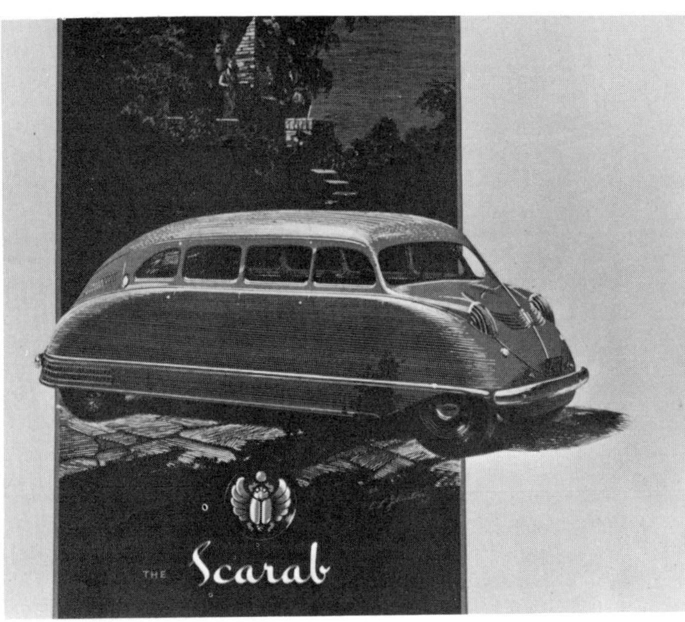

One of the few advertisements brought out by its backer, William B. Stout, shows the 1936 Scarab with estate setting in the background. The Scarab was to have sold for approximately $5,000. Some historians have tried to compare the Scarab with the Sterkenberg, with the insinuation that the Tjaarda car influenced William Stout. Actually, the Scarab was an outgrowth of Stout's proposed Skycar, a novel rear-engine airplane that was supposed to fly as easily as a plane. The Skycar was developed in 1931, but by 1932 the craft had landed, and Stout was busy converting the novel flying car into a car that just looked as if it could fly. By the time the Sterkenberg was released to the public, the Scarab was well under development, and any similarities between the two cars must be chalked up to the coincidence of two automotive geniuses operating on parallel tracks. If any actual vehicles were direct descendents of the Scarab, one would have to be the Gar Wood buses that were produced in 1936 on Ford chassis and were used successfully by the Dearborn Coach Lines for years. Another outgrowth of the Scarab was the Railplane, an ultra-modern self-powered railway car capable of 100-plus MPH speeds.

The 1936 Scarab had a Ford V-8 engine mounted in the rear. Three cars were supposed to have been built. Today, one rests in the storage area of Harrah's Auto Museum in Sparks, Nev., awaiting a complete restoration, and another is in the Detroit Historical Museum. Suspension was by coil springs and airplane-type shock absorbers. It is often claimed that W.B. Stout did not really intend to manufacture the Scarab, but only threatened production in order to scare the automotive industry into adopting some of his inventions.

A rear view of the 1936 Scarab gives evidence of its rear cooling technique with a grille design flowing upward into the roof. Passenger seating could be arranged at the driver's discretion, with divan seating for seven passengers.

Stearns - Knight

The Stearns Knight was produced by an independent anufacturer. The company was the F. B. Stearns Co. ie car was built from 1912 through 1930. The factory adquarters were in Cleveland, Ohio.

The 1930 Stearns Knight cars had 8-cylinder Knight eeve valve engines which developed 127 HP at 3000 PM. The engine displacement was 385 cubic inches. ie fuel supply came from a 24-gallon tank. Mechanical akes were used for the model run. The wheelbases for ese cars were 126 inches and 134 inches in the Series 8-90 and 145 inches in Series J8-90. Both series used 00 x 19-inch tires.

A total of 8 body styles were available ranging from ,500 for a 2-passenger H 8-90 Coupe up to $5,800 for e Series J8-90 Limousine for 7 passengers.

With the depression taking its bites more each day and earns Knight prices staying in the higher bracket, the mpany couldn't cope with it any longer, and at the end 1930 ceased production.

With sales being so low, figures are not available for 30.

A smart-appearing Close-Coupled Sedan for five was this H-8-90 1930 Stearns Knight. The fender wells and wire wheels were available at extra cost. It weighed 5,072 lbs. and sold for $5,500 in standard form.

The 1930 Stearns Knight illustrated was a 7-passenger model. It was available in the 134 and 145-inch chassis. This example happens to be the 134-inch model weighing 5,262 lbs. and selling for $5,600. The same model in Limousine fashion brought $5,800.

This is the 1930 Stearns Knight 5-passenger Coupe, which was available in the "H-8-90" Series. It weighed 5,023 lbs., and sold for $5,500. The wheelbase for this car was 126 inches.

This was considered the best seller of the 1930 Stearns Knight line. Equipped as it is shown, on the 126-inch chassis, it weighed 5,108 lbs. and sold for the same price as all the other body styles in the H-8-90 Series – $5,500. Wire wheels and fender well spares were available at extra cost.

A sporty version of the H-8-90 Stearns Knight. This is the Cabriolet Roadster, available on the 137-inch wheelbase, weighing 4,815 lbs. and selling for $5,500. The deluxe equipment shown included wire wheels, sidemount equipment, sidemounted mirrors, and luggage rack, all at extra cost. The car was equipped with a rumble seat.

Studebaker

The Studebaker was a product of the Studebak Corporation of America. The car had been manufacture as a self-propelled vehicle since 1902. The home factor was in South Bend, Indiana.

Studebaker entered 1930 with three separate series Dictator, Commander, and President. Within the Dictat and Commander Series a 6-cylinder or 8-cylinder engi was available. The President Series offered only the Eigh

The Dictator's engines developed 68 HP in 6-cylind and 70 HP in 8-cylinder form. Both engines had maximum 3200 RPM. These cars had 14-gallon fu supplies like the Commander models. The wheelbase w 115 inches with 5:50 x 19-inch tires as was Commanders.

The Commander in 6-cylinder version developed 75 H at 3000 RPM and displaced 248 cubic inches. A 8-cylinder Commanders used a 250 cubic inch engine 80 HP at 3600 RPM. Their wheelbase was 120 inche The President models used a 115 HP engine of 337 cub inches and turned at 3200 RPM. The fuel supply w from a 16-gallon tank. The Presidents wheelbase was 12 inches on the regular models with 6:00 x 20-inch tire The top of the President line was the same as the regul President except it used 6:50 x 19-inch tires and had 135-inch wheelbase.

Altogether, Studebaker offered 50 models among i three series. Prices ranged from $1,045 for a 2-passeng Dictator 6 Coupe to $2,495 for a President Limousin 7-passenger Sedan.

For the calendar year, Studebaker sold 51,640 car which placed them in 11th sales position.

For 1930, this Studebaker Dictator 8 Club Sedan proved to be a very popular car with the public. It weighed 2,990 lbs. and sold for $1,195. Its running mate, the Dictator 6, was available for $1,085 and only weighed 20 lbs. less than the Eight. Sidemounts and wire wheels were optional at extra cost, as was the trunk and trunk rack.

The 1930 Studebaker President 8 on the 125-inch wheelbase weighed 4,045 lbs. A 5-passenger model, it sold for $1,765. Optional equipment at extra cost included sidemounts, luggage rack, and wire wheel equipment.

A very classic-appearing Studebaker for 1931 is this President State Convertible Victoria, which weighed 4,130 lbs. and sold for $2,050. Full leather interior was standard on this model.

This was Studebaker's Dictator 8 Sedan for 1931. It is equipped with the standard wooden spoke wheels which were losing ground with the public in preference for the modern wire wheels. Basically it was the same offering as the Dictator 6 except for its 8-cylinder engine that developed 81 HP at 3200 RPM. This model as an Eight weighed 3,155 lbs. and sold for $1,150.

931

The 1931 models were offered as a Six and three lines ›f Eights.

The Dictator 6 had a 205 cubic inch engine with a naximum of 70 HP at 3200 RPM. It used a 14-gallon fuel ank. The tire size was 5:25 x 19 and the wheelbase neasured 114 inches.

The Dictator 8 offered the same specifications as the ;ix except that its engine was 221 cubic inches and it leveloped 81 HP at 3200 RPM.

The Commander 8 had a 250 cubic inch engine with 01 HP at 3200 RPM. It used a 17-gallon gasoline tank. 'ire size on this series measured 6:00 x 19 inches. Its vheelbase was 124 inches.

Studebaker's prestige offering for the year was the 'resident 8 which had a 337 cubic inch engine that leveloped 122 HP at 3200 RPM. The fuel tank held a :0½-gallon supply. They used 6:50 x 19-inch tires and :ame on two wheelbases of 130 inches and 136 inches. Aechanical brakes were used throughout the line. Free-vheeling was offered and a synchro-mesh transmission ılso was used on all models.

Studebaker sales for the year placed them in 10th ›osition by selling 48,921 cars.

The 1931 Studebaker Eight State Coupe for four is shown with its optional at extra cost wire wheels and fender well equipment. In base form it weighed 4,200 lbs., came on a 130-inch chassis, and sold for $2,050. The President Eight engine developed 122 horsepower.

This was the 1931 Studebaker Eight President State Victoria for five. It came on the 136-inch wheelbase, weighed 4,275 lbs., and sold for $2,350.

The 1931 Studebaker Eight Four Season's Roadster is shown with the world famous Ab Jenkins at the wheel. The inscription beneath the door states "Free wheeling Studebaker President – World Champion Car." This model weighed 4,130 lbs. and carried a 130-inch wheelbase. The price was $1,950.

Studebaker's most expensive model for 1931 was the President Eight State Limousine on the 136-inch wheelbase chassis, weighing 4,580 lbs. It sold for $2,600. This was a 7-passenger car, available either as a sedan or as a limousine with glass partition.

Studebaker

For 1932 this Studebaker Dictator Eight Sedan came on a 117-inch wheelbase and sold in base form for $1,030. This example was a car put into demonstrator use for the Freeman, Schaus, Freeman Co. dealership of South Bend, Indiana. Note the new 1932 models on the salesfloor in the background. Whitewall tires, sidemounts, wire wheels, twin trumpet horns and luggage rack were all extra equipment.

1932

Studebaker was beginning to be a real eye catcher by 1932, having new bodies with high appeal for the American car buyer. Safety glass was now being used throughout all models as standard equipment. Silent synchro-mesh transmission, free-wheeling, and automatic shock absorbers were standard items in all models.

Cars came in four series this year: A Six beginning at $840, Dictator 8, Commander 8, and President 8. The Six carried an 80 HP engine (3200 RPM) and had a 15-gallon fuel supply. The cars rode on 5:50 x 18-inch tires and had a 117-inch wheelbase.

The Dictator 8 used the same wheelbase, carried the same tire size, reached 3200 RPM in its 8-cylinder engine, but had 5 more horses as an Eight. It also had a 15-gallon tank.

The Commander came with a 101 HP 8-cylinder block (3200 RPM). It used 6:00 x 18-inch tires, a 17-gallon fuel supply, and had mechanical brakes as did all Studebakers. These models had a 125-inch wheelbase.

Top of the line was the President 8, using a 122 HP engine at 3200 RPM. These models used 6:50 x 18-inch tires, had a 20½-gallon fuel capacity, and a 135-inch wheelbase. Altogether, 48 body styles were shown in the 1932 catalogue. The company had the privilege of selling 44,325 Studebaker and Rockne cars for the year, placing them in the Number Six slot.

A well equipped 1932 Studebaker Six Convertible Roadster on the 117-inch chassis. Special equipment on this car includes whitewall tires, special steel molded chromed artillery wheels, twin horns, twin spot lamps, and accessory parking lamps which were not included in the Studebaker Six line. This model sold in base form for $890.

The 1932 Studebaker Commander St. Regis Brougham, displayed on a showroom floor, apparently was a used vehicle, as other non-Studebakers are shown in the background. Note the remains of a painted white sidewall tire. This model when new sold for $1,350. A Regal St. Regis Brougham also was available for $1,445.

Virtually the same car as the 1932 Studebaker Six is this Commander Eight Convertible Coupe which claimed a 101 HP engine and a longer wheelbase of 125 inches. It sold for $1,350. The chromed artillery spoke wheels were a popular Studebaker option.

933

For 1933, with Pierce Arrow no longer under their ontrol, Studebaker came out with four beautiful lines. 'hey had the 117-inch wheelbase Six from $840 to 1,120; the Commander Eight on the same wheelbase for 1,000 to $1,300, the President Eight ranging from $1,325 o $1,650 on a 125-inch wheelbase, and the new Speedway resident Eight, formerly known as the President Eight, vhich sold for $1,625 to $2,040 on a 135-inch wheelbase.

All of these cars were equipped with Bendix vacuum-ype power-operated brakes which were mechanical. Also, he Stromberg automatic choke was used on all models, s were automatic shock absorbers, ball bearing shackles, nd flexible metal springs. Lubrication points were lessened o only four places, which required attention only every ,500 miles.

In the horsepower race, the Studebaker 6 gave 85 at 200 RPM. The Commander 8 had 100 at 3800 RPM; 'resident 8 had 110 at 3600 RPM, and the Speedway 'resident 8 came out with 132 HP at 3400 RPM.

Tire sizes were 5:50 x 17 for the Six, 6:00 x 17 for the 'ommander, 6:50 x 17 for the President, and 7:00 x 17 or the top of the line Speedway President Series.

Fuel tanks on the Six and Commander 8 were 14 allons. While the President 8 used a 17½-gallon tank, the peedway President had a 20½-gallon tank. A total of 8 models were available among these four series. tudebaker held Sixth Position, with Rockne sales helping o move 43,024 cars.

A Studebaker Commander Eight Coupe, nicely equipped with full decor, sold for $1,350. In Regal fashion it brought an additional $90 to the price with a fancier interior package. The golf bag door was standard on the rumble seat equipped coupes.

Studebaker offered this President Eight Convertible Sedan in both Convertible Sedan and State Convertible Sedan models. Both rode on the 135-inch chassis. The Convertible Sedan sold for $1,820 and the State model was $1,925. Note the parking lamps are of the same contour as the headlamps.

Studebaker's most expensive car for 1932 was the 7-passenger President Eight State Limousine which sold for $1,995. It used a 135-inch wheelbase and employed the 8-cylinder engine which developed 122 HP at 3200 RPM.

In 1933, Studebaker offered this Dictator 6 Convertible Sedan on the 117-inch wheelbase for $1,015 in base form. This example is equipped with the optional at extra cost sidemounts which most all cars in this body style were equipped with. Also, note the accessory spot light and the chrome spoke wheels.

Studebaker

This 1933 Studebaker 5-Window Coupe is on the 117-inch Commander Eight chassis. This was a rumble seat version that sold for $1,050 and weighed 3,250 lbs. Note the storage facility on the right quarter panel and the two step plates on the right rear fender.

1934

In 1934, Studebaker offered the public three series A Dictator Six with 88 HP at 3600 RPM, the Commande Eight with 103 HP at 4000 RPM, and the President Eigh delivering 110 HP at 3600 RPM. Mechanical features were an aluminum head with a 6.3:1 compression ratio aluminum pistons, oil filter, crankcase ventilating system automatic manifold heat control, automatic choke, and water thermostat. The Eights were equipped with Bendix brakes and the Six used Steeldraulic brakes. Both systems were mechanical.

All 6-cylinder models rode on 5:50 x 17-inch tires leaving the 6:00 x 17s to the Commanders, and 6:50 x 17 to the Presidents. Free-wheeling, a Warner unit, was stil available. Fuel supplies varied: The Dictators used a 14½-gallon tank, Commanders and Presidents used 17½ gallon fuel supplies.

The Dictator had a 114-inch wheelbase; the Commande came on a 119-inch chassis, and the President rode on a 123-inch wheelbase.

Paul G. Hoffman, the new president, helped give the shot in the arm that the company needed. Six million dollars were made available by interested bankers a Hoffman's request, and this saw the firm come out of the depression quite nicely.

Lowest priced car this year was the Dictator 6 Rega Coupe for $725. Prices continued upward to $1,145 fo the Regal Sedan in the President line. A total of 28 model were available.

A total of 46,103 cars were sold, placing Studebake in 9th Position for the calendar year.

This is the 1933 Studebaker President St. Regis Brougham on the 125-inch wheelbase. It sold for $1,385. This example weighed 3,660 lbs. Note that only one tail lamp was used on this model. The built-in trunk was standard equipment.

A 1933 Studebaker Speedway President Eight State Sedan. The 7-passenger car on a 135-inch wheelbase, sold for $1,940. Only the Limousine topped this model in price at $2,040. Sidemount tires were optional.

The 1933 Studebaker Speedway President Eight State Roadster, on the 135-inch wheelbase, sold for $1,790. This was a Studebaker Rockne dealer driveaway campaign from the South Bend factory. Rocknes follow the Speedway Roadster. The Rockne immediately behind the Roadster is being towed by the Studebaker, and wears a heavy shield for protection against flying gravel.

Studebaker offered this special sedan in all three series for 1934 and referred to it as the Regal Land Cruiser Sedan. This example is painted in a special two-tone paint that was used in the Dictator Series. It sold for $745.

Studebaker's lowest priced Roadster for 1934 was this Dictator Six for 4 passengers. It developed 88 HP at 3600 RPM. A price of $695 was charged for this model.

A 1934 Studebaker Commander Eight Regal Land Cruiser Sedan came with fender skirts and sidemounted tires as standard equipment. It sold for $945 and in the President line sold for $1,145, which was the most expensive Studebaker for the year. Note the unusual rear windows which were very similar to the Pierce Silver Arrow, which had been associated with Studebaker. For the era, this was a very advanced styled car.

Studebaker's lowest priced sedan for 1934 was this 6-cylinder Dictator which weighed 2,900 lbs. and sold for $695 in base form. Studebaker's totally new styling is very evident in this photo.

Appearing almost the same as the Dictator was this 1934 Commander on a 119-inch chassis. It used the 8-cylinder engine developing 103 HP at 4000 RPM. The sidemount tires were optional equipment at extra cost on this Roadster. It sold for $895. Both this and the Dictator models used a rumble seat for extra passenger space.

The 1935 Studebaker Dictator Custom Sedan came on a 114-inch wheelbase and continued to use the 6-cylinder engine which developed 88 HP at 3600 RPM. The lines were quite similar to the 1934 cars, only rounded out somewhat. The Dictator did not offer the trumpet horns mounted under the headlamps as did the President.

The 1935 Studebaker Eight President Custom Sedan came on a 123-inch wheelbase and sold for $1,330. It was the most popular model in the President line. The built-in trunk was standard equipment, as was the covered rear spare.

Described as a business model, this 1936 Studebaker St. Regis Brougham sold well to business firms that required economical transportation in their fleets. It helped Studebaker in the sales race for the year to receive the 9th Position. Sidemounts were a rare accessory. The rear seat of this model could be quickly removed so that the entire rear area could be used to carry packages or sample cases.

A dealer display of 1936 Studebakers shows the Dictator Business Coupe in the foreground with its unusual rear windows, which Studebaker used on the coupes in 1936-1937. It sold for $695. To the left is a 1936 Studebaker truck and to the right is a Dictator Sedan. Studebaker was beginning to reintroduce two-tone paints on many of the models at this time. It proved successful, too.

1935

In 1935, the company brought out three new models the Dictator, Commander, and President body typ These cars featured new hydraulic brakes, independen sprung front wheels, and more plush interiors. Overdr was standard on the President as the leading feature sales. The grille treatment was of a long narrow des extending nearly to the windshield. The new mod headlamps were well in keeping with the streamlir bodies. Each series employed deeply skirted fend

The Dictator Six came with an 88 HP engine at 36 RPM. The 114-inch wheelbase car used 6:00 x 16-ir tires and a 14½-gallon fuel tank. Dictator Sixes came 13 body styles ranging from a 3-passenger Coupe $695 to the Dictator Land Cruiser for $885.

The Commander models used a 107 HP engine 3800 RPM. These cars rode on a 119-inch chassis us 6:50 x 16-inch tires, and had the same fuel supply as Dictators. The 8-cylinder Commander came in 11 bo types starting with the 3-passenger Regal Coupe for $9 and ending with the Commander 8 Land Cruiser Sec for $1,085.

The President models, all being 8-cylinder cars, ca with a 110 HP engine at 3600 RPM. They used a 12 inch wheelbase with a tire size of 7:00 x 16. All Preside used a 17½-gallon gasoline tank. There were also 11 mod in the President line beginning with a 3-passenger Cou for $1,245 ranging to the Regal Berline Sedan for $1,4

Studebaker lost two places in sales this year going do to 11th by selling 49,062 cars for the calendar r

A rare model even when new was the 1935 Studebaker President Eight Regal Roadster which sold for $1,325. Full leather was standard equipment for the open models in this series. Actually, since this model had roll-up windows, it should be called a convertible, not a roadster.

Studebaker

36

'or 1936, Studebaker brought out two models, the :tator Six and President Eight with attractive new lines. e exterior of both models showed a beautiful die-cast rome grille, divided windshield, and a nicely appointed ıvered hood. The Coupes came with an unusual "Bat-ıg" style rear window. Additional equipment for the :tator, at extra cost, included overdrive with free-eeling, Startix, independently sprung front wheels, and hair upholstery. The President also came with overdrive optional equipment. Additional features, available arately or as a group, included extra tail lamp, dual rns, banjo steering wheel, cigar lighter, second sun visor, l full chrome wheel covers.

'he Dictator used a 90 HP engine at 3400 RPM while sidents came with 115 HP at the same RPM. Tire size s 6:00 x 16 for a Dictator and 6:50 x 16 optional on a sident. The wheelbase was 116 inches for a Six and 5 inches in the Eight. Fuel capacity was an 18-gallon ık for each series. Both series used hydraulic brakes. ven models were available in each series, with the :tator Six Coupe selling for $695. A President Touring ınk Sedan went for $1,065.

tudebaker received Ninth Place in sales for the year, :h 85,026 sales.

Posed in front of the Studebaker factory in South Bend is this handsome 1936 Studebaker President Eight Coupe, selling for $945. The optional equipment wasn't included in the base price. Note the unusual "wig-wag" stop light mounted on the rear bumper.

The 1937 Studebaker St. Regis Custom Sedan for 6-passengers offered just a facelifting to already handsome looking cars from the 1936 line. This model sold for $745.

The most popular 1936 Studebaker in the President Eight line was this 6-passenger Touring Sedan which sold for $1,065 in base form. The sidemount tire equipment, metal covers, and full wheel discs were optional at extra cost.

This is the 1936 Studebaker President Eight 2-door Sedan on the 125-inch wheelbase. Its base price was $1,015. It didn't sell as well as the Dictator in the same body style. Again, two-tone paint appears as the fashion for the 1936 models.

The 1937 Studebaker St. Regis Touring Sedan was available in both Dictator and President models. This happens to be the Dictator model which sold for $20 more than the St. Regis Custom Sedan at $765. It also sold far better than the fastback model. Sidemount equipment was a rare accessory for this model.

Studebaker

1937

Studebaker came into 1937 offering two series of cars the Dictator Six with seven models, and the Presider Eight, offering six in the line. Prices ran between $66 for the Dictator Business Coupe for 3 passengers ar $1,065 for a President Eight Cruising Sedan.

Since Studebaker retooled for the 1936 car, the 193 models just received a little streamlined face-liftin Appearancewise, the grille did get a more pointed effe with side louvers extending backward almost to the cow Sound deadening material was used throughout the enti line which helped to keep road noises and engine vibratio from entering the car.

The Dictators used a 90 HP engine at 3400 RPM whi the President Eights had a 115 HP engine at 3600 RPM The Hill Holder option was available in both series, ar 6:00 x 16-inch tires were used on the Dictators whi 6:60 x 16s were employed on the President Eights. A fu supply of 18 gallons was used for both cars. The Dictat wheelbase was 116 inches and the President had 1 inches for its chassis.

Studebaker took the Thirteenth position for the ye by selling only 80,993 cars from its South Bend factor

A well designed coupe was the 1937 Studebaker President which had seating for three or five passengers. This is the rumble seat model as the fender assist pad signifies. It sold for $995. The three-passenger version was available for $965. It offered tremendous trunk space.

A look down on the 1937 Studebaker President Eight Custom Sedan that sold for $1,045. An alligator hood was employed for all 1937 Studebakers, which opened by a twist of the hood ornament. Note the lack of bumper guards which were still classed as an accessory even on President models.

How many of these were ever built? This is a very rare 1937 Studebaker President Eight Touring Cruising Sedan with all the trimmings from fender parking lamps to the rare sun-roof top. It sold in base form for $1,065. Studebaker's sun-roof predated G.M.'s pneumonia hole by two years.

New for 1938 was this Studebaker body, which was offered in three series: the Studebaker Six, the return of the Commander, and the President Eight. This example was the 6-passenger Club Sedan which sold for $933. Note the rounded headlamps which differed from the Commander and President.

This is the 1938 Studebaker Six Cruising Sedan for 6 passengers. It now rode on a 116½-inch wheelbase. The horsepower remained at 90 at 3400 RPM. It was Studebaker's lowest priced sedan for the year, selling at $943.

38

The last Studebaker Convertible Sedan ever to be built was in 1938. In fact, Studebaker built no open cars again until 1947. This body style was available in both Commander and President Series. This example was the President, the most expensive body style available for the year, selling at $1,385.

For 1938, Studebaker underwent another complete body ange, coming out with a very stylish car. It offered three ies known as the Studebaker Six which was minus all luxe trim, the Commander Six and the President Eight. Appearance of the Studebaker Six and Commander re quite similar except for one noticeable feature – ich consisted of the headlamps. On the Studebaker Six ey were just ordinary round lamps placed on top of the ıder catwalks, while Commanders shared their design th Presidents of an oblong shaped lamp tapering to a ınded back.

The Studebaker Six and Commander increased their eelbase ½-inch, making it 116½ inches. The President ed a 122-inch wheelbase.

The engines in the 6-cylinder cars developed 90 HP at 00 RPM. These models rode on 6:00 x 16-inch tires. e famous Hill Holder was made available at extra cost all Studebaker Six models, but was standard on Comınder and Presidents. The President came with five less rsepower now, using a 110 HP 8-cylinder engine at 00 RPM. These models used 6:50 x 16-inch tires or)0 x 16 optional at extra cost. All three series used 18-lon fuel tanks.

Twelve models were available ranging in price from a Coupe for 3 passengers at $843 up to the President ht Convertible Sedan for $1,385. This was the last year ıdebaker built a convertible until 1947.

Sales for the year placed the company in Tenth place h 46,207 units.

Studebaker offered more accessories than most manuturers at this particular time.

A 1938 Studebaker Commander Coupe for 3 passengers sold for $912. The 5-passenger coupe was not available this year, leaving this to the Club Sedan Model. Note the headlamp differences between this model and the Studebaker Six.

A 1939 mid-season offering which helped Studebaker out in sales was this economical Champion Club Sedan which rode on a 110-inch wheelbase and sold for $700. It developed 78 HP at 4000 RPM. The Champions proved to be the Studebaker's most successful Series in the early 1940s.

Getting ready to depart for the Gilmore Economy Run in 1939 is this Studebaker Champion Deluxe Cruising Sedan which sold for $800. This model weighed 2,375 lbs., which was one of the factors enabling Studebaker to be a continual winner in these yearly events.

Studebaker

A rare model is this 1939 Studebaker Commander Station Wagon with body by the Hercules Body Co. Very few of these were turned out in 1939. Studebaker decided to abandon the station wagon trade until 1954 with the Conestoga.

1939

Studebaker's big news, which came in the middle of th year, was the announcement of the "All New Car" whic would help them out considerably in sales for sever years. The car was known as the Champion and was offere in six models ranging from the $660 Business Coupe t the $800 DeLuxe Cruising Sedan. All Champions offere excellent gasoline mileage and won the Gilmore Econom Run. It was one of the overall winners in the class fc several years. The Champion used a 15-gallon fuel tanl offered a 110-inch wheelbase using 5:50 x 16-inch tire

The Commanders rode on 116½-inch wheelbases usin a 6-cylinder 90 HP engine at 3400 RPM. They use 6:00 x 16-inch tires and optional 6:25 x 16s were availabl This series, like the President Eight, used an 18-gallo fuel supply.

All Presidents used the 110 HP 8-cylinder engine at 360 RPM. The tire size for this series was 6:50 x 16. I wheelbase was 122 inches.

For the year, Studebaker offered fifteen models, rangin from the already mentioned $660 Champion to th President Cruising Sedan for $1,110.

Some of Studebaker's mechanical changes for 193 included a new fresh air heating and ventilating syste which was built into the chassis under the driver's sea a new overdrive which allowed the driver to instantl shift to direct drive, and the column gearshift offered i all three series as standard equipment.

Studebaker placed in 8th position and sold 106,47 cars for the 1939 calendar run.

Rarely seen on 1939 Studebakers were sidemount spares. This model is the President Eight Cruising Sedan which weighed 3,440 lbs. and in base form sold for $1,110. It apparently was an early press publication photo, as the front bumper guards and Studebaker bumper nameplate were not ready from the tool and die department.

This is the 1939 Studebaker President Eight Club Sedan which weighed 3,390 lbs. It used the 122-inch chassis and had a price tag of $1,100. This example is equipped with accessory wheel trim rings and center chrome covered discs. Note the interesting and unusual rear quarter window design.

For 1940, the Studebaker Champion offered the lower priced Custom Series and this Deluxe Sedan. Two-tone paint was optional at a slight extra cost. The Deluxe weighed 2,415 lbs. and was offered for $785. The Custom was available for $45 less at $740.

940

For 1940, Studebaker made a nice face-lifting on a body :yle that was two years old for the Commander and resident. The Champion was introduced in March of 1939 nd thus had very few changes.

The Champion continued to offer its advertising claim f last year. That was economy! Having won its class in the ilmore Economy Run and averaging 27¼ MPG in making round trip across the country at an average speed of 0 MPG really helped to sell these little cars. They had a P rating of 78 at 4000 RPM and a cubic inch displace-ent of 164.3 in the 6-cylinder engine. The fuel tank eld 15 gallons. The Champion tire size was 5:50 x 16 ches. They used a 110-inch chassis.

The Commander came with a 6-cylinder engine of 226 ıbic inches developing 90 HP at 3400 RPM. They used an 8-gallon fuel tank. The tire size on Commanders was :25 x 15 inches. Its wheelbase measured 116½ inches.

The President offered an 8-cylinder engine of 250.4 ıbic inches developing 110 HP at 3600 RPM. It also had n 18-gallon fuel supply. The Presidents rode on 6:50 x 16-ch tires and had a wheelbase of 122 inches.

Studebaker offered a total of 15 models ranging in price om the Champion Custom Coupe for $660 as a 3-assenger Coupe to $1,095 for the President Sedan. For ie calendar year Studebaker sold 117,091 cars placing iem in 8th position.

A young star on the road up, the late Judy Garland poses by her new 1940 Studebaker Champion Deluxe Coupe. This car weighed 2,360 lbs. and sold for $740.

The 1940 Studebaker President Eight Sedan is being photographed at Hoover Dam. This was the most expensive regular production model for the year. It weighed 3,420 lbs. an dsold for $1,095 in base form. In this era, Hoover Dam was still known as Boulder Dam.

Studebaker dealers generally had one car wrapped up on their display floor during December, as a typical Christmas gift for the family. This was an advertising promotion for many years. This was an example in December of 1939, with this 1940 President Eight.

The 1940 Studebaker President Eight Coupe used the 122-inch wheelbase and weighed 3,055 lbs. Its base price at South Bend, Ind., was $1,025. A longer wheelbase and a special mesh grille pattern were about the only immediate differences between it and the Commander.

Studebaker

Studebaker had its share of the custom body trade, too, as this example shows. It is one beautiful 1940 President Eight done as a special Convertible Sedan with body by Derham. In all probability it was a one-off model since Studebaker discontinued open models two years before. Note the special windwing deflectors to aid rear seat passengers.

This sharp looking 1941 Studebaker Champion Deluxe Town Coupe for 5 passengers is all decked out with an array of factory approved accessories. The fender skirts were rarely seen on the Champions. The deluxe models offered the fashionable sweep spear two-tone paint beginning at the hood and phasing out at the rear. This model weighed 2,440 lbs. and sold for $790. A three-passenger model also was available weighing 2,340 lbs. and selling for $755.

Another Studebaker Christmas publicity stunt shows this 1941 Commander Sedan ready for a family. It's the 4-door Deluxe Two-Tone Land Cruiser model that weighed 3,150 lbs. and sold for $1,095. The belt line sweep spear was standard on this model.

A nice family car for those with small children was this 1940 Studebaker Commander Club Sedan. It weighed 3,135 lbs. and sold for $925. Note the special paint trim around the window reveals, which was optional.

Studebaker offered this 1941 Skyway Sedan Coupe in both the Commander and President line. This example is on the President's 124-inch wheelbase. It weighed 3,440 lbs. and sold for $1,185. Note this model is well equipped with factory accessories like fender skirts, white sidewall tires, full wheel decor, and the rare fender mounted parking directional lamps. It was only available with a one-piece windshield.

One of the most popular 1941 Studebakers turned out to be this Custom Deluxe Champion Club Sedan which weighed 2,430 lbs. and sold for $760. The two-tone paint was optional at a slight extra cost, as were the whitewall tires.

Studebaker

•41

For 1941, Studebaker again offered the Champion, ommander, and President. Each line was larger than its edecessor. A new body type, the Land Cruiser, designed · Raymond Loewy was available in the Commander and esident Series. It was a 4-door Sedan minus rear quarter ndows and had rear doors opening from the reverse as udebaker did in 1934 and 1935 on a similar model lled the Land Cruiser.

The Champion came with a larger 6-cylinder engine of '0 cubic inches that developed 80 HP at 4000 RPM. The ommander had a 6-cylinder engine of 226 cubic inches at developed 94 HP at 3600 RPM. The President 8 had a ;0 cubic inch engine which developed 117 HP at 4000 PM. The Champion models used a 15-gallon fuel tank hile the Commander and Presidents had 18-gallon pplies.

The Champion wheelbase was 110 inches. Commanders me on a 119-inch chassis, and the Presidents rode on a !4½-inch wheelbase. Champions used 5:50 x 16-inch es and Presidents had 7:00 x 16-inch tires. Commanders d 6:25 x 16s.

A variety of colors were supplied both in one and two- ne treatments with harmonizing upholstery combi- tions. A choice of three kinds of upholstery in eight lors were available in the Champion line. A similar array as found in the other two series. Studebaker's climatizer underseat heater obtained the fresh air out of the left wl ventilator by a duct which ran under the floor.

A total of 27 models had prices ranging from $690 for Champion Custom 3-passenger Coupe to $1,235 for the esident Skyway Land Cruiser 4-door Sedan. The com- ny placed in 9th position from the sale of 119,325 cars r the calendar year.

This was the 1941 Studebaker President Custom Land Cruiser which weighed 3,160 lbs. and sold for $1,030. This model is equipped with the factory fender skirts, and front chrome ornaments which were available at extra cost.

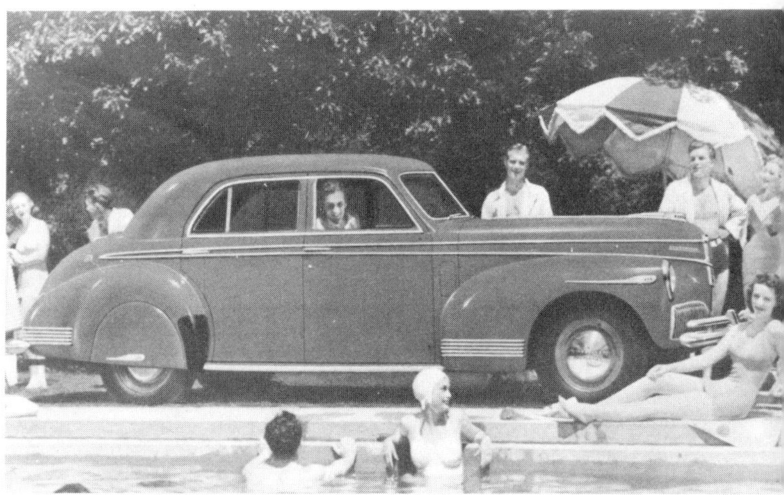

Studebaker's prestige President for 1941 was this Skyway Land Cruiser model which weighed 3,520 lbs. and had a price of $1,235, making it the most expensive model for the year.

Now entering its fourth year of production was this 1942 Studebaker Champion Custom Cruising Sedan. It still used the 110-inch chassis, weighed 2,520 lbs., and sold for $845. In addition to this model was the Deluxe Cruising Sedan for $880. Both models were in high demand with war cries just around the corner.

This was the lowest priced Studebaker for 1942. It was the Custom Coupe, available only as a 3-passenger model. It weighed 2,420 lbs. and sold for $785.

Studebaker

1942

The 1942 models offered an automatic transmissio with the fluid coupling and called it Turbo-matic. It wa available on the Commander and President models only Very few of these ever got beyond the factory doors. Wit the shortage of supplies, all extra equipment was delete in favor of its being used for defense purposes. The tran mission consisted of the coupling, an automatic vacuu operated clutch, and a conventional three-speed tran mission with kick down overdrive. In the new syste the clutch pedal was eliminated and shifting was co siderably reduced. The positions of the gear selector we conventional, however. Second was called the Traffi Range and high known as the Cruising Range. After th car exceeded 15 MPH the transmission shifted into ove drive. If the accelerator pedal was pressed all the wa down, it would be returned to direct drive.

Mechanically, all three series were pretty much th same as last year. The Champion had a 170 cubic inc 6-cylinder engine that developed 80 HP at 4000 RPM. Th Commander had a 226 cubic inch displacement, 94 H 6-cylinder engine at 3600 RPM. The President had a 8-cylinder engine of 250 cubic inches that developed 11 HP at 4000 RPM. The fuel supply of the Champion was 15-gallon tank and the other two series used 18-gallo supplies.

All Champions continued to use 5:50 x 16-inch tire the Commander had 6:25 x 16-inch tires; and th President used 7:00 x 15-inch tires. The wheelbases we 110 inches on the Champion, 119 inches for the Com mander, and 124 inches on the President.

The Studebakers were priced from $785 for the Champ ion 3-passenger Coupe to $1,340 for a President Skywa Land Cruiser Sedan. A total of 26 models were availabl in the three series. All were referred to as Coupes an Sedans in Custom and DeLuxe version.

For the calendar year, Studebaker took the 8th seat b selling 9,285 cars.

Studebaker's most expensive model for 1942 was this Skyway Land Cruiser 4-door Sedan. It weighed 3,540 lbs. and sold for $1,340. Very few were produced as the factory preferred selling the economical Champion. With the gasoline cries being heard, the public also preferred the Champion.

A 1942 Studebaker Commander Deluxe Land Cruiser waits for its train passengers at the Pomona, Cal. depot. This model weighed 3,305 lbs. and sold for $1,175. Whitewall tires were seen on very few actual cars due to war supply shortages. On this model, they would have been an extra-cost option.

All geared up for things to come for the next four years was the B-17 bomber in the background. The 1942 Studebaker President Eight Deluxe style Sedan-Coupe sported a 117 HP engine at 4000 RPM. This model weighed 3,540 lbs. and sold for $1,305.

A popular model for those who enjoyed a sporty looking car was this 1942 Studebaker Commander Skyway Sedan-Coupe. It offered more chrome and stainless than the regular Sedan-Coupe until all bright work was brought to a halt in February of 1942. This example weighed 3,200 lbs. and sold for $1,055. Note the one-piece windshield which the regular line did not have. White sidewall tires were standard on this model until available supplies ran out.

Stutz

The Stutz was a product of the Stutz Motor Car Co. ith headquarters in Indianapolis. The car was built from)13 until 1935.

The 1930 Stutz came with an 8-cylinder overhead valve igine developing 113 HP at 3300 RPM. The cubic inch splacement was 322 inches. The 1930 models were hold-ers at the time from 1929. Stutz was like most other dependent auto manufacturers at this time just waiting see which way the wind was going to blow for them the bottom of the depression.

These cars used 6:50 x 20-inch tires. The wheelbase easured 134½ and 145 inches. All models used Lockheed ydraulic brakes. The fuel capacity was a 20-gallon tank. total of 30 models were displayed in dealer showrooms ith prices ranging from $2,775 for a 5-passenger Coupe $6,985 for the transcontinental Town Car.

Stutz production and sales were so low among its 30 yles that figures were not available.

The people at Stutz claimed this 1930 Monte Carlo was "Strictly European in Every Detail." Actually, this body style was classed as a close coupled five-passenger sedan that came on the 145-inch wheelbase. It sold for $4,495. The body, by Wegmann, was constructed of fabric over a wooden frame.

Stutz brought out this vehicle late in 1929, but it was basically referred to as a 1930 model. It used the 8-cylinder overhead valve engine developing 113 HP at 3300 RPM. This model was photographed at an antique car gathering on a slushy, muddy day, when it definitely should have been indoors.

Stutz introduced this 1930 Torpedo Speedster on the 134½-inch wheelbase. It came with a four-speed transmission, worm drive, vacuum operated hydraulic brakes and a device called "NO BACK" which prevented the car rolling backward. It sold in base form for $3,245. The bad feature of worm drive was that a balky car could not be towed to a start.

In 1930, Stutz presented this new Versailles, which was a five-passenger sedan with a European flow to its lines. It came on the 134½-inch wheelbase and sold for $3,945. Stutz referred to its line of Wegmann bodied cars as its "Chateau Models."

On display for the 1930 New York Salon showing was the Stutz Dual-Cowl Phaeton. Both front and tonneau windshield have been lowered to give a rakish appearance to the sporty model. It came on the 134½-inch chassis and brought a price of $3,945.

Stutz

A late 1930 Stutz that was registered as a 1931 model was this Cabriolet Coupe. It came on the 134½-inch wheelbase and sold for $3,595. Note the Vogue Tyres with the red flags in the white sidewall. Stutz claimed up to 115 MPH top speed for some of its models.

1931

For 1931, Stutz entered the market with only a f refinements from the 1930 cars. The Series LAA, whi was a 6-cylinder car, actually entered the market in l 1930. Some refer to it as a 1930 but actually it was a 19 model which Stutz hoped would help pull them out of t depression. It used a 241.5 cubic inch engine developi 85 HP at 3150 RPM. Its fuel supply was an 18-gallon ta The tire size was 6:00 x 19 and its wheelbase was 12 inches. It was offered in 7 body styles.

In addition to this car were the MA and MB Ser which were practically the same offerings as in 1930. Th used the 322 cubic inch 8-cylinder engine which develop 113 HP at 3300 RPM. The fuel supply was a 20-gall tank. The tire size was 6:50 x 20 inches. The wheelb on the MA and MB models was the same as last ye 134½ and 145 inches.

The prices ranged from $1,995 for a Stutz LAA Cou for five to $7,495 for the 7-passenger Transcontinen Town Car.

Stutz ranked among the miscellaneous cars for the ye as sales were very low.

This 1931 Stutz Series MB Dual-Cowl Phaeton has both the top up and its tonneau cover over the rear compartment. It appeared only on the 145-inch wheelbase and sold for $4,495.

1932

Stutz cars came equipped with custom bodies fro Le Baron, Weymann, Waterhouse, Rollston, Brunn, a Fleetwood.

Prices began in the $1,600 class for a 6-cylinder Cou or Sedan, referred to as Model LAA. These cars carri an 85 HP engine developing 3150 RPM. This series w mounted on a 127½-inch wheelbase, had 6:00 x 19-in tires, and a fuel capacity of 18 gallons.

Second in the series came the SV-16 selling from $2,6 to over $1,000. These were 8-cylinder units developi 113 HP at 3300 RPM. This series used 6:50 x 20-in tires and a 20-gallon fuel supply. Braking was by Lockhe hydraulic. Free-wheeling wasn't available in 1932 for Stu

The DV-32 used a powerplant of 156 HP at 3900 RP Prices started at $3,995 for a 5-passenger Sedan. T DV-32 Bearcat was the only one in this series to carry 116-inch wheelbase. All others used the same two whe bases as the SV-16 – 134 or 145 inches, depending body style. Tire size of the DV-32 was 7:00 x 2

The SV designation stood for Single Valve while t DV meant Dual Valve. Altogether 69 models were list from the LAA to SV-16 and DV-32. Being in limit production, sales figures were not available.

The most expensive 1931 Stutz was the Transformable Town Car with a Fleetwood body. It offered seating for seven passengers on a 145-inch chassis and sold for $7,495. Needless to say very few were sold.

33

This year all body work was done by Le Baron and eymann.

For the year, Stutz made many improvements in its gle and dual valve Eights. These included automatic oke, vacuum-operated clutch control, thermostatically ntrolled hood doors, thermostatically controlled shock sorbers, 3-speed synchro-mesh transmission with a silent cond gear, push button starter, trumpet horns, white ewall tires, and drop center rims. Each of these items re classed as standard equipment.

The prices for the Stutz LLA Six were $1,895 to $2,185 r the Cabriolet Coupe. Five models were available on a 7½-inch wheelbase. At 3100 RPM the engine produced HP. Tire size was 6:00 x 19. It had a fuel supply of gallons.

The SV-16 and DV-32 each carried a 20-gallon supply. e SV-16 used a 113 HP engine at 3300 RPM while the V-32 developed 156 HP at 3900 RPM. These models th used 7:00 x 18-inch tires. These cars all used Lock-ed hydraulic brakes. The SV-16 prices began at $2,695 r a 5-passenger Coupe and rose to $5,895 for the onte Carlo. The DV-32s began at $700 higher and went the same level for each model in the lineup. Fewer odels in the complete line for Stutz were available during 33; still, a total of 55 models were available.

Production was so low, figures weren't available.

For 1931, Stutz did continue a little business abroad. This lower priced "LLA" Series was marketed in England, but only a few buyers were present. The car featured its 4-speed transmission, triplex safety glass, and Zeiss headlamps.

Stutz showed this 1932 Dual Valve Versailles with a Weymann body at its New York Salon in January of 1932. This elegant classic came on a 134½-inch wheelbase, weighed 4,318 lbs. and sold for $4,395. The body was aluminum paneled.

The 1932 Stutz Single Valve 16 7-passenger Sedan Limousine came only on the 145-inch wheelbase. This example weighed 5,275 lbs. and sold for $4,995. The body builder was Le Baron. Note the courtesy lamp above the running board which was common on classics of that era.

This was the 1932 Stutz Prince of Wales Brougham Limousine by Le Baron. It used the 145-inch chassis, weighed 5,215 lbs. and sold for $6,245. The rear quarter was collapsible.

The return in 1932 of the Stutz Bearcat didn't hurt the image at all, even though the buyers weren't there. This D.V. 21 (Dual Valve) Bearcat Speedster came on a 116-inch wheelbase and had a price tag affixed to it for $5,895. The car was guaranteed to do 100 MPH, while the dealers would quickly admit that could far exceed that mark.

Looking just like its 1932 counterpart, this was the 1933 version of the Stutz D.V. 32 Bearcat Speedster. It sold for $700 more than the Single Valve 16 Speedster at $5,795, which was a $100 reduction over the previous year. All Speedsters were guaranteed to have been driven at over 100 MPH by factory personnel before being released to a dealer.

1934

The LLA Series was discontinued and Stutz made o the SV-16 and DV-32. Actually, the only change these two series over 1933 was the gear ratio going fr 4:50 for 1933 to 4:75 in the 1934 cars. Both SV-16 a DV-32 used a 20-gallon fuel tank.

Horsepower on the SV models was 113 at 3300 RP The DV-32 gave 156 HP at 3900 RPM. Both series us 7:00 x 18-inch tires. Wheelbases were 134½ and 1 inches. All cars carried Lockheed hydraulic brakes.

The price of a SV model began at $2,695 as a passenger Coupe. In Monte Carlo form it cost $5,8 A Dual Valve model cost an additional $700 in each mo Many body styles that were available in 1933 no lon were shown. A total of 28 models were listed.

Production was so low, figures weren't available.

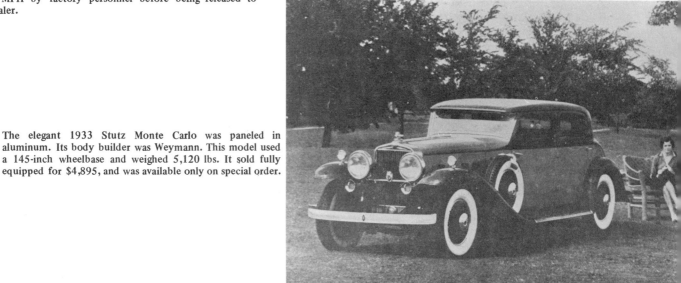

The elegant 1933 Stutz Monte Carlo was paneled in aluminum. Its body builder was Weymann. This model used a 145-inch wheelbase and weighed 5,120 lbs. It sold fully equipped for $4,895, and was available only on special order.

This was a 1933 Stutz Le Baron 6-passenger Sedan known as Model 64. It used the 145-inch wheelbase and weighed 5,346 lbs. It sold for $3,410. Also, using the same chassis was the 7-passenger Limousine, Model 65, which weighed 5,520 lbs. and sold for $3,460.

Brunn did not do very many bodies for Stutz, but this example was a very limited run. It was known as a Patrician Coupe, which was available during the 1932 to the 1935 closing days. Full chrome wheel covers add much style to this handsome vehicle.

35

roducing fewer than 700 cars during the depression, company was finally brought to a close. The few cars ich were built were exactly the same as 1933 and 1934 dels in SV-16 and DV-32 form.

Horsepower was rated at 113 at 3300 RPM in the SV dels and at 156 HP for the DV-32s. 7:00 x 18-inch s were used in both models, with Lockheed hydraulic kes as regular equipment. The fuel supply consisted of 20-gallon tank, on both the 134½ or the 145-inch eelbased cars.

As it was said of H. C. Stutz himself, he made use of rything, never being wasteful. If a part could be made work from a left over year, it was employed for the xt year's cars until the parts were finished. When he d, it was stated "He wore his shoes out evenly." en though Stutz was not with the company after 1919, car that carried his name until 1935 could have the ne note apply to it – "It wore its shoes out evenly, too."

Labeled as a 1934 model, this Stutz 5-passenger Convertible Sedan was cataloged from 1932 to 1935. This was known as Type 42 on the 145-inch wheelbase, which weighed 5,386 lbs. and sold for $3,710.

This 1935 Stutz Cabriolet Coupe came on the 134½-inch wheelbase and was known as Type 27. It weighed 4,865 lbs. and sold for $3,195. Also available was the Type 46 on the 145-inch chassis weighing 5,015 lbs. and selling for $3,660. Both were 4-passenger rumble seat models.

Stutz offered this Type 21 5-passenger Sedan during the 1932 to 1935 days. This example happens to be a 1934 version on the 134½-inch wheelbase. It weighed 5,320 lbs. Its price tag was $2,995.

The 1935 Le Baron 7-passenger Transformable Town Car Type 68 came with the two forward facing auxiliary seats. This example weighed 5,502 lbs. and sold for $5,495. Very few were turned out during the depression days.

Registered as one of the last Stutz cars to be built, this 1935 7-passenger Limousine Type 41 came with forward facing auxiliary seats. It weighed 5,556 lbs. and sold for $3,660. Also available for $200 less was the 7-passenger Sedan weighing 5,346 lbs. It was known as Type 40. Both models used the 145-inch chassis.

Terraplane

Coming on the market as a mid-season car in July of 1932 was the Essex Terraplane. Shown here in Sept. of 1932 was this Essex Terraplane Roadster winning the Pike Peak hill-climb event. Its time was 21 minutes and 21 seconds. This model weighed 2,000 lbs. and sold for $425.

Terraplane was a product of the Hudson Motor Car C with headquarters in Detroit. Actually, this car beg production as a mid-season unit in July 193 referred to as an Essex Terraplane. Through 1932, t Essex name plate was slowly phased out, so that l 1934, Terraplane was the name the public would kno

For the 1934 models, the Terraplane came only as Six, built on two wheelbases. The Standard Six had 1 inches while the DeLuxe used a 116-inch model. T Standard Six came with a 5.75:1 compression rati giving 80 HP at 3600 RPM. The DeLuxe Six can equipped with a cylinder head of aluminum alloy for t combustion chambers and a cast iron top closing t cylinder head water jackets. The 6.25:1 compression rat for this head delivered 85 HP at the same RPM. Besid these two choices, there was also a 7:1 compression rat at an additional charge, giving 89.5 HP.

Tire sizes for the Terraplane were: 5:25 x 17 c Standard models. DeLuxe Terraplanes used 5:50 x 1 and 6:00 x 16s were available at extra cost. All Terr planes used wire wheels as standard equipment. Brak continued to be mechanical. Free-wheeling wasn't availab any longer, but the vacuum-operated clutch was retaine The fuel supply consisted of 11½ gallons. A choice of models ranged from a $585 2-passenger Coupe to $7 for the Convertible Coupe.

Position Five was held this year, showing sales 85,835 cars for the calendar year.

This is the 1933 Essex Terraplane 6 Sedan on the 106-inch wheelbase. It sold in base form for $550. A 113-inch model also was available. That sold for $725.

Hudson, for itself as well as for the Terraplane models, often used celebrities when introducing new models. Shown here is the noted aviatrix Amelia Earhart standing by the new 1933 Terraplane Eight Convertible Coupe. This being an early model, it wears different hood louvers from the late models. It sold for $705.

Some minor changes in the 1933 Essex Terraplane are evident in this late 1933 model. Hood panels now offer vent doors for cooling purposes and fender mounted parking lights are standard equipment. The noted actor and detective author Phillips S. Lord stands proudly by his new Essex Terraplane.

A 1933 Essex Terraplane 8 Sedan was photographed outside the Hudson-Terraplane factory at Detroit. Note the railroad tracks which gave the company immediate access to rail shipment for their cars. This model rode on the 113-inch wheelbase and sold for $725. All four doors opened to the front this year – a design that later day automotive engineers would consider definitely unsafe.

Not only in America was the Terraplane catching on, but in England Lady Astor poses with her 6-cylinder Terraplane Convertible Coupe. Note the right-hand drive and rear mounted license on the right tail lamp bracket. The photo was taken at Cleveland-on-the-Thames, England, home of Lady Astor.

The rare 1933 Essex Terraplane Six panel delivery sold fairly well to small markets, drug firms, and florists. It sold for $440. Note the high mount of the fender well spare. Only on the front right fender was the spare mounted. This truck used the basic body shell of the 2-door coach.

This was the lowest priced 1934 Terraplane. It was the 2-passenger Coupe selling for $585. Being the Standard model, it rode on a 112-inch wheelbase. The grille and hood vent system were different from the Deluxe 116-inch models. Wire wheels were standard equipment but steel pressed wheels were optional at no extra cost.

A 1934 Terraplane Convertible Coupe for 4 passengers was available both in the Standard and Deluxe models. This happens to be the Standard model which sold for $625. The Deluxe was $100 more. Of interest is the placement of the gas filler cap, just below the rumble seat deck.

Terraplane

This 1934 Standard Terraplane Coach used the accessory sidemounted spares. It sold for $630. The Deluxe version cost $685. Note the bumper guards are placed inside the bumper rather than being installed on the out portion. The Standard models came with 5:25 x 17-inch tires.

Terraplane's most popular model for 1934 was this Deluxe 4-door Sedan selling for $690. It came with 5:50 x 17-inch tires, or the owner could order 6:00 x 16-inch tires at no extra cost. This model again had all four doors opening to the front, with rear mounted hinges.

1935

The Terraplane came in both Special and DeLu models using a 6-cylinder engine. The Terraplane DeLu was equipped with a luxurious interior and dash trim, du outside horn trumpets, double tail lamps, and sun viso Radiator and carburetor thermostat, along with automa choke, helped to distinguish this car from the Speci The hood and radiator were long and narrow, similar the Hudson of that year. The seats were three inch wider for front seat passengers. All-steel roof constructic as employed by Hudson, was also found on the Ter plane. Because of the steel roof, the fadio antenna w placed under the running board.

Horsepower ratings for the Terraplane were 88 at 38 RPM, with a 6:1 compression ratio. Also available was t aluminum and cast iron head, raising compression 7:1, yielding 100 HP at the same RPM. Fuel supply wa 15½-gallon tank. The 112-inch wheelbase cars used 6:00 x 16-inch tire. Brake system was still mechanical f the year. Models available for the year amounted to ni ranging from $585 for the 2-passenger Coupe to $725 Convertible Coupe form.

Terraplane gained Eighth Position by selling 101,0 cars for this model run through 3,225 Hudson-Terrapla dealers in the United States. These figures also represe Hudson sales.

Terraplane had a dependable reputation in many cities for taxi service. Shown here was the 1935 Terraplane Sedan in front of the Mathews-Stewart Hudson-Terraplane Dealership where the Checker Cab Co. took delivery of this Special Sedan. This model sold for $655. On a fleet basis the price was reasonably lower. Note the factory spot light this model is equipped with, to aid drivers on nighttime calls.

This 1934 Standard Terraplane Coach used the optional steel pressed wheels. Note the different grille pattern and hood design between the Deluxe 116-inch wheelbase models and the Standard models. This example also has the accessory parking lights, and a canine chauffeur.

936

Terraplanes were sold jointly in Hudson-Terraplane ›alerships. Terraplane resembled the Hudson a great deal is year, and used many of the same new mechanical ›vices such as Duo-Servo hydraulically operated brakes hich worked the rear brakes mechanically if the hydraulic ›stem should fail. Also available was independent sus- ›nsion new to Hudson and Terraplane. The Terraplane ›me with an 88 HP, 6-cylinder engine at 3800 RPM. It ›d a compression ratio of 6:00 with a cast iron head. lso available at additional cost was the high performance uminum head developing 100 HP at 7:00 compression tio.

Fuel supply was a 16½-gallon tank. The wheelbase easured 115 inches; 6:00 x 16-inch tires were used. ight models were in the DeLuxe and Custom Series. ifferences in trim were the only items of change. Price ried from $595 for a 3-passenger DeLuxe Coupe to 745 for the Custom Sedan in Touring Trunk style. Terraplane was in the Eighth Position for sales this ›ar, producing 123,266 cars for the calendar year sales, hich also included Hudson sales.

This 1935 Terraplane Deluxe Convertible Coupe was well equipped with factory fender skirts, twin trumpet horns, and double taillamps as standard equipment. This example sold for $725. Terraplane continued to use its beautiful soaring bird hood ornament, and instituted sharply V-ed bumpers for this year only.

A very rare model was this 1936 Terraplane Station Wagon for six passengers. It appeared only on the Deluxe Chassis. It was available only for the 1936 model run, selling for $700. Even on this model, Terraplane used rear-hinged doors both front and back.

This is the 1936 Terraplane Custom Six Coupe. It was available in both 3 and 5-passenger models. This was a 3-passenger model which sold for $685. A lower priced Deluxe line was also offered beginning at $595. This Coupe is well equipped with the optional at extra cost chrome wheel covers and fender skirts. The 5-passenger model featured a rumble seat instead of vast trunk space.

Terraplane's lowest priced model for 1937 was this 3-passenger Deluxe Coupe for $595. It was an ideal model for businessmen who needed much room to carry their supplies. Apparently, the real estate salesman has just placed his "Open House" sign on this bungalow. For the first time, Terraplane used forward hinged doors.

Terraplane

The 1937 Terraplane Super Brougham came on a 117-inch wheelbase and sold for $680. The Deluxe Brougham offered less chrome trim and a plainer interior and sold for $625.

1937

This was the final year for the Terraplane to be bu as a separate car. Starting with 1938 it was referred to the Hudson Terraplane.

For this model run, a DeLuxe and Super model we offered. The cars were longer, lower, roomier and mo powerful. Front doors were hinged at the front of t door. A new style in fender design started this year Hudson displayed a teardrop fender design which w used for several model runs to follow. The headlamps we bracketed to the radiator shell in place of being mount on the fender catwalks. Rather than the trumpet horns in the past, the 1937 models placed the horns behind t grille. The DeLuxe cars used one horn and the Supers we supplied with twin air horns.

Gone was the rumble seat coupe. The seating of t Business Coupe was ample for three to sit comfortabl

The instrument board differed from previous models that its gauges were placed in a vertical fashion rath than being curved. The ash tray was offered as standa equipment. Available for the Terraplane as in the Huds line was the Bendix automatic clutch with the Electr Hand. Also available was the hydraulic Hill-Hold as optional piece of equipment at extra cost. All Terraplan like Hudsons, had the battery placed under the hoo

Horsepower was 96 at 3900 RPM with 6:25 to 1 rat in the DeLuxe line, with a cast iron head and single dow draft carburetor. The Super models used a dual carburet which was the first 6-cylinder car to employ the syste With this setup, the models developed 101 HP at 40 RPM and performed very well. Both series rode on 11 inch wheelbases using 6:00 x 16-inch tires and a 16½-gall fuel supply.

Thirteen models were available. Seven were catalogu in the DeLuxe line with the remaining six going to t Super Series. Prices ranged from $595 for the 3-passeng DeLuxe Coupe to $745 for the Super Touring Tru Sedan.

Terraplane placed Tenth this year, selling combined wi Hudson, 111,342 units.

This was the 1937 Terraplane Sedan for 6 passengers. It was available in both Deluxe and Super lines, selling for $675 and $725, respectively. This was the last season the car would be known as a Terraplane. The follow-model was referred to as the Hudson Terraplane, before being phased out for the Hudson "112."

A new Terraplane Convertible body style was available for the first time in 1937. It was actually called the Convertible Brougham for 5 passengers, available in the Super line only. It offered year around comfort of a two-door, but could easily be converted to an open model. The canvas panel containing the rear quarter window was easily removed. It sold for $735. This was the company's first approach to the true convertible style popular in the 1940 to 1970 years.

For 1937 this Terraplane Convertible Coupe was available only in the Deluxe line, selling for $650. For 1937, Terraplane, like Hudson, offered the battery placed in the engine room.

Viking

The Viking was a product of General Motors Corp. d classed as the companion car to Oldsmobile. Factory eadquarters were in Lansing, Michigan. The car was built 1929 and 1930.

The Viking sold in the higher price bracket than ldsmobile and offered only a V-8 engine of 259.5 cubic ches which developed 81 HP at 3200 RPM. The cars me on a 125-inch wheelbase and used 6:00 x 18-inch res. The fuel supply came from a 20-gallon tank. All odels used mechanical brakes.

The company offered only three models, a Convertible oupe, Brougham, and Sedan. Oddly enough, all three odels sold for exactly the same price of $1,695. During the model run, G.M. and Oldsmobile realized it ouldn't be wise management to continue producing the r. So with a 29th spot for sales of 2,738 units, another ood car, introduced at the wrong time, had to close s doors.

This 1930 Viking Deluxe Convertible Coupe was the best looking body style available for the year. It sold for the same price as the other models – $1,695 – and weighed 3,510 lbs. Note the golf compartment door in the rear quarter panel. A rumble seat was standard on this model.

Viking offered this 1930 Close-Coupled Sedan for those who preferred an enclosed rear quarter panel giving privacy to rear seat passengers. It also sold for $1,695. It weighed 3,640 lbs. This was Viking's last year. All Deluxe models had as standard equipment the sidemounts and six wire wheels, twin windshield wipers, four Lovejoy hydraulic shock absorbers, a folding trunk rack, and chromed bumpers. Much of this equipment would be considered extra-cost accessories on most other cars.

A 5-passenger 1930 Viking Sedan is here being used in the California Mojave Desert. These gentlemen appear to be checking out their elevation, as the sign proclaims 200 feet above sea level. This model is equipped with the standard wooden artillery wheels. The M-1 license was General Motor's Michigan manufacturing listing.

This 1930 Viking Sedan is equipped with the accessory wire wheels and sidemount tire equipment. It resembles the Oldsmobile a great deal, except it was on a longer 125-inch wheelbase and weighed 3,650 lbs.

Whippet

The Whippet was a product of the Willys Overland C
of Toledo, Ohio. The car was built from 1926 until 19
as the economy package for those years.

The 1930 Whippets had a 4-cylinder engine of 145 cubic inches which developed 40 HP at 3200 RPM. The cars used a 10-gallon fuel supply. The wheelbase measur 103¼ inches. The tire size was 4.75 x 19. Mechanic brakes were used on Whippets.

Nine models were available that ranged in price fro $520 for the 5-passenger Touring and Roadster to $69 for a 5-passenger DeLuxe Sedan.

Whippet sales and production figures were in the 21 position for 1930. Total sales amounted to 17,961 ca Since sales slipped terrifically this year, the Willys Overla Co. decided to cease production of the little 4-cylind car. Total calendar year sales were listed with Willys "6 and Willys Overland which ranked in 6th position fro 69,000 sales.

The 1930 Whippet 2-passenger Coupe weighed 2,269 lbs. and sold for $575. The spare was mounted in the right fender well if the car did not come equipped with bumpers. If two sidemounts were used with bumper equipment, it was all classed as an optional accessory package. A rumble seat was also classed as an accessory, available at extra cost.

Whippet also offered this 1930 4-passenger Roadster for $555. It came on a 103¼-inch wheelbase and weighed 2,190 lbs. The sidemounted spares and canvas tire covers were extra.

This was the lowest priced 1930 Whippet available. It sold for $520 as a 2-passenger Roadster and weighed 2,144 lbs. This car is well equipped with accessories of that era.

The most expensive Whippet for 1930 was this Deluxe 5-passenger Sedan. It weighed 2,459 lbs. and brought a price of $695. This example used the other style of bumper – the round pipe design. This was Whippet's last year of building cars.

This 1930 Whippet wears a two-bar bumper on its Coach body. This 5-passenger model weighed 2,348 lbs. It sold for $575, the same price as the 2-passenger coupe.

Willys

The Willys 6 and 8 were products of the Willys Overland). with headquarters in Toledo, Ohio. The car was anufactured from 1903 through 1942 under different ases of Willys and Overland names. It was again pro-ced from 1952 through 1955 in passenger car style. During the 1930 model run the Willys 6 offered a 6-linder L-head engine of 193 cubic inches. The engine veloped 65 HP at 3400 RPM. The fuel supply came from 10-gallon tank. The brake system was Bendix two-shoe akes with a single cross shaft. The hand brake, which s placed to the left on the floor board, acted on all ur wheels.

The Willys 6 wheelbase was 110 inches and its tire size s 5:00 x 19 inches. Altogether there were eight models the Willys 6 line. Prices began at $695 for the 2-ssenger Roadster and rose to $850 for a 5-passenger Luxe Sedan.

The Willys 8 appeared almost the same as the 6 but came a 120-inch wheelbase using a 75 HP 8-cylinder engine 3600 RPM. It used a 14-gallon fuel tank. Other than ese changes, the cars were quite similar. They were iced from $875 for a 2-passenger Coupe to $950 for the Luxe Eight Sedan.

Willys 6 and 8 placed in the 16th slot with 30,249 cars r the year. Calendar year production is ranked with illys-Knight and Whippet. They were placed in 6th les position from 69,000 sales.

The 1930 Willys Eight Deluxe Coupe seated 5 passengers comfortably. The car came on a 120-inch wheelbase and used a 75 HP engine. Bumper to bumper, the car measured 167 inches.

This is the 1930 Willys Eight Deluxe Sedan which was the most expensive car for the year. It sold for $950. Willys did not sell many eight-cylinder models in 1930.

This was the 1930 Willys Model "97" coupe which sold in base form for $565. The special cloth top and stationary landau irons were available only as extra cost items, as was the welled fender. Demountable rims were standard.

Willys offered this 1930 Model "97" Roadster as the lowest priced car for the year. It came on a 110-inch wheelbase and sold for $495. The two horns, wire wheels, sidemount tires, tire covers, sidemount mirrors and fender parking lamps were all optional equipment at extra cost

Willys

The 1931 Willys Club Sedan came also in each series and oddly enough sold for less than the regular 5-passenger sedan. This model weighed 2,756 lbs. and sold for $625 in the "97" Series.

1931

For 1931, Willys offered two 6-cylinder cars and o 8-cylinder series. The Model 97 was the lowest price of the line. It offered a 193 cubic inch engine developi 65 HP at 3400 RPM. The fuel supply was from a gallon tank. The tire size was 5:00 x 19 inches and it car on a 110-inch wheelbase and was offered in five styl The Willys 98-D was the same car except it was on 113-inch chassis and was available in four models on

The Willys 8-80D had a 245.4 cubic inch 8-cylinc engine of 80 HP at 3200 RPM. They used a 16-gallon fu supply. A 121-inch wheelbase was used for this series, a 5:50 x 19-inch tires were employed.

A total of 13 body styles were catalogued with pric being less in some lines than the previous year. The Moc 97 Roadster for 2 passengers sold for $495, and the t of the line 8-80D DeLuxe Sedan for 5 passengers we for $1,095.

Willys-Willys Overland sold 74,750 units giving th the 6th sales spot for 1931.

Willys offered this 4-door sedan in each of the series for 1931. This happens to be in the Model "97" line, selling for $675 and weighing 2,682 lbs. A rear mounted spare and demountable rims on wood spoke wheels were standard.

Willys used these two 6-cylinder Model "97s" for press release purposes with test drivers and factory representatives showing their durability in a test run. It appears both models have only one fender mounted spare, which was not uncommon for Willys.

The 1931 Willys "98-D" Deluxe Victoria Coupe used the 113-inch chassis. It weighed 2,750 lbs. and sold for $850. This 4-passenger model offered the factory approved side-mount tires, covers, and wire wheels as optional extra cost equipment.

932

Willys Overland made some minor changes in both ›pearance and the mechanical department for 1932. The e of free wheeling was made available on each model. ıe Overland Six engine developed 65 HP at 3400 RPM ıd the Eight had an 80 HP plant at 3200 RPM. The heelbase of the Overland Six consisted of 113-inches and e Eight had a 121-inch wheelbase. Tire size of the Six ıs 5.25 x 18 and Eight used 5.50 x 18s. The fuel systems ere a 13-gallon tank on the Overland Six while the Eight ed a 16-gallon fuel supply. Mechanical brakes by ndix were used on these cars. Body types amounted to 7 in these two series which carried the designation in e Six as Model 6-90, and 8-88 was employed on the verland Eight.

Prices began at $515 for the 2-passenger Roadster and aduated up to $1,095 for the Custom Sedan.

Willys Overland placed in Tenth position with Willys-night, selling 26,710 cars.

The lowest priced Willys Overland for 1932 was this 6-cylinder Roadster selling for $515. Free wheeling was part of the regular equipment on all 1932 Willys Overland cars. This model was available as either a 2-passenger car with trunk or a 4-passenger with rumble seat.

Considered the smartest low-priced car for 1932, according to the Willys Overland Advertising Dept., this 5-passenger Coach weighed 2,765 lbs. and sold for $615. Wire wheels were standard on all models this year.

Willys Overland offered this 1932 6-cylinder Coupe as Model 6-90. It was available in both 2-passenger and 4-passenger models weighing 2,730 and 2,819 lbs. The price of each was $615 and $645, respectively. This year, Willys offered shatterproof glass in all windows as an extra cost option.

This was the 1932 Willys Overland Eight Custom Victoria which came on the 121-inch wheelbase. It was technically called the "8-88." These models offered increased comfort from two-way hydraulic shock absorbers both front and rear. The 8-cylinder cars had six frame cross members, while the 6-cylinder models used five cross members.

A Model "8-88" 1932 Willys Overland Eight Custom Sedan was the most expensive model for the year, selling at $1,095. This was the biggest Willys, built on a 121-inch wheelbase. A somewhat curved vee grille and radiator with trimly designed headlamps and full-crowned fenders made this a very attractive looking car. Among its features were adjustable steering post, free wheeling, dual windshield wipers and roller shades.

Willys

The 1933 Willys "77" Custom Convertible Roadster offered 5:00 x 17-inch tires with steel pressed wheels as standard equipment. This model sold for $430 – the same as the Coupe version. Even in 1933 it was a very rare car.

1933

Willys, being in financial difficulty, went into Feder bankruptcy early in 1933. On February 15, productic stopped. The courts did permit the company to resun production later in the year and 29,918 cars were produc between the two new entries for 1933. These were th Willys 77 and 99.

Nine models were built, five on the 77 model with 100-inch wheelbase, and four on the 99 model whic carried a 113-inch wheelbase and was the 6-cylinder serie Very few of these were ever turned out and the compan discontinued this model at the end of the year to co centrate strictly on the 77 for 1934.

The 4-cylinder model carried a 48 HP engine (32(RPM). It had an 8-gallon fuel supply. The Six carried 13-gallon tank and used an 80 HP engine turning over maximum of 3400 RPM. Free-wheeling was only availab on the Series 99. Both 77s and 99s used mechanic brakes. The Four used a 5:00 x 17-inch tire, while th Six came with 5:50 x 17s. Top speed for the Series was 70 MPH while the Series 99 could produce ten mo MPH.

Prices varied between $430 for a Series 77 Coupe ar $675 for the 99 Sedan.

Willys placed in the 11th sales position for 193

Something new appeared in 1933, with the Willys Model "77." Shown is the lowest priced model for $430. It had a seating capacity for 2 passengers. Its 4-cylinder engine developed 48 HP at 3200 RPM.

Looking practically the same as the 1933 Willys Model "77" are these two 1933 Willys 6 Model "99s." This series was available in four models each, using the 113-inch wheelbase. Kelsey Hayes steel pressed wheels were standard equipment on all Willys.

This 1933 Willys "77" 4-door sedan used the 100-inch wheelbase. It was truly an economy package that saw many families through the depression. The sedan sold for $445 in base form.

A 1933 Willys 6 Custom Sedan Model "99" sold for $675. It was the most expensive model for the year. Most people purchased the Model "77s" in preference to the "99s" because of economy. The 99s engine developed 80 HP at 3400 RPM. This series was built only in 1933.

1934

Being reorganized again, Willys hoped for a better show this year. Basically, this was the same Willys 77 as built in 1933. Appearance changes included porthole vents on the side hood panels, new curved bumpers for the front, and a longer dressed up hood. Wire wheels were available, but at extra cost. The price went up five dollars per model in each of five models that were available.

The engine was a 48 HP 4-cylinder unit of 3200 RPM. It had an 8-gallon fuel tank. Mechanical brakes were used. 5:50 x 17-inch tire was retained, but 5:50 x 17s were available with the wire wheel extra cost package. Top speed for this little car was 70 MPH. It received 25 MPG average driving speed.

A sales position of 16 was given to Willys by selling ,916 cars for the calendar year.

Looking practically the same as the 1933 models, this 1934 Willys "77" Coupe had seating capacity for 2 passengers. It sold for $435. The factory-approved wire wheels were an accessory. For its size, this model offered a surprising amount of trunk space.

1935

For 1935, Willys offered three body styles: coupe, panel delivery, and sedan. There was a $20 difference among these models beginning at $395 for the Coupe and ending at $415 for a Sedan.

The front of the Willys was face-lifted, conforming to the appearance of other 1935 makes. The grille had a more pointed Vee, being slim and high. The hood louvers came in a half circular style with the headlights blending into the fender cat-walk space between hood and fender line.

The 4-cylinder engine was the same as in 1934, giving 48 HP at 3200 RPM. It had an 8-gallon fuel supply. Mechanical brakes were used again this year along with the 5:50 x 17-inch tires. The car averaged 25 MPG and gave a top speed of 70 MPH.

This year's models were available with a special folding trunk fitting into the rear design so completely that it appeared to be a part of the car. It consisted of about ½ square feet of luggage space which made it ideal for a family on vacation, salesmen in business, or whatever.

Willys claimed the 15th position, selling 20,428 cars for the calendar year.

An ideal family car for those on a budget was the 1934 Willys "77" Sedan. It came with an all-steel body with sufficient head and leg room. The price of this example was $450 – an increase of five dollars over 1933 models.

Willys offered this 1935 Panel Delivery for $450. It sold reasonably well to tradesmen who needed low cost transportation in their business. Mechanically, it was the same car Willys had offered in the previous year. Willys rated this truck as a ¾-ton vehicle.

The 1935 Willys "77" 4-door sedan sold for $415. It weighed 2,158 lbs. and was basically the same car as in 1933 and 1934. The wire wheels which this model is equipped with were an accessory. Most all used the steel pressed wheels.

1936

An appointment was made February 25, 1936 tha David Wilson would be made the trustee of the compan with the receivership period coming to an end. The com pany had been under receivership since filing for bank ruptcy early in 1933.

A more attractive design of the small Willys 77 wa made this year with mechanical improvements being a increase in the compression ratio from 5:13 to 5:70, an a vacuum spark device being installed.

The HP was rated at 48 with 3200 RPM. The car use an 8-gallon fuel supply and rode on 5:00 x 17-inch tires Brakes were still of the mechanical type. The car came i two styles on a 100-inch wheelbase. The Coupe, a 2 passenger model, went home for $20 more.

Willys came in 15th in sales by selling 18,824 cars

In 1936, Willys made this pick-up available, and it received favorable comments among automotive tradesmen. It sold for $400 and weighed 2,089 lbs.

Continuing into 1936 was the Willys 77 Panel Delivery, selling for $405, the same as it did in 1935. These models used the same size tires of 5:00 x 17 inches as the regular cars. All Willys commercial cars used the 4-cylinder engine.

Fully restored and resting in Harrah's Auto Museum in Sparks, Nevada is this 1936 Willys "77" Sedan. The same 48 HP engine introduced in 1933 was still being put to work on the 1936 models. This example weighed 2,131 lbs. and sold for $415, being the most expensive car for the year.

937

For 1937, Willys dropped its 77 Series and brought out n attractive new offering with a standard tread size of 6 inches.

These new cars were offered with all-steel bodies, a ounded hood which was something different, and well-laced headlights mounted in the fenders. The fenders wept downward over the wheels, gracefully toward the enter of the car, giving a splash pan effect at the base of ne hood. The hood raised from the center making all arts easy to work on in this 4-cylinder engine room. 'he battery compartment was contained under the hood. 'he hood came directly back to the windshield, making it ecessary to place the ventilating unit on the end of the ood.

The instrument panel displayed all gauges in two eparate chrome plated large dials. One was for the peedometer; the other showed how the car was function-ng. The hand brake was placed to the left of the steering heel and mounted from the cowl. The starter button as located on the instrument board and was of a olenoid type that operated the starter circuit.

Two models were available: a coupe for $395 and a edan for five people at $420. At that time, Willys was merica's only car for under $500.

The engine developed 48 HP at 3200 RPM. The car ad an 8-gallon fuel supply. It used a 100-inch wheelbase. 'ire size was 5:50 x 16 inches. Willys used mechanical rakes during 1937.

The sales picture put Willys in 14th position by selling 6,803 cars for 1937.

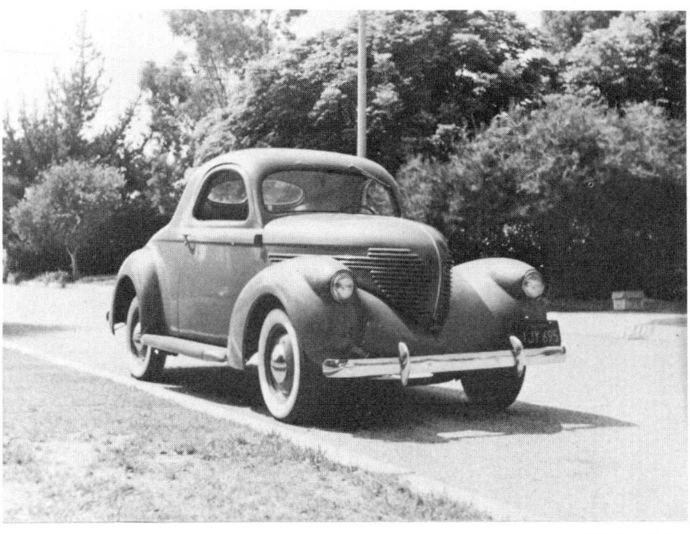

Willys came up with an entirely new car for 1937. This original 1937 Willys Coupe for 2 passengers sold for $395. This example has travelled over 100,000 miles. It is owned by Charles Porter of Santa Barbara, Calif.

This gives an idea of the space provided in the trunk compartment of the 1937 Willys Coupe. It proved to be a fine little car for economy-minded salesmen and businessmen.

The 1937 Willys 4-door Sedan was the more popular body style of the two that were offered. The car still used a 4-cylinder 48 HP engine, as it had done since 1933. The Sedan weighed 2,250 lbs. and sold for $420.

A well-rounded front end was something new that Willys brought out for the year. It was an entirely different looking car from the previous model. Note the clock attachment as an accessory to the rear view mirror. The twin windshield wipers were also optional extra-cost items for the model run. The alligator hood was released by the handle at the base of the hood, and the entire hood, grille and side panels rose as a unit.

Willys

Willys in 1938 offered the Standard, Deluxe and Custom line in the Coupe and Sedan. This 4-door sedan was the Custom model, weighing 2,300 lbs. and selling for $715. The Standard version sold for $573 and the Deluxe brought $624. All models weighed the same, but a better quality of interior fittings and exterior trim were used on the more expensive seires.

In the good old days, Willys advertised that this 1938 Coupe could go 1,000 miles a month, with gasoline costing 18¢ a gallon, for about $7.20 a month. It weighed 2,120 lbs. and sold for $579 in this Custom style. The economy Standard Series was available for $499 and the Deluxe Coupe cost $525.

The Willys continued with the same package it had offered for the past two years, but this model was new and offered for a one-year run. The car was called the Willys Overland and it carried a 4-cylinder engine developing 62 HP at 3600 RPM. The Overland had a 102-inch wheelbase. This 4-door Sedan in the Deluxe line sold for $705.

1938

The company had planned to turn out 125,000 vehicles during the 1938 model run according to sales department directories. However, the picture wasn't that bright, and only 12,110 units were produced.

The models available in passenger car style were more than offered in 1937. A 4-door came in Standard, DeLuxe and Custom style. All were on the same body but just had more deluxe equipment. The Coupe came as an Economy, Standard, and DeLuxe Coupe. Other body styles consisted of small commercial vehicles.

The 1938 models were the same cars as in 1937 with some very minor differences. The models came with bumper guards front and rear as standard equipment and a hood ornament. In 1937 these were optional at extra cost. The additional trim models for 1938 also were the only other noticeable changes.

The horsepower for the year again was 48 at 3200 RPM. These cars again used a 100-inch wheelbase, and 5:50 x 16-inch tires. The fuel tank held 8 gallons. The brake system was of the mechanical type.

Prices ranged from $499 for the 2-passenger Standard Coupe to $715 for the 5-passenger Custom Sedan. Willys came in the 15th position for 1938 calendar year sales with 16,173 cars.

1939

For 1939, the Toledo, Ohio, firm offered the Willys 48 which was the same car offered in 1937 and 1938. But new to the line came the freshly styled Willys Overland 4-cylinder. This name hadn't been seen on Willys for several seasons, but appeared only for the 1939 model run.

Although both lines had basic similarities, numerous changes were offered in the new Overland. Both cars carried the 134.2 cubic inch engine. The Willys continued with its 48 HP engine at 3200 RPM. The Overland developed 62 HP at 3600 RPM. The Overland offered new hydraulic brakes while the mechanical devices were continued for the Willys.

The engine increase in power for the Overland was due to a higher compression ratio of 6:35 in place of 5:70 along with a fixed jet downdraft carburetor. The manifold heat control was automatic rather than manual. The Overland used 14mm spark plugs while the Willys was fitted with 18mm ones.

The appearance changes over the Willys 48 gave the Overland a smart new grille and hood design. It was two inches longer than the Willys models, coming on a 102-inch wheelbase. The Willys continued with 5:50 x 16-inch tires as did the standard Overland, and the Overland DeLuxe employed 6:00 x 16s. The Overlands came with rubber shackles and the Willys 48 had its regular threaded type as used on the 1937 and 1938 models. Both models came with 8-gallon fuel tanks.

A total of thirteen models were available, six in the Overland line and seven for the Willys, Prices ranged from $499 for the Business Coupe on the Willys 48 chassis to $689 for the Overland DeLuxe Sedan.

The company placed 16th in sales by selling 25,383 cars for the calendar year.

1940

For the 1940 model run, Willys offered a Speedway and a DeLuxe Series with three body types: Sedan, Coupe, and Station Wagon (available only in DeLuxe). Both series offered a handsome chrome belt molding which ran from the tip of the hood down the sloping back panel.

The front end appearance was more massive by the elimination of the grille mounted in the hood and its being placed directly beneath the hood opening. The front fenders were redesigned by placing the headlamps flush in the fenders, giving a wider appearance to the car. Running boards were listed as an option. Without them, the car had chromium strips.

The Coupes and Speedway Sedan had a 4.3 rear axle and the DeLuxe Sedan and DeLuxe Wagon used a 4:55 rear axle ratio. The engine continued to develop 62 HP rating at 3600 RPM with a standard compression ratio of 6:4 to 1. A special Coupe in the DeLuxe line was equipped with an aluminum head with a 7 to 1 ratio which was able to give a maximum speed of 80 MPH. Both series used a 10½-gallon fuel tank. The tire size for the Speedway models was 5:00 x 16 inches and the DeLuxe cars used 5:50 x 16-inch tires. This year, both Speedway and DeLuxe cars came with Lockheed hydraulic brakes. The wheelbase was the same as in 1939, which was 102 inches.

A total of five models were available ranging in price from $529 for the 2-passenger Speedway Coupe to $830 for the 5-passenger DeLuxe Station Wagon.

Willys ranked in 16th place for the calendar year from the sale of 26,698 cars.

This is the 1939 Willys Overland Special Coupe which weighed 2,193 lbs. and sold for $610. The Standard Coupe cost $596 and the most expensive coupe for the year was the Deluxe, offered for $689. This example is not equipped with bumper guard equipment, which was an extra cost accessory.

Willys for 1940 offered a trim looking little Station Wagon as the most expensive car for the year. This model had seating for 5 passengers, rode on a 102-inch wheelbase, weighed 2,421 lbs. and sold for $830. Very few were built during the model run.

The 1940 Willys Deluxe Sedan was equipped for the first time with hydraulic brakes. This series used 5:50 x 16-inch tires and had a 10½-gallon fuel tank. This model weighed 2,255 lbs. and sold for $672. With the help of this model, Willys ranked in the 16th spot for the calendar year.

This 1940 Willys Speedway Sedan is well equipped with deluxe equipment such as wheel trim rings, grille guard, twin windshield wipers, and the rare rear bumper wrap around extensions. This model weighed 2,238 lbs. and sold for $596.

Willys

A new title was given to the 1941 Willys. It was now known as the Americar 441. The 4-cylinder engine now developed 63 HP at 3800 RPM. The wheelbase increased two inches, to a 104-inch chassis. This model weighed 2,305 lbs. and sold for $757.

1941

The 1941 model was called the Willys Americar. It was a roomier, smoother, and quieter car than before. The big improvement was a stronger frame. A new intake and exhaust system improved low speed torque, and a new Carter carburetor gave increased fuel economy. Gasoline mileage ran between 21 and 34 MPG depending on the speed driven.

The 4-cylinder, 134.2 cubic inch engine developed 63 HP at 3800 RPM. The fuel tank increased one gallon over last year's model and was a 11½-gallon supply. The tire size was 5:50 x 16 inches. The wheelbase was 104 inches.

A total of 6 models were available, ranging in price from $634 for a 2-passenger Speedway Coupe to $864 in the 6-passenger Station Wagon. For the calendar year, 28,935 Willys Americars left the Toledo assembly line, placing them in the 16th sales position again.

The most expensive 1941 Willys Americar was this 5-passenger Station Wagon which weighed 2,483 lbs. and had a price of $864 attached to it.

1942

Passenger car production ended with this model and didn't resume again for ten years. Production ended in 1955 for the passenger car but did continue under the Willys Overland of Brazil factory at Sao Paulo. The firm name then became Kaiser-Jeep Corp.

For 1942, Willys Americar was basically the same package as offered in 1941 with a few minor differences. A large chrome band divided the grille. Running boards were standard but were optional on the DeLuxe and Speedway line. Plastic was used more extensively in the interior which harmonized well with the car's brown upholstery. More sound deadening insulation was used, especially in the firewall area which gave passengers a quieter, more comfortable ride.

The 4-cylinder engine was 134 cubic inches that developed 63 HP at 3800 RPM. The fuel tank was the same 11½-gallon tank as last year. The tire size was a 5:50 x 16 inches and the wheelbase measured 104 inches. The 1942 models were 29 lbs. lighter than the previous year, which was basically due to substitution throughout the car. It weighed 2,230 lbs. for a 4-door Sedan.

Willys offered one additional model in the 1942 line. It was the Pullman Coupe for 2 passengers which ranked in the higher bracket and sold for $863. A total of 7 models were available priced between a $737 Speedway Coupe for 2 passengers to $1,027 for the 6-passenger Station Wagon.

Willys played a very important role in the defense program this year. Very few cars were produced and production figures are not available.

Looking at the artist's conception of this 1942 Willys Americar 442, it appears the same as the 1941 model. And yet, a large chrome band divided the radiator grille. War-time substitutions required the use of plastic in a great many cases, and the dash components were chiefly made in plastic. This model weighed 2,350 lbs. and had a price increase over the 1941 model. It sold for $890, but few cars were built due to the war-time contract Willys had to fulfill – namely production of that brand new military toy, the Jeep.

Willys - Knight

The 1930 Willys Knight was a product of the Willys verland Corporation with its headquarters in Toledo, hio. The car was manufactured from 1914 through 1932. For this year, the 6-cylinder Knight-engined cars eveloped 53 HP at 3000 RPM in the 70B models and 7 HP at 3200 RPM in the 66-B Series. The 53 HP models ad a 177 cubic inch engine and the 66-B had a 255 cubic ch displacement. The models rode on two wheelbases: 12½ inches for the 70-B and 120 inches on the 66-B. The wer priced 70-B Series had 5:50 x 19-inch tires and the rger models used 6:00 x 19-inch tires. The fuel supply as a 13-gallon tank in the 70-B models and 18 gallons for e 66-B Series. Mechanical brakes were used on the Willys night cars.

Six models were available in the 70-B Series and four the 66-B. Prices ranged from $1,045 for a 4-passenger 0-B model to $1,895 for the 5-passenger 66-B Sedan. he Series 70-B was discontinued at the end of the year. Willys Knight placed in 6th position by selling 67,000 rs during the calendar run. These production figures so include the Whippet, and Willys 6 and 8.

Referred to as the 5-passenger Coupe, this 1930 Willys Knight happens to be on the "66B" chassis of 120 inches. It weighed 3,866 lbs. and sold for $1,895. The trunk and trunk rack were part of the standard equipment as were the sidemounted spares. A novelty was the button at the center of the steering wheel which operated horn, starter and lights.

A 1930 Willys Knight "70B" 5-passenger Coach weighed 2,903 lbs. and was offered in the lower bracket of the "70B" line for $1,045. The wide doors gave ample room for entrance and exit.

This was the 1930 Willys Knight "70B" Rumble Seat Coupe. It came on the 112½-inch wheelbase, weighed 2,916 lbs. and sold for $1,145. The 6-cylinder Knight engine developed 53 HP at 3000 RPM.

Willys - Knight

Willys Knight offered this "66B" 4-passenger Coupe at $1,895, the same price as the other 66B Models. It weighed 3,815 lbs. It developed 87 HP at 3200 RPM from its 6-cylinder engine. A rumble seat was standard on this model.

1931

The 1931 Willys Knight was called the Series 66-D. used the Sleeve Valve 6-cylinder engine of 255 cub inches. The engine developed 87 HP at 3200 RPM. Th car had a 121-inch wheelbase and used 6:00 x 19-inc tires.

With sales slipping this year the company droppe prices by putting the 66-D cars in the price bracket of la year's 70-B Series. The four models sold for $1,095 an if they came with deluxe equipment they were $10 additional.

Willys Knight and Willys sold 74,750 units for the ye which placed them in the 6th position for the calend year.

By far the sportiest model in the 1930 Willys Knight lineup was this "66B" 4-passenger Roadster, available for $1,895. This model weighed 3,592 lbs. and also used the 120-inch wheelbase. Being a sport model, brilliant colors were used to set it off to its best advantages. Top grain leather was standard equipment for this model's interior. A rumble seat was standard equipment, as were the sidemounts and trunk rack.

Being available in both Standard and Deluxe models for 1931, the Willys Knight "66D" was a very impressive looking car. This version is the Deluxe, with sidemount tire equipment, wire wheels, and luggage rack, all part of the Deluxe package selling for $1,195. It weighed 3,582 lbs.

The 1931 Willys Knight Victoria Coupe in the Deluxe style sold for $1,195. Without the special equipment the same model could be purchased for $1,095. The radiator cap was mounted under the hood for the first time, giving the car a touch of modern styling. This model weighed 3,482 lbs. A wide variety of matching color combinations were available.

The most popular model in the Willys Knight "95" Series was this 5-passenger sedan on the 113-inch wheelbase. It sold for $895. The wire wheels were now considered part of the regular equipment.

932

The Knight models were improved in appearance and ad minor mechanical changes. A Warner free-wheeling nit was available on all models at this time. The Six and ight Knight engines developed 60 HP at 3400 RPM and 7 HP at 3200 RPM. The model designations were Knight 5 and Knight 66D. The 95 models had a 113-inch heelbase and the 66D used the 121-inch wheelbase. The re size was 5:50 x 18 on the 95 models and 6:00 x 17 ere used on the 66Ds. A 13-gallon fuel supply was used Knight 95 cars, while the 66Ds employed a 16-gallon nk. Mechanical brakes by Bendix were used in both odels. A total of 9 body styles were used between the vo models.

Prices ranged from $785 for the 2-passenger Roadster night 95 to $1,395 for a Knight 66D 5-passenger Club edan.

The Willys Knight earned only 3,265 sales for the orporation, giving it the 24th position for the year.

Oddly enough, this 1932 Willys Knight "95" Coach sold for less than the Rumble Seat Coupe. Its price was $845 for the 5-passenger model. The "95" models used a 6-cylinder engine of 60 HP at 3400 RPM.

The 1932 Willys Knight "95" Coupe was available either in 2 or 4-passenger style with prices at $845 for the 2-passenger model and $875 for the 4-passenger Rumble Seat Coupe. The wheelbase was 113 inches for the "95" models.

Coming on the 121-inch wheelbase was the 1932 Willys Knight "66D" Custom Victoria Coupe. This model offered good storage. At the left of the rear seat was a convenient parcel shelf and under the rear deck, space was available for larger luggage. The Custom Victoria sold for $1,245. This was the last year for the Knight-engined Willys cars. Ironically, the public continued to refer to Willys vehicles as Willys-Knights right up to World War II.

Windsor

This 1930 Windsor Convertible Roadster was available for $1,995 in base form. This model is equipped with extra cost wire wheels and sidemounted spares with a canvas covered spare tire. The Roadster was photographed with a typical California setting of a Spanish style home with tile roof.

The Windsor was built by the Moon Motor Car Co. wit its factory in St. Louis, Mo. The Windsor was a new c on the market being offered for the first time in 192 Production ceased at the end of 1930.

The 1930 models had an 8-cylinder Continental engir of 286 cubic inches. The maximum brake horsepower w 88 at 3100 RPM. The tire size used was 6:50 x 19 inch and its wheelbase measured 125½ and 141 inches. Hy draulic brakes were used. It had an 18-gallon fuel tan

A total of six body styles were available ranging i price from $1,995 for five of the models to $2,245 fo the 7-passenger Sedan.

Strange as it may seem, the Moon car was discontinue shortly before this time because of a lack of sales with price tag considerably less than the Windsor. The compan kept hoping that this being their new luxury car, it wou be a success. It wasn't, and production ended during 193

The plant was used to build the Ruxton from Jun 1930 until it stopped production in November of 193

Windsor sales were so low it was placed among th miscellaneous makes for 1930.

Shown here are two 1930 Windsor models – the 5-passenger sedan on the left and the Custom Brougham on the right. Both used the 88 HP engine at 3100 RPM. Each model sold for $1,995. They were considered the luxury vehicles of the Moon Motor Company.

A pair of 1930 Windsors – the Convertible Roadster discussed here – and the most expensive model of the year, a 7-passenger Town Sedan nicely equipped with steel disc wheels, landau irons, and carriage lamps. This model sold for $2,245. Very few Windsor cars were sold during their few months of production in 1930.

Airmobile

The 1937-1938 Airmobile used a 4-cylinder O.H.V. air-cooled engine. It developed 57 HP at 3700 RPM. The proposed price was to have been $550. Only one car was built. It is fully restored today, and is on display at the Harrah Auto Museum in Reno, Nev.

The Airmobile, a unique 3-wheel vehicle, was built in Rochester, N. Y., in 1937-1938 by the Lewis American Airways Co. The head of this organization, Paul Lewis, was a man who had a reputation as a successful promoter of unusual mehcanical devices.

The car was first put into the planning stages in 1934. One pilot model was the only vehicle ever produced by the company. It reached its final development stages in the spring of 1937 and was called a 1938 model.

The car used a horizontal 4-cylinder overhead valve air-cooled engine with finned aluminum cylinders and iron cast crankcase. It developed 57 H.P. at 3700 RPM. It had a 15 gallon fuel supply, and the engine averaged 40 miles per gallon. The wheelbase was 126 inches, while the tire size was 5:50 x 16. The car used 2-wheel hydraulic brakes on the front only, and apparently had no brakes on the lone rear wheel.

The projected price for these cars was in the vicinity of $550. A convertible, a pickup truck, and a panel delivery truck were also proposed, in addition to the prototype 2-door sedan. By the time all of the plans were well developed, World War II had reared its head. As a result, plans for future development fell through.

After the war, Preston Tucker took over the facilities of Air-Cooled Motors for his new car. Air-Cooled Motors was the original home of the Airmobile. Today, the one and only Airmobile ever produced, a cute little red-orange vehicle, resides in Harrah's famed auto museum in Reno, Nev.

Albinita

The Albanita was chiefly an experimental one-off car that General Motors turned out during the 1933-34 season. Actually, it was one of many experimental cars that G.M. turned out during the 1930s. The vehicle not only aided G.M., but got Chrysler to rush with their 1934 Airflow models. This car used Dubonnet suspension up front, with coil springs in the rear. A Ford V-8 engine was used in road-testing the Albanita. Note the similarity in the grille to that used on the 1937 Chevrolet. The car had very definite European lines.

American Steam

The American Steam Automobile Co. of Newton, Mass., manufactured a few automobiles from 1926 through 1931. The car offered twice the acceleration of a gasoline car, plus elimination of clutch and gearshift. Smoothness and silence were its main features. This vehicle happens to be one of the last produced in 1930-31. The steam car operated on kerosene and delivered about 10 miles per gallon. Oil mileage was about 1,000 miles per gallon. It weighed in the 4,000 lbs. category and sold in the $2,000 to $3,000 price range. The company used rebuilt Stanley Steamer engines which operated as good as new.

Arrow Plane

This happens to be a 1932 Arrow Plane. It was built under the auspices of Lyman Voelpel of Chicago. The car used a Model A engine. Its streamline design led the way for future companies to try similar styles, none of which proved too successful during the 1930s.

Bremar

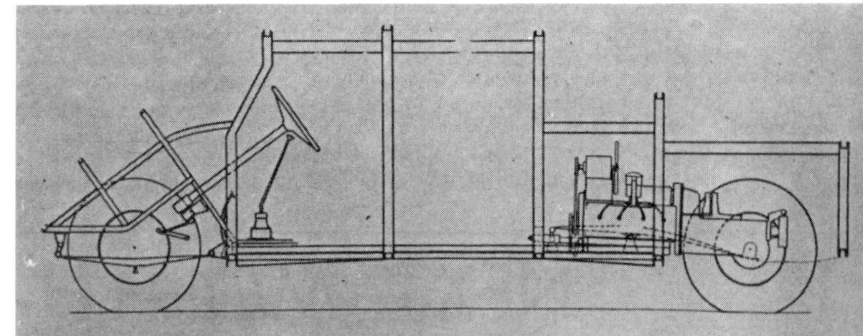

The 1932 Bremar was strictly an experimental car with a rear engine. The name Bremar was coined from the first syllable of the name Proter Bremard whose idea it was to build the car, with the help of William McCalla of Detroit. The factory office was to have been in Detroit, with assembly being in Sydney, Ohio. Three cars were to have been displayed at the 1932 New York Auto Show. Whether any ever got that far it is not known. This is the only photo available. Production was to have been on a limited custom built basis. Amos Northrup of aviation fame did the honors on the design. The body was to have consisted of a light wooden frame with a thin metal covering.

Borntraeger

The 1932-33 Borntraeger was built by a Chicago battery industrialist at a cost of $2,000. It took two years to build. The little front drive speedster used a four-cylinder, air-cooled motorcycle engine, had a wheelbase of 66 inches, an overall length of 83 inches, tread of 41 inches, had 16 x 4-inch tires, a height of 26 inches, and a weight of 500 lbs. Four wheel brakes were used and its top speed was 70 MPH. It does not appear that this car was ever intended for production, even though its name appears in lists of American makes of cars.

Coleman

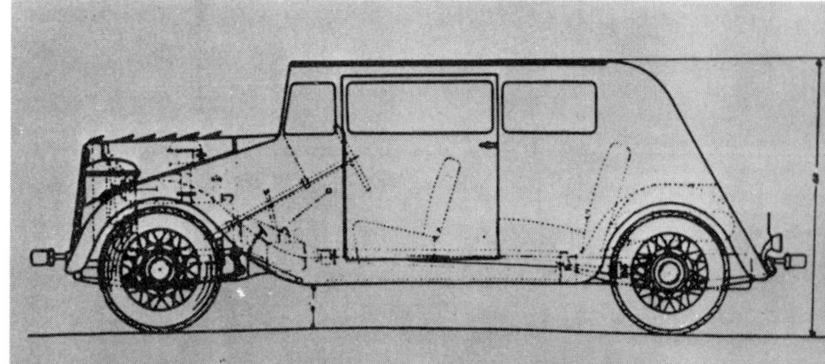

In 1933 a party by the name of Coleman, from Colorado, built this one-off automobile. It was powered by a Ford V-8. The front axle arched over the engine, helping to lower the motor in the frame. The side panels were completely flat. Production never went beyond the pilot model.

Consolidated

Consolidated Motors Corp. of Lima, Ohio, had plans in 1934 to build a passenger car of streamlined design that would be capable of a speed of 100 MPH. It is very doubtful if the automobile ever got beyond the drawing board. Unfortunately, a photo of the proposed make is not available. The same company also intended to reactivate the Garford truck, with assembly of both being in the old Relay Axle plant.

Corsair

This one-off automobile was the 1938 Phantom Corsair built for Rust Heinz at a cost of $24,000. It was built by Bohmann and Schwartz of Pasadena, Calif. This automobile used a Cord V-8 Lycoming engine and front wheel drive.

The Corsair, sometimes known as The Phantom Corsair, was a .one-off vehicle built by Bohmann and Schwartz of Pasadena, Calif. The car was built for Rust Heinz, son of H. J. Heinz of food fame. Heinz designed the car for his personal enjoyment, and had plans for Bohmann and Schwartz to build future models on this design; but, unfortunately, he was killed during the manufacture of this car.

The Corsair contained a Cord front-wheel-drive transmission and a Lycoming engine. The fuel supply was 22 gallons. Tire size was 7:00 x 16 inches. The seating would take four in front seat comfortably. The car came fully equipped including air conditioning, soundproofing and tinted glass of dark green bullet proof safety plate. Taxable horsepower was not released but the car was able to obtain a top speed of 122 MPH.

In later years the car was owned by Herb Shriner of radio and television fame who also was killed in a car accident (not in the Corsair, however). Today, it resides in the Harrah Auto Museum in Reno, Nevada.

Cummins Diesel

This 1935 Cummins Diesel is actually a 1935 Auburn Convertible Sedan. The diesel engine was 400 lbs. heavier than the Auburn engine and the 4-cylinder version ran about 30 M.P.G. Its top speed was 80 M.P.H. Oddly enough, insurance companies were skeptical of the car for fire hazards and would not insure it. The car is shown prior to its test run from New York to California with designer C. L. Cummins at the wheel.

The Cummins Diesel Co. built the diesel engine for this 935 Auburn Convertible Sedan. The Cummins Diesel Co. s located in Columbus, Inc., and is still in business nanufacturing diesel truck engines.

This was strictly experimental, using the diesel engine n this car. The 4-cylinder engine turned a maximum of 200 RPM. All other components were the same as the egular 1935 Auburn. It had 6:50 x 16-inch tires. Bendix ydraulic brakes were used, and a 20-gallon diesel fuel ank was employed.

Detroit Electric

The Detroit Electric Co. had been in business from 1907 through 1939. During the remaining years of the company's existence, which includes the era covered by this book, production was very limited. The factory was located in Detroit. This example combines the graceful lines, and sturdiness of any gas car of that time, yet offered ease of control, flexibility, and excellent riding qualities. The weight was extremely low, giving good balance from the help of extra duty batteries between the front and rear compartment. The Detroit Electric was custom built and finished to each customer's wishes.

A 1931 Detroit Electric made its debut later than most conventional models, coming out in late spring of 1931. The front passenger seats of this model faced forward instead of backward as in previous models. This particular model had a top speed of 35 MPH. It was priced at $4,250. Another model was available later in the year at the same price.

An example of the 1932 Detroit Electric resembled most gasoline passenger cars for the year. A.O. Dunk, President of the firm, claimed there was a considerable demand for this type of car, especially among older women. The remaining models resembled this design quite a bit. Due to the lack of a streamlined body and limited range and speed, the buyers just weren't there by the late thirties. From 1935 to the end of production in 1938, Detroit Electrics used the exterior sheetmetal of contemporary Dodges, and in fact, looked identical to Dodge cars.

De - Vo

Late in 1936, Norman De Vaux intended to build another car chiefly for export using his name once again, only spelling it differently. This time it was to be called the De Vo. The company was to be the De Vo Motor Car Corp. of Maryland. The car was to have been a four-cylinder, five-passenger sedan on a 102-inch wheelbase. The company was to use the Continental Red Seal engine. Whether any cars actually were ever built is doubtful.

Doble

One of the last series of cars from the Doble Steam Motor Car Corp. included this handsome 1930 model. The company reorganized in 1922 under the above title, and continued production of sorts until 1932 when the depression killed it for good.

The last of the classic Dobles was the 1932 Series E Convertible Coupe shown above. The company began production in 1913 under the direction of Abner Doble in Waltham, Mass. After the reorganization in 1922, the remaining cars were produced in Emeryville, Calif. The production figures between 1924 and 1932 of the Series E and F Dobles was 42. Prices ranged between $8,000 and $11,000 with a ready buyer for each car the factory turned out. However, perfectionist production methods contributed to the company never turning a profit. The Doble reportedly was almost automatic in its operation, and capable of tremendous power and speed.

Doodlebug

The Doodlebug began life in 1932 as an experimental car for Reo Motor Car Co. Its chief engineer was H.T. Thomas who spent his spare hours trying to develop an inexpensive car for the company to distribute. By summer of 1933, the car was completed. But Reo was now looking for a company from which they could buy rights for engines and other running gear, as they weren't in a position to tool up on a large scale for just experimentation. The engine that was chosen was a 4-cylinder Hercules 1xB that developed 20-25 HP. A conventional Reo 3-speed transmission with synchro-mesh was put into service. The clutch and gearshift were operated by push-pull cables, and the controls were of the conventional type. The engine was in the rear. It used two radiators, one at each side. Air entered louvers and exited through panels on the decklid. The car gave excellent gas mileage and had good performance with a top speed of 60 MPH. The Doodlebug unfortunately was a one-off creation that was to have sold for $400. If the timing had just been right it may have helped Reo linger on in the passenger car field for a few more years.

Dymaxion

The 1933 Dymaxion experimental car weighed only 1,800 pounds. Only three examples were ever built. Using a Ford V-8 engine, it was to have sold for $2,500.

Actually, the Dymaxion never did get underway for roduction, but being of such a rare type it is shown here. : consisted of a three wheel airplane fuselage of duralium nd balsa. The car's backers were Buckminster Fuller, an ıventor, and W. Starling Burgess, a yacht designer. The ıree cars which were manufactured were completed in the ld Locomobile plant in Bridgeport, Conn. This futuristic ar was road tested on the Locomobile Proving Grounds nd did better than 120 MPH. It could get as much as 0 MPG and weighed 1,800 lbs. The car steered from the ear and was powered by a Ford V-8 engine which eveloped 75 HP at 3800 RPM.

The car seated three persons, and was to have been elivered for approximately $2,500 when production was) have started late in 1933. However, the company ran ut of funds before the unusual car could be put on the ıarket. The original car crashed on a test run, killing two ulf Oil Corp. executives.

Griffin

In 1930, a man by the name of R.A. Griffin, in San Diego, Cal., decided he would start to manufacture a 3-wheel automobile. From this venture came the one and only Griffin car. It was powered by a 4-cylinder motorcycle engine. The frame was of oak, and rubber aircraft straps were used in place of springs. Oddly, this was an idea that was tried on numerous experimental cars in the 1930s – almost totally without success. Unusual features of the Griffin were its use of motorcycle wheels, and its large single front door for the driver – much like the post-war European bubble cars. Unlike the Arrowhead, the Griffin featured a full rear window, and side doors for the rear passengers.

Elcar - Lever

This Elcar-Lever automobile was officially introduced in July of 1930 but was referred to in the trade as a 1931 model. The Elcar Motor Co. of Elkhart, Ind., and Lever Motor Corp. of Delaware merged and became known as the Lever Motors Corp. of Indiana. For the time, the two companies operated as divisions of the merged company until the Elcar line of cars was discontinued in mid-1931. This model is the same as the Elcar 130, using the 7-passenger body on the 130-inch chassis. The Lever engine was the only difference.

A 1931 Elcar-Lever Model 130 7-passenger Phaeton used the 130-inch wheelbase. This was the final year for the joint name to be used. Beginning with the 1932 models, the car was known only as the Lever, with its production to take place in the Kissel Industries plant in Hartford, Wis. The name Lever was used because of the Lever motor which powered the car. The designers of this engine stated that its power was increased by a lever between the piston and crankshaft in a manner that the piston stroke was twice that of the crankshaft stroke. Late in 1932 a new front-wheel-drive car was to be built on a 134-inch wheelbase. The engine was to be an 8-cylinder, developing 110 horse-power at 2400 RPM. Some authorities of front drive cars feel this was to have been a revival of the Ruxton or a car closely resembling it. Whether any ever got beyond the drawing board is not known. A catalog was printed showing future plans, however, for the 1933 Lever.

Harris

Benjamin F. Harris, a Chicago engineer, poses proudly with his one-off Harris Front Drive Special, which he built as a hobby in his spare time from 1935 to 1937. Certainly far more of a "hot rod" than an actual make of car, the Harris has nevertheless found its way into accepted lists of American car makes, and for that reason only is being included in this book. The single seat car was never intended for production. It was powered by a 92 cubic inch V-8 that had a bore and stroke of 2.2 inches by 3 inches and that produced 32 horsepower at 3200 RPM. Its total weight was 1,500 lbs., and it was claimed the car would achieve 90 MPH in high and 110 MPH in overdrive. It had an 86-inch wheel-base. In appearance it was not unlike Sir Malcolm Campbell's famed record-breaking Bluebird.

Howard

The name of Howard was used on at least 10 different automobiles from 1895 to 1930. This one came from the Howard Motors Corp. of Detroit. It was in business from 1928 to 1930. The company sold cars only overseas or on a special order basis in the U.S. through the parent Howard Motors International of New York. It was a relatively conventional assembled light car usually using the Continental Red Seal Six and Lockheed hydraulic brakes. Domestic prices ranged from $700 to $2,000, though very few cars were sold in the U.S. Both 6 and 8-cylinder cars supposedly were available, with horsepowers ranging from 30 to 100, Supposedly too, a full range of body designs were available. Production figures on this car are not available, but it seems that very few were sold either in this country or in whatever overseas markets these cars were designed for.

Hamlin

The Hamlin-Holmes, or Hamlin, as it was known after 1930, was an unusual series of cars produced by a company that managed to remain in business from 1919 to 1930 without ever really getting into production. One of the most successful Hamlins was this front-wheel-drive racing car which was built in 1925 and which performed well enough to be entered in the 1926 Indianapolis 500 Mile race. This particular car used a Model T Ford chassis and a Fronty Ford engine, plus the Hamlin front-drive unit and suspension. Oddly, the car was sponsored by the Chevrolet Brothers. Jack McCarver managed to qualify at 86.4 MPH, which was fast enough to give the car 25th starting position out of 28 entrants. McCarver completed 23 laps before a broken connecting rod forced his retirement. The car never again raced seriously, but was rebuilt constantly by the company, and often was displayed as a Hamlin promotional vehicle right up through 1930.

Bearing 1929 Colorado license plates is this 1930 model Hamlin. The front view shows the two-axle drive system, which allowed the weight of the car to be carried on the dead lower axle while the front-wheel-drive was through the much smaller upper axle. This prototype was fitted with a 4-door sedan body and later displayed front end sheet metal that obviously had been purchased from the Gardner Motor Co., which also was experimenting with a front-wheel-drive car of its own.

Another front view of the last experimental Hamlin shows the unusual suspension system employed by this manufacturer. Because of the front-wheel-drive, the engine had to be set far back, resulting in the long fan shaft for the forward mounted radiator. Unlike Cord, Hamlin mounted its radiator ahead of the front-wheel-drive unit. During its lifetime, Hamlin bought bodies and sheetmetal from Moon, Cleveland, and Gardner, and thus resembled all of those cars at one time or another. By 1930, the Harvey, Ill., company seemed at the threshhold of success with this model, but the depression spelled the end of the venture. Throughout its life, the Hamlin was known for its exceptionally low center of gravity and for its excellent handling characteristics.

Hoffman

Another attempt at a front-wheel-drive prestige car was the Hoffman, produced in 1931 by the R.C. Hoffman Co. of Detroit. A total of two drivable prototype cars were built, both powered by Lycoming Straight-Eight engines. The wheels were carried on dead axles, in the same manner as used on the Hamlins, with much smaller front driving axles transferring power from the engine to the road. In addition, torque arms were used as an aid to the front suspension. The body work on these attractive cars was by Baker-Raulang. Apparently, no financial backing could be found for these cars, and the company folded. In retrospect, it appears that this could have been a successful make of car, had it been born in a better economic environment. Baker-Raulang, incidentally, was a producer of fine electric cars prior to World War I.

L. & E.

The L. & E. car was an interesting West Coast make that managed to stay in business officially from 1922 through 1932, and even then, managed to market some cars as late as 1936. Known as "the car without axles," the L. & E. was the product of the Lunderlius and Eccleston Co. of Los Angeles. In appearance, the 1930 models somewhat resembled Franklins, and it is possible that Franklin sheet-metal was used extensively on the later bodies. The 1930 cars seem to be the most successful by the company, and corporate plans included the construction of a large factory at Long Beach. However, the depression knocked out this idea, and the car officially died in 1932 – though "new" L. & E. models were reported to have been advertised as late as 1936.

View of L & E
chassis showing
front spring
suspension

A detailed view of the L. & E. suspension system shows the workings of the "car with no axles." The wheel hubs were supported by four transverse springs at each end. The rear wheels were driven by a short spline shaft having double universal joints between the hubs and the sprung differential, which was attached to a frame cross-member. The large reduction in unsprung weight was supposed to provide a far superior ride and excellent handling. L. & E. claimed that this particular chassis was six years in the experimental stage, during which time it was driven a distance of 500,000 miles.

Kirchoff

A very rare car is this 1930 Kirchoff Speedster that was built in Pasadena, Calif. This automobile was a handbuilt one-off vehicle, which used a Miller Special engine and had a front-wheel drive transmission. It is sometimes referred to a Miller Special.

Littlemac

The Littlemac is another one of those pesky makes of cars that keeps cropping up, with little to substantiate that serious automotive production was ever contemplated. Produced by the Thompson Motor Co. of Muscatine, Ia., the cars were supposed to sell for $435 in 1930 and 1931. Apparently, the company felt it had a market among former Model-T Ford buyers who were not impressed with the new and more expensive Model A. However, it appears the buyers were even less impressed with the Littlemac. The car reportedly was powered by the old Continental 130-cubic inch 4-cylinder engine, which had been used in Durant's Star, a car that ceased production in 1928. Reports state that the car had a relatively short wheelbase, woodspoke wheels, 2-wheel brakes, and a 3-speed transmission. Overall, the description matches the Star of 1928, which sold for $445, or $10 more than the Littlemac, and prompts one to wonder if the Littlemac was not simply a thinly disguised Star with production simply being a run-off of unused Star components.

Mathis

The 1931 Mathis was introduced as a part of Durant Motors of Lansing, Michigan. This car was a development of the French Mathis. With a similar design, it came on a 96-inch wheelbase, using 4:00 x 18-inch tires. Disc wheels were standard equipment. The 4-cylinder Continental L-head engine had a bore and stroke of 2.75 x 3.25 inches. The engine used aluminum pistons. Its developed horsepower was rated at 32 at 3200 RPM. Only a 2-passenger Coupe was produced to be sold for $455. A Convertible Coupe was to have been produced but never got beyond the prototype state. The car was displayed at the 1931 New York Auto Show from Jan. 4 to 11 and at the Detroit Auto Show Jan. 18 to 25 and was to have been in dealer's hands by April of that year. Whether ot not any additional models were built is not certain.

McQuay - Norris

McQuay-Norris which also was started in 1932. The McQuay-Norris firm of St. Louis, Mo., was chiefly in business as a piston company that specialized in pistons, rings, bearings, and pins. This company had the Hill Auto Body Co. of Cincinnati, Ohio, build six automobiles chiefly for advertising purposes for their company. These identical cars all used stock Ford V-8 engines and rode on Ford chassis. One vehicle was completed in 1932 with the other five being finished by 1934. These cars were in constant use from 1934 through 1940. The whereabouts of these six novel cars hasn't been determined at this date. Though further production of these novel little cars could probably have been made successful, McQuay-Norris didn't seem interested in continuing the program, and the idea ended after the last car was finished. Apparently, Hill Auto Body, which designed and built the cars, either wasn't interested in the project, or had no further manufacturing rights under the contract with McQuay-Norris.

Miller

This car is found on lists of American automobiles under different names – Miller and Kirchoff. Actually, it is a 1930 Miller Special with a one-off body that was turned out at the Kirchoff Body Works in Pasadena, Cal. The Harry Miller Company produced cars in limited numbers in 1917, 1923, and 1930. This particular car was built specially for a wealthy sportsman in Santa Barbara, Calif. The automobile came with front-wheel-drive and a V-8 engine that was equipped with a supercharger. It was capable of doing 135 MPH. The body used no steel but was made of Duralumin. The fenders and panels were of aluminum. The car's disappearing top and deck lid were considered novel at that time. Miller was nationally famous as a race car builder, but the firm would also build an occasional passenger car chassis, such as this one.

Morrison

In 1935, Willard L. Morrison of Buchanan, Mich., made plans to build a car of novel design. A very modernistic streamlined body was to be used. Its tapered design would allow a three-passenger front seat and a more narrow rear compartment allowing room only for two rear seat passengers. The windshield was to set higher and further back than in many regular cars. The steering wheel was to be under the cowl and forward of the windshield, as a safety factor. The spare tire was so placed that it would help alleviate all shock if the car were in an accident. The gasoline tank had an unusual feature – to prevent the possibility of gasoline being stolen from the tank, the filler cap could be opened from the inside only. The Morrison was to use a Ford V-8 engine. However, all other parts were specially built. It is doubtful if any cars ever got beyond the prototype stage, or if they even got that far. No known pictures exist of the Morrison.

Mercer

Mercer attempted to revive its old name in 1931, after being out of the automobile business since 1925. This new car was to come in eight body styles with custom built bodies by Merrimac. The factory was to be in Elkhart, Ind., in the old Elcar Motor Car plant. The Mercer's mechanical features included a Continental eight-cylinder engine that developed 140 HP. Its cubic inch displacement was 322 cubic inches. The car was to feature automatic radiator shutters with thermostatic circulating control, duplex carburetion, four point rubber mounting, and Delco Remy electrical system. The car's exterior trim was well done on the models that did get to the completed stage. Fender parking lamps were provided and fender wells for the spare tires were standard equipment. Both side and top cowl ventilator doors were provided with louver doors in the hood. Unfortunately, the two prototypes that made it to the auto shows were about the only cars to be seen, and whether these survive today, historians cannot ascertain.

Pribil

The Pribil Safety Air Car of 1936-37 was to be the compact car and trailer unit that was to make trailers of its day obsolete. The Pribil used a 30 HP Continental engine which drove the rear wheels through a regular clutch and transmission. The Pribil's rear wheels were so close together, a differential wasn't needed. The maximum speed was 50 MPH. General Jumbo tires were standard equipment, and the brakes were hydraulic. The car weighed 2,400 pounds and had a 140-inch wheelbase, giving sleeping accommodations for two on a davenport that fit across the rear of the compartment. Movable chairs with the davenport allowed for eight people to sit comfortably. The car was to have been built in Saginaw, Mich. Whether any cars other than the prototype were completed isn't known.

Approximately 40 years ahead of its time, the Pribil Safety Air Car today would be considered a mini-motor home or mini-camper. Besides sleeping accommodations for two, standard equipment was to have included an ice box, folding table, and camping utensils. The tear-drop shaped car was intended for production, but funds ran out before the prototype was completed – in fact, it is not certain if the prototype ever reached a drivable stage.

Pitcairin

In 1935, the Pitcairin Autogyro Co. of Philadelphia, Pa., had plans for building a two-passenger autogyro which was driven through the rear wheel and steered by the front wheels. The car could unfold its three wings taking off from the ground. It cost $12,000 and could attain a speed of 20 MPH on land and 100 in the air. When roadable, the wings folded and pointed back over its tail. Probably this could have been classed as an early day helicopter. In 1960, plans were made to try and revive the Autogyro, but nothing further ever came of it. Note the 1935 Dodge sedan in the background. How many of these Autogyros were produced is not known.

Parker

Another of the one-off hobby cars that entered the lists of American makers was this Parker car which was built between 1934 and 1936. Harry S. Parker of Ellsworth, Maine took a notion to build his own car. His components centered chiefly around a 1933 Terraplane Six. He lengthened the chassis frame to increase the wheelbase to 128 inches. The Parker's frame was steel covered with oak over which were laid metal panels of 24 gauge iron. The car was capable of doing 85 MPH. It had a seating capacity for four people. Parker never had any ideas of producing this car for sales.

Raulang

Raunch and Lang Corporation of Chicopee Falls, Mass., were the builders of this gas-electric car they called the Raulang. It was built during 1929-1935 and sold principally as a taxi-cab. They used a Willys Knight engine and chassis which had the transmission and clutch removed. It had a generator and electric motor supplied by General Electric, with the conventional engine hooked to the generator. The firm claimed the car was started and controlled by accelerator and brake, except for reverse, where a small lever had to be operated to reverse the electric motor. The company felt the simplicity of operation by eliminating the gearshift and clutch pedal were the biggest advantages. It was capable of doing 45 MPH.

Tjaara

The experimental 1934 Tjaarda was used chiefly for experimental purposes for the Lincoln Zephyr, which was scheduled for its debut in late June of 1935. The Tjaarda caused a sensation at the Century of Progress exhibition in 1934. The Tjaarda-designed, Briggs-built rear engined car was commissioned by Edsel Ford in an attempt to study possible innovations for the proposed "small Lincoln." The first Tjaarda model was this rear-engined, unit body creation. A later model, used for track testing, had large airscoops under the rear quarter windows and did away with the strange experimental headlights. Seen from the side, the Tjaarda show car displays its radical streamlining. The device on the roof is a periscope replacing the rearview mirror. In 1935, this car was joined at the exhibition by a less radical front-engine of very similar design, but having a longer hood, less rear sweep, and no tailfin.

Sterkenburg

Built in 1931, the Sterkenburg was a fantastically advanced car. And, though it was destined to fail by itself, it did give birth to several other advanced vehicles, and in a sense, led to the eventual Lincoln-Zephyr. The radically streamlined car was designed by John Tjaarda, shown here with the vehicle. Tjaarda claimed that the rear engine design was the only style that made sense, as it abolished heat, fumes, sounds and smell. The car would have used a pressed steel frame and low-slung 4-door, 5-passenger body, with bucket seats in front and a rear bench seat. Power would have been by a Ford V-8. Though Tjaarda demonstrated the advantages of this car on many occasions, financial backers could not be convinced to take a chance on such a wild proposal, and thus production never got under way. Tjaarda used many of the design features of this car on his Tjaarda show car, and this in turn led to the styling of the much more conventional Lincoln Zephyr. The Sterkenburg Motor Co. had its plant (as such) in Detroit, but this one car seems to have been its total production.

Roamer

The Roamer had been in business from 1916 through 1930. The company had different organization names during the years, such as Adams-Montant, Barley Motor Car Co., and in 1923 was reorganized as the Roamer Motor Car Co. Its main headquarters were in kalamazoo, Michigan, at the time of demise. The car was often referred to as the American Rolls Royce both because of its front appearance and the quality with which it was built. The final Roamers used straight eight Continental engines of 226 and 299 cubic inch displacement. This example was the final year. Shown here is a 7-passenger limousine called the "120." Note the side windshield eaves. Production figures are not available for the 1930 Roamer.

Waterman

The Arrowbile or Waterman Arrowbile of 1937 was a product of the Waterman Arrowplane Corp. of Santa Monica, Calif. Its founder was Waldo Dean Waterman, who had built a number of unconventional aircraft in the 1930s. The Arrowbile used a Studebaker Commander 6 engine. The craft was meant to be used both on highways and in the air. The Studebaker Corporation agreed in 1937 to sell the Arrowbile at $3,000 each. Many Studebaker dealers were to handle the franchises throughout the country and they would also service it. Studebaker's first contract was for five crafts for demonstration purposes. If enough demand was there, then plans would continue into 1938. However, in 1938 the depression took a turn for the worse and the public didn't show enough interest to suit Studebaker officials, and the company backed out of the proposed plan. Note the partial view of a 1937 Studebaker parked next to the new Waterman Arrowbile in 1937, with its 1937 California license plate.

About the author

Most people do research for their book for several years, but in my case I've been collecting and recording for over 40 years.

It all started when I was about 18 months old and an aunt brought me a Tootsie Toy car from Lake Arrowhead, Cal. She asked my parents, "I wonder if Jim is too young for this toy? Let's take it home and see what he does with it."

Well, they did just that – and couldn't get it out of my hand. Every Sunday morning after Church, if I'd been good through the week, I could go into the local drug store and get another one. This went on for some while until we all thought I'd left my first childhood. Strangely enough, I went into my second childhood much sooner than most people, and today I have roughly 1,200 choice scale model automobiles ranging from a 1949 Oldsmobile, which is worth about $200, up to current models of today. This happens to be just one phase of my automobile collecting.

My Day always would take me to the Auto Shows in Los Angeles, starting in 1937. (I've only missed one tc date since then.) We would also go to our local car dealers in Pasadena each year where the salesmen would give me the latest brochures of each make. It hurts me to think how most of these wound up between a pair of scissors. What I've spent to replace some of these books in the past few years!

I also remember calling the dealers to have them bring out their latest model for a demonstration. Being just a little kid, my voice sounded like a woman's, so the salesman would come to the door asking for Mrs. Moloney. My Mother, not knowing anything about this at first, was very innocent until one day she felt it was time to bring it to a halt. When a DeSoto salesman knocked at our door, my mother asked me to appear. Was I in seventh heaven when the good-natured salesman gave me a complete demonstration up into some steep hills in back of where we lived in order to show me how Fluid Drive worked. Since that day I've always had a soft spot for a DeSoto.

Always tinkering with the family car in high school was fun until the time when Dad was to come home and see parts strewn all over the driveway.

My first car was a 1947 Olds Coupe which was two years old when I got it, but must have had way more miles than the normal car of two years of age should have. We never got along too well right from the first day. But still, like any teenager, I sure was proud of it. It used so much oil a friend of mine used to kid me that I should throw a pig in the crankcase to help it.

After finishing high school, I went to Pasadena City College for two years where I wasn't quite sure what I wanted to do. Advertising seemed like a favorite, but there just wasn't a particular area to get into as far as automobiles were concerned. I also knew I had to have a visit with Uncle Sam for a time before anything was to take place.

Upon graduating from Pasadena City College, I entered the University of Southern California where I had enough

credits toward completion of a degree as an elementa school teacher. I always liked kids so I felt this was a go avenue to explore. Before completing school I was draft and had one semester to finish upon my discharge fro the Army.

After graduating from U.S.C. in January of 1956, I we to work for the Chevrolet Division of General Motors Los Angeles. My position was in the New Car Distributi Center where we set up the allotments for the 144 Ch rolet dealers in the L.A. zone. I worked there until o tragic day in April of 1957 when I was involved in a ve serious auto accident. Fortunately, I lived and can grateful to God I'm still here. After 2½ years of bei hospitalized, I was able to go back to work and do wh I'd been prepared to do before. I started teaching scho in Monrovia, Cal., where I lived for five years. At th time I decided I'd prefer to live in my favority city of cities I've ever visited – Santa Barbara, Cal.

Here we are 14 years later with the book I've dream of completing for all of you to enjoy. Possibly, you w browse through it many times. As a fourth grade teach today, I know how kids like picture books. After all, c buffs are really overgrown kids, so maybe there are a f photos that will bring back some memories for y between the years of 1930 and 1942.